lonely planet

Thailand

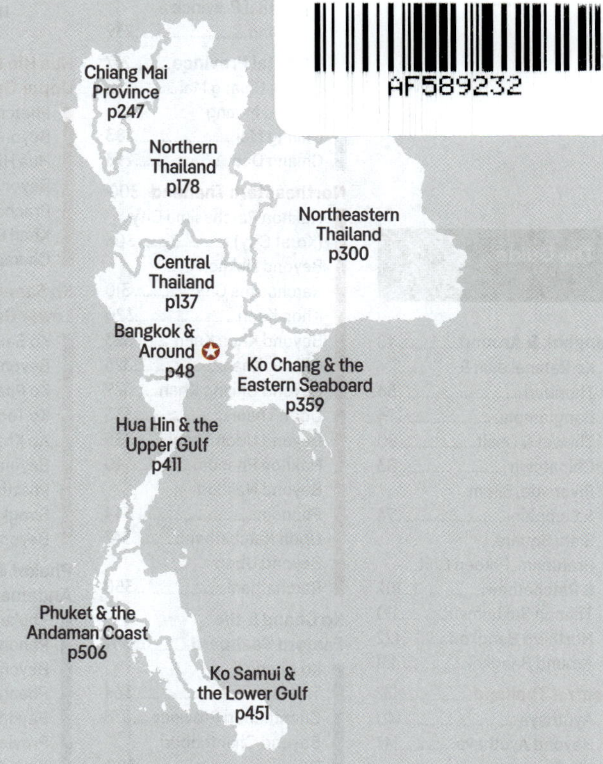

David Eimer, Austin Bush, Philipp Meier, Chawadee Nualkhair, Aydan Stuart, Choltanutkun Tun-atiruj

CONTENTS

Plan Your Trip

The Guide

Wat Chang Rob (p242), Kamphaeng Phet Historical Park

Canal tour, Bangkok (p48)

Ko Chang (p364)

Toolkit

Storybook

NAKORNTHAI/SHUTTERSTOCK

Mekong River, Nong Khai (p338)

THAILAND

THE JOURNEY BEGINS HERE

Travelling around Isan was a reminder that there's always more to discover in Thailand, no matter how much time you spend here. Bangkok has been my home for 10 years, yet exploring the northeast took me back to my first trip to the kingdom 25-odd years ago, when the combination of white-sand beaches, jungle-covered mountains and the glorious street food made me realise I'd landed in paradise.

This time around it was the majestic Mekong that was the revelation. Whether it was the sun setting in an explosion of pinks and reds above the river in Chiang Khan, watching the boats bobbing on the current while cycling the promenade in Nakhon Phanom, or eating dancing shrimp on the riverside beaches of Ubon Ratchathani, I couldn't believe I had waited so long to come here. If this is your first trip to Thailand, we believe you'll be feeling the same soon enough.

David Eimer

David is a Bangkok-based journalist and writer who enjoys exploring Southeast Asia's least-seen regions. He wrote the Northeastern Thailand chapter.

My favourite experience is driving Hwy 211 in Loei Province, following the Mekong as it winds towards **Nong Khai** (p338) with the lush hills of Laos looming in the background.

WHO GOES WHERE

Our writers and experts choose the places which, for them, define Thailand.

FROM LEFT: KETSIRI YINDEE/SHUTTERSTOCK, PHILIPP MEIER/LONELY PLANET, ONAPALMTREE/SHUTTERSTOCK

Mae La-Na (p192) is a remote Shan village in a mountain valley. Apart from a raw natural beauty, there's a sense of timelessness; it's one of my favourite corners of the world.

Austin Bush

@bushaustin

Austin is an American food and travel writer and photographer who tends to focus on food. He wrote the Northern Thailand and Ko Chang & the Eastern Seaboard chapters.

Visit Trang; check out the little-known waterfall of **Nam Tok Phan** (p576). Cascading through the forest with raw power, the pools splash in a wicked crescendo as you approach.

Philipp Meier

linkedin.com/in/writerphilippmeier

A fan of independent travel, Philipp is a Phuket-based travel writer specialising in round-ups and features that centre on Thailand. He wrote the Phuket & the Andaman Coast chapter.

I love Bangkok's **Chinatown** (p83): its heritage, its colour and its food combine to create a brew that's intoxicating and always changing.

Chawadee Nualkhair

@bangkokglutton

Chawadee Nualkhair is a food writer based in Bangkok. Her cookbook Real Thai Cooking *will soon be followed by* Thai Food Stories. *She wrote the Bangkok & Around and Hua Hin & the Upper Gulf chapters.*

FROM LEFT: BALAZSSEBOK/SHUTTERSTOCK, HUW PENSON/SHUTTERSTOCK

Mallika RE 124 (p159) is a living, breathing recreation of life in Thailand circa 1905. Everything there was authentic, and wandering the streets in traditional dress felt like stepping into another era.

Aydan Stuart

@aydanstuart

Aydan is a writer and creative based in Chiang Mai. He wrote the Central Thailand and Chiang Mai Province chapters.

Ko Tao (p478) really stole my heart; it hasn't lost its soul or charm despite being one of the most popular islands in Thailand. Nature still hums here but what really sets it apart is the people.

Choltanutkun Tun-atiruj

linktr.ee/choltanutkun

Choltanutkun is a Thai writer covering travel, culture and politics since 2016. She lives in Bangkok. She wrote the Ko Samui & the Lower Gulf chapter.

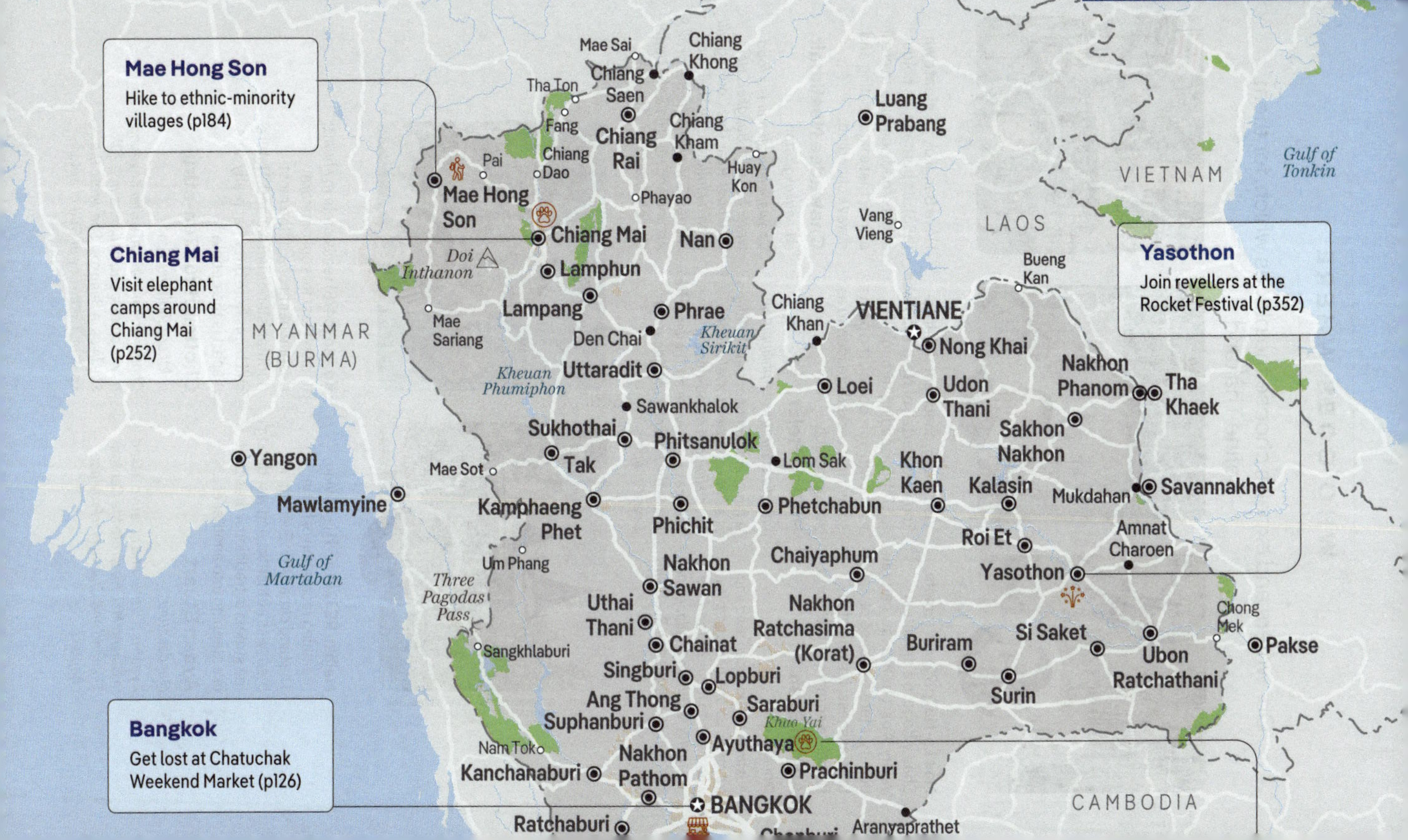

Mae Hong Son
Hike to ethnic-minority villages (p184)

Chiang Mai
Visit elephant camps around Chiang Mai (p252)

Yasothon
Join revellers at the Rocket Festival (p352)

Bangkok
Get lost at Chatuchak Weekend Market (p126)

Mae Sai
Chiang Khong
Tha Ton
Chiang Saen
Fang
Chiang Rai
Chiang Kham
Luang Prabang
Pai
Chiang Dao
Huay Kon
Mae Hong Son
Phayao
VIETNAM
Gulf of Tonkin
Vang Vieng
LAOS
Chiang Mai
Nan
Doi Inthanon
Lamphun
Bueng Kan
Lampang
Phrae
Chiang Khan
VIENTIANE
Mae Sariang
MYANMAR (BURMA)
Den Chai
Kheuan Sirikit
Nong Khai
Uttaradit
Kheuan Phumiphon
Loei
Udon Thani
Nakhon Phanom
Tha Khaek
Sawankhalok
Sukhothai
Phitsanulok
Sakhon Nakhon
Yangon
Tak
Lom Sak
Khon Kaen
Mae Sot
Kalasin
Mukdahan
Savannakhet
Mawlamyine
Kamphaeng Phet
Phichit
Phetchabun
Roi Et
Amnat Charoen
Gulf of Martaban
Um Phang
Chaiyaphum
Yasothon
Three Pagodas Pass
Nakhon Sawan
Uthai Thani
Nakhon Ratchasima (Korat)
Chong Mek
Si Saket
Chainat
Buriram
Ubon Ratchathani
Pakse
Sangkhlaburi
Singburi
Lopburi
Surin
Ang Thong
Saraburi
Suphanburi
Khao Yai
Ayuthaya
Nam Tok
Nakhon Pathom
Kanchanaburi
Prachinburi
BANGKOK
CAMBODIA
Ratchaburi
Aranyaprathet

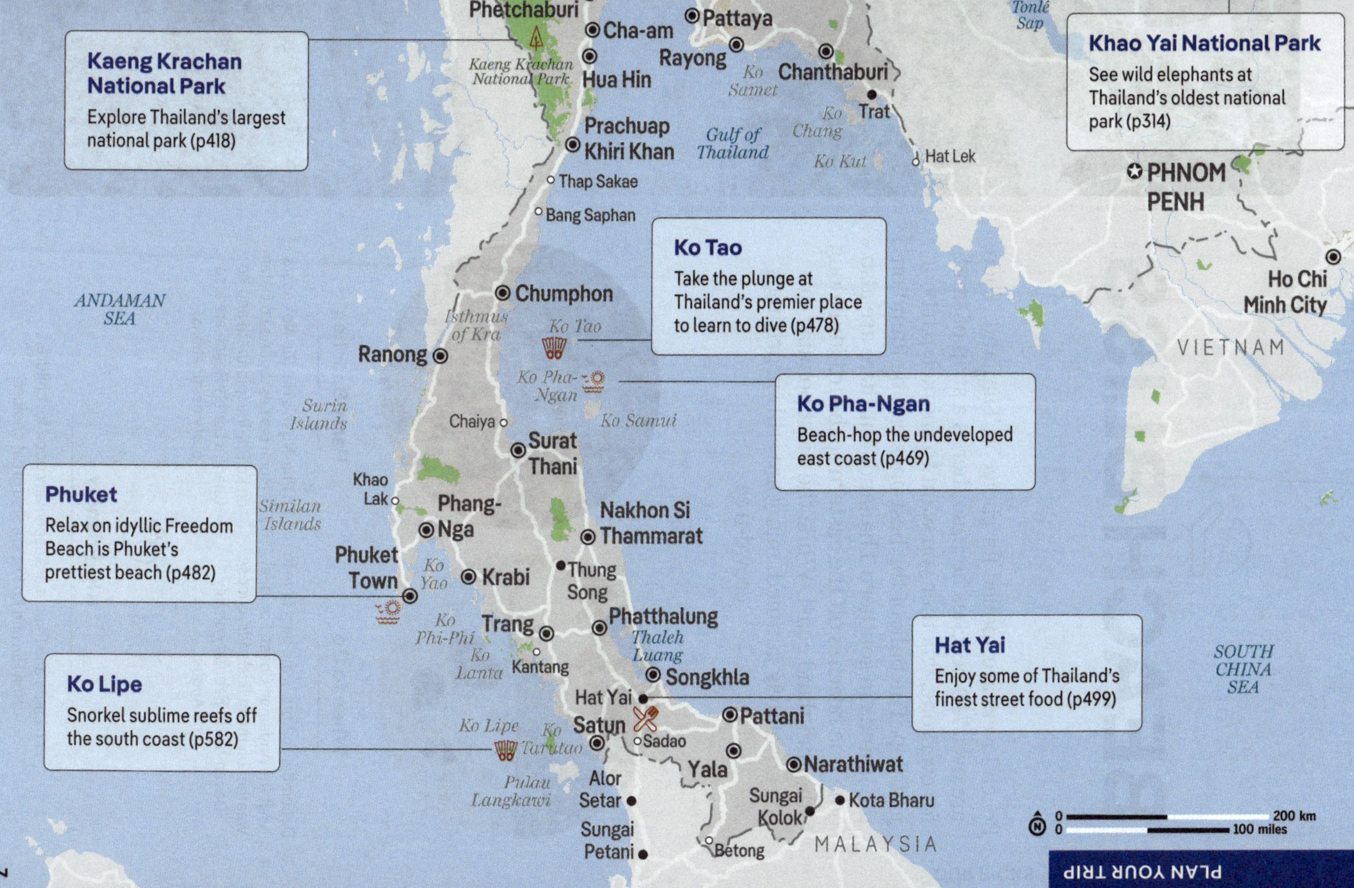
Kaeng Krachan National Park
Explore Thailand's largest national park (p418)
Khao Yai National Park
See wild elephants at Thailand's oldest national park (p314)
Ko Tao
Take the plunge at Thailand's premier place to learn to dive (p478)
Ko Pha-Ngan
Beach-hop the undeveloped east coast (p469)
Phuket
Relax on idyllic Freedom Beach is Phuket's prettiest beach (p482)
Hat Yai
Enjoy some of Thailand's finest street food (p499)
Ko Lipe
Snorkel sublime reefs off the south coast (p582)
Phetchaburi
Cha-am
Hua Hin
Kaeng Krachan National Park
Pattaya
Rayong
Chanthaburi
Ko Samet
Trat
Ko Chang
Ko Kut
Hat Lek
Gulf of Thailand
Prachuap Khiri Khan
Thap Sakae
Bang Saphan
Tonlé Sap
PHNOM PENH
Ho Chi Minh City
VIETNAM
ANDAMAN SEA
Chumphon
Isthmus of Kra
Ko Tao
Ranong
Ko Pha-Ngan
Ko Samui
Surin Islands
Chaiya
Surat Thani
Khao Lak
Phang-Nga
Similan Islands
Nakhon Si Thammarat
Phuket Town
Ko Yao
Krabi
Thung Song
Ko Phi-Phi
Trang
Phatthalung
Thaleh Luang
Ko Lanta
Kantang
Songkhla
Hat Yai
Ko Lipe
Ko Tarutao
Satun
Sadao
Pattani
Yala
Narathiwat
Pulau Langkawi
Alor Setar
Sungai Kolok
Kota Bharu
Sungai Petani
Betong
MALAYSIA
SOUTH CHINA SEA
0 200 km
0 100 miles

BEACH BLISS

Beach lovers are spoiled for choice in Thailand. There are over 740 beaches here, so there's a strip of sand for everyone, whether you want to snorkel, party or just flop. The bulk of the best ones can be found on the islands in southern Thailand, but there are also some fine beaches off the eastern seaboard and along the mainland coast. While the most popular can be absolutely jammed, many are still surprisingly crowd-free.

When to Go

December to April is the best time to visit the Andaman Coast. For ideal weather on the gulf islands, choose December to February or July and August.

Party Beaches

Ko Pha-Ngan's Hat Rin Nok hosts Full Moon parties, but Ao Lo Dalam on Ko Phi-Phi (pictured) and Ko Chang's Lonely Beach are also party destinations.

Kid-Friendly

Ko Lanta and Phuket are especially good for children. Hua Hin and Ko Kut are also great choices.

FROM LEFT: FLORIAN AUGUSTIN/SHUTTERSTOCK, GORAN_SAFAREK/SHUTTERSTOCK, ARTEM EVDOKIMOV/SHUTTERSTOCK

Hat Freedom (p512)

BEST BEACH EXPERIENCES

Hang from the limestone crags above ridiculously photogenic ❶ **Hat Railay West** (p561) or just laze on the glorious white sand.

Watch the sun go down at idyllic ❷ **Hat Freedom** (p512), perhaps Phuket's most beautiful beach.

Contemplate the serene turquoise waters lapping the soft sand of ❸ **Hat Sunrise** (p582) on Ko Lipe.

Beach-hop by long-tail boat along Ko Pha-Ngan's undeveloped east coast. ❹ **Hat Yao** (p476) is our pick for supreme tranquillity.

Wander the wide and long beaches of ❺ **Ao Khanom** (p485). Visit during the week and you might have them to yourself.

ETHICAL ELEPHANT ENCOUNTERS

FROM LEFT: STEVE CUKROV/SHUTTERSTOCK, PLOYPEMUK/SHUTTERSTOCK, MASSDON/SHUTTERSTOCK

Nearly everyone who comes to Thailand wants to see elephants. Thankfully, there are now an increasing number of places where you can get up close with Thailand's national animal in an ethical way that spares these gentle giants the pain and stress that comes from the circus-like shows that some so-called elephant sanctuaries still put on. Avoid anywhere that offers elephant rides. It's also possible to spot wild elephants in a number of national parks.

How Many Elephants?

Around 300,000 elephants once roamed Thailand. Poaching and habitat loss reduced wild numbers to around 3000 to 3600, plus 3500 to 4000 so-called domesticated elephants.

White Elephants

Under Thai law, all white – really albino – elephants are the property of the king. Most live at Lampang's Thai Elephant Conservation Centre (pictured).

Beasts of Burden

Elephants acted as the tanks of Thailand's ancient armies and hauled timber through the forests until logging was banned in 1989.

Elephants, Kuiburi National Park (p431)

BEST ELEPHANT EXPERIENCES

Search for elephant herds at ❶ **Kuiburi National Park** (p431), the premier place to spot pachyderms in the wild.

Feed the rescued elephants at ❷ **Phuket Elephant Sanctuary** (p515) and then watch as they wander the forest, bathe and hang out.

Spend a day walking with the happy pachyderms at ❸ **Chai Lai Orchid** (p594) in the mountains of Chiang Mai Province.

Hang out with the many elephants at the ❹ **Mae Sa Elephant Camp** (p291), which is conveniently close to Chiang Mai.

Travel to far northern Thailand where you can sleep in the jungle amid elephants at the ❺ **Anantara Golden Triangle Elephant Camp & Resort** (p211).

TEMPLE-HOPPING

Thailand has the world's second-largest population of Buddhists, and Buddhist traditions are an integral part of local life. Exploring the 40,000-plus temples here – some of which are genuine architectural wonders – offers insights into Thailand's past, but also the present. And the fact that temples are always busy with worshippers really brings them alive.

BEST TEMPLE EXPERIENCES

Tour Chiang Mai's ❶ **old city** (p252), with temples dating to the 13th century and the Lanna Kingdom.

Climb the steep stairs at ❷ **Wat Arun** (p66; pictured left) for supreme views over Bangkok's historic district and Chao Phraya River.

Visit ❸ **Phanom Rung Historical Park** (p318), Thailand's most significant Khmer temple complex, perched atop an extinct volcano.

Catch the cable car to ❹ **Phra Nakhon Khiri Historical Park** (p414), where temple spires skewer the Phetchaburi sky.

Marvel at the 77m-high *chedi* (stupa) over ❺ **Wat Phra Mahathat Woramahawihaan** (p490), southern Thailand's most important temple.

FROM LEFT: DANIEL_FERRYANTO/SHUTTERSTOCK, KAWEE SU/SHUTTERSTOCK

Dress Appropriately

Thailand's temples are sacred spaces, so visitors need to dress accordingly. Wear anything too revealing and you may be barred from entering.

Making Merit

A key aspect of Thai Buddhism is making merit: performing good deeds. Giving food to monks or donating to temples are common ways of making merit.

World Heritage Sites

Some of Thailand's most ancient temples can be found in Ayuthaya and Sukhothai, both of which are UNESCO World Heritage sites.

WAYPOINT TRIP/SHUTTERSTOCK

Yasothon Rocket Festival (p352)

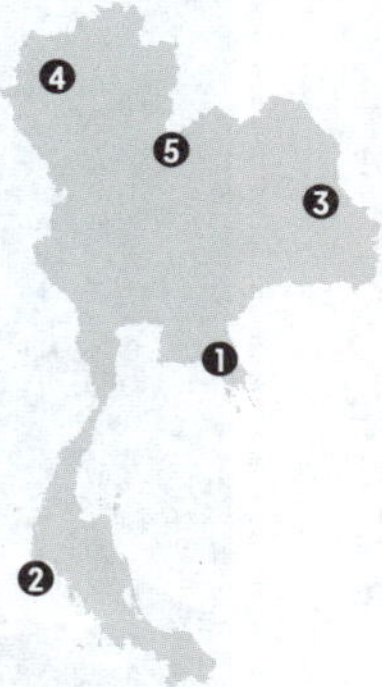

BEST FESTIVAL EXPERIENCES

Tuck into stinky durian at ❶ **Chanthaburi Fruit Festival** (p382), an introduction to Thailand's array of tropical fruit.

Abstain from meat as people parade with pierced cheeks during Phuket's ❷ **Vegetarian Festival** (p523).

Duck as homemade rockets soar into the sky at the ❸ **Yasothon Rocket Festival** (p352) in northeast Thailand.

Release bad karma in a lantern and welcome a brighter future during Chiang Mai's ❹ **Yi Peng Festival** (p251).

Wake the dead at ❺ **Pee Ta Khon** (p331), an Isan festival where revellers dress like the spirits they hope to rouse.

FESTIVAL FUN

Festivals are when Thais come out to play. Almost all non-religious festivals involve a lot of partying and eating, so joining in is a great way to get to know the locals. The biggest festivals are the nationwide Buddhist holidays, but there are many quirky local ones that celebrate everything from fruit to ghosts.

Songkran

The Thai New Year (13 to 15 April), known as Songkran, starts with locals washing Buddha images, before descending into a three-day water war.

Loy Krathong

This charming and highly photogenic festival takes place every November and sees Thais praying for forgiveness by setting lanterns afloat on waterways across the country.

DREAM DIVING

Thailand is an excellent place for underwater adventures, whether you're a newbie scuba diver or a veteran. The water is crystal-clear and bathtub-warm, while the sea is packed with marine life, including whale sharks and manta rays. Ko Tao, Phuket and Ko Chang are key diving hubs, but dive operators are scattered across the islands and on some parts of the mainland. Snorkellers, too, will find plenty of colourful reefs to explore just offshore.

FROM LEFT: MATYAS REHAK/SHUTTERSTOCK, JOHN BACK/SHUTTERSTOCK, SUMMER PARADIVE/SHUTTERSTOCK

Learn to Dive

Ko Tao is Thailand and Southeast Asia's scuba-diving school (p480), with more than 50 dive operators ready to get you qualified in just under four days.

When to Dive

Ko Tao can be dived virtually year-round, with brilliant visibility in July and August. November to April is diving season on the Andaman Coast.

Where to Dive

Try the Surin or Similan Islands on the Andaman Coast, or Ko Tao, Ko Chang and Ko Pha-Ngan in the Gulf of Thailand.

HTMS *Chang* wreck (p371)

BEST DIVING EXPERIENCES

See manta rays, whale sharks and turtles off the ❶ **Surin Islands** (p548), one of Southeast Asia's top diving spots.

Dive with whale sharks at ❷ **Sail Rock** (p476) off Ko Tao, the Gulf of Thailand's premier dive site.

Snorkel the beautiful reefs off the southern coast of ❸ **Ko Lipe** (p582) and the nearby islets.

Explore the wreck of ❹ **HTMS *Chang*** (p371) and its artificial reef 30m below the surface off Ko Chang.

Try freediving off the north coast of ❺ **Ko Pha-Ngan** (p476) and learn how to dive to 20m without any equipment.

OUTDOOR ADVENTURES

Whether it's trekking, kayaking, white-water rafting, ziplining, rock climbing, surfing or kiteboarding, Thailand has it covered. This is a great country for thrill-seekers or anybody who likes to be active outside. Northern Thailand's mountains offer splendid hiking routes, while the islands are the place for most water sports and the best rock climbing. If you're a newbie to any of the above, there are plenty of operators waiting to show you how it's done.

FROM LEFT: LAKKANA SAVAKSURIYAWONG/SHUTTERSTOCK, GUITAR PHOTOGRAPHER/SHUTTERSTOCK, RAWF8/SHUTTERSTOCK

Rainy Season Blues

Hiking in the rainy season (June to October) is no fun, but it is prime time for rafting. Check to make sure the weather doesn't affect your activity.

Sustainable Trekking

For hikes to ethnic-minority villages, pick operators who promote sustainability and responsible tourism. Reputable ones are all involved in the communities they visit.

Motorbike Touring

Northern Thailand has some very dramatic roads to drive by motorbike. Try the legendary Mae Hong Son Loop.

Railay (p560), Krabi

BEST OUTDOOR EXPERIENCES

Hike through the hills to isolated ethnic-minority villages around ❶ **Mae Hong Son** (p184) in far northern Thailand.

Launch yourself down the world's longest zipline roller-coaster at ❷ **Jungle Flight** (p284) in Chiang Mai Province.

Climb up or abseil down the limestone formations that rise out of the sparkling sea at ❸ **Railay** (p560).

Raft the rapids of Mae Nam Pai outside ❹ **Pai** (p196) or kayak down the river.

Learn to surf on the gentle waves of ❺ **Hat Kata** (p512) in Phuket, perfect for beginners and kids.

NATURAL WONDERS

Thailand is home to 156 national parks, as well as wildlife sanctuaries and forest parks, covering almost 31% of the country's territory. They're by far the best places in the kingdom for wildlife spotting, with elephants and rarely seen tigers roaming some of them. They're also home to unique flora, waterfalls, caves and lots of lush tropical jungle. Plunge into them for a taste of the natural splendours on offer in Thailand.

National Park Accommodation

Most national parks offer basic bungalows and campsites, where tents can be hired. Some parks also have a simple restaurant.

Marine National Parks

Some of the most beautiful national parks are offshore: there are 22 marine national parks in Thailand, mostly made up of ocean and uninhabited islands.

E-Ticketing

Book national-park tickets in advance with the QueQ app. You can also book park accommodation in advance via the national-park website.

FROM LEFT: ANAKE SEENADEE/SHUTTERSTOCK, YANA YERMAK/SHUTTERSTOCK, PORNPRASIT PANADA/SHUTTERSTOCK

Nam Tok Haew Suwat (p316), Khao Yai National Park

BEST NATIONAL PARK EXPERIENCES

Trek into the jungle at ❶ **Khao Yai National Park** (p314), where wild elephants, gibbons, deer, bears and waterfalls await.

Make the legendary hike to the heart-shaped summit plateau at ❷ **Phu Kradueng National Park** (p329) in Isan for sky-spanning views and awesome star-gazing.

Dive into ❸ **Kaeng Krachan National Park** (p418) outside Phetchaburi, Thailand's largest national park and one of Southeast Asia's best-preserved wildlife habitats.

Kayak or raft through the canyons at ❹ **Op Luang National Park** (p195) in Chiang Mai Province, where there are also waterfalls.

Come to ❺ **Similan Islands Marine National Park** (p547) for super snorkelling, dreamy white-sand beaches and tons of marine life.

SUCCULENT STREET FOOD

There's no better country for street food than Thailand. Not only are the flavours mind-blowing and the prices super-cheap, but food stalls can be found everywhere and are open from early morning till late at night. Every region has its own unique take on street eats, so follow the example of the locals and get eating.

BEST STREET-FOOD EXPERIENCES

Make tracks for Bangkok's ❶ **Chinatown** (p83), a smorgasbord of dumplings, noodles, curry and seafood.

Chomp your way through the vast array of eats at ❷ **Seven Save One Night Market** (p306) in Nakhon Ratchasima (Korat), the northeast's biggest night market.

Be introduced to Shan cuisine and other ethnic-minority food at Mae Hong Son's ❸ **Walking Street Market** (p186).

Check out southern Thai flavours at night markets in ❹ **Hat Yai** (p500), a contender for street-food capital of Thailand.

Slurp boat noodles with locals at food stands in ❺ **Ayuthaya** (p140), the historic home of this simple yet fulfilling dish.

FROM LEFT: SUWIT CHANAAIYARAT/SHUTTERSTOCK, IMTOEY/SHUTTERSTOCK

Isan Everywhere

The holy trinity of northeastern (Isan) cuisine – *gai yang* (grilled marinated chicken), *som tam* (spicy papaya salad; pictured) and *kow nee o* (sticky rice) – dominate food stalls across Thailand.

Markets

Thailand's markets are fine places to find quality street food; Thais aren't happy shopping unless they know that their favourite dishes are within easy reach.

Gourmet Street Food

Some street-food places are so good that they have Michelin stars. Expect to queue for the most popular places.

Chatuchak Weekend Market (p126), Bangkok

MARKET MADNESS

Plunging into Thailand's highly atmospheric markets, with buyers and vendors crammed together and all manner of items for sale, is an essential experience. There's a buzz to shopping here – the locals take it seriously – and there are some fantastic bargains to be had, as well as excellent souvenirs to be acquired.

BEST MARKET EXPERIENCES

Buy antiques or meerkats at Bangkok's ❶ **Chatuchak Weekend Market** (p126), the world's largest open-air market.

Join Hua Hin's hipsters at ❷ **Cicada Market** (p427), with artisans selling wares, music and food.

Watch farmers bartering for buffaloes at ❸ **San-Pa-Tong Buffalo Market** (p261) near Chiang Mai.

Pick up local handicrafts and traditional fabrics, including prized local silk, at buzzing ❹ **Ton Tann** in Khon Kaen. (p320)

Hunt for precious stones at Chanthaburi ❺ **Gem Market** (p380), with buyers from all over Asia.

Smile Please

Bargaining is a must at most markets (although food items are an exception). Haggle with a smile on your face for the best results.

Does It Fit?

Most markets don't have changing rooms. If you're lucky, vendors will point you towards the nearest toilets to try on an item of clothing.

REGIONS & CITIES

Find the places that tick all your boxes.

Chiang Mai Province

THE ROSE OF THE NORTH

This is northern Thailand's beating heart, where ancient and modern cultures intertwine and the street food, night markets and Michelin-starred restaurants are a foodie's dream. Beyond Chiang Mai are mountains and mystical temples, as well as ethical elephant sanctuaries where you can get up close with Thailand's national animal.

Northern Thailand

RUGGED MOUNTAINS, CULTURAL WONDERS

The north's jungle-covered mountains are a playground for genuine adventure; home to Thailand's most iconic waterfalls, rushing rivers and mysterious caves. A mosaic of ethnic minorities live here, and treks to their villages reveal Thailand's transnational roots, just as a visit to ancient Sukhothai offers insights into how Thailand the nation emerged.

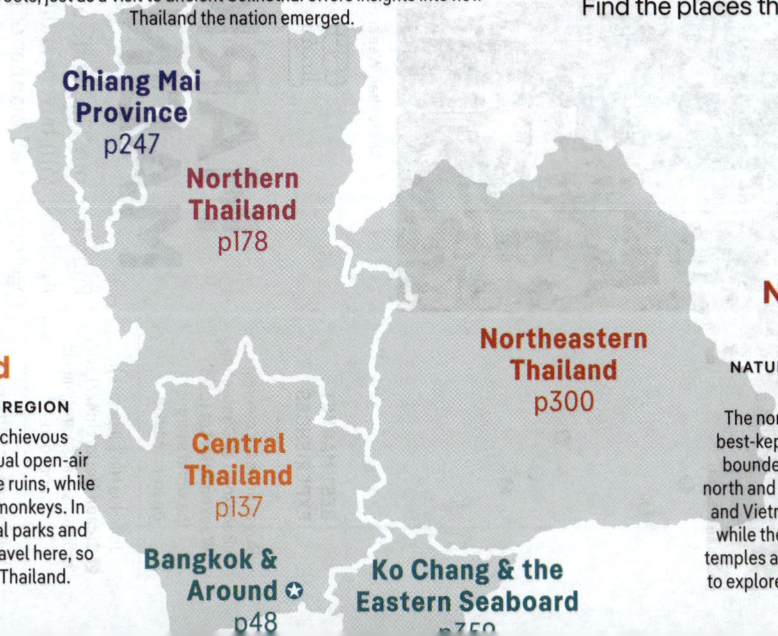

Chiang Mai Province p247

Northern Thailand p178

Northeastern Thailand p300

Central Thailand p137

Bangkok & Around ✪ p48

Ko Chang & the Eastern Seaboard

Central Thailand

THAILAND'S MOST UNDERRATED REGION

Ancient cities, national parks and mischievous monkeys mingle here. Ayuthaya is a virtual open-air museum with dozens of evocative temple ruins, while Lopburi is overrun by sacred macaque monkeys. In contrast, lush Kanchanaburi has national parks and sobering WWII sites. Fewer foreigners travel here, so you can experience a more authentic Thailand.

Northeastern Thailand

NATURE, FOOD, HISTORY AND MEKONG SUNSETS

The northeast, or Isan, is Thailand's best-kept secret, a little-seen frontier bounded by the Mekong River in the north and east. Thai, Laotian, Cambodian and Vietnamese influences blend here, while there are superb national parks, temples and the ruins of ancient empires to explore. You might be the only visitor.

Hua Hin & the Upper Gulf

BEACHES, MOUNTAINS, FORESTS AND CULTURE

Domestic tourists flock here for long, wide beaches, fine seafood restaurants and national parks. Hua Hin is a mix of city sophistication and seaside resort, while Pranburi and Prachuap Khiri Khan have family-friendly beaches. For a different experience, ancient Phetchaburi has temples and royal palaces, and Thailand's largest national park is nearby.

Hua Hin & the Upper Gulf
p411

Bangkok & Around

THAILAND'S EVER-CHANGING CAPITAL

Bangkok wows visitors with a supreme combination of glittering temples, royal palaces, restaurants ranging from high-end to street food, world-class pampering, markets and megamalls. And did we mention the rooftop cocktail bars with panoramic views and a thriving LGBTIQ+ scene? Just beyond Bangkok are riverine islands, canal-side villages and floating markets.

Ko Chang & the Eastern Seaboard

BEAUTIFUL BEACHES AND NATURE NEAR BANGKOK

The eastern seaboard has islands and superb seafood, and offers the chance to immerse yourself in provincial life. Ko Chang tempts with beaches, dense forest and timeless fishing villages. On the mainland, historic Chanthaburi is known for its gems and fruit, or head to atmospheric Trat for a reminder of old Thailand.

Phuket & the Andaman Coast
p506

Ko Samui & the Lower Gulf
p451

Phuket & the Andaman Coast

THAILAND FOR BEACH LOVERS

Phuket is Thailand's largest island, but beyond its superb beaches, flashy resorts and world-class restaurants are other drop-dead gorgeous islands like stunning Ko Lipe, family-friendly Ko Lanta and backpacker favourite Ko Phi-Phi. Travel to the mainland for sleepy provincial towns and national parks packed with wildlife, waterfalls and caves.

Ko Samui & the Lower Gulf

BEACH PARTIES, WELLNESS AND SOUTHERN FLAVOURS

Come here for three spectacular islands. Superstar Ko Samui has gleaming beaches and wellness resorts, Ko Pha-Ngan hosts the world-famous Full Moon parties, and Ko Tao is paradise for scuba divers and rock climbers. In addition, there are pink dolphins and near-empty mainland beaches at Ao Khanom and buzzing night markets in Hat Yai.

ITINERARIES

Bangkok & Around

Allow: 7 days **Distance**: 483km

Explore buzzing Bangkok and then head west to historic Kanchanaburi, famous for its WWII sites, and nearby Erawan National Park, which is packed with waterfalls and wildlife. From there, travel through central Thailand's rice fields to the ancient temples of Ayuthaya, before ending your tour at Khao Yai National Park.

1 BANGKOK 2 DAYS

Hit the major sites in **Bangkok** (p48), including iconic Wat Arun (pictured) and superb Wat Phra Kaew and the Grand Palace, before dinner in Chinatown and a cocktail with a view at a rooftop bar. If it's the weekend, Chatuchak Weekend Market is an essential shopping stop. Alternatively, escape the urban sprawl by cycling around the artificial island of Bang Kachao, Bangkok's 'green lung'. Make sure to fit in a massage to relax you for the journey ahead.

2 KANCHANABURI 1 DAY

Catch the scenic train or take a minivan to **Kanchanaburi** (p150), the site of the infamous Thailand–Burma Death Railway (pictured) and the bridge immortalised in the movie *The Bridge on the River Kwai*. Tour the museums and moving war cemetery here. Consider a rafting excursion on Mae Nam Kwae, or head 30km east to Mallika RE 124, a photogenic recreation of a traditional 19th-century village, before you retire to your riverside resort.

3 ERAWAN NATIONAL PARK 1 DAY

It's a short drive from Kanchanaburi to **Erawan National Park** (p155). Just 500m past the park headquarters is the spectacular, seven-tiered Nam Tok Erawan (pictured), where you can swim in crystal-clear water. It's easy to reach the first three tiers; after that it's a steep 2km climb to the higher ones. The park is home to masses of wildlife and you'll see monkeys around the falls.

4

AYUTHAYA 1 DAY

From Kanchanaburi drive through lime-green rice fields to **Ayuthaya** (p140), the capital of ancient Siam and a UNESCO World Heritage site. Hire a bicycle to tour the dozens of atmospheric ruined temples, stopping at Wat Mahathat, once Siam's most revered temple. Head to the riverside for a delicious lunch of boat noodles or grilled river prawns, both local specialities. For a different angle on Ayuthaya, take a boat tour along the river surrounding the old city.

5

KHAO YAI NATIONAL PARK 2 DAYS

Your final stop is **Khao Yai National Park** (p314), east of Ayuthaya. The park is home to herds of wild elephants, as well as bears, rare birds, barking deer and many gibbons. A night safari is your best chance of spotting elephants, or else overnight in the park to be up early when the pachyderms head to the salt licks. Spend a day hiking to waterfalls, which really gush in the June to October rainy season.

TAKE PHOTO/SHUTTERSTOCK

Wat Phra That Doi Suthep (p266), Chiang Mai

ITINERARIES

Northern Thailand

Allow: 7 days **Distance**: 240km

Loop through the lush mountain scenery of northern Thailand, starting in Chiang Mai, the historic heart of the region, then heading north to the backpacker haven of Pai and the caves of Pang Mapha before ending in Mae Hong Son, a remote hill town that's home to a myriad of minority peoples.

1

CHIANG MAI 2 DAYS

Tour some of the hundreds of old city temples in **Chiang Mai** (p252), as well as the museums. Then eat your way through the night markets (pictured), food stalls and Michelin-starred restaurants. Head to a nearby ethical elephant camp or learn how to prepare northern Thai cuisine at a cooking class. Finish with a night out in the hip bars of Nimmanhaemin Rd.

Detour: *Near Chiang Mai is* ***Doi Inthanon****, Thailand's highest mountain. It's an easy two- to three-hour hike to the summit, or explore the trails, temples, villages and waterfalls.*

2

PAI 2 DAYS

Minivans whisk people northwest to **Pai** (p194), a mountain town with a hippie vibe that has become an essential traveller stop. Pai is the sort of place where you can learn how to be a circus performer, attend any number of yoga classes or find inner peace via vegan baking or pottery classes. If you're after thrills, try rafting the rapids of Mae Nam Pai (go for the tipsy tubing if you're feeling lazy). Alternatively, head to the nearby hot springs and waterfalls or visit villages of ethnic-minority peoples. In the evenings, join everyone else at the eateries and bars along Pai's walking street (pictured).

FROM LEFT: EVGENY ERMAKOV/SHUTTERSTOCK, PLOYPEMUK/SHUTTERSTOCK

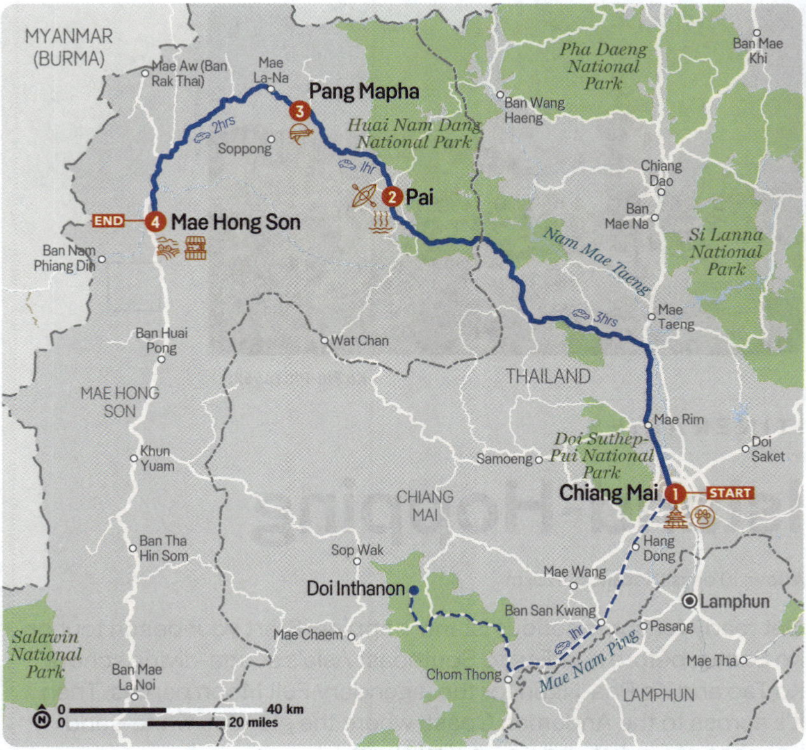

3

PANG MAPHA ⏱1 DAY

Just northwest of Pai is **Pang Mapha** (p191), also known as Sop Pong. This sleepy little district is riddled with limestone formations that are home to over 200 incredibly old cave systems (pictured); prehistoric artefacts have been found in some of them. You can glide through the most-visited cave on a bamboo raft – look out for the ancient teak coffins that perch here – or contact Cave Lodge, where local spelunkers organise in-depth explorations of the caverns, as well as going in search of the caves that are still being discovered here.

4

MAE HONG SON ⏱2 DAYS

Mae Hong Son (p184) is one of Thailand's most fascinating destinations, a crossroads of cultures and ethnicities that feels very different to other Thai towns. Check out Wat Chong Kham, which looks more like the shrines found in nearby Myanmar than any Thai temple, and in the evening head to Walking Street market for a taste of minority cuisines and handicrafts. Treks to outlying minority villages (pictured) are more authentic than the ones offered elsewhere in northern Thailand and offer a fine introduction to the area's cultural complexity. There are rural homestays if you want to really immerse yourself in local life, or try meditation at a forest temple.

BANJONGSEAL324SS/SHUTTERSTOCK, NUWATPHOTO/SHUTTERSTOCK

LAURIN/SHUTTERSTOCK

Ko Phi-Phi (p562)

ITINERARIES

Island-Hopping

Allow: 10 days **Distance**: 423km

Get ready for some serious island-hopping. Start your beach tour on Ko Samui, before heading to Southeast Asia's scuba-diving school Ko Tao and Ko Pha-Ngan for the legendary Full Moon parties. Then it's across to the Andaman Coast, where the glorious white-sand beaches of Phuket and Ko Phi-Phi await.

1 KO SAMUI 2 DAYS

On **Ko Samui** (p456) superb beaches line the east and north coasts, and resorts and spas offer world-class pampering. Tour the beaches by motorbike. Catch a west-coast sunset, or search for waterfalls in the interior. For nightlife, head to Chaweng, Lamai (pictured) and Fisherman's Village.

***Detour:** Take a day tour to **Ang Thong Marine National Park** for sublime seascapes and, with luck, sea turtles while snorkelling.*

2 KO TAO 2 DAYS

Ko Tao (p478) is Thailand's scuba-diving hub; you can dive almost year-round because the water is warm, the marine life plentiful and the coral reefs colourful. It's also a top spot for rock climbing and bouldering. At Jansom Bay, climb before descending to snorkel the crystal-clear water. There's a pumping bar scene at night on the west coast; the less-developed east coast has cute beaches, and peace and quiet.

3 KO PHA-NGAN 1 DAY

Divert to **Ko Pha-Ngan** (p469), a short boat ride from Ko Tao, to join thousands of revellers at the monthly Full Moon parties (pictured) on Hat Sunrise. Even if it's not full moon, there are other raves staged on Pha-Ngan. Away from the party scene, luxuriate at west-coast wellness centres or beach-hop by long-tail boat up the secluded east coast, with gorgeous hidden bays.

FROM LEFT: ALEX TIHONOVS/SHUTTERSTOCK, DIVERDAN/SHUTTERSTOCK, PARKPOOM KOTCHARAT/SHUTTERSTOCK

0 50 km
0 25 miles
MYANMAR (BURMA)
Namtok Ngao National Park
Lang Suan
Ranong
CHUMPHON
Pha To
Kapoe
RANONG
Chaiya
SURAT THANI
Surat Thani
Ao Ban Don
Don Sak
Khanom
Ao Khanom
Sichon
Khuraburi
PHANG-NGA
Chiaw Lan Lake
Khao Sok National Park
THAILAND
Khian Sa
Takua Pa
Khao Lak/ Lam Ru National Park
Thap Lamu
Adaman Sea
Phang-Nga
Plaiphaya
4½hrs
Khao Luang National Park
Khao Luang
Khiriwong
Nakhon Si Thammarat
Lan Saka
Gulf of Thailand
Ban Khok Kloi
Ao Phang-Nga
KRABI
Thung Song
NAKHON SI THAMMARAT
Hua Sai
Ao Nang
Krabi
Phuket Sea
Ao Nang
Klong Thom
4 Phuket
Patong
Phuket Town
1-2hrs
END
5 Ko Phi-Phi
TRANG
PHATTHALUNG
SONGKHLA
Phatthalung
2 Ko Tao
1hr
1½hrs
3 Ko Pha-Ngan
Ang Thong Marine National Park
2hrs
1½hrs
1 Ko Samui
START

4

PHUKET 3 DAYS

Head back to the mainland for the bus ride to **Phuket** (p512), Thailand's largest and most glamorous island, where the beaches are alluring crescents of white sand and the restaurants and nightlife range from sophisticated to raucous. Explore historic Phuket Town, kayak around the stunning limestone formations of Ao Phang-Nga, or hop a speedboat for superb snorkelling in the Similan Islands.

5

KO PHI-PHI 2 DAYS

End your island-hopping by catching the ferry to **Ko Phi-Phi** (p562), a tiny, jungle-topped island with curvy bleached beaches. It has a splendid viewpoint to hike to, decent diving and snorkelling, as well as uninhabited Ko Phi-Phi Leh to visit by long-tail boat, where *The Beach* was filmed. At night Ao Lo Dalam turns into a vast, open-air nightclub. For a more relaxed experience, try the tranquil east coast.

PABOUV/SHUTTERSTOCK, ALEXANDRE.ROSA/SHUTTERSTOCK

PHILIPYB STUDIO/SHUTTERSTOCK

Mekong River, Nong Khai (p338)

ITINERARIES

Mekong River & Northeast

Allow: 7 days **Distance**: 970km

Follow the mighty Mekong on a tour of the little-seen northeast (Isan). Begin in charming Chiang Khan before heading east on Hwy 211 to Nong Khai, separated from Laos by the Mekong. Move south to Vietnamese-influenced Nakhon Phanom and holy That Phanom, then west to bustling Ubon Ratchathani and historic Phanom Rung.

1

CHIANG KHAN 1 DAY

Start in delightful **Chiang Khan** (p326), a Mekong-side town of traditional wooden houses in the far north of Loei Province. The sunsets are superb here, but check out the nearby Chiang Khan Skywalk for horizon-spanning daytime views of the Mekong and Laos. The nightly market sprawls down Chiang Khan's walking street and offers food and handicrafts stalls, as well as artists and musicians.

2

NONG KHAI 1 DAY

Nong Khai (p338), a border town that sits opposite Laos on the banks of the Mekong, is a longtime traveller hangout and there are super sunset views from the laid-back cafes and restaurants along the river. October sees tens of thousands of locals gathering to watch the mysterious Naga Fireballs, when balls of flame shoot up in the sky above the Mekong.

3

NAKHON PHANOM 1 DAY

Bicycle-friendly **Nakhon Phanom** (p340) is a riverfront town with striking views across the Mekong to central Laos. It's also home to a vibrant Vietnamese community; Ho Chi Minh spent two years living here. Cycle the promenade along the Mekong (pictured) and visit Ho's former home. The weekend night market has Thai and Vietnamese choices and is among the best in Isan.

FROM LEFT: CHAIKOM/SHUTTERSTOCK, AMNAT30/SHUTTERSTOCK, PHICHET CHAIYABIN/SHUTTERSTOCK

4 THAT PHANOM ⏱1 DAY

Continue to peaceful **That Phanom** (p344). Devout Buddhists make the pilgrimage to Wat Phra That Phanom (pictured), Isan's holiest temple, to pray to the Buddha relics believed to be enshrined within the 53m-high stupa here. There's also a fun market by the Mekong.

Detour: *Head southwest to* ***Yasothon*** *to spend a day at the riotous Rocket Festival, held in May or June.*

5 UBON RATCHATHANI ⏱2 DAYS

West of the Mekong is **Ubon Ratchathani** (p347), a university city with a small-town vibe. Kick back in Ubon for a few days; there's a Thai country music scene, good restaurants and lively bars, and a few riverside beaches to laze on. Beyond Ubon is the excellent and little-visited Pha Taem National Park (pictured), home to some of Isan's most stunning waterfalls.

6 PHANOM RUNG ⏱1 DAY

Perched atop an extinct volcano, **Phanom Rung** (p318) is the most impressive Khmer temple complex in Thailand. The temple was built between the 10th and 13th centuries to honour the Hindu god Shiva and the setting is awesome, with views over the surrounding rice fields and Cambodia's Dangrek Mountains visible in the far distance. Best of all, the ruins are usually crowd-free.

SUN IMAGE/SHUTTERSTOCK, I VIEWFINDER/SHUTTERSTOCK, MRMICHAELANGELO/SHUTTERSTOCK

ITINERARIES

Temples, Beaches & National Parks

Allow: 7 days **Distance**: 224km

Take in one of Thailand's most culturally significant towns, go wildlife spotting and kick back by the beach on this tour of the upper gulf. Start in historic Phetchaburi and then swoop into Kaeng Krachan National Park. After that, head to the beaches of Hua Hin and end in pretty Prachuap Khiri Khan.

1 PHETCHABURI 2 DAYS

Phetchaburi (p414) should be on every traveller's list: a traditional town of riverside markets and teak houses that's also home to royal palaces, temples and caves. Life moves at a slower pace here, so go with the flow and spend a couple of leisurely days visiting the temples and the former summer palace atop the hill at Phra Nakhon Khiri Historical Park (pictured). Foodies can take tours exploring Phetchaburi's unique culinary heritage, including the aromatic fruit and sweet desserts the town is known for. Just watch out for the brazen monkeys that live here.

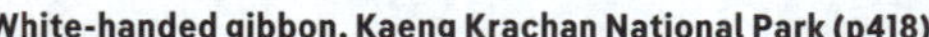

White-handed gibbon, Kaeng Krachan National Park (p418)

2 KAENG KRACHAN NATIONAL PARK 1 DAY

Spend a day at UNESCO World Heritage site **Kaeng Krachan National Park** (p418), Thailand's largest wildlife wilderness. There's a ton of flora and fauna, including elephants, gibbons and masses of rare birds and butterflies. The highlight for many visitors is the hike to 11-tiered Nam Tok Pala-U, one of Thailand's most photogenic waterfalls with a pool at the bottom that's fine for swimming. But you could also walk the nature trails or take a boat ride on the reservoir here. You can stay in park accommodation or hire a tent to camp, but day trips from Hua Hin are perfectly possible.

3 HUA HIN 2 DAYS

Thailand's original beach resort, **Hua Hin** (p421) has been pulling in the locals since the 1920s, including the royal family. Visitors continue to flock here for the wide, long and safe beaches (pictured) and quality seafood eateries. Hua Hin is a fun mix of big-city sophistication (great markets and malls) and old-fashioned seaside fun (donkey rides on the beach). It's especially good for families, as there are tons of activities to keep kids of all ages busy: everything from extravagant water parks to bike tours. This is also Thailand's best spot for kiteboarding and golf courses.

4 PRACHUAP KHIRI KHAN 2 DAYS

Pretty **Prachuap Khiri Khan** (p434) is delightfully relaxed, with crowd-free white-sand beaches looking out on tranquil bays and limestone karst formations reminiscent of those found on the Andaman Coast. Climb the hill at the north of town for tremendous views out to sea or inland to the mountains on the Myanmar border. Prachuap has old wooden shophouses too and some great seafood restaurants, while national parks and picturesque coastal villages are close by.

Detour: *Spend a day exploring **Kuiburi National Park**, which offers perhaps the best opportunities in all Thailand for spotting wild elephants.*

WHEN TO GO

Thailand is a year-round destination. You're guaranteed sunshine even during the rainy season, although the monsoon does restrict some activities.

Thailand's high season corresponds to the November to February cool season, when the landscape is lush and temperatures are comfortable. Christmas and the Western New Year holiday are the busiest time of year. April and May are the hottest months of the year and can be a trial if you're not used to tropical heat, although sea breezes provide some respite on the islands.

The June to October rainy season normally sees short, intense bursts of precipitation. Some hotels shut down on the islands, and there are fewer ferries and rougher seas, but much of the country gets only intermittent showers. If you're prepared to put up with some rain, the rainy season is a great time to visit because of the lack of crowds.

Accommodation Lowdown

Hotel prices drop dramatically on the islands during the June to October rainy season. There are also bargains elsewhere at this time of year. Prices are highest from November to March.

I LIVE HERE

BANGKOK FLOODS

Raenuka Fangtong is a Bangkok native who works in corporate affairs

Floods are part of life in Bangkok, like the traffic jams. We always expect flooding in the rainy season, but the 2011 floods were so severe I think people wondered what will happen in the future. It was especially bad for people who live in houses; they were piling up sandbags outside their doorways. Most Bangkok people expect another big flood will happen before long. I think it'll be worse than 2011.

FROM LEFT: CINDHYADE/SHUTTERSTOCK, RUSLANKPHOTO/SHUTTERSTOCK

Rainy season, Bangkok (p48)

HEATING UP

Thailand is getting hotter. On 28 April 2024, Sakhon Nakhon Province experienced 47.7°C, the highest-ever temperature recorded in the kingdom. But the country has also become more prone to floods, with serious flooding occurring across the country in the last few years.

Weather Through the Year

January	February	March	April	May	June
Avg. daytime max: **28°C**	Avg. daytime max: **29.2°C**	Avg. daytime max: **30.5°C**	Avg. daytime max: **31.5°C**	Avg. daytime max: **31°C**	Avg. daytime max: **30.2°C**
Days of rainfall: **2**	Days of rainfall: **2**	Days of rainfall: **4**	Days of rainfall: **7**	Days of rainfall: **16**	Days of rainfall: **16**

MONSOON SEASON

Thailand's rainy season is dictated by the southwest monsoon, which sweeps out of the Indian Ocean and heads northeast across Thailand from the Andaman Sea. Ranong, on the Andaman Coast, is especially affected and sees more rain than any other province.

Nationwide Festivals

With 15% of the population claiming Chinese ancestry, **Chinese New Year** is widely celebrated. Cities with large Thai-Chinese communities – Bangkok (p48), Chiang Mai (p252), Hat Yai (p500) – are good places to experience it. **January/February**

By far the biggest festival of the year is **Songkran** (p281), the Thai New Year. It's a three-day party that starts out with the washing of Buddha statues at temples, before descending into watery chaos. **April**

Visakha Buscha is the most significant Buddhist festival, commemorating the Buddha's birth, enlightenment and passing. Locals visit temples to make merit, while in the evening there are candlelit processions. **May/June**

Charming **Loy Krathong** festival sees Thais praying for forgiveness by launching origami-like boats illuminated by candles into rivers and seas across the country. **November**

I LIVE HERE

BURNING SEASON

Marisa Marchitelli is a Chiang Mai resident and director of *Smoke: A Crisis in Northern Thailand* *(marisafilmsthailand.com)*

After a few years in Chiang Mai I noticed it was hard to breathe during smoky season and that's when I decided to make a film about it. There's more public awareness now and everyone has adjusted their behaviour – they have air purifiers and wear masks – but the problem hasn't changed. March is the worst month; you stay inside if you can. People hibernate in smoky season.

Regional Festivals

No one knows if the **Naga Fireballs** (p339) are a hoax or a genuine phenomenon, but tens of thousands gather in Nong Khai to watch balls of flame shoot into the sky above the Mekong River. **October**

The three-day **Pai Jazz & Blues Festival** (p201) sees Thai and international musicians taking to public stages and makeshift venues across Pai, a bohemian, backpacker hub in northern Thailand. **July**

Phuket Town hosts the **Phuket Vegetarian Festival** (p523; pictured right), nine days of Taoist-inspired spiritual cleansing that involves firewalking, self-mutilation and, of course, abstaining from meat. **October**

Wonderfruit (p397) is Thailand's premier music and arts festival, with performances and cultural events with an emphasis on sustainability and wellness. Think Glastonbury or Coachella, only staged outside Pattaya. **December**

IT CAN GET COLD

It's always cooler in the mountains of northern Thailand, and visitors will need a jacket at night during the November to February cool season. Sakhon Nakhon in northeast Thailand and Doi Inthanon, Thailand's highest mountain, have both occasionally recorded subzero temperatures.

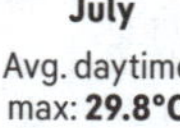

July	August	September	October	November	December
Avg. daytime max: **29.8°C**	Avg. daytime max: **29.6°C**	Avg. daytime max: **29.3°C**	Avg. daytime max: **29°C**	Avg. daytime max: **28.9°C**	Avg. daytime max: **27.7°C**
Days of rainfall: **17**	Days of rainfall: **20**	Days of rainfall: **21**	Days of rainfall: **18**	Days of rainfall: **6**	Days of rainfall: **1**

FROM LEFT: SERGII FIGURNYI/SHUTTERSTOCK, VALERIE MACON/AFP VIA GETTY IMAGES

Longboats, Hat Phra Nang (p561), Krabi

GET PREPARED FOR THAILAND

Useful things to load in your bag, your ears and your brain.

Clothes

Light clothes Light, loose-fitting clothes will be most comfortable in the tropical heat. It's worth bringing one jacket that can double as a raincoat and keep you warm in higher elevations and on air-conditioned buses (or in movie theatres). Bring something smart if you plan on fine dining or clubbing in Bangkok or Phuket. Almost all clothing, including Western brands, is widely available in Thailand and relatively cheap, but finding bigger sizes can be a challenge.

Boots/shoes Flip-flops, known as 'slippers' in Thailand, are standard footwear on and off the beach, but wear shoes or trainers for high-end places or if you're planning on a lot of walking. Bring hiking boots if you're going trekking.

Hats The tropical sun is intense even when there is cloud cover. Wearing a wide-brimmed hat is a good idea.

Manners

Smile Thai culture does not value confrontation. Arguing and raising your voice are frowned upon and regarded as embarrassing.

Monarchy Disrespecting the royal family is a criminal offence. Avoid making disparaging comments about royalty and steer clear of discussions about politics.

Relax Life runs at a different pace in Thailand. So slow down and go with the flow.

READ

A History of Thailand (Chris Baker/Pasuk Phongpaichit; 2009) The best general introduction to the history of Thailand.

Bangkok Wakes to Rain (Pitchaya Sudbanthad; 2019) Acclaimed novel that reveals Bangkok's past and present.

Very Thai: Everyday Popular Culture (Philip Cornwel-Smith; 2005) Decode Thai-ness with the help of this fun, informative guide.

Simple Thai Food: Classic Recipes from the Thai Home Kitchen (Leela Punyaratabandhu; 2014) How to cook Thai classics.

Words

Sa-wat-dee 'Hello.' The speaker ends their sentence with *krap* (for men) or *ka* (for women). Saying *krap* or *ka* is also the common way to answer 'yes' to a question or to show agreement.
Lah gorn 'Goodbye.'
Chai/mai 'Yes/no.'
Kor 'Please.'
Korp kun 'Thank you.' Always say *krap* or *ka* after this.
Kor a-pai 'Excuse me.' The speaker ends with *krap* or *ka*.
Kor toht 'Sorry.' Use *krap* or *ka* after this.
Sa-bai dee mai 'How are you?' Say *'sa-bai dee krap/ka'* – 'I'm feeling good' – as the response.
Kun cheu a-rai 'What's your name?'
Pom/dì-chan cheu 'My name is...' End with *krap* or *ka*.
Kun poot pah-sah ang-grit dai mai 'Do you speak English?'
Pom/dì-chan mai kow jai 'I don't understand.' End with *krap* or *ka*.
Yòo tee nai 'Where's...?'
Lee·o sai/kwah 'Turn left/right.'
Tee yoo keu a-rai 'What's the address?'
Kee·an long hai dai mai 'Could you please write it down?'
Hai doo (nai paan tee) dai mai 'Can you show me (on the map)?'
Mee horng mai 'Do you have a room?'
Yahk ja seu 'I'd like to buy...'
Yahk ja chow rot mor-đeu-sai 'I'd like to hire a motorbike.'
Tow-rai 'How much is it?'
Paang bai 'That's too expensive.'
Lot rah-kah dai mai 'Can you lower the price?'
Pom/di-chan mai gin 'I don't eat...' End with *krap* or *ka*.

WATCH

The Rescue (Elizabeth Chai Vasarhelyi/Jimmy Chin, pictured; 2021) Documentary about a football team trapped in a Thai cave.

How to Make Millions Before Grandma Dies (Pat Boonnitipat; 2024) Comedy about a scheming grandson.

Uncle Boonmee Who Can Recall His Past Lives (Apichatpong Weerasethakul; 2010) Cannes winner about ghosts that haunt us.

Last Life in the Universe (Pen-Ek Ratanaruang; 2003) Tale of love and violence in Bangkok.

Pee Mak (Banjong Pisanthanakun; 2013) Hugely successful romantic comedy/horror mash-up.

LISTEN

The Sound of Siam: Luk Thung, Jazz & Molam in Thailand 1964–75 (compilation; 2010) Great introduction to Thai country/folk music.

Thailand's Most Wanted (Thaitanium; 2005) Thaitanium are the original gangsters of Thailand's booming hip-hop scene.

Made in Thailand (Carabao; 1984) Thailand's longest-running and best-loved rock band fuses socially conscious lyrics and Western sounds.

Cyantist (Atom Chanakan; 2017) Singer-songwriter who has turned out a string of sweet pop hits.

CHABEE.INTANAI/SHUTTERSTOCK

Seafood *dom yam*

THE FOOD SCENE

Food is a massive part of Thai identity and the locals are immensely proud of their fiery and flavourful cuisine.

Thailand has it all when it comes to food: incendiary curries, super seafood, endless rice and noodle dishes, fusion specialities that blend local tastes with those of neighbouring countries, and tropical fruit so luscious that some towns hold festivals in its honour. This bounty is available to everyone, everywhere. You don't have to walk far in Thailand to find a food stall or simple restaurant offering delicious eats at bargain prices.

Unsurprisingly, Thais spend much of their time eating or thinking about the next meal. Food is central to family and social life and no gathering is complete without an array of food to nibble on. Sharing a meal with the locals is one of the best ways to get to know them.

To experience the full gastronomic glory of Thailand, familiarise yourself with the dishes of its various regions and ethnic groups. But wherever you are in the country, you'll find the classic dishes that define Thai cuisine. We hope you're ready to eat.

Curries & Soup

Gaang is often translated as 'curry', but it actually describes any dish with lots of liquid and can thus refer to soups, as well as the classic chilli-paste-based curries for which Thai cuisine is famous. Typical ingredients used to create that fiery paste include chilli, galangal, lemongrass, kaffir-lime zest, shallots, garlic, shrimp paste and salt, all mashed and pounded together.

Best Thai Dishes

LARB
A northeastern classic: spicy and seasoned minced pork or chicken salad.

GGANG KEE O WAHN
Known outside Thailand as green curry; features a coconut-milk base.

SOM TAM
Spicy papaya salad. A northeastern favourite now eaten everywhere.

Also falling into the soupy category is *dom yam*, the famous Thai spicy-and-sour soup. Fuelling the fire beneath *dom yam*'s often velvety surface are fresh *prik kee noo* (tiny chillies) or, alternatively, half a teaspoonful of *nam prik pow* (roasted chilli paste). Lemongrass, kaffir-lime leaves and lime juice give *dom yam* its characteristic tang.

Salads

Standing alongside curries in terms of Thai-ness is the ubiquitous *yam*, a hot and tangy 'salad' based around seafood, meat or vegetables. Lime juice provides the tang, while abundant chilli generates the heat. Most *yam* are served at room temperature, or just slightly warmed by any cooked ingredients. The dish functions well as part of a meal or on its own as *gap glaam*: snack food to accompany a night of boozing.

Rice

To eat in Thailand is to consume rice, and throughout most of the country a meal is not acceptable without this staple. Rice is so central to Thai food culture that the most common term for 'eat' is *gin kow* (literally, 'eat rice') and one of the most common greetings is *gin kow reu yang*? (Have you eaten rice yet?)

Kow mok

FROM LEFT: PPKPL/SHUTTERSTOCK, ANIRUT THAILAND/SHUTTERSTOCK

Rice is a vital part of the economy, too. Thailand has the fifth-largest amount of land dedicated to rice production in the world and is the third-biggest exporter of rice globally, while rice farmers make up over two-thirds of the people who work in agriculture. The northeast and central Thailand are the main rice-growing areas, with jasmine rice cultivated in the northeast and white rice in central Thailand.

Durian

TROPICAL FRUIT

Thailand excels in the fruit department. Mangoes *(ma moo ang)* alone come in a dozen varieties that are eaten at different stages of ripeness. Other common fruit include pineapple *(sapparot)*, papaya *(ma la gor)* and watermelon *(daang moh)*, all of which are sold from ubiquitous vendor carts and accompanied by a dipping mix of salt, sugar and ground chilli.

Other delicious fruit includes lychee *(lin jee)*; longan *(lam yai)*, which resembles a mini-lychee; fragrant mangosteen *(mang kut)*, the queen of Thai fruit; pomelo *(soom oh)*, which is like a grapefruit on steroids; and rambutan *(ngo)*, a hairy shell containing sweet translucent flesh. But the most notorious fruit of all is the durian *(tuu ree an)*, thanks to its intense flavour and pungent odour, which can suggest everything from custard to onions.

DOM YAM
Sour and spicy soup of vegetables, fish, seafood or meat.

KHAO SOI
This northern Thai dish is a rich curry noodle soup.

KOW MOK
Thai version of biryani: golden rice and chicken with a sweet-and-sour dip.

BA MEE
Wheat-and-egg noodles served with roast pork and/or crab. A food-stall staple.

PAT TAI
Fried rice noodles with egg, tofu and shrimp (or meat), often called *pad Thai*.

Pat tai

Sticky, or glutinous, rice is also grown in northern and northeast Thailand.

Fusion Cuisine

Many Thai dishes have been influenced by the cuisines of neighbouring and nearby countries. The iconic *som tam* and *lahp* salads and *khao soi* noodle soup have their origins in Laos and Myanmar, respectively, but there's also a strong Cambodian flavour to Thai food, with both countries sharing a love of sour fish soups and curries featuring coconut milk. Some staples of Vietnamese cooking have also been adapted to Thai tastes, such as *khao ji*, the Thai take on the banh mi sandwich, while it's been claimed that *pat tai* has its roots in Vietnamese noodle dishes

But it's China and India that have had the most impact on Thai food. Chinese immigrants introduced the wok to Thailand and many classic food-stall dishes are a fusion of Thai and Chinese cooking. These include *kow kah moo*, a braised pork leg and rice; and *kow man gai*, a chicken and rice dish that migrated to Thailand from the Chinese island of Hainan.

Indian-influenced dishes include the rich and mild curry *gaang mat sa man*, the grilled skewers of meat served with a peanut-based dipping sauce known as *sade* (or satay) and *ma da ba roh dee*, the Thai version of roti, served with a savoury or sweet filling.

Stir-Fries & Deep-Fries

Pat (stir-fries) were introduced to Thailand by the Chinese, and many cling to their Chinese roots, such as the ubiquitous *pat pak bung fai daang* (morning glory flash-fried with garlic and chilli).

Tort (deep-frying in oil) is mainly reserved for snacks such as *gloo ay tort* (deep-fried bananas) or *po pia* (egg rolls). Exceptions are *gai tort* (deep-fried chicken), found everywhere, and *pla tort* (deep-fried fish).

Nam Prik

More home than restaurant food, *nam prik* are spicy chilli-based dips. Typically eaten with rice, vegetables and herbs, they're also among the most regional of Thai dishes – you could probably pinpoint the province you're in simply by looking at the *nam prik* on offer.

VEGETARIANS & VEGANS

Visitors will find vegetarian and vegan eateries in cities and major tourist destinations. Buddhist charitable groups across the kingdom also operate vegetarian eateries, which are normally very cheap, while the annual Vegetarian Festivals held in October (Phuket stages the biggest celebration) see people abstaining from meat and other animal products for nine days.

But vegetarianism is still a minority taste in Thailand. Around 15% of Thais identified as vegetarian in 2025, although their numbers have increased dramatically in recent years. Most restaurants will offer a few vegetarian dishes (although there's no guarantee that they haven't been cooked in the same wok as meat). The phrase 'I'm vegetarian' in Thai is *pom gin jair* (for men) or *di chan gin jair* (for women). Loosely translated this means 'I eat only vegetarian food', which includes no eggs and no dairy products – in other words, total vegan.

Specialities

Insect Eats

Normally served with soy sauce and pepper.

Bamboo worms *(rot doo an)* Excellent beer snack; good introduction to bug dining.

Silkworms *(nhon mai)* Soft and mushy; normally fried with kaffir-lime leaves.

Grasshoppers *(tak ka tan)* Good and crunchy; remove wings and legs before consuming.

Crickets *(jing reed)* Soft centre; remove legs before eating.

Red ant eggs *(kai mot daeng)* White in colour with a sour, lemony flavour. Often used in salads and omelettes.

Noodle Dishes

Noodles *(goo ay)* can be served in a soup or dry and fried.

Goo ay dee o look chin Common dish: rice noodles in clear broth with pork or fish balls. Choose your noodles, from *sen lek* (thin) to *sen yai* (wide).

Pat see ew Wide rice noodles fried with pork or chicken and greens.

Goo ay dee o kaang Thai-Muslim rice noodles with a curry broth, often garnished with tofu, hard-boiled egg and peanuts.

SAWARIN PAKDEEPHON/SHUTTERSTOCK

Kow dom mat

Ka nom jeen Combines thin rice threads and a mild, curry-like broth. Served with fresh veggies.

Sweet Treats

Generally for breakfast or a snack.

Korng wahn Literally 'sweet things' such as grated coconut, coconut milk, rice flour, cooked sticky rice, tapioca, mung-bean starch, boiled taro and fruit.

Ka nom Like European pastries. The most popular are bite-sized *kow dom ga ti* and *kow dom mat* – sticky rice grains steamed with *ga ti* (coconut milk) and wrapped in banana leaf.

Kow nee o ma moo ang Best-known Thai dessert: mango with sweet sticky rice.

MEALS OF A LIFETIME

Samrub Samrub Thai (p96) Fine dining at a Bangkok restaurant where the menu ranges across Thailand's regions.

Samuay & Sons (p334) Udon Thani eatery offering northeastern fusion flavours with local ingredients.

Blackitch Artisan Kitchen (p274) The seasonally themed menu at this Chiang Mai spot features rare ingredients.

Mae Luang Phen (p191) Northern Thailand's greatest BBQ shack is by the side of the road in Mae Sariang.

Hidden Hut Cafe & Eatery (p565) Top Thai food at this atmospheric place close to Ko Lanta's old town.

Aunt Miau Curry Rice (p484) Unassuming Ko Tao restaurant that's a local fave for its fiery southern Thai dishes.

THE YEAR IN FOOD

MARCH

As the weather heats up, Thais turn to cooling dishes like *kow chae* (pictured): moist chilled rice served with sides of fresh veg and deep-fried fish balls. Try it in Phetchaburi, where the dish originated.

APRIL

This is the prime time of year for fruit. In April, mangoes, mangosteen, lychees (pictured), rambutan, papaya and durian are bursting with juice and flavour.

AUGUST

Thailand is blessed with a multitude of mushrooms *(het)*, used in salads, soups and stir-fries. They burst out of the ground in rainy season. Head to north and northeast Thailand to find the tastiest.

DECEMBER

Tamarind is a vital ingredient in Thai cooking, popping up in everything from *dom yam* to *pat tai*, as well as in chilli pastes. Tamarinds can be either sweet or sour and this is the best month for them.

TOP LEFT: FOOD IS LOVE/SHUTTERSTOCK; ABOVE FROM LEFT: AKACHAI STUDIO/SHUTTERSTOCK, PADA SMITH STOCKPHOTO/SHUTTERSTOCK, WARANON8327/SHUTTERSTOCK, RUBEN PH/SHUTTERSTOCK

FROM LEFT: KOSOL PHUNJUI/SHUTTERSTOCK, TEERASAK KHUNRACH/SHUTTERSTOCK

Kayaking, Ang Thong Marine National Park (p467)

THE OUTDOORS

Thailand is a magnificent place for outdoor adventures, whether it's hiking the mountains of the north, rafting through canyons or cycling the plains.

Thailand is so associated with dreamy beaches that it's easy to forget just how dramatic its other landscapes are, and how well they lend themselves to everything from biking to white-water rafting. There are dramatic mountains riddled with rivers and caves in the north, thick jungle teeming with wildlife to the west, while almost one-third of the country is now made up of national parks and protected areas, so it's never been easier to access all that beauty.

Cycling

Thailand's road network is the most developed in Southeast Asia, making cycling a great option for exploring the country in a sustainable way. An ever-increasing number of locals are biking these days, so there are plenty of bicycle rentals and bike shops, as well as many bicycle-tour operators. And if you get tired of cycling, buses, trains and planes will transport bikes for a small fee.

The ancient and flat cities of Ayuthaya and Sukhothai are perfect for exploration by bike, as are Chiang Mai and Chiang Rai and the riverine islands of Bang Kachao and Ko Kret close to Bangkok. Some islands and coastal areas, such as Ko Tarutao and Hua Hin, have cycling paths. Serious mountain bikers should head to Chiang Mai Province for trails galore. Early morning is often the best time to take

More Outdoor Fun

BIRDWATCHING
Thailand is a twitcher's paradise. **Kaeng Krachan National Park** (p418) near Phetchaburi is the top spot.

GOLF
There's crazy golf at **Pai Bamboo Mini Golf** (p198) or head to the **Royal Hua Hin Golf Course** (p424) for a serious round.

KAYAKING
Explore the bays and offshore islands of **Ko Lipe** (p582) or paddle karst formations at **Ao Phang-Nga National Park** (p541).

FAMILY ADVENTURES

Take to water slides and ziplines at **Grand Canyon Water Park** (p285) just north of Chiang Mai, where there are loads of lifeguards.

Spend a day observing and walking with the elephants at **Chai Lai Orchid** (p594) outside Chiang Mai.

Kayak the gentle waters of **Ang Thong Marine National Park** (p467) before monkey spotting on the islands.

Glide above the jungle on the ziplines at **Thai'd Up Adventures** (p554) outside Krabi town; suitable for kids over 100cm tall.

Bike around Bangkok's green lung, **Bang Kachao** (p131), exploring the gardens and looking out for giant lizards.

Make the family-friendly hike to **Nam Tok Khlong Plu** (p371) on Ko Chang, a waterfall with a pool for swimming.

to the roads, when the traffic is light and it's not too hot.

Rafting

Hiking through the jungle and mountains during the rainy season (June to October) can be a challenge, but it's the best time of year to take to the rushing rivers of northern Thailand. White-water rafting is a serious adrenaline blast and there are many places to experience it, whether you're a rookie or a veteran rafter.

Mountain town Pai is one of few places where you can raft year-round on rapids that vary from class I to class IV. Alternatively, make for Nan, northern Thailand's least-visited province, where Mae Nam Nan Wa offers the most exciting and challenging white-water rafting anywhere in the country. If you're in southern Thailand, it's also possible to raft rapids in Krabi and Phang-Nga.

Bang Kachao (p131)

Trekking

Thailand has some of the best trekking in Southeast Asia. Not only is the scenery spectacular, but there are also plenty of ethical trekking companies to make sure you don't get lost in the mountains. Chiang Mai is the jumping-off point for hikes to Doi Inthanon, Thailand's highest peak, where there are numerous trails to follow, and the little-visited hills of Chiang Dao.

Further north, Mae Hong Son and Chiang Rai are the start line for treks into steep, forest-covered mountains that are home to remote ethnic-minority villages, rivers and waterfalls. Make sure you organise your trek with an operator who is involved with the communities you'll be visiting.

If you don't have the time or energy for a multiday trek, head to one of Thailand's 156 national parks, which offer relatively easy nature trails to ramble along. There are also good hiking opportunities on the larger islands, Ko Chang and Phuket in particular.

KITEBOARDING
Hua Hin (p421) on the mainland or **Ko Samui** (p456), **Ko Pha-Ngan** (p469) and **Phuket** (p514) are the places with favourable winds.

ROCK CLIMBING
Get involved in Thailand's booming rock-climbing scene at **Railay** (p561) or **Ko Tao** (p478).

SURFING
There's modest surf on the Andaman Coast. **Hat Kata** (p512) on Phuket is Thailand's surf central.

ZIPLINING
Soar through the air at **Pong Yaeng Jungle Coaster & Zipline** (p291) outside Chiang Mai, where there are numerous ziplines.

ACTION AREAS

Where to find Thailand's best outdoor activities.

Hiking

1. Chiang Rai (p207)
2. Mae Hong Son (p185)
3. Doi Inthanon (p292)
4. Khun Nan National Park (p230)
5. Ko Chang (p364)

Cycling

1. Ko Yao Noi (p530)
2. Chiang Rai (p207)
3. Nakhon Phanom (p340)
4. Bang Kachao (p131)
5. Chiang Mai (p284)

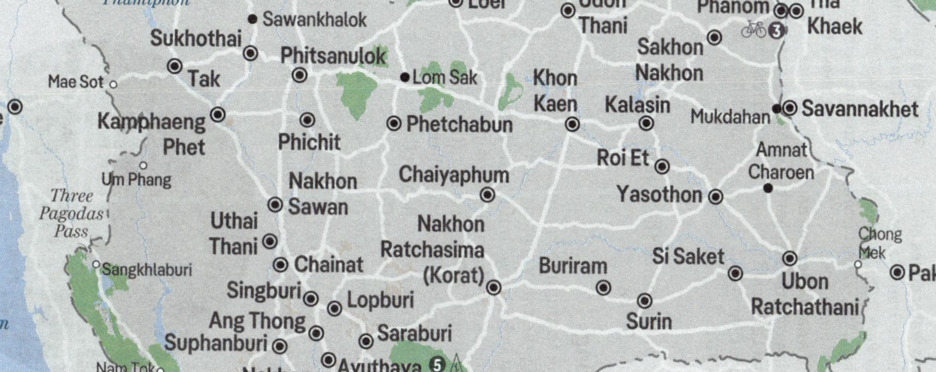

National Parks
1 Kaeng Krachan National Park (p418)
2 Kuiburi National Park (p431)
3 Khao Sok National Park (p511)
4 Surin Islands Marine National Park (p548)
5 Khao Yai National Park (p316)
Kayaking/Rafting
1 Pai (p199)
2 Ao Phang-Nga National Park (p541)
3 Ko Lipe (p582)
4 Ang Thong Marine National Park (p467)
5 Ko Talabeng (p568)
Snorkelling/Diving
1 Ko Tao (p480)
2 Similan Islands Marine National Park (p547)
3 Phuket (p514)
4 Ko Chang (p364)
5 Ko Lipe (p582)
Phetchaburi
Cha-am
Hua Hin
Pattaya
Rayong
Chanthaburi
Ko Samet
Trat
Ko Chang
Ko Kut
Hat Lek
Tonlé Sap
PHNOM PENH
Ho Chi Minh City
VIETNAM
Prachuap Khiri Khan
Thap Sakae
Bang Saphan
Gulf of Thailand
Chumphon
Isthmus of Kra
Ko Tao
Ko Pha-Ngan
Ko Samui
ANDAMAN SEA
Ranong
Surin Islands
Chaiya
Surat Thani
Khao Lak
Similan Islands
Phang-Nga
Nakhon Si Thammarat
Phuket Town
Ko Yao
Krabi
Thung Song
Ko Phi Phi
Trang
Phatthalung
Thaleh Luang
Ko Lanta
Kantang
Songkhla
Hat Yai
Satun
Sadao
Pattani
Ko Tarutao
Ko Lipe
Pulau Langkawi
Yala
Narathiwat
Alor Setar
Sungai Petani
Sungai Kolok
Kota Bharu
Betong
MALAYSIA
SOUTH CHINA SEA
0 200 km
0 100 miles

THAILAND

THE GUIDE

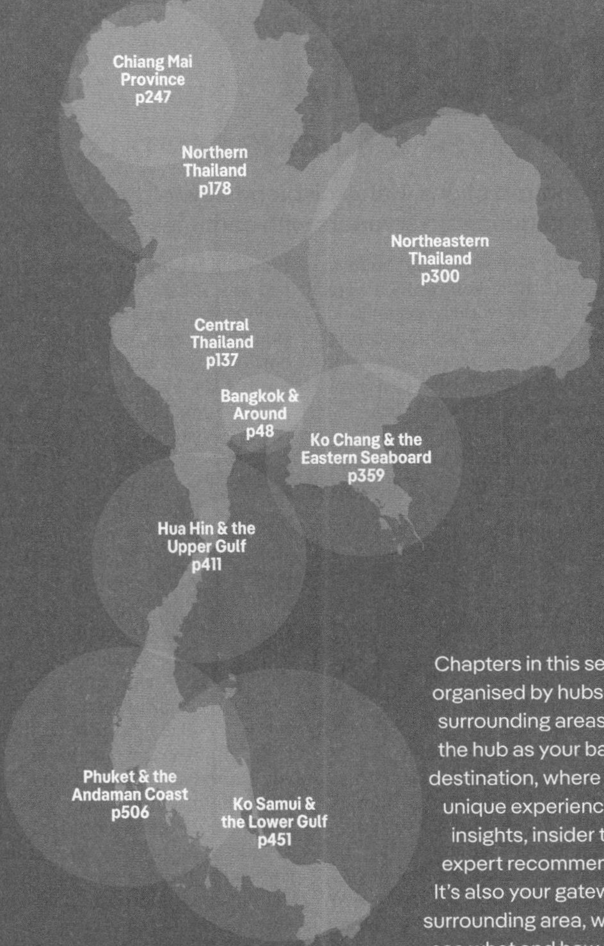

Chapters in this section are organised by hubs and their surrounding areas. We see the hub as your base in the destination, where you'll find unique experiences, local insights, insider tips and expert recommendations. It's also your gateway to the surrounding area, where you'll see what and how much you can do from there.

AYUTHAYA HISTORICAL PARK (P142)
JULIA MOUNTAIN PHOTO/SHUTTERSTOCK

Researched by
Chawadee Nualkhair

Bangkok & Around

THAILAND'S EVER-CHANGING CAPITAL

A mass of contradictions, Bangkok blends the old with the new, juxtaposing glittering skyscrapers with centuries-old temples.

Spanning roughly 1550 sq km and home to 10 million people, Bangkok ranks among the largest cities in the world by population. Little wonder, then, that Thailand's capital is frequently used as a mere transportation hub, a necessary stop on the way to a tropical island or rural idyll. But while bristling with traffic jams, bouts of hazy air pollution and numerous twisty alleyways, Bangkok still bears a soft heart underneath its tough exterior. All you need is a little research.

Called Krung Thep in Thai, Bangkok is known as the City of Angels, becoming the kingdom's capital in what is now known as Thonburi after the fall of Ayuthaya in the 18th century. The capital shifted to the eastern side of Chao Phraya River at the ascension of Rama I, where its heart has remained ever since. It has hosted many of Thailand's most important historical events: reforms during the reign of Rama V, the fallout from WW II and the Vietnam War, the 1997 Asian financial crisis and numerous coups. Along the way, it has expanded in all directions, welcoming a quarter of Thailand's population and integrating communities from all corners of the globe.

What some may see as Bangkok's biggest curse – its densely packed sprawl – can also be its greatest blessing. For centuries, Thais have proven adept at adapting to the times, and their capital city is no different. Bangkok offers something for everyone, be it the bon vivant on the hunt for the next big party, the history buff in search of great stories, the foodie with hopes of an exciting discovery, or the shop-till-you-dropper seeking the next bargain. Even better, you can be all of these people here. Bangkok's chameleonic nature encourages flexibility and experimentation, occasionally testing your limits – especially when it comes to the heat. Bring a hat and sunscreen, and know that an ice-cold drink is always around the corner.

ARTAPARTMENT/SHUTTERSTOCK

THE MAIN AREAS

For places to stay in Bangkok and around, see p134

SOMBOON RUNGAREE/SHUTTERSTOCK

Left: Siam Paragon (p103); Above: Wat Suthat (p74)

Find Your Way

There's no two ways about it: Bangkok is massive. If you have limited time, a good rule of thumb is to concentrate on a handful of neighbourhoods. If you're a Bangkok newbie, this means Banglamphu, Ko Ratanakosin and Chinatown. If you're looking for something different, the area around central Bangkok holds worthwhile diversions.

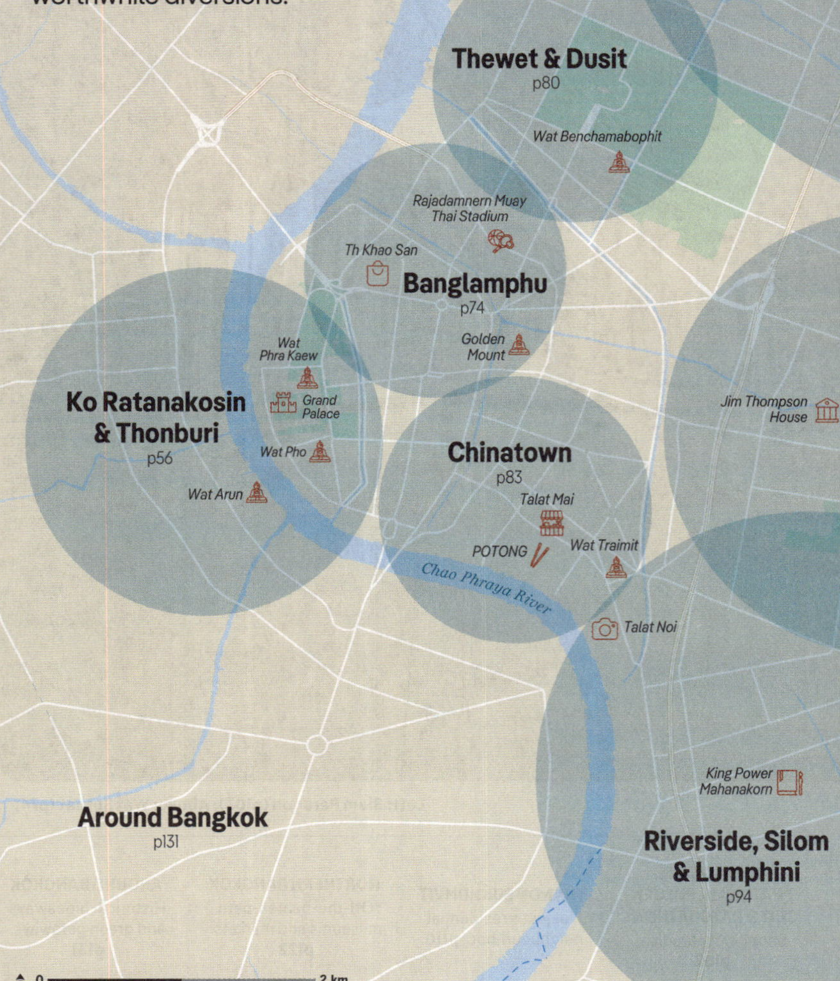

Chatuchak Weekend Market

Museum of Contemporary Art (7.8km)

Northern Bangkok
p122

Siam Square, Pratunam, Phloen Chit & Ratchathewi
p102

Siam Paragon

Thanon Sukhumvit
p110

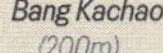

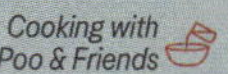

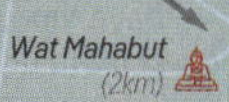

TAXIS, MOTORBIKES & TUK-TUKS

Taxi drivers have become more temperamental and frequently refuse to use their meters, meaning Grab or Bolt (the Southeast Asian equivalents of Uber) may be better options. Thrill-seekers can opt for motorcycle taxis if pressed for time, while tuk-tuks – touristy to be sure – can be fun for short stretches if there's little traffic. Always negotiate the price beforehand.

CANAL BOATS & RIVER BOATS

Avoid traffic jams by taking a *klorng* boat along Saen Saep Canal, which runs from Minburi to the Old Town. Another canal boat, the Khlong Phadung Krung Kasem boat service, can take you from Hua Lamphong Station Pier to Thewarat Market Pier.

FROM THE AIRPORT

Suvarnabhumi International Airport has taxis as well as Grab and Bolt, but the Bangkok Airport Rail Link can connect you to both Skytrain (BTS) and Metro (MRT). If you land in Don Mueang, take the Don Mueang Airport Train to town.

SKYTRAIN & METRO

Also known as the BTS and MRT, respectively, these systems now stretch to remote crannies of the city and are set to expand further. Besides both airports, the BTS also services Krungthep Apiwat Railway Station, Chatuchak, Thonburi and the mostly residential neighbourhoods of Lardprao and Ramkhamhaeng. A pass on one does not work on the other, but the MRT does take Visa.

Plan Your Days

The hardest thing about planning a day in Bangkok is choosing where to go. The temples are a no-brainer, but leave time for markets, massages and, of course, food.

MAZUR TRAVEL/SHUTTERSTOCK

Stupa, Wat Phra Kaew (p62)

Day 1

Morning

- Start your trip with the Big Two: the Emerald Buddha at the **Grand Palace** (p62) and the Reclining Buddha at **Wat Pho** (p57). Carve out some time for a massage at the **Wat Pho Thai Traditional Massage School** (p57).

Afternoon

- After lunch, explore the charms of Banglamphu, particularly the **Golden Mount** (p74), **Wat Suthat** (p74) and the area around **Sao Ching-Cha** (p77). Leave some time for a traditional (and refreshing!) *nam kaeng sai* (Thai shaved ice).

Evening

- End your day with a relaxing evening on **Th Charoen Krung** (p100), either at the historic **Mandarin Oriental Hotel** (p134) or at an open-air riverside spot such as **Jack's Bar** (p99).

YOU'LL ALSO WANT TO...

There is a lot more to Bangkok than temples and shopping. If you have time, try out something off the beaten track.

CATCH A MUAY THAI MATCH

Grab a seat at **Rajadamnern Muay Thai Stadium** (p79), where many of the giants of Thailand's most famous sport frequently exchange elbows, knees and wits.

EXPLORE A HISTORIC COMMUNITY

Stroll through **Kudi Chin** (p70), settled by the Portuguese after the fall of Ayuthaya. Learn about their history at the **Baan Kudichin Museum** (p72) and try a Thai-Portuguese sweet.

LEARN HOW TO COOK THAI FOOD

Book a class at **Cooking with Poo & Friends** (p117) or *Chef's Table*-featured **Bo.lan** (p117), where traditional Thai techniques are melded with friendly hands-on instruction.

Day 2

Morning

- Take in a dose of local history at the **Ancient City**, located on Bangkok's outskirts, or, if it's between August and October, head out on a **whale-watching excursion** (p133) around Thailand's Upper Gulf.

Afternoon

- If you're not whale watching, spend some time on the Thonburi side of the river, nosing out oddities at the **Siriraj Medical Museum** (p69) or decompressing at **Chao Phraya Sky Park** (p68).

Evening

- After the sun sets, **Chinatown** (p83) really comes alive. Explore its **street-food spots** (p86) or spend the entire evening at Michelin-starred **POTONG** (p87).

Day 3

Morning

- Even if you're not a shopaholic, a visit to **Chatuchak Weekend Market** (p126) – Southeast Asia's biggest – makes sense. Even better, it's sprinkled with foot-massage parlours and cafes. If it's not the weekend, head to **Siam Square** (p102) instead.

Afternoon

- If you're not already there, take the train to Siam Square, where you can spend your afternoon at the **Bangkok Art & Culture Centre** (p106) and the **Jim Thompson House** (p105). Refresh with a drink at Jim Thompson's **OSS Room**.

Evening

- Why not end your visit at **Thanon Khao San** (p77), the OG of all of Bangkok's nightspots?

PAMPER YOURSELF

It would be a shame to miss out on a good Thai massage. Luckily, Bangkok is chock-full of **spas** (p117) that cater to every preference, from no-frills to all-out luxe.

GET LOST IN ANOTHER LAND

The northern side of Th Nana is a maze of Middle Eastern and African eateries, particularly in **Little Arab Town** (p113; aka Sukhumvit 3/1).

HAGGLE IN LITTLE INDIA

Phahurat, also known as **Little India** (p88), is one of Bangkok's centres for textiles. Of course, it's also ground zero for Indian food. Grab a street-side samosa before perusing the wares at **India Emporium** (p88).

TAKE IN SOME NATURE

The revamped **Benjakitti Park** (p114) offers copious greenery, ample walkways and a sparkling lake. If you want to go further afield, there's always **Bang Kachao** (p131), the lungs of Bangkok.

HELP ME PICK:

Bangkok's Temples

Any traveller to the City of Angels would be forgiven for being intimidated by the sheer number of wat (temples) in Bangkok – after all, there are more than 400 of them. As such, it's easy to feel a bit templed out by the end of your visit. To make things easier, here are some choices to consider – from historically important touchpoints and breathtaking architecture to quirky destinations that provide real insight into Thai life.

Where to go if you love ...

Historically important monuments

Grand Palace (p73) Every tourist who has been to Bangkok has at least felt *some* pressure to visit this important sight, home to Thailand's venerated Emerald Buddha. What Westminster Abbey is to London and what the Blue Mosque is to Istanbul, the Grand Palace is to Bangkok – instantly recognisable and forever intertwined with Thailand's image.

A beautiful place to relax

Wat Pho (p57) Frequently open until 9pm, this temple compound houses the famous Reclining Buddha, as well as a Thai massage school that's said to be the birthplace of the art. Older than even Bangkok itself, Wat Pho takes up over 80,000 sq metres and is home to more than 1000 Buddha images. But the real draw here is the smiling 46m-long golden Reclining Buddha, captured resting on his side on his journey into nirvana.

Taking stunning photos

Wat Arun (p66) Also known as the 'Temple of the Dawn', this temple sports a distinctive *chedi* (stupa) that makes it an instantly recognisable riverside landmark. A favourite with young Asian tourists who flock here for photos in traditional Thai dress, Wat Arun is arguably most beautiful in the late afternoon, especially just as the sun starts setting at around 5pm, when you'll have ample fodder for your Instagram feed.

Making a wish that might come true

Erawan Shrine (p107) Many Thais – and quite a few non-Thais – believe so sincerely in the wish-granting powers of this shrine that a cottage industry has popped up around it. Adding to the allure are Thai dancers performing to a live band, which is hired when someone's wish has come true. Make merit to the four-faced Phra Phrom if you feel worthy.

Quirky glimpses into Thai life

Wat Mahabut (p121) Out in the eastern suburbs of Bangkok is a temple housing a shrine to arguably Thailand's most famous ghost, Mae Nak. Many Thais believe that making merit to her will not only aid in fertility and childbirth, but also provide inspiration for finding winning lottery numbers. As a result, the shrine is packed before the 1st and 16th of every month, when the government lottery is drawn.

KRISHNA.WU/SHUTTERSTOCK

Wat Arun (p66)

HOW TO

Wear appropriate attire All temples require visitors to cover their shoulders and legs, although the Erawan Shrine's standards are not as exacting.

Donate money There are usually boxes in the main halls if you feel moved to donate to the temple you're visiting. The money goes to general upkeep, and any amount is appreciated.

Make merit There is no need to bring your own incense, flowers or candles. Everything you need to make merit will be sold at the temples.

Avoid scams Unofficial guides at the entrance are typically best avoided, as are 'guides' driving tuk-tuks and promising discounts at the gem stores of various relatives.

Behaving Respectfully

It can be tricky to navigate staying respectful of Thai culture while still participating in rituals that Thai people take seriously. The most important thing to remember is that monks cannot be touched by women; to greet monks, instead use the simple and commonplace *wai* (palms-together Thai greeting with the head bowed). Thais frequently wear white thread bracelets after their visit to a temple, showing they have been blessed by a monk. If you desire one, simply ask a monk for his blessing, typically performed by sprinkling holy water on you.

When it comes to making merit at places such as Erawan Shrine, it's best to do as the locals do and behave sincerely without putting your own stamp on things (making offbeat offerings, for instance). Also be mindful of other people and their offerings, flowers and figurines; these are not to be touched (this includes spirit houses, which are placed in front of many buildings and are meant to accommodate the local spirits of the land).

Often, vendors at smaller temples will sell live turtles, eels and birds in cages. These animals are meant to be freed by the merit-maker into the air or into a nearby waterway. Many of these animals will be recaptured and resold the next day. While it may seem a cruel fate, it's important to remember that this is a religious ritual.

Ko Ratanakosin & Thonburi

THE BIRTHPLACE OF BANGKOK

TOP TIP

If you don't get seasick, this area is best explored by boat, either via the **Chao Phraya Express Boat** *(chaophrayaexpressboat.com; 14-33฿)* or a private hire, with long-tail boats available to hire *(200-500฿)* online or at the piers of Tha Tien, Tha Chang or IconSiam.

The historic neighbourhoods of Ko Ratanakosin and Thonburi are where Bangkok was born. Separated by Chao Phraya River, they are home to the capital's most significant sights, including temples, palaces and museums. At the same time, glimpses of a gentler, more old-fashioned way of life can be found among their narrow alleyways, from street vendors grilling rice cakes to school children on their way home.

Ko Ratanakosin is bordered by Chao Phraya River to the west and canals to the east. It became the capital of then-Siam in 1782, and is home to Wat Pho and Wat Phra Kaew – both among Thailand's most important religious sites – while the imposing Grand Palace is a symbol of the Thai monarchy's ongoing power. Residential Thonburi, opposite Ko Ratanakosin on Chao Phraya's western bank, is intersected by canals, while the iconic spire of Wat Arun rises above the spot where the city that would become Bangkok was founded.

GETTING AROUND

Neither the Skytrain (BTS) nor the Metro (MRT) stop at Ko Ratanakosin, but you can reach the area via the boat on the **Saen Saep Canal Boat** *(transitbangkok.com/khlong_boats.html)*, which leaves from piers including Thong Lor and Witthayu and disembarks at Panfa Leelard (the end of the line). You can also take the MRT to Sam Yod and then hop on a tuk-tuk or motorbike taxi from there.

Thonburi is serviced by several BTS stops, including Saphan Taksin (where you can take the free IconSiam or Millennium Hilton boat shuttles across the river). You can also take the MRT Blue Line from Siam to Bang Wa, right in the heart of Thonburi.

MIRAIYUKI/SHUTTERSTOCK

Reclining Buddha, Wat Pho

Where the Reclining Buddha Sleeps

Finding tranquillity at Wat Pho

Wat Pho *(watpho.com; 300฿)* covers 8 hectares, and it needs to, because this sprawling compound is home to the magnificent Reclining Buddha, the largest collection of Buddha images in Thailand, the country's first centre for public education, and the national headquarters for the teaching and preservation of traditional Thai medicine, including Thai massage.

On the western edge of the complex is the **Temple of the Reclining Buddha**, the highlight of Wat Pho. The statue is the biggest in Bangkok and seems slightly too big for the pavilion that houses it. A common public ritual here is to place coins (representing alms) in the series of metal bowls placed in a long row to the rear of the Buddha statue. If you don't have enough coins on you, an attendant will provide you with change for bigger denominations of cash.

Dress in long skirts/trousers and sleeved shirts when you visit, and note that shoes must be taken off to enter the temple. (You'll be given a reusable plastic bag at the entrance, in which you place your shoes and carry them with you during your visit. Once outside, deposit the bag in one of the collection vats.) Wat Pho is open daily from 8am to 6pm.

MASSAGE AT WAT PHO

The preservation of Thai massage was a mandate legislated by Rama III when the tradition was in danger of extinction, and **Wat Pho Thai Traditional Massage School** is the most famous centre for massage training in Thailand.

Located just outside Wat Pho itself, the school teaches all aspects of Thai massage and offers courses ranging from 30 hours (over the course of five days) to 200 hours (over the course of four weeks). Prices start at 15,000฿ and go up to 53,000฿.

Inside the compound of Wat Pho, at the eastern edge, is the **massage pavilion** where weary travellers can have their aches and pains eased. Prices start at 320฿ for a 30-minute foot massage.

EATING NEAR WAT PHO: OUR PICKS

Sixth 6th: Reasonably priced lunches next to Wat Pho, with crowd-pleasing portions of Thai faves including papaya salad and *dom yam* soup. *10.30am-4.45pm* ฿

Rongros: Also known in Thai as 'House of Flavors', this is a popular spot with a view of nearby Wat Arun; it's lauded in the *Michelin Guide* for its green curry. *11am-3pm & 5-10pm* ฿฿

Pad Thai Kratong Thong by Ama: Good prices, with a focus on Thailand's most famous dish; a convenient location between the Royal Palace and Wat Pho. *10am-5.30pm* ฿

Horsamut: Fancy-pants Thai by the river with local seafood caught sustainably from independent Thai fisherfolk. *11am-11pm* ฿฿฿

Wat Pho

Walk Through the Big Buddhas of Wat Pho

The logical starting place is the main *wi hahn* (sanctuary), home to Wat Pho's centrepiece, the immense **1 Reclining Buddha**. In addition to its enormous size, note the **2 mother-of-pearl inlay** on the soles of the statue's feet. The interior walls of the *wi hahn* are covered with murals that depict previous lives of the Buddha, and along the south side of the structure are 108 bronze monk bowls; for 20฿ you can buy 108 coins, each of which is dropped in a bowl for good luck.

Exit the *wi hahn* and head east via the two **3 stone giants** who guard the gateway to the rest of the compound. Directly south of these are the four towering **4 royal chedi**.

Continue east, passing through two consecutive **5 galleries of Buddha statues** linking four *wi hahn*, two of which contain notable Sukhothai-era Buddha statues; these comprise the exterior of **6 Phra Ubosot**, the immense ordination hall that is Wat Pho's second-most noteworthy structure. The base of the building is surrounded by bas-relief inscriptions, and inside is the notable Buddha statue, **7 Phra Buddha Deva Patimakorn**.

Wat Pho is often referred to as Thailand's first university, a tradition that continues today in an associated traditional Thai medicine school and, at the compound's eastern extent, two **8 massage pavilions**.

Interspersed throughout the eastern half of the compound are several additional minor *chedi* and rock gardens.

OASIZZ/GETTY IMAGES

ILLUSTRATION BY MICHAEL WELDON

VICHAN SRISEANGNIL/GETTY IMAGES

6 Phra Ubosot
Built during the reign of Rama I (r 1782–1809), the imposing *boht* (ordination hall) as it stands today is the result of renovations dating to the reign of Rama III (r 1824–51).

7 Phra Buddha Deva Patimakorn
On an impressive three-tiered pedestal that also holds the ashes of Rama I is this Ayuthaya-era Buddha statue originally brought to the temple by the monarch.

8 Massage Pavilions
If you're hot and footsore, the two air-conditioned massage pavilions are a welcome way to cool down while experiencing high-quality and relatively inexpensive Thai massage.

KISZON PASCAL/GETTY IMAGES

SAMART BOONYANG/GETTY IMAGES

❶ Reclining Buddha

Modelled around a brick core 46m long and 15m high, and finished in plaster and gold leaf, Wat Pho's Reclining Buddha is an imposing reminder of the Buddha's passing into nirvana (the Buddha's death).

❺ Buddha Galleries

The two series of covered hallways that surround Phra Ubosot feature no fewer than 394 gilded Buddha images, many of which display classic Ayuthaya or Sukhothai features.

❹ Royal Chedi

Decorated in coloured tiles in a classic example of Ratanakosin style, these four *chedi* are meant to represent the first four kings of the Chakri dynasty.

❷ Mother-of-Pearl Inlay

The 108 auspicious *lak sa na* (physical characteristics of the Buddha) are depicted on the soles of the feet of the Reclining Buddha.

IMAGE SOURCE/GETTY IMAGES

❸ Stone Giants

These huge granite figures – with depictions ranging from Chinese opera characters to Marco Polo – originally arrived in Thailand in the 19th century as ballast aboard Chinese junks.

KAMPEE PATISENA/GETTY IMAGES

HIGHLIGHTS
1 Grand Palace
2 Wat Arun
3 Wat Pho
4 Wat Phra Kaew

SIGHTS
5 Baan Kudichin Museum
6 Bang Luang Mosque
7 Kian Un Geng Shrine
8 Museum Siam
9 National Museum
10 Royal Barges National Museum
11 Santa Cruz Church
12 Siriraj Medical Museum

ACTIVITIES
see 16 Wat Pho Thai Traditional Massage School

SLEEPING
13 1905 Heritage Corner
14 Arun Residence
15 Chakrabongse Villas
16 Royal ThaTien Village
17 Theatre Residence
18 Uncle Loy's Boutique House

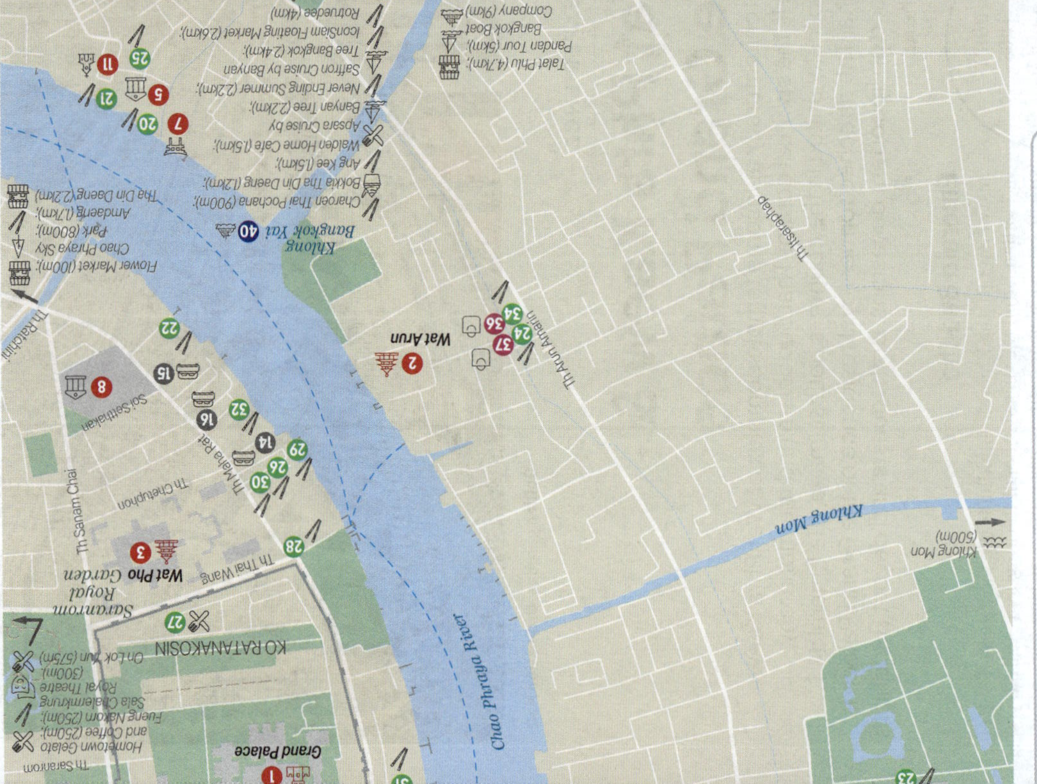

EATING
19 342 Bar
see 26 All Meals Sawasdee
see 5 Baan Sakulthong
20 Caf Kudeejeen
21 Helo Nomsod
22 Horsamut
23 Kaenkrung
24 Khon Mamuang
25 Macaroni by Chris
26 Manee Thai Food
27 Old Town Cafe Bangkok
28 Pad Thai Kratong Thong by Ama
29 Rongros
see 8 Siam Origins
30 Sixth 6th
31 Somtum Der (Tha Thien)
32 Supanniga Eating Room, Tha Tien
33 Wang Lang Market
34 Wat Arun Fried Pork Rice

SHOPPING
35 Amulet Market
36 Little Princess Wat Arun Costumes
37 Na Som Thai Costumes
38 Sense of Thai: Thai Costume Rental

TRANSPORT
39 Phra Chan Pier
40 Rajinee Pier

SHUTTERTHEP/SHUTTERSTOCK

Golden garudas, Ordination Hall

TOP EXPERIENCE

Wat Phra Kaew & the Grand Palace

The architecturally awesome temple complex of Wat Phra Kaew (1783) is the spiritual core of Thai Buddhism and the monarchy, symbolically united in the country's holiest image, the Emerald Buddha. The attached former royal residence of the Grand Palace is still used on important occasions. Both tourists and devout Buddhists flock here.

DON'T MISS

- Emerald Buddha
- Ordination Hall
- *Ramakian* Murals
- Mythical Beings
- Chakri Mahaprasat
- Dusit Hall
- Borombhiman Hall

Emerald Buddha

Just 66cm tall, the Emerald Buddha is the most sacred object in Thailand, and the very symbol of the kingdom. At first, you might fail to spot the diminutive image sitting high above the pilgrims and worshippers who crowd out the Ordination Hall that houses it. Crafted out of semi-precious green jasper (rather than emerald), the Emerald Buddha first appeared on record in 15th-century Chiang Rai in northern Thailand. Stylistically, it seems to belong to the Thai artistic periods of the 13th to 14th centuries.

Because of its royal status, the Emerald Buddha is ceremoniously draped in monastic robes. There are three robes: for

PRACTICALITIES

● 500฿ ● 8.30am-3.30pm ● royalgrandpalace.th

the hot, rainy and cool seasons. The robes are still solemnly changed by the king at the beginning of each season.

Ordination Hall

The spectacular ornamentation of the Ordination Hall, both inside and out, does a good job of distracting visitors from paying their respects to the Emerald Buddha within it. Check out the gold leaf and glass mosaics adorning the exterior walls, the coloured glazed tiles on the roof and the painted murals depicting scenes from the life of the Buddha in the hall's interior.

Ramakian Murals

Lining the walls of the 2km-long cloister that defines the perimeter of the complex are 178 wonderfully vivid and intricate murals depicting the entire *Ramakian* (the Thai version of the *Ramayana*, an ancient Hindu epic).

The murals begin at the north gate and move clockwise around the compound, telling how the hero Rama (the green-faced character) joins forces with Hanuman, the monkey king (the white monkey), to rescue his bride, Sita (the topless maiden), after she's kidnapped by the evil king Ravana (the character with numerous arms and faces). Battles and intrigue follow until it all ends happily.

Mythical Beings

Every entrance to Wat Phra Kaew is guarded by a pair of giant *yaksha* (ogre-like attendants who are commonly seen standing watch over Buddhist temples in Thailand). Other mythical beings to look out for here are the graceful *kinaree* (half-swan, half-woman creatures) and grimacing Hanuman (mischievous monkey-like deities).

Chakri Mahaprasat

Just to the west of the temple complex is the Grand Palace, a compound of over 100 buildings. Only four are open to the public, the most impressive of which is the triple-winged Chakri Mahaprasat or Grand Palace Hall, a striking blend of Italian Renaissance and traditional Thai architecture.

Dusit Hall

The cruciform Dusit Hall, built in traditional Thai style, is one of the more elegant palace buildings. Once a venue for royal audiences, the hall is now where the king and members of the royal family lie in state ahead of their funerals. Look out for the mother-of-pearl throne situated close to the centre of the hall.

Borombhiman Hall

Located at the eastern end of the complex, Borombhiman Hall is a French-inspired neo-Renaissance structure that was the most modern building in the Grand Palace when it was completed in 1903. It served as Rama VI's residence until 1925. Today, visiting heads of state sometimes stay here; the hall can only be viewed through its iron gates.

ROYAL HAREM

Until Rama VI ended the practice of polygamy, Thai kings housed harems in the inner palace, which was guarded by female sentries. The intrigue of this cloistered community was fictionalised in the 1953 novel *Four Reigns* by Kukrit Pramoj, a great-grandson of Rama II and former Prime Minister of Thailand.

TOP TIPS

- Get here at opening time to avoid the crowds and the midday heat.
- Wear long skirts/ trousers and sleeved shirts.
- Buy tickets online at least 24 hours before your visit.
- English-speaking guides can be hired at the ticket kiosk. Audio guides in a number of languages are also available.
- While there's always a crush of people in and around the Ordination Hall and the Emerald Buddha, the cloisters that contain the *Ramakian* murals are mercifully quiet and shady.
- There are accessible toilets for the disabled, and free wheelchairs.
- Grand Palace tickets include a free *khon* performance at Sala Chalermkrung Royal Theater (p68), accessible via a free shuttle.

ANTONIO D'ALBORE/GETTY IMAGES

ALEXEY STIOP/GETTY IMAGES

❶ Murals of the Ramakian

These wall paintings, which begin at the eastern side of Wat Phra Kaew, often depict scenes more reminiscent of 19th-century Thailand than ancient India.

❺ Emerald Buddha

Despite the name, this diminutive statue (it's only 66cm tall) is actually carved from nephrite, a type of jade.

❷ The Death of Thotsakan

The panels progress clockwise, culminating at the western edge of the compound with the death of Thotsakan, Sita's kidnapper, and his elaborate funeral procession.

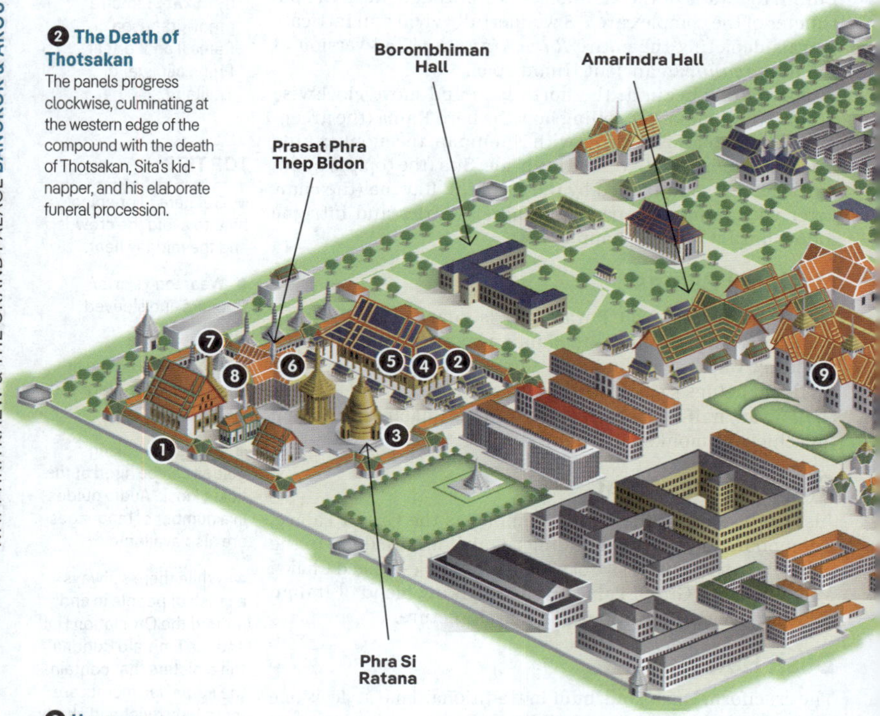

Borombhiman Hall

Amarindra Hall

Prasat Phra Thep Bidon

Phra Si Ratana

❽ Hanuman

Rows of these mischievous monkey deities from Hindu mythology appear to support the lower levels of two small *chedi* near Prasat Phra Thep Bidon.

❸ Yaksha

Each entrance to the Wat Phra Kaew compound is watched over by a pair of vigilant and enormous *yaksha*, ogres or giants from Hindu mythology.

❻ The Three Spires

The elaborate seven-tiered roof of Phra Mondop, the Khmer-style peak of Prasat Phra Thep Bidon, and the gilded Phra Si Ratana *chedi* are the tallest structures in the compound.

PETRONILO G. DANGOY JR./SHUTTERSTOCK

ZZVET/GETTY IMAGES

Wat Phra Kaew & Grand Palace

Explore Bangkok's Premier Monuments to Religion & Regency

The first area tourists enter is the Buddhist temple compound generally referred to as Wat Phra Kaew. A covered walkway surrounds the area, the inner walls of which are decorated with the **1 murals of the Ramakian** and **2 the Death of Thotsakan**. Originally painted during the reign of Rama I (r 1782–1809), the murals, which depict the Hindu epic the *Ramayana*, span 178 panels that describe the struggles of Rama to rescue his kidnapped wife, Sita.

After taking in the story, pass through one of the gateways guarded by **3 Yaksha** (guardian demons) to enter the inner compound. The most important structure here is the **4 boht** (ordination hall), which houses the **5 Emerald Buddha**.

Head east to the so-called Upper Terrace, an elevated area home to the **6 spires of the three primary chedi**. The middle structure, Phra Mondop, is used to house Buddhist manuscripts. This area is also home to several of Wat Phra Kaew's noteworthy mythical beings, including beckoning **7 Kinaree** and several grimacing **8 Hanuman**.

Proceed through the western gate to the compound known as the Grand Palace. Few of the buildings here are open to the public. The most noteworthy structure is **9 Chakri Mahaprasat**. Built in 1882, the exterior of the hall is a unique blend of Western and traditional Thai architecture.

ALINA_ZAINEA/GETTY IMAGES

7 Kinaree
These graceful half-swan, half-women creatures from Hindu-Buddhist mythology stand outside Prasat Phra Thep Bidon.

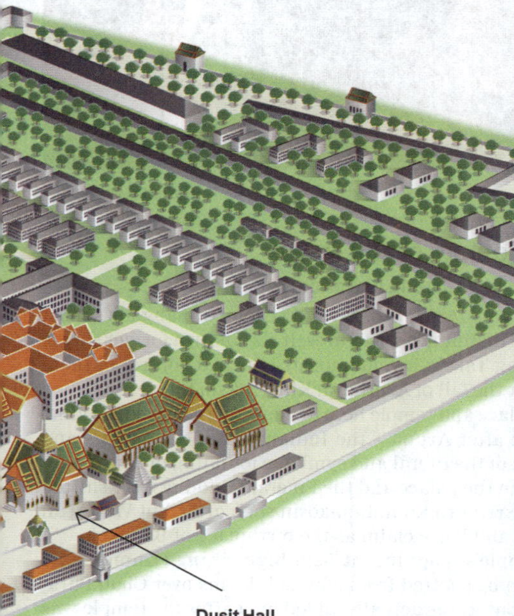

4 Boht (Ordination Hall)
This structure is an early example of the Ratanakosin school of architecture, which combines traditional stylistic holdovers from Ayuthaya with more modern touches from China and the West.

DESIGN PICS/BLAKE KENT/ GETTY IMAGES

9 Chakri Mahaprasat
This structure is sometimes referred to as *fa rang sai cha dah* (Westerner in a Thai crown) because each wing is topped by a *mon·dop*: a spire representing a Thai adaptation of a Hindu shrine.

ILLUSTRATION BY MICHAEL WELDON

DRESSING UP AT WAT ARUN

Thanks to the popularity of the 2018 Thai TV series *Buppesannivas*, many Thais and non-Thais have shown up at Wat Arun in traditional Thai dress, hoping to recapture the vibe of the TV show via impromptu photoshoots at the temple. This has led to a proliferation of costume rental companies and photographers in the area. If you wish to join in the fun, don't worry: Thais are quite happy to see foreigners dressed up in traditional outfits.

Some popular costume rental shops include **Na Som Thai Costumes, Little Princess Wat Arun Costumes** and **Sense of Thai: Thai Costume Rental**; they also include hair, makeup and photography services. The average costume rental cost is around 200฿ per person for three hours.

GREETING MOL/SHUTTERSTOCK

National Museum

At the Temple of the Dawn

Stunning views among historical relics

Wat Arun *(wat-arun.com; 200฿)* is one of Bangkok's most iconic and distinctive structures. It stands on a former shrine where King Taksin ceremoniously clinched control of then-Siam after the fall of Ayuthaya. King Taksin then established a royal palace and temple here to house the Emerald Buddha, naming it after Aruna – the Indian god of the dawn – and in honour of the literal and symbolic founding of a new Ayuthaya. Both the palace and the Emerald Buddha were shifted across the river to Ko Ratanakosin soon after, but Wat Arun remained and has a claim as the birthplace of Bangkok.

The temple's magnificent 82m-high *prang* (Khmer-style tower) can be spotted from afar as it looms over Chao Phraya River, but it was actually added long after the temple was founded, with construction beginning during the first half of the 19th century by Rama II (whose ashes are interred here) and later completed by Rama III. Steep steps lead to the top, from where there are amazing views of the river and the surrounding area.

Visitors should wear long skirts/trousers and sleeved shirts. The temple is open daily from 8am to 6pm.

EATING NEAR WAT ARUN: OUR PICKS

Supanniga Eating Room, Tha Tien: Just across from Wat Arun; spectacular views and good Thai food. *11am-10pm Mon-Fri, from 10am Sat & Sun* ฿฿

Kaenkrung: A 12-minute walk down the road from Wat Arun takes you to this Isan-influenced restaurant. *noon-10pm Thu-Mon* ฿฿

Wat Arun Fried Pork Rice: Every Thai's childhood favourite: garlicky fried pork on rice; located close to the temple. *5.30am-8pm* ฿

Khon Mamuang: Reasonable prices for well-made Thai dishes such as *pat see ew*, green curry, and mango sticky rice. *10.30am-8pm Sun-Fri, from 9am Sat* ฿

Explore Thai History at its Museums

Places of learning

With its motto of 'Play and Learn = Joy', **Museum Siam** *(musemsiam.org; 100฿)* is a surprisingly fun stop for the museum-phobe. Blending plenty of information with numerous interactive displays, the museum is housed in an Italian-designed neoclassical building that once served as the Ministry of Commerce. The museum was founded in 2007 with the purpose of exploring Thailand's national identity and culture, with a particular focus on making said exploration both engaging and accessible to young people.

That means a variety of interactive media exploring definitions of 'Thainess' – namely, how the clothing, customs and cuisine of Thailand have developed – via a series of rooms. There are also exhibits on architecture, music, TV, pop culture, religion, ethnic minorities, relations with Thailand's neighbours and the impact of the West on Thailand. The result is a highly satisfying and worthwhile trawl through Thai identity. Audio guides are available, and the museum is open from 10am to 6pm and is closed Mondays.

A more traditional approach to learning can be found at the **National Museum** *(museumthailand.com; 200฿)*, housed in the former palace of Rama I's viceroy, Prince Wang Na. The palace became a museum in 1874 courtesy of Rama V, and today three permanent exhibitions are spread over several buildings. The main exhibition, the Gallery of Thai History – Archaeology, features some of the country's most beautiful Buddha images and sculptures of Hindu gods. Also interesting is the Gallery of Thai Traditional Arts, with everything from handicrafts and textiles to puppets and royal regalia on display. English-speaking guides can be booked in advance, and the museum is open from 8.30am to 4pm Wednesday through Sunday.

Buddhist Bling

Peruse talismans at the Amulet Market

Buddhist Thais love their amulets – talismans that can bring good luck and offer spiritual protection from the slings and arrows of everyday life. Not surprisingly, they are big business in Thailand, with some fetching over US$1 million. Most devout Buddhists, be they young or old, rich or poor, have at least one amulet, believing them to offer either physical or mental protection, depending on what type of amulet it is.

HISTORY OF SOUTHERN THAI FOOD IN THONBURI

The area around Siriraj Hospital is a great place to sample southern Thai food, the theory being that the cuisine took root here because the nearby train station served southern destinations. As a melting pot for the country, Bangkok lured ambitious Thais from all corners of the kingdom, including those from the south, who brought with them their herb-inflected, seafood-focused and addictively spicy cuisine. Commonly described as 'soldiers' rations', southern Thai cuisine is thought to have featured such intensely fiery flavours in order to more easily fill empty stomachs with rice, eaten to counteract the spice. The descendants of the first southern Thai cooks who set up shop in Thonburi can still be found cooking here today.

EATING LUNCH NEAR MUSEUM SIAM: TOP SPOTS

Siam Origins: On the Museum Siam grounds, this cafe serves great Thai food and can do a special seven-course set menu with advance notice. *9am-7pm* ฿฿

Manee Thai Food: Veggie-friendly spot serving quick Thai dishes such as stir-fried noodles in soy sauce, fried rice and holy basil stir-fry. *10.30am-7pm Thu-Tue* ฿

All Meals Sawasdee: Cheap and cheerful spot on Tha Tien that's popular with Thais and backpackers; serves *pat tai* and mango sticky rice. *9.30am-7pm* ฿

Somtum Der (Tha Thien): An outpost with branches in NY and Tokyo, this spot specialises in dishes such as corn salad with salted egg. *11am-10pm* ฿฿

LEARNING ABOUT KHON

The Thai classical dancers enacting scenes from the *Ramayana* – an Indian epic that has been incorporated into Thai culture – undergo rigorous training from a very young age, including bending back their fingers while their bones are still malleable in order to make hand gestures deemed beautiful enough to perform. Although their faces may stay serene (or hidden entirely by masks), their quick hand and foot movements, almost constantly bent knees, and athletic lifts require strength, endurance and whole a lot of flexibility. Those who are interested in this demanding but beautiful art can apply for a place in a five-day intensive *khon* workshop and/or a three-week training **residency** *(artsonlocation.net; from 8000฿)*.

Bangkok's **Amulet Market**, located along Th Maharat and Th Phra Chan and running south from **Phra Chan Pier**, offers curious visitors the chance to delve into the arcane world of amulets and the obsessives who collect them. As for the amulets themselves, they are usually miniature Buddha statues enclosed in a glass locket. The market is open daily from 7am to 5pm.

The Art of Khon

Catch a traditional Thai dance performance

Khon, considered the crown jewel of Thai performing arts, showcases classically trained dancers, ornately beautiful costumes and breathtaking set pieces. Performances – often based on scenes from the Hindu epic the *Ramayana* – are held at the historic **Sala Chalermkrung Royal Theatre** *(salachalermkrung.com)*, where tickets are free if you purchase a 500฿ entrance ticket to the Grand Palace (p73). Three 25-minute performances are held at 1pm, 2.30pm and 4pm on weekdays. A free shuttle bus can take you from the Grand Palace to the theatre.

Exploring Thonburi's Best-Kept Secret

Bridging the gap between east and west

In 1992 plans for Bangkok's very first electric train line, which would bridge the eastern and western banks of the city, were abandoned due to finance issues. This left a derelict construction site towering over Chao Phraya River. City officials decided to turn lemons into lemonade by transforming the site into a public park, dubbed the **Chao Phraya Sky Park**, which opened in June 2020 – when Thailand was in the throes of the COVID-19 pandemic. As a result, news of a splashy park with unparalleled views of Chao Phraya River was lost in the ether, resulting in what is now considered the neighbourhood's best-kept secret.

Modelled after New York City's High Line, two 280m paths (one for walkers, the other for cyclists) perch in the middle of Phra Pokklao Bridge, flanked by traffic on both sides and offering 360-degree views of Bangkok. Concrete bleachers set among picturesque foliage line both pathways, making it a spectacular spot for the tens of locals who journey here at sunset. Because of construction on the Chinatown side, the park is more accessible from Thonburi via Chaloem Phra Kiat Forest Park and is wheelchair-friendly.

EATING NEAR SALA CHALERMKRUNG: SNACKS

On Lok Yun: This extremely popular old-school cafe serves Thai coffee and breakfasts, but you'll have to brave a long line for a seat. *5am-4.30pm* ฿

Fueng Nakorn: Find this collection of sweets vendors on the 1st floor of the Old Siam Plaza. *9am-8pm* ฿

Old Town Cafe Bangkok: Vintage vibes with great coffee, banh mi and croissants, and creative coffee drinks. *10am-6.30pm Wed-Sun, from 2pm Tue* ฿

Hometown Gelato and Coffee: A cute sweets spot popular with young Thais; it serves creative ice-cream dishes such as their *kanom kai* gelato set. *9.30am-6pm* ฿

Chao Phraya Sky Park

'Undiscovered' Bangkok

An underrated part of the capital

There are plenty of sights to behold in Bangkok Noi (literally, 'Little Bangkok'), which includes the heavily trafficked areas around Wat Arun, but also encompasses tranquil waterside neighbourhoods that provide glimpses of Bangkok as it might have been 50 years ago.

A standard Bangkok Noi attraction is the **Siriraj Medical Museum** *(200฿)*, where the body of a serial killer was once kept preserved but has since been cremated following complaints. All the same, for those with morbid curiosities, there is plenty to satisfy, including two-headed foetuses, cancer-ridden organs and grisly crime-scene evidence. In spite of the occasionally harrowing exhibits, the museum is very popular, especially with visitors with an interest in forensic medicine beyond the occasional episode of *CSI*. Curators detail real cases, providing a wealth of information on how crimes get solved. It's open from 10am to 4pm Wednesday through Sunday.

Only an 18-minute walk from the museum is an attraction for both historians and sailors: the **Royal Barges National Museum** *(100฿)*. Here, the barges used in ceremonial processions – a tradition dating back to the Ayuthaya era – are kept

BUILDING BRIDGES

With construction beginning in 1929, **Phra Phutthayodfa Bridge** was named after Phutthayodfa Chulalok, who would later go on to become Rama I. It was opened to the public in 1932 as a bascule bridge, meaning it featured a double-leaf lifting mechanism to allow boats to pass through. Although the lifting mechanism is no longer in use, the distinctive bascule bridge structure and seafoam green colour make the bridge – referred to as the Memorial Bridge by English speakers – a popular destination for both locals and tourists at dusk, who like to document their visits on social media. Only a few metres away, the neighbouring **Phra Pokklao Bridge** (home to the Chao Phraya Sky Park) was built in 1982 to alleviate some of the cross-river traffic from the Memorial Bridge.

EATING NEAR CHAO PHRAYA SKY PARK: LUNCH

Ang Kee: A Hong Kong-style cafe boasting the best pork chops in town and excellent fried rice. *9am-4.30pm Tue-Sun* ฿฿

Amdaeng: This well-hidden riverfront hotel has a small restaurant with good views; it's popular during events such as New Year's. *8am-8pm* ฿฿

Charoen Thai Pochana: An old-style Thai-Chinese shophouse eatery specialising in solid stir-fries, oyster omelettes and steamed sea bass. *11.30am-9pm* ฿฿

Walden Home Cafe: A twee spot for coffee that illustrates the neighbourhood's gentrification; is also dog-friendly. *8am-5pm* ฿

PORTUGUESE CONTRIBUTIONS TO THAI FOOD

When Portuguese traders came to Siam in the 1700s, little did the Siamese know how their cuisine would change. On the traders' boats were ingredients that would transform Thai cuisine: peanuts, corn, papaya, potatoes, pineapples, guava, cashew nuts, pumpkin and tomatoes. Perhaps most crucially, they also brought with them chillies from Africa, broadening the way the Siamese would season their dishes. They also brought sweets, including *fios de ovos* and *ovos mole* (originally made from leftover egg yolks, as Portuguese nuns starched their habits with egg whites). These desserts would become the Thai *foy tong* (golden threads) and *tong yip* (golden drops), while Portuguese marzipan fruit became *ka nom chup*.

RATT_ANARACH/SHUTTERSTOCK

in the museum, which is tucked down a winding alley close to the entrance to a naval base. Eight barges, particularly *Suphanaphong* (the king's personal vessel), feature intricate carvings and colourful glass inlay. The barges can be seen in action during the Royal Barge Procession, which is a rare occurrence – the last one was in 2019, to celebrate the coronation of Rama X. The museum is open from 9am to 5pm.

Explore a Multi-Ethnic Community

Walk the alleyways of Kudi Chin

Strangely overlooked by many tourists, this charming, historic neighbourhood is an example of three different communities (Portuguese, Chinese and Muslim) living together in harmony for generations. Founded during the reign of King Taksin following the fall of Ayuthaya, **Kudi Chin** (also occasionally spelled Kudeecheen) housed loyal Portuguese troops. Later, when an influx of Chinese and Muslim communities came

EATING IN BANGKOK NOI: OUR PICKS

342 Bar: Wonderful rooftop views mixed with a quirky vibe and easy-to-eat pastas, burgers and French fries. *4pm-midnight* ฿฿

Little Pine Cafe: Cute spot with hearty open-faced sandwiches, pastries and homemade ice cream. *10am-5pm Wed-Sun, from 1pm Tue* ฿

Panlom Bangkhun Non: Make your reservation on Facebook and enjoy a traditional Thai menu crafted from the owner's family recipes. *reservation only* ฿฿฿

Combine Cafe & Gallery: A slick, friendly space in an old house, with a focus on simple meals and coffee in a tranquil, green-filled setting. *8am-6pm Tue-Sun* ฿

Canal tour (p72), Bangkok Noi

to Bangkok, they were also invited to settle here. The result is an interesting mix of Thai, Portuguese, Chinese and Muslim architecture and food offerings, all tucked away among winding, picturesque walkways.

The neighbourhood's name originally comes from 'Kadichin', which was the name of the riverside Chinese shrine Giang An Geng. The Portuguese who moved to this part of the city in the 1700s were then called the *Kadichin farang* (*farang* meaning Westerners), which eventually morphed into 'Kudichin', used to describe anything that fused Thai and Portuguese elements. As a result, every trip to the area starts with a look at **Santa Cruz Church** (aka Wat Kudichin), built in 1770 on land granted to the Portuguese by King Taksin. The oldest Catholic church in the city, it was originally built in teak but burned down and was replaced by the current neoclassical brick structure.

There are other religious sites in the neighbourhood worth noting: the Hokkienese **Kian Un Geng Shrine** is one of

THONBURI'S MARKETS

Chin Chongtong is the owner of **Chili Paste Tour** *@chilipastetour*

Thonburi has many great markets. **Talat Phlu**, **Wang Lang**, **Tha Din Daeng** and **Khlong Lat Mayom** are all markets [...] that I include on some of my food tours.

The market for me is real life. There is an exchange of both suffering and happiness, and learning to live and adapt. It's a joy to help share it with foreigners. Everywhere I've travelled in Thailand, it doesn't matter if it's a big city or a small village, I must go to the market first. It is the best way to learn about the food, and also local people and how they live.

EATING IN THONBURI: OUR PICKS

Rotruedee: A great Thai bistro with a cosy shophouse feel – a viable option for food lovers tired of the usual Thai fare. *10am-9pm* ฿฿

IconSiam Floating Market: The floating market on the ground floor of IconSiam is home to a plethora of indoor food vendors. *10am-10pm* ฿

Never Ending Summer: Still a popular spot for traditional Thai food in a riverside setting; get the (admittedly non-Thai) Burmese tea leaf salad. *11am-10pm* ฿฿

Bokkia Tha Din Daeng: Try refreshing shaved ice desserts featuring *tubtim grob* and *selim*; in the *Michelin Guide*. *10.30am-7pm Mon-Sat, to 8pm Sun* ฿

BEST BANGKOK RIVER CRUISES

Manohra Cruises: This might just be the most high-end river cruise out there, with good food served on picturesque, well-kept wooden boats.

Saffron Cruise by Banyan Tree Bangkok: Another hotel-chain offshoot, Saffron boasts a hand-painted boat showcasing Siamese fighting fish, an open-air rooftop bar and a four-course dinner.

Chao Phraya Princess: Offering world-class dinner experiences, this longtime operator sports seven cruise ships in its fleet, all for various occasions.

Chaophrayacruise: The newest player in the Bangkok river-cruise sweepstakes claims to have the most modern ship.

Apsara Cruise by Banyan Tree: Stylishly repurposed rice barges feature a four-course Thai fine-dining experience.

Thonburi's oldest shrines, built in honour of the Goddess Guanyin; while **Bang Luang Mosque**, with its distinctive white facade, blends Thai and Muslim design elements.

Of course, no trip to the neighbourhood is complete without a visit to the **Baan Kudichin Museum** *(baankudichin museum.com)*, located in a charming shophouse with a relaxed cafe on the ground floor. To get to Kudi Chin, head to the Sanam Chai MRT station and walk to **Rajinee Pier**, from where you can take a cross-river ferry to the pier in front of Santa Cruz Church. All of these sites are free to enter.

A River Runs Through This

Cruise Bangkok's many canals

Once generously criss-crossed by waterways, Bangkok has since filled in many of its canals with concrete in an effort to 'modernise'. Luckily, some *klorng* (canals) remain, and watching scenes of day-to-day life unfold along them is one of the city's great pastimes – for half the day at least, before heat exhaustion sets in.

Chao Phraya River and its tributaries, especially on the Thonburi side, are particularly picturesque, bristling with greenery, stilt houses and temples. Canoes, rice barges and long-tail boat taxis ply the waters, and fish can be spied along the banks, nibbling on algae (it's best to not touch them). Of course, many tour operators have risen to the challenge of chartering boats for customers, including **Pandan Tour** *(thaicanaltour.com; from 2000฿)*, the **Bangkok Boat Company** *(bangkokboat.com; 500฿)* and **Bangkok Canal Tours** *(thairivercruise.com; including guide, welcome drink & buffet 1100฿)*. Most tours navigate calm and verdant **Khlong Bangkok Noi**, residential **Khlong Mon** and **Khlong Bangkok Yai**, which are dotted with markets and temples. On weekends, there's also the option to stop at **Taling Chan Floating Market**, a great time-saving option for visitors who want to experience a good floating market without taking the two-hour drive south to see it.

EATING IN KUDI CHIN: OUR PICKS

Baan Sakulthong: Probably the most famous restaurant in Kudi Chin, serving 'royal Thai' cuisine; reservations essential. *10am-4.30pm Tue-Sun* ฿฿

Caf Kudeejeen: A cafe next to the river serving dishes such as shrimp *pat tai*, roast pork over rice, and sweet *longan* sticky rice pudding. *9am-8pm Sat & Sun* ฿

Macaroni by Chris: An oddly named restaurant featuring Thai-Portuguese fusion dishes. *10am-6pm Tue-Sun* ฿

Helo Nomsod: This riverside restaurant serves Kudi Chin's best-known dish: rice noodles topped with a mild minced chicken curry. *10.30am-6pm Wed-Mon* ฿

STROLL THE SIGHTS OF KO RATANAKOSIN

The majority of Bangkok's essential sights are in Ko Ratanakosin, where the seeds of the capital city were first sown.

START	END	LENGTH
Chang Pier	Wat Arun	4km; two hours

Start at ❶ **Chang Pier**. Follow Th Na Phra Lan east, with a quick diversion to ❷ **Silpakorn University**, Thailand's premier fine-arts and architecture university. Continue east to the main gate into the ❸ **Grand Palace** (p62), which shares its compound with the hallowed Wat Phra Kaew temple (p62), consecrated to the Emerald Buddha.

Return to Th Maha Rat and proceed north through an enclave of herbal apothecaries and amulet sellers. On your right is ❹ **Wat Mahathat**, one of Thailand's most-renowned Buddhist universities. Turn left into narrow Trok Maha That for great people-watching at the intriguing ❺ **Amulet Market** (p68). Winding north through the market, Buddhist talismans give way to food vendors before you reach ❻ **Thammasat University**, known for its law and political-science departments.

Exit at Phra Chan Pier, cross Th Na Phra That and continue east to ❼ **Sanam Luang**, the 'Royal Field' that's also a park. Cross the park and continue south along Th Ratchadamnoen Nai to Bangkok's city pillar shrine, ❽ **Lak Meuang**.

Head south along Th Sanam Chai and turn right onto Th Thai Wang to reach the entrance of ❾ **Wat Pho** (p57), home of the Reclining Buddha. Catch the cross-river ferry from adjacent Tien Pier to ❿ **Wat Arun** (p66).

On the grounds of the **Amulet Market** (p68), you might find a fortune teller or two. The 'fortune-telling school' is only a few steps away.

Sanam Luang, a rare green space, was originally used for royal cremations.

The best time to visit **Wat Arun** (p66) is around 5pm, when you can take photos during magic hour before it closes at 6pm.

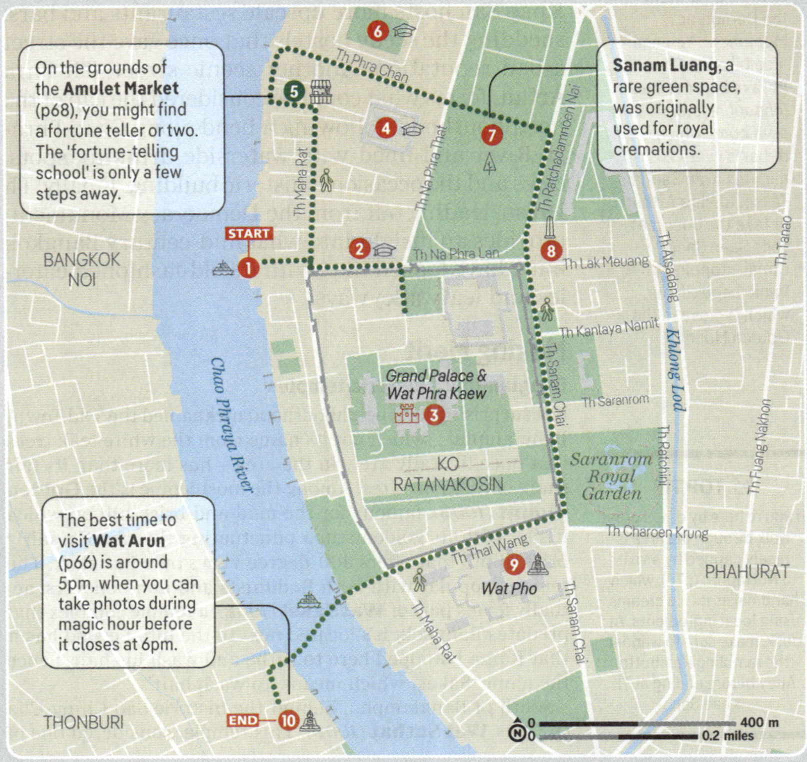

Banglamphu

BANGKOK'S MOST CHARMING QUARTER

GETTING AROUND

You can take the Metro (MRT) to Sam Yod and hop in a tuk-tuk from there for around 200฿ to the area around the Democracy Monument. You can also take the **Chao Phraya Express Boat** *(chaophrayaexpress boat.com)*, which departs every 20 minutes from Saphan Taksin to Phra Arthit; or take the boat that sails Saen Saep Canal, stopping at Panfa Leelard Pier, which is close to the Golden Mount.

TOP TIP

If you're here by day, a great walk through the area is nicely capped by a visit to Nuttaporn (p78), which handmakes its ice creams using local ingredients. At dusk, make sure to wander the rambling Rambuttri Alley before ending at Th Khao San.

Even die-hard Bangkokians idealise the neighbourhood of Banglamphu, which forms the northern end of Ko Ratanakosin. Bordered to the west by Chao Phraya River, and liberally sprinkled with unexpected green spaces and rakish old buildings, Banglamphu is a walker's paradise.

It's little wonder, then, that it also harbours the traditional entry point for foreign travellers to Thailand: Th Khao San (aka 'Backpackers' Road'). Today, Khao San hosts more upscale restaurants and bars, shedding the seedy hostels that once gave the street a bad reputation. Another scenic street, Th Phra Arthit, forms what could be considered the cap of the neighbourhood, following a bend along Chao Phraya River and lined with waterside drinking spots, cafes and the occasional historic building. Finally, Th Dinso, leading out from the Democracy Monument, provides an insight into what mid-century Bangkok must have looked like, with its old-fashioned eateries and leafy alleyways.

Making Merit

Banglamphu's historic temples

Not surprising for a neighbourhood nicknamed the 'Old Town', Banglamphu – which got its name from the white teak trees that once liberally grew in the area – has more than its fair share of religious sites. Among the most iconic is the **Golden Mount** *(100฿)*, famous for the mud-and-brick hill on which it sits, with its golden stupa punctuating the top of a fairly brisk climb that offers 360-degree views over Bangkok. The temple, popular with both Buddhists and non-believers, actually forms part of **Wat Saket** *(100฿)*, a temple complex that predates Bangkok; it's located next to the hill. Legend has it that Rama I stopped here to bathe and wash his hair, hence the name 'Saket', which means 'to wash hair'.

South of Banglamphu, behind the historic Sao Ching-Cha (p77), is **Wat Suthat** *(100฿)*. This temple, considered one of

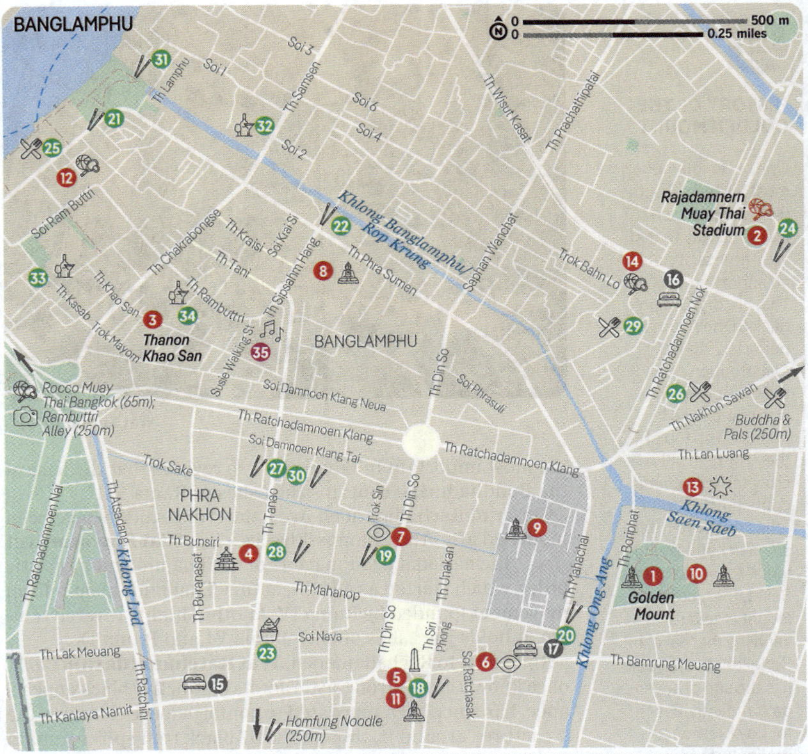

BANGLAMPHU

HIGHLIGHTS
1 Golden Mount
2 Rajadamnern Muay Thai Stadium
3 Thanon Khao San

SIGHTS
4 San Chao Por Sua
5 Sao Ching-Cha
6 Thanon Bamrung Meuang
7 Thanon Dinso
8 Wat Bowonniwet
9 Wat Ratchanatdaram
10 Wat Saket
11 Wat Suthat

ACTIVITIES
see 12 Jaroenthong Muay Thai Gym
12 Muay Thai Street
13 Sangmorakot Muay Thai Academy
14 Thanomsak Boxing Gym

SLEEPING
15 Bhuthorn
16 Nanda Heritage
17 Niras Bankoc

EATING
18 Absorn Thai Bistro
19 Arawy Vegetarian Food
20 Jay Fai
21 Karim Roti-Mataba
22 Khao Tom Bowon
23 Kor Panit's Sticky Rice
24 Likhit Kai Yang
25 Nai Soie Beef Noodle
see 15 Nuttaporn
26 Paengrum's Books & Cafe
27 Pak Mor Phu-Phan
28 Saw Nah Wang
29 Seven Spoons
30 Sky High
31 Somsong Phochana

DRINKING & NIGHTLIFE
32 Adhere the 13th Blue Bar
33 Fu Bar
34 Happy Bar

ENTERTAINMENT
35 Brick Bar

EATING NEAR BANGLAMPHU'S TEMPLES: OUR PICKS

Absorn Thai Bistro: A cheaper, more accessible place to try a crab omelette and *dom yam gung* than its more renowned neighbour, Jay Fai. *9.30am-midnight* ฿

Jay Fai: In the shadow of the Golden Mount, this celebrity chef has been churning out great wok dishes for decades; lines are now hours long. *9am-7.30pm Wed-Sat* ฿฿฿

Homfung Noodle: Great *dom yam* broth noodles in this spot, right next to Wat Suthat. *10am-7pm Thu-Tue* ฿

Khao Tom Bowon: This longtime rice-porridge institution across from Wat Bowonniwet claims to have been the first in Bangkok to stir-fry morning glory. *3.30-9pm* ฿฿

HISTORY OF THE GOLDEN MOUNT

One of Banglamphu's most visited sites, the Golden Mount isn't just a fun way to test your fitness, it's also an important part of Thai history. Dating back to the Ayuthaya period (1290–1769), construction of the Golden Mount was completed by Rama V. The top of the 77m-high hill is crowned by a *chedi* containing Buddha relics received from a *chedi* in Kapilavastu, India. Alongside Wat Saket, the Golden Mount is said to serve as the 'navel of Bangkok'. Every year, it is the site of seven days of festivities for Loy Krathong (typically held in November), when old grudges and sins are carried away by the river, and the slate is wiped clean for the new year.

AMNAT30/SHUTTERSTOCK

Wat Suthat (p74)

the most important in Bangkok, is so revered that the base of the Buddha image contains the ashes of Rama VIII.

Closer to Rachadamnoen Ave – the street said to have been modelled after the Champs-Élysées – lies **Wat Bowonniwet** *(free)*, the national headquarters of the Thammayut monastic order, which started as a 19th-century Thai Buddhism reform movement founded by Rama IV. Another highly revered temple, it holds the ashes of both Rama VI and Rama IX.

Right next to Rachadamnoen, **Wat Ratchanatdaram** *(20฿)*, once known as the 'Iron Castle' for its distinctive black appearance, has since been renovated to conform more closely to the structures around it, though the 37 black iron spires remain (representing the 37 virtues required to reach enlightenment).

Charming Old Town

Travel to a gentler time

Visitors to Banglamphu can be forgiven for never leaving the neighbourhood; with its beautiful wooden buildings, interesting alleyways and general chilled-out atmosphere, the so-called 'Old Town' makes traffic jams and air pollution seem like afflictions from a different era. Ratanakosin-era architecture – known for its lattice-edged roofs and mix of Eastern and Western styles – coexists alongside glittering temples and the occasional mid-century building, making for diverting wanders shaded by trees and the occasional peek of a river or canal.

EATING IN BANGLAMPHU: LUNCH

Sky High: This old-fashioned rice-porridge shop dates back to the 1940s and has a suitably heady retro atmosphere. *10am-midnight* ฿฿

Saw Nah Wang: This unassuming open-air shophouse serves what may be the best *mee pad grachate* in the city. *9am-9pm Thu-Tue* ฿

Arawy Vegetarian Food: One of the oldest Thai vegetarian eateries in Bangkok is housed in an open-air shophouse. *7.30am-7pm* ฿

Somsong Phochana: Serves hard-to-find Thai dishes, including Sukhothai noodles and fermented rice noodles with pineapple and shrimp. *11am-1.30pm & 4-9.30pm* ฿

Perhaps most illustrative of the Old Town feel is **Thanon Dinso**, which branches out south from Rachadamnoen Ave and runs almost horizontally through the centre of the neighbourhood. Shady and lined with rickety shophouses, Dinso – which means 'pencil', named after the items made by craftspeople here – can serve as a half-day walk for the consummate foodie, with well-known restaurants rubbing shoulders with ancient mobile carts. The street ends with City Hall on the left. Although it's unlikely to be of much interest to you (aside from its restrooms), the two signs in front of City Hall show off Bangkok's full name, recognised by the *Guinness Book of World Records* as the longest city name in the world.

Meanwhile, the 30m-high **Sao Ching-Cha** is a relic from a bygone era, when young men competed to swing high enough to reach a bag of gold suspended from a pole during Hindu Brahmin ceremonies. The ceremony was discontinued in 1935 after some fatalities. The monument is also home to the 8m bronze Buddha image Phra Si Sakayamuni, the largest surviving one of its kind from the Sukhothai period.

Finally, in front of Wat Suthat stretches **Thanon Bamrung Meuang**, which is lined with shops selling everything a Buddhist temple needs, from golden Buddha figures to candles, monks' robes and even coffins.

THANON KHAO SAN IN POPULAR MEDIA

There's a reason why visitors to Bangkok feel compelled to check out this 410m street in the Old Town. After all, it has starred in movies, TV series and books. Of course, there is Alex Garland's *The Beach* (1996), a book about a jaded young traveller in search of utopia amid the chaos of the big city (which later became a movie starring Leonardo DiCaprio). It also served as a backdrop to the misadventures of *The Hangover Part II* (2011), to some of the real-life crimes of French serial killer Charles Sobhraj in the Netflix series *The Serpent* (2021), and to detective Sonchai Jitpleecheep's murder investigation in John Burdett's *Bangkok 8* (2003).

Head to Backpacker Central

Follow in the footsteps of backpackers past

Thanon Khao San is perhaps the most high-profile product of the age of independent travel, a 400m-long street that gives its name to the most famous backpacker enclave in the world. Even if they're not staying in the area, many travellers come to join the party and see for themselves why Th Khao San has been immortalised in books and movies.

On busy nights, as many as 50,000 people visit Khao San, turning the slender street into a beach-less version of the Full Moon parties on Ko Pha-Ngan. EDM pounds out and travellers sink buckets of alcohol while food stalls, hair-braiders, henna tattooists, T-shirt sellers, and touts for bars and massage parlours take up almost every inch of available space. If this sounds like your personal version of hell, no worries: there's more to Khao San than just the street itself. The alleyways – Rambuttri, Phra Arthit and Samsen – surrounding it are the breezy bossa nova to Khao San's insistent EDM. It's here that you'll find traditional wooden homes, shophouse restaurants, laid-back music venues and most of the area's accommodation.

DRINKING AROUND KHAO SAN: LIVE MUSIC

Adhere the 13th Blue Bar: An intimate jazz and blues spot that's one of Bangkok's top live music bars; a convenient location on Th Samsen. *7pm-1am* BB

Brick Bar: Ska and reggae reign at this mammoth bar that can accommodate up to 1000 guests, with a mostly Thai crowd. *6pm-2am* BB

Happy Bar: A longtime favourite among Bangkok expats, this tiny but crowded spot bills itself as the 'real rasta bar' on Rambuttri Alley. *4pm-2am* BB

Fu Bar: This funky spot's claim to fame is the excellent three-piece live band; there's Guinness on tap. *5pm-midnight* BB

SAMPLE STREET FOOD IN THE OLD TOWN

Take a bite – or several – of the street-food offerings in historic Old Bangkok.

START	END	LENGTH
Karim Roti-Mataba	Nuttaporn	2km; 40 minutes

Start your tasting trail of Banglamphu at historic Thai-Muslim shophouse 1 **Karim Roti-Mataba**, where the *roti* (flatbreads) and *mataba* (stuffed flatbreads) are made fresh daily.

Turn left out of the shophouse onto Th Phra Arthit. Just past a Rattanakosin-era mansion and with a distinctive smell of stewing beef, you'll find 2 **Nai Soie Beef Noodle**, where tender strips of beef (and blood) are served in bowls of soupy noodles; this spot draws gaggles of tourists.

Turn left into Chana Songkhram Alley – a charming narrow lane lined with offbeat shops – to reach Rambuttri Alley. This pleasant tree-lined street is home to a peaceful temple and all manner of mobile vendors. From here, it's a 10-minute walk to 3 **Thanon Khao San** (p77), a frequent backdrop in books and movies. Food-wise, there's not much here for lunch when it comes to famous Thai dishes, but Th Tanao, just four minutes away across Rachadamnern Ave, harbours plenty. Stop at 4 **Pak Mor Phu-Phan** for a good *kai kata*, or 'egg in a pan'. Suitably refreshed, stroll down the street to the famous 5 **San Chao Por Sua** shrine, home to a tiger god and a favourite with Chinese visitors.

From here, it's only a stone's throw to 6 **Nuttaporn**, where a group of taciturn women churn homemade ice cream on a daily basis. They'll let you know what toppings are best for your ice cream.

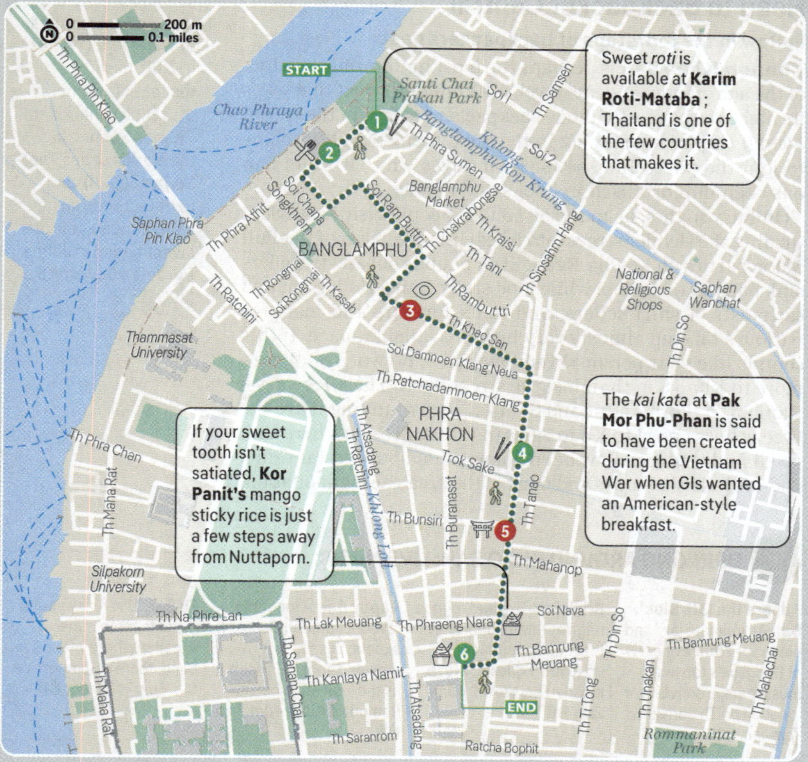

Sweet *roti* is available at **Karim Roti-Mataba**; Thailand is one of the few countries that makes it.

The *kai kata* at **Pak Mor Phu-Phan** is said to have been created during the Vietnam War when GIs wanted an American-style breakfast.

If your sweet tooth isn't satiated, **Kor Panit's** mango sticky rice is just a few steps away from Nuttaporn.

Of course, Khao San wasn't always a destination. The street itself dates back to 1892, when it was known for its rice market; in fact, *khao san* means 'milled rice'. During the 1980s, traders who visited asked to rent rooms, spurring entrepreneurial Thais to open businesses that would cater to them. This is when Khao San's reputation as a cheap spot for accommodation was launched. Later in the 2000s, hipster Bangkokians would 'rediscover' the street, opening up quirky establishments that gradually phased out the cheap hostels. Today, post-COVID, Khao San is back to a soundtrack of duelling EDM tracks and bucket drinks – proof that you can't keep a good party down.

The Art of Eight Limbs

Up close and personal with muay Thai

A night of *muay Thai* at **Rajadamnern Muay Thai Stadium** *(rajadamnern.com; tickets from 1500฿)* can feel a lot like attending an American sporting event: flashing lights, pulsing music, a hyperactive MC, and lots of ads for pizza and burgers. But once the bell clangs and the traditional Thai music kicks in, you're reminded that you are in Thailand – even if the fighters in front of you may not all be Thai.

Known as the 'Art of Eight Limbs', *muay Thai* is said to have been developed by Siamese soldiers who often had to engage in hand-to-hand combat in war. The 'eight limbs' are the striking points of the sport: fists, elbows, knees and shins. Besides jabs and uppercuts, fighters utilise 'clinches', which enable them to grab onto their opponent to land a knee or elbow; and 'sweeps', which allow them to use their legs to knock their opponent down. All the while, sweat sprays as the band plays, with the music building to a frenzy until the bell clangs to signal the end of the round.

Rajadamnern Stadium, built in 1945, bills itself as the 'oldest *muay Thai* stadium in the world'. Different days of the week host different events, with Mondays to Wednesdays typically featuring weaker fighters. Thursdays, Fridays and Saturdays are the big-ticket nights, with Thursdays and Fridays showcasing traditional *muay Thai*, while Saturdays add entertainment *muay Thai* (similar to MMA) to the mix. Spectators can pay anywhere from 1500฿ per person for a concrete bleacher (bring a cushion) to 3500฿ and upwards for VIP seats, which include unlimited snacks, soft drinks and beer. Although buying tickets online is encouraged, you can still rock up to the box office a few hours ahead of time to make your selection.

BANGLAMPHU'S BEST MUAY THAI GYMS

Strap on the gloves and live out those Jean-Claude Van Damme dreams at these *muay Thai* gyms.

Sangmorakot Muay Thai Academy: Serious *muay Thai* followers come here at 3pm to watch skilled fighters practise.

Jaroenthong Muay Thai Gym: This spot is recommended for both beginners and intermediate fighters.

Rocco Muay Thai Bangkok: This gym has skilled instructors and a focus on fitness.

Thanomsak Boxing Gym: For *muay Thai* newbies, this spot offers a great entry into the sport if you don't know where to start.

Muay Thai Street: For those who already love *muay Thai*, this well-equipped gym is where to meet like-minded people.

EATING AROUND RAJADAMNERN STADIUM: OUR PICKS

Likhit Kai Yang: This longstanding joint does northeastern Thai-style grilled chicken and sticky rice. *9am-7.30pm* ฿฿

Seven Spoons: This spot draws a crowd from the nearby UN building with its Mediterranean cuisine. *11am-2.30pm & 5-9.30pm* ฿฿฿

Paengrum's Books & Cafe: This tiny spot serves eggs, toast and sausages (plus coffee) in a charming bookshop cluttered with retro knick-knacks. *9am-6pm, to 6.30pm Sat* ฿

Buddha & Pals: Officially a jazz club, they also offer good open-faced sandwiches, Brittany-inspired crepes and filling soups. *10am-midnight Tue-Sun* ฿฿฿

Thewet & Dusit

ROYAL RESIDENCES AND A RIVERSIDE COMMUNITY

GETTING AROUND

Dusit is right next to the river, so getting to it via **Chao Phraya Express Boat** *(chaophrayaexpress boat.com)* is a snap. The river boat can be accessed from the Saphan Taksin Skytrain (BTS) stop, after which you can take a 40-minute boat ride to Thewet Pier. If you take the Metro (MRT), the closest stop is Hua Lamphong, after which you can take a taxi or motorbike to Dusit and Thewet. Within the two districts, taxis, motorbikes and tuk-tuks are available.

TOP TIP

There's very little tourist infrastructure in Dusit, but there are a few riverside restaurants in Thewet, and food stalls generally congregate around the flower market.

The twin neighbourhoods of Thewet and Dusit came into being in the 19th century, when Bangkok's boundaries began to expand north and east of Ko Ratanakosin. Dusit is now the administrative heart of Thailand – home to government offices and the Dusit Palace, a vast compound currently closed to the public that contains the present-day residences of the royal family. The wide boulevards and European-style mansions (most now official buildings) were inspired by what Rama V saw on a tour of European capitals in 1897.

Thewet, in contrast, is a small riverside neighbourhood that's essentially an extension of Banglamphu, which lies just to the south. It takes its name from a historic canal bridge constructed during Rama V's reign and is best known for its large fresh-produce market, which sits close to Chao Phraya River. While Thewet is a quiet area, especially at night, you're just a short hop from lively Th Khao San.

JACK SUVARNABHUMI/SHUTTERSTOCK

Wat Benchamabophit Dusitwanaram

HIGHLIGHTS
1 Wat Benchamabophit Dusitwanaram

SIGHTS
2 Dusit Palace Park
3 Wat Thevarat Kunchorn

SLEEPING
4 Baan Tepa Boutique House
5 Casa Nithra
6 Phra-Nakorn Norn-Len

EATING
7 Kaloang Home Kitchen
8 Krua Apsorn
9 Rat Na Yot Phak 40 Years
10 Steve Café & Cuisine

TRANSPORT
11 Thewet Pier

Temple Traditions

Finding tranquillity at riverside temples

Because the twin neighbourhoods of Dusit and Thewet are essentially viewed as a place where civil servants go to work, they don't see as many tourists as their neighbouring districts. This is a shame, since Dusit in particular possesses a quiet, laid-back charm that is absent from the street-side hurly-burly of Silom and Sukhumvit. That charm extends to **Wat Benchamabophit Dusitwanaram** *(20฿)*, also known among locals as 'Wat Ben' and built by Rama V after he decided he wanted a royal temple near his residence at Dusit Palace. Of all of the temples in Bangkok that could have been chosen, it is here that Rama V's ashes are interred, even though the temple is considered relatively new. Wat Ben is also called the 'Marble Temple', with the ordination hall fashioned out of white marble imported from Italy. Its graceful symmetry is now regarded as a classic example of modern Thai Buddhist architecture. Although somewhat popular with tourists – who arrive early in the morning when the resident monks parade to receive alms between 6am and 7.30am – Wat Ben gets nowhere near the crowds of temples such as Wat Pho and Wat Suthat.

Another underrated temple is **Wat Thevarat Kunchorn** *(free)*, a riverside temple in Thewet dating back to the pre-Ratanakosin days that was successively expanded and renovated by later kings. The ordination hall was constructed during the reign of Rama III and modelled on the hall housing

HOME OF THAILAND'S KINGS

No history of Thailand's monarchy is complete without a mention of **Dusit Palace Park**, built in the early 1900s by Rama V and inspired by European palaces. Comprising 6.5 hectares of gardens and royal residences, Dusit Palace has now mostly been turned into museums, which are currently under renovation. **Vimanmek Royal Teak Mansion** was the first permanent residence built in Dusit and is possibly the world's biggest golden teak structure, blending European neoclassical architecture with traditional Thai style. Meanwhile, the **Abhisek Dusit Throne Hall**, built to receive foreign dignitaries, fuses Victorian gingerbread style with Moorish and Thai elements. As of writing, you can walk around the plaza grounds only.

AALEKSANDER/SHUTTERSTOCK

Vimanmek Royal Teak Mansion

the Emerald Buddha at Wat Phra Kaew (p73). Interior murals depict stories from Buddhist lore, and there's a collection of Buddha statuary from the Ayuthaya period (1290–1769). Worshippers here often leave a monk's robe as an offering. Best of all, you can get here via boat, disembarking at Thewet Pier. The temple is open daily from 9am to 5pm.

EATING IN DUSIT & THEWET: OUR PICKS

Krua Apsorn: This unassuming restaurant is something of a local institution, specialising in delicious lotus stem curry. *10am-7.30pm Mon-Sat* ฿฿

Steve Café & Cuisine: The Thewet branch of this popular restaurant offers decent Thai food with great riverside views. *10am-10pm* ฿฿

Rat Na Yot Phak 40 Years: Renowned Thai-Chinese noodles (flat rice noodles served in a gravy sauce) in this traditional, open-air shophouse setting. *9am-9pm* ฿

Kaloang Home Kitchen: Right next to the river, this open-air eatery – part of a hotel – specialises in Thai seafood. *11am-10pm* ฿฿

Chinatown

A HISTORIC NEIGHBOURHOOD FINDS NEW LIFE

The history of Chinatown – called Yaowarat by locals – is intertwined with that of modern Bangkok. Once situated in the area now known as Sampeng, the current heart of Chinatown is Th Yaowarat, considered the cultural nexus for Bangkok's burgeoning Chinese–Thai community, most of whom are of Teochew descent. By day, it's a bustling warren of activity, criss-crossed by food vendors bearing snacks on mobile carts and motorbikes transporting goods. By night, the neon lights flicker on, and Chinatown's party atmosphere ramps up as guests throng its streetside eateries, sampling everything from super-spicy squid to sweet-filled buns. Always known for its street food and fresh markets, Chinatown has undergone something of a renaissance in the past few years, particularly around Th Songwat and Th Nana, now home to trendy restaurants, shops and bars. All the same, the heartbeat of Chinatown's heritage thumps soundly as the birthplace of Thai street food.

TOP TIP

The most beautiful time to visit Chinatown is at dusk, when the neon lights come on and everything is bathed in a purple light. If you plan on doing a street-food crawl, start with a fortifying drink at Shanghai Mansion (p134), a hotel where you'll also find decent bathrooms.

Eat Your Heart Out

Chinatown's most distinctive restaurants

Bangkok's Chinatown is not only the birthplace of Thai street food (where Chinese immigrants sold snacks canal-side as people went about their day). It's also the birthplace of Thai restaurants in general. Before the arrival of the Chinese en masse in the 18th and 19th centuries, Thais cooked and entertained at home. As chef and food-history scholar David

Continued on p87

GETTING AROUND

The easiest way to get to Chinatown is by Metro (MRT), exiting at Wat Mangkon station. If you don't have a particular place in mind, take the Plang Nam Rd exit, which will land you straight in the thick of things. Take the scenic route (via water) by boarding the **Chao Phraya Express Boat** *(chaophrayaexpressboat.com)* at Saphan Taksin and getting off at Ratchawong Pier, a short walk from Th Yaowarat. By bus, use lines 1, 4, 7, 25, 53 or 73. You can always take a taxi if you're not concerned about traffic.

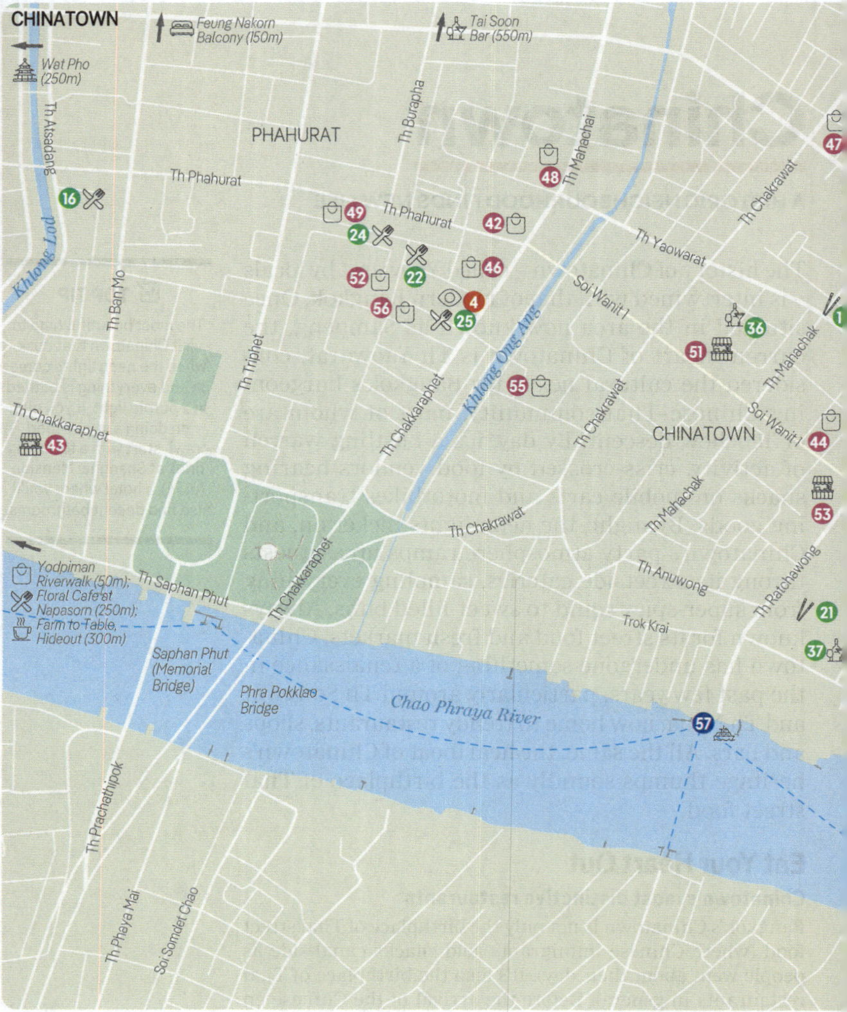

CHINATOWN

Feung Nakorn Balcony (150m)
Tai Soon Bar (550m)
Wat Pho (250m)
Yodpiman Riverwalk (50m); Floral Cafe at Napasorn (250m); Farm to Table, Hideout (300m)
PHAHURAT
CHINATOWN
Th Atsadang
Khlong Lod
Th Ban Mo
Th Phahurat
Th Burapha
Th Mahachai
Th Chakrawat
Th Yaowarat
Soi Wanit 1
Th Triphet
Th Chakkaraphet
Khlong Ong Ang
Th Mahachak
Th Chakrawat
Th Saphan Phut
Th Anuwong
Th Ratchawong
Trok Krai
Saphan Phut (Memorial Bridge)
Phra Pokklao Bridge
Chao Phraya River
Th Prachathipok
Th Phaya Mai
Soi Somdet Chao

HIGHLIGHTS
1 POTONG
2 Talat Mai
3 Wat Traimit

SIGHTS
4 Little India
5 San Chao Mae Guan Yin
6 Wat Mangkon Kamalawat
7 Yaowarat Chinatown Heritage Center

SLEEPING
8 Luk Hostel
9 Mustang Blu
10 Shanghai Mansion

EATING
11 Baan Trok Tua Ngork
12 Chop Chop
13 e-Ga Lab
14 HAGOW Yaowarat
see 35 Hua Seng Hong
see 46 India Emporium Food Court
15 Jae Lee Vegan
16 Kem-Kon Vegan
17 Kiew's Pie
18 Krua Phon La Mai
19 Lod Chong Singapore
20 NAAM 1608
21 Nai Ek Roll Noodle
22 Punjab Sweets
23 Punsuk Vegetarian
24 Royal India
25 Samosa Corner
26 Samsara
27 So Vegan
28 SongViet at SongWat
29 Tia Sua Restaurant
30 Urai Braised Goose
31 Yim Yim

DRINKING & NIGHTLIFE
32 Asia Today
33 Bukowski & Co.
34 Chaidim Tea House
35 Double Dogs Tearoom
36 Glass Half Full Bar & Cafe
37 Hex Bar
38 Jip Eu
39 K. Mui Kee Teahouse
40 Teens of Thailand
41 Tep Bar

SHOPPING
42 China World
43 Flower Market
44 Hong 265
45 I'm Chinatown
46 India Emporium
47 Khlong Thom Center
48 Mega Plaza Saphan Lek
49 Phahurat Market
50 Road of Cinnamon
51 Sampeng Lane
52 Sanguansook Store
53 Talat Gow
54 Talat Khlong Thom
55 Venezia Textile
56 Yong Panich

TRANSPORT
57 Ratchawong Pier

A TASTE OF CHINATOWN'S STREET FOOD

Eat your way through some of Chinatown's most beloved foodie stops, from curry on rice to hot charred noodles.

START	END	LENGTH
Jek Pui	: Bua Loy Nam King	1.5km; 30 minutes

Start in the shadow of Wat Mangkon Kamalawat (p88), where 1 **Jek Pui** has been serving their Chinese-inflected style of curry on rice for decades. The grandmother – who helped her father sell curries from the bamboo pole on his back – still holds court in the kitchen, cooking vats of yellow and green curries every day.

Suitably fortified, take a five-minute walk to 2 **Jay Eng Mu Sate**, where the char-grilled chicken, pork, beef and squid satay are considered the best in the neighbourhood.

Double back from Jay Eng to the 100-year-old rice-porridge shop 3 **Jay Suay**, popular with chefs for the tea-smoked duck and clear soup with pickled plum. But if you fear getting too full, cross Th Charoen Krung towards busy Th Plang Nam and 4 **Krua Phon La Mai**, which is popular for its range of fried noodles served on hotplates.

If you have space, continue towards Th Yaowarat and turn right. Across the street, you'll find 5 **Guay Jab Ouan Pochana**. This shop has served its unique style of peppery and clear pork-noodle soup for over 50 years, gaining it a Michelin Bib Gourmand. If you're not a fan of pork innards, just order the pork meat.

To finish off your ambulatory dinner, take dessert at 6 **Bua Loy Nam King**, where the namesake dish – rice flour dumplings stuffed with black sesame seeds in a hot ginger broth – is homemade every day.

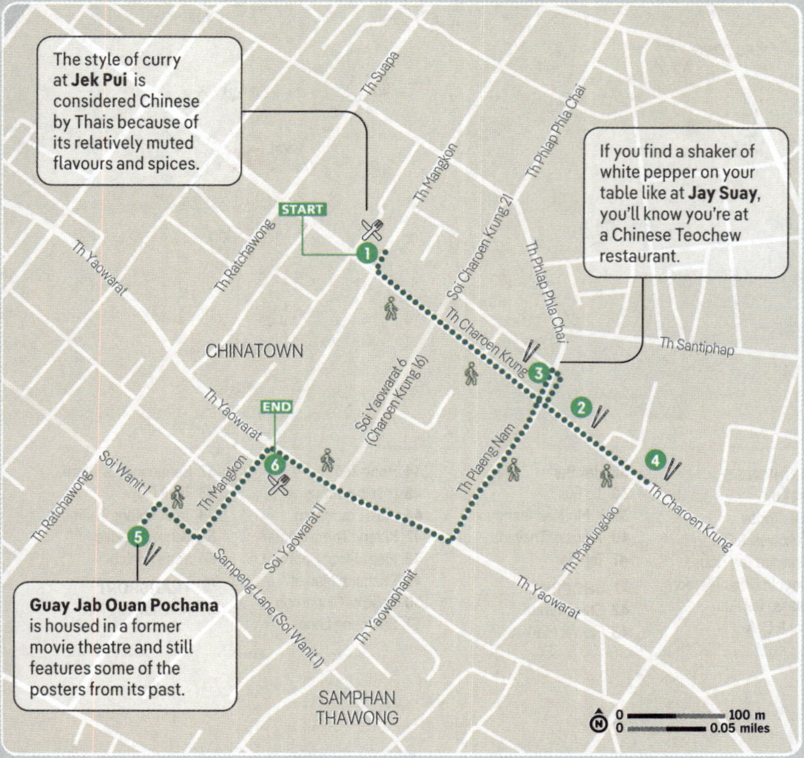

The style of curry at **Jek Pui** is considered Chinese by Thais because of its relatively muted flavours and spices.

If you find a shaker of white pepper on your table like at **Jay Suay**, you'll know you're at a Chinese Teochew restaurant.

Guay Jab Ouan Pochana is housed in a former movie theatre and still features some of the posters from its past.

Continued from p83
Thompson explains it, the homes of Chinese immigrants were too small to accommodate kitchens, so some Chinese converted their living quarters into places where they could cook and sell food to their countrymen and women. And *voilà*, the first restaurants were born.

This means that having a meal in Chinatown isn't just about enjoying delicious food; it's also about sampling a bit of history. Foodies who want to taste Thai-Chinese food as it was in the early 1900s should check out the century-old **Yim Yim** *(062 396 4255)*, tucked off the main drag in a quiet alleyway and offering a menu and decor that haven't changed since its inception.

For an updated look at the traditional Thai-Chinese 'cookshop', David Thompson's **Chop Chop** *(chopchopbkk.com)* on Th Yaowarat provides a lovingly retro experience, replete with hard-to-find dishes.

Classic dim-sum parlours are a dime a dozen here, but arguably the most low-key and local spot is **Hua Seng Hong** *(huasenghong.com)*, also on Th Yaowarat. And if high-end foodery is what you're hankering for, Michelin-starred **POTONG** *(restaurantpotong.com)* provides a glimpse into the future of Thai-Chinese food by mining the family heritage of Chef Pam Pichaya Soontornyanakij. Make sure to book ahead!

Ascending to the Temple of the Golden Buddha

The gateway to Chinatown

If you decide to walk from Hua Lumphong Train Station to Chinatown, you'll know you're close to the action when you start smelling incense, star anise and cinnamon in the air. These smells also mean you're in the vicinity of **Wat Traimit** *(100฿)*, known as the Temple of the Golden Buddha thanks to the solid-gold Buddha image that is the main draw to visitors. Said to have been discovered in 1955 underneath a plaster shell, the 3m-tall, 5.5-tonne image was discovered when it fell from a crane while being moved within the temple compound, revealing the Sukhothai-style treasure within. Scholars speculate that the image, which may date as far back as the 13th century, was hidden for fear of Burmese marauders taking the golden statue to their homeland. Today, its presence has rendered the once-neglected Wat Traimit into Chinatown's

WHAT IS A COOKSHOP?

Thai TV personality Chef McDang has detailed how during the reign of Rama V, royal palaces and aristocratic houses employed Hainanese chefs, considered the best in the region, to cook their idea of Western cuisine for European guests in a bid to look *sivilai* (civilised). This charm offensive resulted in fusion dishes that can still be spied on menus today, including pork chops in cornstarch-thickened gravy with cow peas; beef tongue stew, eaten with white bread and butter; and thin slices of steak served alongside a salad with a sweet dressing. The descendants of these Hainanese chefs eventually opened their own restaurants, which became the height of glamour in mid-century Bangkok; today, only a handful of these cookshops remain.

DRINKING IN CHINATOWN: TEA

Double Dogs Tearoom: A wide selection of teas in a calm setting not too far from the Wat Mangkon Metro station. *11am-6pm Thu-Mon* ฿฿

JIp Eu: Enjoy a real slice of Chinatown life at this cafe, mostly patronised by an older clientele and offering a wide range of teas. *8am-5pm Mon-Sat* ฿฿

K. Mui Kee Teahouse: The owner is frequently on-hand to provide insight into the many teas on offer. *10am-6pm Mon-Sat, 11am-2.30pm Sun* ฿฿

Chaidim Tea House: A selection of promising organic tea grown mostly on Thai plantations, with a few selections from China and Japan. *10am-5pm Tue-Sun* ฿

OTHER CHINATOWN TEMPLES

Although Wat Traimit is one of Chinatown's biggest draws, it's not the only one. **Wat Mangkon Kamalawat** *(free)*, after which the Chinatown Metro (MRT) stop is named, is traditionally considered the heart of Chinatown and plays an integral role during the Chinese New Year (January and/or February) and the Chinese–Taoist Vegetarian Festival (October). Unlike Wai Traimit, Wat Mangkon is built in the Chinese style, with tiled roofs, dragon motifs and a pavilion dedicated to the Chinese goddess Mae Guan Yin (the reason why a sizeable number of Chinese–Thais abstain from eating beef).

A temple dedicated solely to Mae Guan Yin is **San Chao Mae Guan Yin** *(free)*, an incongruously beautiful spot on Th Charoen Krung.

most important Buddhist shrine. The statue's surroundings – in the impressive four-storey marble Phra Maha Mandop – reflects its importance to the neighbourhood.

On Phra Maha Mandop's 2nd floor, the **Yaowarat Chinatown Heritage Center** *(100฿)* details the birth and evolution of the neighbourhood, right up to the present day. The museum depicts what life was like for Chinese immigrants arriving in the capital in the late 18th century before branching out into the community's assimilation into the Thai populace. Today, 15% of Thailand's population is descended from Chinese immigrants, making it the world's biggest overseas Chinese community. Wat Traimit is open daily from 8am to 5pm.

Explore Little India

Get lost in Phahurat

One of Chinatown's most underrated corners, Phahurat – also known as Little India – offers a vibrant glimpse into one of Bangkok's most interesting communities. Little India was born in the late 19th century when Rama V, recognising the importance of Indian traders to the local economy, invited them to settle in the parcel of land situated between Chinatown and the Old Town. Today, this neighbourhood offers a dizzying array of goods unavailable anywhere else in the city, as well as some excellent Indian food, making it the perfect lunchtime stop or full-on afternoon activity.

Just turn right when leaving Exit 1 of Sam Yod Metro (MRT) station, and a seven-minute walk will take you to Little India. You can choose to plunge straight into the fray along Th Chakkraphet, or dip a dainty toe by entering **India Emporium**, where everything sold on the street outside can be found, but on a smaller scale, and in air-conditioning. Peruse shops bursting with saris, *kajal* and henna before indulging in a quick snack on the top floor. Better yet, grab a streetside samosa from the **Samosa Corner** cart next to India Emporium before hurtling into the adjacent alleyway, where Little India's grocery stores and a handful of sweets shops reside. Hard-to-find spices such as curry leaves and cardamom pods vie with *gulab jamun* and *jalebi* for your attention, and if you go all the way to the end, you'll find yourself in **Phahurat Market** (*facebook.com/taladphahurad*), known for its byzantine, twisty walkways and vendors selling everything from stick-on bindis to incense.

EATING AROUND CHINATOWN: VEGETARIAN

Ruyi Vegetarian: This vegan spot close to Hua Lumphong Train Station is lauded for its realistic takes on deep-fried crab and chicken with cashew nuts. *10am-9pm* ฿฿

Punsuk Vegetarian: Thai vegan standards compete with vegan sushi stuffed with cabbage, carrots and cucumber at this eatery near Wat Mangkon. *6am-2.30pm & 4.30-8pm* ฿

So Vegan: Just as the name says, this restaurant in the 'I'm Chinatown' mall serves vegan versions of favourites such as wonton soup and Thai curries. *10am-8pm* ฿

Jae Lee Vegan: Find extremely reasonable renditions of Thai street-food favourites in a casual setting. *8am-5.30pm* ฿

STROLL LITTLE INDIA & SAMPENG

These markets are the perfect playground for visitors seeking just a taste of Chinatown's chaotic market life.

START	END	LENGTH
Th Vanich 1 (Saphan Han Bridge)	GaCha Tea House & Cafe	1.1km; 20 minutes

Start at Saphan Han Bridge, and you'll find yourself on the walking street known as 'Hua Met Alley' or 1 **Thanon Vanich 1**. The entire street feels like a maze of narrow tunnels – in actuality small alleys lined with shops and vendors, with carts constantly moving in all directions.

On the opposite side of the bridge is 2 **Salim Porncharoen**. This is the perfect place to try the *salim*, a Thai dessert of brightly coloured, delicate vermicelli in sweet coconut syrup and shaved ice.

Southeast along Th Vanich, you'll find 3 **Jae Buay Saphan Han**, where you can stop *for poh pia sod* – a Thai snack of fresh, hand-wrapped spring roll topped with a thick, savoury brown sauce.

Further southeast along Th Vanich, proceed to where it meets Th Mangkon. Look up to admire the facade of the iconic gold shop, 4 **Tang Toh Kang**. The building features a beautiful blend of Chinese-influenced architecture, carefully preserved by the owners.

As the street grows quieter towards the edge of the neighbourhood, you'll find 5 **GaCha Tea House & Cafe**, a cosy teahouse offering a range of beverages – from vegan milk tea to iced coconut-water coffee. If the owner has stepped into the back for a rest, just ring the bell for service.

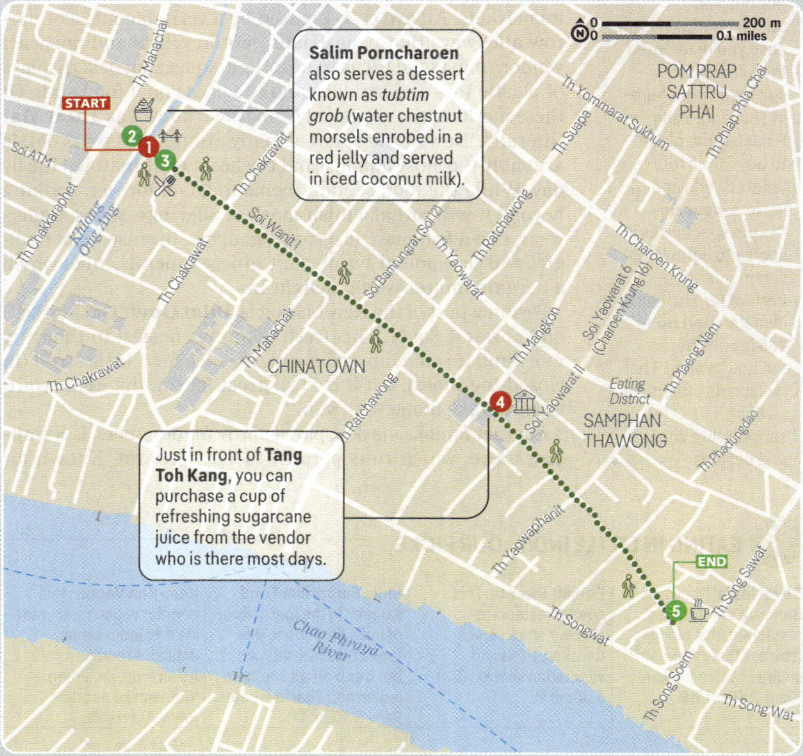

Salim Porncharoen also serves a dessert known as *tubtim grob* (water chestnut morsels enrobed in a red jelly and served in iced coconut milk).

Just in front of **Tang Toh Kang**, you can purchase a cup of refreshing sugarcane juice from the vendor who is there most days.

GREAT SHOPS FOR DESIGNERS IN CHINATOWN

Tawn C is a fashion designer and TV personality. *@tawn_c*

The Little India (p88) and Sampeng areas have long been a creative playground for hobbyists and designers alike. **Sanguansook Store** is a longstanding sewing-supply shop where you'll find vintage buttons, ribbons and upholstery tassels. In case you're tempted to have a custom suit made right here in Thailand, **Yong Panich** is the place to buy fabric for tailored suits and jackets. **Venezia Textile** specialises in linen and lightweight summer fabrics – perfect for Thailand's climate – and **Hong 265** is considered the holy grail by Thai fashion designers for all kinds of sewing supplies like zippers and buttons.

STRIPPEDPIXEL.COM/SHUTTERSTOCK

Fabric for sale, Sampeng Lane

Markets Galore

Shop Chinatown's crooked alleyways

One of the most eye-catching features of Chinatown by day is its markets. All are criss-crossed by a veritable maze of narrow alleyways that pedestrians, motorcyclists and pushcart vendors must take turns to negotiate, squeezing past displays of plastic toys and sandals, and the occasional food stall. Of these markets, the section of Chinatown known as **Talat Mai** (literally, 'New Market', but actually around 200 years old) is arguably the most famous, and the heart of Chinatown life by day. While the food section seems to go on forever, walking beyond it will reveal a mish-mash of offerings: shoes, underwear, dried fish maw, electronic gadgets, incense, paper effigies and ceremonial sweets for Chinese funerals, all of which a bargain hunter would delight in.

Forming part of the New Market is **Talat Gow** ('Old Market') on Yaowarat Soi 11. This fresh market is busiest in the early morning; if you're up and about, it's nice for a little stroll (in closed-toe shoes), but it isn't so great for finding items you'd want to take home with you.

Another famous market, particularly for designers, is **Sampeng Lane**, which runs parallel to Th Yaowarat. Known for

EATING IN LITTLE INDIA: OUR PICKS

Royal India: Known as Bangkok's first Indian restaurant, this place features tasty standards such as butter chicken. *10am-9.30pm* ฿฿

Punjab Sweets: This combo restaurant-grocery store serves delicious *dosa* and vegetarian snacks. *8am-6.30pm* ฿

India Emporium Food Court: On the fourth floor of India Emporium, this food court has shrunk, but it still offers southern Indian and Thai favourites. *9am-5.30pm* ฿

Kem-Kon Vegan: This popular vegan restaurant in Little India serves delicious renditions of Asian food, including Vietnamese noodles. *10am-10pm* ฿฿

its wholesale prices, Sampeng heaves with deals on fabrics, accessories, ready-made clothing, and other bits and bobs including tassels and buttons. Once considered the 'original Chinatown', Sampeng once contended with a difficult reputation as a den of iniquity but is now more popular for its lively atmosphere than its illicit activities.

Chinatown by Night

Savour Bangkok's buzziest streets

Bangkok is full of interesting neighbourhoods that enjoy flares of newfound interest after bursts of gentrification. For the past few years, that neighbourhood has been Chinatown, with said gentrification fuelled by the recent opening of the Wat Mangkon Metro (MRT) stop and a smattering of hot hotel and restaurant launches. Luckily for Chinatown, the arrivals have done little to alter its spirit: creative, colourful and cheerful, with just a tinge of chaos.

No mention of Chinatown nightlife is complete without discussing Th Nana, a newly revived street lined with trendy bars and restaurants (just make sure not to confuse it – and your taxi driver – with Th Nana on Sukhumvit, which is a notorious red-light district). This street is renowned for the atmospheric, rickety-looking shophouses that run alongside it. The OGs of the street remain **Tep Bar** *(tepmahanakhon.com)*, a self-described 'cultural bar' that regularly features live classical Thai music, and the oddly named **Teens of Thailand** *(@teens_of_thailandaround)*, which offers a wide selection of gin cocktails. Finally, **Asia Today** *(@asia_today_bar)* is beloved for its neon-lit interiors and great drinks made from Thai ingredients.

Having more recently undergone a nightlife facelift, Th Songwat is practically bursting with new bars and restaurants juxtaposed with traditional shophouses and trendy graffiti. Some standouts include the Shakespeare & Company–influenced **Bukowski & Co** *(086 996 0095)*, with its hipster living-room vibe, creative drinks and prime location on top of Bad Poutine, which serves the Canadian dish to Thai tastes. Another is **Hex Bar** *(@hexcocktailbar.chinatown)*, a speakeasy hidden behind a knick-knacks shop. Next to the river are two dueling restaurant-bars, **NAAM 1608** *(naam.1608)* and longstanding **Samsara** *(facebook.com/samsarabkk)*, which is easier to find now that it's not hidden behind a wall of hubcaps.

BEST SHOPS IN CHINATOWN

Because Chinatown isn't *all* about food.

I'm Chinatown: A decent mix of chain restaurants, independent shops, chemists and noodle vendors, plus good bathrooms (for this part of town).

China World: Located at the end of Th Yaowarat, this is where you get your coffee fix, an air-conditioned stroll and a bathroom break.

Mega Plaza Saphan Lek: Sort of an everything-store for die-hard shopping aficionados with toys, fabrics, IT gadgets and even old DVDs on sale.

Road of Cinnamon: This cute shop features everything Th Songwat-related.

Khlong Thom Center: This three-storey building sells cheap electronics and clothes; it's next to Talat Khlong Thom.

EATING IN CHINATOWN: SNACKS

Lod Chong Singapore: Known as *cendol* in Malaysia, these green noodles in coconut milk are popular throughout Southeast Asia. *10.30am-9.30pm Fri-Wed* ฿

Kiew's Pie: Open 130 years, this place specialises in Chinese-style savoury hand-sized pies (nearly impossible to get elsewhere in Thailand). *8.30am-4.30pm* ฿

HAGOW Yaowarat: Chinese-Thais love these deep-fried dumplings stuffed with shrimp, made to dip into a sweet-and-spicy sauce. *10.30am-10pm* ฿

Nai Ek Roll Noodle: An exemplary version of the dim sum standard – flat rolled noodles – is made here using dough studded with tiny shrimp. *8am-midnight* ฿

RENOVATING CHINATOWN'S HISTORY

It's not uncommon to hear of a 90-year-old undergoing a facelift, but few facelifts have been as successful as the one undergone by 90-year-old **Baan Trok Tua Ngork**. Owned by the Assakul family and located in a once-unsavoury part of Chinatown, the five-storey building has served as a family home, chilli paste factory and workers' hostel. Today, it is home to two popular restaurants – serving Mexican and Shan cuisine, respectively – and a painfully cool bar, Messenger Service. The renovation manages to preserve the traditional shophouse facade while giving the interior an extensive upgrade, retaining the original tiled floors and narrow staircase but adding a glass ceiling and a (somewhat tiny) elevator.

ALMONFOTO/SHUTTERSTOCK

The Market that Never Sleeps

Visit Bangkok's Flower Market – at any time

Bangkok's **Flower Market** (locally known as Talat Pak Khlong, or 'Market at the Mouth of the Canal') is a 24-hour wholesale market that's considered one of the largest flower markets in the world. Its sheer size, beautiful mix of colours, pleasant smells and vibrant energy have turned it into a low-key tourist attraction, especially at night. The exuberant profusion of lilies, orchids, roses and gerberas make this a must for any flower lover, but even visitors without a flower fetish will enjoy watching the efficient workings of the market, with florists hard at work on their arrangements at all hours of the night and deliverymen on their motorbikes or on foot, busy pushing bundles of flowers on carts.

In its past life, the area served as a trading post as early as the Ayuthaya period. It then became a floating market during the time of Rama I. A century later, it was turned into a fish market, where fresh seafood – caught in Samut Sakhon

EATING ON TH SONGWAT: OUR PICKS

e-Ga Lab: This modern cafe wows Gen Zers with its Instagram-friendly surrounds and decent Thai food, including *khao kluk prik gluea*. *8.30am-6pm* ฿

Tia Sua Restaurant: An old-timey dim-sum parlour, this spot serves great goose wings, clams and exemplary stir-fried greens. *11.30am-9.30pm* ฿฿

SongViet at SongWat: Vietnamese-style noodle soups, stuffed noodles and desserts rule at this cheerful spot inspired by Hanoi street food. *10am-8pm Tue-Sun* ฿฿

Urai Braised Goose: Specialising in Chinese-style goose, this spot is popular with both youngsters and the old guard. *10am-1pm & 4-7pm Mon-Sat, 10am-1pm Sun* ฿

Flower Market

Province and transported to Bangkok via Chao Phraya River – was sold. Later, the wares shifted to produce after nearby residents complained of the fishy smell, prompting an increasing number of flower vendors to move here. In 2016 the government moved much of the flower market indoors (which, in this case, means a covered awning between two buildings), but the market has since spilled over into another, uncovered street. Both streets are busiest between 2am and 3am, when the fresh flower deliveries arrive.

The Flower Market is close to Wat Pho (p57), so it's reachable via a short walk or tuk-tuk ride from the temple, but the best way to get here is by boat. The **Chao Phraya Express Boat** *(chaophrayaexpressboat.com)* leaves Saphan Taksin regularly and stops at Yodpiman Pier. Here, you can find the **Yodpiman Riverwalk**, with its many shops and cafes. The Rattanakosin-inspired development is worth a look, as it's the longest riverside walkway in the area. Just behind the Riverwalk is the Flower Market.

PUANG MALAI

You'll frequently come across these flower garlands in Thailand. They are often made of white jasmine buds strung together to form a diminutive loop, with tassels of colourful red roses or pink lotus flowers. While these garlands are certainly beautiful, they're not meant to be worn on the body; they often serve as decorative items in the home, usually to be placed on a tray in front of a Buddha image. You'll see them sold on the streets at busy intersections, placed in front of photos of deceased loved ones, or left as offerings at shrines. Necklace-like strands of jasmine buds are also frequently bought by drivers and placed around their car's rearview mirror as a way to ask for protection from Mae Yanang, the Thai goddess of journeys.

DRINKING AROUND THE FLOWER MARKET: TOP SPOTS

Glass Half Full Bar & Cafe: This pleasant, laid-back bar makes sure to snag return customers with its good drinks and karaoke. *10am-1am Tue-Thu, from 7pm Wed* ฿฿

Tai Soon Bar: An achingly cool beer bar, Tai Soon boasts a wide range of stouts and IPAs for beer nerds. *1pm-1am* ฿฿

Farm to Table, Hideout: This charming, leafy spot has good coffee, as well as rice dishes and handmade gelato. *9am-7pm* ฿

Floral Cafe at Napasorn: This beautiful coffee spot is tucked away on the 2nd floor of a florist. *9am-7pm* ฿฿

Riverside, Silom & Lumphini

BANGKOK'S BUSINESS AND ARTS CENTRE

GETTING AROUND

Public transport-wise, this is one of Bangkok's best-served areas. This is a good thing, because the area is also home to a lot of the city's traffic jams. To see most of the major sights, take the Metro (MRT) to Lumphini or Silom, or the Skytrain (BTS) to Saladaeng, Chong Nonsi or Saphan Taksin (for Th Charoen Krung). If you don't mind traffic, you can also hail a taxi or ride app, or take bus 504 from Rajdamri and disembark on Th Silom.

If you're a fan of glitz and glam, Silom is where to go. The twin thoroughfares of Th Silom and Th Sathorn are home to most of Thailand's heavy-hitting business headquarters and skyscrapers. This is also where you'll find the places encouraging you to spend the most money, so you're sure to find the city's finest restaurants, bars, hotels and art galleries and, of course (this being Bangkok), a high-end shop or two.

But luckily it's not all skyscrapers in this part of town. The area also boasts Bangkok's largest park, Lumphini, while Chao Phraya River hugs Bangkok's Riverside district as it spreads north towards Chinatown. You can also explore Bangkok's oldest official road, Charoen Krung – home to some of the city's most famous and historic buildings – while discovering newly rejuvenated neighbourhoods along the way.

A Historic Riverside Market

Melding old and new

Asiatique *(asiatiquethailand.com)* gives itself the somewhat-unwieldy moniker of 'the largest riverside lifestyle tourist landmark in Thailand', and it's not lying. Located on the site of the original port warehouse of the East Asiatic Company, this night market is further south along Chao Phraya River from the Saphan Taksin Skytrain (BTS) station. Besides shops, a Ferris wheel and a wealth of eateries, there's Jurassic World: The Experience and a Mystery Mansion ride. The market is open daily from 11am to midnight.

DRINKING IN TALAT NOI: OUR PICKS

Citizen Tea Canteen: Specialising in Thai traditional milk tea, this spot is fronted by an interesting orange-and-black checkered facade. *10am-5pm Thu-Tue* ฿

Soul's Cafe: Next to So Heng Tai House, serving iced coffee and tea, plus fruit juices and Italian sodas. *10am-6pm Mon-Thu, to 7pm Fri, from 9am Sat, to 6pm Sun* ฿

Blacksmith Cafe: A decent coffee shop that's popular for its Oreo milkshake and espresso yuzu honey drink. *8am-5pm Mon-Sat* ฿

Mother Roaster: Take the stairs to the 2nd floor, where special filter coffees from Colombia and India will please any coffee snob. *10am-5pm* ฿

HIGHLIGHTS
1 King Power Mahanakorn
2 Lumphini Park
3 Talat Noi

SIGHTS
4 Antique Turtle Car
5 Bangkokian Museum
6 Kathmandu Photo Gallery
7 Sathorn Unique Tower
see 1 SkyWalk at King Power Mahanakhon
8 Tang Contemporary Art

ACTIVITIES
9 Neilson Hays Library

SLEEPING
10 Everyday Hostel
11 kokotel
12 LUXX
13 Mandarin Oriental
14 Siam Heritage

EATING
see 26 Charmgang
15 Commons Sala Daeng
16 Jay So
17 Jua
18 Ruenton
see 31 Sam Lor
19 Samrub Samrub Thai
see 14 Thanon Thaniya

DRINKING & NIGHTLIFE
20 Beef BKK
21 DJ Station
22 EA Rooftop at the Empire
23 Maxwell Onsen
24 Mod Kaew Wine Bar
25 Moon Bar
26 Mother Roaster
see 1 Ojo Bangkok
27 Sky Bar
28 Smalls
29 Stranger Bar
30 Vesper
31 Viva & Aviv

ENTERTAINMENT
32 Patpong

THE SHRINES OF TALAT NOI

One of the most interesting things about Talat Noi is its Chinese communities. The Hokkien Chinese formed the backbone of the community from the 19th century onwards, turning the neighbourhood into a major trading area. Evidence of strong Hokkien influence can be found in the **Chow Sue Kong Shrine**, one of the oldest Hokkien-Chinese temples in Talat Noi. Built around 1804, it holds the statue of Chinese doctor Chow Sue Gong, who is said to have tested his herbal cures on himself. Unfortunately, this was how he died.

Another big community was the Hakka Chinese, who were famed for their blacksmithing abilities. The **Rong Kuek Shrine** facing the river is a popular place to visit during Chinese New Year.

Getting to Know Talat Noi

Perusing Bangkok's coolest neighbourhood

Somewhere in the nebulous borderlands between Chinatown and Th Charoen Krung is the dynamic neighbourhood of Talat Noi, whose name literally means 'Little Market'. Originally a port where immigrants to the city arrived during the reign of Rama I, Talat Noi has been home to Portuguese, Chinese, Vietnamese and Khmer communities. It gradually morphed into a Chinese neighbourhood as it contained the spillover from nearby Sampeng (p90). The neighbourhood also became known for its blacksmiths, turning it into a mostly blue-collar area that eventually served as a centre for car parts production – an industry that lives on in some corners today. You can catch business in action in the area known as **Sieng Gong**, a more than 70-year-old neighbourhood by Soi Wanit 2 where a clutch of auto-parts manufacturers can be seen welding away.

The hipster children of some of these longtime businesses have sought to reinvigorate their family fortunes by cleverly repurposing their business headquarters or former homes into tourist attractions. Among the most successful is **Hong Sieng Kong** *(facebook.com/HongSiengKong)*, a riverside antiques shop that has been turned into a cafe/restaurant/gallery by its enterprising owners.

Another similar business model is **Photohostel & Photocafe** *(photohostel.com)*, a cafe/hostel carved out of a 200-year-old former liquor warehouse. Then there's **So Heng Tai House** *(facebook.com/Sohengtai)*, another two-century-old Hokkien-Teochew building that calls itself the 'oldest Chinese courtyard house in Thailand'.

Artistic Leanings

Surveying Bangkok's arts scene

Bangkok's contemporary art scene continues to evolve at pace. More than 80 galleries and art spaces participated in the city's latest **Galleries Night** *(galleriesnights.com)*, while the biannual **Bangkok Art Biennale** *(bkkartbiennale.com)* is going from strength to strength. On a smaller scale, the more independently minded **Mango Art Festival** *(mangoartfestival.com)*, founded in 2022, is held annually, and is Asia's first and only festival that combines art, design and performance.

A longtime stalwart of the Bangkok art scene, **Tang Contemporary Art** *(tangcontemporary.com)* in River City, just off Th Charoen Krung, highlights both emerging and established

EATING AROUND SILOM: OUR PICKS

Samrub Samrub Thai: This Michelin-starred restaurant is helmed by Prin Polsuk, considered one of today's best Thai chefs. *5.30-11pm Tue-Thu, to midnight Fri & Sat* ฿฿฿

Jay So: This longtime northeastern Thai vendor serves delicious green papaya salad and grilled chicken. *11am-5.30pm* ฿

Ruenton: This restaurant in the Montien Hotel has undergone a recent revamp but still serves the best chicken rice in the city. *11am-9.30pm* ฿฿

Thanon Thaniya: Patronised by Bangkok's Japanese community, this is an entire street lined with restaurants serving everything from sushi to ramen. *hours vary* ฿

MAODOLTEE/SHUTTERSTOCK

Hong Sieng Kong

Asian artists, and has built a reputation as one of the most progressive galleries in Asia. **Gallery VER** *(galleryver.com)*, south of Th Silom, is another essential stop and was co-founded by Rirkrit Tiravanija, one of Thailand's most famous contemporary artists who is known for his interactive installations. Established as an artist-led enterprise, this gallery seeks to forge a stronger connection between the artist and the audience by cutting out the traditional 'gallery owner'.

Photographer Manit Sriwanichpoom established **Kathmandu Photo Gallery** *(kathmanduphotobkk.com)* in 2006, and it remains Bangkok's only gallery wholly dedicated to photography. Considered Thailand's most famous photo-artist, Sriwanichpoom is especially known for his *Pink Man* series, which critiques modern Thai consumerism.

Distinctive Buildings in the Area

A neighbourhood's history through its architecture

Simply passing by some of the area's most interesting buildings will give you a good insight into how architecture has changed in Bangkok. **Neilson Hays Library** *(neilsonhays library.org; 100฿)*, housed in a splendid 1922 neoclassical building designed by Italian architects, is one of the city's best-preserved historic structures. It also acts as the repository for one of the city's biggest collections of English books. Note the domed rotunda and the H-shaped reading room, which makes for a cool and quiet retreat from Bangkok's frenetic

INTERESTING LOCAL ARTISTS TO CHECK OUT

Top Changtrakul is an artist and co-founder of the **Mango Art Festival**. *@mangoartfestival*

There are several artists I like. One of them is Amnaj Wachirasut. I admire his work because it doesn't feel forced – he just lets the artworks be, and this reflects his personality as well. Another artist I like is Somyot Hananuntasuk. Once you look beneath the surface, you'll feel the strong emotions and passion behind his paintings. An up-and-coming artist I admire is Parinot Kunakornwong. I like his work because he is pushing the language of art. It feels like he's constantly exploring how far he can go – redefining what art is by taking a different path to investigate its meaning.

DRINKING AROUND SILOM & SATHORN: OUR PICKS

Vesper: A slick, comfy setting with inventive cocktails, this bar is a stalwart on the 'Asia's 50 Best Bars' list. *5.30pm-2am* ฿฿฿

Mod Kaew Wine Bar: There's also food at this bar, but the specialty here is of course the wine, particularly the natural ones. *4pm-1am* ฿฿฿

Viva & Aviv: A riverside bar with good drinks and great views; popular with the after-work crowd as well as tourists looking to laze by the river. *noon-10pm* ฿฿

Smalls: Just off Sathorn, this is a longtime favourite among the city's chefs and artists because of its relatively late hours; there's also live music. *6pm-2am Wed-Mon* ฿฿

BANGKOK'S INFAMOUS GHOST TOWER

Featured as the setting in the Thai horror movie *The Promise* (2017), **Sathorn Unique Tower** is one of Bangkok's most infamous sights. An unfinished skyscraper from the 1990s that looms over its neighbourhood, some believe it's haunted due to its unlucky location close to a graveyard. A casualty of the 1997 Asian Financial Crisis, Sathorn Unique remains unfinished because the high cost of finishing it is comparable to the high cost of demolishing it, making it an enduring relic of one of Thailand's most difficult economic periods. Today, rumours about supernatural sightings, on-site suicides and a bizarre murder plot involving the tower's architect add to the sinister mystique. Alas, it is illegal to enter.

streets. The library hosts the **Bangkok Literature Festival** (*bkklitfest.com*) every November, as well as monthly classical music concerts; there's also an attached cafe.

Meanwhile, the **Bangkokian Museum** *(facebook.com/Bkk Museum; free)* consists of three houses dating from the 1930s to the 1960s that have been frozen in time. Once the home of a prosperous Bangkok family, the museum is packed with beautiful wooden furniture, porcelain and other detritus from the mid-20th century. It's a strange but informative experience touring the museum – it feels as if you're going through the possessions of a deceased relative with hoarding issues. Cheerful volunteers are on hand to explain things in English.

To embody Bangkok's current era, look no further than **King Power Mahanakorn** *(kingpowermahanakhon.co.th; from 880฿)*, a modern paean to steel and glass with a distinctive facade that some Thais liken to cheese being nibbled on by mice. The crowning feature of this building, literally, is the **SkyWalk**, an open-air glass-floored balcony suspended 78 floors above the ground.

A Modern-Day Oasis

Making the most of Lumphini Park

Lumphini Park is central Bangkok's most popular park. Occupying a chunk of the main business district and named after the Buddha's birthplace in Nepal (Lumbini), Lumphini's 58 hectares are where thousands of people come every day in search of an outdoor escape in the heart of the city. Despite this, the park rarely feels crowded and is one of the capital's most tranquil spots.

There's an artificial lake (which visitors can boat on) surrounded by broad, well-tended lawns where tai chi is practised, while the 2.5km of paths are busy in the morning and evening with joggers and walkers. (Cyclists are technically only allowed to use the park between 10am and 3pm.) There are also wooded areas, a kid's playground, exercise machines, a basketball court, statues, a concert venue and even a public library.

Lumphini is home to a fair amount of flora and fauna, too. The park attracts birdwatchers, especially during migratory seasons when many different species can be seen. But by far the most famous inhabitants are the startlingly large monitor lizards – some over 2m long – that swim in the lake and can be seen strolling and sunbathing on the surrounding lawns.

DRINKING AT ROOFTOP BARS: OUR PICKS

Sky Bar: Yes, it was in *The Hangover Part II*. But you're unlikely to get into any trouble so long as you follow the bar's strict dress code (no open-backed shoes or shorts). *5pm-12.30am* ฿฿฿

Moon Bar: The original Bangkok rooftop bar offers panoramic views and pricey drinks. *5pm-1am* ฿฿฿

Ojo Bangkok: In the Mahanakorn Building, it's a Mexican restaurant, but it has a bar, and you can access the rooftop from the restaurant. *11.30am-2.30pm & 5.30-11.30pm* ฿฿฿

EA Rooftop at the Empire: A more recent entrant in the rooftop-bar game, this spot has beautiful surroundings. *11.30am-2.30pm & 5pm-midnight* ฿฿฿

The lizards are uninterested in humans. Don't feed them, it makes them aggressive.

Originally a royal reserve, Lumphini was declared a public space in 1925 by Rama VI, making it Bangkok's first official park. Both the Lumphini and Silom stations on the Blue Line of the Metro (MRT) are close to the park, which is open daily from 4.30am to 9pm.

Patpong A-Go-Go

A red-light night on Silom

For good or bad, Bangkok's red-light districts are now part of the city's tapestry. Take a trip to Soi Cowboy or Nana Plaza (p120), the current red-light zones for foreigners, and you'll encounter tour groups and visitors who are there for the spectacle, not the sex.

Before Soi Cowboy and Nana took off, it was Patpong in Silom that was infamous for its go-go clubs and sex shows. Patpong began to acquire its seedy reputation from the late 1960s, when American soldiers on leave from the Vietnam War began to visit Bangkok. By the 1980s Patpong was synonymous with the Bangkok sex industry and a backdrop for movies such as *The Deer Hunter* (1978), as well as a near-compulsory stop for many visitors to Bangkok.

These days, Patpong is a shadow of itself, with the COVID-19 pandemic the final nail in the coffin for many of the bars and clubs, although a touristy market does set up here nightly. But it's still worth a stroll for its historical importance to the city alone; after all, how did a rice field from 100 years ago turn into one of the world's most notorious red-light districts?

Unfortunately, a museum dedicated to outlining Patpong's interesting history recently closed, but it's a fascinating story that involves the Thai-Chinese community, Thai police and government, David Bowie and the CIA. Long story short, the CIA was a tenant in one of the buildings owned by the Thai-Chinese Patpongpanich family in the 1960s, from where it was conducting operations to destabilise its enemies during the Cold War. This culminated in the Vietnam War, which led to an influx of American GIs in the area – specifically Patpong. In 1969 a former Air Force officer opened the Grand Prix Bar, Bangkok's first official go-go bar. Needless to say, many more bars followed, and the celebrities came with them, including David Bowie, Jean-Claude Van Damme and the cast of *The Deer Hunter*.

BEST LGBTIQ+ VENUES IN BANGKOK

DJ Station: Bangkok's OG gay club still has a good mix of locals and foreigners. Similar clubs are nearby.

Beef BKK: This is a big player in the LGBTIQ+ nightlife scene alongside G.O.D.

Maxwell Onsen: Currently the hottest gay sauna in town (pun intended), followed closely by Krubb Bangkok Social Club & Sauna.

Stranger Bar: Also known as 'House of Drag Queens', you'll find nightly drag shows at 10.30pm and a fun vibe.

Commons Sala Daeng: A place to pre-game before the real party begins.

EATING ON TH CHAROEN KRUNG: OUR PICKS

Jack's Bar: Right on the river next to the Shangrila Hotel, Jack's is a Thai-style spot with good dishes, great atmosphere and interesting local characters. *11am-midnight* ฿

Jua: A popular and modern *izakaya* with sleek, minimalist interiors. The Japanese-style mac and cheese is recommended. *6pm-midnight* ฿฿

Charmgang: A well-known restaurant with excellent curries and regional specialties that are hard to find elsewhere. *6-9.30pm Mon-Fri, noon-2pm & 6-9.30pm Sat & Sun* ฿฿฿

Sam Lor: A contemporary take on the Thai-style *kub klaem*. Especially recommended is the viral take on the traditional Thai omelette. *6-10.30pm Wed-Mon* ฿฿฿

WALKING TOUR

Talat Noi & Charoen Krung

The neighbourhoods of Talat Noi and Charoen Krung are home to some of the most interesting sights to be found in modern-day Bangkok. From rejuvenated riverside haunts to modern creative landmarks, a new generation of Bangkokians are taking parts of their heritage and adapting them to a wider audience. This walk starts where Talat Noi meets Chinatown and ends at one of Charoen Krung's most historic buildings.

1 Hong Sieng Kong

The fascinating antiques-shop-turned-cafe of Hong Sieng Kong (p96) is a great example of how the next generation are tailoring their family business to a new world. On the walk from Hua Lumphong to the cafe, you'll see the distinctive *Transformers* statue and sections of the auto-parts district on Soi Wanit 2.

The Walk: Turn right upon leaving Hong Sieng Kong and head towards Soi Duang Tawan. Take the next right to pass the Antique Turtle Car on the way to So Heng Tai.

2 So Heng Tai House

The former family residence of So Heng Tai (p96) has seen better times, but it still offers a great opportunity to explore the oldest Chinese-style courtyard home left intact.

The Walk: It's only one minute to your next stop from here. Turn left and continue on Trok San Chao Rong Kueak towards Rong Kuek Shrine (p96). Turn left where the street meets the river and head down an alleyway famous for its street art.

SOMBAT MUYCHEEN/SHUTTERSTOCK

So Heng Tai House

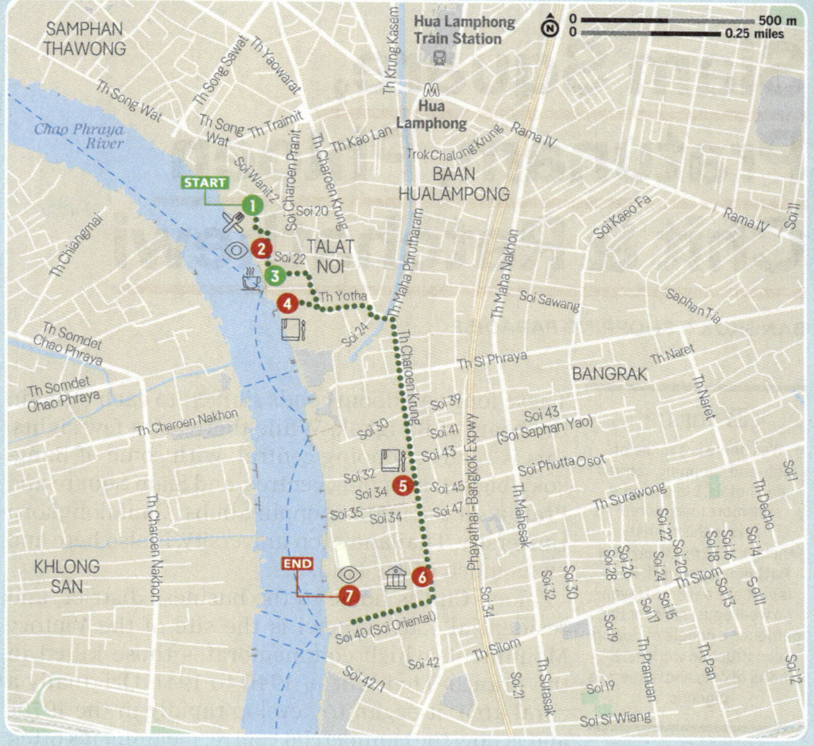

3 Mother Roaster

This popular cafe (p94) looks like a dilapidated shophouse on the ground floor. Walk up the flight of stairs (helpfully pointed out by graffiti) to the cafe on the 2nd floor.

The Walk: Turn left at Mother Roaster to Soi Wanit 2. Turn left again and you'll see Siam Commercial Bank on your right.

4 Siam Commercial Bank

Arguably Bangkok's most beautiful bank, it's also Thailand's first locally owned and operated one. It's still a working bank, so be respectful.

The Walk: Head back onto Soi Wanit 2 and turn left at the *Transformers* statue (Bumblebee). Walk to Th Charoen Krung. Once you pass Charoen Krung 32, you'll see an imposing brutalist building that is the Central Post Office.

5 General Post Office

This is still a working post office, considered a historical landmark for its Art Deco-inspired architecture – with its own merch store to boot.

The Walk: Turn right from the post office and walk just four minutes south on Th Charoen Krung until you find a red-brick building on your right that was the original location for Central: The Original Store.

6 Central: The Original Store

Built in 1950, this was Bangkok's original department store, ushering in a post-WWII era of peace and prosperity.

The Walk: Proceed to Charoen Krung 40, where you'll turn right to head in the direction of the Mandarin Oriental.

7 Mandarin Oriental

The Mandarin Oriental (p134) marks the end of your walking tour, and where better to finish than at Bangkok's first hotel (with air-conditioning)?

Siam Square, Pratunam, Phloen Chit & Ratchathewi

BANGKOK'S SHOPPING PARADISE

TOP TIP

Yes, there is a tonne of high-end shopping centres and hotels, but consider the more unexplored nooks in this touristy enclave. The relatively new **Pathumwananurak Park** is virtually deserted (even on weekends) save for the gardener, a couple of dozing construction workers, a handful of cats and numerous pigeons.

These four neighbourhoods sit next to each other in the heart of Bangkok. While there are a few sights, this is really shopping central, with some of Bangkok's biggest shopping centres, and Siam Square and Pratunam the main shopping hubs. Chulalongkorn University, Thailand's top university, is also here and owns much of the land.

Phloen Chit is home to the business district, and residential Ratchathewi is the site of the Victory Monument, which commemorates those killed in the Franco–Thai War of 1940 to 1941. Originally a rural area, it began to develop rapidly in the 1970s and is now the commercial centre, meaning it's often the location of political protests. Yet even with all of the glitzy shopping centres and high-end hotels, you'll find numerous unexpected sights that provide a glimpse into the real Bangkok. The area also has tons of accommodation, making it an excellent base.

Shopaholics Unite

Happiness can indeed be bought

Say 'Siam' to any Bangkokian, and the first thing they will think of is shopping. Bangkok's very own shoppers' paradise is its answer to Singapore's Orchard Rd, featuring a line of malls

GETTING AROUND

There is an embarrassment of riches when it comes to public transport in this area, which is arguably Bangkok's most beloved neighbourhood for Bangkokians. The Siam Skytrain (BTS) stop is a major hub here, where the Sukhumvit and Silom lines meet. The Sukhumvit Line also goes direct to Phloen Chit, Chitlom, Ratchathewi and the Victory Monument. For a more interesting route, consider taking the Saen Saep Express Boat, which stops at Chitlom, Pratunam and Saphan Hua Chang (you need to transfer to another boat at Pratunam to take the Saphan Hua Chang route).

TANG YAN SONG/SHUTTERSTOCK

Siam Paragon food court

all geared towards a slightly different audience. Meanwhile, across the road from the shopping centres is a square-sized network of lanes rimmed by independent shops and casual eateries, interrupted by the occasional tutoring service (it is university land, after all).

The biggest shopping centre to greet you as your Skytrain trundles to its stop is **CentralWorld** *(centralworld.co.th)*, also the largest shopping centre of the nationwide Central Department Store empire. The sprawling complex follows a one-size-fits-all approach to shopping, covering 830,000 sq metres of land and housing over 600 stores. Not surprisingly, the area in front of CentralWorld is where Bangkok's biggest public New Year's party is held – the local equivalent of Times Sq.

Siam Paragon *(siamparagon.co.th)*, meanwhile, remains the grande dame of the block, anchored by big-ticket luxury stores such as Hermès and Chanel. However, its main draw is on the ground level, where an enormous food court and restaurants cover the entire floor. If you have young children in tow, they will be wowed by **Sea Life Bangkok Ocean World** *(visitsealife.com; adult/child 1550/801฿)*, which serves as home to hundreds of fish species. Booking online is slightly cheaper than buying tickets in person.

Next door, **Siam Center** *(siamcenter.co.th)* is a longtime magnet for nearby university students and youngsters, and

WAIT, WE'RE NOT DONE SHOPPING

That's just the major shopping centres; here are the rest.

Pratunam Market: This is bargain-hunter central, and Thailand's largest clothing market.

Platinum Fashion Mall: Located on nearby Th Petchburi, this place is Ground Zero for true bargain-hunters.

Gaysorn Village: Further east from Platinum is Gaysorn, which has undergone a recent renovation and includes an entire building devoted to food.

Central Chidlom: Where Bangkok's old money still shops.

Central Embassy: Situated on the former British embassy grounds, this shopping centre is notable for its basement food court and top floor, which consists of a large bookshop cleverly incorporated into various restaurants.

EATING THAI IN SIAM: OUR PICKS

Somtam Nua: A popular Isan restaurant, this northeastern specialist draws lunchtime queues for its grilled chicken and papaya salad. *11am-9pm* ฿฿

Erawan Tea Room: A Thai place to head to when comfort is paramount; it may not have the most authentic food, but it does have great service. *10am-10pm* ฿฿

Ban Khun Mae: A longtime favourite that serves reliables Thai dishes, including tapioca balls stuffed with pork and steamed rice-flour dumplings. *11am-10pm* ฿

Paste: Excellent high-end Thai cuisine in a hushed setting. The char-grilled pork with tomato relish is recommended; reservations essential. *noon-3.30pm & 6-11pm* ฿฿฿

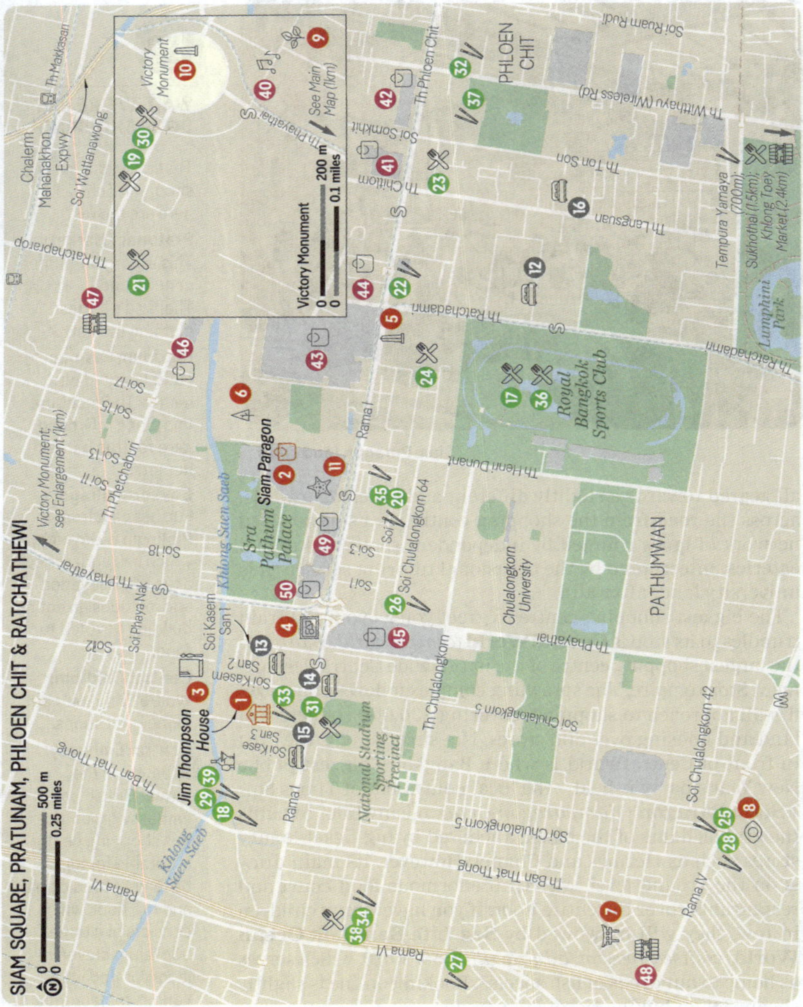

EATING NEAR SIAM SQUARE: OUR PICKS

Inter: Serving students since 1981, this longtime eatery is known for its Thai-Chinese dishes, including fried rice and oyster omelettes – whatever is cheap and cheerful. *11am-8.30pm* ฿

SOMA: Owned by Thai chefs Chalee Kader and Weerawat Triyasenawat. Supercharged versions of traditional dishes such as *pad kaprao* (holy basil stir-fry) and river prawns. *11am-3pm & 5-11pm* ฿฿฿

Baan Dalaa by Angkana: A pretty, greenery-filled spot with great decor and eye-pleasing Thai dishes including pomelo salad and rice noodles slathered in curry. *11am-10pm* ฿฿

Karemeen & Sobereen: This family-owned open-air eatery next to the canal specialises in smoothies and papaya salad. *9am-5.30pm* ฿

HIGHLIGHTS
1 Jim Thompson House
2 Siam Paragon

SIGHTS
3 Baan Khrua
4 Bangkok Art & Culture Centre
5 Erawan Shrine
6 Pathumwananurak Park
7 San Chao Mae Thapthim Saphan Lueang
8 San Chao Pho Suea
9 Santhiphap Park
10 Victory Monument

ACTIVITIES
11 Sea Life Bangkok Ocean World

SLEEPING
12 Hansar
13 Lit Bangkok Hotel & Residence
14 Lub d
15 Siam@Siam
16 Urbana

EATING
17 Anantara Siam
18 Baan Dalaa by Angkana
19 Baan Kuay Tiew Ruathong
20 Ban Khun Mae
21 Boat Noodle Alley
22 Erawan Tea Room
23 E-San Bangkok
24 Grand Hyatt Erawan
25 Hi Nakorn Pochana
26 Inter
27 Jeh O Chula
28 Jok Sam Yan
29 Karemeen & Sobereen
see 31 Le Pla Daak
30 Pa Yak Boat Noodle
see 31 PARADAi
see 44 Paste
31 Pu Tie Shrimp Wonton Noodles
32 Sanguan Sri
33 SOMA
34 Somboon Seafood
35 Somtam Nua
36 St Regis
37 Thai Niyom
38 Thanon Banthat Thong

DRINKING & NIGHTLIFE
see 31 Booms
39 OSS Room

ENTERTAINMENT
40 Saxophone Pub & Restaurant

SHOPPING
41 Central Chidlom
42 Central Embassy
43 CentralWorld
44 Gaysorn Village
45 MBK Center
46 Platinum Fashion Mall
47 Pratunam Market
48 Sam Yan Market
49 Siam Center
50 Siam Discovery

includes a wealth of local designers. **Siam Discovery** *(siamdiscovery.co.th)*, located right beside it, features niche brands and is aimed at a more avant garde crowd. Finally, across the street sits the **MBK Center** *(mbk-center.co.th)*, ground zero for cheap electronics and a well-regarded food court.

A Legacy in Thai Silk

A visit to Jim Thompson's house

This jungly compound of wooden homes packed with exquisite art and furniture is the essential sight in the area. It's the former home of **Jim Thompson** *(jimthompsonhouse.org; 250฿)*, an American silk entrepreneur and art collector who first came to Thailand at the end of WWII as a member of the Office of Strategic Services (the forerunner of the CIA).

Thompson settled in Bangkok after the war, when his neighbours' handmade silk caught his eye and piqued his interest. He sent samples to fashion houses in Milan, London and Paris, gradually building a steady worldwide clientele and helping to revive the Thai silk industry.

In addition to textiles, Thompson also collected parts of various derelict Thai homes and had them reassembled at the compound in 1959. Some of the homes were brought from the old capital of Ayuthaya; others were pulled down and floated across the *klorng* from Baan Khrua (p106). One striking departure from tradition is the way in which each wall has its exterior facing the house's interior, thus exposing the wall's bracing system. Thompson's small but splendid Asian art collection and his personal belongings are also on display in the main house.

THE MYSTERY OF JIM THOMPSON'S DISAPPEARANCE

When Jim Thompson disappeared in 1967 while in Malaysia's Cameron Highlands, it sparked worldwide publicity. And after his sister was murdered in the US later the same year, the conspiracy theorists went into overdrive. Was Thompson targeted by business rivals? Did he encounter a hungry tiger? Were his former employers at the CIA unhappy at his increasingly vocal criticism of US policy in Southeast Asia? All that can be said is that no trace of Thompson's remains has ever been found. His life (and disappearance) are now fodder for Reddit threads and documentaries. Today, Jim Thompson House leans into speculation about his death by naming its bar the **OSS Room**; Office of Strategic Services, the CIA's precursor.

HOW THE BACC CAME TO BE

For 14 years, the Thai Artists' Network petitioned the government to build a contemporary art centre that was accessible to the general public – both in location and in content. What better place, artists reasoned, than Siam, the traditional nexus for Bangkok's youth?

Unfortunately, land deemed ideal for the museum had been earmarked for another shopping centre, leading to a public hearing that included artists laying down 4000 of their artworks across a span of 4km. Plans for the shopping centre were scrapped in 2002, and in 2008 the BACC finally opened its doors to the public, years after the idea was first floated (in 1994).

AMNAT30/SHUTTERSTOCK

Silk production, Siam Square

The compound is open daily from 10am to 6pm. All visitors must join one of the frequent 45-minute tours that are held in a variety of languages.

Culture Vulture

Visit the Bangkok Art & Culture Centre

The large, light-filled **Bangkok Art & Culture Centre** *(BACC; bacc.or.th)*, with a central atrium, nine floors and 3000 sq metres of gallery space, has become one of the more significant players in Bangkok's contemporary arts and culture scene. With an emphasis on demystifying the arts and introducing them to the general public, it stages rotating exhibitions from Thai and foreign artists, as well as film screenings, theatre and music performances, and educational events. The centre also contains shops, private galleries, cafes and an art library, making it a good pit stop if you're visiting the shopping centres nearby. It's open from 10am to 8pm and closed on Mondays.

Unearthing Generations of Tradition

Historic canal-side neighbourhood

It's a treat to discover the wooden homes and winding alleys of **Baan Khrua** amid the urban sprawl of Ratchathewi. Occupying both sides of Khlong Saen Saeb, the neighbourhood dates to the turbulent late 18th century, when Cham Muslims from Vietnam fought with Rama I against a Burmese army

DRINKING & EATING IN BACC: TOP SPOTS

Booms: Located in the BACC, this is the centre's most popular coffee spot; expect to bump into artists in desperate need of caffeine. *10am-7pm Tue-Sun* ฿

PARADAi: This dessert spot features both coffee and local handcrafted chocolate – a winning combination. Especially popular is its chocolate ice-cream parfait. *10am-8pm Tue-Sun* ฿

Pu Tie Shrimp Wonton Noodles: A cute spot on the 2nd floor serving decent bowls of shrimp wonton noodles, as well as its Hong Kong–style BBQ pork. *10am-8pm Tue-Sun* ฿

Le Pla Daak: Named after Thai anchovies in the Isan dialect, this eatery features a number of northeastern Thai dishes, including papaya salad and sticky rice. *11am-8.30pm Tue-Sun* ฿

and were rewarded with this land east of the then nascent capital of Bangkok. The immigrants brought silk-weaving traditions with them, and the community grew when the residents built Khlong Saen Saeb to connect to Chao Phraya River. Jim Thompson, whose former home (p105) is on the south side of Khlong Saen Saeb, employed residents to produce the silk he sold around the world. A few workshops still make silk today. Baan Khrua remains mostly Muslim, with some small mosques amid the alleys that straggle away from the canal; it's peaceful and great for a wander.

A Hindu & Buddhist Landmark

Visiting the four-faced Brahma

Occupying prime real estate at the southeastern corner of Ratchaprasong intersection, the **Erawan Shrine** is one of Bangkok's most recognisable landmarks. It is also something of a tourist draw, attracting an estimated million visitors a year who, like the Thais, make offerings to each side of the shrine in a silent petition to the Hindu god Brahma to grant them their wish. This makes Erawan Shrine the most visited religious site in Bangkok.

Built after a series of mishaps during the construction of the Erawan Hotel, the shrine is Hindu and centres around a four-faced statue of Brahma, referred to as Phra Phrom by Thais. Traditionally the god of builders, Phra Phrom's four faces symbolise east, west, north and south, illustrating the god's ability to see everything in Heaven and on Earth.

Vendors conveniently offer candles, flower garlands, incense and gold foil – the bare necessities for praying at the Erawan Shrine – right outside of the entrance for around 1000฿, though adding on to that with elephant figurines, coconuts and soft drinks will of course cost you extra. Visitors make their offerings to each side of the shrine in a clockwise direction, lighting a candle and three sticks of incense at each side and repeating their prayer every time. Visitors whose wishes have been granted traditionally pay for live Thai dancers to perform to live music; the frequency of these performances adds to locals' beliefs that praying here works.

The shrine's popularity can be a double-edged sword: in August 2015 a bomb exploded close by, killing 20 people and damaging the shrine. It was repaired and reopened just two days later.

ERAWAN SHRINE

Trude Renwick is a lecturer in Architectural Studies at the University of Manchester.

The Erawan Shrine is a landmark that is hard not to stop and admire. However, most visitors remain unaware of the foundational role that this shrine has played in the development of this bustling commercial centre. The Erawan Shrine was established in 1956 as a solution to problems that were encountered in the construction of the Erawan Hotel. The power of this shrine has grown alongside the numerous malls that have sprouted around it. Political protests and clashes in the Ratchaprasong intersection, and even attacks on the shrine, have added to its auspiciousness. The shrine has become so famous that a replica was installed outside of Caesar's Palace in Las Vegas.

EATING SUNDAY BRUNCH BUFFETS: OUR PICKS

Grand Hyatt Erawan: A sprawling affair offering oysters, fresh seafood, roast beef and a sizeable dessert section on the ground floor. *noon-2.30pm* ฿฿฿

Anantara Siam: Describing itself as 'arguably the best Sunday brunch in Bangkok', this hotel includes Veuve Clicquot Champagne and live music. *noon-3.30pm* ฿฿฿

St Regis: This brunch offering on the 12th floor has the added benefit of stunning views over the city. *12.30-3.30pm* ฿฿฿

Sukhothai: The OG of massive Sunday brunches, they now only offer it on select Sundays, so call ahead to book on the ground floor. *noon-3pm* ฿฿฿

DEVELOPMENT GONE WRONG

Philip Cornwel-Smith is the author of *Very Bangkok* and *Very Thai.*

Banthat Thong Rd emerged as a vibrant dining hub. Then rents and prices soared, quality fell, and mega-eateries teetered when tourism dropped in 2025. It was just another unplanned boom-bust in the pattern of Bangkok's bar strips and night markets. Emulating Singapore by purging streets of traders, officials view street food as a tourism lure. Yet they overlook why street food exists: to nourish Thai communities affordably. Banthat Thong first grew by drawing vendors evicted from Sam Yan by Chulalongkorn University's property arm. Short-term redevelopment again trumped long-term support of public interest and Thai food heritage. The real lesson of Singapore is to provide cheap hawker centres that preserve culture while feeding all.

ARTAPARTMENT/SHUTTERSTOCK

San Chao Pho Suea

Where Three Roads Meet

Untangling the enigma of Sam Yan

Originally a blue-collar Thai-Chinese neighbourhood known for the trading of used car parts, Sam Yan has since undergone a dramatic transformation, much of it at the hands of its landlord, Chulalongkorn University. The famous street-food mecca of Suan Luang Market was razed in favour of a shopping centre and park, and its famous fresh market, **Sam Yan Market** – an upscale cousin to Khlong Toey Market (p116) – was downsized in favour of Samyan Mitrtown, a mixed-use project melding retail, office and condo spaces. Sam Yan Market remains open, still selling excellent duck and fresh produce.

All the same, there are glints of heritage among the malls, jogging trails and wedding-dress shops. Chinese shrine **San Chao Mae Thapthim Saphan Lueang**, in spite of pressure from the university to close, remains open to the public from 8am to 6pm, with volunteers happy to guide visitors through the process of properly paying respects. Another popular shrine, **San Chao Pho Suea**, also has helpful staff and signs that explain the right way to ask for blessings.

EATING IN SAM YAN: OUR PICKS

Jeh O Chula: Waits here usually last an hour, but you are given a number in the queue, so you can dip out and make it back in time for your table. *3.30pm-midnight* BB

Somboon Seafood: Go to the place that once gave Sam Yan a reputation as Bangkok's seafood capital; get the stir-fried crab in curry sauce. *11am-9pm* BB

Jok Sam Yan: This spot serves one of Bangkok's most famous bowls of Chinese-style congee. *5-9.30am & 3-8pm* B

Hi Nakorn Pochana: Called 'Nai Hi' by regulars, this is another old-timey seafood stalwart from Sam Yan's glory days. *11am-9pm* BB

In an attempt to cash in on Bangkok's reputation for street food, Chulalongkorn helped to develop **Thanon Banthat Thong**, a street-food rival to Chinatown that's lined with independent vendors, famous street-food vendors from elsewhere, and still other vendors displaced by gentrification. To many, it's a fun getaway and the chance to try many street-food vendors in one place. To others, it's a soulless simulation of Thai street food with no heritage or tradition to back it up. Recently, Th Banthat Thong has made the news due to the lack of Chinese tourists (towards which many of its vendors are geared), resulting in low sales for many of its vendors. All the same, some longtime places remain busy.

THE BIRTHPLACE OF SOM TAM THAI

In the mid-20th century, Bangkok was a growing city in need of labour from other parts of Thailand. Entrepreneurial northeastern Thais arrived en masse on the hunt for job opportunities in the capital. Arriving via bus to Victory Monument, some Isan-ers saw a business opportunity in selling northeastern Thai food to their own compatriots. A line of *som tam* vendors soon appeared, selling the Isan-style green papaya salad along with grilled meats and sticky rice. Alas, Bangkokians who tried the dish hated the *plaa rah* (fermented Thai anchovy) in it, so a new dish was born: *som tam Thai*, which incorporated ingredients that central Thais would love, including peanuts, palm sugar and dried shrimp.

Nosh Around the Victory Monument

Exploring one of Bangkok's busiest neighbourhoods

Known mostly for the WWII-era monument at its centre, the Victory Monument neighbourhood is more than it seems. Markets, street food, buzzy pubs and scurrying travellers: this area has it all, and showcases Bangkok's on-the-go spirit.

Of course, there's the Victory Monument itself, a 1941 nationalist salute to Thailand's victory over France in the Franco-Thai War (1940–41). The roundabout surrounding it hosts a sprawling daily night market offering everything from T-shirts to ice cream. This is also where buses travel to and from all corners of Thailand, making it great for people-watching. An ideal spot for said people-watching – or to just munch on your street food in peace – is nearby **Santhiphap Park**, a carpet of green amid a bona fide concrete jungle.

A few steps northeast of the monument is the famous **Boat Noodle Alley**, where a string of vendors specialises in soup noodles said to have been originally sold in boats on Bangkok's canals. The broth – which includes animal blood, cinnamon and star anise – results in a rich, complex taste combining Chinese and Thai flavours. Because of their history, boat noodles are often served in tiny bowls, meaning between three and four bowls are needed for a full meal. The most popular places to sample this dish are **Baan Kuay Tiew Ruathong** and **Pa Yak Boat Noodle**.

Southeast of the Victory Monument is what might just be Thailand's most famous jazz club, which is nearing its 40th anniversary: **Saxophone Pub & Restaurant** *(saxophonepub.com)* holds nightly live music performances ranging from acoustic to jazz and blues.

EATING IN PHLOEN CHIT & CHITLOM: OUR PICKS

E-San Bangkok: A northeastern Thai-style *izakaya* in one of Bangkok's newest developments. *noon-10.30pm Mon-Sat* ฿฿฿

Sanguan Sri: A Bangkok culinary institution that's still in its original humble setting, among the modern skyscrapers of Wireless Rd. *9am-3pm Mon-Sat* ฿

Thai Niyom: Enjoy Michelin-starred cuisine at relatively friendly prices – something that's hard to find in this neighbourhood. *11am-9pm* ฿฿

Tempura Yamaya: In the basement of the somewhat new shopping centre of One Bangkok, this Japanese restaurant draws a line of 60+ patrons daily. *10am-10pm* ฿฿

Thanon Sukhumvit

NIGHTLIFE, DINING AND MASSAGE

TOP TIP

It can be fun to check out the neighbourhood's ever-evolving roster of upscale restaurants, bars and shopping centres, but for a taste of the real Bangkok, head to the canal, most accessible from Thonglor, Asoke or behind the Ital-Thai building at the intersection of Th Sukhumvit 39 and Th Petchburi. The canal walkways make for a diverting stroll.

Stretching all the way to Cambodia, Th Sukhumvit – Thailand's longest highway – was once considered a mostly residential backwater. Today, Th Sukhumvit's glitzy cafes, restaurants and bars rival those of Th Silom and Th Sathorn, and its side streets are home to a host of international communities: Middle Eastern, African, South Asian, Korean and one of the biggest Japanese expat communities in the world. As a result, the international offerings on Th Sukhumvit are second to none, numbering among the very best in Thailand and, in some cases, the world.

Still, there are pockets of a more down-to-earth Bangkok tucked away amid the glamour. Along the canals sit riverside communities and good street food, and even on the northern ends of Th Ekamai and Th Thonglor – where much of the city's most expensive real estate is – you'll find shophouse vendors that have been there for generations. Further east, following Bangkok's outward creep, quirky temples and unexpected hideaways await.

Fusing Past with Present

Lanna culture and modern Thai art

Part of the Siam Society, **Kamthieng House** *(thesiamsociety.org)* is a mid-19th-century teakwood house brought to the capital from Chiang Mai. A beautiful specimen of northern Thai architecture, the house was reassembled in Bangkok

GETTING AROUND

Sukhumvit is well served when it comes to public transport options. Besides taxis, tuk-tuks, motorbikes and ride apps, there's a Skytrain (BTS) stretching all the way to the next province, Samut Prakan, and a Metro (MRT) that serves still-mostly residential Lardprao to the north. Along similarly residential Ramkhamhaeng to the northeast, the **Saen Saep Canal Boat** *(transitbangkok.com/khlong_boats.html)* runs through the city, stopping at Thonglor and Asoke. If you'd prefer the bus, numbers 2 and 511 run along Sukhumvit, while the 40 hits Ekamai and Nana.

AMNAT30/SHUTTERSTOCK

Kamthieng House

in 1963, with its reconstruction taking two years. The compound consists of two connected teakwood houses raised on pillars and with verandas, as well as a separate kitchen and granary. It was built for a prince of Muang Chae and passed down through the matrilineal line (in keeping with northern Thai culture) before it was gifted to the Siam Society, which celebrated its 120th anniversary in 2024.

Unfortunately, the house is currently closed for renovation, but the Siam Society has held behind-the-scenes tours showcasing its restoration, which aims to strengthen the ancient home's foundations. It should be reopened to the public by the end of 2026.

To study a different kind of art, head to the tucked-away **SAC Gallery** *(sac.gallery)*, housed in a large white building on Sukhumvit 39. This is one of the largest, most ambitious art spaces in Bangkok. SAC has a mission to promote Thai artists – especially painters – but also shows artists from elsewhere in Southeast Asia. Spread over four floors, it was founded by a Thai real-estate mogul and noted collector of Asian contemporary art. SAC normally shows two different exhibitions at any one time, rotating every couple of months. It's open from 11am to 6pm Tuesday through Sunday.

FRIENDSHIP THROUGH UNDERSTANDING

Dr Navamintr Tom Vitayakul, co-owner of **Ruen Urai** and council member of the **Siam Society Under Royal Patronage**. *@tom_vitayakul*

When I was 15, my father gave me a lifetime membership to the Siam Society as a birthday present. He knew that I appreciated the arts, history, and nature, and the Siam Society is an organisation that promotes knowledge of the culture and natural history of Thailand and neighbouring countries.

This is the first internationally minded organisation that uses English as its main language to disseminate knowledge on the culture and natural sciences of Thailand and Southeast Asia. It's not just for academics, but for everyone. It's very important because when you understand your own culture and others' cultures, you have a better relationship.

EATING ON THONGLOR & EKAMAI: STREET FOOD

Nomjit: A decades-old northeastern Thai eatery with excellent green papaya salad. *10.30am-8pm Mon-Sat, to midnight Sun* ฿฿

Wattana Panich: Now in its third generation, this stewed beef vendor is famous for its 50-year-old broth that's reheated every day. *10am-7pm* ฿

Mae Somporn: Across from Thonglor Police Station, Mae Somporn serves different types of curry on rice for breakfast and lunch. *5am-3pm Mon-Sat, from 6am Sun* ฿

Lung Cheay Egg Noodles: Delicious egg noodles with pork are served at this longstanding vendor; open til late. *6pm-3am* ฿

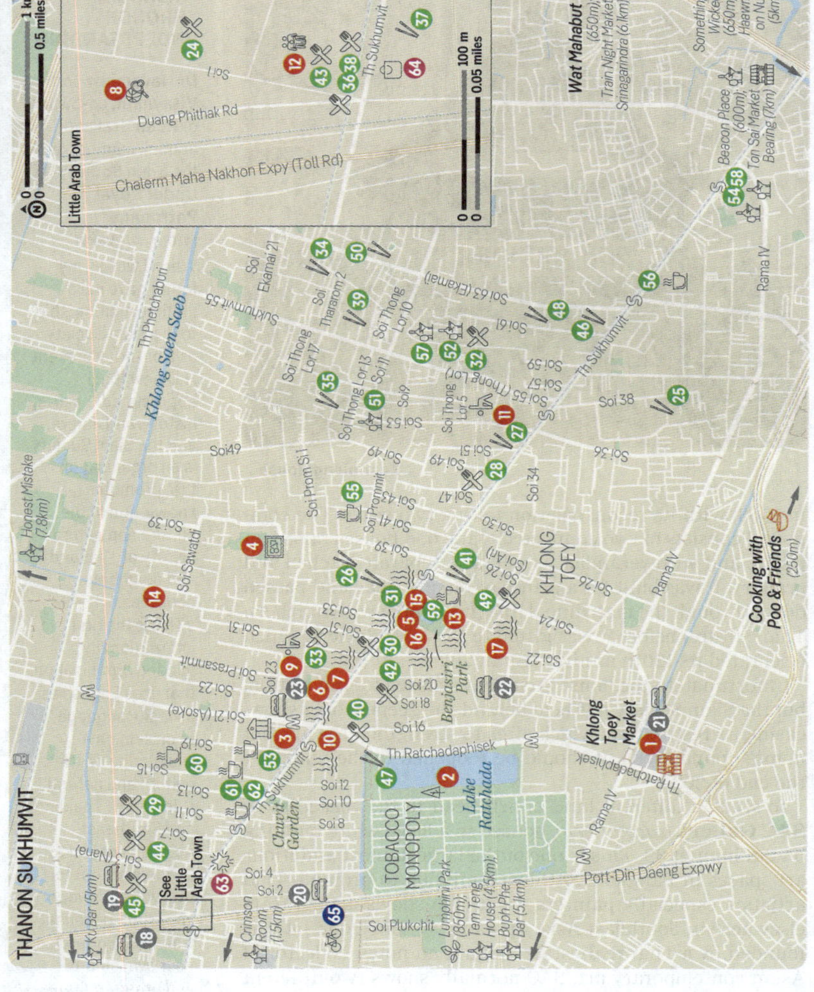

Step into Another World

Exploring Little Arab Town

The section of Th Nana north of Sukhumvit (aka Sukhumvit 3) has a far different reputation from its southern counterpart, though it does share south Nana's penchant for bright lights and dizzying activity. Perhaps because the road is named after longtime landlord and prominent Thai-Muslim businessman Lek Nana, north Nana has been the de facto centre for all Middle Eastern and African businesses in Bangkok. That means north Nana hosts a mouthwatering array of

HIGHLIGHTS
1 Khlong Toey Market

SIGHTS
2 Benjakitti Park
3 Kamthieng House
4 SAC Gallery

ACTIVITIES
5 Anastasia Miaray
6 Divana Massage & Spa
7 Footmaster
8 Grace Bowling Alley
9 Green Room Yoga
10 IDA Salon
11 Iyengar Yoga Bangkok
see 7 Let's Relax
12 Little Arab Town
13 Nuad Thai Training
14 Oasis Spa
15 Po Thai Traditional Massage School (Sukhumvit)
16 Take Care Beauty Salon
17 Trendi @24 Hair Beauty Massage

SLEEPING
18 Ad Lib Bangkok
19 AriyasomVilla
20 Atlanta
21 Fig Lobby
22 House by the Pond
23 Tints of Blue

EATING
24 Al-Saddah
25 Baan Somtum
26 Bankara Ramen
27 Bo.lan
28 Broccoli Revolution
29 Daniel Thaiger
30 Easy Burger
31 Gold Curry
32 Homeburg
33 Kaek Kao Kua
34 Lung Cheay Egg Noodles
35 Mae Somporn
36 Mahmoud Shawarma
37 Nana Seafood
38 Nefertiti
39 Nomjit
40 Prime Burger
see 59 Ringer Hut
41 Rung Rueang Pork Noodle
see 7 Sai Nam Phueng Noodle Shop
42 Saras
43 Shahrazad
44 Soho Pizza
45 Taye Ethiopian Restaurant
46 Teppen
47 Took Lae Dee
48 Toritama
49 Vistro
50 Wattana Panich

DRINKING & NIGHTLIFE
51 #Find the Locker Room
52 Bar Vagabond
53 Bitter Brown
54 Cielo Sky Bar & Restaurant
55 Eden Dispensary & Cafe
56 Fat Buds
57 J.Boroski
58 Little Wine Bar
59 Siam Green
60 SOL Coffee Asoke
61 Vivin Asoke
62 WWAPORTAL

ENTERTAINMENT
63 Nana Plaza
see 23 Soi Cowboy

SHOPPING
64 Souky

TRANSPORT
65 Bangkok Forest Cycling

restaurants, tucked-away shisha lounges, and possibly more oud and perfume shops per square metre than in the rest of Bangkok combined.

An offshoot of Sukhumvit 3 – literally – is **Little Arab Town**, filled almost exclusively with Middle Eastern businesses. Once a dark, bare-bones alleyway dominated by roadside shisha lounges, the area has seen something of a makeover in recent years and is now done up in lots of glass and reflective surfaces, somewhat similar to an airport (but open-air). The shisha lounges have been shooed away from public view and are now hidden on second floors, drastically changing the look of longstanding restaurants such as **Nefertiti** *(@nefertitibangkok)*

WHAT TO BUY IN NORTH NANA

Nana can be a shopper's paradise, as long as you're not easily overwhelmed. The entrance to Sukhumvit 3 remains flanked by as-yet-uncleared street vendors (remember to haggle) hawking everything from slightly rude T-shirts to sex toys and what they say is Viagra. This adds to the neighbourhood's wonderfully chaotic air. The street proper is lined with shawarma vendors – lending the street the smell of grilling meat – and a surprising number of men's sandals purveyors. Most striking, of course, is the sheer volume of oud and perfume shops. (You know you're in Nana when even the Skytrain station has a perfume shop.) We recommend only purchasing this fragrant wood from spots where the varieties are displayed.

EATING IN NORTH NANA: INTERNATIONAL FARE

Shahrazad: Arguably the neighbourhood's most famous eatery, this longstanding restaurant serves a mix of Egyptian, South Asian and Thai dishes. *9am-2.30am* ฿฿

Taye Ethiopian Restaurant: Great food with friendly service and homemade *injera* in a comfortable, family-owned restaurant. *11am-11pm* ฿฿

Al-Saddah: Delicious Yemeni cuisine, including a whole goat or lamb with all the fixings. Special seats enable you to enjoy your meal seated on the floor. *24hr* ฿฿

Mahmoud Shawarma: The reason why Th Nana smells like deliciously char-grilled meat? It's this outdoor vendor. *3pm-4am* ฿

GETTING THE MOST FROM BENJAKITTI PARK

Andrew Hiransomboon is an ultra-marathon runner and the founder of **Andy's Chili Crunch**. *@andyschilicrunch*

Benjakitti is now over 700,000 sq metres of walking, jogging and biking paths through engineered wetlands, plus it houses various activities housed in old tobacco-drying warehouses – all free. There is also a skateboard park, balance bike course, exercise areas and playgrounds. App-based shared bikes can be found at docks near park entrances, while equipment such as balls and racquets (of varying quality) can be checked out for free. Bookings for pickleball and badminton can be made through the CSTD app, but frankly easier than trying to navigate the app is showing up 30 minutes early to get in line for one of the walk-in courts.

TAKE PHOTO/SHUTTERSTOCK

Benjakitti Park

and giving the street a more family-friendly vibe. Adding to that is the addition of the neighbourhood's own answer to 7-Eleven – the bright and cheery **Souky** *(facebook.com/souky official)*, which has everything you'd expect from a convenience store, plus halal products and hard-to-find spices.

Perhaps most surprising is the existence of what is surely Bangkok's most tucked-away bowling alley (and pool tables), located in the northern side of the lobby of **Grace Hotel** *(gracebangkok.com)*. At **Grace Bowling Alley**, you can buy a game for 200฿ (socks and shoes provided) and even a bottle of Singha (for extra). Best of all, it's open from 4pm to 5am.

It's Easier to be Green

Getting pumped up at Benjakitti Park

Once a somewhat-neglected expanse of land centred around a seldom-visited lake, **Benjakitti Park** has undergone a major revamp, with land from a former tobacco business incorporated to form the largest park on Th Sukhumvit. What used to be a big lawn for the Queen Sirikit Convention Centre has been updated to include a forest park, elevated walkways, an outdoor recreation area and health park spreading over 72 hectares.

DRINKING NEAR ASOKE: COFFEE

SOL Coffee Asoke: A local chain specialising in modern, minimalist interiors and good coffee; this spot really heats up at lunchtime. *7am-4pm Mon-Fri, 8am-5pm Sat & Sun* ฿

WWAPORTAL: Part of a city-wide chain, this shop offers a wide selection of coffees and some sweets in a sparkling white setting. *8am-8pm* ฿

Bitter Brown: A longstanding favourite among local office workers, with good coffee, and popular breakfast and lunch options. *8am-8pm Mon-Fri* ฿฿

Vivin Asok: A rapidly expanding chain of cafe/grocery/bistro spots, Vivin's hybrid model enables you to take home the coffee beans that you're enjoying. *8am-9pm* ฿฿

This has led to a surge in enthusiasm among Bangkokians, with its thoroughfares liberally dotted by joggers, cyclists and walkers at sunrise and sunset, all taking advantage of an additional 10+ tracks earmarked specifically for them. Visitors without a bicycle can conveniently rent one nearby at **Bangkok Forest Cycling** *(bangkokforestcycling.com; two hours 350฿)*.

BENJAKITTI PARK–LUMPHINI PARK WALKWAY

Around 1.3km from Benjakitti Park is **Lumphini Park** (p98), central Bangkok's other big chunk of green space. The two parks are connected by an elevated walkway that starts at the southwest corner of Benjakitti.

Besides the original lake encircled by a 1.6km jogging and walking trail, the 1.7-km-long Skywalk over the newer forest park will take you past different types of local flora, as well as native wetlands. There is a concerted effort to attract different types of birds to the area – all the better to attract accompanying birdwatchers – and a museum is slated to join the open-air amphitheatre as a recent addition to the park. Even better, there is now a dog park in which to walk your dog (as of yet still a rarity in the city) and a shady spot for picnics by the lake. Finally, children can enjoy the resident playground, and there are free fitness machines along the paths.

Have a Little Class

Learning opportunities on Sukhumvit

Sukhumvit's large expat community has led to a lot of interesting English-language classes becoming available, ranging from the traditional (massage and food) to the more Western-skewed (rock climbing).

For a neighbourhood with so many massage parlours, there are, naturally, quite a few massage schools. The most well-known include the Sukhumvit branch of Wat Po's **Po Thai Traditional Massage School** *(watpo-school.com; 5-day course 9500฿)*, which is the branch of the famous massage school that started it all; and **Nuad Thai Training** *(nuadthaischool.com; four-hour beginner course 4000฿)*. Courses range from 30 hours for a grounding in the basics to 165 hours to become a professional masseuse.

THE STORY BEHIND COOKING WITH POO

The neighbourhood of Khlong Toey, just a block away from Th Sukhumvit, has been home to a slum that's considered one of Bangkok's biggest. In 2007 Saiyuud 'Chompoo' Diwong ('Poo') was one of its thousands of inhabitants, facing a dire shortage of rice and a need to supplement her income selling food from her house. Enter Australian Anji Barker, a fellow resident of Khlong Toey. Banding together with a group of friends, she helped Poo open her own cooking class – a daunting endeavour for Poo, who did not have any English. Today Cooking with Poo has a team, and even a published cookbook that has sold millions of copies. Best of all, the school's continued success brings more visitors to Khlong Toey.

EATING ON SUKHUMVIT: VEGETARIAN

Broccoli Revolution: One of the original upscale vegetarian eateries on Sukhumvit, with Thai, Burmese and Western dishes. *8am-9pm* ฿฿

Vistro: Plant-based pizza, Chinese noodles, a selection of dumplings and numerous Thai dishes served in a comfortable, airy space. *10.30am-9pm* ฿฿

Kaek Kao Kua: Really good vegan *khao soi*, egg noodles and Sukhothai noodles in an outdoor setting (beware of the dog). *11am-7.30pm Fri-Wed* ฿

Saras: Veg Indian food in a food court, with delicious dishes at reasonable prices – to make up for the nondescript ambience. *11am-11pm Mon-Fri, 8am-11.30pm Sat & Sun* ฿

A MORNING STROLL THROUGH KHLONG TOEY

Spend a typical morning at the market that keeps Bangkok's restaurants and vendors well stocked.

START	END	LENGTH
Lao Za	Khun Thing Sai Mai Roti	1km; 30 minutes

Do as the vendors do and have breakfast on the periphery before diving into work. One popular place is longstanding noodle shop 1 **Lao Za**, famous for its homemade fish meatballs. Our favourite order is the *sen mee* (rice vermicelli) with fish broth and meatballs.

Afterwards, turn left to your next breakfast stop – the famous hotpot vendor 2 **Heng Chun Seng**. Although it's famous for its beef hotpot, an underrated dish is the soup noodles, with your choice of beef cuts for 60฿. If you don't like beef, they have pork versions. Alas, there are no veggie versions.

Then, turn right into the alleyway and go straight towards 3 **Khlong Toey Market**. It's a sensory overload: goods are piled high;, porters wend their way through crowds with overfilled baskets; customers haggle with vendors. Once you hit a dead end, turn left and make your way through the market – past Burmese food stalls, IT vendors and sweets shops – towards the intersection of Th Ratchadaphisek and Th Rama IV, to find 4 **Khun Thing Sai Mai Roti**, where women work tirelessly to make paper-thin flatbreads stuffed with spun sugar. Although it's tempting to ask for a *roti* straight off the griddle, they don't do that here. Instead, get a pack to take home.

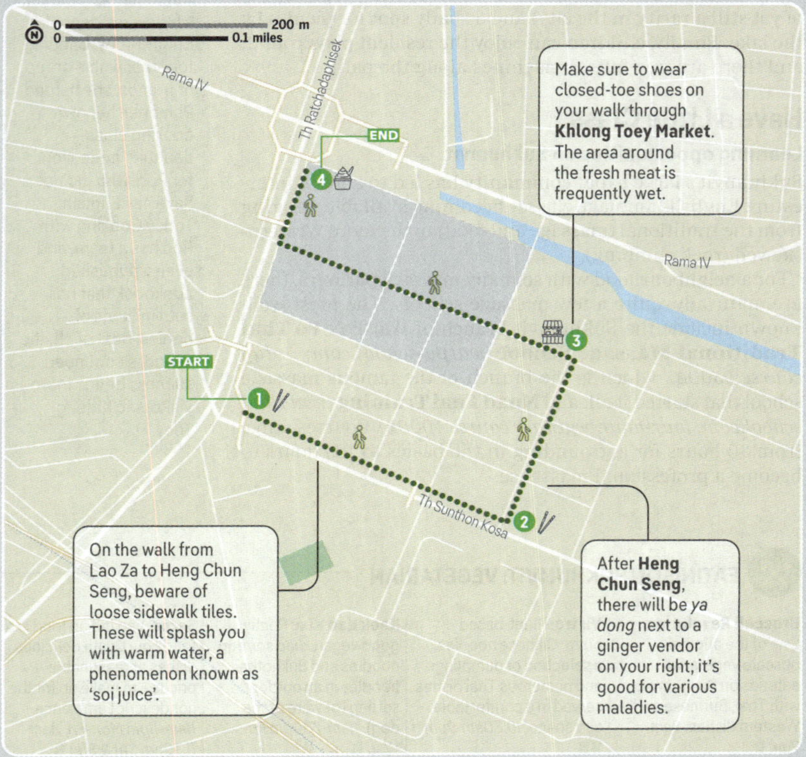

As for food, the long-running **Cooking with Poo & Friends** *(cookingwithpoo.com; 1800฿)* has been operating since 2007 out of Khlong Toey. Classes include learning how to make some of Thailand's best-known dishes, plus a tour of nearby Khlong Toey Market. If you want to move beyond the basics, you can join a three-day Thai food masterclass by pioneering restaurant **Bo.lan** *(bolanedu.com; price available on request)* of *Chef's Table* fame.

As for yoga, you can try a range of classes from yin yoga (in which holding a pose for a long time helps boost flexibility) to more dynamic ashtanga at the **Green Room Yoga** *(thegreenroomyoga.com; from 550฿)*. If you prefer a different approach, you can learn Iyengar yoga (in which props are encouraged to help achieve the 'ideal' yoga pose) at **Iyengar Yoga Bangkok** *(iyengar-yoga-bangkok.com; weekend class 1250฿)*, which includes special courses such as backbend workshops.

Holistic Heaven

Better yourself in body and mind

In parts of this area – particularly around Th Sukhumvit 24 – a newbie visitor would be forgiven for assuming that entire streets are devoted solely to spas and massage parlours. All of Thailand's major massage and spa chains maintain at least one outlet here, if not a handful, and the neighbourhood is also rife with luxury spa names (not to mention hotel spas). To be thoroughly refreshed, **Let's Relax** *(letsrelaxspa.com; two-hour Thai massage 1200฿)* is popular for its no-frills/high-quality approach to Thai massage, but if you can't be bothered to change your clothes into the requisite Thai massage pyjamas, a good foot massage can be had at the aptly named **Footmaster** *(footmaster.co.th; one hour 600฿)*.

The most well-known luxury spa in the area is probably **Oasis Spa** *(oasisspa.net; two-hour Thai massage 1700฿)*, beloved for its peaceful garden setting and many treatment options. The masseuses are skilled, if a bit overzealous at times in ironing out stubborn knots with thumbs of steel. Meanwhile, **Divana Massage & Spa** (*divanaspa.com; one-hour aromatherapy massage 1850฿*) offers a somewhat more stereotypically 'relaxing' experience, with packages emulating the beauty programmes of 'ancient brides-to-be' as well as anti-ageing packages utilising pomegranate and mangosteen. Some of these options will allow you to easily while away the afternoon in herbal-scented bliss.

BEST PLACES TO PRIMP ON SUKHUMVIT

Take Care Beauty Salon: This multistorey salon is actually a one-stop shop for nails, haircuts, brow shaping and lash extensions.

Trendi @24 Hair Beauty Massage: It doesn't look like much, but the brow waxing here is very good and reasonably priced.

Anastasia Miaray: This longstanding eyebrow-waxing salon has branches worldwide and also sells its well-known brow beauty products here.

Lelé Studio: If the idea of water jets encircling your head for an ultra-thorough wash sounds like fun, then the home of the original hair spa is for you.

IDA Salon: If a big change – especially with hair colour – is on the cards, this is where to go.

EATING ON SUKHUMVIT: JAPANESE

Toritama: Good *yakitori* joint with an authentic Japanese feel serving skewers and *izakaya* standards, including grilled rice balls. *5pm-midnight Mon-Sat* ฿฿฿

Teppen: A fun *izakaya* on a street next to busy Th Ekamai, this restaurant specialises in *wara-yaki* (hay-smoked fish or meat). *5pm-midnight* ฿฿฿

Bankara Ramen: Bankara specialises in *tonkotsu* featuring a rich pork broth, but they also have miso and shoyu ramen, plus tasty sides. *11am-10.30pm* ฿฿

Ringer Hut: This Nagasaki-based chain mostly serves *champon*, udon and ramen noodles. *11am-10.30pm* ฿฿

BANGKOK'S OTHER SPEAKEASIES

Crimson Room: Inspired by *The Great Gatsby*, this luxurious bar is on Th Lang Suan and has live jazz Tuesday through Saturday.

Tem Teng House: A quirky live music space located inside an old building in Chinatown.

Honest Mistake: On Th Phaholyothin, this spot is inspired by 1930s–1940s Bangkok, when Chinese gangs ruled parts of the city.

Buph Phe Bar: This bar is hidden in Chinatown behind a fake vending machine.

Ku Bar: A longtime speakeasy in the Old Town that genuinely confused people when it first opened.

Rise of the Speakeasy

Sukhumvit's spate of speakeasy bars

Bangkok is full of bars, many of them with interesting concepts and well-curated ingredients. But there is a subset of bar openings in recent years that highlights a somewhat newish trend in local mixology: the bar that wants you to work at finding it.

Some of these bars are actively hidden, requiring would-be guests to solve a puzzle like Indiana Jones trying to save his father's life. Others are simply in out-of-the-way spots, discernible only if you happen to be walking by. Regardless of which you prefer, Th Sukhumvit is studded with these establishments.

The most famous of these speakeasies is probably **#Find the Locker Room** *(@findthelockerroom.bkk)*, which is hidden behind a wall of school-like lockers. Inside is a lugubriously appointed, dimly lit bar straight out of Central Casting, with drinks inspired by Pokémon and the original Nike Air Max. Less difficult to get into is longtime speakeasy stalwart **J.Boroski**, which is simply out of the way, located at the end of a nondescript alley. Here, you won't find a menu, just a painfully handsome hipster asking what type of drink you prefer (refreshing or spirits-forward?). If you'd like a Japanese spin on the speakeasy, there's **Bar Vagabond**, found in the basement of a seemingly abandoned house. Besides impeccably made cocktails, you'll also find Japanese dishes here.

Up in Smoke

Navigating Thailand's cannabis scene

In June 2022 Thailand became the first country in Asia to legalise cannabis, a much-anticipated decision that followed Thailand's legalisation of marijuana for medical purposes in 2018. The move led to some 1200-odd dispensaries opening along Th Sukhumvit, perhaps because so many foreigners live and stay here. Unfortunately, faced with pressure from other governments, Thailand has attempted to walk back its free-wheeling approach to weed with new restrictions, muddying the waters for what is and is not allowed in Thailand as a result.

Proponents of more controls fear unfettered cannabis sales will spark addiction and crime, or just make young people lazy. The proposed restrictions are set to affect up to 18,000 licensed marijuana sellers in Thailand, according to Thai PBS.

DRINKING AROUND ON NUT: OUR PICKS

Beacon Place: This plaza is full of small bars, including nightlife institution Cheap Charlie's. *5pm-1am Tue-Sun* ฿

Cielo Sky Bar & Restaurant: A rooftop bar with strong cocktails, this is a sophisticated standout in a neighbourhood full of pubs. *5.30pm-1am* ฿฿

Little Wine Bar: A couple of reasonably priced wine-by-the-glass options in an intimate space that seems miles away, vibes-wise, from nearby W Market. *5pm-midnight* ฿฿

Something Wicked: Bangkok's only voodoo-inspired cocktail bar, with 'potions' such as caramel apple martini. *7pm-2am Tue-Sun* ฿฿

NELSON ANTOINE/SHUTTERSTOCK

Cannabis shop, Thanon Sukhumvit

A new amendment to Thailand's cannabis law makes it illegal to smoke marijuana on the premises of the cannabis store, unless the seller is a licensed medical practitioner. In the future, a doctor's prescription may be needed to purchase marijuana for symptoms such as insomnia and migraines. The amount sold may also be controlled and the quality regulated, but as of writing, sellers say the situation remains unclear. No changes are currently being enforced, but the uncertainty has led to a precipitous drop in sales.

That means legitimate cannabis outlets are still allowed to operate, including **Eden Dispensary & Cafe** *(edenbkk.com; from 300฿)*, which bills itself as providing 'cannabis for successful stoners'. Open for nearly a year, the store sells clothing, coffee and cocktails, as well as various locally grown cannabis strains. Another reputable seller is **Siam Green** *(siamgreenco.com; price upon enquiry)*, which maintains outlets throughout the city, including in Chinatown and Silom. **Fat Buds** *(fatbudsweedshop.com; 3g 900฿)*, has three locations, including Sukhumvit Soi 77.

CANNABIS IN THAILAND

Stephen Yuan is the owner of **Eden Dispensary & Cafe.** We believe that there are people who can smoke regularly and be successful. Eden offers a less stigmatised environment for cannabis that is less stereotypical. We like to think that everyone here is cannabis positive. Here, we look to build a community – we hold get-togethers and movie nights, work out together – our goal is to create a community of successful stoners. We are supportive of the regulatory changes. We just wish for equal enforcement. We are more interested in making sure that we have the best and cleanest cannabis in the city. The biggest negative impact of the law has been on tourists and consumers. That's the part that most of us are very upset about.

EATING ON SUKHUMVIT: BURGERS

Daniel Thaiger: This was arguably the first place to usher in Th Sukhumvit's burger craze; try the Mr Steve burger. *10am-10.30pm* ฿฿

Prime Burger: A longstanding favourite, the bestsellers here are the New York and the Stockholm, as well as the seriously good curly fries. *10.30am-3am* ฿฿

Easy Burger: This spot specialises in smash burgers, with buns made in-house. Get the hard-to-find pimento cheese burger. *11am-3am* ฿฿

Homeburg: Bangkok's first (and only) burger *omakase* chef's bar, which features creative takes on tacos and cheesecake. *5-10pm Mon, Thu & Fri, 2-10pm Sat & Sun* ฿฿฿

THE HISTORY OF THANON NANA

One of Bangkok's busiest roads, Th Nana is the name for Sukhumvit Sois 3 and 4, which are spread out on either side of Th Sukhumvit. Frequently confused with another Th Nana in Chinatown, this Th Nana is named after Thai-Indian businessman Lek Nana, the one-time Landlord of Bangkok who owned much of the area. Th Nana's popularity took off during the Vietnam War in the 1970s, when it became a popular hangout with American GIs. Today, it remains a major nightspot, but with different characteristics: southern Nana has a red-light district; northern Nana is known as the centre for Middle Eastern and African businesses, drawing so many people from that region that there's now a Little Arab Town (p113).

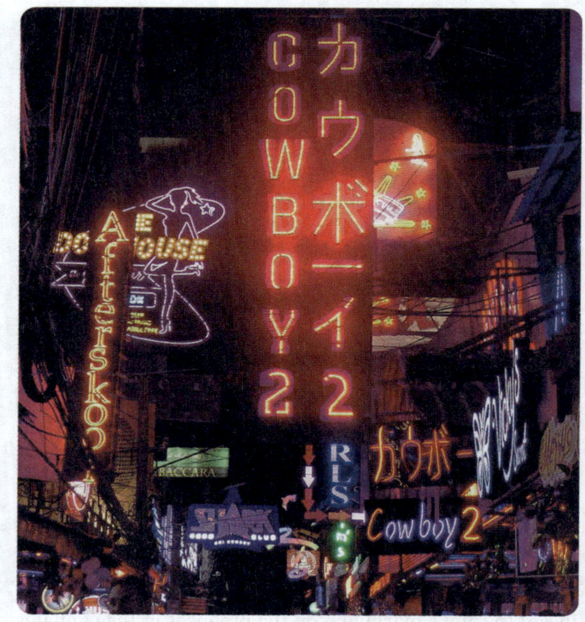

ERICAPOWELL39/SHUTTERSTOCK

Soi Cowboy

Red-Light Bangkok

Cowboy and Nana nightlife

Bangkok has long been associated with sex work. As far back as 300 years ago, visitors were shocked by the immorality they were witnessing. By the end of the 19th century, Chinatown was known for its bars, brothels, nightclubs and dance halls. The scene moved to Silom after WWII, with Patpong's sex shows acquiring worldwide infamy in the 1980s.

Now Th Sukhumvit is home to Bangkok's red-light zones for foreigners (the locals have their own areas), with the action centred on **Soi Cowboy** and **Nana Plaza**. Cowboy is a narrow street of flashing neon lined with go-go bars and beer bars where the staff are all female and the customers all men. Nana Plaza is bigger, with open-air bars surrounded by three floors of go-go bars and clubs.

EATING ON SUKHUMVIT: LATE-NIGHT PICKS

Took Lae Dee: The traditional go-to for late nights, this Thai-style diner is never closed. Another plus: you can go shopping after eating! *24hr* ฿

Gold Curry: A late-night staple of Japanese-style curry, with crowd-pleasing variations that include katsu cutlet stuffed with cheese. *24hr* ฿

Nana Seafood: Thai seafood available 24 hours? Only in Bangkok. Satisfy your late-night river-prawn-and-lobster cravings in this open-air shed. *24hr* ฿฿

Soho Pizza: On the traditional party street of Sukhumvit 11, this spot stays open until (almost) dawn. *9am-5am* ฿฿

On any night, both areas are packed out, but many of the visitors are here as tourists rather than customers. Bangkok's red-light areas are now as much of a sight as any museum or temple.

Both Soi Cowboy and Nana are strictly monitored by the Bangkok authorities.

Sukhumvit on the Fringes

Experiencing Sukhumvit's frontier spirit

In a way, upper Sukhumvit (beyond Sukhumvit 63, or Th Ekamai) really is like the frontier of Bangkok – moving in sync with the capital's gradual creep all the way out to Samut Prakan, the next province. If you hop on the newish Yellow Line Metro (MRT) from Samrong to Lardprao, you'll pass through Sukhumvit as it must have appeared in the 1970s, replete with a couple of rice paddies.

This retro spirit can be found in spades at **Wat Mahabut** in On Nut, home to the shrine of Mae Nak Phra Khanong. Legend has it that Mae Nak was a young woman who lived on the canals close to the shrine. Pregnant when her husband went off to war, she and her baby died in childbirth. Alas, she did not realise she was dead and greeted her husband with their baby upon his return. The husband's neighbours had to intervene, telling him he was living with ghosts, leading him to eventually flee to Wat Mahabut, where she could not enter. Angered, she wreaked havoc on the canal-side community until a powerful monk captured her spirit in an earthenware jar and threw it into the canal.

Visitors – mostly local – come regularly to the shrine, centred around a statue of Mae Nak and her baby. Some give presents to her and/or the baby in hopes of becoming pregnant or of being exempted from military service. The temple becomes especially busy before the 1st and 16th of every month – lottery days in Thailand. People come with baby powder to tease out numbers from the bark of the two tree trunks in the shrine (baby powder is helpfully sold for 10฿), and if they do find numbers, lottery vendors are conveniently right there (80฿ for a pair of tickets).

HOW ON NUT IS CHANGING

Dylan Eitharong is the chef-owner of **Haawm On Nut**.

On Nut is gentrifying, but in this neighbourhood, there are still canal houses; if you walk down to the temple, you can still walk along the canal, and you can go to old-style Bangkok houses where the boats can come up in the front of the house.

Give it another five years and On Nut will go the route of Ekamai or maybe Phra Khanong...Phra Khanong is the next gentrification area, with a lot of brunch places and pretty coffee shops. What's really interesting...we have a lot of Muslim Thais and mosques here. Phatthanakan is the area here that's still heavily Muslim... there's an Indonesian population that's settled here, with good Indonesian restaurants.

EATING ON SUKHUMVIT: THAI FOOD

Sai Nam Phueng Noodle Shop: In an alleyway between Sukhumvit 18 and 20 are delicious chicken-wing noodles from a longtime vendor. *8am-2pm* ฿

Rung Rueang Pork Noodle: *Michelin Guide*–mentioned pork noodles in a *dom yam* broth on Sukhumvit 26. *8am-5pm* ฿

Haawm On Nut: A supper club, or a Thai restaurant run from the owner's house? The menu changes frequently to reflect the seasons. *reservation only, closed Sat-Mon* ฿฿฿

Baan Somtum: Sukhumvit residents love this northeastern Thai restaurant, which blends good Isan food with air-conditioned comfort. *11am-10pm* ฿฿

Northern Bangkok

FOR SHOPAHOLICS AND FAMILIES

TOP TIP
There's more to northern Bangkok than just Chatuchak. To get to the other destinations listed here – which are all fairly spread out – it's a good idea to rent a car or hire a taxi for the day.

Northern Bangkok covers a mammoth area and includes many of the 50 districts that comprise the capital (as well as many of the city's local residents). The region is set to get even bigger as Bangkok's northern boundaries push into central Thailand, gobbling up areas that were farmland a few years ago. A great thing about visiting northern Bangkok is that it offers an insight into the lifestyle and culture of the surrounding provinces without requiring you to leave the city. Few travellers stay here, although there's no shortage of accommodation, and newly expanded Skytrain and Metro lines have made it easier to access. All the same, almost everyone visits Chatuchak Weekend Market, an essential sight whether you're a retail enthusiast or a reluctant shopper. Also worth a trip is Chang Chui, an artsy and largely tourist-free market. There are also many local restaurants that are more authentic and regional than those further south.

Quirky Collections

A mecca for secondhand collectors

Papaya *(papaya-studio.com)* features a mindboggling collection of 19th- and 20th-century artefacts, occupying three floors of a warehouse-sized space. The collection includes stained-glass lamps, antique phones, 1960s beer signage, superhero statues, Piaggio scooters, typewriters, movie projectors, love

GETTING AROUND

Northern Bangkok is now well served by public transport, accessible via the Metro (MRT) and the newish Yellow Line (an overground train that is officially part of the Metro, but only accepts the Skytrain's Rabbit cards). If you are more northeasterly (in the direction of Minburi), you can use the Saen Saep Express Boat to get into downtown Bangkok. You can also take the 501, 71 or 38 bus from Lardprao to Sukhumvit. While it's easy to get to Chatuchak, Chang Chui and MOCA using public transport, it's harder to get to Papaya without using a taxi or ride app.

MARIUS KARP/SHUTTERSTOCK

Museum of Contemporary Art

seats, TV sets, VHS players, wall clocks, shopfront mannequins, lampshades, a huge collection of crucifixes, a few dolls that might be haunted, and some seriously cool mid-century furniture. Once popular mainly with American and Japanese customers, Papaya is gaining traction with local Thais since moving to its new location in 2022.

Getting Artsy-Fartsy

Bangkok's finest art space

The **Museum of Contemporary Art** *(MOCA: mocabangkok.com; 300฿)* is Bangkok's most important contemporary and modern art gallery, although you wouldn't guess it from its peculiar location by the side of an expressway in the city's northern reaches. It's also one of the biggest galleries for contemporary art in Asia, and inside it's an impressive, light-filled, minimalist white space spread over five floors.

MOCA is where hip international artists such as Banksy and Jacky Tsai stage their Bangkok shows – it's worth checking to see who MOCA is exhibiting (book in advance for big-name artists). There are also permanent collections featuring some of the most renowned Thai artists (both painters and sculptors) from the last 100 years, and galleries devoted to photography, *kohn* masks and shadow puppets. The 5th floor has a small collection of work by foreign artists. MOCA is open Tuesday to Sunday, from 10am to 6pm.

HOW THAILAND'S BIGGEST ANTIQUES STORE BEGAN

Papaya is the brainchild of Supoj Siripornlert, whose nickname is 'Tong'. As he recalls on Papaya's website, he has loved antiques all his life, once spending all of his money on antiques at the age of 14. These purchases, he says, marked the beginning of Papaya. The store officially opened in 1977, supplementing Tong's other career as a furniture designer and builder. Today, Papaya counts among its clients the Siam Hotel. Although Papaya is a store in name, in reality, it's a showcase of Tong's antiques collection – one he continues to add to via semi-regular trips to Europe. In this way, Papaya can be considered more of a musem, but a museum in which everything can be touched.

EATING IN LARDPRAO: OUR PICKS

Baan Sen Sai: Good *khao soi* (northern Thai curried egg noodles), refreshing iced drinks and boat noodles served in a comfortable setting. *10am-9pm* ฿

Wood Cafe: A stylish spot that serves a range of international dishes, including Italian–Thai pasta; but the real specialty here is the cake. *10am-7pm Wed-Sun* ฿฿

Tawandang Brewery: A fun beer hall with good northeastern Thai food and live *mor lam* (northeastern Thai music) performances. *5pm-1am* ฿฿

B-Story Garden Cafe & Restaurant: An interestingly decorated, high-ceilinged space that feels like Miss Havisham's conservatory. *10am-10pm* ฿฿฿

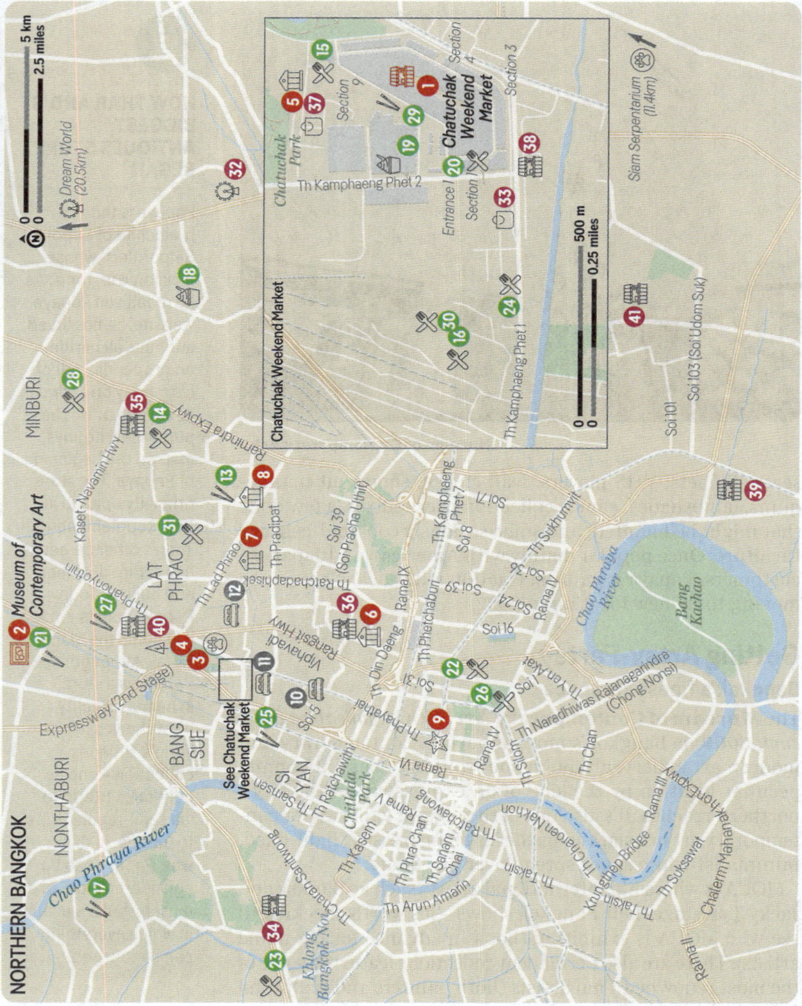

NORTHERN BANGKOK

EATING IN NORTHERN BANGKOK: OUR PICKS

Krua Jaidee: Basic but quality Thai seafood, including prawns baked in glass noodles and fish *larb* (spicy minced salad). *11am-2pm & 4-10pm Mon-Fri, & 4-10pm Sat & Sun* ฿

Somtum Nong Rejoice: Billing itself as sellers of 'Bangkok's spiciest *som tam*', this spot also serves less fiery renditions of their spicy dishes. *11am-10pm* ฿฿

Chaophraya Antique Cafe: In the rainy season, Chao Phraya's waters flood the outside terrace and attract diners who want to eat their food in knee-deep water. *11am-9pm* ฿฿

Prik Yuak: Once an outdoor eatery in Chatuchak, this restaurant has taken over more glamourous surroundings in a former school nearby. *11am-9pm* ฿฿

HIGHLIGHTS
1 Chatuchak Weekend Market
2 Museum of Contemporary Art

SIGHTS
3 Bangkok Butterfly Garden and Insectarium
4 Chatuchak Park
5 Children's Discovery Museum
6 INVESTORY Investment Discovery Museum
7 Kunawong House Museum
8 Papaya

ACTIVITIES
9 Sea Life Bangkok Ocean World

SLEEPING
10 Josh Hotel
11 Pillow & Bread
12 Woodstory Boutique Hotel

EATING
13 Baan Sen Sai
14 B-Story Garden Cafe & Restaurant
15 Café Ice
16 Chamlong's
17 Chaophraya Antique Cafe
18 Chocolate Ville
19 Coco JJ
20 Duck Noodle
21 Krua Jaidee
22 La Monita
see 23 Na-Oh Bangkok
23 Olive Kitchen
24 Pasta District Chatuchak
25 Prik Yuak
26 Smokin' Pug
27 Somtum Nong Rejoice
28 Tawandang Brewery
29 Toh-Plue
30 Vegetarian Society in Chatuchak
31 Wood Cafe

ENTERTAINMENT
32 Siam Amazing Park

SHOPPING
33 About Herbs Natural
34 Chang Chui
35 Hua Mum Night Market
36 Jodd Fairs Ratchada
37 Mixt Chatuchak
38 Or Tor Kor Market
39 Ton Sai Market Bearing
40 Train Market Dan Neramit
41 Train Night Market Srinagarindra

Bangkok's Hipster Market

Get eclectic at Chang Chui

Chang Chui *(changchuibangkok.com)*, formally known as Chang Chui Creative Park, calls itself both a creative space and a night market. Centred on an abandoned airplane that now houses a fine-dining restaurant, you'll find performance spaces, installations and an art gallery here, but also vintage clothing stores, craft beer bars, many restaurants, mellow live music and even a hipster barber shop. It's an almost exclusively Thai scene, with few foreign visitors, and it feels rather more sophisticated than other night markets in Bangkok.

The plane that looms over the market is an old Lockheed Tristar that has been artfully converted into the high-end **Na-Oh Bangkok** *(naohbangkok.com)*, which has live jazz on Saturdays and a posh tasting menu; reservations are essential. There are also numerous food stalls and Thai restaurants, as well as **Olive Kitchen** *(facebook.com/olivekitchenthailand)*, which combines craft beer with pizza, pasta and artisanal sausages.

Spanning 18 different structures – all made from discarded objects and around which more informal vendors cluster – the market is open 11am to 11pm Tuesday to Sunday, but not many places operate during the day. To experience the market properly, come on a weekend evening after 5pm.

Chang Chui is located on the Thonburi side of Chao Phraya River in Bang Phlat. To get here by public transport, take the Metro (MRT) Blue Line to Bang Yi Khan and then hop in a taxi for the final 3km.

NORTHERN BANGKOK'S OTHER NIGHT MARKETS

Train Market Dan Neramit: Located in the former Dan Neramit amusement park, a fairy-tale castle still stands over this laid-back market.

Jodd Fairs Ratchada: Further south along Th Ratchadaphisek is this popular market. Here you'll find rolled ice cream, squid shots and scorpions.

Hua Mum Night Market: This sees few foreigners and has lively bars and restaurants; it's located just past Lardprao.

Train Night Market Srinagarindra: Another bustling night market with all the expected bells and whistles: antique tchotchkes, vintage decorations, and food and drink.

Ton Sai Market Bearing: A more laid-back vibe pervades this night market, where street food, iced coffee, tea and live music reign.

MICHAELNERO/SHUTTERSTOCK

TOP EXPERIENCE

Chatuchak Weekend Market

The largest weekend market in the world is a vast warren of 15,000-odd shops and stalls, and with every conceivable item on sale, it's one of Bangkok's most popular excursions. Once you're inside, it can seem like there's no order or escape, but the market is organised into coherent sections. The clock tower is a handy landmark.

DON'T MISS

- Antiques, Handicrafts & Souvenirs
- Clothing & Accessories
- Eating & Drinking
- Housewares & Decor
- Massage & Coffee
- Plants & Gardening

Antiques, Handicrafts & Souvenirs

Sections 1 and 29 are the place to go for bronze religious statues, old LPs, Thai musical instruments and other random antiques with religious motifs. If you like to collect old watches and Japanese-style denim, head to Section 1, Soi 35. Antique ceramics, and old masks and carved doors can be found in Section 26, at places such as **Product of Gargoyle** and **Raan Jipata Antiques** on Soi 1. Also on Soi 1 is **House of Lamp**, with – you guessed it – lamps, and knobs for drawers (this one is more for decor, but stores will occasionally bleed into other sections here). Next to popular **Tik's Cafe** in Section 9 (great for a breather), you'll find *kohn* masks, Buddha figures (they can be bought if they are small and show the whole figure) and baby-sized *muay Thai* gear.

Clothing & Accessories

Clothing dominates much of Chatuchak. Sections 2 to 4 deal in new and used clothing for every Thai subculture, from punks to cowboys. Sections 5 to 6 do used clothing, while 9 to 11 and 21 to 26 sell new clothing. Of particular interest is Section 6, Soi 59, where you'll find cheap-but-stylish runners, hand-tooled leather belts and used cowboy boots. Further afield, Section 9, Soi 13 sells well-crafted straw handbags, and **G-Shop** in Section 21, Soi 28 sells bohemian dresses made of Indian fabric. A similar vibe can be found at **Le Plaacard**, made with Thai fabric, and **Moaré** on Soi 48. **Bells_Shopp** in Section 23, Soi 32 offers Issey Miyake–style pleated pants and dresses; **Inky** in Section 23, Soi 31 offers more tailored shirts and shorts.

As for jewellery, you can find pretty earrings and crystal necklaces at **Hindo** in section 24, Soi 33, or have fun at a silver jewellery workshop at **Origin Ag** in Section 22, Soi 30.

Eating & Drinking

Food stalls set up shop between Sections 6 and 8 and also close to Entrance 1. Veteran standouts include Ice Cube by **Café Ice**, a Western-Thai joint that does good *pat tai* and tasty fruit shakes; and **Toh-Plue**, which has all the Thai standards. In front of Section 20, a line forms outside of **Duck Noodle** at noon, and for the original coconut ice cream at **Coco JJ**. If you are vegetarian, you can find food at **Vegetarian Society in Chatuchak** or **Chamlong's**. And if you only want a chocolatey snack, there's **Alp Bakery** in Section 21, Soi 28. Finally, **Mixt**, an air-conditioned mall behind Section 27 with lots of 100฿ shops inside, also holds some eateries, as well as clean bathrooms.

Housewares & Decor

Sections 15, 19 and 20 specialise in all manner of housewares, from plastic buckets to expensive brass woks. This is a particularly good spot to stock up on inexpensive Thai ceramics, from celadon to the traditional rooster-themed bowls from Lampang. Find traditional Thai ceramics at **Jirada Benjarong** in Section 17, Soi 10 or **JJ Benjarong** in Section 19, Soi 6. **Bangsai Shop** in Section 9, Soi 13 offers a plethora of wooden cookware, and there are charming straw baskets and dish covers (a traditional Thai item to hold off flies) in Section 8, Soi 14. Finally, you can sniff all the hand-poured natural soy candles at **Teakwood Essence** in Section 13, Soi 11 to find your favourite.

Massage & Coffee

A foot massage is a great (and air-conditioned) way to ease the strain of a day's shopping. There are massage shops throughout Chatuchak – their promoters will likely find you. Another way to ease stress is to stop for a coffee: we like **Heart Rock Coffee** in Section 18, Soi 26; **Section 25 Coffee Corner** (which is air-conditioned); and **Coffee Drip Talen** in Section 1, Soi 35.

Art, Paintings & Fragrances

Section 7 is an open-air art gallery, from traditional religious paintings to contemporary pieces. Popular collage artist Pariwat Anantachina *(@big_pariwat)* of Pariwat Studio, who specialises in Bangkok-themed murals, has moved to **Mixt** mall.

Saisalang in Section 15, Soi 10 produces Thailand-themed scents that make good souvenirs, as do **About Herbs Natural**, who also make pain relievers and mosquito spray.

DON'T GET CRANKY

Chatuchak rage is a common phenomenon brought on by crowds, heat and hunger. With so many people pushing past, and the market being outside and lacking air-con, it's easy to lose it. Hydrate and snack regularly, get one or two foot massages, and/or head to nearby **Mixt** or **Chatuchak Park** to escape the retail frenzy.

TOP TIPS

- Chatuchak is also known to locals as 'Jatujak' or 'JJ'.
- Reach the market via the Mo Chit Skytrain (BTS) station or the Kamphaeng Phet/Chatuchak Park Metro (MRT) stations.
- A few shops are open on weekdays, but the market really gets going on Friday night when vendors start setting up.
- Spend a full day here, but arrive early to beat the heat.
- Maps and toilets are scattered throughout the market.
- If you like food, check out nearby **Or Tor Kor Market**, Thailand's finest fresh market.
- An information centre (not always staffed) and ATMs are near the northern end of Soi 1, Soi 2 and Soi 3.

Where to Find Everything in Chatuchak...

Chatuchak is the world's largest weekend market, a fact that can be both exhilarating and daunting. It's easy to find yourself overwhelmed by row upon row of goods, seemingly arranged haphazardly. Instead of trying to see everything, save your energy by heading to the sections that interest you the most. Late mornings and afternoons see fewer visitors and cooler temperatures. Comfortable shoes and a good backpack are a must.

Market Key

1 Green Plants and gardening

2 Purple Pets and pet products

3 Blue Home goods, decor and handicrafts

4 Pink Antiques and books

5 Yellow Clothing and accessories

TOP TIPS

➡ Jot down the stall number if you see something you might want to come back for as shops in the same section tend to look the same.

➡ Take frequent breaks with a stop for a chilled drink or a reviving foot or body massage right in the market.

❸ Home goods, decor and handicrafts

CKTRAVELS.COM/SHUTTERSTOCK

❹ Antiques and books

RADIOKAFKA/SHUTTERSTOCK

❺ Clothing and accessories

MICHAELNERO/SHUTTERSTOCK

GREAT CHILDREN'S DESTINATIONS

Bangkok Butterfly Garden and Insectarium: This free-admission 'insect zoo' houses a butterfly garden and lamphu trees, whose roots attract fireflies.

Sea Life Bangkok Ocean World: The largest aquarium in Southeast Asia covers 10,000 sq metres and holds 5 million litres of water.

Kunawong House Museum: This informative museum in a repurposed house details how Thai art has evolved over time.

Siam Serpentarium: Hiding nuggets of information through interactive exhibits, this museum houses more than 70 types of snakes.

INVESTORY Investment Discovery Museum: Through a series of interactive exhibits, this museum shows children how to invest their money.

QUALITY STOCK ARTS/SHUTTERSTOCK

Siam Amazing Park

Bangkok for Children

Fun for kids

Northern Bangkok has the biggest cluster of kid-oriented sights. All can be accessed via taxi or ride app from the Mo Chit Skytrain (BTS) station or the Chatuchak Park Metro (MRT) stop.

At the **Children's Discovery Museum** *(bkk-cdm.com; free)*, located conveniently close to Chatuchak Weekend Market, learning is well disguised as fun. The interactive exhibits range in topic from construction to culture, although we suspect most kids will be drawn to the Dino Detective Zone, where they can dig in sand to find and reassemble dinosaur bones. There are also a couple of good playgrounds here.

Siam Amazing Park *(siamamazingpark.com; adult/child 1000/850฿)* is Thailand's premier amusement park, occupying 47.7 hectares in northeast Bangkok. Some of the rides are a little dated now, but the water park has the biggest wave pool in the world and is deservedly popular. There are also roller-coasters here, as well as rides specifically for small children, plus lots of eating options. On weekdays, the park is often fairly quiet. Book online for discounted tickets.

Another amusement park in the area is **Dream World** *(dreamworld.co.th; 1000฿)*. While it's also looking its age a tad, the big draw is Snow Town, a snow and ice village where kids can sled down a snow slope. It's a a real novelty for local children, who love it (warm clothing is provided). There's also a big water park to cool off in at the end of the day. It's cash only here.

EATING IN BANGKOK: KID-FRIENDLY FOOD

Smokin' Pug: Close to Bangkok's shopping centres, this homey spot serves barbecue with great key lime pie. *5-11pm* ฿฿

Chocolate Ville: Billing itself 'the first theme park restaurant in Bangkok', it specialises in chocolate (plus pizza and Thai food). *3pm-midnight Mon-Fri, from 2pm Sat & Sun* ฿฿

La Monita: This Tex-Mex restaurant is still going strong, with various branches throughout the city, but the best one is in Ploen Chit. *11am-10pm* ฿฿

Pasta District Chatuchak: In Chatuchak Market, it serves up different pasta dishes that are crowd pleasers for picky children. *11am-9pm Tue-Sun* ฿

Around Bangkok

DAY TRIPS AND OPEN SPACES

Bangkok is ringed by five provinces: Nakhon Pathom, Nonthaburi, Pathum Thani, Samut Prakan and Samut Sakhon. Along with the capital, they make up the Bangkok Metropolitan Region, home to around 15% of Thailand's population. Some areas are now effectively suburbs of Bangkok, but others retain a more rural feel, making them ideal for a day trip or weekend retreat from the city.

Bang Kachao, an artificially created island in Samut Prakan with a fun market and a great botanical garden and park, is the easiest and perhaps the most popular option for an escape from Bangkok. There's also the Ancient City, modelled after an Ayuthaya-era Thai town that's within easy reach via Skytrain; an island housing an ancient community specialising in unique pottery; and, further afield, Phetchaburi and Samut Songkhram piers, from which whale-watching excursions depart.

GETTING AROUND

You won't be able to reach all of the destinations mentioned here by public transport, but you can reach the Ancient City (most of the way, at least) on the BTS. The MRT Purple Line will also take you most of the way to Ko Kret. Bang Kachao can be accessed from various piers throughout the city, but the most accessible activity is whale watching, since the tour operator will likely pick you up.

Pedal Pushers

Ko Kret and Bang Kachao by bike

Bang Kachao, a lush artificial island known as Bangkok's green lung, is a great place to escape the capital's urban sprawl. Much of Bang Kachao is essentially a wetland, with the interior a maze of canals criss-crossed by elevated concrete pathways. These pathways are a lot of fun to navigate by bike, which explains the **bike rental shops** *(per hour 30-80฿; bring photo ID)* that greet you no matter which pier you choose to leave from. Nature lovers can delight in the greenery, interesting birds and occasional glimpse of a monitor lizard, and coffee snobs can enjoy stopping at the different cafes that freckle the island. Finally, there is the **Bang Nam Pheung Market** on weekends, located along a canal where noodle vendors have set up shop for customers to enjoy the view. To get here, take the ferry from either Khlong Toey or Bang Na piers for between 10฿ and 20฿ (keep the slip given to you after paying for when you return).

TOP TIP

Even if you'll only spend half a day in your chosen destination (like Ko Kret), budget a whole day for the commute (half of the adventure) and for unwinding afterwards, as being out and about around Bangkok can be tiring. Whale watching is a whole-day event.

THE POTTERY OF KO KRET

Ko Kret's most famous souvenirs are its pottery, crafted by the Mon community and immediately recognisable by the intricately carved terracotta. As a result, you'll find a lot of working kilns set alongside the island's walkways. While, like everything else, quality will vary from potter to potter, all are made from the red clay gathered from the bottom of Chao Phraya River, feature hand-carved design motifs such as lotus flowers and leaves, and are shaped by the use of traditional kick-wheels. Many pottery workshops will also allow visitors to shape their own pottery on the kick-wheel for an extra fee. Best of all, the hand-thrown pottery here is on the whole more reasonable than elsewhere in Thailand.

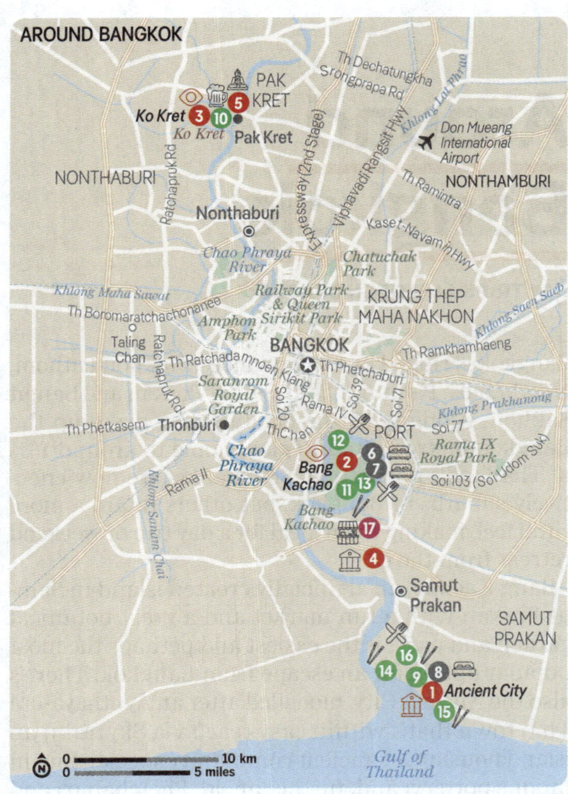

HIGHLIGHTS
1 Ancient City
2 Bang Kachao
3 Ko Kret

SIGHTS
4 Erawan Museum
5 Wat Poramai Yikawat

SLEEPING
6 Baanrongmai Canal Front Cafe & Homestay
7 Bangkok Tree House
8 Rimkhobfa Urban Resort

EATING
see 7 Bangkok Tree House
9 Camp Moo Kata
10 Chitbeer
11 Coconut Lane
12 Deep in Bangkrachao
13 Hiddenwoods Cafe
14 Krua Boonlert
15 Rabieng Ta-Le Restaurant
16 White Rabbit Restaurant

SHOPPING
17 Bang Nam Pheung Market

EATING & DRINKING ON BANG KACHAO: OUR PICKS

Bangkok Tree House: One of Bang Kachao's first green hotels, its cafe has refreshing drinks, including great iced herbal teas. *8am-11pm* ฿

Coconut Lane: Another hotel with a nice cafe and a charming terrace, with coconut drinks as well as 'blue milk' – infused with butterfly pea extract. *10am-6pm Thu-Mon* ฿

Deep in Bangkrachao: This out-of-the-way spot (handwritten signs point the way) offers food and drink along an elevated pathway. *7.30am-9pm* ฿

Hiddenwoods Cafe: A chi-chi eatery with lots of windows and blonde wood; you can find pasta, drinks – and e-scooter rentals. *10.30am-6.30pm* ฿

Another fun cycling destination is **Ko Kret**, an island in Chao Phraya River known for its Mon community, who have passed down the art of pottery from generation to generation. The island is home to twisty walkways that are perfect for biking. There's also **Wat Poramai Yikawat**, an ancient temple with a leaning stupa, constructed at Rama IV's request in 1721. Finally, there's popular **Chitbeer**, one of Bangkok's original craft beer bars. To get here, take the Metro (MRT) Purple Line to Nonthaburi Civic Center, a taxi to Wat Sanam Nuea, and then a ferry to Ko Kret. Alternatively, you can take the **Chao Phraya Express Boat** *(chaophrayaexpressboat.com)* to Nonthaburi and hire a long-tail boat to Ko Kret (around 200฿ return).

Out on the Water

Communing with the whales

Whale watching is particularly good during the rainy season when anchovies fill the oceans, drawing everything (including local Bryde's whales) that likes to feed on them. A couple of tour operators provide day-long excursions that include breakfast, lunch and an English-language guide. We recommend **Bangkok Whale Watching by Parinya** *(facebook.com/bangkokwhalewatching; per person 2000฿)* and **Wild Encounter Thailand** *(facebook.com/wildencounterthailand, per person 2000฿)*. Hotel pickups can be arranged, and Wild Encounter guarantees a free excursion if your first one doesn't result in any whale sightings. Days usually start at 9am and end around 3pm or 4pm.

Travelling Back in Time

A trip to the Ancient City

Also known as 'Muang Boran', the **Ancient City** *(muangboranmuseum.com; adult/child 700/350฿)* calls itself 'the world's largest private outdoor museum', focusing on showing 'traditional Thai lifestyles' to the masses. Covering about 300 hectares, the scope of the project – the brainchild of businessman Lek Viriyahbhun – is vast, with a replica of a floating market and park zones spanning the different regions of Thailand.

The nearby **Erawan Museum** *(adult/child 400/200฿)* is famous for the three-headed elephant statue at its entrance; it's the first and largest hand-carved sculpture in the world.

The Ancient City is open from 9am to 7pm and is reachable by taking the Skytrain (BTS) Green Line to Kheha, the end of the line.

HOW TO SPOT A WHALE

Jirayu Ekkul is the CEO of **Wild Encounter Thailand**.

Normally we look at two things when out on the water: the blowhole when the spurt is coming out of the water, which we can see from 1–2km away, and the whale's head popping up – it's about 2–3m high and looks like a black dot coming up out of nowhere. You need really good eyes to see it. Once we spot them, we motor closer to the spot, and at about 200–300m away, people start getting excited. I've seen whales countless times; I've been working in this industry for 15 years, but we are extremely excited every time we see them. This is our passion.

EATING AROUND THE ANCIENT CITY: OUR PICKS

Krua Boonlert: A lively restaurant with all the dishes Thais like, including fried whole fish and German pork knuckle. *10.30am-11pm* ฿฿

Rabieng Ta-Le Restaurant: A 12-minute drive from the Ancient City, you'll find Thai seafood with an ocean view. *11am-9pm Fri-Sun, to 8pm Mon-Thu* ฿฿

Camp Moo Kata: Find Thai barbecue at reasonable prices at this lively outdoor venue. *5pm-midnight* ฿฿

White Rabbit Restaurant: Steak, Japanese-style curry and pasta are served at this popular spot, just a 15-minute drive from the Ancient City. *10am-8.30pm* ฿

Places We Love to Stay

฿ Budget ฿฿ Midrange ฿฿฿ Top End

Ko Ratanakosin & Thonburi

Map p60

Royal ThaTien Village ฿ This spot charges extremely reasonable prices for a two-star hotel that's located right in the middle of everything.

Arun Residence ฿฿ With a stunning view of Wat Arun from its rooftop, this riverside hotel is within walking distance of everything in this historic neighbourhood.

Theatre Residence ฿฿ A super-charming spot with a pool on the Thonburi side of the river.

Uncle Loy's Boutique House ฿฿ Also on the Thonburi side, this stylish boutique hotel is cloaked by its humble name.

1905 Heritage Corner ฿฿฿ These two stylishly appointed converted shophouses in a charming Sino-Thai neighbourhood host well-appointed rooms inspired by the Rattanakosin era.

Chakrabongse Villas ฿฿฿ This luxurious boutique hotel was once the grand former residence of Thai royalty.

Siri Sala Private Thai Villa ฿฿฿ A beautiful and traditional wooden house in Bangkok Noi (you might recognise it from *The White Lotus*) that accommodates up to 12 guests.

Banglamphu

Map p74

Niras Bankoc ฿ Billing itself as a 'cultural hostel', this converted shophouse is close to the boat pier of Saen Saep Canal and within walking distance of the river.

Nanda Heritage ฿฿ A stylish spot made partially out of old wood; it has its own restaurant and is close to the Grand Palace.

Bhuthorn ฿฿ Like staying in a homestay, this hotel boasts only three rooms, all comfortably appointed with thoughtful touches.

Thewet & Dusit

Map p81

Phra-Nakorn Norn-Len ฿ Imaginatively attired rooms with air-conditioning and en suite bathrooms, a Thai restaurant and coffee shop, and an airport shuttle at an extra charge.

Baan Tepa Boutique House ฿ A beautifully serene spot within walking distance of the major sights.

Casa Nithra ฿฿ Within walking distance of the Grand Palace, Wat Po and Th Khao San, this comfortable hotel sports all the expected amenities.

Siam ฿฿฿ If you feel like a splurge, this longtime hotel on the banks of Chao Phraya River has private pool rooms and wonderful views.

Chinatown

Map p84

Luk Hostel ฿ This modern hostel has clean dormitory-style rooms, high-ceilinged shared rooftop spaces, a Thai restaurant and evening entertainment.

Shanghai Mansion ฿฿ Right in the middle of things on Th Yaowarat, this stylish hotel has live music nightly and a restaurant with good Peking duck.

Feung Nakorn Balcony ฿฿ This is a bright, stylish spot with reasonably priced rooms.

Mustang Blu ฿฿฿ High-end style for those who want to splash out while staying in the neighbourhood.

Riverside, Silom & Lumphini

Map p95

Everyday Hostel ฿ This spot has clean and reasonably priced rooms in the middle of town.

kokotel ฿ Well-priced rooms in a bright, clean setting.

LUXX ฿฿ This longtime boutique hotel charges affordable rates in an expensive part of town.

Siam Heritage ฿฿ The Siam is a stylish spot with a great rooftop bar and pool.

Mandarin Oriental ฿฿฿ The grande dame of the Bangkok hotel scene; if you stay here once, they'll remember you forever.

Siam Square, Pratunam, Phloen Chit & Ratchathewi

Map p104

Lub d ฿ Still going strong after all these years, this hostel is close to all sorts of public transport.

Lit Bangkok Hotel & Residence ฿฿ Convenient location, spacious rooms, free wi-fi and just steps away from the Skytrain station.

Urbana ฿฿ Only a short walk from CentralWorld and Lumphini Park, this stylish hotel has both studios and apartments, plus an infinity room and fitness centre. Car-rental services are available at the front desk.

Siam@Siam ฿฿ Stylish, moderately priced and close to public transport, this place is a steal.

Hansar ฿฿฿ Only a short walk from Siam Square, this hotel makes up for its lack of name recognition with great service and wonderful views.

Thanon Sukhumvit

Map p112

Atlanta ฿ With both fan-cooled and air-conditioned rooms, a stay here is a step back in time to 1950s Bangkok.

House by the Pond ฿ Rooms start at under 1000฿ per night, making this spot a bargain; it's tucked down a backstreet.

Tints of Blue ฿฿ Reasonably priced rooms with a rooftop pool in a convenient area.

AriyasomVilla ฿฿฿ A beautiful oasis in a busy part of Bangkok, with a good pescatarian restaurant.

Ad Lib Bangkok ฿฿฿ A great lobby and brunch, with spacious, well-designed rooms and a rooftop pool.

Fig Lobby ฿฿฿ This quirky spot next to Khlong Toey Market has interestingly decorated rooms, a spa, fitness centre, terrace and swimming pool. There's also a restaurant, bar and massage service.

Northern Bangkok

Map p124

Pillow & Bread ฿ A charming hostel close to the Saphan Kwai Skytrain station with air-conditioned rooms and shared bathrooms. There's also a common room, board game room, garden area, washing machine and, in keeping with the name, bread and jam with coffee or tea for breakfast.

Woodstory Boutique Hotel ฿ Rooms with the expected private bathrooms and city views, alongside the more unexpected convenience mart, coffee shop and express check-in and check-out.

Josh Hotel ฿฿ Clean and reasonable, this hotel also hides a bar in room 75.

Around Bangkok

Map p132

Rimkhobfa Urban Resort ฿฿ Set in the neighbouring province of Samut Prakan, this tiny resort is a deal with big rooms, saltwater swimming pool, indoor pool and international restaurant. It's close to the Ancient City.

Bangkok Tree House ฿฿ The OG of eco-conscious hotels in Bangkok, on Bang Kachao with a great view over the river.

Baanrongmai Canal Front Cafe & Homestay ฿฿ Charming rooms next to a canal on Bang Kachao with well-kept surroundings and a good restaurant. Also a spa, hot tub and water-sports facilities.

TANAWAT CHANTRADILOKRAT/SHUTTERSTOCK

Shanghai Mansion, Chinatown

For places to stay in central Thailand, see p177

LEMARET PIERRICK/SHUTTERSTOCK

Above: Phra Pathom Chedi (p164); Right: Damnoen Saduak Floating Market (p171)

Researched by
Aydan Stuart

Central Thailand

THAILAND'S MOST UNDERRATED REGION

Despite having as many gems as other parts of the country, central Thailand is surprisingly overlooked aside from the odd day trip out of the capital.

Central Thailand consists of 22 mostly low-key and untouristed provinces, and this is just what makes this region so charming. Aside from the better-known spots like Ayuthaya, Thailand's majestic former capital city, and Kanchanaburi, home to most of the country's wartime history, this underrated region is brimming with unexpected things to do – as long as you can get past the miles of industry that act as a buffer between natural reaches and capital concrete. Take Ratchaburi, a rural spot often overlooked but packed with everything from floating markets and themed days out to pottery and farmstays – if you know where to look.

Many of central Thailand's provinces are places most travellers couldn't name, let alone find on a map, but those who venture here are rewarded by warm, authentic Thai experiences that few others get to see. Yet it is exactly because of its underrated and 'untouristy' standing that this glorious region (which can sometimes, admittedly, be inconvenient to travel through) is ripe for discovery.

For Bangkokians, central Thailand is a playground for weekend trips and family adventures: trips to waterfalls, museums, theme parks, ancient cities and wayward wineries are all on the roster. And with the capital always just a few hours away, it makes adventure here a little more accessible, provided you don't mind the odd busy highway and long, scenic drives to get there.

AB_PRODUCTION/SHUTTERSTOCK

THE MAIN AREAS

AYUTHAYA
The first capital, royal roots and great river prawns. p140

KANCHANABURI PROVINCE
Mountains carved by a dark Death Railway past. p150

RATCHABURI PROVINCE
A playground for families with iconic floating markets. p167

Find Your Way

Surrounding the capital, a decent amount of city connections can be found, although the freedom of car or bike exploration is still a more attractive choice, allowing for last-minute detours and access to remote destinations.

Kanchanaburi Province, p150

Although best known for the infamous Death Railway, this sprawling province reveals a world of waterfalls, mountains and living ancient cultures beyond the cuttings and tracks.

Ayuthaya, p140

Thailand's ancient capital city, now a spiritual patchwork of stunning Buddhist architecture, riverside hotels and famous cuisine. A favourite among Bangkok day-trippers.

Ratchaburi Province, p167

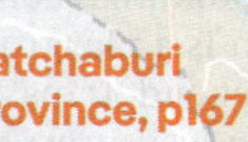

The westernmost province separating the southern stretch of central Thailand from the central plains, where families connect with nature and history lingers in surprising ways.

CAR

If you're up for a road trip, there's no better region in which to do it, with affordable car rental and plenty of scenery-filled roads that lead to many of the country's most unseen spots.

TRAIN

Although a little dilapidated (which only adds to its charm), the State Railway connects the entire country via sprawling routes that all have to pass through central Thailand first. Hop on and off as you please.

KP SUVANNASUK/SHUTTERSTOCK

St Joseph Catholic Church (p146), Ayuthaya

Plan Your Time

This region's highlights are well spread out, so build your plans around long road trips and strategic overnight stays to make sure you can fit the best bits in.

Weekend in Ayuthaya

● While you can day trip to Ayuthaya from Bangkok, it's better to stay the night and sample it all. Exploring the **historical park** (p142) is a given, but a few hours at the **Japanese enclave** (p145) or checking out Thailand's first **Catholic church** (p146) are close seconds. Round it off with a **dinner cruise** (p140) and you'll see how good it gets.

East for a Week

● Head east towards Kanchanaburi and Ratchaburi. A full week gives you ample time to see most of it. Zigzag your way by car or train through **floating markets** (p171), dress up at living museums **NaSatta Park** (p176) and **Mallika RE 124** (p159) before venturing deep into **Mon territory** (p159), following the tragic tracks of the **Death Railway** (p150).

SEASONAL HIGHLIGHTS

FEBRUARY

The tail end of the cold season promises good weather for trips to **Sangkhla Buri** (p161). Great for camping and cabin trips.

APRIL

The hottest time of year. If you're here in May, you can wallow in the mud during **Buffalo Conservation Day** (14 May).

JUNE

Monsoon season, with lots of short, heavy rains. Touristy spots are less crowded and **Erawan Falls** is beautiful.

DECEMBER

Cooler days begin, meaning tourists flock to Ratchaburi, Kanchanaburi and the **Ayuthaya World Heritage Fair** (p143).

Ayuthaya

ANCIENT RUINS | RIVER CRUISES | GRILLED DELICACIES

TOP TIP

The easiest way to reach Ayuthaya from Bangkok is by train. Located on both the northern and northeastern line (before they diverge), you can easily stop here for a few days before taking the sleeper train further afield. Third-class seats cost as little as 40฿, with scenic views along Chao Phraya River.

Founded in 1351, Ayuthaya is often described as the first capital of Thailand. Then just a burgeoning city state, it would eventually become the capital of Siam. A magnificent city, it was governed by powerful kings that saw value in diplomacy, trade and religious freedom over conquest and control. It thrived for centuries, attracting peopl from the world over to settle within its influence. However, by 1767 tensions with the Burmese came to a head, and Ayuthaya was invaded, sacked and burnt to the ground. Much of the city was abandoned or destroyed, but what remains of this old kingdom's beautiful architecture now attracts tourists and scholars. Aside from historical sites, the city is bubbling with local culture and markets. As it's only an hour from Bangkok, it's a perfect spot for both day-trippers and those seeking a taste of Thailand's ancient history without straying too far from the modern-day capital.

See the Ancient City by River

Ride the kingdom's ancient waterways

One of the best ways to enjoy Ayuthaya is seeing its temples and ancient waterways by boat. Coming from Bangkok, you can skip the train and opt for a slow boat with **Sabai Sabai Bangkok** *(sabaisabaibangkok.com; adult 2900฿)*, the only company to provide a city-to-city boat trip. This five-hour journey (running Friday to Sunday) takes you on a meandering

GETTING AROUND

The best way to explore Ayuthaya is by bicycle or tuk-tuk, as most of the main temples and ruins are far apart. Rent a bicycle for as little as 50฿ per day; try opposite the train station. Boat-shaped tuk-tuks are unique to the city and worth riding in at least once. Hourly rates are set by local authorities (per hour 300฿). If you travel further afield, ride-hailing apps can be useful, but negotiate with the driver to wait for you, as the app's hailing catchment is still relatively close to the city centre.

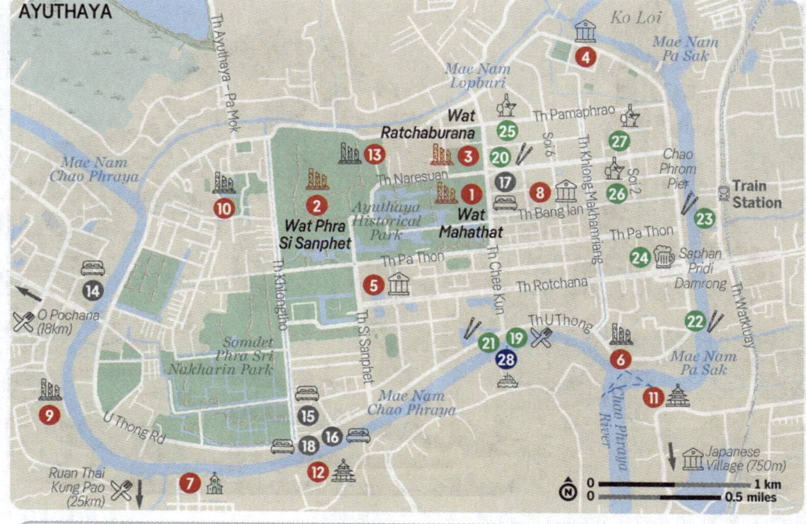

HIGHLIGHTS
1 Wat Mahathat
2 Wat Phra Si Sanphet
3 Wat Ratchaburana

SIGHTS
4 Chantharakasem National Museum
5 Chao Sam Phraya National Museum
6 Pom Phet Fort
7 St Joseph Catholic Church
8 Thai Boat Museum
9 Wat Chaiwatthanaram
10 Wat Lokayasutharam
11 Wat Phanan Choeng
12 Wat Phutthaisawan
13 Wat Thammikarat

SLEEPING
14 Ayothaya Riverside House
15 Baifern Homestay
16 iuDia Hotel
17 One Dhatu
18 Sala Ayutthaya Boutique Hotel

EATING
19 Baan Mai Rim Num
20 Boran
21 Civilize Ayutthaya
22 Pae Krung Kao
23 Tarn Ayutthaya

DRINKING & NIGHTLIFE
24 Brown Ale Ayutthaya
25 Earthling Craft
26 Khaosan Bar Ayutthaya
27 Planet Earth Bar & Eatery

TRANSPORT
28 Sampao Lom Ferry Pier

tour up Chao Phraya River and back from the country's capital to the city rivers of Ayuthaya. Once out of Bangkok, the river is mostly peaceful, with sights of interesting temples, riverbank homes and locals going about their business by boat, buffalo and bike.

The ride is technically unguided, but local staff are at hand to answer questions, point out landmarks – such as Bangkok's Wat Arun (p66) – and share personal insights along the way.

Continued on p145

DRINKING IN AYUTHAYA: FUN BARS

Brown Ale Ayutthaya: Stylish bar specialising in craft beer, with taps of both local beer and imported ales, stouts and IPAs on rotation. *5pm-midnight*

Khaosan Bar Ayutthaya: This is where the tourists come – along with some fun-loving locals who keep the vibe high. *5pm-2am*

Planet Earth Bar & Eatery: A fun local haunt serving cocktails and beers alongside a number of other bars that make up the Naresuan Soi 2 strip. *6pm-2am*

Earthling Craft: A coffee bar that turns cocktail bar at night, serving classics and custom-made mixes. *8.30am-midnight Sun-Fri, from 9am Sat*

LLEEKINS/SHUTTERSTOCK

Wat Mahathat

TOP EXPERIENCE

Ayuthaya Historical Park

From 1351 to 1767 the Kingdom of Ayuthaya was a thriving hub of trade, culture and diplomacy. Today, its ruins are among Thailand's most important heritage attractions. A 'park' only in name, there are over 50 archaeological sites scattered across the city, with temples and monuments both inside the ancient walled 'island' and along the banks of Chao Phraya River.

DON'T MISS

- Wat Mahathat
- Wat Ratchaburana
- Wat Chaiwatthanaram
- Wat Lokayasutharam
- Wat Yai Chai Mongkhon
- Wat Phutthaisawan
- Wat Phanan Choeng

Wat Mahathat

Ayuthaya's most photographed temple ruin is no doubt Wat Mahathat – famous for its sandstone Buddha's head entangled within the protruding roots of a bodhi tree. As the city's most ancient temple, it was once a gilded seat of spiritual power, housing the kingdom's most treasured Buddhist relics. At the fall of Ayuthaya in 1767, the temple was set ablaze by Burmese attackers. Legend has it that the bodhi tree emerged from the ashes, gently wrapping around the decapitated Buddha head, preserving it and the spirit of the site for centuries to come.

PRACTICALITIES

- Entrance for temples within the historical park cost 80฿ each (300฿ for a day pass). Most others are free or by donation.

Wat Ratchaburana

Founded in 1424 by King Borom Rachathirat II on the cremation site of his brothers who died fighting for the throne, this remains as one of the city's best-preserved sites. If you aren't afraid of heights, small spaces or bats, climb inside its *prang* (Khmer-style stupa) to see Thailand's largest crypt, adorned with intricate frescoes depicting scenes from the Buddha's past lives. While many valuable artefacts were stolen from the crypt during the mid-20th century, some were recovered and are now displayed at the nearby Chao Sam Phraya National Museum.

Wat Chaiwatthanaram

Built in 1630 by King Prasat Thong to honour his mother, Wat Chaiwatthanaram was conceived as a replica of the Angkor temple and still stands majestic today, overlooking the city from across the banks of Chao Phraya River. At its centre stands a towering 35m *prang*, surrounded by smaller satellite *prang* and rows of headless Buddha statues that echo the kingdom's turbulent past. Especially stunning at sunset, it's best admired from a riverboat.

Wat Lokayasutharam

Although mostly ruins, this temple is worth the detour to bear witness to one of Ayuthaya's most striking sights: an open-air, 42m-long reclining Buddha statue. With a gentle smile and one hand propping up his head, the statue was once in remarkably good condition. However, a recent preservation project has left it clean and reclad – replacing its ancient charm with a finish that makes it look like a brand-new construction against the crumbling hexagonal pillars of the *ubosot* (prayer hall) behind.

Wat Yai Chai Mongkhon

Although the origins of this temple date back to the early Ayuthaya period, its name and towering *chedi* (stupas) come from the reign of King Naresuan, who in 1592 defeated the Burmese army at Nong Sarai by killing the Burmese crown prince in single-handed combat on elephant. To celebrate this victory, it is believed the temple's main *chedi* was enlarged, giving way to a new temple name: the Great Temple of Auspicious Victory.

Wat Phutthaisawan

Technically outside Ayuthaya, located on the west bank of Chao Phraya River, this incredibly preserved temple marks the site at which King Ramathibodi I first settled before founding the Kingdom of Ayuthaya in 1351. The temple's striking white *prang* survived Burmese sacking and stands in good condition inside an ancient compound. Today the temple is still active, with resident monks, new buildings and ancient ruins unapologetically intertwined.

AYUTHAYA WORLD HERITAGE FAIR

Each December, Ayuthaya celebrates its UNESCO World Heritage status with a spectacular week-long celebration that transforms the historical park into a glowing festival ground, complete with traditional dance performances, shadow puppetry, handicraft markets and historical reenactments. However, the real highlight comes after dark, when a dazzling sound-and-light show projects Ayuthaya's rise and fall onto ancient temple ruins. The date changes each year, so check the calendar to time your visit.

TOP TIPS

- Many riverside temples can be enjoyed from a boat – and are especially stunning when lit up at night.
- Rent a bicycle opposite the train station to see the historical park temples. Temples further away deserve a tuk-tuk ride.
- Chat with monks in English and learn to meditate at Wat Mahathat every Friday from 1pm to 6pm, free of charge.
- Tuk-tuk hire is set at 300฿ per hour, up to 1500฿ for five hours. If charged more, check prices against the 'tourist police' price list.

MUSEUMS

Thai Boat Museum Private museum full of wooden boats, many of which still ply Thailand's rivers.

Pom Phet Fort The walls of this weathered 1580 fortress once served as Ayuthaya's primary line of defence.

Chao Sam Phraya National Museum Displays Ayuthaya's most impressive treasures, including royal gold, jewellery, utensils and Buddha statues.

Chantharakasem National Museum Antiques and relics from the Ayuthaya era forward, housed within the grounds of a royal palace.

Wat Phanan Choeng

Built in 1324, several decades before the city of Ayuthaya was officially founded, this temple remains one of the city's most revered and actively used temples. Though there are few remaining ruins, its main attraction is the nearly 20m-tall golden Buddha image, housed in a richly decorated prayer hall. One of the oldest in Thailand, the image is said to have been spared by the Burmese army, bringing tears to all who lay eyes on it. The temple also features shrines dedicated to Chinese deities, offering a rare blend of spiritual traditions under one roof.

Wat Phra Si Sanphet

While many ruins in Ayuthaya are awe inspiring, few capture the imagination like Wat Phra Si Sanphet. Three wonderfully intact stupas line up to form one of the city's most iconic views – one that can be enjoyed from both the ground and from lofty vantage points thanks to its rare status as one of the few temples you're allowed to climb.

Wat Thammikarat

Although less maintained than other major temples due to its location outside the official historical park, this ancient ruin is still used by monks today, offering a curious combination of new and old structures to admire. The temple ruins are best known for a striking lion-adorned *chedi*, and for lion statues that circle it. The active temple features a statue depicting a golden Buddha head inside a lotus flower and a resident community of roosters – both real and decorative.

LOVELYPEACE/SHUTTERSTOCK

Wat Phra Si Sanphet

Continued from p141
Snacks and refreshments are included in the price, with an option to stop at Bang Pa-In Palace (p147) just south of Ayuthaya or at the **Sampao Lom Ferry Pier** in town. The return journey is just as memorable, arriving in Bangkok just after sunset to scenes of glittery, light-filled cityscapes. And if you can't get enough of life on the water, the company has a number of liveaboard boats that keep to the Bangkok area.

Once in Ayuthaya itself, there are even more chances to get out on the water in the form of dinner cruises, river tours and ferry crossings. Although a number of companies operate boat tours in the city, the most active is **Ayuthaya Boat & Travel** *(ayuthaya-boat.com; 035 244 558)*, which covers a range of excursions – the best being its rice-barge dinner cruise, which sets off at 12.30pm and 7.30pm daily (1500฿ per person, minimum two, maximum 15 guests, private hire available). Enjoy set menus of Thai cuisine and take in the romantic atmosphere of the ancient city, passing temples, churches, fortresses and communities that have stood, survived and thrived through hundreds of years of kingdoms, sackings, coups and wars. If eating on the water is not your cup of tea, **Ayuthaya Boat Trip** *(ayuthayaboattrip.com; 085 919 9054)* hasd a great selection of small one- to three-hour boat trips that include stop-offs at Wat Phutthaisawan (p141), Wat Chaiwatthanaram (p143), Wat Phanan Choeng and other riverside landmarks for around the same price.

Visit the Historic Japanese Enclave

Study ethnic history dressed in a kimono

Ayuthaya was once regarded as one of the most cosmopolitan cities in Asia thanks largely to a culture of openness, diplomacy and religious freedom – something quite unusual for the era. Welcoming traders, missionaries, travellers and diplomats, a thriving international community emerged, resulting in Dutch, French, English, Persian, Portuguese, Moor, Malay, Chinese and Japanese enclaves and communities flourishing outside the city walls.

The **Japanese Village** *(facebook.com/japanesevillage.aya; adult/child 50/20฿)* is a relic of this period. A well-kept Japanese garden and museum tells the story of Ayuthaya's golden age of trade and community in Thai, Japanese and English. There's enough to keep you busy for an hour or more, and the two main buildings both have displays and mini-theatres. Traditional *yukata* outfits (adult/child per hour 100/50฿) and

THAILAND'S SCENIC TRAIN ROUTE NORTH

The State Railway of Thailand plays a significant role in connecting major cities, towns and tourist destinations. The railway system offers several classes – depending on passenger preference and budget – with differing levels of comfort and amenities. Many train routes out of Bangkok pass through Ayuthaya on one of the country's more scenic track segments, and in recent years there has been an improvement in the train system with the launch of Scenic Routes, where travellers can buy a special ticket and join a day-trip tour with the State Railway. For more information click on 'Trips by Train' on the *railway.co.th* homepage.

EATING IN AYUTHAYA: FAMOUS PRAWN RESTAURANTS

Baan Mai Rim Num: The thick menu of seafood and by-the-kilogram river prawns make this a must-try spot for any crustacean fan. *10.30am-9pm* ฿฿฿

Ruan Thai Kung Pao: A riverside favourite serving fresh produce straight from the river. The charcoal-grilled prawns sell out fast. *10am-5.30pm* ฿฿฿

O Pochana: Established 75 years ago, O Pochana earned a Bib Gourmand for its legendary – and affordable – local food and seafood. *9am-6pm* ฿฿฿

Pae Krung Kao: Open for over 50 years, this living legend continues to serve some of the best grilled river prawns in the city. *10am-8pm* ฿฿฿

ELEPHANT WELFARE

Short elephant rides near Ayuthaya's main temples are available, but for the elephants' wellbeing, it's best to avoid these, as walking on hot concrete roads is bad for the elephants, and carrying humans on their backs every day can damage their spines. Instead, do your research (p616) and opt for an elephant sanctuary with a good track record. While there are plenty of ethical elephant sanctuaries in Thailand, where the elephants are rescued and taken care of after they have been abandoned or injured, there are also some questionable ones out there too. Chiang Mai, Phuket and Kanchanaburi are the most reliable regions for ethical elephant tourism.

kimonos (per hour 200฿) can be rented on-site from the ticket office, perfect for anyone who loves a good themed photoshoot.

The Japanese are thought to have first arrived in the region during the reign of King Naresuan (1590–1605), but it wasn't until the late 16th or early 17th century, after the first fall of Ayuthaya, that the community really thrived. The village is located a few kilometres south of the city on historical land once shared by foreign settlements on both banks of Chao Phraya River. At its peak, the village was home to over 1500 permanent Japanese residents.

Throughout the year, the village hosts a handful of Japanese festivals, such as the Hanami Festival in February and the Tanabata Festival in July – complete with activities, games, markets and performances. Fun for all the family, they offer a refreshing change from the usual Thai holiday calendar.

Gain a Different Religious Perspective

Visit Thailand's first Catholic church

Although most religious sites in Ayuthaya are Buddhist, the city is also home to **St Joseph Catholic Church** *(085 903 7289)* – the very first Catholic church ever built in Thailand. Established by Bishop Pierre Lambert de la Motte in 1666, the church was authorised by King Nari the Great as part of his welcoming policy towards foreign religions and diplomatic ties, particularly with the French.

Funded by the French Mission Étrangères de Paris, it served as a religious and cultural hub for the growing community of European missionaries and settlers who flocked to Asia in the 17th century. First made of wood then upgraded to brick some 20 years later, the original structure was eventually destroyed in the 1767 Burmese invasion but was rebuilt and restored over the centuries and now stands cathedral-like along the banks of Chao Phraya River.

Its bright yellow facade, colourful interiors, stained-glass windows and the entombed sarcophagi of the founding bishop and his successor (the first vicar apostle of Siam, Bishop Louis Laneau) make it a popular pilgrimage site for Catholics across the world. Mass is held every day (5.30pm weekdays, 6.30pm Saturday, 8.30am Sunday) and is open to all who wish to witness the service. If ceremony is not your thing, next to the church there's a small **museum** *(free)* with exhibitions on the church's history, Catholicism in Thailand and important relics such as the first ever Thai-French-English dictionary, published in 1903 by the Catholic Mission.

EATING IN AYUTHAYA: OUR PICKS

U-Khao Restaurant & Cafe: Thai dishes with a modern twist that still have an authentic taste but always excite the palate. *10.30am-7.30pm Wed-Mon* ฿฿

Civilize Ayutthaya: Serving both authentic Thai and fusion specials, this somewhat unassuming restaurant is a great riverside option. *11am-9pm* ฿฿

Boran: Served from an old teak house, the regionally specific menu transports diners into the past via both setting and flavour. *8am-9pm* ฿฿

Tarn Ayutthaya: A reinvention of Thai food served from a distinctive floating raft upon which is a cherished building of local heritage. *11am-10pm* ฿฿

Beyond Ayuthaya

Far beyond ancient walls exists a playground of history and exploration, with places that are off the beaten track, yet easy to reach.

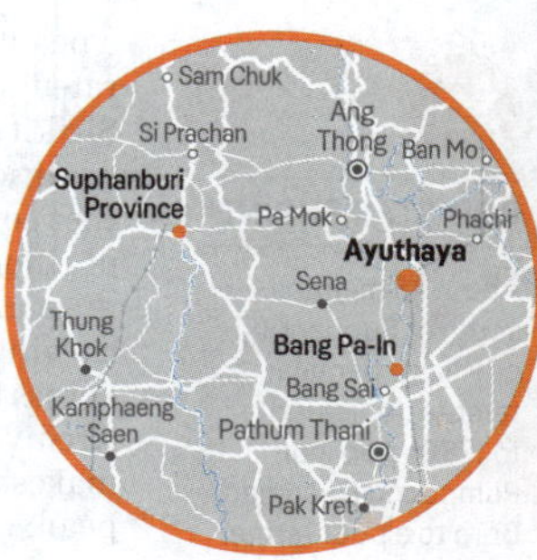

Places

Central Thailand's history doesn't end at Ayuthaya. It doesn't begin there either. Scattered beyond the ancient capital are a number of quiet riverside villages and long-forgotten towns that were once described as 'golden, fertile lands' by wandering Indian monks and traders. These lesser-known places, often overlooked by guidebooks and travellers, are where myth and mystery still echo through the landscape. From royal palaces to hermit kingdoms, and communities that live and breathe ancient traditions, the wider region offers a different kind of discovery – ones shaped by faith, folklore and the slow rhythm of rural life. While the roads are a little dustier, they lead to some of the more unexpected corners of Thailand's fertile, golden lands.

GETTING AROUND

While buses do connect most major towns, timetables are rarely followed and chasing bus stops can leave you stranded. Hiring a driver to get you to each location is by far the easiest option, and can be arranged through any reputable tour agency. If you have an international driver's licence you can choose to rent your own wheels and explore more freely. While fewer options are available, renting a car in Ayuthaya tends to be cheaper than those in Bangkok, and means you don't have to navigate the confusing and often dangerous capital-city roads.

Bang Pa-In

TIME FROM AYUTHAYA: **30MIN**

Thailand's most 'Eurasian' royal palace

Bang Pa-In village is a popular pit stop when driving from Bangkok to Ayuthaya. While here, visit **Bang Pa-In Palace** *(tourismthailand.org; adult 100฿)*, a grand palace meshing architectural styles. Constructed in the 17th century, the palace was revived by 19th-century kings who added eclectic European fixings, a Chinese-style orange-and-red-striped observatory and a 'floating' Thai pavilion. The Summer Palace has the option of English-speaking guides who tour the complex with you, sharing stories and secrets you'd miss without their presence. The stunning **Wat Chumphon Nikayaram** right next door is also worth a visit, as is **Wat Niwet Thamaprawat** – Thailand's only Buddhist temple designed in the style of a Christian church – which is located on the river island opposite the palace grounds. **Ayuthaya Boat & Travel** *(ayuthaya-boat.com; 035 244558)* offers tours that depart via the train station *(15 minutes; several times daily; 26฿)* and return to Ayuthaya via long-tail boat. That said, the trip is easy to manage on your own without a guide.

Gaze at the kingdom's most ancient art

Just across Chao Phraya River from Bang Pa-In Palace (although it's quite a detour to cross the bridge) sits the **Arts of the Kingdom Museum** *(artsofthekingdom.com; adult 150฿)*,

POP-STAR SHRINE

About 45 minutes south of Suphanburi city lies a peculiar temple dedicated to 1980s pop icon Pumpuang Duangjan. Born to a poor farmer and unable to read, she memorised lyrics and sang in local competitions before being discovered by a famous Luk Thung singer (a type of country pop unique to Thailand) at just 15. Rising to fame, she blended traditional tunes with electronic beats that went on to define the era. Sadly, her life was cut short at 30 with lupus – now often called 'Pumpuang's disease' in Thailand. Today, her hometown temple, **Wat Thap Kradan**, serves as her final resting place, with sprawling shrine-like displays of memorabilia and photos honouring her megastar legacy.

a beautifully designed museum and garden compound decorated with art collections created by craftspeople of the Queen Sirikit Institute. The museum showcases Thailand's finest traditional crafts under one roof. Most work on display is either commissioned from or donated by rural artisans – many of whom come from humble farming backgrounds but show great artistic prowess. Expect to see gold-and-silverware, wood carving, damascene, beetle-wing inlay, enamel and basketry across two main collections: the Highlight Collection and the Archive Collection. Open Wednesday to Sunday, the museum makes for a serene, nature-filled detour that feels almost European; think multi-language audio guides, a small cafe and the usual gift shop. And if you happen to hold on to your Grand Palace (p62) tickets, you can flash them to get in for free.

Suphanburi Province

TIME FROM AYUTHAYA: **1HR**

Learn the way of the buffalo

Suphanburi Province is among Thailand's top five rice-producing zones, and here you'll find a rather unique conservation village dedicated to the MVP of Thai agriculture – the buffalo. A love letter to Thailand's rural roots, the **Thai Buffalo Conservation Village** *(facebook.com/buffalovillages; adult/child 150/100฿, combo tickets 320฿)* offers a comprehensive and educational day out that gets you up close and personal with Thailand's second most mighty beast. The centre consists of a series of traditional wooden houses, makeshift farms maintained with old-world technology and walkways that snake between shady ponds filled with buffaloes in various stages of bathing and sunbathing. Daily buffalo shows and farming demonstrations (twice daily, 100฿ per show) are the main attractions, while the special 'smiling buffalo' trick charms kids and first-timers alike. And yes, you can even hop on a buffalo for a ride through the paddy fields – slow, muddy and unforgettable. Guest rooms are available.

Discover dragons and their descendants

Built initially to celebrate 20 years of Thailand–China diplomatic relations, this one-of-a-kind dragon-themed attraction is like walking into a fantasy world that sits somewhere between the two countries. The towering four-storey dragon statue at **Dragon Paradise Park** *(035 526211; 99฿)* is an unmissable landmark on the skyline of Suphanburi city, which reveals itself to be home to a surprisingly detailed museum of Chinese history and heritage in various languages. An impressive multimedia exhibition provides guided journeys through thousands of years of heritage while dedicated rooms and sections cover everything from Chinese settlers in the Ayuthaya period to the rulers of the many Chinese dynasties of the pre-Communist era. Although most guides are in Thai, they also provide English and Mandarin audio guides for foreign tourists at no extra cost. Aside from the attraction itself, the space also acts as a shrine to the local Thai-Chinese community, often packed with people making

AVETPHOTOS/SHUTTERSTOCK

Buffaloes, Suphanburi

offerings, seeking fortunes and ringing bells that are said to communicate directly with the gods.

Uncover U Thong's hidden history

Although Suphanburi city is quite under the radar, it boasts a rich history dating back to ancient times, and was an important city during the Ayuthaya period. Twenty minutes east of the main city is a small town called U Thong, which is home to some of the region's most interesting history. A repository for some of this history is the **U Thong National Museum** *(035 551 021; 150฿)*, which features many of the region's archaeological and cultural finds. The main hall displays city artefacts ranging from the prehistoric era to modern day, along with some stunning Dvaravati-style Buddha statues. Outside, you can explore reconstructed Lao Song homes and learn about the daily life, traditions, clothing and tools of this ethnic group. Like most museums in Thailand, displays vary in quality, but it's the other spots around town that make this worthy of the detour. A few kilometres west you'll find the **Suphanburi Sky Walk**, a safe but precarious glass pathway that hugs the cliffs of **Wat Khao Tham Thiam** – where you'll also find a massive 108m Buddha statue called Luang Pho U Thong carved out of the rock itself. There's also an ancient *chedi* ruin in case you need a fix after your tour of Ayuthaya. And for the adventurous types, a small nature trail (search for Uthong Ancient City Nature Trail) can be found nearby. It leads to the top of the cliff from the other side, passing a number of almost obscured ancient ruins that promise spectacular views across the otherwise flat landscape beyond.

Further west still you'll find **Phra Ruesi Park**, a temple-like tourist attraction (open 8am to 5pm) dedicated not to monks or the Buddha, but local hermit legends. Claiming to be the world's first dedicated hermit park, expect an immersive dive into the ways of traditional *ruesi* – Thai ascetic sages believed to have achieved enlightenment through rigorous meditation and self-discipline.

AYUTHAYA'S FAMOUS GRILLED RIVER PRAWNS

Few dishes capture Ayuthaya's heritage quite like the giant river prawns, freshly caught and grilled daily throughout the region. Once prized by the royal courts that ruled the ancient kingdom, these lobster-like critters are iconic to the region. Once grilled, their buttery, almost custard-like heads make for some incredible flavour, best enjoyed as a dip for the meaty tail section while still warm. Today, restaurants across the land grill them low and slow over charcoal, letting the natural oils caramelise until the shells blister. Although a simple dish, they carry with them centuries of history. If you can handle the heat, double dip into spicy seafood sauce.

Kanchanaburi Province

WAR HISTORY | NATURAL SECLUSION | FAMOUS WATERFALLS

GETTING AROUND

The easiest way to explore this province is with a car. Rental cars are relatively inexpensive and easy to acquire from Bangkok or Kanchanaburi city, but you can also have your hotel organise a car and driver if you prefer to ride as a passenger. In town, tuk-tuks and taxis can move you around easily, while the main train line (which still follows the path of the Death Railway) begins its journey from Thonburi Station, Bangkok.

TOP TIP

Kanchanaburi Province is large and sprawling, with highlights scattered throughout. You could spend weeks here if you had the stamina, so it's best to pick one area and explore it in full. For example, stay in the city and day trip to nearby highlights or head far west and make camp near the border.

The city of Kanchanaburi was only established in the late 18th century. However, its land and geography tell a story that dates back much further. History tells us that it was once home to the culturally rich Mon people of the Dvaravati kingdom, whose descendants are still found thriving in the northwest corner of the province. Over time its land stood as an important mountainous defence against the invading Burmese during the Ayuthayan and Rattanakosin periods before becoming a theatre of war in WWII, occupied by the Japanese who forced prisoners of war and local labourers to construct the Thailand-Burma Railway – better known as the Death Railway. Since the release of Pierre Boulle's novel *The Bridge on the River Kwai*, which was subsequently adapted for film, the Death Railway has become a major tourist destination, offering insights into its troubled past and a handful of stunning national parks, waterfalls, riverside resorts and hidden trails. Today, the iconic bridge still stands as a testament to its poignant history.

Cross the Bridge Over the River Kwai

Ride the infamous Death Railway

Kanchanaburi has long been shaped by war. From King Naresuan's battles with the Burmese to the fall of Ayuthaya centuries later, it has been a key battleground for many kingdoms and rulers. Thankfully, peace has reigned for nearly a century, with the last major conflict unfolding during WWII when it was seized by Japanese forces, who used prisoners of war and Asian forced labour to construct the infamous Death Railway.

Heavily damaged by Allied bombing, the bridge remained in disrepair until it was restored by the State Railway of Thailand (notice the square steel frames replacing the original curved design), completed in 1958. The bridge gradually became popular during the 1960s following the release of the film *The Bridge on the River Kwai*.

PAKPOOM PHUMMEE/SHUTTERSTOCK

Tham Krasae Station

Today, visiting the 'Death Railway' is a popular day trip for locals and international travellers alike. Whether you're crossing the iconic bridge on foot, riding the historic train from Bangkok or tracing the tracks through lush river valleys towards Myanmar, it's a journey packed with history, atmosphere and unforgettable views.

Riding the train from Bangkok (Thonburi Station) to the train station in Nam Tok, a small town some 60km west of the bridge, costs just 100฿ per person and takes around four to five hours. Most of that time is spent simply getting out of the sprawling capital. Given the most scenic part is the Kanchanaburi–Nam Tok leg, most people opt to find other ways to Kanchanaburi then board at the bridge station itself.

Most passengers hop off early at **Tham Krasae Station**, a spot that overlooks a portion of track that hugs the cliff above the Wamop Viaduct. It's a popular spot for exploring, with a nearby cave and freedom to walk along the precariously laid cliffside tracks. However, a more rewarding ride can be enjoyed from the terminal station of **Nam Tok**, where you can grab a good seat without the crowds (choose the right-hand side for the best river views) and ride the train back into the city, with the most scenic stretches unfolding before you. Trains depart Nam Tok at 5.20am, 1pm and 3.30pm, the first two going all the way to Bangkok while the last one terminates in Kanchanaburi.

WHAT HOLLYWOOD GOT WRONG

Kanchanaburi first captured international curiosity thanks to the film *The Bridge on the River Kwai* (1957), which left a string of misconceptions in its wake. For starters, the river that the bridge crosses is pronounced 'khwae' (say 'where' with a 'k' at the start) not 'kwai' as the movie suggests. The wartime bridge didn't cross Mae Nam Khwae either. Although the railway ran adjacent to it for much of its length, it actually crossed Mae Khlong – Pierre Boulle's book had it wrong. However, following the film's success and tourists keen to see 'the bridge over the River Kwai', local officials renamed the river Khwae Yai ('yai' means 'big') to match the story's setting and avoid tourist disappointment.

EATING IN KANCHANABURI CITY: OUR PICKS

MAP P154

Dedthodsaphak: Dangle your legs in the water and enjoy local Thai cuisine, served Kanchanaburi style along the Mae Khlong riverside. *10am-9pm* ฿฿

Dan Gak Lao: An understated Isan and Lao food spot with delicious, freshly made food opposite the River Kwai Bridge Resort. *11am-10pm* ฿

Keereetara Riverside: A new development by neighbouring 'Keeree Tara', serving fancy Thai fare. Incredible river views. *10am-10pm* ฿฿

Taraburee: While many places are by the river, few are actually on it. This place doubles down with rafts and river cruise fresh fish dinners. *11am-10.30pm* ฿฿

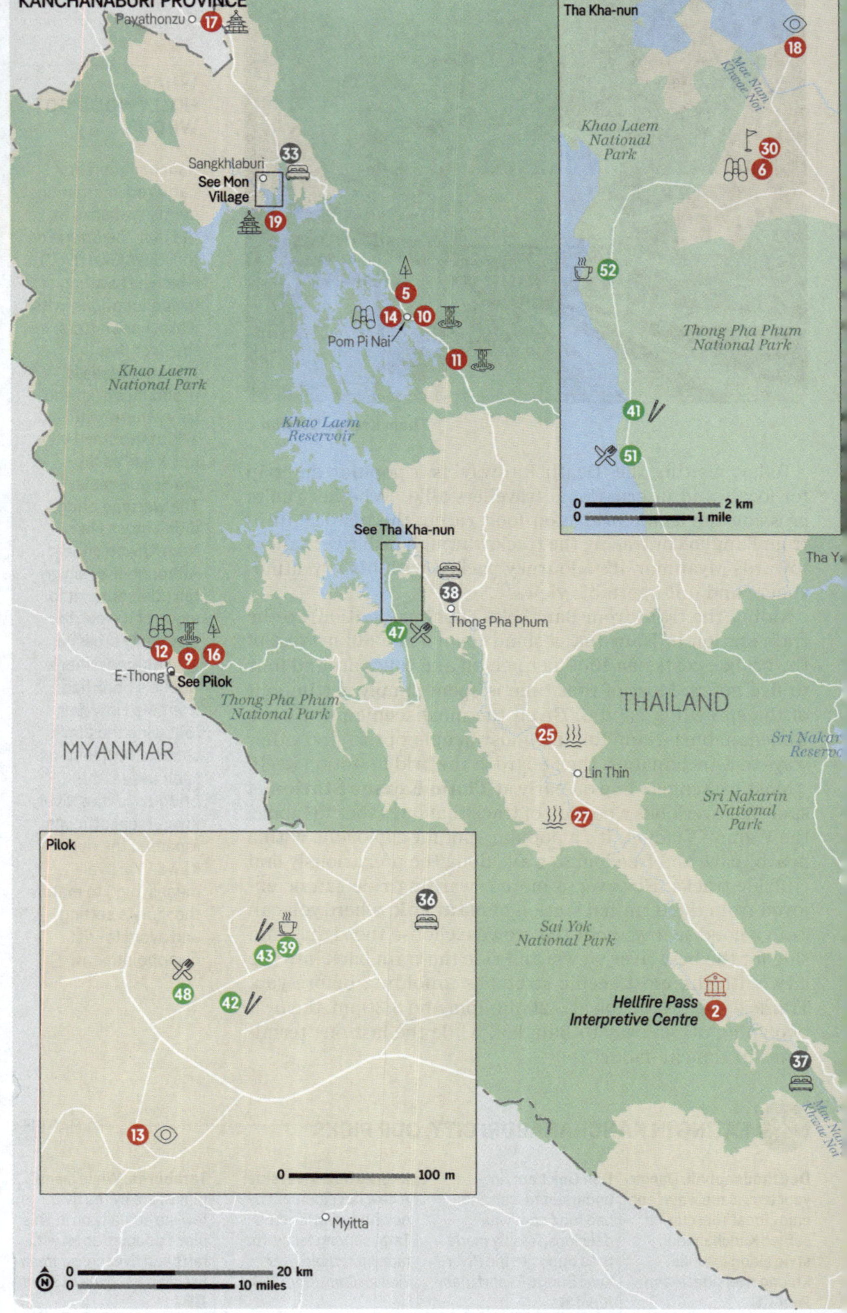
KANCHANABURI PROVINCE
Payathonzu
17
Sangkhlaburi
33
See Mon Village
19
5
14
10
Pom Pi Nai
11
Khao Laem National Park
Khao Laem Reservoir
See Tha Kha-nun
38
Thong Pha Phum
47
12
9
16
E-Thong
See Pilok
Thong Pha Phum National Park
MYANMAR
THAILAND
25
Lin Thin
27
Sri Nakarin National Park
Sai Yok National Park
Hellfire Pass Interpretive Centre
2
37
Myitta
0
20 km
0
10 miles
Tha Kha-nun
18
Khao Laem National Park
30
6
52
Thong Pha Phum National Park
41
51
0
2 km
0
1 mile
Pilok
36
43
39
48
42
13
0
100 m

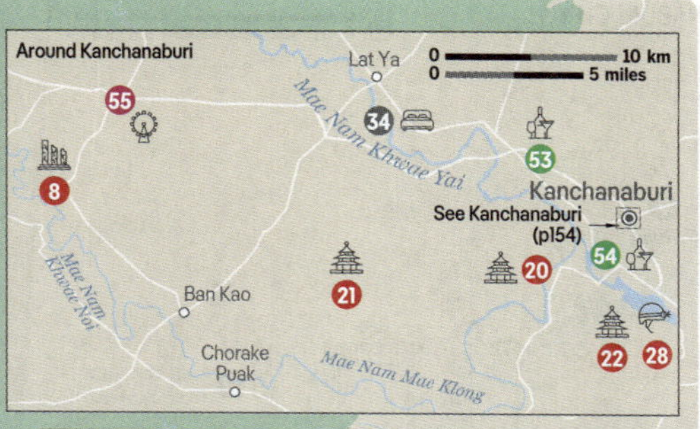

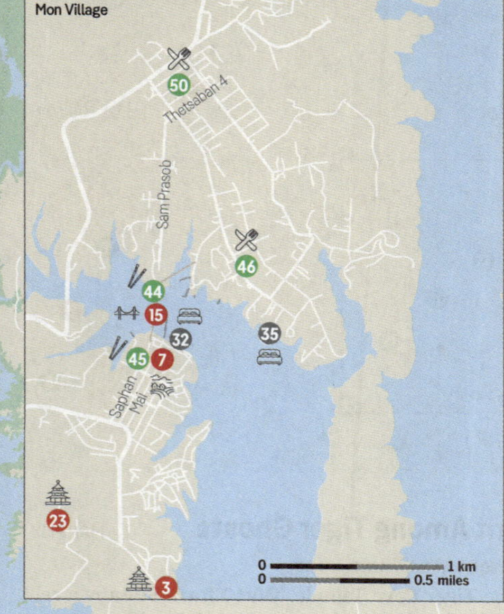

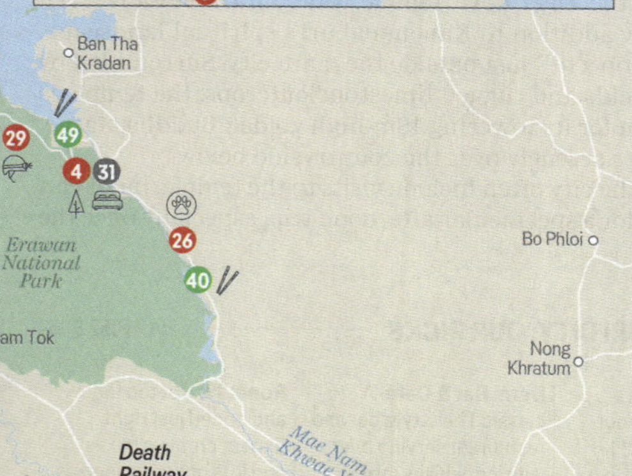

HIGHLIGHTS

1 Death Railway Bridge
2 Hellfire Pass Interpretive Centre

SIGHTS

3 Chedi Phuttakhaya
4 Erawan National Park
5 Khao Laem National Park
6 Khao Laem Skywalk
7 Mon Village
8 Muang Sing Historical Park
9 Nam Tok Jokkradin
10 Nam Tok Kra Teng Cheng
11 Nam Tok Kroeng Krawia
12 Nern Sao Thong Viewpoint
13 Pilok Mine
14 Pom Pi Viewpoint
15 Saphan Mon
16 Thong Pha Phum National Park
17 Three Pagodas Pass
18 Vajiralongkorn Dam
19 Wat Tai Nam
20 Wat Tham Khao Pun
21 Wat Tham Pu Wa
22 Wat Tham Suea
23 Wat Wang Wiwekaram

ACTIVITIES

24 Elephant Haven
25 Hin Dat Hot Springs
26 Khao Nam Pu Nature and Wildlife Education Center
27 Lin Thin Hot Springs
28 Tam Kaew Kanchanapisek
29 Tham Phra That
30 Vajiralongkorn Dam Golf Course

SLEEPING

31 Erawan National Park Accommodation
32 MonStay Resort
33 Nature Club Resort
34 Oriental Kwai Resort
35 P Guesthouse
36 Pilok MyHome
37 River Kwai Jungle Rafts Floating Hotel
38 Thongphaphum River

EATING

see 31 Bann Ton Nam
39 Cafe Bossa
40 Halal Kitchen
41 Kawarin Local Kho-Leam
42 Khrua Sut Daen
see 31 Khunpol Erawan Coffee
43 Krua Jaeni E-Tong
44 Mao Deep Bar and Restaurant
45 Mon Restaurant
46 Ounrak Vegetarian
47 Phae AomZuk
48 Ran Tungsten
49 Ruaen Thara Restaurant
50 Sangkhla Buri Walking Street
51 Songtaew Cafe
52 SudTangRak Coffee

DRINKING & NIGHTLIFE

53 Check in Kan
54 Derm Bar & Café

ENTERTAINMENT

55 Mallika RE 124

JEATH WAR MUSEUM

Founded in the 1970s, the **JEATH War Museum** was the first museum in Thailand to document the horrors of the Death Railway. The museum name – an acronym of Japan, England, Australia, Thailand, Holland – honours those involved in the railway construction during the war. The museum has recently relocated to the opposite side of the river, a place where the original bridge building camp was erected. Part of this move includes a rehash of its previous exhibitions, now focusing more on the people, prisoners and struggle they endured over the old site's halls of weapons and war memorabilia. Although officially reopening just after this book goes to print, by the time you're reading it the legendary museum should be back in action.

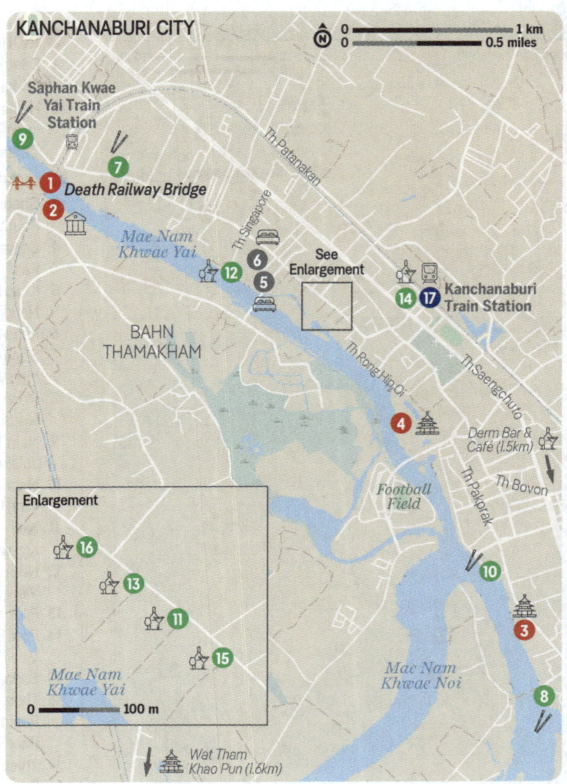

Make Merit Among Tiger Ghosts

MAP P152

Visit the famous Wat Tham Suea

Known as the Tiger Cave Temple, **Wat Tham Suea** is a relatively new addition to Kanchanaburi's spiritual landscape, perched atop a hill just outside the main city. Surrounded by lush rice fields and rugged limestone outcrops, the temple is best known for its towering 18m-high golden Buddha statue, which gazes serenely over the countryside below.

Tours of the city often include visits to the temple, but it can also make for a spectacular afternoon trip, especially once the

DRINKING IN KANCHANABURI CITY: OUR PICKS

MAP P152 & 154

Get Drunk for 10 Baht Bar: An unpretentious watering hole on the River Kwai Rd, with drinks as cheap as the name suggests. *5.30pm-midnight*

Ecko Superclub: A smaller version of your typical Bangkok EDM club, complete with live music, DJs, neon lights and booze by the bucket. *8pm-2am Wed-Sat*

Derm Bar & Café: A classic Thai-style bar and restaurant serving beer with ice, whisky mixers and a decent menu of drinker-friendly food. *5pm-midnight*

Room89: Not too fancy and priced just right. Expect creative mixes and lots of fun, as long as you're as adventurous as the barman. *11am-midnight Thu-Tue*

HIGHLIGHTS 1 Death Railway Bridge **SIGHTS** 2 JEATH War Museum 3 Wat Chaichumphon 4 Wat Thaworn Wararam **SLEEPING** 5 Good Times Resort	6 Revolution Hostel **EATING** 7 Dan Gak Lao 8 Dedthodsaphak 9 Keereetara Riverside 10 Taraburee **DRINKING & NIGHTLIFE** 11 Aussie Rules Bar	12 Barrub 13 Bojangles Sports Bar and Grill 14 Ecko Superclub 15 Get Drunk for 10 Baht Bar 16 Room89 **TRANSPORT** 17 Kanchanaburi Train Station

midday heat begins to subside. To reach the Buddha statue and main temple complex, most people opt to climb the 157-step walkway that leads to the top of the hill, passing a striking mix of Thai and Chinese architectural styles on the way. At the top, ornate shrines, pagodas and stupas are adorned with intricate designs that offer a breathtaking reward, blending spiritual ambience with photo-worthy highlights. If you can't face the climb, a small tram lets you skip the steps for a fee.

The temple gets its name from a cave near the summit that, according to local legend, was once home to a deadly tiger. Monks who scaled the hill to meditate claimed to hear the roars from within and often purported to find footprints at the cave opening. And while the claims were never corroborated, they were convincing enough for Thailand's official Buddhist monastic council to approve the building of a temple on the site. Today, the elusive tiger is certainly long gone, but remains a powerful symbol of strength and protection, drawing Buddhists from across the country in search of blessings and spiritual protection.

Across the highway, there's another cave-inspired, hilltop temple that sees far fewer tourist feet. **Tam Kaew Kanchanapisek** may lack the grandeur of Wat Tham Suea, but it promises a quieter, more local experience with equally breathtaking views. A large white-and-gold Buddha statue overlooks the area next to a towering golden stupa, though the real highlight is the cave itself – lined with crystal-like quartz formations and a peaceful Buddha shrine found in the inner chamber.

Thailand's Most Beautiful Waterfall

MAP P152

Hike and swim Erawan National Park

Erawan National Park *(thainationalparks.com/erawan-national-park; adult/child 300/150฿)* is 65km north of Kanchanaburi and is easily reachable by bus, tour operator or private car. The park offers an incredible adventure through the Thai jungle, winding past striking emerald-green pools, lush nature trails and breathtaking waterfalls.

Swimming in the pools and splashing waterfalls is an undeniable highlight of any visit, with seven tiers to explore spanning a 2km hike that follows the river upstream. While the lower levels are easy to reach, the upper tiers require a

HOW TO SEE ELEPHANTS UP CLOSE

While Erawan Falls and the surrounding national parks are home to a fair few wild elephants, it's unlikely you'll see them first hand when exploring the more touristic zones. Wild elephants generally avoid humans too, unless there's food or the scent of a female attracting an angry bull in musth – in both cases, keep your distance. If you really can't go without seeing an elephant while in Kanchanaburi, the nearest place is **Elephant Haven** *(elephanthaventhailand.org; half-day adult/child 1500/750฿)*, which houses mainly ex-riding elephants that are in retirement or rescued. However, if you have more time to spend and plan a trip north, then read about how to visit elephants ethically on p616.

KANCHANABURI CITY'S WARTIME HISTORY

Delve into the history of Thailand's wartime past through WWII museums, war cemeteries, temples and the odd abandoned building.

START	END	LENGTH
Death Railway Bridge	Kanchanaburi Thai Paper Mill	3km; four hours

Luckily, most of the major historical attractions are in one area. Starting at the 1 **Death Railway Bridge** (p150), enjoy the sights then hop on the train and take one stop to 2 **Kanchanaburi Train Station**. Cross the road past the park and check into the 3 **Death Railway Museum and Research Centre** *(tbrconline.com; 9-4pm, adult/child 160/80฿)*, where you'll find a in-depth and somewhat interactive exhibition on wartime history. Adjacent you'll find the 4 **Don Rak Kanchanaburi War Cemetery**, with close to 7000 graves for Commonwealth and Dutch POWs who died under the Japanese occupation. A respectful walk takes around 30 minutes.

For a change of scene, head towards the river and explore the grounds of 5 **Wat Thaworn Wararam**, a beautiful Chinese-Vietnamese Buddhist temple on the banks of the river, built by Vietnamese refugees in 1881. As afternoon passes by, make a beeline for the newly built 6 **Kanchanaburi City Skywalk** for sweeping views of three converging rivers before passing 7 **Lak Meuang**, ending the day at the 8 **Kanchanaburi Thai Paper Mill**, a now-abandoned industrial powerhouse built by a German engineer in 1935 and used to print bamboo pulp banknotes during the war.

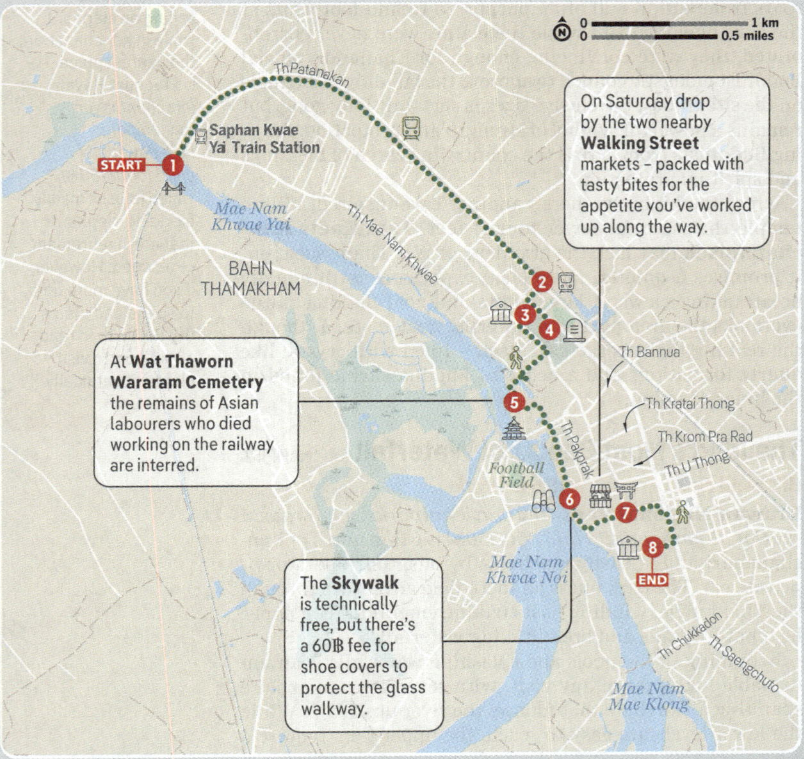

On Saturday drop by the two nearby **Walking Street** markets – packed with tasty bites for the appetite you've worked up along the way.

At **Wat Thaworn Wararam Cemetery** the remains of Asian labourers who died working on the railway are interred.

The **Skywalk** is technically free, but there's a 60฿ fee for shoe covers to protect the glass walkway.

bit more preparation – bring water, sunblock and good shoes to enjoy it safely.

The emerald pools are famous for their peculiarly clear, still water and resident fish community. The fish are so tame you can touch them – in fact, they may approach with the express purpose of nibbling off your dead skin. And while the falls are free to explore without a guide, all visitors must check in, deposit all food and drink (apart from water), and at all times when in the water wear a life jacket (20฿ for two hours, but extra hours are rarely counted). Areas not designated for swimming are clearly marked, while lifeguards monitor each pool throughout the day.

It's a short but sweaty walk from the park's visitor centre to the start of the falls, one that can be avoided by spending 20฿ on a golf-buggy ride along the forest trails. The park also offers bicycles for hire (20฿ per day), although these are not entirely useful unless you plan on seeing other parts of the park aside from the waterfall.

Ranger-led walks (prices vary) are the other popular park activity, with forested hiking trails and visits to hidden gems such as **Tham Phra That**, a shimmering limestone cave formation hidden in the jungle. Tigers, elephants, sambar, gibbons, red giant flying squirrels, king cobras and hornbills call the park home – although don't expect to see them at the waterfalls. If you decide to stay overnight, early-morning excursions are your best bet to see wildlife – but nothing is guaranteed in such dense forests. Bungalows and tents can be booked in advance at the visitor centre or online, alongside the walks.

Spot Wildlife Up Close & Personal

MAP P152

Mammal spotting at Khao Nam Pu

Khao Nam Pu Nature and Wildlife Education Center *(089 551 9835; portal.dnp.go.th)* is located on the edge of Khao Salak Phra Wildlife Sanctuary, just before Erawan Falls. Inside the centre, wild animals are bred for research purposes, and there are educational nature trails with informative signs to provide insight into the western forest ecosystem.

While the centre itself definitely gives off a more scientific vibe than other waypoints in the area, it does make an effort to provide some hands-on insight into Thailand's wildlife conservation efforts. While the centre's river-fed forest gardens offer a fun stroll, the banteng roaming the land are the true

BEST KANCHANABURI TEMPLES

Aside from Wat Tham Suea, there are several other iconic temples worth visiting in Kanchanaburi if you have the time.

Wat Tham Pu Wa: A stunning Khmer-era temple that looks almost new thanks to recent renovations, with a cave network full of Buddha images and friendly monks who run meditation retreats.

Wat Chaichumphon: More shrine than temple, this creation depicts a heavenly boat drawn by a man on horseback galloping through the waves. Popular for cremations.

Wat Tham Khao Pun: Another cave temple (there are lots of these in Thailand), this one with a labyrinth of nine chambers that were commandeered by the Japanese during the war and used as an underground military hospital.

DRINKING IN KANCHANABURI CITY: OUR PICKS

MAP P152 & 154

Aussie Rules Bar: A popular backpacker haunt on the main strip filled to the brim with pool tables and Aussie-style drinking games. *9am-12.30am*

Barrub: A riverside spot for Thais, serving the usual drinks and food options to live music and the hum of evening conversation. *10am-midnight*

Check in Kan: Another Thai-style city nightclub serving a steady stream of live bands (often big names) and visiting Bangkok DJs. *7pm-midnight*

Bojangles Sports Bar and Grill: The city's largest sports bar, with a mix of foreigners and locals catching up on football, rugby and motorsports. *7am-10pm*

TOP EXPERIENCE

Hellfire Pass Interpretive Centre

Northwest of Kanchanaburi city, the infamous cutting known as Hellfire Pass was the largest on the Thailand–Burma Railway, and the most deadly for those forced to construct it. Today's memorial centre and walking trail pays tribute to the victims – Australian, Allied POWs and Asian forced labourers – and is run and operated by the Australian Department of Veterans' Affairs in cooperation with the Thai Government.

LAPETITEVANI/SHUTTERSTOCK

TOP TIPS

- The centre is a place of solemn commemoration and reflection; respect the ground it occupies.
- The hike can take longer than expected; come prepared.
- An alternative, easier route to/from the memorial obelisk can be found behind the toilets.

PRACTICALITIES

- dva.gov.au/thailand
- 034 919605
- 9am to 4pm
- Free entry

The Main Gallery

The indoor gallery and interpretive centre commemorates those who worked on the railway and explores the stories that they have to tell. Deeply moving video interviews with returned prisoners of war play on repeat alongside museum-like displays explaining the horrors of what happened along the Death Railway. Over 12,000 POWs and 90,000 Asian forced labourers perished due to brutal conditions, starvation, disease and mistreatment at the hands of the Japanese.

The Konyu Cutting Walk

From the interpretive centre, a short 45-minute walk takes you along the old railway track and through the Konyu Cutting – a 600m stretch nicknamed 'Hellfire Pass' after its hellish torchlit construction resembling Dante's *Inferno*. Audio guides share powerful stories alongside flags, tokens and memorials left by visiting families and veterans. At the end, a memorial obelisk stands in solemn tribute to those who died.

The Hike to Hintok Road

A longer three-hour walk along the track, through Hintok Cutting and back again, is also possible. Audio-guide waypoints can be found along the way; however, there are no staff or shuttle services available, so bring water and prepare for a hike.

highlight. These red, wild cows are bred by the centre for the purpose of education, research and conservation.

There are also two nature-study trails that can be enjoyed. **Trail 1** is focused on plant species and wildlife, taking approximately three hours to hike in total. **Trail 2** is shorter (around one hour) and passes through different natural features such as streams, waterfalls, plains and hills.

Transport Yourself to 1905 Thailand

MAP P152

Roleplay life in a time past

Part museum, part theme park, part living interactive experience, **Mallika RE 124** *(mallika124.com; adult/child 250/120฿)* is one of Thailand's most underrated cultural attractions, so much so it's often skipped on regular tour routes and online guides. It's set in 1905 during the reign of King Chulalongkorn (Rama V). Visitors are transported to a living slice of history – complete with a breathing village community of people, vendors, performers and nobles.

While not mandatory, dressing up in traditional Thai attire (200฿ to 300฿) makes the experience far more immersive, and a lot more fun besides. Once suited up, your journey through the city gates begins aboard a rickshaw (30฿ to 100฿), pulled by park performers dressed as Chinese immigrants who lived under royal patronage at this time. Inside the 'city', vendors peddle wares, craft goods and serve food the old-fashioned way – using traditional tools, techniques and recipes of old. No shortcuts can be seen, and everything seems to be handmade on-site.

Even the money used in the park is authentic to the era: trade in Thai baht for replica antique holed coins from the Ayuthaya and Sukhothai eras, strung together on a handy length of string.

Beyond browsing, snacking and shopping, each entry includes a complimentary workshop and a free serving of mango sticky rice. Stay long enough and you can catch the evening *khon* performance, or go all in with a seat at the noble's table for a traditional banquet-style dinner (advance booking required).

APRIL 1ST IS NO JOKE IN THAILAND

While the rest of the world associates April 1st with pranks and practical jokes, Thailand marks the day for another, more meaningful reason: the anniversary of the official abolition of slavery in Siam. The year 1905 was an auspicious one under the reign of King Chulalongkorn (Rama V), who is heralded for his Abolition of Slavery Act, formally ending the centuries-old practice. In the Thai calendar abolition took place in year 124 of the Rattanakosin Era (RE), which ended following the Siamese Revolution in 1932, and which accounts for the name of Mallika RE 124. Uniquely, most slaves in Thailand were not foreigners, but fellow Thais, often indebted peasants or those born into servitude.

Thailand's Most Famous Mon Village

MAP P152

And the world's second-longest wooden bridge

Head west out of Kanchanaburi (about three hours, but well worth the jaunt) and you'll eventually stumble across a village with a slower pace of life that's rather unique. The

EATING NEAR ERAWAN FALLS: OUR PICKS

MAP P152

Ruaen Thara Restaurant: Great atmosphere, excellent service and affordable prices. The fish is fresh and cooked well. *7am-9pm* ฿฿

Bann Ton Nam: A perfect spot to grab lunch before heading to the falls. Classic Thai fare served generously. *9am-8pm Thu-Tue* ฿฿

Khunpol Erawan Coffee: A good spot for families with everything from *pat tai* and fried rice to banana split and iced cocoa. *9am-5pm Mon-Fri, to 9pm Sat & Sun* ฿

Halal Kitchen: Beef noodles, biryani and halal versions of Thai favourites found within a small Muslim community near the falls. *9am-6pm* ฿

THREE PAGODAS PASS

Named after three small *chedi* (or pagodas) built on the Thai side of the Thai–Myanmar border, **Three Pagodas Pass** has served as a major trade route and military gateway between the two nations for centuries. Likely erected in the Ayuthaya period – then recovered and redesigned in 1929 by Phra Sri Suwan Khiri, the then-ruler of Sangkhla Buri district – these three towering waypoints sit beside a lively border crossing with markets on either side selling mainly Burmese craft, textiles and gems. While tourists used to be allowed to cross, the border is currently closed. Luckily, the majority of the market sits on the Thai side to capture the tourist dollar.

LOVELYPEACE/SHUTTERSTOCK

Wat Wang Wiwekaram

imaginatively titled 'Mon Village' is home to an ethnic group that once played a major role in shaping early Southeast Asian culture. Today their peaceful way of life has merged with modern society to a point, but their traditions and styles are palpable and easily identifiable.

The village – found in the Sankhla Buri district of Kanchanaburi Province – still has a number of stilted wooden homes and other Mon-style architectural wonders, most notably **Wat Wang Wiwekaram**, whose architecture stands in contrast to other Thai temples. A handful of homestays and small restaurants offer a glimpse into Mon life through food, performance and cultural activities – varying depending on season and availability. One tradition you can count on, however, is the morning alms-giving rituals that take place between 6.30am and 7am. Locals dress in traditional Mon attire and line narrow village lanes waiting for monks, offering food and flowers in exchange for blessings. Monks can often be seen walking across **Saphan Mon** – the world's second-longest wooden bridge, an incredible sight any time of day.

In the 1980s construction of the Vajiralongkorn Dam flooded much of this culturally rich region, submerging entire villages and centuries-old temples. Today, only a few peek above the water's surface, including Wat Sri Sawaan and the aptly named 'Underwater Temple', **Wat Tai Nam**. **Boat trips** *(round trip 4-6 people 500฿)* from the Mon Bridge take you right up to the ruins, although during monsoon they're often fully submerged. Conversely, in the dry season waters recede, allowing you to explore on foot from the dried reservoir bed.

Nearby, the **Chedi Phuttakhaya** is said to enshrine sacred relics of the Buddha, which Luang Pho Uttama, a revered local monk, had brought over from Sri Lanka. At the front of the pagoda, there are two Mon-style lion statues guarding the long staircase that leads up to the square base of the pagoda, where the sacred relics are enshrined.

Explore the King's Reservoir

MAP P152

Where nature and humanity intertwine

If you do decide to make your way to the Mon Bridge, a great waypoint along the road is **Khao Laem National Park** *(adult/child 200/100฿)*. Spanning a massive area surrounding one of Thailand's largest, and most interesting, reservoirs (now dubbed the Vajiralongkorn Reservoir after the current king), the space is best known for its dramatic landscapes, limestone mountains and an abundance of wildlife.

However, despite the park's size, only a few spots are frequented by visitors given its a fair few hours from Kanchanaburi city. At its southernmost tip is **Vajiralongkorn Dam** holding the water at bay – an impressive feat of engineering that has become a landmark in the region. Along the same road that continues onto Pilok Mine (p162), you can stop and climb the **Khao Laem Skywalk** *(60฿)* or play a round of golf at the **Vajiralongkorn Dam Golf Course** *(034 598030; 9 holes 200฿)*, as long as the King isn't here using it himself.

Further north along Rte 323, **Nam Tok Kroeng Krawia** is the second most popular waterfall waypoint – a beautiful spot with lots of little falls amid green pools and gnarly tree roots. Set within the national park itself, the same fees must be paid to enter but give you access to all in-park locations, so it's worth holding onto your ticket if you plan on doing more than one stop.

Just past the falls is the park's visitor centre where you can stop to hire a ranger to guide you to the arguably more impressive **Nam Tok Kra Teng Cheng**. With nine levels, this waterfall requires a moderate trek up a challenging 4km trail to see all it has to offer, so allow yourself a good few hours to complete the circuit. For bird lovers, rangers can also arrange visits to the 32-hectare Kroeng Krawia Swamp nearby – a lush haven for tropical birdlife, especially active during the cool season.

Camping is allowed at both the waterfalls, the swamp and the visitor centre, but the best spot to pitch a tent is at **Pom Pi Viewpoint**. Overlooking the lake, it offers stunning sunset views and a peaceful atmosphere. Locals like to park cars, pitch tents and enjoy dinner over gas stoves; however, there are also a fair number of basic bungalows available if you'd prefer a roof over your head.

WHY I LOVE KANCHANABURI

Aydan Stuart, Lonely Planet writer

The journey out to Kanchanaburi is not the nicest of trips, but once in the wild landscapes, all those negative travel blues quickly melt away. For me, heading past the city and along Rte 323 towards the hills was an absolute pleasure during the years I spent living in Bangkok – a green getaway lined with waterfalls, hot springs, campsites and hidden treasures. When the weather is just right, there's nothing better than booking a cabin in the foothills far away from any technology, waking up to mist-covered mountain views and the distant toot of the Death Railway train reminding you exactly where you are, and just how remarkable it is to be able to return here in peace.

EATING IN SANGKHLA BURI: OUR PICKS

MAP P152

Mon Restaurant: This Mon Village spot serves up authentic congee breakfasts from hand-me-down recipes. *5.30am-10am* ฿

Mao Deep Bar and Restaurant: Fantastic views of the Mon Bridge and the best spot in town for affordable but delicious Thai food and cocktails. *10am-8pm* ฿฿

Ounrak Vegetarian: Thai veg eatery operated by the Unrak Foundation. Food made by refugees and orphaned kids in vocational training. *7.30am-8pm* ฿

Sangkhla Buri Walking Street: The city's daily dose of street food and market shopping with a distinct Mon twist. As local as a walking street can get. *2-10pm* ฿

THE FOREST SPIRITS OF THONG PHA PHUM

Thong Pha Phum's mountains hold more than mist, mines and trees – if you talk to the locals, the hills are threaded with stories of *phi pa*, forest spirits believed by Karen and Mon communities to guard woodland, rivers and ancient groves. Even today, hunters and hikers ask permission to the ghosts before entering the forest, leaving offerings at spirit posts and travelling quietly so as not to disturb the unseen. The nearby Pilok Mine itself takes its name from the term *phi-lok*, which means to be haunted. Miners claimed to hear voices in the dark and tools moving on their own. These stories are commonplace among Thais, especially those who live in the forests themselves.

Old Mines & Villages, New Homestays

MAP P152

A pre-war settlement as old as time

Kanchanaburi shares a long western border with Myanmar, though only a handful of roads cut through the rugged, mountainous terrain that divides the nations. One of these roads (although now stopping short on the Thai side) leads to the village of **Ban I-Tong** – a misty hilltop village that was once shaped by cross-border trade.

In its heyday, Ban I-Tong was a booming mining settlement home to over 600 workers and their families, all drawn to the rich tin and tungsten fortunes found in **Pilok Mine**. Today, the mine lies silent – nothing more than a derelict monument to an industry almost forgotten. However, the village has quietly re-emerged as a fog-shrouded tourist destination for those in search of stillness, natural escapes and fresh mountain air.

The mine ruins are open to explore, scattered with old machinery, trucks and equipment from a bygone era, slowly rusting away. The mine itself was closed with explosives, but a small garden with manicured ponds remains as a memory to the once lively mine operation. Don't miss the tradition of hanging wooden message tags along the Pilok Mine Bridge.

Stays here are basic but welcoming, with a small village market and a handful of local cafes and eateries to explore. A small road leads from the village up to **Nern Sao Thong Viewpoint**, which offers spectacular views out over Myanmar, although it's sometimes closed due to tensions across the border.

It's best to visit this remote corner of Thailand with the help of a guide or directly through your homestay of choice – both of which can help arrange transport that will comfortably navigate to the village along a winding 75km road (with over 400 curves taking around two to three hours from Kanchanaburi city). Most trips include a stop at **Thong Pha Phum National Park** and **Nam Tok Jokkradin** – the latter a stunning single-tier waterfall hidden within the park, which is great for a mid-journey swim.

Soak in Hot Springs, Riverside

MAP P152

It's never too hot for hot springs

Discovered by the Japanese during their construction of the Death Railway of Thailand during WWII, **Hin Dat Hot Springs** *(034 531048; adult/child 50/20฿)* became a waypoint for the various officers of the colonial occupier. Fast

EATING & DRINKING IN THONG PHA PHUM: LAKESIDE SPOTS

MAP P152

Songtaew Cafe: A popular waypoint for those heading up towards Pilok Mine that serves fresh coffee, the odd pastry and fill-you-up food. *8.30am-5pm* ฿

Kawarin Local Kho-Leam: Floating houseboat-style restaurant attached to a lakeside resort that serves fish-forward central Thai cuisine. *11am-8pm* ฿฿

SudTangRak Coffee: Sip on coffee, real matcha and other heart-warming drinks from atop an imitation double-decker bus parked adjacent to the reservoir. *6am-7pm* ฿

Phae AomZuk: Strong curries and spicy Thai dishes served on the roof of floating houses, made with fish you can catch yourself. *stays required* ฿฿

SUMETH ANU/SHUTTERSTOCK

Ban I-Tong

forward to modern times and the naturally warm, 55°C water has been reclaimed by locals and transformed into the province's most famous – and most picturesque – hot-spring destination.

Easily found on the side of Rte 232 (some two hours straight west from Kanchanaburi city), the spring features three public pools, each offering different heat levels, plus a fourth reserved exclusively for monks. Set alongside the jungle-edged Khwae Noi River, the main pools use river water to help balance the heat (one hot, one medium and one lukewarm – ideal for kids), with steps leading directly into the river for that perfect hot-cold therapy experience.

The mineral-rich water is believed to help treat a variety of ailments, with signs listing conditions like rheumatism, gout, vitamin B1 deficiency and even stress. However, if you're not fond of the water, you can skip the pools and pamper yourself with a Thai or foot massage for a few hundred baht instead. Just down the road, you'll also find **Lin Thin Hot Springs** *(facebook.com/LinthinHotSprings; adult/child 50/30฿)*, a solid alternative with less jungle and more of a community-pool feel, with foot bathing troughs and several pools but no river bathing. Locals will happily debate which spring comes out on top.

THE LAND OF RICH CIVILISATION

Under the shells and rubble of WWII, Kanchanaburi has a deep, archaeological history that goes back millennia. For centuries, the region has been a rich source of sites alluding to ancient cultures and civilisations. Some, like the **Muang Sing Historical Park**, still sit above ground to this day, with evidence suggesting that the ancient Kanchanaburi cities were likely powerful trading outposts as far back as the 12th century. Under the ground, even older evidence is found, sharing whispers from the ancient Mon and Dvaravati kingdoms of old. Further back still, you'll find ancient trilobite fossils peeking up from limestone shore trails in places like Thong Pha Phum National Park and Erawan National Park (p155).

EATING & DRINKING IN BAN I-TONG: OUR PICKS

MAP P152

Ran Tungsten: Coffee by morning, grilled meats by afternoon. Don't forget to leave your name on their chalkboard wall. *9am-8pm* ฿

Cafe Bossa: Town centre coffee served by a giggly owner who isn't afraid to try out new concoctions, for better or for worse. *8am-6pm* ฿

Krua Jaeni E-Tong: A beautifully decorated lunch and dinner spot serving fresh hot food with extra helpings of wild boar and spicy salad. *11am-8pm* ฿

Khrua Sut Daen: Cold weather in Thailand causes severe cravings for *moo kra-ta*, a Korean BBQ-style dinner that is best enjoyed here. *7am-8pm* ฿

Beyond Kanchanaburi Province

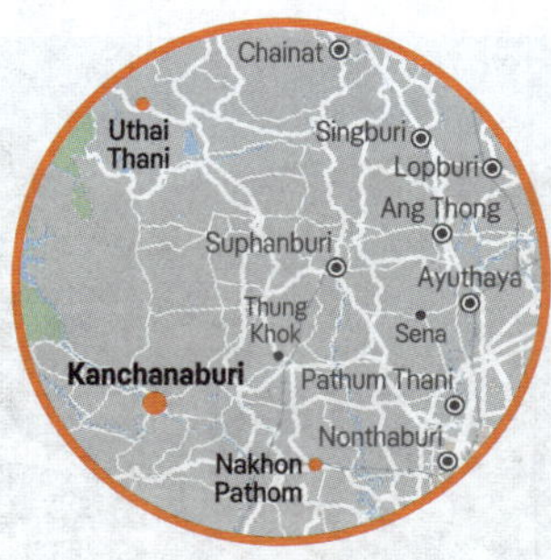

While Kanchanaburi has lots to offer, a few distant districts and neighbouring provinces are equally worth attention.

Places

GETTING AROUND

Finding your way around the furthest reaches of eastern Kanchanaburi and its neighbouring provinces can be a complicated task. While some destinations sit on major highways (with frequent bus routes), many are a little more off the beaten track. The best solution is to either hire your own transport and explore on your own terms, or rely on a tour company – many of which are happy to accommodate custom itineraries from the back of a minibus.

Kanchanaburi Province shares borders with Myanmar to the east, Ratchaburi to the south, Uthai Thani to the north and Nakhon Pathom to the east – all of which are regions of glorious natural beauty and peaceful living that see far fewer tourists than most other parts of Thailand. Sparsely populated, exploring these neighbours can sometimes feel like you're the only one around, but that only adds to the unique experiences you'll uncover. From the world's second-largest stupa to wildlife sanctuaries and ancient temples, exploring beyond central Thailand's far-flung fringes means you'll catch plentiful glimpses of authentic ways of life, along the way sharing your experience with city-living Thais in search of a quick nature fix.

Nakhon Pathom

TIME FROM KANCHANABURI: 1½HR

The world's second-largest stupa

Halfway between Kanchanaburi and Bangkok, you'll pass through the small province of Nakhon Pathom, home to a city of the same name. This city was one of Siam'st' earliest cities, although today is far more industrial-focused with main highways lined with endless factories and distribution centres.

Yet detour off the main routes and you'll still find a land that echoes the spiritual and cultural stories of Thailand's past. **Phra Pathom Chedi** defines this history with a towering 120m-tall stupa that can be seen from all directions. Its name in Sanskrit roughly translates to 'first monument', an indication of its ancient status among Thailand's religious structures. As one of the tallest Buddhist monuments in the world, it comes second only to Shwemawdaw Pagoda in Bago, Myanmar (and only by 5m). It dates back to the Mon Kingdom of Dvaravati and was constructed at some point between the 6th and 8th centuries.

Exploring the site is a calm and rewarding experience; one often paired with tours to Kanchanaburi. You can easily spend a few hours admiring the stupa, walking the grounds and

AMNAT30/SHUTTERSTOCK

Night market in front of Phra Pathom Chedi, Nakhon Pathom

visiting the various shrines and prayer halls that are dotted around the temple compound. Also of interest are a number of Chinese sculptures carved from a greenish stone that came to Thailand in 19th-century Chinese junks.

Monks can be seen meditating and offering blessings to observing devotees, with the temple itself enjoying bragging rights of being only one of six temples in Thailand with the highest rank of Rachavoramahavihan – likely due to the fact Rama VI's ashes are interred in the base of the standing Sukhothai-era Buddha statue, Phra Ruang Rochanarit.

Uthai Thani

TIME FROM KANCHANABURI: **3HR**

Huai Kha Khaeng Wildlife Sanctuary

Aside from temples and cultural landmarks, wildlife sanctuaries can earn UNESCO World Heritage status too, with Thailand's largest being the **Huai Kha Khaeng Wildlife Sanctuary** *(065 480 1138; khakhaeng@hotmail.com; adult/child 200/100฿)*. This sanctuary is part of a protected area spanning over 4045 sq km and home to more wild elephants and tigers than anywhere else in the kingdom. Thankfully, its easily accessible on the road just before the entrance to Erawan's waterfalls.

CHEDI VS STUPA VS PRANG

Not all stupas are the same. The three terms *chedi*, stupa and *prang* are often used interchangeably, but they do have distinct meanings when it comes to Thai religious architecture.

Chedi: The Thai term for what is generally called a 'stupa' in English. Defined by a bell-shaped structure, they often house Buddhist relics and are distinctly Thai.

Stupa: A broader, international term that originates from Sanskrit. It refers to dome-like Buddhist structures much like Thailand's *chedi*. All *chedi* are stupas, but not all stupas are *chedi*.

Prang: Distinctive Khmer-style towers with a steep, square, corn-cob like form. Originating from Hindu structures, the design was adapted into Buddhist temples with Khmer or Ayuthaya influences.

EATING IN NAKHON PATHOM: OUR PICKS

Banrimbung: Classic Thai fare served atop floating rafts just out of town. Its fresh fish curries and soups are a local fave. *10am-10pm* ฿฿

Nai Chua Roasted Pork: Simple but absolutely delicious roasted pork on rice and stewed pork noodles. Always busy, so runs out fast. *9am-3pm* ฿

Ali's Kitchen: A nice alternative to Thai food, serving rich Indian-Pakistani curries, breads and sides at unbeatable prices. *10am-9pm* ฿

Full Moon Restaurant & Camping: Thai favourites served with cold beer, live music and open-air seating, camping style. *5pm-midnight* ฿฿

BEST TEMPLES OF UTHAI THANI

If you make it into Uthai Thani, add a few temples to your journey for maximum Thai-style tourism.

Wat Sangkat Rattana Khiri: Famous for its unique architecture, featuring a combination of Thai, Chinese and European styles. The golden hues and intricate wood carvings attract visitors.

Wat Tham Khao Wong: This uniquely structured temple an hour or so out of Uthai Thani city resembles traditional Thai houses and is built from teak wood. The main monastery is on the 4th floor.

Wat Uposatharam: Located on Tha Po island, this temple (aka Wat Bot) was built in 1781. Inside the monastery, you'll find a Sukhothai-style Buddha statue with ancient murals on the walls.

NART COOMPANTHU/SHUTTERSTOCK

Tiger, Huai Kha Khaeng Wildlife Sanctuary (p165)

Together with **Thungyai Naresuan Wildlife Sanctuary** *(westernforest.org/en/areas/thung_yai_naresuan.htm)* at the southern tip of Tak Province, this site makes up the largest protected wildlife area in mainland Southeast Asia. Much of the flora and fauna found here are rare, endangered or endemic and include some species found nowhere else in the world. The sanctuary is also home to over 270 unique bird species, including hornbills and red-headed vultures.

The sanctuary is massive, and exploring it is no mean feat. Far away from any major city or highway, private transport is the way to go here. It's also not your usual tourist attraction. While there are a number of treks, jungle stays and tours offered (advance booking required), it's mainly visited by professionals – students, birdwatchers, researchers, veterinarians and the like.

That being said, rangers are happy to take you into the depths of the forest for glimpses of rare banteng (a type of wild cattle), tapirs, elephants and big cats (leopards are most commonly seen) along stunning nature trails that disappear as far from civilisation as you can get. Everything you do must be accompanied by a ranger, with the exception of the visitor centre watchtower, which overlooks forest and savannah scenes that almost guarantee sights of big mammals peacefully grazing. Plan to spend at least two days here to fully explore. Visits must be booked a minimum of 15 days before you arrive, so be sure to plan ahead.

Ratchaburi Province

FAMILY DAY TRIPS | CULTURAL PARKS | ACCESSIBLE NATURE

Straddling space between Kanchanaburi in the north and Phetchaburi to the south, Ratchaburi is a popular day-trip destination for families, thanks mostly to the accessible attractions that pepper the mostly natural landscape. Closest to Bangkok, you'll find floating markets shared with neighbouring provinces, a thriving pottery trade (Thailand's traditional water jars originate here), shadow puppetry, a mix of forest- and farm-themed escapes, camping and dining. Add in a vibrant food scene, cosy communities and a fair dose of cultural heritage and you have a destination that's easy to reach, refreshingly unexpected but still quintessentially Thai.

GETTING AROUND

Like many central provinces, getting around Ratchaburi is easiest if you have your own transport. Car rentals from the capital or in Ratchaburi city are equally easy to navigate. If you prefer to stay on public transport, regular buses and minivans connect the capital and the province, from where you can take other buses and minivans to major sub-districts around town, such as Suan Phung and Damnoen Saduak.

TOP TIP

If taking the sleeper train south to the islands, forgo a busy Bangkok rush through traffic to the main train station and hop on a bus to Ratchaburi instead. Spend a few days here exploring then board the train headed south from the calm, relaxed and easy-to-navigate Ratchaburi central station.

Learn all about Thailand's Dragon Jars

The story of the Ratchaburi ong

Pottery Legend *(Ruang Kong Ong; 084 141 5465; facebook.com/potterylegend; adult/child 380/200฿)* is a theme-park-style museum that celebrates the 100-year history of the region's signature dragon-decorated Ratchaburi *ong*, or jar – a centuries-old ceramic tradition imported by Chinese traders in the early 1900s.

When traders discovered the clay in Ratchaburi matched the quality of their homeland's, they began making Chinese-style jars here in Thailand and taught locals how to throw massive jars, decorating them with ornate depictions of dragons. Over time, the tradition became entrenched in the local culture and economy, placing Ratchaburi firmly on the map. Originally made for storing water, fermenting food, liquor and fish sauce, they're now mostly used as decorative items enjoyed by kings and common folk alike.

The museum includes a tour of the site, with history and traditions explained in either English or Thai (English needs advance booking to ensure a translator is present, no added cost). Tours run 10am, 1pm and 3pm daily. Part of the tour

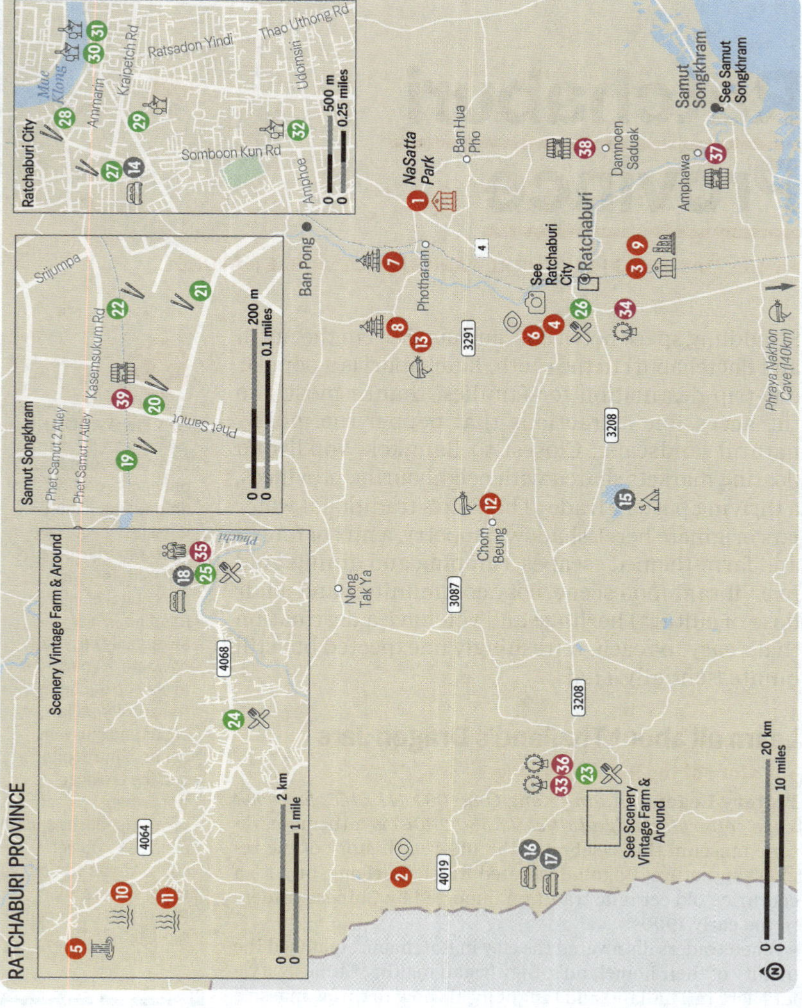

includes a live demonstration by one of the jar spinners – a team who still throw jars to this day, combining modern processes with tradition to ensure they keep up with demand.

Standard entry gets you the tour, but workshops cost extra, with a few packages offering combinations for various group sizes. Kids can paint jars and take them home on the day, while bigger kids and adults can try their hand at throwing their very own Ratchaburi clay jar, which is then fired in traditional ovens, glazed and posted to your home address several weeks later (extra fee for international postage, breakages possible).

HIGHLIGHTS
1 NaSatta Park

SIGHTS
2 Alpaca Hill
3 Ban Khu Bua Museum
4 Hin Khao Ngu Park
5 Nam Tok Kaew Chan
6 Phu Pha Raet
7 Wat Khanon
8 Wat Khao Chong Phran
9 Wat Khlong Suwankhiri

ACTIVITIES
10 Bore Klueng Hot Spring
11 Suan Phun Onsen
see 6 Tham Cham
see 6 Tham Chin
12 Tham Chomphon
see 6 Tham Fa Tho
13 Wat Tham Nam

SLEEPING
14 Centara Life Wisma Hotel
15 Huai Mai Teng Camping
16 La Toscana
17 Phapok Eco Resort
see 35 Scenery Vintage Farm Hotel
18 Swiss Valley Hip Resort

EATING
19 Ban Rod Fai Mae Klong
see 34 Cowboy Cafe Ratchaburi
20 Gong Meng Chan Ba Mee Kiao
see 35 Honey Scene Kitchen
21 Khao Gaeng Pa Auan
22 Maya Thai Restaurant
23 Morning Glory the Bakery House
24 Mount to Mouth
25 Oliva View De'Cafe
26 Ong Mang Korn Noodle
27 Ros Jeen Restaurant
28 Rtee Kopi

DRINKING & NIGHTLIFE
29 Juk
30 Kacha Craft Bar
31 Mellow Bar
32 WhereHouse Bar

ENTERTAINMENT
33 New Land
34 Pottery Legend
35 Scenery Vintage Farm
36 Suanphung Highland

SHOPPING
37 Amphawa Floating Market
38 Damnoen Saduak Floating Market
39 Mae Klong Railway Market

Markets Among Ruins

Ban Khu Bua ancient city

Fifteen minutes south of Ratchaburi city, a small but significant ancient city stands in ruins. This fascinating archaeological site is the remnants of a flourishing Dvaravati-era Mon settlement and was once regarded as a significant religious settlement in the region, dating back to before the Ayuthaya Kingdom. Today the site covers a small area of ruins, mostly found within temple grounds, including well-preserved brick stupas, weathered figurines, stucco reliefs and stone tables with Indian-style art. This dates it to a time when Buddhism was first brought to the Southeast Asia region.

While the village is relatively inactive during the week, half-day tours of the 44 documented ruins (you'll not see them all) can be arranged through tourist-friendly hotels and Bangkok-based tour operators like **Asia King Travel** *(asiakingtravel.com)*, often bundled with nearby highlights like the floating markets of Damnoen Saduak (p171) and Amphawa (p171). Weekends, however, offer a wholly different experience, defined by traditional markets and cultural dance performances that draw crowds to **Wat Khlong Suwankhiri**.

Open from 9am to 6pm (Saturday and Sunday), the market is packed with traditional snacks, handicrafts and other bits and bobs. A small stage hosts performances by community groups, kids and musicians, while the temple ruin acts as a centrepiece for people picnicking on the grassy knoll that surrounds it. The nearby **Ban Khu Bua Museum** also opens at this time (it's usually closed during the week, despite official

THE ORIGINAL WATER COOLER

Before plumbing and refrigeration, large earthenware jars *(ong)* were used to collect rainwater and store it over the dry months. Not only did these jars keep the water fresh, they also maintained a cool temperature throughout the year – important during a time without ice and air-conditioning. First imported from China by merchants making detours from the Silk Road, many Thai families still use *ong* to store water today, although its importance has diminished over the last half century, much to the dismay of some 50 *ong* manufacturers in Ratchaburi alone, who continue preserving this quiet but essential craft.

A LITTLE POCKET OF PEACE

Nana Rattanamung, Car Coffee owner

Once a spot for some serious rock-blasting, this hidden alcove known as Phu Pha Raet (aka Rhino Hills) was lost for many years before it was rediscovered. Now, it's my favourite pocket of peace. Just me, my van, good coffee and no phone signal. The quarry lake is some 30m deep and rumour has it there's still a couple of old cars and a jumbo drill sleeping at the bottom of it. Don't jump in though, swimming's banned and for good reason. I see rocks fall in from the hills every day, though they don't seem to get any smaller.

VESPA_FOTO/SHUTTERSTOCK

Hin Khao Ngu Park

opening times suggesting otherwise) and provides a somewhat basic overview of the area's main temple ruins, most of which is in Thai. Get there by car, taxi or better still jump on the early train and head one stop south from Ratchaburi station to Ban Khu Bua station.

A Secret Corner of Khao Ngu

Hin Khao Ngu Park's hidden spots

Step out of the city and swing by **Hin Khao Ngu Park**, a beautiful flooded quarry that has been transformed into a mountain park. Limestone karsts rise dramatically from a serene lake where paddle boats (per hour 50฿) zip and zoom across the otherwise still waters. A small nature trail begins with an equally small suspension footbridge, with boardwalks that purposely wind past the best viewpoints, while wild monkeys flirt with visitors in hope of snacks.

While not jaw-dropping in beauty, the caves and hidden alcoves nearby are arguably the park's most intriguing highlights. **Tham Cham**, **Tham Chin** and **Tham Fa Tho** are the three main caves, all located within walking distance of the

EATING IN RATCHABURI: CITY CENTRE

Ros Jeen Restaurant: Chinese-Thai city restaurant serving banquet-style dishes in a red-lantern-lined family-friendly setting. *11am-9pm* ฿฿

Rtee Kopi: Chinese dim sum and southern Thai *kopi* (coffee, bread and eggs) made fresh every morning next to the city museum. *6.30am-3.30pm Thu-Tue* ฿

Ong Mang Korn Noodle: Authentic Ratchaburi noodles inspired by Chinese traders, served in ceramic *ong*-style pottery bowls. *8am-5pm* ฿

Cowboy Cafe Ratchaburi: Wild West-themed spot serving steaks, chicken and pork knuckle alongside Thai soups and stir-fries. *10.30am-10pm* ฿฿

main quarry. That said, having your own wheels will save you from a sweaty trek between the caves. Inside, Ayuthaya-era Buddhist stuccos carved into the cave walls offer a striking reminder of life before the era of industrialisation.

However, **Phu Pha Raet** might just be the park's best-kept secret, tucked down a small track that leads to a less-known section of the flooded quarry. Limestone karsts tightly tower on either side, with still green water snaking its way through the middle, disappearing behind an unknown corner. It was once a popular water-sport destination, but visitors can now only enjoy the water with their eyes following some dramatic rock falls in recent years.

Thankfully, a small minivan-turned-cafe offers a welcome oasis from the outside world, where fresh lattes are enjoyed in a mobile-signal dead zone by white-collar workers catching a break and curious tourists alike.

RATCHABURI'S BEST CAVES

Tham Chomphon: Although smaller than Phraya Nakhon Cave (p430) in Hua Hin, this cave is just as impressive. After squeezing through its smaller passageways, you'll be greeted by a stunning Buddha statue basking in striking rays of sunlight entering through a cathedral-like opening in the ceiling.

Wat Khao Chong Phran: While the temple is a little lacklustre, its cave and the thousands of bats that emerge every evening at dusk are true natural wonders.

Wat Tham Nam: A natural grotto filled with flowing water and moss-clad walls that has since been transformed into a serene underground temple. Few tourists find the time to visit.

Out-of-City River Shopping

Central Thailand's famous floating markets

A stone's throw from Ratchaburi, you'll find a number of floating markets that are among Thailand's most authentic. **Damnoen Saduak Floating Market** *(7am-1am)* is probably the country's most famous, with its kaleidoscope of wooden long-tail boats vying for prime canal positioning to sell to locals and tourists, both on boats and along the banks. Private **motorboats** *(per person 400฿; minimum four people)* can be rented, with a journey around the canals taking between one and two hours, depending on how much shopping you do. However, most visitors opt for the traditional **paddle boat** *(per hour 1000฿; seats four to five people)* for a more authentic experience. And while it can feel a little overrun with tourists at times, it offers a rare glimpse into how most markets used to flow during Thailand's 'Venice of the East' era.

By afternoon, head 30 minutes south or Ratchaburi into the neighbouring province of **Samut Songkhram**, where you'll find **Amphawa Floating Market** *(2-9pm)*, an equally impressive floating market, which floats on the tidal Mae Khlong River. Close to the sea, the seafood is a highlight. The market now takes up more of the river's edge than it does of the actual water, but during high tide boats re-emerge, carrying with them a myriad of local flavours – mostly food – as well as the odd souvenir or trinket.

DRINKING IN RATCHABURI: BARS

Mellow Bar: Probably the city's chillest bar, serving secret cocktails and hoppy drinks from the underpass of Thanarat Bridge. *5pm-midnight*

WhereHouse Bar: Live jazz and indie bands play tunes in this discreet craft-beer bar with vinyl records and stylish-looking people. *5pm-midnight*

Kacha Craft Bar: A cool little bar in the city's old town that attracts more hip than hipster. Great for dates, quiet drinks and cold beers. *9am-11pm Tue-Sun*

Juk: A funky, retro bar that turns into a club later in the evening. It has live bands every night plus a regular lineup of special events. *5pm-midnight*

THE ORIGINS OF THAI SHADOW PUPPETRY

Although the origins of Thai shadow puppetry can be first traced to the trade routes of southern Thailand, *nang yai* (literally 'large hide', named after the leather they are cut from) is one of Ratchaburi's most precious traditions, given it is one of the few places to keep the practice alive. Today, **Wat Khanon** stands as one of the last places in the country where this art is still performed. It houses more than 300 original, intricately carved cowhide shadow puppets and a cohort of students who are passionately committed to preserving the craft. Weekend practice shows are often open to the public, offering a rare glimpse behind the curtain of Thailand's storytelling past.

ANNA KRIVITSKAYA/SHUTTERSTOCK

Cross the footbridge in the middle of the market and find a small kiosk on the west side of the canal that sells private boat rides (per hour 500฿) and group river tours to five temples along the river (per person 50฿). You can also find similar priced tickets at **Municipal Amphawa Pier**. If you're there at sundown, the group tour turns into a firefly tour. As you gently drift along the river, thousands of fireflies light up along the banks in a magical display. Sightings are not always guaranteed, but are best during the rainy season (May to October) and on moonless nights.

A Market on the Train Tracks

Thailand's very own train market

In the same province as Amphawa Floating Market, you'll also find Thailand's famous train market, **Mae Klong Railway Market** – often referred to as Talad Rom Hup ('umbrella pull down market' in Thai).

EATING IN SAMUT SONGKHRAM: TRAIN MARKET

Maya Thai Restaurant: Thai food served at the far end of the train market. A safe bet if the roadside isn't doing it for you. *7.30am-5.30pm* ฿฿

Ban Rod Fai Mae Klong: One of the better haunts found within the train station itself. While it caters mainly to tourists, it's also the one locals go to as well. *8am-4pm* ฿

Gong Meng Chan Ba Mee Kiao: Generous servings of Chinese-style noodles in clear broth, topped with pork dumplings and red pork. *8.30am-5.30pm* ฿

Khao Gaeng Pa Auan: Pre-made curries served over rice, with combo deals for two, three and more options per plate. Queues likely, it's that good. *6.30am-4.30pm* ฿

Mae Klong Railway Market

Reminiscent of Hanoi's Train Street, this unique market straddles a tight train line, with vendors constantly pulling back their market stalls and sun-shading umbrellas every time a train passes through. With over half a dozen 'crossings' a day, it's easy to catch sight of a train coming or going, trundling at a walking pace through the dense market packed with tourists, wares, sun-warmed seafood and camera-wielding influencers.

Trains depart every two to three hours between 6.20am and 5.40pm. For up-to-date schedules check Richard Barrow's *thaitrainguide.com* (the best for English details) or confirm at the station when you arrive. Tours are easily organised from Ratchaburi or Bangkok, but DIY travellers can take Bangkok's rail network to Maha Chai, cross the river by ferry to Ban Laem Station and hop on the market-bound train to Mae Klong.

EXPLORE THAILAND BY TRAIN

Richard Barrow, Thai rail tourism expert

If you're new to Thai trains, plan one overnight sleeper (saves a hotel) and one unhurried daytime leg, then fill gaps with 3rd-class hops. Book sleepers and daytime expresses up to 180 days ahead. Same-day 3rd-class tickets with open windows are fine for short local rides – a good way to meet Thais and buy from vendors who hop on selling meals, drinks and snacks. Go west to Kanchanaburi for 'Death Railway' history (p150), north as paddy fields give way to hills, or south for quick ferry links to Samui and Koh Pha Ngan. Watch for limited steam runs and weekend excursion specials.

EATING IN SUAN PHUNG: TOP DINNER CHOICES

Honey Scene Kitchen: Thai and Western comfort food served in an American farmhouse-style setting overlooking a sheep farm. *11am-9pm* BB

Oliva View De'Cafe: A popular spot for influencers. It serves specialty coffee, pizzas, Thai food, and desserts almost as beautiful as the views. *9am-9pm* BB

Morning Glory the Bakery House: European-style bakery famous for its pastries, scenic mountain views and cute rabbit farm. *9am-5pm* BB

Mount to Mouth: Pre-bookable barbecue dinners served in a beautiful outdoor camp-style setting overlooking the hills. *4.30-11pm Thu-Mon* BB

ROAD TRIP

A Family Tour of Suan Phung

Suan Phung district is probably the most popular Ratchaburi Province destination among Thai holidaymakers seeking a nearby getaway from the busy streets of Bangkok. It's home to a range of camping spots, farms, wineries, hot springs and European-style hotels. Attractions are mainly geared towards families, but are fun for solo travellers too. This area is best enjoyed over a couple of days.

1 Suanphung Highland

Drive an hour west from Ratchaburi on Rte 3208 until you reach Suan Phung district and enjoy the walk up the hill to Suanphung Highland. Explore a green landscape filled with beautiful flowers before a series of enclosures let you feed chickens, rabbits, goats, horses and a family of giraffes. Nearby **New Land** is also great for kids, with miniature trains, sheep, archery, go-carts and mini-ATVs.

The Drive: Take a left at New Land and follow Rte 4068 for less than 10 minutes.

2 Scenery Vintage Farm

Another family favourite, Scenery Vintage Farm is a theme-park-style farm destination that looks something between an American farmhouse and a fantasy village. Tickets include vouchers for farm-themed fair games, lamb feeding, horse riding, carousel rides and the Scenery Show – where prized sheep breeds show off their intelligence. Adults can partake in ATV trips and a special package that allows you to frolic with the farm's friendliest sheep dogs.

NOR GAL/SHUTTERSTOCK

Camping, Suan Phung

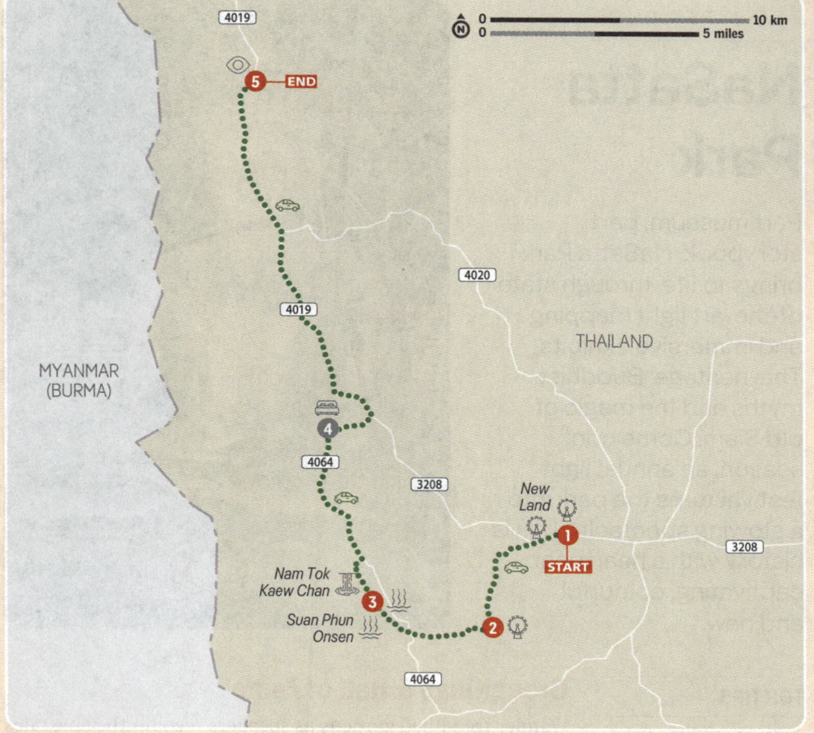

The Drive: Follow Rte 4068 westward for five minutes and take a left at Ban Huai Phak School junction.

3 Bore Klueng Hot Spring

Bore Klueng Hot Spring is a soothing waypoint where you can unwind and rejuvenate your skin in mineral-rich waters. Foot bathing is free, but use of the communal pools and earthen tiled springs costs between 30฿ and 50฿. Out back, you'll find a trail that crosses a jungle-covered footbridge towards **Nam Tok Kaew Chan**. If you prefer something more private, the **Suan Phun Onsen** has bamboo huts equipped with spring-fed *onsen* tubs and overnight stays.

The Drive: Follow Rte 4064 to where it joins Rte 3208.

4 La Toscana

Italian architecture meets Thai hospitality at La Toscana, an idyllic Tuscan village-style resort that boasts brick villas, manicured garden mazes, Roman-style pools and wood-fired BBQ nights. Overnight stays (p177) are required to enjoy all the facilities and activities.

The Drive: Head north from Suan Phung district along Rte 4019.

5 Alpaca Hill

If you plan onward travel to Kanchanaburi, Alpaca Hill is a worthy waypoint. It's the first, and largest, alpaca farm in Thailand. It's so popular you need to book a visit in advance. Limited to just 200 guests a day, activities include feeding, petting, photos, tree planting, tea picking, pony rides, lamb feeding, treasure hunts and cosplay opportunities.

TOP EXPERIENCE

NaSatta Park

Part museum, part storybook, NaSatta Park brings to life, through state-of-the-art light mapping and immersive exhibits, Thai heritage, Buddhist myths and the magic of old Siam. Come cool season, an annual light festival turns the park into a glowing spectacle. This is history with a heartbeat – captivating, colourful and new.

SOMBAT MUYCHEEN/SHUTTERSTOCK

TOP TIPS

- Thai costumes can be rented before you enter the park, for some added authenticity.
- The park can help reserve a taxi for two hours after you arrive.
- From November to April, the light festival transforms the park into a wonderland. It requires a separate ticket (adult/child 300/200฿), but is worth every penny.

PRACTICALITIES

● nasatta.com ● 032 383 333 ● 9am-3.30pm Tue-Fri, 9.30am-4pm Sat & Sun ●adults/children under 90cm 200฿/free

Great Kings & Hall of Fame

Wander tree-lined gardens as speakers recount the epic tales of Thai kings before stepping into a mid-century Thai house populated with a maze of life-sized dioramas, wax figures, and installations that showcase Thailand's national heroes, literary icons and cultural legends.

Three-Era Temples

Reconstructed temples from the Ayuthaya, Sukhothai and Thonburi eras come to life through immersive light mapping while multilingual narration recounts tales of the Buddha's enlightenment, the defeat of demon Mara, and the rise and fall of ancient kings.

Cave of the Ruthless Bandit

Step cautiously into the cave of Angulimala, a feared serial killer who claimed the lives of 999 souls before transforming from ruthless bandit to devoted Buddhist disciple. Retold through light, sound, and wax artistry.

Thai House Village

Explore a village of authentic Thai homes, built from original materials. Each home is a living museum, with period furniture and belongings that demonstrate Thailand's diverse cultures.

Places We Love to Stay

฿ Budget ฿฿ Midrange ฿฿฿ Top End

Ayuthaya

Map p141

Ayothaya Riverside House ฿ This wonderful guesthouse offers simple, traditional sleeping across an old Thai-style house and a wooden boat (some with fans and shared bathroom; some air-con).

Yimwhan Hostel and Cafe Ayutthaya ฿ Simple beds set on pallets in minimalistic rooms. It's above a coffee shop, so good java is guaranteed. Just near Wat Yai Chai Mongkhon.

Baifern Homestay ฿฿ Authentic homestay experience with lovely rooms, a garden and a tasty, invitingly priced Thai restaurant on-site.

iuDia Hotel ฿฿ Resort-feel accommodation that overlooks the river and on the opposite riverbank Wat Phutthaisawan is beautifully lit up at night. Incredible breakfasts but lacks any dinner service.

One Dhatu ฿฿ Three-star hotel that feels like it deserves at least four. Beautifully appointed rooms with lots of gold. Wide guestroom windows overlook Wat Mahathat.

Sala Ayutthaya Boutique Hotel ฿฿฿ Stepping inside is reminiscent of entering the city's ruins, thanks to maze-like brick alcoves, sleek rooms and a stylishly minimalist pool.

Kanchanaburi

Map p152 & 154

Revolution Hostel ฿ A hub of backpacker fun with an ethos that brings people together. Free family dinners each night and social activities most days, plus a ton of excursions that are more on the fun side of adventure.

Erawan National Park Accommodation ฿ Plain riverside bungalows in the heart of wild nature. Book well in advance via the park website, or camp with a rented tent from the visitor centre.

Thongphaphum River ฿ A great waypoint on the journey up to the Mon Village. No more than a room with a river view, but it's close to restaurants and shops in Thong Pha Phum.

Pilok MyHome ฿ Simple but clean and slightly more modern than other accommodation in Pilok village. Close to the lake, the mine, and the main roads where food and markets prevail.

P Guesthouse ฿ Features plenty of affordable rooms right by the river. It also offers views of Put Tha Kaya Pagoda.

MonStay Resort ฿ Simple rooms overlooking the reservoir and, if you get the right room, views of the Mon Bridge.

Nature Club Resort ฿฿ If you want a real getaway, this is your place, with only rivers and mountains for company.

River Kwai Jungle Rafts Floating Hotel ฿฿ Jungle-based, electricity-free (lamp-lit) sustainable bamboo floating lodge. Accessible by long-tail boat (hourly from the pier).

Good Times Resort ฿฿ Busy and buzzing riverside resort with live-music dinners. Operated by a big tour operator in the city, making it an easy one-stop shop.

Oriental Kwai Resort ฿฿฿ Sumptuously decorated and furnished cottages among semi-wild gardens. Conveniently 13km northwest of town, 1.5km off the road to Erawan National Park. Book well ahead.

Ratchaburi

Map p168

Huai Mai Teng Camping ฿ Camping spots overlooking a beautiful lake. Hot in summer but beautiful in winter months, with almost guaranteed views of fog over the water and freedom to do as you please on site.

Centara Life Wisma Hotel ฿฿ Budget resort in the heart of the city. Rooms are clean and spacious, and there's an all-day-dining restaurant.

Scenery Vintage Farm Hotel ฿฿ Attached to the farm-style theme park (p174), with minimal but on-theme rooms ranging from small studios to larger hot-tub rooms and garden villas.

Phapok Eco Resort ฿฿ Simple well-maintained eco-resort, with everything from panoramic mountain views from private villa balconies to smaller rooms that ooze sustainable luxury.

Swiss Valley Hip Resort ฿฿฿ Converted farmhouse vibes with flagstone flooring, standalone bathtubs and private villa pools.

La Toscana ฿฿฿ Tuscan-style resort set among untamed mountains. Thematically out of place but exceptionally well put together and feels like Europe.

Samut Songkhram

Hometown Hostel ฿ Fun and laid-back hotel stays that see travellers and Thais come together over drinks, coffee and roadside barbecues.

Buffalo Amphawa ฿฿ A buffalo ranch, but this one's clean, modern and stylish and with no smelly animals in sight. Think bamboo thatched villas, green water pools and surrounding paddy fields.

Damnern Pawa Resort ฿฿฿ A riverside hotel surrounded by coconut plantations that has a strong focus on activities and excursions to nearby attractions designed for kids and adults alike.

Researched by
Austin Bush

Northern Thailand

RUGGED MOUNTAINS AND CULTURAL WONDERS

Thailand's northernmost provinces are vast and hard to navigate. For many, that's what makes them so special.

Northern Thailand's natural beauty makes it a region ripe for exploration. From lofty mountain peaks that offer breathtaking vistas to dense jungles awaiting discovery, the region presents a seemingly endless playground for those seeking adventure. This is where Thailand's most iconic waterfalls, mysterious caves and important rivers can be found, all of which contribute to the region's enchanting natural allure.

But northern Thailand is more than just a haven for nature enthusiasts. Its historical ties to the legendary Lanna Kingdom and its mix of cultures have created a rich tapestry of diverse people and traditions that have profoundly shaped not only the region, but the country as a whole. Set foot into the ancient city of Sukhothai, the birthplace of Thailand, and be transported back into a time almost forgotten. Head towards the borders, and the influences of Shan and Yunnanese cultures will leave you questioning what country you're in. And high in the mountains of Chiang Rai, a seamless blend of hill-tribe life and agricultural innovation never cease to amaze.

And while the region's laid-back pace offers respite from the hustle and bustle of Bangkok, the north's charming provincial capitals and tiny villages also offer delightful surprises for even the most seasoned Thai traveller. Simply put, northern Thailand has it all.

NAKORNTHAI/SHUTTERSTOCK

THE MAIN AREAS

MAE HONG SON PROVINCE
Wild mountains and diverse cultures. p184

PAI
The backpackers' paradise. p196

CHIANG RAI PROVINCE
The artistically inclined, northernmost province. p203

LAMPANG PROVINCE
Cosmopolitan architecture and horse-drawn carriages. p219

For places to stay in northern Thailand, see p244

JULIA SMITH-VIDAL/SHUTTERSTOCK

Left: Sukhothai Historical Park (p240); Above: Pai (p196)

Find Your Way

Northern Thailand's roads are a sprawling, often winding blend of highways and mountain passes. Buses connect all major cities but heading into the hills can be tricky without your own set of wheels. Luckily, an abundance of rental shops means getting around independently is now easier than ever.

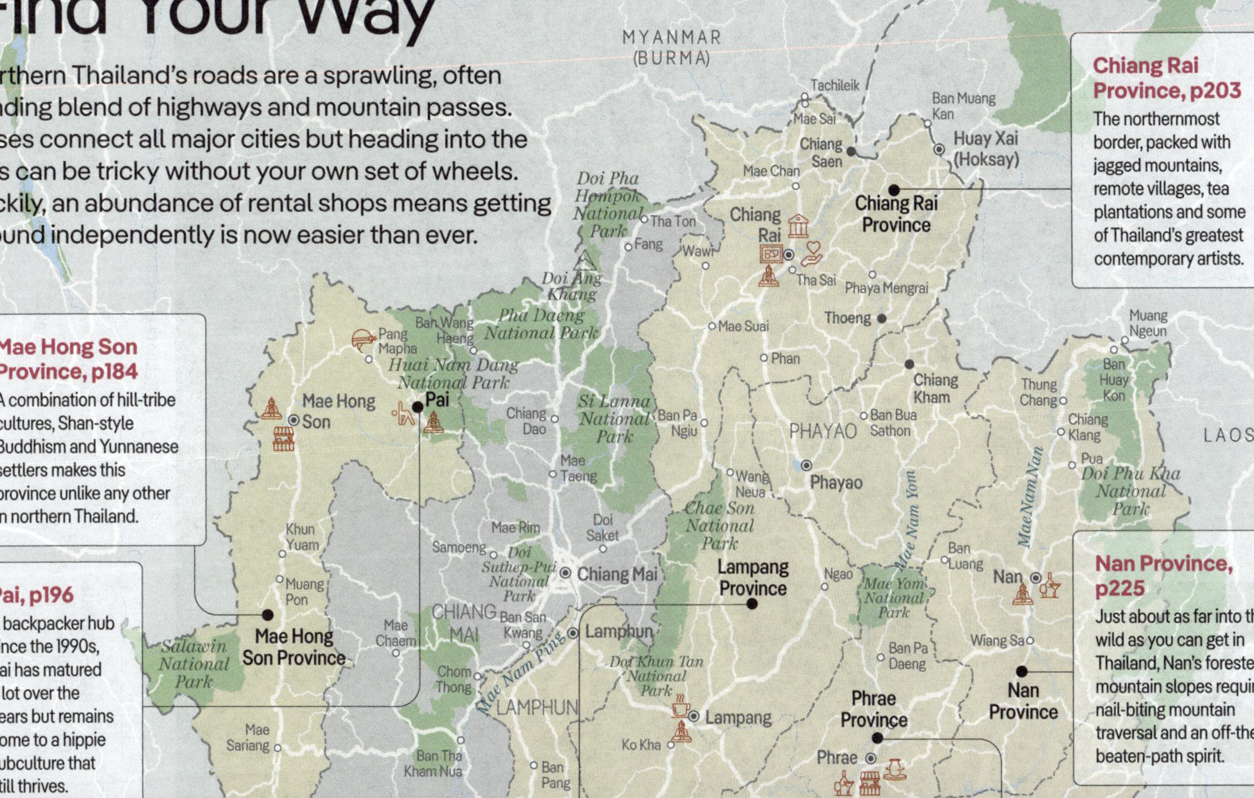

Chiang Rai Province, p203
The northernmost border, packed with jagged mountains, remote villages, tea plantations and some of Thailand's greatest contemporary artists.

Mae Hong Son Province, p184
A combination of hill-tribe cultures, Shan-style Buddhism and Yunnanese settlers makes this province unlike any other in northern Thailand.

Pai, p196
A backpacker hub since the 1990s, Pai has matured a lot over the years but remains home to a hippie subculture that still thrives.

Nan Province, p225
Just about as far into the wild as you can get in Thailand, Nan's forested mountain slopes require nail-biting mountain traversal and an off-the-beaten-path spirit.

AIR

Just about every provincial capital in northern Thailand has an airport, but only a handful were operating at press time; be sure to check in advance.

CAR & MOTORBIKE

Your own wheels are by far the best way to explore, with the freedom of discovery that scheduled routes can't provide. Even modern scooters are powerful enough to get you most places. Stay vigilant for dangerous drivers and always wear a helmet.

BUS & SORNG TAA OU

Whether it's a two-storey coach or a cramped minivan, there's typically some kind of bus headed where you want to go. If there's no bus, there's bound to be a *sorng taa ou* (passenger pick-up truck), although the going can be slow.

Lampang Province, p219
Often skipped by tourists, Lampang is where you can find beautiful architecture and a unique culture that caters to both old and new generations.

Sukhothai Province & Beyond, p239
The first Thai kingdom that led to modern-day Siam (the old name for Thailand) and a must for any history buff or travel influencer.

Phrae Province, p233
Once the heart of the region's teak trade, Phrae is now a sleepy, charming province that's beloved for handicrafts and food and drink.

Plan Your Time

Given its enormous size, the north is best tackled in sections, leaving you with more to discover on your next trip. Do as the locals do; don't rush and take your time.

NOKKAPOOD1977/SHUTTERSTOCK

Wat Mae Lan Nuea (p237)

A Day Away from Chiang Mai

- Most trips to northern Thailand start and end in **Chiang Mai** (p247), but if you have a day or so to kill, neighbouring **Lampang Province** (p219) provides an easy, worthwhile escape.

- Head east and stop in to see the best elephant vets in the world at **Friends of the Asia Elephant Hospital** (p219), or to ascend to the floating pagodas at **Wat Chaloem Phrakiat** (p224). Continue into town, where you can wander among the charming architecture of Lampang's **Kad Kongta historic district** (p222), or paint your own 'chicken bowl' at the **Dhanabadee Ceramic Museum** (p221) – all of this before heading back to Chiang Mai in time for dinner.

SEASONAL HIGHLIGHTS

The vast number of cultures and traditions in the north means there are many festivals and celebrations on the Buddhist calendar.

FEBRUARY

Pour yourself a cup at Baan Rak Thai's **Tea Festival** (p188), celebrating the harvest with tea tastings and Chinese-style revelry.

MARCH

Witness freshly ordained novice monks paraded around town by their fathers at **Poy Sang Long** (p186) in Mae Hong Son.

APRIL

Find **Songkran** festivities wherever you are. This nationwide water fight rings in the Thai New Year.

A Good Few Days

- Given the distances between provinces, it can be wise to hone in on a particular region of Northern Thailand. For an experience that links adventure and people, head west into **Mae Hong Son Province** (p184) and explore its many natural and cultural waypoints before looping back into Chiang Mai via Doi Inthanon.

- If history's your thing, look south to the three UNESCO World Heritage historical parks in **Sukhothai, Si Satchanalai** and **Kamphaeng Phet** (p240).

- Alternatively, for a bit of everything, head north to **Chiang Rai Province** (p203), where you can sample Thailand's best **tea** (p213), organise a **trek** (p207) to a hill-tribe village, stop in at a **gallery** (p209) or experience one of the country's rarest **massage therapies** (p208).

A Week or More

- If you've got a bit more time and an aversion to planning, rent yourself a car and let fate decide your journey by driving off into the region's little-known east, with only a few waypoints to guide you.

- Start in **Phrae Province** (p233), whose provincial capital seemingly has **teak houses** (p234) on every street corner and some excellent food, and whose **rural villages** (p237) boast heaps of charm. Then disappear into **Nan Province** (p225), Thailand's final frontier, home to two of the country's most **epic roads** (p231) as well as remote **rural outposts** (p230), where you're likely to be the only foreign face.

JULY
Make your way to Pai for the annual **Pai Jazz & Blues Festival** (p201).

OCTOBER
Witness the incredible speeds and hilarious hijinks of Nan's infamous **Longboat Race Festival** (227).

NOVEMBER
Head to the hills around Khun Yuam, in Mae Hong Son Province, where during this time of year **wild sunflowers bloom** (p189).

DECEMBER
Celebrate cool temperatures and Thai Yai culture at Mae Hong Son's **Perd Meng Tai Festival** (p185).

Mae Hong Son Province

CULTURE | WILDERNESS | OPEN ROADS

GETTING THERE & AROUND

Mae Hong Son Province's notoriously winding, hilly roads are best explored via a hired motorcycle or car. Yellow *sorng taa ou* connect the province's villages and cities, although waits can be long and the going is slow. More comfortable minivans connect the larger cities, although belligerent driving is sometimes an issue here.

Three daily buses connect Bangkok and Mae Hong Son's bus station – a whopping 16-hour, overnight trip. From Chiang Mai, frequent minivans and buses run the Mae Hong Son Loop, a winding, hilly and, for some, vomit-inducing voyage. Minivans run the route north, via Pai, while buses go south, via Mae Sariang.

Mae Hong Son is remote, misty and mysterious, a melting pot of cultures, languages and traditions seemingly preserved in amber in Thailand's northwest corner. Steep forest mountains shape the striking landscape in which villages and towns are blanketed in mountain fog for half the year, and slash-and-burn smoke for the other. Getting here can be a challenge for even the most seasoned drivers, with just a few winding mountain highways connecting it to the outside world.

These days, the word is out about Mae Hong Son's natural splendours – its waterfalls and caves especially – and the province is now on the tourist trail. But the vast majority of visitors don't make it much further than Pai (p196), leaving plenty of space for those who do venture to the province's less visited areas. So straddle a motorbike and get ready to tackle those turns.

Follow the Shan Trail

Discovering the best of local life

The Thai Yai or Shan people are a predominant ethnic group in Mae Hong Son Province and have influenced the region in almost every way. From food to clothing, architecture to traditions, stepping into Mae Hong Son is like stepping into another country, and it's possible to spend a day stopping in at various Thai Yai cultural sites.

Early risers can enjoy mist-covered mountain sunrises from **Wat Phra That Doi Kong Mu**, the Shan-style temple that towers over the city. Fill up on traditional Thai Yai dishes (p192) at the morning market (p186) before stopping into the **Living Museum**, which has charming old photos of the city and displays on local culture. A short walk away is **Wat Jong Klang**, with its century-old glass *Jataka* paintings and a tiny 'museum' with 150-year-old wooden dolls from Myanmar that depict some of the agonies of the wheel of life, and its neighbour **Wat Jong Kham**, both perched at the edge of the **Chong Kham Reservoir**, a focal point for Tai Yai festivities. At night they light up, casting a mystical reflection on the waters below. If you're in the city in December, don't miss the **Perd Meng Tai Festival**, a weeklong celebration of Thai Yai culture, which includes food, dance and handicrafts.

Welcome to the Jungle

A nature walk in Mae Hong Son

Drive – or even walk – a few minutes in just about any direction from Mae Hong Son's provincial capital and you'll encounter rugged hills and intact forest, natural areas that can be approached either by guided visits or independent exploration, a wonderful way to spend a half-day or more.

Our favourite local guide to the region's nature is **Chan** *(naturewalksthai-myanmar.com)*. A Thai Yai native of Mae Hong Son with decades of experience, his hikes range from day-long nature walks to multiday journeys across the province. He can also organise more specific excursions, such as birdwatching trips or the orchid-viewing tours he conducts from March to May.

Alternatively, have a taste of the area's natural beauty by tackling the **Mae Sakut Nature Trail** *(100฿)*, part of **Nam Tok Mae Surin National Park**. In a relatively easy 5km loop, you'll encounter bamboo forests, teak woods, waterfalls, wildflower fields (in season) and viewpoints. The trailhead is about 7km north of Mae Hong Son town, along the same

TOP TIP

Mae Hong Son can be downright chilly during the winter; don't forget to bring a jumper if you're visiting during this time of year.

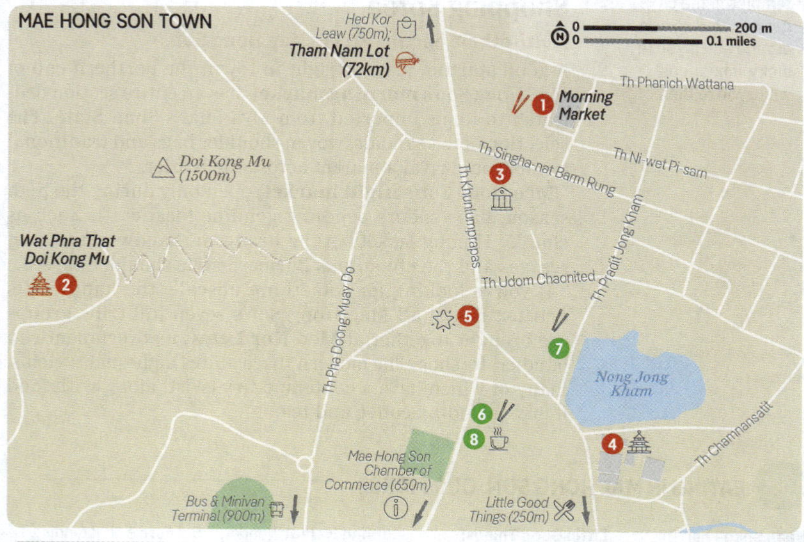

HIGHLIGHTS
1 Morning Market
2 Wat Phra That Doi Kong Mu

SIGHTS
3 Living Museum
4 Wat Jong Klang

ACTIVITIES
5 Rosegarden Tours

EATING
6 Bai Fern
7 Night Market

DRINKING & NIGHTLIFE
8 LOLA

POY SANG LONG FESTIVAL

A typical Buddhist belief is that if you are ordained, you bring good merit to yourself and your family. For centuries, the Shan people have celebrated this belief by ordaining young boys as novice monks. Boys and their fathers dress in extravagant colourful outfits and are paraded around town before finishing the weeks-long ordination process. The festival takes place late March or early April, but finding exact dates can be hard. Most Shan temples in the city get involved so ask around and if you're lucky, it happens while you're there.

TREETRAISIT UP/SHUTTERSTOCK

Viewpoint near Wat Phra That Doi Kong Mu (p184)

road that leads to Fern Resort (p244); proceed about 200m past the resort to the roadblock where you're expected to park your vehicle and pay the entry fee.

Shopping Spree

Multi-ethnic handicrafts in Mae Hong Son

A good starting place is right in town: the northern end of Mae Hong Son's **morning market** has an entire section dedicated to items imported from Myanmar's Shan State. The selection of felt sandals, woven shoulder bags and traditional outfits could rival a market across the border.

Mae Hong Son's **night market**, open only during the high season, has vendors peddling genuine local crafts such as chunky Hmong jackets, Akha headgear, handwoven cotton scarves and the ubiquitous Burmese-style shoulder bags.

If you're looking for something upscale, the handicrafts and textiles of all Mae Hong Son's seven hill-tribe groups are brought together at **Hed Kor Leaw**, a government-run handicrafts shop. The modern space unites high-quality items, many of which have a contemporary twist, along with food items, including coffee and tea.

EATING IN MAE HONG SON: OUR PICKS

Baan Song Thai: This cafe, located 4km south of Mae Hong Son, has a brief list of delicious local dishes as well as coffee drinks and baked goods. *8.30am-4pm* ฿

Little Good Things: Almost certainly the most sophisticated eatery in Mae Hong Son. Come for vegan baked goods and snacks. *10am-4pm Tue-Sun* ฿

Morning Market: Vendors at the northern end sell local fare such as *too a poo un*, noodles in a thick split-pea porridge with deep-fried 'Burmese tofu'. *7-11am* ฿

Bai Fern: Longstanding restaurant with Thai Yai and Thai dishes, and plenty of meat-free options, too. *11am-2pm & 5-9pm* ฿฿

And outside of town, Mae Hong Son's so-called 'longneck villages' – Huay Pu Keng and Huay Sua Thao – essentially function as rural markets. In some cases, the items sold are made by the villagers themselves, and it's possible to see them at work, weaving or shaping bracelets.

Get Muddy

Mae Hong Son's sloppy spa experience

Phu Klon Country Club *(phuklon.co.th)* is touted as Thailand's only mud treatment spa. Indeed, the geothermal mud spring here is one of only three known sources in the world, putting it in the same elite category as the much more well-known Dead Sea. Discovered by a team of geologists in 1995, the mineral-rich, odourless mud is pasteurised and blended with herbs before being employed in various treatments – it's a lot of fun to get your entire body smeared with the stuff. There's thermal mineral water for soaking, Thai-style massage is available, and there's also a selection of mud-based products for sale. It's located in Mok Champhae, a beautiful rural area around 20km north of Mae Hong Son.

Bridge Club

Cross Thailand's longest bamboo bridge

One of the biggest draws in the Mae Hong Son area for domestic tourists is the **Su Tong Pae Bridge**. Located 13km north of the provincial capital, near Mok Champhae, it takes the form of a 500m-long bamboo bridge – allegedly the country's longest – that spans a stream and vast paddies to reach a Shan temple. Visit during the wet season and those fields will be waterlogged and thick with emerald stalks of rice; come during the dry season and the fields are dry and golden. Either time of year it's a beautiful scene, and the bridge is still used by monks every day, who cross it at around 6am to collect alms.

Visit Hill Tribes Responsibly

Trek in Mae Hong Son with a good conscience

Mae Hong Son is the most ethnically diverse province in the country, with 68% of its population made up of seven hill tribes: Karen, Lahu, Lisu, Lua, Miao, Chinese Yunnan and Pa-O. Additionally, trekking in Mae Hong Son Province is not as commercialised or large-scale as in Chiang Mai, making the province arguably the most intriguing in northern Thailand for this type of cultural tourism.

Yet despite the diversity, the most touted hill-tribe villages to visit in Mae Hong Son are those of the so-called 'longneck' tribe. These villages, originally populated by Kayan refugees from Myanmar, charge entry fees and in the past have been accused of being 'human zoos'. In many visits over the years, we haven't witnessed this type of behaviour first hand, but the villages can resemble rural marketplaces.

Huay Pu Keng *(250฿)* is the most popular 'longneck' village, although it's probably also the most commercial-feeling. It's

IT CAN GET SMOKY

Between late January and early April, northern Thailand is plagued by toxic levels of smoke, blanketing the region in a thick layer of smoke and dust particles (often referred to as PM2.5 because they have a diameter of 2.5 micrometres or less) caused by forest fires and slash-and-burn agriculture. Despite attempts to reduce its impact, the problem persists, leaving a usually beautiful destination without fresh air for months. If you plan to visit during this time, beware that air quality may be bad, affecting your health and the views. If you get caught in the worst of it, it's advisable to wear an N95 mask to protect your lungs.

reached via a 20km-long, beautiful, well-paved road that's worth the drive alone. A better option is **Huay Sua Thao** *(250฿)*, populated by a mix of peoples, including the Kayan. The village is best reached by a boat (800฿) from the pier at Ban Huay Dua. English-speaking **Aye Maung** *(093 191 2920)* acts as a coordinator, and can help organise activities in the village ranging from homestays to making brass bracelets.

If you want to go deeper, the city's best trekking guide is **Chan** *(naturewalksthai-myanmar.com)*, a native of Mae Hong Son who leads both day-long nature walks and longer treks across the province. Ju at **Rosegarden Tours** also gets good feedback, and outfits such as **Tour Merng Tai** *(tourmerngtai.com)* and **Thailand Hill Tribe Holidays** *(thailandhilltribeholidays.com)* can also arrange tailored treks and hill-tribe visits.

And if you're taken by the handicrafts of the province's minority groups, head to Hed Kor Leaw (p186), a government-initiative handicraft shop in Mae Hong Son that has a small but appealing mix of textiles and food items.

A LOCAL PERSPECTIVE

Maprang, a Kayan resident of Huay Sua Thao, shares her daily life.

I was born in Myanmar. I moved here 36 years ago; I came here when I was six. We lived at a refugee centre for two years, then we moved here.

I sell things and I also grow sesame and soybeans. Visitors here have to pay 200฿, which goes to the entire village. But if people buy things from me, I get to keep that money. These days it's mostly foreign tourists; Thais only come in the high season. Some days nobody buys anything from me – there's a lot of competition!

We like that tourists come here. If they didn't, the village would be very quiet. Even if people don't buy things, we still want them to come.

A Taste of China in Ban Rak Thai

Sipping tea in Thailand's Yunnan

Tucked against the Myanmar border nearly 50km north of Mae Hong Son is Ban Rak Thai. Established by Yunnanese soldiers fleeing the 1949 communist revolution in China, the village's food, architecture and culture are still very much rooted in its Chinese past. Many residents still speak Chinese dialects to this day and are proud of their heritage. These cultural elements and the village's unique setting, typically shrouded in mist as if it were a city in the clouds, make it well worth a day trip or overnight stay.

The main industry here is tea, with its founders sharing their expertise to create some of Thailand's best-quality oolong, jasmine and green teas. Today there are numerous places to taste the golden nectar, with each shop offering to brew a fresh pot right in front of you through a ceremony known as Gong Fu Cha. Every February, the **Tea Festival** turns the village into celebration mode, with tastings, plantation trips, free food and revelry.

Aside from tea, locals also produce wine from plums, grapes and other fruit that is best enjoyed with a traditional Yunnanese meal overlooking the reservoir. The same reservoir is where picturesque **sightseeing boat rides** can be chartered from 350฿.

The best time to visit Baan Rak Thai is the cold season (November to February), when the temperatures can drop as low as 12 or 13 degrees C. The village's high altitude (1200m) also means weather can change in an instant, so best to pack a coat when out and about. If you visit during the rainy season, you'll be treated to the most luscious green landscapes of the year, but thick dense clouds can often hang around for days, obscuring any chance of a view. Weather permitting, the neighbouring village of Pang Oung is a nice daytime getaway with a pine-tree forest perfect for winter picnics.

SCOTT BIALES DITCHTHEMAP/SHUTTERSTOCK

Ban Rak Thai

If you do plan to stay the night, cottage-like guesthouses make up most of the accommodation; however, given the influx of tourists in recent years, new developments are slowly changing the village landscape. It's worth checking with your hotel if they have any planned construction before arriving, especially during the low season.

Outpost Town

Explore little-visited Khun Yuam

Once a busy trading post – the border with Myanmar's Kayin State is only 35km away – **Khun Yuam** was a key Japanese army base during WWII. Now it's a small and somnolent hillside town located between Mae Hong Son and Mae Sariang. As such, it makes a pleasant break from more visited destinations – you are likely to be the only foreigner in town.

Khun Yuam's main attraction is the **Thai-Japan Friendship Memorial Hall** *(100฿)*, which details the village's role as a Japanese military outpost during WWII. It's an impressive museum for such a small town. After watching a brief film (with English subtitles) on the history of Khun Yuam, you'll find displays and artefacts on the Japanese presence in Khun Yuam, as well as local history and culture. Some of the Japanese soldiers stayed in Khun Yuam and married local women; the last Japanese soldier who settled in the area died in 2000.

Waterfalls & Sunflowers

Rural delights outside of Khun Yuam

Head southwest of Khun Yuam, where beautiful **Wat To Phae** sits on the banks of Mae Nam Yuam. Aside from an impressive Myanmar teak *wi hahn* (sanctuary) and a Mon-style *chedi* its main attraction is an exquisite 150-year-old embroidered and sequinned tapestry that originated from Myanmar. A small viewing platform here looks over beautiful tiered rice fields.

Alternatively, head northeast from town to to the wild Mexican sunflower fields that turn the Hmong village of

WHY I LOVE MAE HONG SON

Austin Bush, Lonely Planet writer

I've been to just about every corner of Thailand, but Mae Hong Son is by far my favourite place in the country. Why is it so special to me? I love the mix of cultures that make the province a little bit Thailand and a little bit Myanmar. I love its ruggedness – steep mountains, windy roads and a remoteness that, even today, make it hard to reach. I'm drawn to the potential for exploration that the region holds; of villages not connected to any road, distant footpaths, unexplored caves. And with its tiered rice fields, karst cliffs and, in winter, hillsides blanketed by the purple, pink and orange teak tree leaves, it's also just plain drop-dead gorgeous.

LIVE THAT LOCAL LIFE

The small, incredibly picturesque Thai Yai village of makes for one of Thailand's most off-the-beaten-track homestay experiences. Around 15 different families take part in the **Muang Pon Homestay Program** *(080 431 7555)*, which charges visitors 400฿ and includes food, board and activities from traditional handicrafts to cooking local delicacies and helping on the farm. The locals are welcoming and eager to share their knowledge but be aware that few speak much English.

Muang Pon is about 12km south of Khun Yuam; any Mae Sariang- or Chiang Mai-bound bus can drop you off there.

H.DUFF/SHUTTERSTOCK

Ban Mae U Khaw bright yellow every November. Continue along the same route to **Nam Tok Mae Surin** *(200฿)*, part of Mae Surin National Park and, at 100m, one of Thailand's highest free-fall waterfalls.

Get Off the Beaten Track

Side roads and jungles of Mae Sariang District

Located at the southern end of Mae Hong Son Province, Mae Sariang is an established stop on the Mae Hong Son Loop (p194). Although most travellers do a night before heading east towards Chiang Mai, the town, with its charming riverside vibe, comfy hotels and an excellent northern Thai restaurant, has left many changing their plans to stay longer. And the surrounding countryside provides even more excuses to linger.

Located just east of Mae Sariang is **Salawin National Park** *(200฿)*, which spans 722 sq km of protected land in Mae Sariang and Sop Moei districts. The park is covered with teak and Asian redwood, and is home to what is thought to be the second-largest teak tree in Thailand.

Within the park's bounds, at the end of a 50km winding, beautiful mountain road, is the riverside trading village of **Mae Sam Laep**. Populated by Burmese refugees, the town has a raw, border-town feel. If you have your own wheels (or can stomach the *sorng taa ou*), it's a great day trip.

If you want to go even deeper, Mae Sam Laep acts as a launching point for **boat trips** *(500-2000฿)* along the Salawin River, which acts as the border between Thailand and Myanmar. Trips pass through untouched jungle, unusual rock formations along the river and, occasionally, dips into Myanmar's Karen State. It's possible to charter boats from the pier at Mae Sam Laep.

Nam Tok Mae Surin

A Ghost in the Cave

Mae Hong Son's mysterious Pii Man

A stone's throw from Pai (p196) is the district known as **Pang Mapha**, a rugged border area home to over 200 cave systems that cut through the mountain landscape. For millennia these caves have played an important role in the ecosystem and cultures found in the hills, and these days provide several days – or more – of distraction for adventure-seeking visitors.

Of all the caves in Pang Mapha, **Tham Nam Lot** is the most accessible. It's one of the largest known caves in Thailand, with a total length of 1600m, impressive stalagmites, ancient teak coffins and a wide stream running through it for 600m. The cave's three main chambers can be visited via a **guided bamboo raft tour** *(600฿)*, although during the rainy season only one chamber is accessible. The cave known as **Tham Pii Man**, located just past Pangmapha Hospital, has more of these teak coffins, most dating back over 2000 years. Access is via an unmaintained path up a steep hillside and rickety stairs to reach this sequence of three shallow caves, where you'll find ancient coffins carved from solid teak logs. The name 'Pii Man'

PANG MAPHA'S CAVES

The caves in Pang Mapha District are of great antiquity, with remains of prehistoric hunting tribes found across the area. Of the 200 caves explored, more than 35 have been found to contain prehistoric tools, 12 have rock art depicting scenes of people and animals, and 85 contain ancient teak coffins. In more recent years, Dr Rasmi Shoocongdej discovered the remains of a woman who lived some 13,640 years ago in Tham Lot Cave, and in 2017 she found a new Pii Man cave that is said to have the full remains of more than 100 individuals in lacquered and painted coffins – although this cave is still closed to the public.

EATING & DRINKING IN MAE HONG SON PROVINCE: OUR PICKS

Gee Lee: This long-standing restaurant in Ban Rak Thai serves delicious Yunnanese-style Chinese dishes. *9am-9pm* ฿฿

Mae Luang Phen: Northern Thailand's greatest grill shack is found by the side of the road in Mae Sariang. *8am-6pm* ฿

Noodle Soup House: Located at the top of a mountain in the Black Lahu village of Ban Jabo, it can likely lay claim to the country's best noodle shop views. *7am-4pm* ฿

LOLA: Delicious single-origin coffee drinks served by chill Karen dudes in Mae Hong Son. *7.30am-3.30pm Mon-Fri, 8am-4pm Sat & Sun* ฿

A TASTE OF THAI YAI

Thai Yai or Shan food takes ingredients and influences from neighbouring Myanmar.

Kaeng hang le: Pork belly in a curry seasoned with tamarind and a masala-like spice mixture.

Khang pawng: Vegetables in batter seasoned with turmeric and fermented soybeans, deep-fried until crispy.

Khao kan jin: Rice mixed with pork blood, wrapped in a banana leaf, steamed and drizzled with garlic oil.

Khao mun muay: Shan 'doughnuts' made from sticky rice flour sprinkled with sesame seeds and drizzled with raw sugarcane syrup.

Too a poo un: A noodle soup in which the broth takes the form of a thick, yellow porridge made from split peas.

MERCEDESS/SHUTTERSTOCK

Tham Nam Lot (p191)

translates to 'large spirit', with legends of tall, cave-dwelling beings once inhabiting the area. And for biology nerds, Tham Mae La-Na, in the village of the same name, is where you can go to capture a glimpse of an eyeless, waterfall-climbing fish that is found in only two caves in the world, both in Pang Mapha District, although this isn't a cave for casual visitors.

If all this appeals, book a few nights at **Cave Lodge** and get face to face with owner and archaeological enthusiast John Spies, a key player in many of Thailand's archaeological cave expeditions. The lodge offers board and various adventure tours such as kayaking, trekking and cave exploration. Spies's book, *Wild Times*, is ostensibly an autobiography but also serves as a page-turning guide to the region.

And if you like the area, go even deeper via a day trip with **Mook's Hill Tribe Crafts & Tours** *(mookshilltribecrafts.com)*, which operates out of Muang Phaem, a scenic, remote-feeling Karen village 6km east of Cave Lodge.

Little Eden

Rural bliss in the village of Mae La-Na

Set in a picturesque mountain valley just off the main Mae Hong Son Loop near Pang Mapha, **Mae La-Na**, a tiny, remote Shan village, feels like it's been cut off from the rest of the world. A beautiful rural setting, accommodation and a host of natural attractions mean it's a wonderful place to hide out for a few days.

The most famous local attraction is **Tham Mae La-Na**, a 12km-long cavern with a stream running through it. Although local guides are willing to take people inside, in reality the cave lacks the appropriate infrastructure to support visitors, who run a serious risk of permanently damaging delicate cave formations and disturbing the habitat of sensitive cave fish. A better bet is to check out nearby **Tham Pakarang (Coral Cave)** and **Tham Phet (Diamond Cave)**, both of which feature good wall formations. Guides can be arranged at the main village shop and petrol station. Some of the caves may not be accessible during the rainy season.

If you're inspired to stay, located at the edge of the village, **Maelana Garden Home** *(081 706 6021)* takes the form of basic, fan-cooled rooms and a few very rustic A-frame bamboo bungalows. Authentic Shan meals can be prepared. Call ahead – transport can be arranged from Rte 1095 or Soppong – or ask for the owner, Khun Ampha, at the village shop/petrol station, and she'll pick you up.

Off-Piste

Get your boots dusty in the countryside around Mae La-Na

The village of Mae La-Na is a good base for some inspiring walks. Some of Mae Hong Son's most beautiful scenery is within a day's ramble, and there are several Red and Black Lahu villages nearby. Indeed, to reach Mae La-Na you'll need to pass through **Ban Jabo**, a Black Lahu village dramatically positioned between karst cliffs and a mountaintop. The former is home to a cave with prehistoric coffins and the latter is home to a string of homestays and cafes with astounding views over the countryside.

It's also possible to walk a 15km half-loop all the way from Mae La-Na to Tham Lot. Khun Ampha, the owner of Maelana Garden Home, can provide a basic map.

Finding Solace in a Forest Monastery

Master your vipassana breathing technique

Finding spirituality is not an uncommon objective for travellers to Thailand, but only the most serious seekers of enlightenment should head for **Tum Wua Forest Monastery** *(wattamwua.com)*. Open to everyone, from absolute beginners to those well versed in the practice, the retreat offers free board as well as two vegetarian meals per day in exchange for upkeep and meditative learning.

Visitors must stay for a minimum of two nights, and must follow a strict daily timetable that starts at 5am and ends at 8.30pm. The abbot, alongside a number of English- and Thai-speaking monks, offers spiritual guidance in mindfulness and breathing each and every day. For the very determined, they can even train you in the art of silent meditation where you don't speak for your entire stay.

Not a hotel, this place is a serious meditation retreat that is only suitable for those willing to partake fully. Yet unlike some more traditional temple retreats, this monastery tones down its Buddhist teachings in place of inclusivity, welcoming people from all religions and allowing use of phones and technology, making for a unique and balanced experience that is tailored to the foreign traveller.

Getting here is relatively easy and requires no prior booking. There's a bus stop at the entrance of the monastery that sits between Mae Hong Son and Pang Mapha, allowing you to simply arrive, check in, trade your jeans for robes and submit to a new way of life.

WHAT IS VIPASSANA?

Vipassana is an ancient Indian meditation practice that focuses on self-transformation through self-observation. A meditative state is achieved by paying close attention to bodily sensations, thoughts and emotions. Buddhists believe that cultivating awareness of these things can ultimately reveal the true nature of existence – a key step on the journey towards enlightenment and liberation from suffering.

For non-Buddhists, *vipassana* has become a popular tool for those who practise yoga and mindfulness, proven to reduce stress and enhance emotional wellbeing, helping people find inner peace and opening doors to personal self-discovery.

ROAD TRIP

Mae Hong Son Loop

Touring the northern provinces on motorbike can be a thrilling experience, with the Mae Hong Son Loop taking the crown as a true rite of passage for backpackers and adventure enthusiasts alike. With 1864 twists and turns, this 600km route is an exhilarating way to witness northern Thailand first hand, beckoning those seeking an off-the-beaten-path experience.

1 Chiang Mai

You can tackle the loop clockwise or anti-clockwise, but heading north through Mae Rim and then Pai has shorter legs at the start to get you used to the road.

The Ride: Before you head out, check your bike's tyres, brakes and oil. Then do a few loops of the city to get familiar with your machine.

2 Pai

As you reach your first stop, stop at Pai Canyon (p201) and **Pai Memorial Bridge** so you don't need to loop back on yourself. Book into a guesthouse and explore Pai (p196) as you please. And if you're already feeling sore, a dip in the Sai Ngam Hot Springs (p198) can help ready you for the days ahead.

The Ride: Head north from Chiang Mai via Rte 107 until you reach Mae Taeng. Then take a left onto either Rte 3009 or Rte 1095 and let the winding climb into the mountains guide your way.

O.KEMPPAINEN/SHUTTERSTOCK

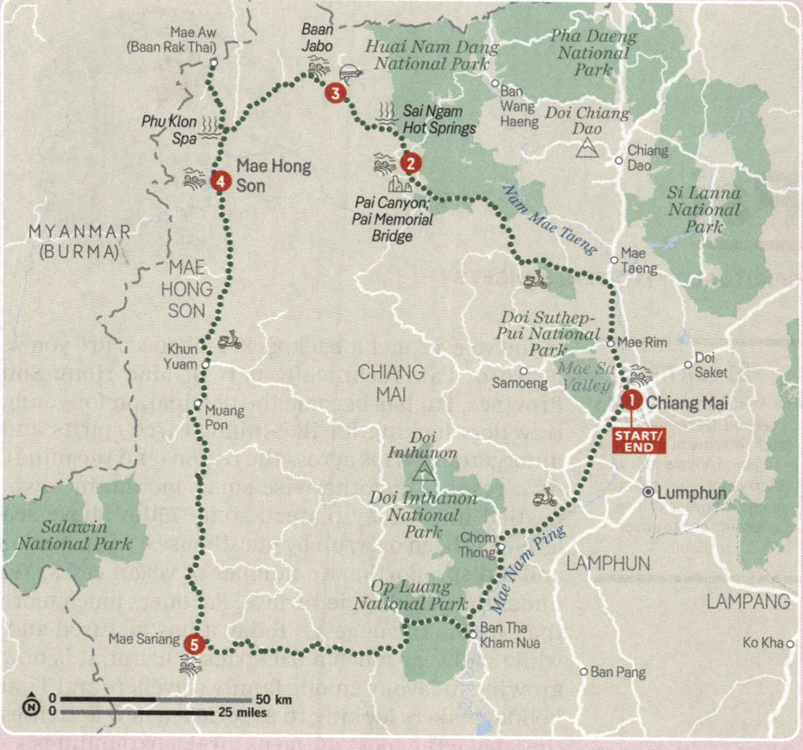

❸ Pang Mapha

On day two, detour to Tham Nam Lot (p191), a cave famous for its 30m-high chambers, 2000-year-old teak coffins and prehistoric human remains. A guided tour includes a bamboo-raft ride inside the cave. Nearby, Tham Pii Man (p191) houses more coffins, and legends of giant monsters. End your day at a homestay in Ban Jabo (p193), a Black Lahu village with awe-inspiring vistas and locally farmed coffee.

The Ride: Things get a little steeper here. As you snake through the mountains, take detours left and right depending on what catches your eye.

❹ Mae Hong Son

This is when the road really starts to get fun – winding but not too steep. On the way into town, detour to Ban Rak Thai (p188) or visit Phu Klon Country Club (p187) for a mud bath and hot-spring *onsen* to loosen tight muscles. Be sure to stop by the **Mae Hong Son Chamber of Commerce** for a (preemptive) certificate of completing all 1864 curves for 60฿.

The Ride: Winding, spectacular and hair-raising. Completing your journey along Rte 1095 to the city is only half the journey. The best is yet to come.

❺ Mae Sariang

Attractive riverside town Mae Sariang has a warm and friendly population. On the way here, you'll pass Khun Yuam (p189), a once-busy trading post that was commandeered by the Japanese during WWII. There's a turn-off back to Chiang Mai via Rte 1263 that takes you up and over Doi Inthanon (p292), Thailand's highest mountain. To complete the full loop, traverse **Op Luang National Park**.

The Ride: Rte 108 promises the best vistas of the trip as you meander through green landscapes of jagged mountain ranges and rolling rice-paddy plateaus.

Pai

SPIRITUALITY | WATER | SUNSETS

TOP TIP

The air in Pai during burning season (December to March) is some of the worst in Thailand. Vistas turn into blurry nothingness and many businesses close, choosing escape over revenue.

If you've ever met a backpacker, chances are you've heard of Pai. Technically part of Mae Hong Son Province, Pai has become the destination for young travellers looking for like-minded free spirits and unforgettable trips across the region (and the mind). As a result, this otherwise small mountain town, nestled in a valley plateau some 750m above sea level, has been overrun by guesthouses, yoga studios and a disproportionate number of vegan cafes. Yet under the hazy hippie surface, Pai offers much more than its image suggests. Today it has matured and, while still very much a backpacker haunt, it is now growing in favour among family travellers and Thai holidaymakers looking to experience new activities that make the most of the natural surroundings.

Hobby Hub

Learn a new skill in Pai

Gaining notoriety in the 1990s as a stopover for backpackers, Pai quickly evolved into a busy town of dreadlocked locals and tie-dyed Westerners looking to escape reality and find themselves. Although the scene has evolved a lot since then, its hippie-trail-leaning origins can still be felt, and you'll still see lots of ads posted around town for a variety of workshops that stray from the mainstream – keep your eyes peeled for these.

GETTING AROUND

'Downtown' Pai is entirely accessible on foot. To explore the surrounding countryside, several outfits in Pai hire motorcycles. For a car, you're best off hiring one in Chiang Mai. There's usually a couple of motorcycle taxis near Pai's bus station, and *sorng taa ou* can be chartered to destinations outside the city centre. Prempracha Transport operates frequent minivans between Chiang Mai's Arcade Bus Station and Pai, a trip of around five hours. Or you can hire an off-meter taxi or Grab car for a pre-agreed sum. Take car-sickness prevention.

Alternatively, hire a motorcycle or car in Chiang Mai, keeping in mind that the journey has exactly 762 turns, and most are tight hairpins or steep cliffside arches that are best ignored while passing.

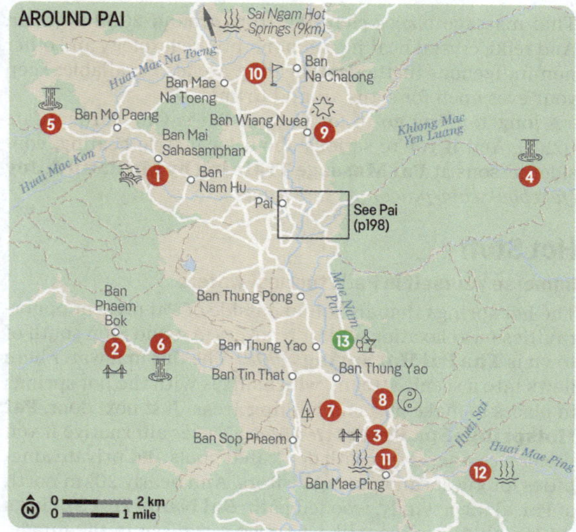

SIGHTS
1 Ban Santichon
2 Kho Kuso Bamboo Bridge
3 Memorial Bridge
4 Nam Tok Mae Yen
5 Nam Tok Mo Paeng
6 Nam Tok Pembok
7 Pai Canyon
8 Pai International Meditation Center
11 Pai Hotsprings Spa Resort
12 Tha Pai Hot Springs

ACTIVITIES
9 Harmony Hub
10 Pai Bamboo Mini Golf

EATING
see 1 Mitraphap Pai

DRINKING
13 Two Huts

Some of the more established venues include **Harmony Hub** *(harmonyhub.space)*, where you can spend your day finding inner peace with owners Clem and Sushi doing art classes, ink therapy, vegan baking and pottery. Alternatively, get one-on-one with the 'mother' via a kombucha-fermentation class at **Good Life Dacha**. Or during the high season, hone your tightrope skills at the **Pai Circus Hostel**.

A Place for Healing

Massage out those kinks in Pai

If you've arrived in Pai saddle-sore from the Mae Hong Son Loop (p194), you're in luck. The town is one of the best places in Thailand to alleviate pain. There are plenty of traditional

A TASTE OF YUNNAN

Mae Hong Son (as well as Chiang Rai and Chiang Mai) Province is home to communities of Yunnanese Chinese who fled their homeland after losing the civil war in 1948.

Gai dam: 'Black' chicken is a common ingredient in Chinese-Yunnanese cooking.

Mantou: Steamed buns.

Mu phan pii: Strips of pork belly steamed with pickled vegetables.

Mu nam kang: 'Dewdrop pork' is air-dried pork loin, delicious when stir-fried with green chillies.

Pa tong ko: Deep-fried fingers of dough, often paired with soy milk for breakfast.

Yam bai chah: A salad made from young, fresh tea leaves.

EATING & DRINKING IN PAI: OUR PICKS

Larp Khom Huay Poo: The house special is *larb koo a*, a take on the minced-meat 'salad'. Pair with sticky rice, bitter herbs and an ice-cold beer. *9am-8pm* ฿

Mitraphap Pai: One of a handful of restaurants serving Chinese cuisine in Ban Santichon, the Yunnanese village around 6km west of Pai. *9am-8pm* ฿

Malamong Art Cafe: Refreshing, delicious herbal teas and other drinks and healthy snacks. *10am-10pm* ฿

Jikko Bar: Mega-friendly bartenders and all around a far more sophisticated bar than you'd expect to find in Pai. *5pm-midnight* ฿

FAMILY FRIENDLY

Ban Santichon: This Yunnanese village is almost a theme park, with traditional Chinese clay houses, faux castle walls, a Ferris wheel, dress-up photos and archery.

Pai Bamboo Mini Golf: Thirteen holes tackled with tennis balls and bamboo clubs.

Harmony Hub: (p197) Sign the kids up for a ceramics lesson here.

Good Life Dacha: (p197) The square adjacent to this restaurant has a playground where kid-centred activities are often happening.

Kho Kuso Bamboo Bridge: (p200) Located outside of Pai, this expansive rural area is great for family exploration.

Thai massage places charging from around 200฿ an hour. And reiki, crystal healing, acupuncture, reflexology and other non-indigenous methods of healing are also available; keep your eyes open for signs around town.

A longstanding go-to for yoga in Pai is Om Garden Cafe (p201). And if you're serious about local-style healing, consider lessons at **Pai Massage Training by Mr Bann & Joy** *(facebook.com/paicomfortmassage)*.

Hot Stuff

Immerse yourself in Pai's thermal waters

The hot springs that are found outside of Pai present opportunities for relaxation and/or recovery. Around 8km south of town is **Tha Pai Hot Springs** *(60฿)*. The thermal water here flows into a scenic stream, which mixes with the hot springs in places to make pleasant bathing areas. Just next door, **Pai Hotsprings Spa Resort** *(100฿)* is a clever alternative if you prefer a cleaner setup with dedicated pools and private amenities for guests and paying visitors. And nearly 20km north of Pai, along a windy, wooded path, **Sai Ngam Hot Springs** (p194; *200฿)* is almost like an open-air *onsen* in the jungle, although the water is warm rather than hot.

Market Day

Burn baht at Pai's bustling places of commerce

Every evening, the streets of central Pai transform into a **walking street**, with vendors selling food (with lots of meat-free and vegan options), clothes, souvenirs and knick-knacks. It's one of the city's biggest draws, and is open year-round, but is far busier during high season (from November to February).

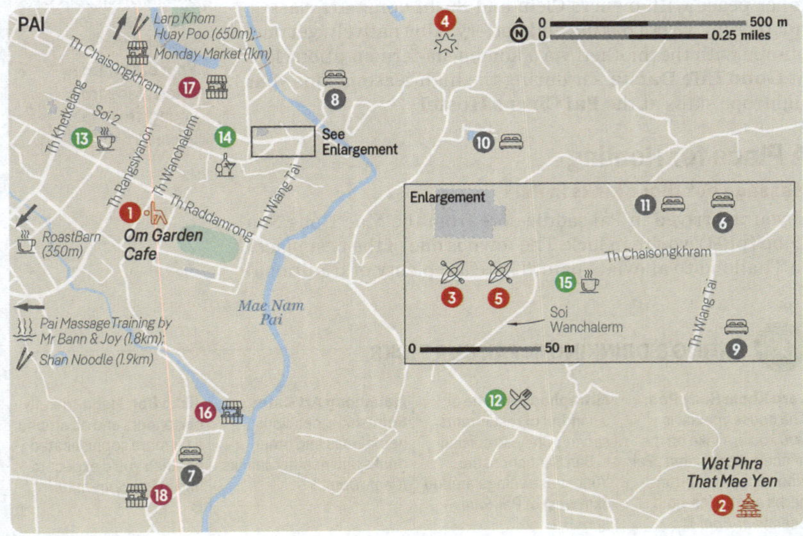

Pai, like all larger villages in Mae Hong Son Province, also hosts a revolving market oriented towards locals. The **Monday Market** unfolds just east of Pai's airport, and brings together hill-tribe vendors selling produce grown in the hills, Shan villagers selling bowls of noodles and deep-fried snacks, and traders selling items imported from Myanmar. On Wednesdays, a similar **market** unfolds southeast of the village centre.

And on Saturday mornings, a foreigner-centred **Community Market** pops up in the square across from Good Life Dacha. Expect homemade pickles and baked goods, used clothing, and vegetarian and vegan food.

Rolling on the River

Tubing and rafting in Pai

The Pai River is no longer just a languid backdrop to the village. Love it or hate it, tubing has finally made its way to Pai and floating down the river in an inflated inner tube, alcohol in hand, is the name of the game. At various waypoints along the river, the whole flotilla is stopped and ushered into bars where live DJs, BBQ parties and drinks on demand keep spirits high. The water is shallow enough for kids to safely join, and there are staff stationed along the river to ensure nobody gets injured. Tipsy Tubing usually runs every Tuesday and Friday (paused during the rainy season), with chalkboards on Pai's walking street keeping a tally of those signed up, garnering much excitement among passing crowds.

If you're looking for adventure rather than a buzz, why not see the jungle through a misty spray of white-water rapids? Outfits such as long-established **Thai Adventure Rafting** *(thairafting.com)* and **Pai Adventures** *(paiadventures.com)* conduct one-day and multiday expeditions along the Mae Nam Pai spanning over 60km of inaccessible jungle between Pai and Mae Hong Son, and passing as many as 60 rapids from class I to class IV.

Be Present

Check in at Pai's biggest meditation centre

If you're drawn to the more local style of spirituality in Pai, consider a stint at the **Pai International Meditation Center** *(paimeditationcenter.org)*. The flashy (by Pai standards), expansive park-like compound, located southeast of town, just across from the entrance to Tha Pai Hot Springs, focuses on Theravada-style meditation and Buddhist education. A team of

PAI ACCOMMODATION CHEAT SHEET

At one point, Pai was thought to be home to more than 500 hotels and guesthouses. Its place on the backpacker trail has led to many options in the lower and mid range, while its popularity among middle- and upper-class Thai tourists has led to several fancier places, meaning that just about any type of traveller is covered.

If you've come to Pai to party, consider a stay 'downtown'. You can walk just about everywhere, and you'll have easy access to bars, restaurants and the market, although it can be noisy.

If you've come to Pai with notions of an idyllic, rural stay, look in the approximate 3km ring that surrounds the town, although you'll need to hire a motorcycle to get around.

HIGHLIGHTS
1 Om Garden Cafe
2 Wat Phra That Mae Yen

ACTIVITIES
3 Pai Adventures
4 Pai Circus Hostel
5 Thai Adventure Rafting

SLEEPING
6 Hotel des Artists
7 Nolo Hub Pai
8 Pai Country Hut
9 Pai Village Boutique Resort
10 Pairadise
11 Rim Pai Cottage

EATING
see 16 Good Life Dacha
12 Jerk Spot

DRINKING & NIGHTLIFE
13 Chatchai Coffee Farming & Roaster
14 Jikko Bar
15 Malamong Art Cafe

SHOPPING
16 Community Market
17 Pai Walking Street & Night Market
18 Wednesday Market

PAI DRINKING CHEAT SHEET

Chaisongkhram Rd, the main east–west strip in downtown Pai, is home to the town's most sophisticated bars, especially at its eastern end, as well as some scruffier backpacker bars. With the vendors from the walking street market selling a variety of foods, it's a great place to bar-hop.

Head south from here, along the road that parallels the river, and you'll find a string of bars with more of a live rock-and-roll and pool table vibe.

Cross the bridge and head east and things get trippy; this is the realm of open-air bars and late-night dance parties in the woods. Continue along the road that leads to Tha Pai Hot Springs to find the string of open-air sunset bars such as Two Huts.

MERCEDESS/SHUTTERSTOCK

Pai Canyon

seven foreign and Thai Buddhist monks provides instruction in English. Both absolute beginners and hardened *vipassana* veterans are welcome, and there are two daily sessions of drop-in meditation as well as seven-day meditation retreats, which include accommodation; check Instagram or the website for schedules for both when you're in town.

Cascade City

Waterfall enthusiasts, behold Pai

The hills surrounding Pai are home to numerous waterfalls, which are at their best after the rainy season (October to early December). **Nam Tok Pembok** *(200฿)*, 8km west of Pai, has a secret trail that leads to deeper pools higher up the river. Combine a dip with a visit to the nearby **Kho Kuso Bamboo Bridge** *(30฿)*, a charming, bucolic network of elevated bridges spanning streams and rice fields. Around 10km northwest of Pai is **Nam Tok Mo Paeng** *(100฿)*, an impressive and beautiful multi-tiered cascade unfortunately surrounded by some ugly contemporary infrastructure. Nonetheless, there are charming little hang-outs perfect for cooling off in the water, with a handful of vendors selling sweet drinks. And **Nam Tok Mae Yen** is worth a visit, particularly after the rainy season (from October to early December). The waterfall is a couple of hours' walk down the rough road east of Pai; the trailhead is near the entrance to Wat Phra That Mae Yen.

Sundown Spots

Take in the sunset in Pai

Pai's natural beauty is often shrouded by the town's buzzing energy, but with so much in close proximity it would be a crime not to see it. And the latest trend in town is taking in this beauty at sunset. Operators even lead sunset tours to various locations outside of town, but if you've got your own wheels, it's easy to experience on your own.

Pai Canyon steals the show with grand views from its narrow, elevated trails, but beware of the loose sandy terrain and sheer drops on either side, especially at sunset when high-season crowds tend to jostle for the best views.

For human-made alternatives, the Big Buddha at **Wat Phra That Mae Yen** offers arguably the most impressive sunset perch in the area. But for something a bit more lively, head to **Two Huts**, an open-air bar with lounging platforms overlooking the beautiful Pai valley. There's a social, festive vibe where people play music, throw Frisbees and enjoy picnics and drinks until the stars come out. There are several similar places along this strip, but Two Huts was the most popular at research time.

The Rhythms of Pai

Attend the Pai Jazz & Blues Fest

If you're stuck in Pai at the start of rainy season, you may stumble upon **Pai Jazz & Blues Festival** – a three-day music event that turns this sleepy town into a roaring festival city. With a strong emphasis on music hopping, a ticket (200฿) will get you entry to all participating venues playing host to Thai and international music performances. Starting in 2017, the festival grows bigger every year.

Cafes, restaurants, bars, hotels and resorts turn into make-shift concert halls for talented musicians over the three-day event, some of whom begin playing dulcet tones of smooth jazz and emotive blues as early as 11am. On Friday and Saturday, a main stage is erected in town for headline performances.

In 2025 over 30 artists descended on the city, attracting fans who overflowed onto the small village roads outside the bars. Entry to venues is free with an event ticket, but you're expected to buy some food or drink while you enjoy the show. Given the small size of Pai relative to the size of the event, booking accommodation in advance is crucial. The town is often booked to bursting during the event.

FROM INVERLOCH TO PAI

Somchai Khan-asa, founder of Pai Jazz & Blues Fest.

I was first inspired to create a jazz festival in Pai after attending a small jazz festival in the seaside town of Inverloch, Australia. The whole city came together, with stages, street performances and music played in restaurants and bars across town. Pai was the perfect location for this dream, always full of foreigners and locals who appreciate art and music. As the event turned six this year, I turned 60. I like to imagine what the 30th Pai Jazz & Blues Festival would look like. For anyone who loves a small-town vibe and the melancholy sound of blues and jazz – you must come at least once.

EATING & DRINKING IN PAI: OUR PICKS

Shan Noodle: Located just beyond Pai Massage Training by Mr Bann & Joy, this homebound places serves delicious local noodle dishes. *8am-5pm* ฿

Jerk Spot: Serving warm-ya-heart Jamaican favourites like jerk chicken and rice and peas. *noon-8pm Thu-Tue* ฿

Om Garden Cafe: Meat-free and vegan meals, smoothies and light bites, but it'd be a shame if you missed the carrot cake. *8.30am-5pm Tue-Sun* ฿

RoastBarn: Located in a warehouse just outside of 'downtown' Pai is this sophisticated-feeling, award-winning roastery and cafe. *8am-4pm* ฿

MINI PAI LOOP BY MOTORBIKE

If you're intimidated by the 600km of the Mae Hong Son Loop, consider hiring a motorcycle and exploring the lush countryside surrounding Pai.

START	END	LENGTH
Chatchai Coffee	Two Huts	45km; eight hours

Kick-start your trip with a piccolo latte made with local beans at 1 **Chatchai Coffee Farming & Roaster** in Pai.

Head around 10km southwest to 2 **Nam Tok Pembok** (p200), the waterfall reached by a windy, hilly and slightly rough in parts road. After splashing around, continue a tiny bit further to the 3 **Kho Kuso Bamboo Bridge** (p200) and soak in the beautiful countryside.

Return to Rte 1095 and head 15km north to 4 **Ban Santichon** (p198), the Yunnanese village where you can take in the foreign vibe and enjoy a Chinese-style lunch.

Sufficiently refuelled, head south along Rte 1095 to scramble atop the cliffs at 5 **Pai Canyon** (p201). Follow this with the obligatory selfie at the 6 **Memorial Bridge** (p194), a rite of passage for Thai visitors to Pai.

If it's cool out – or your butt's feeling sore – hit the thermal waters of 7 **Tha Pai Hot Springs** (p198). At this point, it should be late afternoon, so head north to one of the open-air bars along Rte 4024 such as 8 **Two Huts** (p201), to take in the glorious Pai sunset.

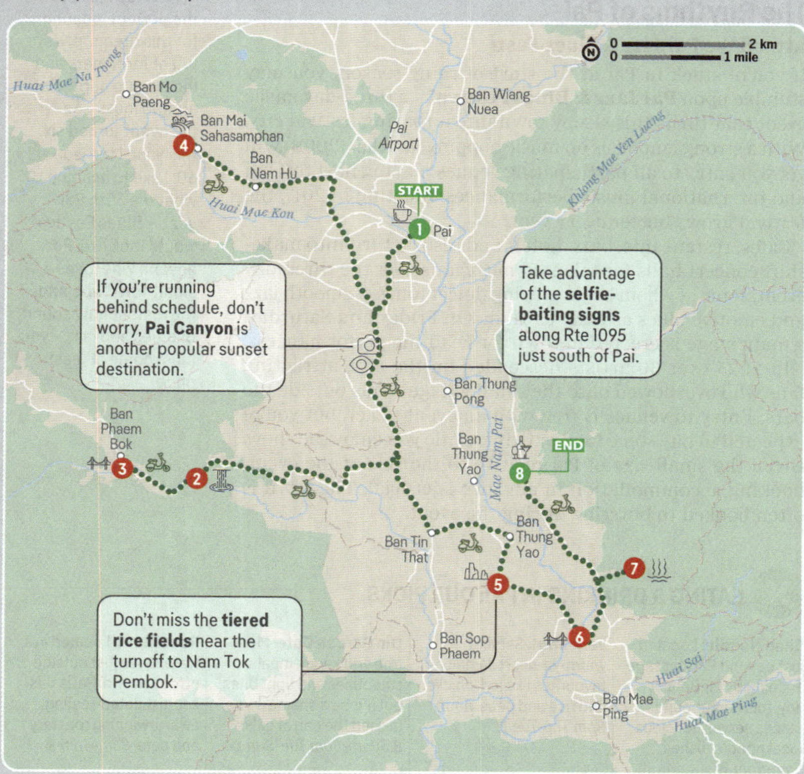

Chiang Rai Province

TEA & COFFEE | ART | REMOTE VILLAGES

Thailand's northernmost province, Chiang Rai is full of destinations that practically force intrepid travellers to detour from the tourist path.

The provincial capital bursts at the seams with art, commerce and creative flair. Alternatively, venture beyond the city limits to discover epic mountain ranges, vast Mekong River floodplains and wild borderlands ripe for exploration. From the mystical northern border that's home to the Golden Triangle where Thailand, Myanmar and Laos collide, to ancient cities that straddle the mighty Mekong, Chiang Rai links the present and the past. And there's also the province's lush countryside, where rolling hills, iridescent rice paddies, and bountiful tea and coffee plantations paint a breathtaking backdrop for outdoor adventure.

GETTING THERE & AROUND

Buses connect the major towns of the province. Most provincial buses depart from Chiang Rai's old Terminal 1, and some from the newer Terminal 2 (which handles interprovincial routes; regular buses run from Chiang Mai and other provincial capitals multiple times a day).

Car or motorbike rental is a much more efficient way to get around the province. Chiang Rai Airport rentals are the most competitive.

The provincial capital is mostly walkable, but you can hail a cab using the Grab app or call for a metered taxi from **Chiang Rai Taxi** *(053 773477)*. Tuk-tuks can be hailed for a bartered fee.

Chiang Rai Airport has flights to/from Bangkok.

White, Blue & Black

Chiang Rai's colour-coded temples

There's no denying Chiang Rai is a vibrant and colourful city, not least because of the sheer volume of artists and talented architects that have found the province to be their very own canvas. Three temples (of sorts) stand out among the rest, each one encompassing its own unique style, which are best seen in person by way of a motorcycle or taxi tour of all three in one day.

The White Temple, formally known as **Wat Rong Khun** *(100฿)*, and located around 15km south of the provincial capital, is agreed to be one of Thailand's most astonishing buildings, completely white and intricately designed from top to bottom with carvings, inscriptions and statues that have an eerie story to tell. Constructed in 1997 by the internationally renowned Thai artist Chalermchai Kositpipat, this temple-sized art piece reflects humanity's greed, desire and destruction, juxtaposing it against Buddhist symbology. Inside, the mood changes, where brightly coloured murals and paintings of contemporary scenes and pop-culture icons (hi, Keanu Reeves

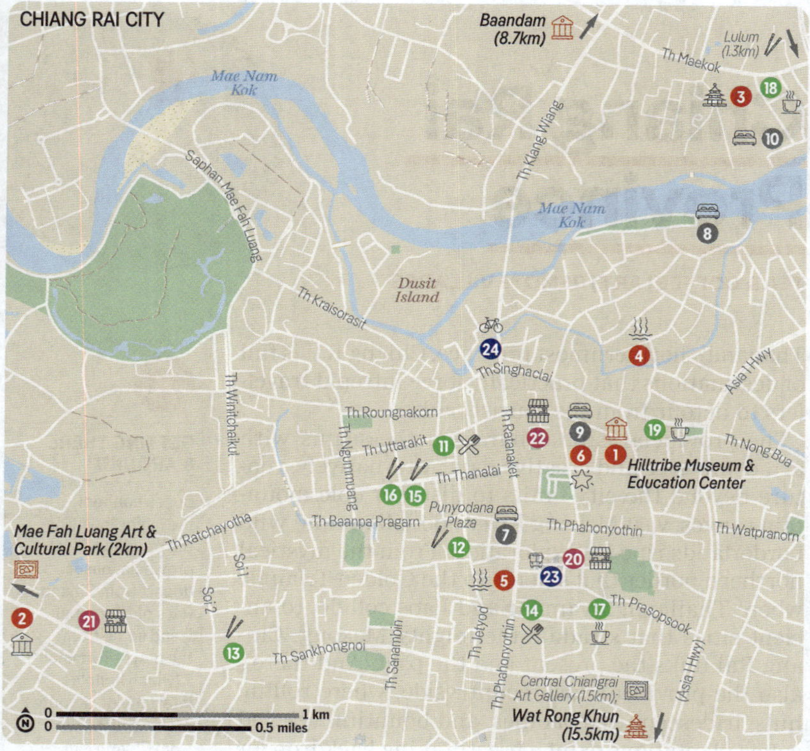

CHIANG RAI CITY

Baandam (8.7km)
Lulum (1.3km)
Th Maekok
Mae Nam Kok
Saphan Mae Fah Luang
Th Klang Wiang
Mae Nam Kok
Dusit Island
Th Kraisorasit
Th Singhaclai
Asia 1 Hwy
Th Winitchaikul
Th Roungnakorn
Th Ngummuang
Th Uttarakit
Th Ratanaket
Th Thanalai
Hilltribe Museum & Education Center
Th Nong Bua
Punyodana Plaza
Th Baanpa Pragarn
Th Phahonyothin
Th Watpranorn
Mae Fah Luang Art & Cultural Park (2km)
Th Ratchayotha
Soi 1
Soi 2
Th Prasopsook
Th Sankhongnoi
Th Sanambin
Th Jetyod
Th Phahonyothin
(Asia 1 Hwy)
Central Chiangrai Art Gallery (1.5km);
Wat Rong Khun (15.5km)
0 1 km
0 0.5 miles

and Michael Jackson) stand out against the glittering white. Don't miss the compound's all-gold toilet cubicles.

Next on the list is **Wat Rong Suea Ten**, or the Blue Temple. Located in town, and ditching the usual red, golds and greens of traditional temple design, this one has adopted an entirely indigo approach, with every wall, pillar, ceiling and statute painted a stunning shade of royal blue. Inside, visitors come in droves to pray to the magnificent pure-white Buddha statue illuminated in bright blue light. Like the White Temple, its construction is relatively new, created by none other than Chalermchai's own student. Look closely and you'll see lots of similarities.

DRINKING IN CHIANG RAI: BEST CAFES

Kalae Coffee: This Chiang Rai cafe has its own plantation near Mae Sai, in Chiang Rai Province, and beans are also roasted in-house. *8am-5pm*

Couple Cups: Pint-sized cafe in Chiang Rai serving coffee blends that use Thai beans. *7.30am-5pm Mon-Fri, 8am-5pm Sat & Sun*

1:2 Chiangrai Brew: Smell your coffee while it's being roasted at this minimalist-feeling former warehouse in the provincial capital. *8am-5pm*

LOCAL Coffee: Located south of Chiang Rai on the way to the White Temple is this tiny, friendly coffee bar that centres local beans. *8am-4pm Mon-Sat*

HIGHLIGHTS
1 Hilltribe Museum & Education Center

SIGHTS
2 Oub Kham Museum
3 Wat Rong Suea Ten

ACTIVITIES
4 Baan Gita
5 Monmueang Lanna Massage
6 PDA Tours

SLEEPING
7 Bed & Bike Poshtel
8 Legend of Chiang Rai
9 Nak Nakara Hotel
10 Riva Vista

EATING
11 Evening Market
12 Khao Soi Phor Jai
13 Nam Ngiao Pa Suk
14 Namngiew Panual
15 Rosprasert Muslim Food
16 Si Biao Panich Bakery & Breakfast

DRINKING & NIGHTLIFE
17 1:2 Chiangrai Brew
18 Bike Coffee
19 Couple Cups
see 12 Kalae Coffee

SHOPPING
20 Night Bazaar
21 Thanon Khon Muan
22 Walking Street

TRANSPORT
23 Bus Terminal 1
24 Fat Free Bike Shop

Last on the list is **Baandam** *(80฿)*, the sprawling residence and brainchild of the late legendary artist Thawan Duchanee, located 10km north of Chiang Rai. Despite being dubbed the 'Black Temple', it is actually the only place on this list that is not a temple, although the main art hall could easily be mistaken for one. Enter to explore a complex of halls, huts and structures all painted black and furnished from floor to ceiling in buffalo antlers, deer pelts and crocodile skins. Phallus-filled bathrooms and breast-shaped echo chambers add humour to this otherwise dark living museum.

TOP TIP

Chiang Rai Province is home to some of the more intriguing border crossings in Thailand, but these are subject to closures. Be sure to check in advance if the border you want to cross is actually open.

Exploring the City's Many Markets

Get your fill of food or souvenirs

Founded in 1262 by King Mengrai as he expanded his Lanna Kingdom, from the start Chiang Rai was destined to be a hub for travelling traders. Today, that trade-city energy continues to exist, now in the form of large shopping districts and even larger weekend markets that give Bangkok's places of commerce a run for their money.

Saturday's **walking street** is the city's largest pop-up market, taking over Thanalai Rd from 5pm until late. Here you'll find vendors peddling everything under the sun, from clothing and toys to handicrafts. You could also stitch together an entire meal from the food items sold here, which range from regional snacks and sweets to international-leaning junk food. While the market runs, the nearby city square comes alive with music concerts, events and a type of Thai line dancing led by the city's elders who just can't resist grabbing your arm and pulling you in. Escape the mayhem by making a beeline to the **clock tower**, which lights up and 'dances' to music on the hour between 7pm and 8pm.

EATING IN CHIANG RAI: OUR PICKS

Locus Native Food Lab: Refined, upscale takes on northern cuisine by a chef from the region. West of Chiang Rai, reservations required. *5.30-10pm Mon-Sat* ฿฿฿

Namngiew Panual: This semi-concealed gem serves a mix of Vietnamese and northern Thai dishes. *9.30am-9pm Fri-Wed* ฿

Nam Ngiao Pa Suk: This popular place does big bowls of *ka nom jeen nam ngee o* (broth of pork or beef and tomatoes over rice noodles). *9.30am-2.30pm Tue-Sun* ฿

Lulum: This riverside restaurant can boast a fat menu of northern Thai dishes and seating on a floating dining room. *10.30am-8.15pm* ฿

NORTHERN NOSH

Some must-try northern Thai dishes.

Gaang ho Leftover curry, vegetables and herbs fried with glass noodles and pickled bamboo.

Kaab moo Deep-fried pork crackling, an obligatory pairing with northern Thai-style dips.

Khao soi Wheat and egg noodles in a curry broth.

Larb koo a Literally 'fried *larb*', this dish takes the region's famous Thai minced-meat 'salad' and fries it with a mixture of dried spices.

Naam Fermented raw pork, a sour delicacy that tastes much better than it sounds.

Nam prik num Green chillies, shallots and garlic that are grilled then mashed into a stringy and spicy paste.

Nam prik ong Another Thai-style dip, this one combining minced pork, fermented soybeans and tomatoes.

Sai oo a A grilled pork sausage seasoned with fresh herbs.

ANIRUT THAILAND/SHUTTERSTOCK

Performers at Thanon Khon Muan market

Come Sunday evening, things tone down a notch with the **Thanon Khon Muan** market on San Khong Noi Rd. Here you'll find more traditional wares and cuisines, as well as a regular Lanna culture show that rotates performances throughout the year.

The least interesting of the lot is Chiang Rai's **Night Bazaar**, with its permanent market shops selling typical tourist souvenirs and its beer garden open every night.

The Ways of Mountain Tribes

Engage with Northern Thailand's minorities

Hill tribes are ubiquitous in the north, and Chiang Rai has one of the country's largest hill tribe populations, second only to Mae Hong Son. While their cultures are mostly celebrated, many are still stuck in a cycle of deadlock bureaucracy and dwindling natural resources that leave many with little to no opportunities.

Thankfully the rise of responsible tourism means people are now supporting local communities in ways that benefit rather than exploit. To learn about the issues surrounding northern Thailand's minority groups, a good starting point is Chiang Rai's nonprofit **Hilltribe Museum & Education Center** *(pdacr.org; 100฿)*, which offers a somewhat outdated crash-course in Thailand's tribes and the issues they face. A visit begins with a 20-minute slide show on Thailand's hill tribes, followed by a self-guided exploration among exhibits that include the typical clothing of six major tribes, examples of bamboo usage, folk implements and other anthropological objects. Videos and exhibitions come in Thai, English, French, German and Japanese, with deeper-dive videos into harder topics on request.

Once informed, now it's time to hit the hills. **PDA Tours**, also based at Hilltribe Museum & Education Centre, organises day trips and trekking for groups of up to 12 that visit various Akha, Hmong, Karen and Lisu villages in Chiang Rai Province. We did a day walk with them and had a great time slashing through jungle, visiting waterfalls and eating an Akha-style lunch. Sustainably minded hill-tribe village visits, homestays and trekking excursions in Chiang Rai Province can also be arranged via **Thailand Hill Tribe Holidays** *(thailand hilltribeholidays.com)* or **Akha Hill House** *(akhahill.com)*.

If you don't want to go the guided route, simply hire some wheels or charter a taxi and head to **Ban Ruam Mit**. Located 20km northwest of Chiang Rai, the name translates as 'mixed village', and is an accurate description of this riverside community that's home to ethnic groups including Thai, Karen, Lisu and Akha. It's as simple as basing yourself at a local guesthouse and heading out on self-guided day walks along the numerous country roads and trails, although some knowledge of Thai will help.

Rural Escape

Experience the countryside without leaving city limits

Cross to the northern side of Mae Nam Kok and the vibe quickly shifts. Although still part of Chiang Rai city proper, the atmosphere is rural, and a string of low-key destinations make the area an ideal destination for a lazy bike or motorcycle ride.

After spanning Chiang Rai's Mae Fah Luang Bridge (located just northwest of the city centre), turn left on Thawirat Soi 5. The north side of this road is home to a handful of small, cliffside caves outfitted with Buddha statues, most of which can be visited by ascending a few steps. Continue along the same road for 3km more and you'll reach **Wat Tham Phra**, a cavern by Mae Nam Kok containing a tiny but active Buddhist temple, a lone monk and numerous cats. The temple was one of several destinations on a visit to the region by King Rama V in the early 20th century. There's a riverside Buddhist monument on a large rock and even a riverside walking/bicycling track. On the opposite bank of the river is **Chiang Rai Beach**, a popular destination for bathing during the hot season.

Touring the City on Two Wheels

Cycling tours around Chiang Rai Province

Chiang Rai, with its endless rice paddies, jutting hills and paved roads, has an excellent landscape for any type of rider.

Chiang Rai Bicycle Tour *(chiangraibicycletour.com)* is the city's best cycling operator with a wide range of tours. Highlights include tea plantations, buffalo trails, mountain biking down waterfalls, long-tail boat rides and hot springs, all within riding distance of the city. It offers trailers, baby seats, tandems and child-sized bikes for families and larger groups. It also goes further afield with multiday tours spanning 40km to 60km per day over gravel and road routes that

SO YOU WANT TO DO A TREK?

A trek to a hill-tribe village is something of a rite of passage for many visitors to northern Thailand. Yet expectations and reality don't always align. For starters, these days, many of northern Thailand's ethnic minorities live in modern homes, and hill-tribe dress isn't so different from standard Thai – or Western – clothing.

That said, the day-to-day lives of the region's minority groups are most likely different from yours. Standards of hygiene when it comes to food preparation or bedding are likely to be unlike what you grew up with. There's little privacy in a hill-tribe village. And the day begins very, very early in the morning. If you acknowledge these elements and roll with them, you're likelier to have a good time on your trek.

CHIANG RAI'S COFFEE SCENE

Lee Ayu Chuepa is the founder of **Akha Ama Coffee**, which serves coffee grown in remote Akha villages in Chiang Rai Province. *@akhaamacoffee*

I've been involved with coffee since I was about 18 years old. At that time, coffee wasn't something that was given value by the community.

I started by making people in the area drink coffee; they used to drink instant coffee! I told them about aromas and body, and asked them to describe what they tasted. They learned very quickly. The coffee started to get better and evolve.

Chiang Rai coffee is really bright and refreshing, with lively acidity and good body. There's a full range of choices. It's floral, fruity or citrusy – bergamot, which really amplifies the refreshing, crisp acidity.

often loop as far away as the Golden Triangle (p211) and even into Laos via Chiang Khong (p217).

If you're a cyclist looking for a tribe, **Bike Coffee** is the best place to meet other cyclists and get the lowdown on exciting routes. It's a cafe and community hub, conveniently located next to Blue Temple. **Fat Free Bike Shop** has bikes for rent and can organise custom tours by appointment, while apps like Bikemap and Strava have a handsome range of routes that can be ridden independently. Just rent a bike, clip in your shoes and let the road take you.

If you're starting from Chiang Mai, **Spice Roads** *(spiceroads.com)* has cycling tours that connect the two provinces, avoiding highways and busy roads for a scenic route left largely unseen by regular road travel.

Fire-Fuelled Wellness, Lanna-Style

Experience a traditional fire massage

Yam Khang is a massage technique found only in Chiang Rai and Chiang Mai, first adapted by the Lanna people who incorporated oils, herbs, medicines and unorthodox massage postures. Despite a recent revival, the number of places that perform this fiery massage can still be counted on two hands.

The word *khang* is the local name for the sharp end of an iron plough that holds almost spiritual significance to farmers in the region. The tool itself is often revered as magical and sacred, seen as something that helps grow good rice and feed the world. The iron alloy is also known for its mineral properties that are said to treat disease. In the past, parents would soak the *khang* in water and give it to children who had a sore throat, while town doctors believed the healing heat from a warmed *khang* would penetrate deeper than other metals. Today, retired *khang* are used for the Yam Khang massage, which is believed to leach iron into the oils and add additional benefit to the patient.

Hong Hom Paya *(facebook.com/P.Putan)*, known in English as the Wisdom Learning Center & Lanna Medical Treatment, is one of few locations that not only perform, but also teach this ancient practice. Hidden in the outskirts of Chiang Rai city, this monk- and nun-led commune focuses on the traditional healing techniques of Lanna through community learning and experiences for visitors. The massage, performed entirely with the feet, starts with the therapist preparing a charcoal fire that warms a *khang* and a bowl of oil. When ready, a pole is used to balance while a foot is dipped into the oils, tapped on the *khang* to heat and set it alight, then quickly applied to the body to transfer heat and pressure to the back, legs and arms.

The laid-back approach is contagious so expect to lose hours to what is advertised as a one-hour massage. It also offers other northern Thai treatments such as *tok sen* massage, sand burial, chicken-coop steam therapy and even a local form of chiropractic bone alignment.

SUPALEKA_P/SHUTTERSTOCK

Cyclist, Chiang Rai

Dive into the Art Scene

Ancient and contemporary art in Chiang Rai

As the home of two internationally acclaimed artists, Thawan Duchanee and Chalermchai Kositpipat, the host of 2023's Thailand Biennale, as well as an aspiring contingent of arts, Chiang Rai is slowly working towards becoming a world-class art city, and it's possible to spend a full day hopping between galleries and museums.

If you already have the White, Blue and Black Temples (p203) ticked off your list, head to the **Mae Fah Luang Art & Culture Park** *(maefahluang.org/en/mae-fah-luang-art-and-cultural-park; 200฿)*, the city's other large-scale art piece. This vast, meticulously landscaped compound includes antique and contemporary art, Buddhist temples and other structures. **Haw Kaew** has a permanent collection of mostly teak-based artefacts and art from across the former Lanna region, as well as a temporary exhibition room. **Haw Kham**, a temple-like tower built in 1984 from the remains of 32 wooden houses, is arguably the park's centrepiece. The immense size of the structure, with its Buddha image seemingly hovering over white sand (the latter imported from Ko Samet) and its sacred, candlelit aura, culminates in a vibe not unlike the place of worship of an indigenous cult.

CHIANG RAI'S BEST SPAS

Monmueang Lanna Massage: Inner-city spa with midrange prices and treatment packages that incorporate local herbs and precious metals.

Salabran: 'Bathe' in natural enzymes and sweat out toxins in a fermented-rice-bran bath that naturally sits at 40°C.

Museflower Spa: Wellness retreat west of Chiang Rai city centre; multiday yoga and meditation packages also available.

Baan Gita: B&B and wellness space offering self-care through holistic therapies and massage. Laughter yoga, too.

Anantara Golden Triangle Elephant Camp & Resort: For a more luxurious Yam Khang experience, guests can enjoy the same treatment as it's included in the price of a room.

EATING IN CHIANG RAI: OUR PICKS

Khao Soi Phor Jai: Serves mild but delicious bowls of the eponymous curry noodle dish, as well as a few other northern Thai staples. *7am-3.30pm* ฿

Rosprasert Muslim Food: Shophouse restaurant by the mosque on Th Itsaraphap; Thai-Muslim favourites, like Thai-style chicken biryani. *7am-8pm Mon-Sat* ฿

Si Biao Panich Bakery & Breakfast: Handsome wooden building housing an old-school Thai-Chinese cafe. Lots of breakfast options. *7.30am-1pm Wed-Mon* ฿฿

Evening Market: Self-caterers: consider Chiang Rai's evening market, which has lots of local dishes to go. Located near the old clock tower. *3-7pm Tue-Sun* ฿

A MILLION RICE FIELDS

The Lanna Kingdom (Lanna means 'million rice fields') once covered most of northern Thailand and parts of Myanmar, Laos and southern China. Its final capital city was Chiang Mai, built in 1296, with earlier capitals dotted across the north. During its existence, it was host to a key trading route that connected China's Silk Road with Myanmar seaports. After centuries of vibrant cultural expansion, the kingdom was invaded and became a Myanmar vassal state before being liberated by Siam and eventually dissolved into provinces of respective countries by the late 1800s. Lanna culture has seen a revival in recent years, with old traditions, languages and practices brought back from extinction, now a defining feature of northern Thailand culture.

SAIKOSP/SHUTTERSTOCK

Oub Kham Museum

In town, the **Oub Kham Museum** *(300฿)* is a somewhat zany private museum that houses an impressive collection of items from virtually every corner of the former Lanna Kingdom. The items, some of which truly are one of a kind, range from a monkey-bone food taster used by Lanna royalty to an impressive carved throne from Chiang Tung, Myanmar. Guided tours (available in English and included in the entrance fee) are obligatory and include a walk through a gilded artificial cave holding several Buddha statues, complete with disco lights and fake torches! The grounds of the museum are equally kitschy and include a huge golden *naga* (a mythical serpent-like being with magical powers), waterfalls and fountains.

For a taste of today, the two-storey **Chiangrai Contemporary Art Museum** showcases art collections from the Chiang Rai Artist Fund, Thai Artist Exhibition and international artists. It is also an artistic hub, with restaurants, shops and art workshops. And Chiang Rai's mall even has a gallery: **Central Chiangrai Art Gallery** has a permanent exhibition with work from Thai artists to buy and take home.

EATING IN CHIANG RAI PROVINCE: OUR PICKS

Sue Hai: Specialities at this Chinese restaurant in Doi Mae Salong include local mushrooms fried with soy sauce and flash-fried local greens. *8am-9pm* ฿

Salima: Tasty Muslim-Chinese dishes in Doi Mae Salong, including a rich Yunnan-style beef curry and a deliciously tart, spicy tuna and fresh tea leaf salad. *9am-8pm* ฿

Khao Soi Islam: An old-school, Muslim-run, delicious *khao soi* (wheat noodles in a curry broth) shack just outside of Mae Sai. *7am-5pm* ฿

Khao Soi Sipseongbbanna: Chiang Khong's take on *khao soi* replaces curry broth with clear soup topped with rich, spicy minced pork. *8.30am-3.30pm* ฿

A Legacy of Opium

Visit the Golden Triangle

In historical terms, the Golden Triangle refers to an area stretching thousands of square kilometres into Myanmar, Laos, Thailand and China's Yunnan Province, within which the opium trade was once prevalent. From the early 20th century to the 1980s, this region was the world's biggest grower of *Papaver somniferum*, the poppy that produces opium. Poverty and lack of infrastructure and governance in the largely rebel-controlled areas meant that growing poppies and transporting opium proceeded virtually unchecked, eventually making its way around the world as refined heroin.

Today, the Golden Triangle essentially refers to the village of Sob Ruak, where Thailand, Myanmar and Laos kiss borders in the middle of the Mekong River. It's a bucket-list destination for many, but one that often leaves travellers feeling a little underwhelmed with its megaphone-led group tours, souvenir stalls and tour buses. A better approach is to spend a half-day learning about the history of the opium trade at the village's two museums.

One kilometre north of Sob Ruak, the Mae Fah Luang Foundation has established the 5600-sq-metre **Hall of Opium** *(120฿)*. The multimedia exhibitions include a fascinating history of opium, as well as engaging and informative displays on the effects of opium abuse on individuals and society. And in Sob Ruak, the small but informative and recently renovated **House of Opium** *(50฿)* features historical displays pertaining to opium culture. Exhibits include the various implements used in the planting, harvesting, use and trade of the *Papaver somniferum* resin, including pipes, weights and scales.

If you want to linger, boat trips out over the water can be chartered from booths at **Phra Chiang Saen Si Phaendin**, the massive Buddha statue overlooking the junction of boundaries, but they no longer stop at any visa-free destinations in Laos or Myanmar. The conspicuous casinos on the Laos side can technically be reached, but authorities and locals both advise against it, calling it a hive of illegality run by immune mafia cartels.

Sleep in a Bubble among Elephants

Staying at the Anantara Golden Triangle Elephant Camp

As one of only two five-star resorts in the area (the other being **Four Seasons Tented Camp**), **Anantara Golden Triangle Elephant Camp & Resort** is the Golden Triangle's golden star. Looking out near where the Ruak meets the Mekong, it boasts Lanna-inspired architecture designed by the legendary Thai architect Mom Tri, and authentic northern Thai experiences from spa treatments to sunset soirees. But what makes this place noteworthy is the work it does to help preserve and support elephants through its very own Golden Triangle Asian Elephant Foundation (GTAEF), setting a benchmark for elephant welfare across Asia.

THE MIGHTY MEKONG

As the world's 12th-longest river (sixth-longest in Asia), the Mekong originates in the Tibetan Plateau and flows some 4350km through China, Myanmar, Laos, Thailand and Cambodia before reaching the sea at the Mekong Delta in Vietnam. This vital waterway sustains over 70 million people by providing food and irrigation for rice cultivation over vast swaths of land known as 'Asia's Rice Bowl'. For locals, it has immense religious significance, evident through elaborate Loy Krathong festivals and obsession with the elusive Naga Fireballs, believed to be the breath of a mythical river serpent. Unfortunately, deforestation and hydropower-dam construction upstream now pose a grave threat to the river's future and the lives of millions who depend on it.

DO RIGHT BY THE ELEPHANTS

John Roberts, Group Director of Sustainability & Conservation, Minor Hotels and Director of Elephants & Conservation, GTAEF, shares his ideal sustainable elephant attraction.

Elephant experiences have improved a lot, with many places trying hard to improve standards for the elephants. If you want to see elephants, go for those audited by organisations such as Asian Captive Elephant Standards or Global Spirit. Even if not fully accredited, opening their doors to scrutiny is good evidence they are trying their best to do it right. Failing that, look for space, green areas to roam, natural habitats and other elephants to socialise with. What's important is how elephants are treated behind the scenes, which, if hidden from view, is probably a bad sign.

Its award-winning elephant camp lets guests observe and connect with elephants in their natural environment, learn about customs and be taught by live-in elephant vets. Proceeds from each stay go towards their care while the foundation works hard to assist captive elephants, improving elephant welfare and overall conservation across the region. GTAEF also offers free veterinary care to any elephant in the region and conducts regular research and welfare training projects off-site.

Its high price point is money well spent for those who can afford it, with up-close and personal experiences with the resort's more than 20 pachyderms that include walk-alongs, accompanying mahouts going about their daily tasks, and informal courses in elephant education. Or you can go all in and spend a night sleeping among the elephants in a dusk-to-dawn jungle bubble.

Myanmar by Proxy

The Thai side of Mae Sai

Thailand's northernmost town, **Mae Sai**, is best known as a border crossing to the Myanmar town of Tachileik and the captivating Shan State that extends beyond. Unfortunately, at press time non-locals were no longer allowed to cross the border here. Despite this, the Thai side still offers a taste of Myanmar, making it a fun place to spend a couple of hours for those interested in Thailand's neighbour.

Get your bearings at **Wat Phra That Doi Wao**, a hilltop temple with a **skywalk** *(50฿)* that grants amazing views over Mae Sai and across the border. In line with Chiang Rai's other colour-themed temples, Wat Phra That Doi Wao is done up almost entirely in purple.

Back on ground level, it's fun to explore the various market *sois* that snake under and out from the Mae Sai border crossing itself. There's lots of Burmese housewares, medicine, clothing and produce for sale here, culminating in an atmosphere that's very much like a village in Myanmar's Shan State. Soi 4 is home to a small gem market, while scattered among the lanes vendors sell Shan and Burmese food.

A Taste of China

Cross-cultural borders at Doi Mae Salong

To experience China without a visa, head to **Doi Mae Salong**, an atmospheric village perched among the back hills of Chiang Rai. Spanning unique cultural legacies, delicious food and Thailand's premier tea plantations, it's a great place to escape for a few days and try your hand at self-guided exploration.

The culture of Yunnan, in southern China, is dominant here as the village was settled by Chinese soldiers fleeing the communist revolution in 1949. Locals talk in a mix of tribal, Thai and Chinese dialects and the food here is distinctly more Chinese than Thai. The **Chinese Martyr's Memorial Museum** and the **Tomb of General Tuan** do a good job in recounting this history. From the village's highest peak you'll find **Phra**

KLANARONG CHITMUNG/SHUTTERSTOCK

101 Tea Plantation

Borommathat Chedi, located 1500m above sea level where it overlooks rows of tea plantations as far as the eye can see.

Every morning, a tiny but busy and vibrant **morning market** convenes at the T-intersection near Shin Sane Guest House. The market attracts town residents and hill peoples from the surrounding districts and is worth waking up early for.

The best time to visit Doi Mae Salong is debatable. During the rainy season (July to October) the tea is bushy and green, while winter (November to January) brings lower temperatures and Himalayan cherry blossoms, which line the roads into the village with striking *sakura*-pink flowers.

Thailand's 'Must-Tea' Destination

Cop a cuppa at Chiang Rai's tea plantations

When Chinese soldiers fled to Thailand in 1949, they brought with them a fondness for drinking – and the know-how to grow – tea, a legacy that persists in and around Doi Mae Salong.

Notable estates near town include the **101 Tea Plantation**, where you can taste some of the world's best oolong teas, and **Wang Put Tan Tea Plantation**, which took Grand Gold for its 'Khiri Black Tea' in the World Green Tea Contest 2021, and which has a lovely elevated platform for sipping.

If you don't have a night to spend in the hills, the district of Mae Chan is a little closer to the provincial capital and is where you can find **Choui Fong Tea**, arguably Chiang Rai's most popular tea plantation, and where you'll find sweeping terraced tea fields, interactive harvesting activities and countless tea blends to try out.

DOI MAE SALONG'S TOP TEAS

Oolong #17: Known as winter tea; harvested on winter mornings when the dew is present, absorbing into the leaves.

Oolong #12: The region's most award-winning tea, with a mild and refreshing taste. Locals call it Jin Xuan.

Red oolong: Red, slightly sour tea with naturally low caffeine. Made by extended fermentation of oolong #12 leaves.

Osmanthus oolong: Gentle blend of oolong tea and the white flowers of the osmanthus shrub; earthy yet floral aroma.

Bai Yai green tea: Taken from older trees, this everyday leaf has a green-tea taste with all the health benefits.

Jin Xuan black tea: Oolong #12 is fermented, resulting in a dark cup with rich and nutty tea bloom notes.

KHUN SA

Undoubtedly the single most infamous player in the Golden Triangle drug trade was Khun Sa. From the late 1960s, Khun Sa's private army, ex-KMT fighters in Doi Mae Salong and other warlords in the region formed a partnership that would eventually claim a virtual monopoly of the world's opium trade.

In 1988, after having been the victim of two unsuccessful assassination attempts, Khun Sa offered to sell his entire crop of opium to the Australian government for A$50 million a year, claiming that this would essentially end the world's entire illegal trade in heroin. He made a similar offer to the US, but he was dismissed by both. With a US DEA bounty of US$2 million on his head, in 1996 Khun Sa gave himself up to Burmese officials. They refused to extradite him to the US and Khun Sa died a free man in Yangon in 2007.

CHANCHAI DUANGDOOSAN/SHUTTERSTOCK

Phu Chi Fah

In Khun Sa's Footsteps

Hide out like a drug lord in Ban Thoet Thai

Located in a narrow river valley about 20km north of Mae Salong, **Ban Thoet Thai** is a multi-ethnic village with a remote, border-town vibe and an infamous recent past. It's delightfully off the beaten track, and makes a fun escape for a night or two.

The village is best known for having served as one of the bases of Khun Sa, the most notorious of the Golden Triangle's narco-warlords. Between the 1960s and '80s, the half-Shan, half-Chinese Khun Sa commanded a 20,000-strong army and dominated the opium and heroin trade in the Golden Triangle, a largely lawless region straddling the borders of Thailand, Myanmar, China and Laos. Rough displays on the so-called Opium King can be found at his former headquarters, today known as **Khun Sa Old Camp**, located about 500m north of the market area up a winding track. You'll probably have to ask for the key from the groundskeeper, and don't miss the VIP Parlour with its creepy life-sized model of Khun Sa.

Ban Thoet Thai was also allegedly the first settlement of Akha in Thailand. Today, it's also home to many Shan and Chinese, as well as Thai Lue, Lahu, Hmong, Lua and Lisu, and its **morning market** is one of the more exotic in the region, with items from the surrounding jungles, vendors selling Shan dishes, and ingredients trucked over from Myanmar and China.

Where the Sky Meets the Earth

Seek serenity atop Phu Chi Fah

Towering over Laos like a pulpit in the sky is **Phu Chi Fah**, a peak in the Doi Pha Mon mountain range. Its name, which translates to 'the mountain that points to the sky', alludes to its iconic shape.

At 1628m above sea level, the views are breathtaking. Although open all day, most visitors opt for an early-morning hike to catch the sunrise and witness morning mist blanket the land below. From 5am, *sorng taa ou* at the trailhead take you most of the way for 80฿, stopping a mere 400m before the summit. The hike takes around 20 minutes and can get steep in places, so be sure to go equipped as there are no shops if you run out of water. The trail is closed during the rainy season when it's dangerously slippery and leech-infested.

Geographically, the peak technically crosses the Laos border, although it can only be accessed from the Thai side. A small border marker marks the spot where you can take pleasure stepping into Laos without a visa. If you're there between February and March, the **Phu Chi Fah Forest Park**, which you walk through to reach the summit, erupts in a cascade of white cherry blossoms.

Coffee Country

Explore the mountaintop attractions of the Doi Tung area

Red and barren just half a century ago due to severe deforestation and militia-led opium production, the mountain range of Doi Tung, in far-northern Chiang Rai Province, is now home to a lush, fertile and thriving farm community that is both peaceful and prosperous.

Pioneering this change was the Doi Tung Development Fund – a royal project that aimed to free ethnic tribes from poverty through education, infrastructure and alternative crop production. While travelling in Thailand, look out for the **Doi Tung** *(doitung.com)* brand. It's best known for its coffee and macadamia products, which continue to fund the development of this community today, and are harvested from the mountain's almost four million nut and coffee trees.

Tourism now plays a big part in this area, and there's a spread of places to see and visit across the mountainside, all of which require your own wheels to reach. These include the 900-year-old temple **Wat Phra That Doi Tung**. **Doi Tung Royal Villa** *(90฿)*, originally a residence for the Princess Mother to oversee the project, now a museum dedicated to her. Near the ticket booth is a small **Hill Tribe Market** selling handicrafts, clothing and locally sourced produce that's also worth checking out. There's also a **Doi Tung Cafe**, or you can make your visit a sleepover by booking a room in the **Doi Tung Lodge**.

And further north is the **Mae Fah Luang Arboretum** *(90฿)*, where old opium fields have been replanted with native flora and other rare species.

Retrace Thailand's Famous Cave Rescue

The place where the Wild Boars were saved

You saw it on the news, now visit where it all happened. **Tham Luang Cave**, the very cave that in 2018 trapped 12 young boys and their football coach (dubbed the Wild Boars), triggering a race against time to save their lives that drew worldwide attention, is now open to visitors.

THE GIANT MEKONG CATFISH

The Mekong River stretch that forms a border of Chiang Rai Province is a traditional habitat for the *plaa beuk* (giant Mekong catfish, *Pangasianodon gigas* to ichthyologists), the largest freshwater fish in the world. A full-size *plaa beuk* can measure 2m to 3m in length and can weigh up to 300kg. Although the adult fish have only been found in certain stretches of the Mekong near Chiang Khong, it's thought that the fish begin life in China's Qinghai Province (where the Mekong originates) on the Tibetan Plateau and swim all the way to the middle Mekong, where they spend much of their adulthood. Today, the *plaa beuk* is on the Convention on International Trade in Endangered Species (CITES) list of endangered species, and the fishing of it has been banned since 2006.

RECAPPING THE RESCUE

In 2018 the world watched as a dramatic rescue mission unfolded at Tham Luang Cave. Inside, a group of 12 boys and their coach were trapped, forced deeper and deeper inside by rising water from heavy monsoon rain.

The ensuing rescue operation – deemed one of the most challenging and complex in history – involved a multinational team of expert divers, rescuers and volunteers who, over 17 days, managed to locate the boys some 3km deep inside the cave, supply them with food and ultimately guide them to safety through dozens of flooded passages.

The successful rescue mission amazed the world, showing the true power of human resilience, determination and collaboration.

Local officials have spent the last few years improving the site to make it suitable for tourists, creating an immersive experience that takes you into the first few chambers of the cave, sharing stories of heroism and fast-thinking ingenuity along the way. Thick power and communication lines used in the rescue have been preserved as a memory, along with the table, chairs and whiteboard used by the rescue team in the back cavern. At its entrance, a small collection of artefacts, including the boys' bikes and backpacks, still remains.

Of all the caves in Thailand, this one is especially well maintained with handrails on the pathways, soft lighting tucked behind rocks and a pleasant absence of guano. Entrance to **Tham Luang Khun Nam Nang Non National Park** is free, but visitors must pay for a shuttle bus that runs between the car park, cave entrance and **Kun Nam Emerald Pool**.

Outside, the easily missed memorial statue to the only person to perish during the mission – former Navy SEAL Saman Kunan – is a solemn tribute in what was otherwise a flawless rescue operation.

The cave is closed during the wet season, from July to September.

The Good Old Days

Time travel to ancient Lanna in Chiang Saen

The calm riverside town of **Chiang Saen** may not look much on a map, but it's actually an ancient capital of the almighty Lanna Kingdom, a regional empire founded in the 12th century that once stretched as far north as Xishuangbanna in China. Evidence of this ancient kingdom is still visible today in Chiang Saen via rugged stone *chedi,* temple ruins and earthen city ramparts littering the landscape, making it a smart overnight stay to break up a journey across Chiang Rai Province.

The somewhat dated and dusty **Chiang Saen National Museum** *(120฿)* is the natural starting place to grasp the local history, granting access to an impressive display of artefacts from the ancient kingdom, along with more modern exhibitions on hill tribes and the Mekong River.

Practically next door, **Wat Chedi Luang** has a 58m-tall Lanna-era *chedi* that is in surprisingly good condition given its age, and a *vihara* with a modern roof, the latter giving a perspective on what these structures would have looked like back in the day. A short walk away, the compound that includes **Wat Pa Sak** *(80฿)* is home to Chiang Saen's most impressive ruins. Although they may not compete with the likes of Sukhothai (p240), they offer a rare glimpse into the past. The name means 'Temple of the Teak Forest' and was coined by the founder of Chiang Saen, King Saen Phu, who planted 300 teak trees when it was built. There are also admission-free ruins scattered through the town, such as **Wat Athi Ton Kaeo**, **Wat Roi Khong** and **Wat Pha Khao Pan**, and about 2.5km northwest of town on a hilltop, the remains of **Wat Phra That Chom Kitti** and **Wat Chom Chaeng**.

MUSICPHONE/SHUTTERSTOCK

Wat Pa Sak

For something more modern, south of town, **Wat Phra That Pha Ngao** houses a breathtaking, contemporary teak and gold *hor trai* (manuscript depository) and a **skywalk** *(30฿)* that boasts views extending to the Mekong River and beyond.

Border Vibes

Straddle two countries in Chiang Khong

Perched on the Mekong River, **Chiang Khong** was historically an important market town for local hill peoples and for trade with northern Laos. Travellers have long passed through this settlement en route to and from Laos.

Since 2013, when a bridge over the Mekong River connecting Chiang Khong to Huay Xai in Laos was opened, fewer people are spending the night here. Nevertheless, there's still a small backpacker scene with quite a number of guesthouses and a few breezy, riverside restaurants. Head south of town to Hat Khrai, where the giant Mekong catfish (p215) used to be caught. Take in the campy monuments to the fish, order a Beerlao and watch the Mekong River roll by at riverside **Baan Pheung Rim Khong** restaurant. And on Wednesdays and Saturdays during the tourist season (from around November to May), Chiang Khong's main drag hosts a **walking street** market, which has a decent selection of local eats.

If you're collecting passport stamps, the Lao city of **Huay Xai** makes an easy visit for its French stronghold, Fort Carnot; Wat That Suvanna Pakham; and Muangkeo Market.

The bridge has made river travel largely an anachronism, but boats still run the nine-hour or two-day trip (depending on what kind of boat you book) to Luang Prabang – that is, unless more dams on the Mekong are built.

GETTING TO LAOS FROM CHIANG KHONG

Crossing the border into Laos at Chiang Khong is a breeze. The friendship bridge opens from 6am to 10pm and is rarely busy, taking just minutes to pass through immigration each side. If you are travelling by foot, note that shuttle buses across the river stop running at 8pm and walking across is prohibited. Laos visitor visas cost US$30 regardless of duration (one day up to 30 days maximum).

These days, non-locals are no longer allowed to cross the Mekong via boat at the old Bak Ferry Terminal long-tail boat crossing located in Chiang Khong town.

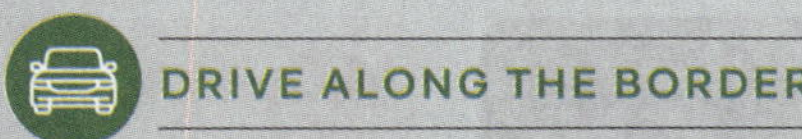

DRIVE ALONG THE BORDER

Steer along Route 1149, Thailand's high-altitude border road.

START	END	LENGTH
Mae Sai	Mae Sai	80km; six hours

Head south from ❶ **Mae Sai** and turn right on Tessaban Soi 5, which eventually turns into Rte 1149. Ascend astoundingly sharp turns and steep roads to reach ❷ **Ban Pha Mi**, a mountaintop village with a handful of coffee shops and homestays.

Continue south along the road, which functions as the border and passes Thai and Myanmar military checkpoints, to ❸ **Ban Pha Hee**, another sky-high village with more coffee shops and grand views over the Myanmar wilderness. South of here you'll start entering the various linked attractions that make up Doi Tung, a string of royally-initiated development programmes.

The first you'll reach is the ❹ **Mae Fah Luang Arboretum** (p215), where old opium fields have been replanted with native flora and other rare species. Continue south to ❺ **Doi Tung Royal Villa** (p215), the former residence of the current king's grandmother, where there's a small hill-tribe market selling handicrafts and food.

Wind down to Rte 1, turn left, and make a stop at ❻ **Tham Luang Cave** (p215), where in 2018, 12 young boys and their football coach were trapped for 15 days.

Continue north, back to Mae Sai, where you can close with a Burmese meal or stay a night before heading elsewhere.

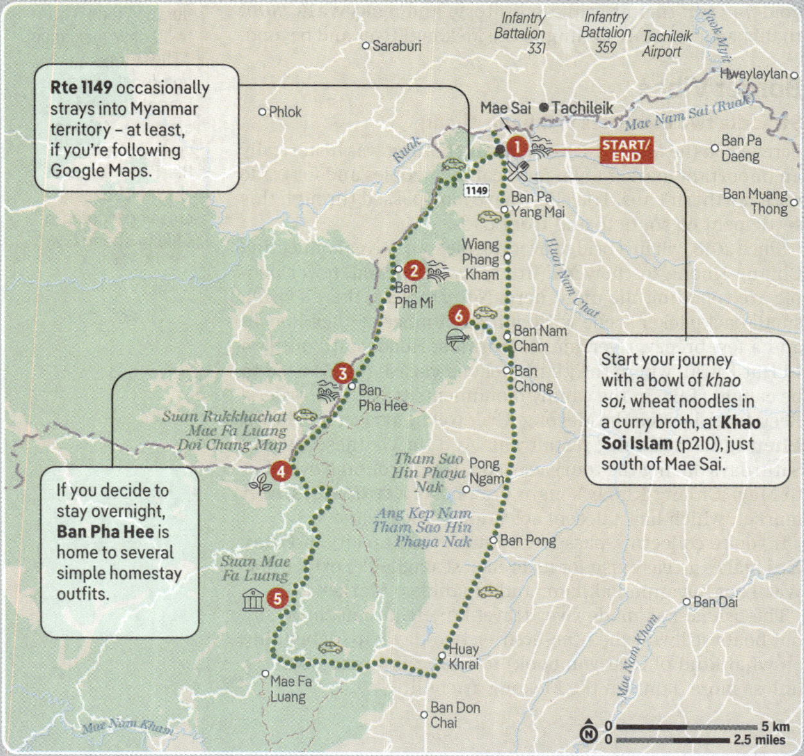

Rte 1149 occasionally strays into Myanmar territory – at least, if you're following Google Maps.

Start your journey with a bowl of *khao soi*, wheat noodles in a curry broth, at **Khao Soi Islam** (p210), just south of Mae Sai.

If you decide to stay overnight, **Ban Pha Hee** is home to several simple homestay outfits.

Saraburi
Phlok
Infantry Battalion 331
Infantry Battalion 359
Tachileik Airport
Hwaylaylan
Mae Sai
Tachileik
Mae Nam Sai (Ruak)
START/END
Ban Pa Daeng
Ban Muang Thong
Ban Pa Yang Mai
Wiang Phang Kham
Ban Pha Mi
Ban Nam Cham
Ban Chong
Ban Pha Hee
Suan Rukkhachat Mae Fa Luang Doi Chang Mup
Tham Sao Hin Phaya Nak
Pong Ngam
Ang Kep Nam Tham Sao Hin Phaya Nak
Ban Pong
Suan Mae Fa Luang
Ban Dai
Huay Khrai
Mae Fa Luang
Ban Don Chai
Mae Nam Kham
0 5 km
0 2.5 miles

Lampang Province

ELEPHANTS | ARCHITECTURE | CERAMICS

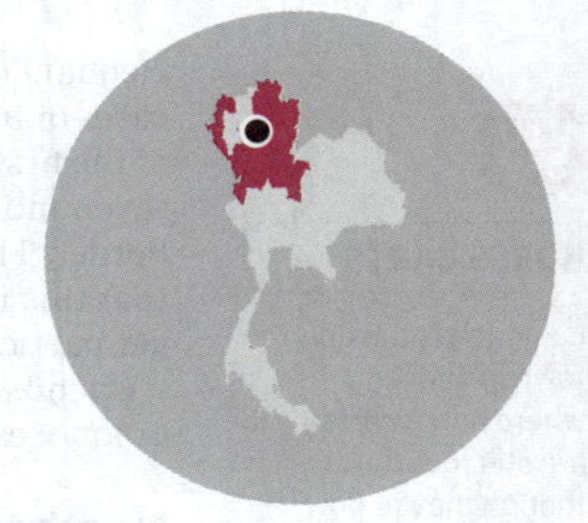

In recent years, Lampang's provincial capital has become a hip hang-out for coffee-drinking domestic hipsters and homecoming graduates looking to make their own city more vibrant. This has given way to a number of stylish venues and accommodation options in Lampang's historical quarter, which is now enjoying a mini-revival as a result. In the hills and valleys beyond, a rugged area formerly associated with logging, elephants and classic northern Thai temples define what tourist trail there is.

While foreigners have yet to discover Lampang en masse, it's home to a delightful mix of history and activities. Just a couple of hours from Chiang Mai, it's perfect for day trips or one-nighters, and a charming alternative to more well-travelled routes.

TOP TIP

If you're visiting Lampang from Chiang Mai, consider taking the train. The short journey cuts through one of the north's most scenic stretches before pulling into Lampang's historic train station.

Pachyderm Infirmary

Visit Lampang's elephant hospital

Rural Lampang Province is home to one of the world's only elephant-centred medical institutions. **Friends of the Asia Elephant Hospital** *(friendsoftheasianelephantfoundation.com)* is at the forefront of research development into elephant-specific healthcare and veterinary training. With a mission to provide healthcare to Thailand's 3000-plus captive elephants, the experts here are some of the best in the world. The centre will treat any sick elephant for free...as long as they can get there. It also operates a special sanctuary that acts as a hospice for old or badly injured elephants and training centre for

GETTING THERE & AROUND

Buses and minivans connect the provincial capital with villages, but the going is slow.

Renting a motorbike in Lampang is a challenge. Car rental is best done from Lampang Airport. There are a few **taxis** *(taxilampang24hrs.com/portal)* and Grab also operates in Lampang.

The bus station is a stop along many northern bus lines and it's easy to get from Lampang to just about anywhere else in northern Thailand.

Lampang's historic train station, built in Lanna-colonial British style in 1915, has semi-regular connections between Chiang Mai and Lampang that pass through some of the region's most beautiful landscapes.

The airport has direct flights to/from Bangkok.

HORSE CARTS

Lampang is the only town in Thailand where horse carts are still found, though they're now exclusively used by tourists. They were probably first introduced by the Shan, who settled in Lampang during the logging era. You can't miss the brightly coloured carts that drip with plastic flowers and are handled by Stetson-wearing drivers, although we don't endorse a ride.

elephant owners and mahouts to help reduce preventable diseases or injury. The hospital was also behind the construction of the first-ever elephant prosthetic leg for Mosha who, at just seven months old, lost a leg to a landmine on the Myanmar border. The hospital is open to visitors, but it's worth noting that this is a working facility; you can't touch or feed or even get particularly close to any of the elephants.

Friends of the Asia Elephant Hospital is located around 40km west of Lampang.

Northern Commerce

Take in the northern Thai pantry at Thung Kwian Market

Located about 30km west of Lampang, **Thung Kwian Market** is an expansive, roadside place of commerce that's a crash course in northern Thai food and handicrafts. At the perimeter, you'll see vendors selling mountains of deep-fried pork crackling, ideally paired with *nam prik num* (roast chilli 'dip') or other northern Thai–style dips. Go deeper, and you'll see butchers preparing buffalo meat and other vendors selling deep-fried silkworms. These aren't entirely unusual items at a northern Thai market, but in the old days Thung Kwian was associated with 'wild' proteins, a trade that these days has been driven underground.

If exotic produce isn't your thing, the market also has stalls selling northern Thai kitchenware, handicrafts and clothing.

Clay & Chickens

Lampang's legacy of ceramics

Lampang is home to clay-heavy soils and has long been an important place for the production of ceramics. Today, without a doubt the most famous ceramic item from Lampang is

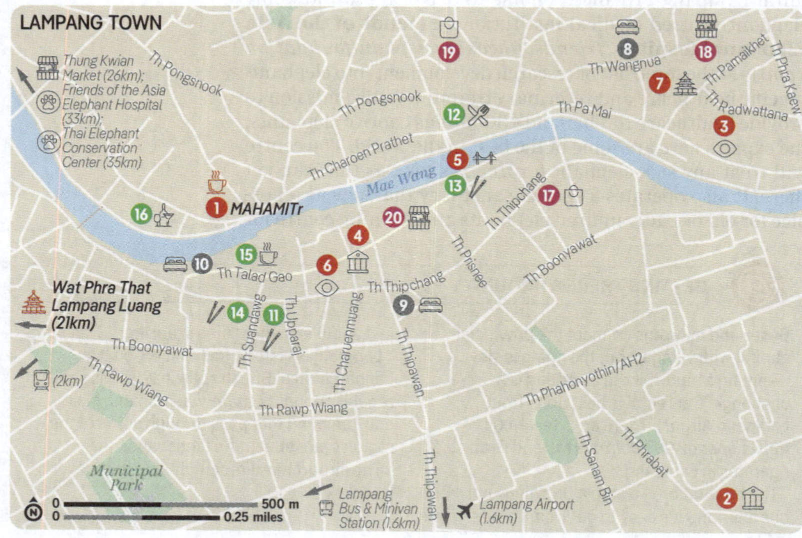

the so-called 'chicken bowl'. Although first introduced by Chinese merchants during the 1950s, the design is now ubiquitous across Thailand. Dhanabadee claims to be the originator of the design in Thailand, and today the company operates a **ceramic museum** *(dhanabadee.com)* with guided tours that span the history of the bowls and demonstrate how they are made. There's an attached workshop where you can paint and fire your own bowl to be sent to a Thai address a few days later and, of course, a gift shop were you can buy all manner of poultry-themed ceramics, including the classic chicken bowl.

If this has piqued an interest, venues for ceramics shopping in Lampang include **Indra Outlet**, the seemingly never-ending showrooms of the city's biggest ceramics producer, and the downright rustic by comparison **Ceramics Market**, located downtown and where cheap wholesale ceramics go for as little as 12฿ a pop.

And if you are in Lampang in December, look out for the city-wide **Ceramics Fair** that runs over the course of two weeks opposite the Big C. Booths and performances showcase the best in Lampang ceramics and offer hefty discounts on their most-prized wares.

13 MARCH: THAI ELEPHANT DAY

The month of March marks the National Thai Elephant Day in Thailand, which both celebrates the crucial role elephants have played in Thai society and promotes awareness around maintaining and improving the wellbeing of the Asian elephant as a whole. The **Thai Elephant Conservation Center**, located west of Lampang, hosts the biggest event every year, where elephants are presented a northern Thai–style buffet of food while monks pray to make merit for the coming year. The centre also proudly houses six royal white elephants that do make the odd appearance...if you're very lucky.

The Lanna School

The epitome of the northern Thai temple

Wat Phra That Lampang Luang, located in rural Lampang Province, is considered one of the most classic and beautiful temples in northern Thailand. The walled compound hides several ancient structures worth exploring.

Enter through a gate that allegedly dates to the 15th century. The lintel features an impressive dragon relief, once common in northern Thai temples but rarely seen today.

The compound's main structure, the open-sided **Wihan Luang**, dates back to 1476 and is thought to be the oldest standing wooden structure in the country. The impressive *wi hahn* features a triple-tiered wooden roof supported by immense teak pillars and early-19th-century *Jataka* murals (showing stories of the Buddha's previous lives) painted on wooden panels around the inside upper perimeter. A huge, gilded *mon dop* (the small square-sided building with a spire) in the back of the *wi hahn* contains a Buddha image cast in 1563.

The Lanna-style **chedi** behind the structure, raised in 1449 and restored in 1496, is 45m high.

HIGHLIGHTS
1 MAHAMITr

SIGHTS
2 Dhanabadee Ceramic Museum
3 Louis T Leonowens Mansion
4 Moung Ngwe Zin Building
5 Ratsada Phisek Bridge
6 Thanon Talad Gao
7 Wat Pratu Pong

SLEEPING
8 Auangkham Resort
9 Hug Lampang
10 Riverside Guest House

EATING
11 Aroy One Baht
12 Evening Market
13 Khanom Jeen Pa Bunsri
14 Sai Ua Mae Jandee

DRINKING & NIGHTLIFE
15 Papacraft
16 Riverside, The

SHOPPING
17 Ceramics Market
18 Cultural Street
19 Khun Manee Rice Cracker
20 Walking Street

WALKING KAD KONGTA & BEYOND

Lampang's riverside is home to ancient neighbourhoods where architecture sheds light on times gone past.

START	END	LENGTH
Papacraft	Auangkham Resort	2km; three hours

Kick off your walk at 1 **Papacraft**, a cafe whose garden-like backyard extends all the way to the Yom River.

From here, head east along 2 **Thanon Talad Gao**, a curious and charming mix of Thai, Myanmar and colonial British architectural styles. Perhaps most notable is the 3 **Moung Ngwe Zin Building**, a shopfront built by a Myanmar teak trader in 1908 to sell Western consumer goods.

If it's mealtime, consider a bowl of *ka nom jeen nam ngee o*, thin rice noodles with a savoury topping of tomatoes and pork, at 4 **Khanom Jeen Pa Bunsri**.

Cross the 1917-era 5 **Ratsada Phisek Bridge** to the north bank of the Yom River. A short walk east is the hidden 6 **Louis T Leonowens Mansion**, once home of the eponymous teak magnate and son of the English teacher depicted in *The King & I*.

Return the way you came and head north via 7 **Wat Pratu Pong**, home to some charming contemporary temple murals. You'll emerge on Th Wangnua, which on Friday evenings hosts the 8 **Cultural Street** market. Close with a much-needed drink at the garden-based cafe at 9 **Auangkham Resort** (p244).

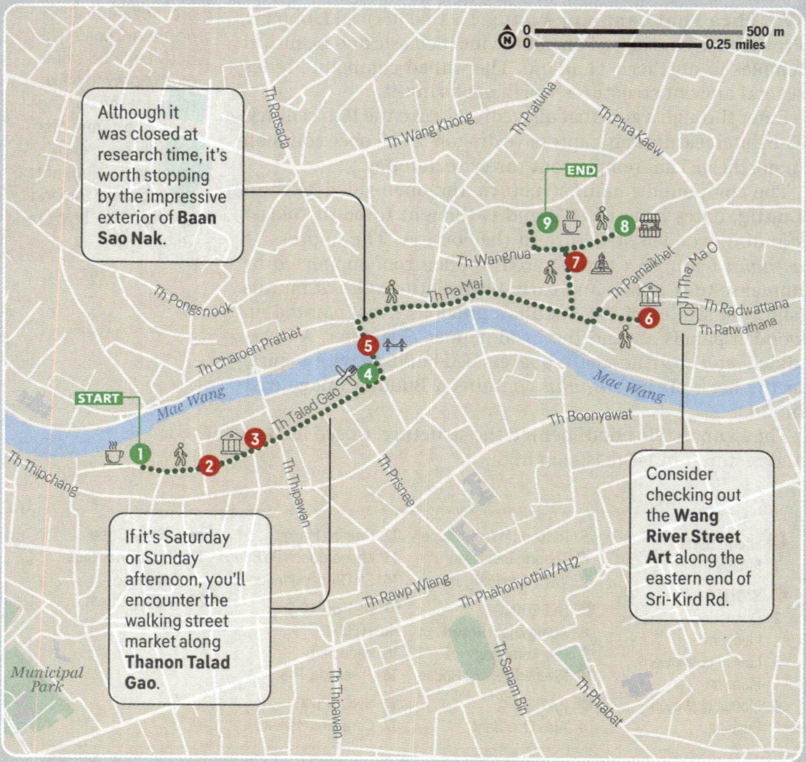

Although it was closed at research time, it's worth stopping by the impressive exterior of **Baan Sao Nak**.

If it's Saturday or Sunday afternoon, you'll encounter the walking street market along **Thanon Talad Gao**.

Consider checking out the **Wang River Street Art** along the eastern end of Sri-Kird Rd.

Wihan Nam Taem, to the north of the *chedi*, was built in the early 16th century and, amazingly, still contains traces of the original murals, making them among the oldest in the country. To the east, the small and simple **Wihan Ton Kaew** was built in 1476. South of the main *chedi*, **Wihan Phra Phut** dates back to the 13th century and is the oldest structure in the compound. The structure just southwest of the *chedi* houses a **camera obscura**. The image is projected (upside down) onto a white cloth and clearly depicts the colours of the structures outside. It was being restored when we visited, and in the past was only accessible to men.

In the arboretum outside the southern gate of the compound there are three sporadically open **museums**. One displays mostly festival paraphernalia and some Buddha figures. Another, called House of the Emerald Buddha, contains a miscellany of coins, banknotes, Buddha figures, silver betel-nut cases, lacquerware and other ethnographic artefacts, along with three small, heavily gold-leafed Buddhas placed on an altar behind an enormous repoussé silver bowl. The third, a small museum, features shelves of Buddha figures, lacquered boxes, manuscripts and ceramics, all well labelled in Thai and English.

Wat Phra That Lampang Luang is located around 20km southwest of Lampang and makes for a fun half-day excursion, especially if combined with nearby Wat Lai Hin (p224); a taxi can be arranged in the city if you don't have your own wheels.

Ancient Graffiti

Witness prehistoric art in rural Lampang

Thais were not, in fact, the first people to inhabit Thailand. Located northwest of Lampang, **Pha Gate Prehistoric Cliff Rock Paintings** is home to more than 1800 prehistoric paintings, forming the largest collection of prehistoric art found in the country. The drawings date from 5000 to 3000 BCE, and miraculously survived the elements on a 580m-high exposed cliff face. They were painted with red ochre and represent anthropomorphic figures, animals (both wild and domesticated), geometric forms and hands. The paintings were allegedly discovered by a mountain-climbing soldier in 1988, and later, human remains, pottery and other tools were also found. The paintings can be admired via an easy, paved 800m path.

In typical Thai style, there's a small market and religious monuments on the grounds.

ROOTED IN TEAK

At the end of the 19th and beginning of the 20th century, Lampang became an important centre for the domestic and international teak trade. A large British-owned timber company brought in supervisors familiar with the teak industry in Myanmar to train loggers from Thailand and Myanmar in the area. These well-paid supervisors, along with independent teak merchants from Myanmar who plied their trade in Lampang, sponsored the construction of more than a dozen temples in the city, a legacy that lives on in several of Lampang's most impressive *wat* and the beautiful antique homes along Th Talad Gao.

EATING & DRINKING IN LAMPANG: LOCAL EATS INTERNATIONAL

Sai Ua Mae Jandee: Look for the rustic stall across from Aroy One Baht, indicated by locals queuing for grilled items and other local dishes. *8am-8pm Mon-Sat* ฿

Khanom Jeen Pa Bunsri: Southwest of Lampang's historical Ratsada Phisek Bridge, this longstanding restaurant does excellent northern-style noodle dishes. *9am-2pm* ฿

Evening Market: Self-caterers or those interested in local eats will want to check out Lampang's evening market. *4-8pm* ฿

Khun Manee Rice Cracker: Lampang is known for its *khao taen*, deep-fried rice cakes seasoned with watermelon juice, drizzled with palm sugar. *8am-6pm* ฿

WAT LAI HIN

Just 6km west of Wat Pra That Lampang Luang is tiny but graceful Wat Lai Hin. The temple is thought to have been built in 1683 by a prince from Keng Tung, in today's Myanmar. Like many other Lanna monasteries, the legend goes that the location was selected by an elephant when it stopped en route from India while carrying a Buddhist relic. Wat Lai Hin is considered another masterpiece of northern Thai architecture, and was a significant influence on the design of the Dhara Dhevi hotel in Chiang Mai, not to mention a film location for the 2001 Thai historical blockbuster *Suriyothai*.

There's an interesting folk museum on the grounds that the monks can unlock for you.

PINKBLUE STUDIO/SHUTTERSTOCK

Wat Chaloem Phrakiat

Ascend to the Floating Pagodas

Unseen Thailand's pièce de résistance

Perched atop some of Lampang's sheerest peaks, **Wat Chaloem Phrakiat** *(adult/child 290/180฿)* stands as a testament to human artisanship and devotion. Otherwise known as the Temple of the Floating Pagodas, this extraordinary temple defies gravity as a series of small pagodas seemingly float above the landscape.

Built in the early 2000s by the hands of esteemed monks and a cohort of dedicated volunteers, these towering structures placed atop death-defying karst peaks pay homage to the royal Rama lineage. The entrance fee includes a white-knuckle *sorng taa ou* shuttle to the trailhead, where 500m of steep steps takes you to the summit, 878m above sea level. While caution is advised with low railings, sheer drops and uneven wooden platforms that jut out over nothingness, the reward for reaching the summit and beholding the marvel of the Floating Pagodas is an experience of awe-inspiring beauty and, for some, great spiritual significance.

Wat Chaloem Phrakiat is located around 60km north of Lampang, and makes a wonderful half-day trip; you'll need your own transportation to reach it.

EATING & DRINKING IN LAMPANG: THAI & INTERNATIONAL

Walking Street: On Saturday and Sunday evenings, the traffic on Lampang's Th Talad Gao is replaced by dozens of food stalls. *4-10pm Sat & Sun* ฿

Aroy One Baht: Tables are always full at this wooden house in Lampang but turnaround is fast. Dishes start at 1฿; no wonder people love it. *4-11pm Wed-Mon* ฿

The Riverside: This expansive wooden bar with a large terrace right by the side of Mae Wang has live music most nights. *11am-11pm* ฿

MAHAMITr: Outside the provincial capital in a riverside location, this sophisticated cafe takes coffee seriously, using only northern Thai beans. *8am-5pm* ฿

Nan Province

HISTORY | ADVENTURE | CULTURE

Nan is often referred to as Thailand's final frontier. As the last province officially incorporated into Siam in 1932 after centuries as an autonomous state, it has its own unique culture.

Beyond Mae Nam Nan Valley is a rugged wildland of mountains, national parks and isolated communities, connected by small mountain roads that inexplicably chose to cut straight over the province's towering mountains instead of finding routes around them. The hills are predominantly populated by the hill people of Mien, with smaller numbers of Hmong, Tai Lue and a number of lesser-known groups that share more culture with Laos and China than they do with Thailand.

From ancient salt wells that draw traders from across the world, to middle-of-nowhere village retreats and a bountiful agricultural scene (including chocolate), there's a lot of fun to be had in these hills.

TOP TIP

The best time to visit Nan Province is from November to February, with mist-covered mountains and single-digit temps. The monsoon is also stunning, albeit more cloudy, but heavy rain can make slippery mountain roads treacherous.

GETTING THERE & AROUND

Car or motorbike rentals are your best bet if you can brave the hills. Transport routes link the provincial capital and destinations such as Pua, but the going is slow.

Most of Nan's city centre can be easily walked. Hotels often supply bicycles. There are motorcycle taxis around the bus station, as well as at local markets and the historical centre.

Not being located on any major transportation routes, Nan takes a bit of effort to reach. That said, there are relatively frequent bus and minivan connections between Nan's bus station and other larger provincial capitals in the north, and it's easy, if time-consuming, to get to Chiang Mai and Chiang Rai.

Tiny Nan Airport, located 3km north of town, operates daily flights to/from Bangkok.

If you've got your sights set abroad, daily minibus routes connect the provincial capital with Ban Huay Kon, a border crossing with Laos, from where it's possible to continue to Xayaboury and then to Luang Prabang.

HIGHLIGHTS
1 Wat Phumin

SIGHTS
2 Khum Chao Ratchabut
3 Nan National Museum
4 Wat Ming Muang

SLEEPING
5 Nan Lanna Hotel
6 Pukha Nanfa Hotel

EATING
7 Evening Market
8 Hot Bread
9 Huean Horm

SHOPPING
10 Nan OTOP Centre

Witness the Whisper

Take in northern Thailand's most famous temple paintings

Wat Phumin, whose murals are now found on everything from knick-knacks at Chiang Mai's night bazaar to postcards sold in Bangkok, is considered northern Thailand's Sistine Chapel.

The Buddhist temple's murals were executed during the late 19th century by a Thai Lue artist named Thit Buaphan, who was commissioned by Jao Suliyaphong, the last king of Nan. Inside the temple, virtually every surface is covered with murals, some of which include political commentary, a rarity in Thai Buddhist art. An example of this is the Khaddhana Jataka, a relatively obscure story of one of the Buddha's lives that, according to Thai historian David K Wyatt in his excellent book, *Reading Thai Murals*, has never been illustrated elsewhere in the Buddhist world. The story, which is on the left side of the temple's northern wall, depicts an orphan in search of his parents. Wyatt argues that this particular tale was chosen as a metaphor for the Kingdom of Nan, which also had been abandoned by a succession of 'parents': the Thai kingdoms of Sukhothai, Chiang Mai and Ayuthaya. At roughly the same time as the murals were painted, Nan was

EATING & DRINKING IN NAN CITY: OUR PICKS

Evening Market: Nan is not a great restaurant town. If you're willing to self-cater, its evening market is excellent, with delicious northern Thai dishes. *3-9pm* ฿

Huean Phukha: Just about every Thai tourist has dinner at this place serving a thick menu of northern Thai dishes, and so should you. ฿ *9am-9pm*

Hot Bread: The lovely couple at this longstanding cafe do international-leaning breakfasts and light meals. *8am-3pm* ฿

Bitter Bar: A disproportionately sophisticated cocktail bar for this corner of northern Thailand. *5.30pm-midnight* ฿

fully incorporated into Siam by King Rama V, and much of its territory was allotted to France. Apparent discontent with this decision can be seen in a scene on the western wall that shows two male monkeys attempting to copulate against a background that, not coincidentally, according to Wyatt, resembles the French flag.

As a whole, the murals are also valuable purely for their artistic beauty, something that is even more remarkable if you step back and consider the limited palette of colours that Thit Buaphan had to work with. The paintings are also fascinating for their fly-on-the-wall depictions of local life in Nan during the end of the 19th century. A portrayal of three members of a hill tribe on the western wall includes such details as a man's immense goitre and a barking dog, suggesting this group's place as outsiders. Multiple depictions of a man wearing a feminine shawl, often seen performing traditionally female-only duties, are among the earliest depictions of *kathoey* (Thai transgender people and cross dressers). And in what must be one of the art world's most superfluous cameos, the artist painted himself, nearly life-sized, on the western wall, whispering in the ear of a woman. Considering that the murals took Thit Buaphan more than 20 years to complete, we'll grant him this indulgence.

Wat Phumin's structure itself is also noteworthy, and takes the form of a cruciform *boht* (ordination hall) that was constructed in 1596 and restored during the reign of Chao Anantavorapitthidet (1867–74). The ornate altar in the centre of the *boht* has four sides, with four Sukhothai-style sitting Buddhas facing in each direction.

WAT NONG BUA

If you liked the murals of Wat Phumin, consider a visit to Wat Nong Bua. Located 60km north of Nan in the Thai Lue village of **Tha Wang Pha**, the temple was built around 1862, and its murals are thought to have been painted by Thit Buaphan, the same artist who painted Wat Phumin, although the work is earlier and more primitive. The scenes depicted are similar, and the murals are also thought to include a self-portrait of the artist, located on the lower right-hand side of the main wall of the temple.

Directly behind the temple is a house where weaving is done and where local textiles are sold.

Pick a Winner at the Longboat Race

Nan's biggest spectacle

Despite the modest size of Nan's main river, the people are obsessed with boats. Throughout the year uncles tinker on hollowed-out vessels that, come October, are flung into the water for the annual **Longboat Race Festival**. An important gathering of local communities, the competition is often fierce, steeped in camaraderie, scandal and hijinks. Long, thin boats sit tightly packed with rows of oarsmen who use all their strength to win prizes, and more importantly, bragging rights.

You'll see just how much effort teams put into both training and decorating their boats. Technique and boat design are passed down through generations, often carefully guarded by families in a bid to preserve their winning formulas.

The three-day festival is held on different dates every year depending on the river's flow, but throughout October you'll likely find dozens of teams from across Thailand training in anticipation of the big day. As the event gets underway, the riverbanks are packed with people, vendors, cultural events and dancing that turn this otherwise quiet city into a hubbub of competition and revelry.

THE NORTHERN THAI SCRIPT

Northern Thai has its own writing system, based on an old Mon script that was originally used only for Buddhist scripture. The script became so popular during the Lanna period that it was exported for use by the Thai Lue in China, the Khün in the eastern Shan State, and other Thai-Kadai-speaking groups living between Lanna and China. Few northerners nowadays can read the northern Thai script – often referred to as Lanna script – and it is mostly used in signage to add a northern Thai cultural flavour.

High Salinity

Witness the origins of salt in Ban Bo Klua

Hidden in the back hills of Nan Province is a peculiar town with an even more peculiar feature. **Ban Bo Klua**, 'Salt Well Village', is named for its two natural saltwater wells, once the only place northern traders could get salt, a resource that has been exploited here for centuries. A thriving community has emerged around it, most recently taking to tourism to bolster its growth. Yet despite becoming a trending destination among Thais during the COVID-19 pandemic, visitor numbers are still low, with even fewer foreign tourists making it here.

A small street connects to the original wells that are surrounded by local traders who extract salt using traditional methods that date back over 800 years. The near-endless supply of mountainous saltwater is hoisted up using a bamboo pulley system, before it's slow-boiled over firepits to evaporate the water and leave salt crystals behind. During Buddhist Lent, from June to October, work is paused. Historically, this salt would be traded with other northern kingdoms, as it was once a primary source of the resource in the region, reaching as far as China. Nowadays it is sold to tourists in neat packaging, sometimes flavoured with various spa scents and mineral additives. There's even now a so-called salt spa in the tiny village.

If salt alone isn't enough of a draw, the beautiful rural setting and access to Sapan (p230) and **Doi Phu Kha National Park** *(adult/child 200/100฿)* are additional reasons to consider an excursion here.

Border Commerce

Visit the international market at Ban Huay Kon

Ban Huay Kon, a tiny village in far-northern Nan Province, is home to a border crossing with Laos, and on Fridays and Saturdays, the community comes alive via a **border market**. The commerce starts on Friday afternoon, when villagers from the Lao side bring items scavenged from the jungle, prepared food, hand-woven textiles and hand-carved household items. It continues again on Saturday morning, when at 8am – when the border opens – vendors literally run to the market area to display their wares. The market is small, but the items sold are fascinating, the next best thing to crossing to Laos.

If you're coming from Ban Bo Klua or Sapan, Rte 1081 passes through remote forested areas, tiered rice fields and tiny

EATING & DRINKING IN NAN PROVINCE: OUR PICKS

Pong Za: The restaurant at Boklua View, in Ban Bo Klua, is the origin of *gai tort makwaen*, chicken deep-fried with a relative of Sichuan pepper. *11am-10pm* ฿฿

Ban Tai Lue Cafe: Combine northern Thai-style noodle dishes with a view over rice fields at this casual restaurant in Pua. *7am-5pm* ฿

Cocoa Valley Cafe: Taste Pua-grown chocolate and other cacao products at the cafe attached to this hotel. *8am-6pm* ฿

Lan Du Dao: Take in the stunning views from Rte 1256 from this roadside cafe, whose name means 'Star Viewing Field'. *8am-6pm* ฿

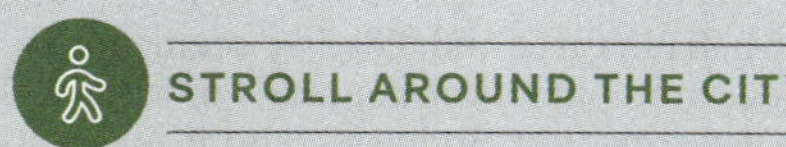

STROLL AROUND THE CITY

A short walk around Nan's historical centre reveals some of the country's most famous temple art, an excellent museum and a royal legacy.

START	END	LENGTH
Wat Phumin	Khum Chao Ratchabut	1km; two hours

Nan's claim to fame is the 16th-century 1 **Wat Phumin** (p226), which features Thailand's only four-way-facing Buddha statue and beautiful murals painted by the legendary Thit Buaphan.

Head north and turn left on Th Suriyaphong, where you'll reach 2 **Nan OTOP Centre**, a one-stop shop for things local including hand-woven cloth, indigo-dyed garments and silver.

Practically next door is the resplendently white 3 **Wat Ming Muang**. Head inside the main structure and spot the influences from Wat Phumin apparent in the contemporary murals here. If it's lunchtime, cross the street for a northern Thai meal at 4 **Huean Horm**.

Head north then east to the 5 **Nan National Museum**, an impressive palace that was home to Nan's last feudal lords. Recently restored, it's one of the better provincial museums in the country, offering a detailed view on Nan's history, ethnic minorities and local handicrafts.

Head north, cross Th Phakong, and seemingly hidden behind the greenery is 6 **Khum Chao Ratchabut**, built in 1866 as a private residence for one of Nan's final independent rulers. The gate is generally left open but visitors can't enter the structure.

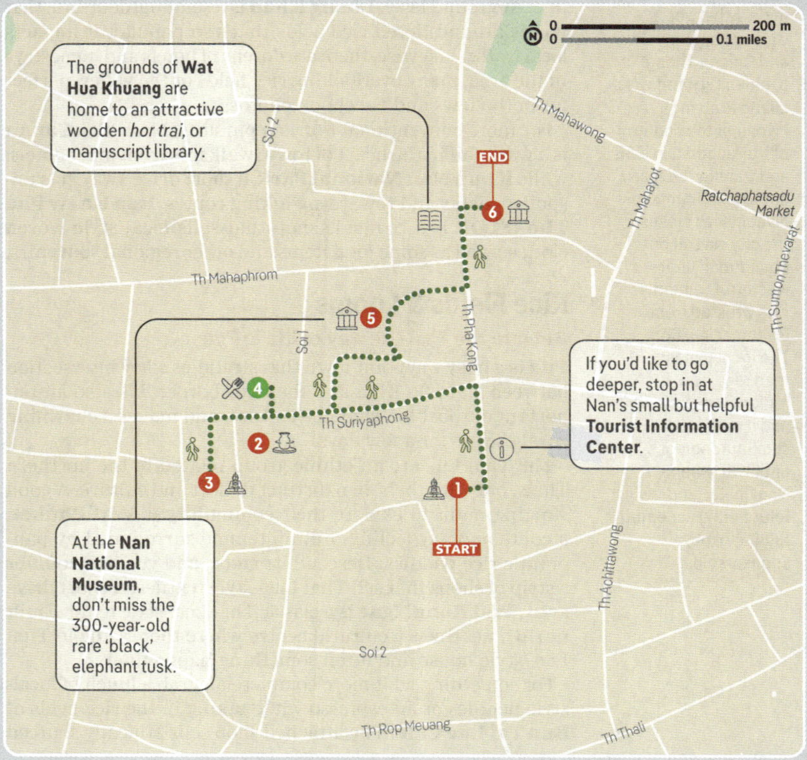

The grounds of **Wat Hua Khuang** are home to an attractive wooden *hor trai*, or manuscript library.

If you'd like to go deeper, stop in at Nan's small but helpful **Tourist Information Center**.

At the **Nan National Museum**, don't miss the 300-year-old rare 'black' elephant tusk.

NAN'S BACKSTORY

For centuries Nan was an isolated, independent kingdom with few ties to the outside world. Towards the end of the 14th century, Nan became one of the nine northern Thai–Lao principalities that comprised the Lanna Kingdom. The city state flourished throughout the 15th century under the name Chiang Klang (Middle City), a reference to its position approximately midway between Chiang Mai (New City) and Chiang Thong (Golden City, today's Luang Prabang). Myanmar took control of the kingdom in 1558 and transferred many of the inhabitants to Myanmar as slaves; the city was all but abandoned until western Thailand was wrested from Myanmar in 1786. The local dynasty then regained regional sovereignty and it remained semi-autonomous until 1931, when Nan finally (and reluctantly) accepted full Bangkok sponsorship.

no-name villages via hairpin turns and 'floating' segments. In 2025 the road was declared one of the country's most beautiful by Thailand's Department of Highways, and it makes a wonderful half-day side trip from Ban Bo Klua or Sapan. When we visited, work was being done to upgrade the road, but it's still subject to landslides and flooding during the rainy season.

Pai for Thais

Experience the domestic escape that is Sapan

If the foreign backpacker crowd heads to Pai, then the domestic alternative – at least when we passed through – is **Sapan**.

Located in rural Nan, just north of Bo Klua, Sapan is a valley village with a river running through it and picture-perfect views. This peaceful community is best visited at the end of the rainy season when early-morning mist and dew-covered rice fields are guaranteed, and is a pleasant place to spend a few nights.

The thing that makes Sapan a uniquely Thai destination is less its landscape and more the attractions that have sprung up in it. The surrounding hills are home to several rustic-chic cafes, where locals take part in selfie-snapping and downing massive iced coffees. In town, the biggest selfie draw is **Yut Vela Cafe**, a hilltop coffee shop near the village temple and overlooking village's rice paddies just above the morning fog line. At ground level, **Lhong Khao** is a semi-outdoor cafe that winds around tiered rice fields that's so popular, it impacts local traffic. Likewise, there are dozens of hotels and homestays in the area, many overlooking rice fields or the valley, perfect for both views and Facebook photos.

For more conventional tourism pursuits, **Nam Tok Sapan** is a waterfall in the heart of town, walkable from most hotels, while **Khun Nan National Park**, a short drive away, has unspoiled vistas and rewarding hiking routes. **Bua Kaew Pha Tho OTOP** is a roadside shop that sells local-style woven cloth as well as some food items and other regional souvenirs.

Rice Fields & Looms

Get into the Thai Lue way of life in Pua

Pua is a busy waypoint town that straddles a key intersection between Nan, Bo Klua and the Laos border. It's also an important outpost for Thai Lue culture, and makes a charming rural escape for a few days.

The Thai Lue are an ethnic group related to the northern Thais, but with their own distinct dialect and culture. A good starting point to explore their community is **Wat Phuket**, a contemporary-feeling, hilltop temple surrounded by panoramic rice paddies. Descend its steps, and you'll encounter a strip of shops that sell Thai Lue–style textiles. A short drive away, **Wat Rong Ngae** is a classic Thai Lue–style temple built in 1767; nearby is a cultural centre where there's an old Thai Lue–style house and often something happening.

For something a bit more commercial, grab a lunch of local-style noodles or an espresso while taking in the rice fields at **Ban Tai Lue Cafe**. The attached shop sells ethically sourced fabrics and clothing made by minority groups from around the region. Featuring weaving styles that originate from Pua, these textiles are considered a symbol of the district – a perfect souvenir gift that's unique to the area and supports local artisans.

If the Thai Lue lifestyle appeals, consider a stay at **DaiDib DaiDee** *(daidibdaidee.com)*, a permaculture farm-stay experience that focuses on preserving and sharing traditional cultures and skills. Spend your days off-grid chilling with buffalo, harvesting food and telling stories around the campfire. The owner is dedicated to simple living so don't expect air-con or power outlets in the wooden cabins. Instead, expect communal showers, a herbal sauna and a solar-power hub (for those who want power).

MAKHAEN

The hills of Nan Province are an important source of the spice known in the northern Thai dialect as *makaen*. An evergreen shrub native to Asia, the petals that surround the berries of *Zanthoxylum limonella Alston* have a citrusy, vibrant aroma, and also provide the same subtly numbing sensation as Sichuan pepper. The fresh berries are preserved in fish sauce and used as a condiment, while the dried spice is a common ingredient in northern Thai-style dishes including *larb*, soups and curries and, more recently, *gai tort makaen*, a regional style of deep-fried chicken.

Star Light, Star Bright

Take in the night sky at Doi Samer Dao

While there are many spots in northern Thailand ideal for stargazing, the National Astronomical Research Institute of Thailand (NARIT) has taken steps in recent years to preserve and protect key stargazing locations through a campaign called 'Dark Sky in Thailand' and promoting stargazing to tourists. There are currently 48 locations registered as dark sky locations, one of which is **Doi Samer Dao** in Nan.

The mountain is part of **Si Nan National Park** *(adult/child 100/50฿)*, known for exceptional stargazing that spans 360 degrees atop its peak. The best time to visit is during Thailand's cold season, from approximately October to February, when the sky is at its clearest.

The park can provide tents, cabins and treks for passing visitors at low prices. It can get busy during weekends and the high season, when makeshift restaurants and rentable tents in neat rows take up much of the hillside, so if you prefer privacy visit on a weekday. Alternatively, several glamping outfits, located just outside the park zone, also operate during this time of year.

Off the Beaten Track

Venture into Ban Sakoen's caves and forests

Head east from Nan on Rte 1148, a winding, well-maintained road particularly popular with motorcycle tourists, and eventually you'll encounter a sweeping valley with a conspicuous karst outcropping; this is **Ban Sakoen**. The area has an appealingly remote, rural vibe, and is home to some natural attractions worth exploring in the form of an overnight stay.

The karst mountain that sets the scene is known as Pha Chang Noi, and is part of **Phu Langka Forest Park**. Technically in Phayao Province, the views of the valley are even more dramatic when seen from a string of cliffside cafes and hotels just west of Ban Sakoen. To see those mountains up close, descend to **Tham Sa Koen National Park** *(adult/child 100/50฿)*. Closed during the wet season, from June to October, the park is home to a large, easily accessible cave, as well as a 1.8km nature walk.

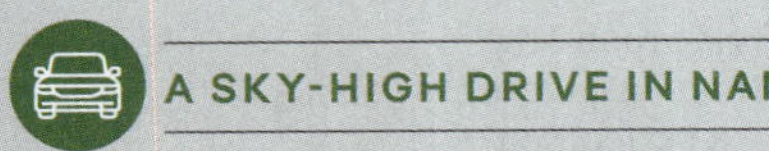

A SKY-HIGH DRIVE IN NAN

Scale some of the most dramatic roads in the country along this province-spanning drive.

START	END	LENGTH
Nan	Tha Wang Pha	200km; three days

Start your journey in 1 **Nan** before joining Rte 1169 into the hills. Just 11km later, stop at the first viewpoint for 360-degree views, as long as the clouds aren't in the way. If you want to have the complete Thai experience, you'll also need to stop for a photo at 2 **Street Number 3**, a point where the bending road resembles – you guessed it – the numeral three.

The next leg crosses a towering mountain range, with sheer drops on each side as the road straddles mountain ridges. Upon reaching the junction with Rte 1333, head north to your destination for the night: the village of 3 **Ban Bo Klua** (p228) or 4 **Sapan** (p230).

The next day, head east along Rte 1256, a road with even more sheer drops and higher mountain ridges. Stop at 5 **Phu Kha Viewpoint** for the best sights of the drive.

Spend a deserved night in 6 **Pua** (p230) before heading back to where it all began in Nan, but first make a stop at 7 **Wat Nong Bua** (p227) to see this classic Thai Lue–style temple with its rustic murals, a counterpart to Wat Phumin.

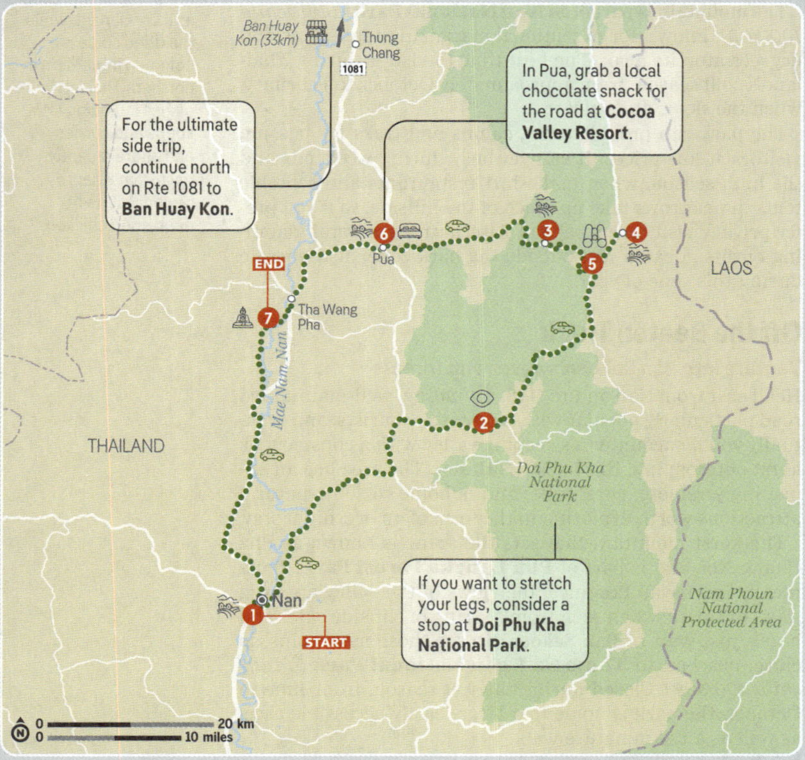

For the ultimate side trip, continue north on Rte 1081 to **Ban Huay Kon**.

In Pua, grab a local chocolate snack for the road at **Cocoa Valley Resort**.

If you want to stretch your legs, consider a stop at **Doi Phu Kha National Park**.

Ban Huay Kon (33km)
Thung Chang
1081
END
Pua
Tha Wang Pha
Mae Nam Nan
LAOS
THAILAND
Doi Phu Kha National Park
Nam Phoun National Protected Area
Nan
START
0 20 km
0 10 miles

Phrae Province

TEAK | INDIGO | RURAL LIFE

Phrae is a city steeped in heritage. From the revered pagoda of Wat Luang, built by the mother of the first ruler of Phrae back in the year 844, to its vibrant textile industry and its majestic teakwood mansions that stand as a testament to the city's power during the trade era, its legacy runs deep among the stories and traditions of the northern Thai people.

Beyond the city, Phrae's natural beauty unfolds across lush rice paddies, meandering rivers and open plains that cut through the mountains, offering an idyllic setting for some of the region's more off-the-beaten-track experiences. Whether you come here seeking moments of peaceful reflection in a rural village, or want to embark on a journey into the land of fermented rice whisky, Phrae promises an authentic experience that feels unlike anywhere else in the north. Warm, cosy and unique…or maybe it's the whisky talking.

TOP TIP

Phrae is a place to savour. Stroll through old city streets and engage in conversations with friendly locals. Enjoy the energy (and food) at its bustling weekend markets. Don't rush; take time to appreciate how special a place it is.

A Legacy of Logging

Witness how teak influenced Phrae's architecture

Following a Shan people's rebellion in 1902 in response to high taxes and demanding Bangkok officials, the last leader of Phrae, Chao Piriyatheppawong, fled to Luang Prabang, leaving a logging trade that was handed over to the British. What followed was an economic boom that gave rise to a whole industry of entrepreneurs who turned the city teak. Today, the legacy of this

GETTING THERE & AROUND

Phrae's provincial capital is small and largely possible to explore on foot.

Phrae's bus station is located in the city centre, and has frequent but slow connections to smaller towns in the province (as well as decent connections with the rest of northern Thailand). If you're in a hurry or want more freedom, you'll probably want your own wheels, although only a couple of places in town rent cars and motorcycles.

A train line crosses through only the southernmost part of Phrae Province – not a very convenient form of inter-provincial transportation for most visitors. Thailand's rail network connects with Phrae Province at Den Chai, 23km south of the provincial capital.

KA NOM JEEN

A ubiquitous dish in Phrae and Nan is *ka nom jeen*: thin, round noodles made from a fermented, extruded rice-based dough. Noodles can come with a variety of soups and curries but here the topping is generally a savoury broth of braised pork ribs, occasionally supplemented with tomato, and often garnished with crispy deep-fried garlic. The dish is often served with optional sides – shredded cabbage, long beans and slices of lime.

time lives on in traditional structures that still stand strong, all of which could be explored on foot in a single morning.

The city's most impressive example is **Vongburi House** *(60฿)*. It was built between 1897 and 1907 for Luang Phongphibun and his wife Chao Sunantha, who once held a profitable teak concession in the city. Inside, many of the house's 20 rooms display late-19th-century teak antiques, documents (including early-20th-century slave concessions), photos and other artefacts from the bygone teak-dynasty era.

The **Forestry Museum**, with its emphasis on teak, was closed for renovation when we were in town but is worth investigating, not least to see it and other charming old buildings in the Forestry School compound. Other notable wood structures in town include **Wichairacha House**, a mansion built in 1898 by Cantonese artisans, and **Wat Jom Sawan,** a teak Buddhist temple built by Shan loggers under the employment of the British Bombay Burmah Trading Corporation and the Danish East Asiatic Company.

If you want to go even deeper, stop by **Gingerbread House Café & Gallery**, a cafe and bed and breakfast run by Teerawut Klomlaew, a passionate historian and cyclist who is more than willing to share stories, offer recommendations and answer questions related to the town. He has made an excellent free

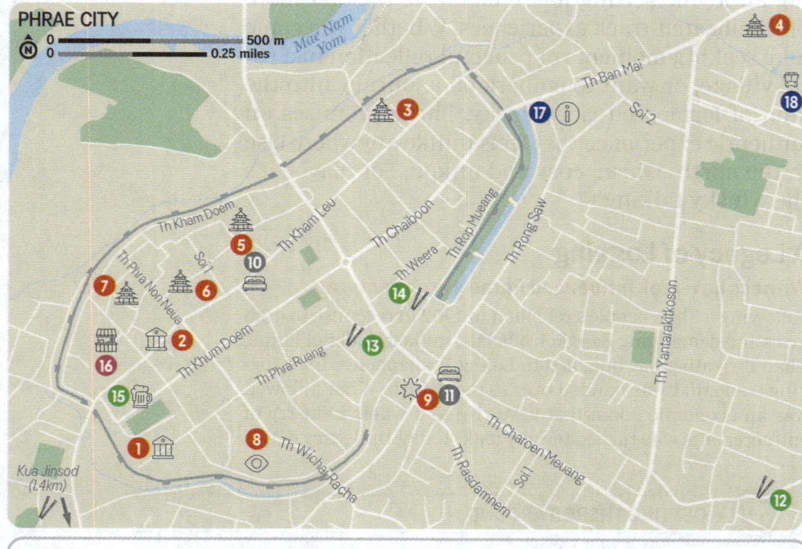

SIGHTS
1 Forestry Museum
2 Vongburi House
3 Wat Hua Khuang
4 Wat Jom Sawan
5 Wat Luang
6 Wat Phong Sunan
7 Wat Phra Non
8 Wichairacha House

ACTIVITIES
9 Gingerbread House Café & Gallery

SLEEPING
10 Huen Him Kong
11 Need a Nap Hostel Phrae

EATING
12 Duang Nate Noodle
13 Night Market
14 Pan Jai

DRINKING & NIGHTLIFE
15 Nomad

SHOPPING
16 Kat Kong Kao

INFORMATION
17 Tourism Authority of Thailand

TRANSPORT
18 Bus Station

map of the city's legacy buildings, and organises semi-regular English Sightseeing Night Tours for larger groups (advance booking required), opening up the teak houses and temples at night for a special audience.

Kind of Blue

Stain your hands getting into Phrae's indigo crafts

Among Thais, Phrae is probably most famous for the distinctive *seua mor horm*, the indigo-dyed cotton farmer's shirt seen all over northern Thailand. The cloth is made in Ban Thung Hong, these days a suburb of the provincial capital, and the place to spend a couple of hours if you're interested in textiles or simply want to do some shopping. The streets here are literally lined with shops selling indigo-dyed clothing, but one of the longer-term producers in Ban Thung Hong is **Mohom Ban PaLuang** *(089 851 3327)*. They still dye their products by hand using real indigo, a process that you may be able to witness behind the small showroom.

Alternatively, if you'd like to get your hands wet, there are a couple of options. With advance notice, **Kaewwanna Natural Indigo** *(081 960 4502)*, located south of the airport, can offer English-language instruction in natural indigo dyeing hand-woven cloth. For something a bit more commercial, **Auntie Ngiem Indigo Dyeing Learning Center**, in Ban Thung Hong, is home to a bunch of local women and a deep vat of indigo. Through a small passageway between two shopfronts you'll find a garden workshop centre that lets you pick out cotton clothing and dye it with your own hands, right then and there. There isn't much English spoken, and it can get a little messy, so wear clothes you don't mind getting accidentally dyed.

LOCAL ADVICE

Phrae is home to a branch of the **Tourism Authority of Thailand** *(facebook.com/tat.phrae)*, which can provide advice, maps and brochures. It's located just east of the centre of town, and English-speaking staff and volunteers are keen to lend a hand.

Another go-to for local insight is Gingerbread House Café & Gallery. The owner has produced a beautifully illustrated map that highlights local attractions, with an emphasis on local building styles, and that could function as the basis for a self-guided architecture tour of the town.

Shopping Spree

Spend your baht locally at Phrae's walking street

Just about every provincial capital in northern Thailand has a so-called 'walking street' market, but Phrae's feels much less commercial and particularly northern, and is a wonderful way to spend a Saturday evening.

If you're around at the weekend, the Saturday-night **Kat Kong Kao** unfolds along the old wooden buildings in the heart of Phrae's old town. It's great for artisan clothing, trinkets and souvenirs, with almost none of the tat you might see elsewhere in northern Thailand. There are also several food stalls, many of them selling dishes specific to the region.

EATING IN PHRAE: OUR PICKS

Duang Nate Noodle: Excellent local-style *ka nom jeen*, thin rice noodles served with a porky, garlicky broth; don't sleep on the desserts. *9.30am-1pm* ฿

Kua Jinsod: The go-to for local-style meat dishes such as northern Thai-style *larb* (spicy, herbal minced-meat salad); just west of the city centre. *9.30am-8pm* ฿

Pan Jai: Pleasant, semi-open-air garden setting that does *ka nom jeen* noodles served with a variety of toppings, and rice dishes. *8am-4pm* ฿

Night Market: This small but lively night market convenes around the Pratu Chai (Victory Gate) intersection every evening. *6-10pm* ฿

HOMESTAYS

In communities across northern Thailand, usually in places too small or remote to have proper hotels, locals have opened up their doors in the form of homestays. Typically, several families host guests on a rotating basis, and a modest fee can include meals and even activities. It's a fascinating insight into local life, although 'local' must be emphasised – hygiene and cleanliness standards may not be what you're used to, communication can be difficult, wake-up calls can be astonishingly early (due to rural traditions but also roosters), and the food can be simple and monotonous. That said, it's a humbling experience to step outside of one's comfort zone for a night or two, and the best way to go beyond feeling like a tourist simply ticking off boxes.

ARTAPORN PUTHIKAMPOL/SHUTTERSTOCK

Wat Phong Sunan

Make Merit Phrae-Style

Phrae's unique and fascinating temples

Any trip to Thailand is bound to involve temples, monks and making merit. There are a few differences with Phrae temples that are worth spending a cool morning to explore.

Wat Phong Sunan is one of the most photogenic and bewildering temples you'll ever visit in Thailand. As you enter, a towering gold tortoise two storeys high ominously greets you. Behind the *ubosot* (chapel), which houses a rare Marnwichai-style Buddha statue and walls painted with Hindu and Buddhist fables, a dense block of miniature golden-tipped white *chedi* make for a brilliant photograph. Across from that, you'll find a giant reclining Buddha statue, a common pose in Phrae that's not often seen at such high frequencies in other provinces. Matching this theme, nearby **Wat Phra Non** has a 1000-year-old reclining Buddha.

Wat Luang is one of Phrae's oldest temples, with a fascinating story to tell. Legend has it that after years of fighting, local leaders and their Myanmar rivals decided to lay down their arms and decide the fate of Phrae by a *chedi*-off. Whoever built the largest *chedi* would be victorious, claiming the city and ending the war. Local leaders eventually won, sending the Myanmar people back for at least a few hundred years. The temple also has an interesting museum that opens sporadically.

Even older still is **Wat Hua Khuang**, built by Mae Chao Chom Come Wong, mother of Phraya Pol (the first ruler of Phrae) in the year 844. The 31m, red-brick *chedi* still stands to this day and is an impressive sight to behold.

If you want to engage directly with Phrae's Buddhist rituals, every Wednesday at dawn, a row of monks emerge from the local temples and head to the old city walls on Th Rop Muang in anticipation of alms. They congregate on the wall, which is now a park (labelled 'Garden & Park' on Google Maps), before walking down to the road where early-morning market stalls appear. To see this magical moment and get involved, arrive early (no later than 6am) with food to donate – rice packets, snacks, water and juice boxes are a good choice – and follow what the locals do as they pay respects, place offerings in the alms bowls and receive blessings. Thai Buddhists are very humble and welcoming, so don't worry about getting something wrong; you'll either be corrected or quietly blessed a little harder.

Mountain Escape

Rural northern Thai life at Ban Na Khu Ha

One of the more touted tourism destinations in Phrae Province these days is **Ban Na Khu Ha**, a village around 40 minutes east of the provincial capital that makes for a fun day trip or overnight escape.

If you'd previously imagined a rural northern Thai village, it probably looked a lot like Ban Na Khu Ha. Follow a winding road through thick jungle to arrive at a string of rustic houses extending along a narrow mountain valley. A good starting point is **Wat Na Khu Ha**, the village temple, which is home to a **bamboo bridge** that extends across tiered rice fields before terminating in a karst outcropping. If you're feeling intrepid, you can continue along a rough, uphill 400m trail to **Pha Sing**, a viewpoint at the top of one of those cliffs. Alternatively, the views at the much more approachable NaKuHa Coffee (p238), overlooking the village at the side of the road, are also pretty impressive.

The stream that runs through Ban Na Khu Ha is a source of *tao*, a type of edible freshwater algae that locals make into a variety of snacks. The principal source of this ingredient is steps from **Mae Daengnoi Homestay** *(089 999 8785)*, a clutch of bungalows in a pretty garden, and one of only a few places to stay in the village.

An Explosive History

Explore the quirky small-town delights of Long

In 1973 a US bomb landed in the village of **Long**, in rural Phrae Province, but didn't explode. Bewildered by this capsule from the sky, locals dug it up and paraded it around the city before donating it to **Wat Mae Lan Nuea**. The bomb was ultimately defused by monks and turned into a bell you can still hit today. Later that year, two more were found, paraded and donated to **Wat Phra That Si Don Kham** and **Wat Na Tum**. This dangerous practice earned the title 'Khon Phrae Hae Ra-bert', which means 'Bomb Parade Phrae People' – a subtle dig at their death-tempting foolishness. A museum at Bomb March Coffee (p238) displays a collection of bomb relics from the era, and owner Mr Tong will tell the story over sweet tea and cake.

If you've made it to Long, consider a stop at **Komol Old Cloth**, a nonprofit centre opened by antique fabric collector Komol Panichphan. Phrae has a legacy of weaving, and the collection here spans ethnic dress from across the region, with examples of styles specifically from Long and silk skirts more than a century old.

Long is located an hour west of Phrae.

SPEAKING NORTHERN

Thailand's regional dialects vary greatly and can even be unintelligible to native speakers of Thai not familiar with the vernacular being spoken. *Gam meuang*, the northern Thai dialect, is no exception and, in addition to an entirely different set of tones to master, it possesses a wealth of vocabulary specific to the north. The northern dialect also has a slower rhythm than Thailand's three other main dialects, an attribute reflected in the relaxed, easygoing manner of the people who speak it.

LOW KOW & SATO

In northern Thailand, rice-based alcohol takes two main forms, both of which are increasingly gaining popularity after decades of having been perceived as provincial or the drink of old men.

Sato is, roughly speaking, rice wine, and is created when when cooked sticky rice is allowed to ferment with the help of added yeasts and sometimes sugars. The result is generally low in alcohol (roughly equivalent to beer), with a cloudy appearance, a slightly sweet, sometimes funky or tart flavour, and some light effervescence.

Low kow, 'white alcohol', is made by taking *sato* and distilling it in a still. The result is closer to a rice 'whisky', and is clear in colour, with a much higher alcohol content.

A Boozy Bastion

Sample rice whisky in Sa-iab

Rice whisky, or *lao khao* as it is locally known, is a popular but potent liquor that varies in taste and palatability. Popular among working classes, Thailand has battled a long love-hate relationship with its existence, with home-distilling illegal and commercial licences tied up in bureaucracy and monopoly market powers. Yet despite the hurdles, Phrae has become the unexpected capital of local distillery culture, giving birth to some of Thailand's most celebrated rice whiskies.

The village and countryside surrounding **Sa-iab**, around an hour north of the provincial capital, is where the magic happens. People in this community have worked for generations turning their cultivated rice and fruits into spirits and wines and the name 'Sa-iab' has become synonymous with northern rice whisky.

Sakthong Distillery, the area's largest producer, is open to visitors and you can stroll around unaccompanied to see the traditional distillation process in action. Balls of sticky rice are left to ferment while wood fires heat vats of liquid, evaporating the alcohol and distilling it into bottles that are then packaged and labelled by hand. **Sakthong Cafe** next door was built to feed and quench visitors. If you're interested in tasting but can't make the trip to Sa-iab, Gingerbread House Café & Gallery (p234) in Phrae carries several products from the region and elsewhere in the province.

Ghost Town

Explore unique geographical formations at Phae Meuang Phi

The landscape of **Phae Meuang Phi** *(adult/child 100/50฿)*, 10km northwest of the provincial capital, is best known for otherworldly columns and rock formations that tower some 30m high, with others that look uncannily like giant mushrooms. Legend has it that an elderly woman got lost in the forest and stumbled upon a well filled with silver and gold. When she sought the help of the local village, the riches had vanished with a trail of giant footprints that led them to discover the canyon, thus believed to be the home of giant forest spirits. Today it's a popular geological attraction that is reminiscent of Turkey's Cappadocia or the sandstone plateaus of Central America, and is a fun way to spend a half-day or so.

EATING & DRINKING IN PHRAE PROVINCE: OUR PICKS

Thongchai Nam Yoy Mae Lan: Just outside of Long, this place specialises in freshly extruded *ka nom jeen* noodles with various toppings. *9.30am-2pm* ฿

Bomb March Coffee: In Long District, a quirky cafe and restaurant with a bomb-themed museum. *8am-5pm* ฿

NaKuHa Coffee: Located just above the village of the same name, with spectacular views and good coffee. *9am-5.30pm* ฿

Nomad: Craft beer, both domestic and imported, in a cosy old wooden house in Phrae's old town. *6-11.30pm* ฿

Sukhothai Province & Beyond

HISTORY | BUDDHISM | RUINS

Most people are drawn to Sukhothai to pay witness to the incredible ruins that make up the former Sukhothai Kingdom – the kingdom that marked the beginning of the Thai people and the kingdom we know today. Flourishing in the 13th and 14th centuries, a golden age turned the vast empty plains that straddle today's northern and central regions into a thriving, culturally rich civilisation reaching far and wide.

Sukhothai's historical city and the historical cities in nearby areas make up Thailand's most-visited ancient sites, transporting visitors to a bygone era where magnificent temples and intricate sculptures stood as beacons of civilisation. Beyond the historical allure, Sukhothai's charming atmosphere and tranquil surroundings make for some of the best destination resort getaways, with many places built in or around the ancient relics of the Sukhothai era.

GETTING AROUND

Sukhothai Historical Park is a destination in itself, making it hard to travel to less-visited adjacent ancient cities. If you want to see them all, either hire a car and drive yourself or arrange a private minibus from your hotel – don't rely on public transport.

PATPITCHAYA/SHUTTERSTOCK

Si Satchanalai Historical Park (p241)

TOP TIP

Avoid the monsoon season, from approximately June to October, when rain can make the historical park grounds squishy and slippery, and can discourage cycling.

HIGHLIGHTS
1 Kamphaeng Phet Historical Park
2 Sukhothai Historical Park

SIGHTS
3 Kamphaeng Phet National Museum
4 Ramkhamhaeng National Museum
5 Si Satchanalai Centre for Study & Preservation of Sangkalok Kilns
6 Si Satchanalai Historical Park
7 Sukhothai Historical Park Central Zone
8 Sukhothai Historical Park Northern Zone
9 Sukhothai Historical Park Western Zone
10 Wat Chang Lom
11 Wat Chang Rob
12 Wat Chedi Jet Thaew
13 Wat Mahathat
14 Wat Nang Phaya
15 Wat Phra Si Iriyabot
16 Wat Phra Si Ratana Mahathat
17 Wat Sa Si
18 Wat Saphan Hin
19 Wat Si Chum
20 Wat Si Sawai

ACTIVITIES
21 Banpraphim Amulet Learning Centre

SLEEPING
22 Le Charme Sukhothai
23 Navarat Heritage Hotel
24 Old City Guest House
25 Ruean Thai Hotel
26 Sisatchanalai Heritage

PINGLABEL/SHUTTERSTOCK

Sukhothai Historical Park

TOP EXPERIENCE

Three Sukhothai-Era Cities

The Sukhothai era hailed the beginning of Thailand as we know it. The dynasty was founded by Si Inthrathit in 1238, and three major cities were established: Sukhothai (the capital), Si Satchanalai (the trade hub) and Kamphaeng Phet (the defender). Today, these UNESCO World Heritage sites are the most significant relics of Thailand's birth.

Sukhothai Historical Park

Sukhothai Historical Park is one of Thailand's most impressive World Heritage sites. The park includes the remains of 21 historical sites and four large ponds within the old walls, with an additional 70 sites within a 5km radius. The ruins are divided into five zones, three of which receive the most visitors, and one would need a car, motorcycle or strong cycling legs to tackle all of them.

The **Central Zone** *(200฿)* is the most popular, and is home to some of the most recognisable Buddhist ruins in Thailand.

PRACTICALITIES

- various entry fees
- opening times vary; generally 6am to sunset

DON'T MISS

- Si Satchanalai Historical Park
- Sukhothai Historical Park
- Banpraphim Amulet Learning Centre
- Ramkhamhaeng National Museum
- Kamphaeng Phet Historical Park

AN ARTISTIC ERA

The Kingdom of Sukhothai flourished from the mid-13th century to the late 14th century, spanning the reigns of nine kings. The kingdom is viewed as the 'golden age' of Thai civilisation, and the religious art – in particular, the pneumatic, almost 'boneless' lines of the Buddha sculptures – and architecture of the era are considered the most classic of Thai styles.

TOP TIPS

- Exterior sections of each park can be seen for free anytime, day or night.
- Temple-appropriate clothing is advised.
- Do not climb on the sacred images, stupas or shrines.
- If you're at Sukhothai Historical Park Friday or Saturday, **Nam Rap Sadet Market** opens part of the ruins for sunset evenings of traditional food by the water, granting free access to the central park from 5pm.
- The 'Reconstructed' placards near most ruins give a helpful idea of what the structures originally looked like.

On Saturday night much of this zone is illuminated and remains open until 9pm. **Wat Mahathat** is without a doubt the most impressive temple ruin, with a towering structure that sparks imagination. **Wat Sa Si** reflects against a beautifully manicured lake while **Wat Si Sawai** features distinct Khmer architecture that tells an unspoken story of cultural crossover. **Wat Traphang Thong** is one of the few ancient ruins that is still a working temple. At 6.20am every morning, people come to give alms on the wooden bridge; a truly magical experience that's impossible to forget. Next door you'll find **Ramkhamhaeng National Museum** *(200฿)*, home to a replica of the famous Ramkhamhaeng Inscription, said to be the earliest example of Thai writing (the real one can be found in the National Museum, Bangkok).

To the south of the Central Zone, locals and traders were said to congregate outside the city walls. Today it is still home to some of their descendants, one of whom runs the **Banpraphim Amulet Learning Centre** *(facebook.com/banprapim)*, a place where real memories (and real amulets) can be made.

The **Northern Zone** *(120฿)*, 500m north of the old city walls, is easily reached by bicycle. A highlight is **Wat Si Chum**, with a stunning depiction of a Buddha peeking at you through the narrow doorway, almost too big for the room it sits in.

The **Western Zone** *(120฿)*, at its furthest extent 2km west of the old city walls, is the most expansive. In addition to **Wat Saphan Hin**, on the crest of a hill that rises about 200m above the plain, several mostly featureless ruins can be found here. A bicycle or motorcycle is necessary to explore this zone.

Si Satchanalai Historical Park

Located some 60km north of the provincial capital, Si Satchanalai Historical Park *(200฿)* oozes natural beauty and historical relevance, strategically set amid forested hills along Mae Nam Yom, making it our favourite of the area's historical parks.

The park is extremely pleasant to explore and is much quieter than Sukhothai Historical Park. Bikes can be rented, which makes traversing the 45-sq-km landscape a little easier in the heat of midday. **Wat Chang Lom** is the park's most impressive temple – you are free to climb it and take in the views from its raised position overlooking the park. Next door, **Wat Chedi Jet Thaew** has brick-and-plaster barred windows designed to look like lathed wood (an ancient Indian technique used all over Southeast Asia). South of here, **Wat Nang Phaya**, built in the 15th or 16th century, a bit later than the other monuments at Si Satchanalai, has intact stucco reliefs sheltered by a tin roof.

While you're here, head east and visit the **Yom River Suspension Bridge** and cross over to see **Wat Phra Si Ratana Mahathat** *(50฿)*, a living temple ruin with a Khmer stupa in the centre that can be climbed.

At one time, more than 200 huge pottery kilns lined the banks of Mae Nam Yom in the area around Si Satchanalai. In China – the biggest importer of Thai pottery during the Sukhothai and Ayuthaya periods – the pieces produced here came to be called 'Sangkalok', probably a mispronunciation of Sawankhalok. The **Si Satchanalai Centre for Study & Preservation of Sangkalok Kilns** *(200฿)*, located 5km north of the ruins, has large excavated kilns and many intact pottery samples.

Kamphaeng Phet Historical Park

The often forgotten third city in neighbouring Kamphaeng Phet Historical Park forms the trifecta of ancient cities that made up the Sukhothai Kingdom. As the kingdom's easternmost garrison, its main purpose was to conduct trade along Mae Nam Ping and protect the capital Sukhothai from invasion by Burmese armies. The park consists of two distinct sections.

The majority of Kamphaeng Phet's ruins are found in the expansive **zone** *(200฿)* located about 1.5km north of the city walls. **Wat Phra Si Iriyabot** has a structure that contains the shattered remains of standing, sitting, walking and reclining Buddha images, all sculpted in the classic Sukhothai style, and **Wat Chang Rob** is buttressed with 68 stucco-covered elephants.

Closer to the modern city, another smaller **zone** *(200฿)* is home to Wat Phra Kaeo, which has an immense reclining Buddha and several smaller, weather-corroded Buddha statues that have assumed slender, porous forms, reminding some visitors of the sculptures of Alberto Giacometti. Nearby, **Kamphaeng Phet National Museum** *(100฿)* offers an impressive account of the city's history and why the city shrine was dedicated to the god Shiva.

BUILDING BLOCKS

The primary building material of many of the religious structures of Kamphaeng Phet and Sukhothai is laterite, a claylike substance found over much of Southeast Asia. When still in the ground, laterite is soft and pliable, but when exposed to light and air it hardens. As is evident today, laterite is extremely porous and must be coated with plaster to give it a smooth look.

CASPER1774 STUDIO/SHUTTERSTOCK

Wat Chang Rob

Places We Love to Stay

฿ Budget ฿฿ Midrange ฿฿฿ Top End

Mae Hong Son Province

Sang Tong Huts ฿฿ A clutch of ecofriendly, fan-cooled, TV-free, bamboo and wood bungalows is set in an expansive forested garden just outside Mae Hong Son.

Riverhouse Hotel ฿฿ The combination of teak and handsome decor – not to mention the riverside location – makes this boutique hotel the best spot in Mae Sariang.

Fern Resort ฿฿฿ This veteran resort outside of Mae Hong Son is one of the pleasanter places to stay in northern Thailand. The 37 wooden bungalows are spaced out for privacy among tiered rice paddies and streams, and are simple but comfortable.

Lee Wine Rak Thai Resort ฿฿฿ Chinese-style huts in a working tea plantation in Ban Rak Thai with panoramic, misty views of the village.

Kanlaya's Thailand ฿฿฿ Luxurious accommodation right at the edge of some of Thailand's wildest jungle in Ban Tham Lot.

Pai

Map p198

Nolo Hub Pai ฿ Hostel with a pool and a distinct party vibe.

Pai Country Hut ฿฿ The bamboo bungalows here are simple and attractive, with inviting hammocks on their small verandas.

Pairadise ฿฿ This neat resort looks over the Pai Valley from atop a ridge just outside town. The bungalows are spacious and all surround a spring-fed pond that's suitable for swimming.

Hotel des Artists ฿฿฿ This former Shan mansion has been turned into one of the most charming boutiques in town.

Pai Village Boutique Resort ฿฿฿ This well-maintained place offers a luxury version of the basic backpacker bamboo bungalow with 38 wooden small, plush huts in an attractive garden.

Rim Pai Cottage ฿฿฿ The tastefully decorated bungalows here are spread out along a secluded and beautifully wooded section of Mae Nam Pai.

Chiang Rai Province

Map p204

Bed & Bike Poshtel ฿ New-feeling, tidy and great-value dorm beds, conveniently situated in the centre of Chiang Rai.

Phu Chi Fah House ฿ Modest rooms near the eponymous mountaintop with simple amenities, lovely hosts and breathtaking views.

Baan Hom Muen Li ฿฿ In the middle of Doi Mae Salong, this place consists of rooms artfully decked out in modern and Chinese themes, some with outstanding views over the surrounding tea plantations.

Pak-Ping-Rim-Khong ฿฿ Clean, comfortable and spacious rooms at this tidy villa compound just across the road from the Mekong River in Chiang Saen.

Nak Nakara Hotel ฿฿ A longstanding, family-friendly midranger in the heart of the Chiang Rai. Recently renovated and located a stone's throw from the weekend market.

Rai Saeng Arun ฿฿฿ Located 22km from Chiang Khong, this ecofriendly resort brings together 14 wooden bungalows in a serene plot of land adjacent to the Mekong River.

Legend of Chiang Rai ฿฿฿ One of Chiang Rai's best resorts, tucked against Mae Nam Kok. The riverside infinity pool and spa are the icing on the comfort-filled cake.

Riva Vista ฿฿฿ Sleek, contemporary rooms in Chiang Rai with wide balconies overlooking the Mae Nam Kok.

Athita ฿฿฿ This new hotel takes the form of sophisticated brick and wood structures that blend in with Chiang Saeng's ruins.

Lampang Province

Map p220

Auangkham Resort ฿฿ The 14 rooms in this Lampang hotel feel bright, big and airy; all have balconies overlooking an attractive garden, and perks such as free use of bicycles and a location steps from Friday's Cultural Street market.

Riverside Guest House ฿฿ Get local in Lampang by staying in a traditional wooden-style structure that backs onto Mae Nam Wang.

Hug Lampang ฿฿ A converted bank with a modern interior that also manages to hold onto the old-world charm of Lampang's market area.

Nan Province

Map p226

Nan Lanna Hotel ฿฿ Tucked in a tiny street behind a temple, an old-timey-feeling structure with spacious rooms with handsome wood furnishings and tile floors.

Boklua View ฿฿฿ Elegant cabins sit atop a raised mountain edge just outside Ban Bo Klua, overlooking the village and river below.

Pukha Nanfa Hotel ฿฿฿ A legacy hotel has been transformed into this charming boutique. Its 14 rooms are cosy and classy, with aged wood accentuated by touches such as local cloth, handicrafts and art.

Kiri Vari ฿฿฿ Located in its own little patch of paradise straddling the river in Sapan, this exceptional resort is perfect for some mountain escapism.

Ban Me Dao ฿฿฿ Climb to the top of Sapan and you'll be greeted by stilted houses with charming jungle views.

Ing Mok Homestay ฿฿฿ Standard rooms with exceptional views over the Ban Sakoen valley.

Phrae Province

Map p234

Huen Him Kong ฿฿ Spacious, modern rooms with enough teak to feel Lanna, and a convenient location right in the middle of Phrae's old town.

SuanGlangNa ฿฿ Surrounded by fields in rural Phrae Province, this thoughtfully designed hotel fits well within its environment. Friendly owners.

Need a Nap Hostel Phrae ฿฿ Contemporary rooms in a renovated building at the edge of Phrae's old town. Lots of communal areas.

Sukhothai Province & Beyond

Map p240

Old City Guest House ฿ This budget complex features a variety of decent-sized wood-panelled rooms, some fan-only, all set around a courtyard steps from Sukhothai Historical Park.

Sisatchanalai Heritage ฿ Capable riverside bungalows next door to Si Satchanalai Historical Park.

Navarat Heritage Hotel ฿฿ The 'heritage' part of this hotel's name is a reference to its original 1970s incarnation. It's been extensively updated since then and the rooms are the best and most modern in Kamphaeng Phet.

Ruean Thai Hotel ฿฿฿ At first glance, you might mistake this eye-catching, hospitable complex in Sukhothai for a Buddhist temple or a traditional Thai house.

Le Charme ฿฿฿ Near Sukhothai Historical Park, an inviting cluster of bright bungalows linked by an elevated wooden walkway, with lush gardens and lotus ponds.

Nak Nakara Hotel, Chiang Rai

For places to stay in Chiang Mai, see p298

JEWNNN_YEEPLD/SHUTTERSTOCK

Above: Wat Umong Suan Phutthatham (p280); Right: Wat Pha Lat (p264)

Researched by Aydan Stuart

Chiang Mai Province

THE ROSE OF THE NORTH

The last capital of the Lanna Kingdom is steeped in history, rich in culture and surrounded by Thailand's most incredible natural wonders.

The province of Chiang Mai is the cultural and historical heart of northern Thailand, where the legacy of the ancient Lanna Kingdom intertwines with a vibrant melting pot of modern-day cultures. Scratch beneath the surface and you'll discover the incredible, far away from the chaotic metropolitan vibes of Bangkok and the tourist-saturated beaches to the south.

The city is by far the main attraction. A bustling hub of connections to everywhere else in the north, it has become the launchpad for some of the country's most exciting excursions. Bustling night markets and a growing number of clubs and bars keeps the city thriving at night, while hundreds of temples and museums all do their part in balancing out modernity with the ancient history and traditions that define Chiang Mai's soul. It's also a well-known foodie heaven, famed for an incredibly diverse range of cuisines, from roadside noodle soups to Michelin-starred journeys at artisan chef tables.

Beyond the city walls, adventure seekers can trek through jungles and zipline over treetops. Whichever way you look, breathtaking landscapes fill the frame, from the imposing Doi Inthanon (the highest mountain in Thailand) to climbable waterfalls, unusual rock formations and mystical forest temples.

In the lowlands, rice-paddy vistas paint the countryside a vibrant hue of green – a testament to the agricultural backbone that holds the province together.

ALEXANDRE.ROSA/SHUTTERSTOCK

THE MAIN AREAS

MUANG CHIANG MAI
Roughly 1000 years of culture within four walls. **p252**

DOI SUTHEP
The spiritual mountain overlooking the city. **p266**

DOI INTHANON
Thailand's highest mountain and jungle playground. **p292**

CHIANG DAO
Towering mountains and hidden gems. **p293**

Find Your Way

Chiang Mai's adventures begin in the city, and often end there, too. Whether you explore snaking city *soi* (streets) or scale steep mountain trails, start from within the city walls, and you'll easily find day trips and overnight jaunts beginning from there.

Chiang Dao, p293

A serene mountain town nestled between lush, dense jungles and sheer mountain cliffs, Chiang Dao is best known for its caves, hot springs and calming, slow-life atmosphere.

Doi Suthep, p266

Chiang Mai's most iconic mountain is home to sacred legends, hill-tribe communities and rich biodiversity, creating a spiritual and natural landmark that defines the city.

Muang Chiang Mai, p252

Rich in history and oozing culture, the city of Chiang Mai is the hub of the north. With so much on offer in such a small area, it's no surprise visitors return again and again.

Doi Inthanon, p292

Ascend into the mountains and scale Thailand's highest peak, where misty forests and waterfalls make for a natural and surprisingly accessible wonderland.

MOTORBIKE

The best way to explore Chiang Mai is on two wheels: it gives you the freedom of discovery without the headache of confusing bus timetables. If you head into the mountains, modern scooters have enough power to get you most places, but beware of overzealous police and dangerous drivers.

ROT DAANG

The ubiquitous red truck of Chiang Mai may get a bad rep for occasionally ripping tourists off, but it's still one of the best ways to get around. Drivers are also the most willing to head out of town to harder-to-reach places – for a price, of course.

CAR

In the city, ride-hailing apps such as Grab and Bolt are the cheapest form of transport. **Chiang Mai Taxis** *(098 823 7385)* still need to be called in advance and often charge more, while rental cars are cheap, easy and convenient if you have an international driving permit.

Plan Your Time

With so much going on in Chiang Mai, it can be hard trying to choose what's best to do. Our advice is to go with the flow as much as possible, fitting in the must-sees whenever it makes the most sense.

BUNYIAM/SHUTTERSTOCK

Food stall in Nimmanhaemin (p277), Chiang Mai

A Day in the City

- Whether you're just passing through or have a full day to see it all, head to the old city to pop into a few **temples** (p258) and sip on **Akha tribe-grown coffee** (p271) for the quickest snapshot of city life.

- If you're into outdoor activities, spend your afternoon getting elbow-deep in **indigo mother** (p263) or forging your own **silver jewellery** (p279) with a theatrical helping of royal **Khantoke dinners** (p272) and traditional Lanna performances.

- Alternatively, spend the afternoon at a **cooking class in the jungle** (p265) before making a detour into the hip district of **Nimmanhaemin** (p277) for a tour of its best bars, be it sipping cocktails at rooftop spots or pouring beer over ice at student haunts.

SEASONAL HIGHLIGHTS

There's a lot going on, with festivals and events – some dating back to the Lanna Kingdom – occurring throughout the year.

JANUARY

Join locals as they celebrate ancient culture and handicrafts from the Lanna era at the **Bo Sang Umbrella Festival** (p262), where parades, workshops and markets take over an entire block of the city.

FEBRUARY

Be amazed by the number of rare and beautiful tropical plants growing in the region as part of the tapestry of colour that is the **Chiang Mai Flower Festival** at **Royal Park Rajapruek** (p269).

MARCH

Avoid the smog season in the mountains (from January to April) and instead join Thais digging for bargains in the ctiy's many **thrift shops** (p282).

A Weekend to Hang Around

● With more time to kill, a good tip is to keep organised, find a theme for each day and run with it. On the first day, you could stick to the city and explore some hidden gems, such as its **art galleries** (p267) and **world-class spas** (p275). On the second, hike to hidden temples on **Doi Suthep** (p266), while on the third, let your adventurous spirit guide you through the hills of **Mae Sa Valley** (p291).

● There's something quite special about visiting a place and coming back with new knowledge: a day trip to **Mae Kampong** (p283) is a great choice, but an overnight stay is better. Especially when paired with **ziplines** (p284) and **jungle trails** (p285) that straddle the peaks nearby.

The Full Tour

● If time is less of an issue, then adopt a slow-life attitude (as the locals do) and spend a few days exploring each corner of the city before heading out into the province to zig-zag your way across northern Thailand.

● Dedicate time to learning the history and crafts of northern Thailand at the city's best **museums** (p276) and creative centres. Make your own **paper umbrellas** (p262) and spend a few days at the pottery kiln with **InClay Studio** (p275), located just outside the city. Then, admire contemporary Lanna art at the **MAIIAM Contemporary Art Museum** (p267) before going rural to soak up the incredible vistas of Thailand's highest mountain, **Doi Inthanon** (p292), or trek to the mighty peaks of **Doi Luang Chiang Dao** (p293).

APRIL
Make rounds of the old town on the back of an open-top tuk-tuk in one of the country's largest **Songkran** (p281) celebrations – the country-wide water fight to celebrate Thai New Year.

JUNE
In an ancient clearing near Wat Doi Kham, see the **Pu Sae Ya Sae** (p287) spirits appeased through the ritual of a sacrificed buffalo – parts of which are eaten raw by a possessed witch-doctor.

NOVEMBER
Release your wishes on a floating lantern along with a thousand others at the magical northern Thai festival of **Yi Peng**, which conveniently coincides with the nationwide Loy Krathong Festival.

DECEMBER
Witness the incredible vistas and spy rare fauna from the hard-to-reach peaks of **Doi Chiang Dao Luang** (p296), a 230-million-year-old limestone massif that is Thailand's third-highest mountain.

Muang Chiang Mai

ANCIENT CITY | COFFEE CAPITAL | ART & CULTURE

TOP TIP

In Thailand, the provincial capital of each province has the same name as the province itself. To differentiate between the two, people use the prefix *muang* to identify the city, which is why many locals refer to Chiang Mai city as 'Muang Chiang Mai'.

The city of Chiang Mai offers a unique contrast of old-world charm and modern flair. Founded in 1296 by King Mengrai as the capital of the Lanna Kingdom, Chiang Mai quickly rose to importance as a cultural and religious centre in what is now northern Thailand, its strategic location on ancient trade routes helping it to flourish.

The mazelike alleys of the historic old city contain hundreds of temples and relics, while bustling night-bazaars, organic markets and the soothing ambience of Mae Nam Ping all add to the allure. Beyond the city centre, a sprawling outer suburb reaches far and wide in all directions. The city outgrows its walls here, adding a touch of modernity that blends with the rustic charm of rural Thailand, evoking the ambience of a remote village populated by artists and innovators. From backpackers and solo travellers to young families and tour groups, there's something for everyone in Chiang Mai, and then some.

GETTING AROUND

Getting around Chiang Mai is easy, with copious tuk-tuk and *rot daang*, and a large number of taxis and ride-hailing apps. The ubiquitous *rot daang* is the easiest and often cheapest option, with shared rides following random routes that depend on the passengers. They'll generally set you back between 10฿ and 30฿, depending on where you get off. Private hire is negotiable, starting at 100฿, with haggling expected.

Although a few bus routes have been established around the main city, they're inconsistent and slow. Ride-hailing apps such as Grab and Bolt are now the standard for both locals and tourists; download the app before you arrive so you can easily connect your bank card to the app to save paying in cash. Alternatively, rent a car or motorbike if you expect to do a lot of moving around; you'll need an international diving licence to keep within the law. Police checkpoints are common, with fines issued for anything from loose helmets to dirty licence plates to tax and driver licence issues.

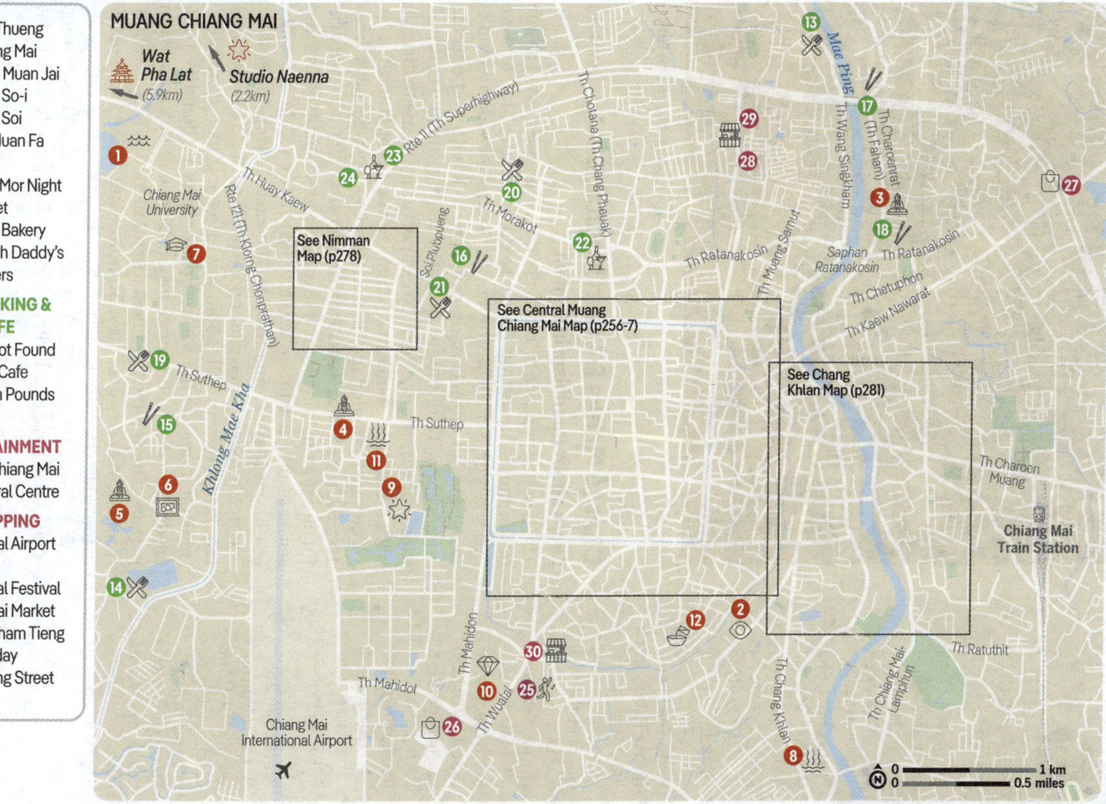

SIGHTS
1 Angkaew Reservoir
see 28 Jing Jai Gallery
2 Khlong Mae Kha
3 Wat Faham
4 Wat Suan Dok
5 Wat Umong Suan Phutthatham
6 Wattana Art Gallery

ACTIVITIES
7 Chiang Mai University
8 Health Land Chiang Mai
9 InClay Studio
10 Old Medicine Hospital
11 Sense Onsen Suandok Wellness & Spa
12 Thai Akha Cooking School

EATING
13 Baristro x Ping River
14 Dinky's BBQ
15 Han Thueng Chiang Mai
16 Huan Muan Jai
17 Khao So-i
18 Khao Soi Lamduan Fa Ham
19 Lang Mor Night Market
20 Nana Bakery
21 Smash Daddy's Burgers

DRINKING & NIGHTLIFE
22 Bar Not Found
23 LISM Cafe
24 Seven Pounds

ENTERTAINMENT
25 Old Chiang Mai Cultural Centre

SHOPPING
26 Central Airport Plaza
27 Central Festival
28 Jing Jai Market
29 Kad Kham Tieng
30 Saturday Walking Street

THE FOUR CITY GATES

Chiang Mai's original city wall was built by King Mengrai in 1296, with only four entrances/exits.

Pratu Chang Pheuak (North): Originally named Hua Viang Gate, this gate was used by royalty to make grand entrances to the city.

Pratu Tha Phae (East): Rebuilt in the 1980s, this gate is a loose replica of what was once the main way in and out of the city for traders and residents.

Pratu Chiang Mai (South): The city's southern gate led to the region's bountiful floodplains and was home to emerging silverware traders who still populate Th Wua Lai.

Pratu Suan Dok (West): Meaning 'Door to the Flower Garden', this gate once led to a royal flower garden where Lanna royalty would relax.

PHICHAK/SHUTTERSTOCK

Monks, Wat Suan Dok

Chat to Monks & Learn Meditation

MAP P253

Learn about Buddhism in English

The popular practice of 'monk chat' is constantly rated as one of the most interesting things to do in Chiang Mai, and we can see why. Set up for foreigners, English-speaking monks take time out of their daily rituals to talk with and educate guests about Thai Buddhism. Enlightening, fun and cultural, these conversations offer a rare opportunity to speak directly with a Buddhist monk in a language you understand.

The most popular monk chat happens on weekdays from 4pm to 7pm at **Wat Suan Dok** *(monkchat.net; free)* – a peaceful city temple known for its stunning royal mausoleum and series of bright white *chedi* (stupas) that contain the ashes of Chiang Mai's Lanna royalty. The casual, drop-in sessions are free, unstructured and open to all, with no pre-booking required. You can talk about anything you like, from questions on monastic life to deep philosophical thoughts. One-on-one sessions and private group chats can be arranged in person. The temple also hosts regular meditation retreats, from one-day sessions most Mondays and Fridays to monthly four-day retreats.

Wat Chedi Luang (p258) and Wat Phra That Doi Suthep (p266) also have monk chats, though their schedules are less

EATING IN CHIANG MAI: KHAO SOI RESTAURANTS

MAP P253, P278 & P281

Khao Soi Lamduan Fa Ham: Popular among locals filling up at lunch, you'll find quick *khao soi* (curried noodles) and thousands of satay sticks on the menu. *8am-4pm* ฿

Khao Soi Pa Pai: A little hard to find but worth the journey for its classic halal *khao soi* with a deeply satisfying broth. *9am-2pm* ฿

Khao So-i: Japanese-themed *khao soi* topped with squid, scallop or Wagyu beef. *10.30am-8.30pm* ฿฿

Khao Soi Nimman: A fun mix-and-match style menu of meat and vegetarian toppings. Expect a queue at all hours of the day. *10am-9pm* ฿฿

fixed. Visit the temples to find out their current schedule and remember to always dress respectfully by covering your shoulders and knees.

Paddle Through the City

MAP P253

Kayaking and paddleboarding

Although it may seem as if the Ping River is underutilised in terms of recreation, a few spots offer easy water access, meaning you can explore the city by way of paddle and oar. A popular jetty for locals is the **Chiang Mai Kayaking Center**, found inside the quiet temple of **Wat Faham**, where you can pick up a kayak and take to the river for just 50฿ a pop. The centre is open from 8am to 8pm.

A number of restaurants and cafes have their own pontoons where you can stop and find refreshments on your trip, while a local Facebook group – **Chiang Mai Kayaking Meetup** – organises regular community-led kayaking outings (also from Wat Faham). And with the late cutoff of 8pm, catching the sunset while kayaking down the river is reason in itself to try.

For the more active, **SUP CNX** *(facebook.com/supcnx; 085 597 9662)* runs daily sightseeing tours down the river via paddleboard, with training and stop-offs included. Various excursions can be chosen, from fun family jaunts *(per person 200฿)* to more intensive routes for experienced hands that cover much longer distances *(per person 700฿)*.

Drive a Tuk-Tuk

A Thai-style adventure

If you've ever wondered what it's like to sit behind the wheel of the country's most famous mode of transport, now's your chance. The **Tuk Tuk Club** *(thetuktukclub.com; 093 000 5492)* is the only company in Thailand that lets you actually drive your own.

After a detailed driving lesson, you'll become 'tuk-tuk approved' and ready to hit the open road on tours which show a side of Thailand that most never get the chance to see. The bumper 11-day tour *(61,000฿)* around northern Thailand has been described by the *Sunday Times* as 'the best driving holiday in the world', and we tend to agree. With professional English-speaking guides leading the way, tours navigate roads less travelled, stop by pristine rivers, share hill-tribe secrets, and fill you full of northern food and fresh mountain coffee.

Continued on p259

SEVEN CENTURIES IN THE MAKING

Founded in 1296 by King Mangrai, the city of Chiang Mai was the capital of the influential Lanna Kingdom, which once spanned as far as modern-day eastern Myanmar, western Laos and southern China. Before Chiang Mai, the kingdom's capital moved from Fang to Chiang Saen to Lumphun to Wiang Kum Kam (p279), a ruin just a few kilometres from the city centre that can still be visited today.

A key trading-hub between ports in China and Myanmar, the city experienced numerous power shifts, including a 16th-century Burmese conquest. It was eventually liberated and integrated into Siam during the 18th and 19th centuries, when the wider Chiang Mai province officially became a province of Thailand.

EATING ON THE RIVERSIDE: OUR PICKS

MAP P253 & P281

River View Bar: Rustic, local feel with an array of Thai food, as well as hotpot and BBQ options. *5-11pm* ฿฿

Sai Ping Bar & Restaurant: Local food, lantern lighting and ice-cold beers in this spot overlooking the river; it's located right next to the bridge. *11am-midnight* ฿

Baristro x Ping River: Creative menus, Instagrammable spaces and top-quality coffee make this a favourite of the city's hipsters. *8am-6pm* ฿฿

Riverside Bar & Restaurant: With good food on the menu, this has been a legendary late-night spot since 1984, with live music and a millennial crowd. *11am-1am* ฿฿

CENTRAL MUANG CHIANG MAI
Th Hutsadisawee
Th Mani Nopharat
Th Si Phum
Th Sanan Kila
Soi 4
Th Wiang Kaew
Th Phra Pokklao
Th Bunreuangrit
Th Singharat
Th Ratwithi
Th Inthawarorot
Th Jhaban
Soi 12
Th Arak
Th Ratchadamnoen
Sunday Walking Street
Soi 8
Th Ratchamankha
Th Ratchamankha
Soi 7
Soi 6
Th Samlan
Soi 3
Soi 6
Th Ratchaphakhinai
Suan Buak Hat
Th Bamrungburi
Th Chang Lor
Kanchanaphisek Park
Th Wualai
Th Thiphanet
Th Nontharam
Th Suriwong

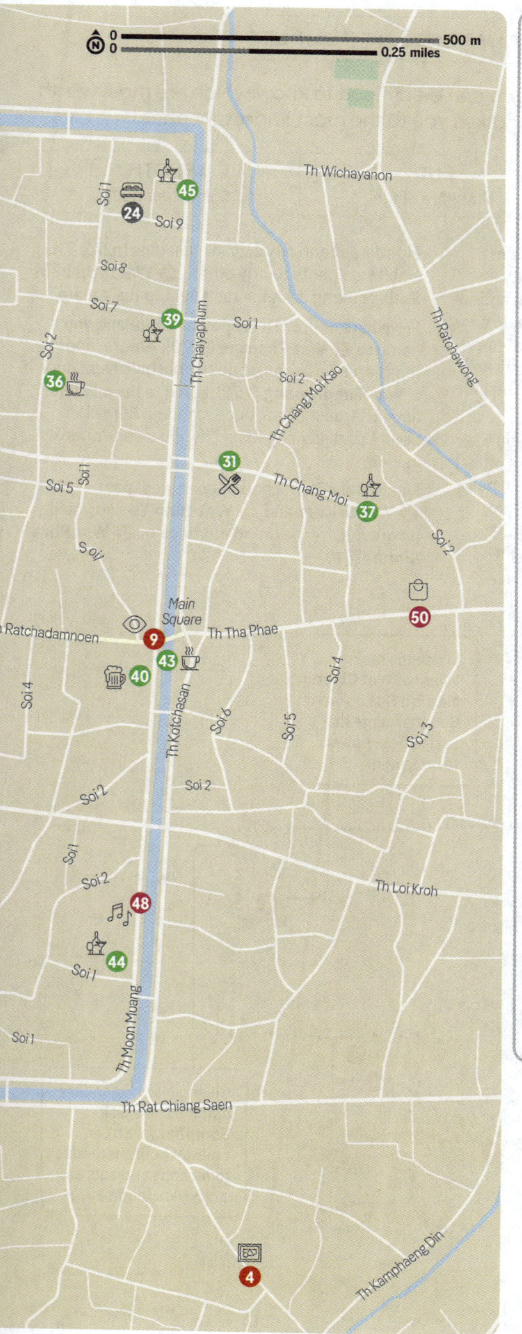

HIGHLIGHTS
1 Sunday Walking Street

SIGHTS
2 Chiang Mai City Arts & Cultural Centre
3 Chiang Mai Historical Centre
4 Dream Space Gallery
5 Lanna Folklife Museum
6 Pratu Chang Pheuak
7 Pratu Chiang Mai
8 Pratu Suan Dok
9 Pratu Tha Phae
10 Three King's Monument
11 Wat Chedi Luang
12 Wat Chiang Man
13 Wat Inthakhin Saduemuang
14 Wat Lok Moli
15 Wat Phantao
16 Wat Phra Singh
17 Wat Si Koet
18 Wat Srisuphan
19 Wat Tung Yu

ACTIVITIES
20 Fah Lanna Spa
21 Makkha Health & Spa Chiang Mai (Colonial Gardens)
22 Oasis Spa

SLEEPING
23 Le Charcoa Hôtel
24 Libra Guest House
25 Nuan Nil Bed and Breakfast
26 Rachamankha Boutique Hotel
27 Tamarind Village

EATING
28 Baan Landai Fine Thai Cuisine
29 Chang Phuak Gate Night Market
30 Chiang Mai Gate Market
31 Downtown Vegan Garden
32 Jok Somphet
33 Reform Kafé

DRINKING & NIGHTLIFE
34 Akha Ama Cafe
35 Deaf Shop
36 Graph
37 HIDELAND
38 Mahoree City of Music
39 NOISE
40 Renegade Craft Beer
41 Sapphic Riot
42 See You Soon Cafe
43 Single Origin Store
44 Sound Up
45 Sriphum Melodic
46 White Rabbit
47 Yoda's CNX Gallery

ENTERTAINMENT
48 Chiang Mai OriginaLive
49 North Gate Jazz Co-Op

SHOPPING
50 Nova Jewelry Collection

CHIANG MAI'S MOST IMPORTANT TEMPLES

With over 300 temples in the city, it can be difficult to know which are most worth stopping to see; this walking tour takes you to the most important ones.

START	END	LENGTH
Wat Lok Moli	Wat Phra Singh	4.5km; four hours

This route is the ultimate way to see the most important temples of Chiang Mai's old city in one fell swoop. Start at 1 **Wat Lok Moli** and pay your respects to the 14th-century *chedi* by pouring water over it using the pulley system. Head through the newly built *viharn* (shrine hall) out front, cross the footbridge and head east for about 600m.

Take a right at Jok Somphet (p268) and you'll find 2 **Wat Chiang Man** (1296), the city's oldest temple. Make sure to walk behind the main hall to see the spectacular elephant *chedi*. Then, follow Th Ratchapakhinai south, turning left on Ratvithi to arrive at the 3 **Three King's Monument** and city's main museums (p276). The small yet spectacularly ornate 4 **Wat Inthakhin Saduemuang** is on the road next to the square.

From here, follow Th Prapokloa south and you'll come to 5 **Wat Phantao** (p270), a more modern temple with a Lanna-style temple hall. Next door is **Wat Chedi Luang** *(40฿)*, home to the city pillar and its largest *chedi*, once standing 85m high before partially collapsing during an earthquake in 1545.

Finally, take Th Rachadamnoen west past 6 **Wat Si Koet** and 7 **Wat Tung Yu** and you'll be greeted by the grand entrance of 8 **Wat Phra Singh** *(20฿)*.

Inside the main *viharn* of **Wat Chiang Man** is a Sri Lankan Buddha image that's said to hold powers to bring rain.

During Songkran, the Buddha image at **Wat Phra Singh** is placed on a float and paraded around the city as people splash it with water.

Chiang Mai's legendary congee shop, **Jok Somphet** (p268), is open 24 hours. It feeds thousands and acts as a citywide landmark.

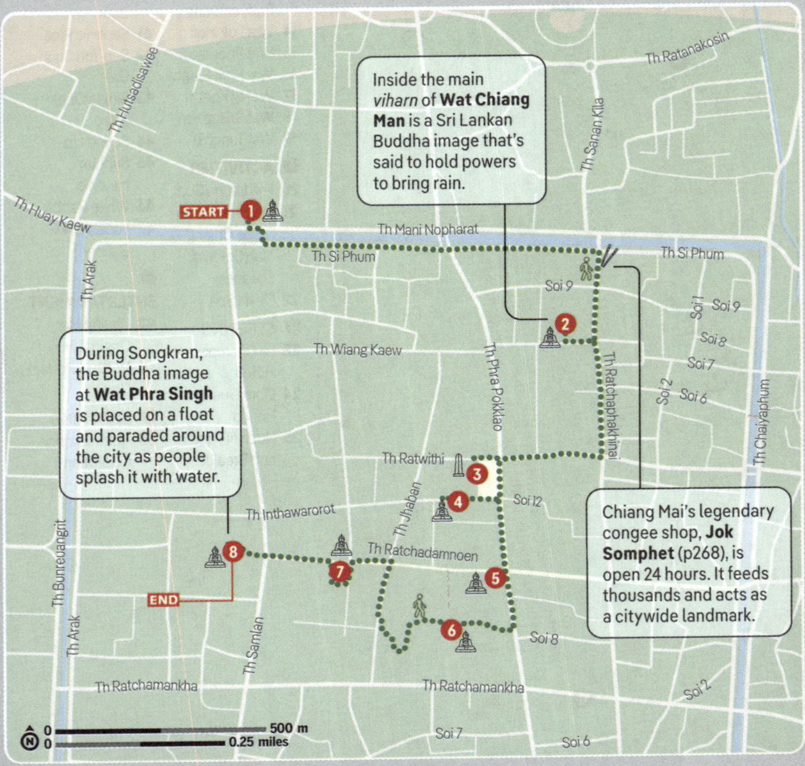

Continued from p255
Shorter trips of five *(25,000฿)* and three *(17,000฿)* days are also available with or without a chauffeur, while their one-day trip *(5700฿)* promises an action-packed three-wheel jaunt around the mountain roads of Mae Wang, where you'll visit temples, raft on rivers and meet elephants. International driving permits are required to drive the tuk-tuk.

Dine on a Golden Barge

MAP P281

A river cruise fit for royalty

Though relatively new to the river, **Anantara Chiang Mai Resort** *(anantara.com)* has joined other long-standing operators in offering dinner cruises that drift past riverside temples, old city houses and lush green banks.

Their golden barge – with motifs blending Thai, Lanna and Burmese styles – is hard to miss as it glistens in the tropical sun. Known as the *Dibba Yana Chitta* ('Heavenly Boat'), this striking vessel was designed by Thai National Artist Chalermchai Kositpipat, the visionary behind the famous White Temple in Chiang Rai.

With just 18 seats, the **Dibba Yana Chitta River Cruise** *(6999฿)* must be booked in advance, but you don't need to be a guest at the hotel to join. On board, indulge in a seven-course Thai tasting-menu by Michelin-starred chefs and wine pairing from Thailand's top vineyards. If you can't fork out such an expense, the hotel's **Jao Ping River Cruise** offers an accessible alternative aboard a traditional scorpion-tail boat, with choices of **morning voyages** *(1800฿)* that include alms-giving to monks and the sampling of local snacks; two types of **afternoon tea options** *(1400–2700฿)*; and a four-course royal Thai dinner **sunset cruise** *(2400฿)*.

The OG of river cruises, **Mae Ping River Cruise** *(maepingrivercruise.com; per person 550฿)* has been floating along for almost 40 years, although today the dinners have all but vanished. Organise charter rides from the pier at **Wat Chai Mongkhon** and stop at an out-of-town village for some riverside *khao soi*. Riverside Bar & Restaurant (p255) fills the gap with a cheap riverboat dinner option *(200฿)* that departs most nights at 8pm.

PEDAL-POWERED ALTERNATIVES

If the revving engine of a tuk-tuk is a little too much for your taste, perhaps a tour of the city on the back of a *samlor* (Thai rickshaw) will be more appealing. Approach any rickshaw driver – most easily found around Pratu Tha Phae (p254) and Wat Phra Singh – and they'll be happy to take you around town, pointing out the sights in simple English. As this traditional mode of transport is in steep decline, it's a great way to support the heritage of the city. **Tamarind Village** *(tamarindvillage.com)* is a hotel that also offers guests rickshaw tours around the old town; these tours come with a guide and are perfect for families and group travellers.

EATING IN CHIANG MAI: NIGHT MARKETS

MAP P253, P278 & P281

Chang Phuak Gate Night Market: Find quick Thai food here, including Cowboy Hat Lady's *kow kah moo* (slow-cooked pork with rice). *5pm-midnight* ฿

Chiang Mai Gate Market: Fresh produce by day and bustling street-food market by night; home to some of the city's most famous quick-cook vendors. *4pm-2am* ฿

Lang Mor Night Market: Filled with cheap and colourful street food, this is where students come after class; closed every 25th of the month for cleaning. *5-9pm* ฿

Kalare Night Bazaar: Tucked in off the main drag of the Night Bazaar, the food here is best enjoyed with a beer and a table. *4-11.30pm* ฿

SUTTIRAT WIRIYANON/SHUTTERSTOCK

Jing Jai market

TOP EXPERIENCE

Chiang Mai's Best Markets

DON'T MISS

- Sunday Walking Street
- Wua Lai Walking Street
- Jing Jai Market
- Coconut Market
- White Market
- Warorot Market
- Bamboo Family Market

PRACTICALITIES

Shopping in Thailand is done almost entirely via a QR payment system linked to local banks. Kasikornbank offers prepaid cards and an accompanying app, **TAGTHAi** *(tagthai.com/easy-pay)* that allows foreigners to pay with ease.

Chiang Mai is home to some of the most intriguing and diverse markets you'll find in Thailand. Here are the main ones.

Sunday Walking Street

Chiang Mai's biggest market *(4pm-midnight Sun)* stretches from Thapae Gate all the way to Wat Phra Singh (p258). Here since the 14th century, it has evolved over generations and now features rows of local artisans, tribespeople, food vendors and talented performers.

Wua Lai (Saturday Walking Street)

At Wua Lai *(4-10pm Sat)* you'll find a wealth of handcrafted goods, trinkets, souvenirs and food stalls that promise an energetic and festival-like energy; it's all set against a backdrop of silver shops that lend an old-world charm.

Night Bazaar

At the Night Bazaar *(5pm-midnight)*, expect more typical tourist tat than your usual market, with the addition of many bars and restaurants giving it a distinct downtown feel. In the centre of it all you'll find the Anusarn Market, home to beer gardens, Thai boxing shows and the odd *kathoey* (Thai transgender and cross dressers') cabaret.

Jing Jai Market

The permanent courtyard of this market *(8am-8pm)* is lined with stalls, concept shops and restaurants; weekends see a morning farmers' market. It has themed market days, such as the vintage market every first Friday of the month.

San-Pa-Tong Buffalo Market

Well off the tourist trail, San-Pa-Tong *(5-11am Sat)* promises a thoroughly Thai experience for a Saturday morning. As one of the largest agricultural markets in the region, farmers come here to trade goods and, more importantly, sell cattle.

Warorot Market

Also known as Kad Luang, Warorot *(4am-6pm)* is the city's main trade hub, founded in 1296 when the city was established. Today, the main buildings house vast food markets, gold shops, fabric shops, tribal handicrafts and fresh flowers. It's also where you'll find Chinatown.

Chang Phuak Gate Night Market

This market *(5pm-1am)* is a true hawker fest, rammed to the brim with Chiang Mai's most famous street-food vendors, including Pretty Pork Lady's Anthony Bourdain-approved stewed pork leg, and a mean *pat tai* vendor.

Chiang Mai Gate Market

As if set up to rival its northern counterpart, the Chiang Mai Gate Market *(5pm-midnight)* on the south wall of the moat offers an almost identical street-food experience, with the added excitement of being right next to the old city's busiest wet market of the same name.

Coconut Market

Set among a working coconut grove, this market *(8am-2pm Sat & Sun)* is where bamboo bridges cross algae-covered ponds and rows of palms frame market stalls selling copious amounts of breakfast snacks and Lanna-style goodies.

White Market

Originally formed by a gathering of Japanese people living in Chiang Mai, the White Market *(3-10pm Fri-Sun)* combines classic Japanese chic with local music, fashion and souvenirs.

Chiang Mai Amulet Market

A quintessentially Thai affair, the Amulet Market is within **Kad Kham Tieng** *(7am-2pm Thu)* and features thousands of Buddhist amulets that are 'lent' to shoppers. (Buddhist law states you can't sell spiritual objects; instead you 'lend' them indefinitely for a predetermined fee.) Prices range from 20฿ to millions of baht.

Bamboo Family Market

A large bamboo amphitheatre houses a zero-waste food and handicraft market *(8am-4pm Sat & Sun)* that supports refugees and ethnic minorities through meaningful employment and cultural exchange. It was created by **SangGaDee** *(sanggadee.com)*, a community-driven initiative that also hosts the odd workshop and exhibition.

A MEETING OF TRIBES

At Warorot Market on Fridays between 5am and noon, you'll come face to face with different tribes trading everything from staple rice grains to the downright bizarre. Known as **Kad Baan Hor** to locals, this market brings together Yunnanese Muslims, Shan tribespeople and local hill-tribes, as well as a curious collection of meats, herbs and spices that are difficult to find anywhere else.

TOP TIPS

- Although many markets have banned plastic bags, they're still prevalent. Bring your own reusable bag and be clear that you don't want a plastic one when vendors prepare your purchases.
- Markets in Thailand usually open quite early to make the most of the cool morning weather. Locals will tell you that the best food and goods are to be found at the crack of dawn.
- The old tourist adage of 'no change for 1000฿ notes' is still going strong. With most residents opting for digital payments, it's now even harder to break big notes, so bring change with you.

MAE NAM PING

King Phaya Mengrai's (also spelt Mangrai) first attempt at building a new capital on the banks of Mae Ping at Wiang Kum Kam lasted only a few years: the city was eventually abandoned due to flooding. But Mae Nam Ping, which runs parallel to the old city, has been both the lifeblood and trade centre of Chiang Mai since the city was first founded. Local merchants once sailed boats up and down the river, through the central plains and into Bangkok in search of salt, fish, clothing and tools. By the 1800s, logging barges populated its banks, while missionaries set up on its eastern flank. Today, there's little action on the river, aside from the odd scorpion-tail dinner boat, fish farm and a handful of tourist activities.

PLOYPEMUK/SHUTTERSTOCK

Bo Sang Umbrella Festival

Make a Paper Umbrella

Where tradition meets tourism

Spend a great day in the city by signing up to a cultural activity that connects you with the craft traditions of northern Thailand. Chiang Mai is famous for its hand-painted paper umbrellas, a handicraft that originated in Bo Sang and San Kampang some 200 years ago. Historically used exclusively by monks and members of the royal court, the umbrellas eventually fell into everyday use.

Villagers in Bo Sang continue to create the umbrellas to this day; you can see them at the umbrella-making centre in **Bo Sang Umbrella Village** *(bosang-umbrella.com; free)*. Watch artisans at work and learn about the umbrella-making process, shop for a special souvenir or try your hand at making one yourself. Kids can enjoy painting umbrellas in the garden out back and joining in the artisan-led workshops. The village is open from 8am to 5pm.

Time your visit for the third weekend of January and you'll catch the **Bo Sang Umbrella Festival** – a colourful celebration of the craft and its community, with markets, activities, parades of umbrella-wielding women on bicycles and traditional music performances all weekend.

DRINKING IN CHIANG MAI: CRAFT BEER

MAP P253, P278 & P281

Grumpy Old Men: Local craft beer 'My Beer Friend' served on tap, alongside a range of international favourites. *5pm-midnight Thu-Tue*

Chiang Mai Craft Beer: Huge collection of bottled craft beer, plus a modest selection of IPA, weizen and stouts on tap. *5pm-midnight*

Chit Hole CNX: Part of a growing network of bars owned by Thailand's first and most politically active craft-beer brewery. *4.30pm-midnight*

Renegade Craft Beer: Rotating taps of craft beers and over 300 bottles to choose from. Wash them down with one of their tasty pizzas. *5pm-midnight*

Turn Your Hands Indigo

MAP P253 & P278

Deep-blue artisanal roots

Once a cornerstone of the local economy, indigo dyeing is a craft that dates back millennia, now found living on at Chiang Mai's **Studio Naenna** *(studio-naenna.com; 053 226 042)* – one of the few places in the city that continues to honour the 2000-year-old process, and a great place for hands-on learning. Activities led by writer and textile historian Patricia Cheesman take place in a hidden, peaceful studio in the foothills of Doi Suthep, alongside decades-old indigo vats of bubbling 'indigo mother'.

Workshops *(from 1000฿)* cover everything from natural dyeing to tie-dye techniques and are bookable online. The studio also hosts the annual indigo harvest workshop – a rare opportunity. Usually taking place towards the end of monsoon season, the workshop allows participants to harvest the plants, pound them to make fresh indigo paste and use it to dye fabrics. Aside from indigo, the studio also runs one-on-one weaving courses (five days for the full course) using traditional Karen backstrap looms and naturally dyed cotton.

Those short on time can visit their studio, **Adorn with Studio Naenna**, in the Nimmanhaemin area and pick up some ready-made fabrics made by the studio's resident artisans.

TRAVEL BY ROT DAANG

Literally meaning 'red trucks', *rot daang* are converted pickup-truck taxis that are ubiquitous in Chiang Mai and have become a symbol of the city. Aside from being cheap forms of transport, you can also hire them for the day and have the driver take you around to numerous sights. Locals tend to hop-on and hop-off for just 30฿ a ride, telling the driver roughly where to drive to. If you're a bigger group, it's easier to book out the full truck for a negotiable price, starting at around 50฿ per person, depending on where you need to go. We say to take advantage of all that space in the cabin and shop Chiang Mai's markets to your heart's content.

Get a Taste for Hill-Tribe Cuisine

MAP P253

Learn how to cook, Akha style

The **Thai Akha Cooking School** *(thaiakhakitchen.com; cooking course 1400฿)* is the first and only cooking school in Thailand that offers an opportunity to experience Akha food and culture from the kitchen. Different from regular Thai fare, Akha food is often healthier, made using ingredients sourced from the jungle.

Both the morning and afternoon courses are run by an English-speaking Thai-Akha chef who makes a real effort to detail all the steps and ingredients to make sure you not only understand what you're making, but also why. Expect to learn traditional Akha techniques and discover new flavours as you work through a menu of 11 dishes. According to the instructors, Akha people say 'There are only three things in the jungle that you can't eat, and nobody knows what they are' – meaning they eat just about everything.

EATING IN CHIANG MAI: VEGAN RESTAURANTS

MAP P256 & P278

Free Bird Cafe: Bold, plant-based takes on curry noodles and other classics, as well as a decent selection of Burmese food. *9am-8pm* ฿

Downtown Vegan Garden: Bright salads, rice bowls and modern vegan interpretations of Thai food, all served in a cozy garden setting. *9am-11pm* ฿฿

Aeeen Japanese Vegan: Clever Japanese-style reimaginations using vegan ingredients. Workshops and dinner events are common here. *11am-5pm Thu-Sun* ฿

Reform Kafé: Serving 100% plant-based food and 100% breaking the rules on what vegan means. Think power bowls, burgers, cakes and craft beer. *9am-10pm* ฿฿

FOREST TRADITIONS

Wat Pha Lat is just one of many Thai temples that follow the Thai Forest tradition, a sub-sect of the Theravada Buddhist tradition, which is the most prominent form of Buddhism practised in Thailand.

This approach emphasises a more austere and contemplative approach to Buddhist teachings, the roots of which can be traced back to the forest-dwelling monks of ancient India, long since exported across Southeast Asia. Monks of the Thai Forest tradition often wear darker, ochre-coloured robes and eat a more strictly vegetarian diet. They live in remote forest monasteries far away from urban centres in order to deepen their meditation practice and cultivate a closer connection to nature.

BANGPRIKPHOTO/SHUTTERSTOCK

Wat Pha Lat

Follow the Monk's Trail

Ancient pilgrimage into the jungle

At the foothills of Doi Suthep – where the back walls of the university and the city zoo meet – you can find a hidden trail that follows a centuries-old pilgrimage path to one of Chiang Mai's most beautiful and unseen temples.

Searching Google Maps for 'Wat Pha Lat Hike (Monk's Trail)' will get you to the trailhead of an ancient pilgrimage route that disappears into the jungles of Doi Suthep, only to emerge at the forest temple of **Wat Pha Lat**. The trail follows a stream that can overflow during the rainy season, meaning it gets rocky and slippery in places. You're likely to meet other tourists and locals on the trail, as well as the odd (often barefoot) monk or two.

Once you reach the temple, you'll be struck by its ethereal beauty and ambience – a true oasis of natural and spiritual splendour. You can easily spend hours exploring, admiring

DRINKING IN CHIANG MAI: HIDDEN COCKTAIL BARS

MAP P253, P256, P278 & P281

Noir CMI: Three dimly lit jazz bars hidden behind a hotel car-park. Think 1960s' speakeasy with *omakase*-style cocktails. *7pm-1am*

Bar Not Found: Funky, fun and brightly lit, this spots feels more friend's living-room than bar, with a pantone-inspired menu to match. *7pm-midnight.*

White Rabbit: Head upstairs, through what looks like an abandoned building, and you'll find one of the city's most sophisticated cocktail bars. *6pm-midnight*

BRINE: Creative cocktails that play on the tastes of vinegar and olive brine, served with a selection of savoury pickled all-sorts. *6.30pm-midnight*

the forested temple ruins or meditating to the gentle murmur of the holy stream you passed on the way up.

The monks at the temple speak reasonably good English and tolerate photo-hungry tourists, but they would much prefer to share their wisdom and beliefs with those who ask. It's important to note that both the trail and temple are significant spiritual places, so appropriate temple clothing that covers your shoulders and legs is a must.

Taxis to and from the trailhead are best booked through a ride-hailing app, as hailing a taxi from the temple isn't always successful. You can also hitch a ride with any *rot daang* that happens to appear. If you're feeling up to the challenge, the trail continues up the mountain all the way to Wat Phra That Doi Suthep (p266).

Learn to Cook in Paradise

Cooking classes in the jungle

Beyond its reputation for amazing northern Thai food, Chiang Mai also gives you the chance to take to the kitchen and immerse yourself in the savoury, spicy and sour world of traditional Thai cooking. And while the city boasts a cooking school for every budget, the real culinary adventures lie with those who have something special to share.

Zabb-E-Lee Thai Cooking School *(zabb-elee-cooking.com; cooking courses 1200฿)* is a rising favourite for those looking to get hands-on with Thai cooking, and is led by friendly, fun-loving cooking instructors in picture-perfect jungle surroundings. The towering bamboo structure that acts as an open-air kitchen feels like something out of a film, while the repertoire of dishes to choose from defies expectation. Morning and afternoon cooking courses include pick-ups, market tours and cooking ingredients for four dishes, a curry paste (that you can take home) and a fresh fruit dessert. Small classes max out at 10 people, keeping the experience intimate. All dishes can be adjusted for vegetarians and vegans.

For a more refined cooking experience, **Grandma's Home Cooking School** *(grandmascookingschool.com; cooking courses 1150฿)* offers both full- and half-day courses that follow traditional recipes and techniques passed down from the owner's grandmother. Aside from the cooking, you'll also learn to mill flour using a millstone, grate fresh coconut, harvest herbs from the organic garden and fire up charcoal stoves in the kitchens of the family's traditional Lanna teak home.

A TASTE FOR LARB

Govit Thatarat, founder of **Review Chiangmai** *(facebook.com/reviewchiangmai)*

If there's one food you should try while in Chiang Mai, it's *larb*. This meat salad is ubiquitous to Thailand, with two versions – northern and Isan styles. **Laab Ton Koi** in the San Sai district may be a bit out of town, but it's where you'll find the best northern *larb*. People rush here every day and can often be seen queuing outside before it's even open. Serving for just three hours (11am to 2pm), I've never *not* seen it overflowing with people waiting, and it even closes early sometimes when people eat the place empty! Sure, it gets a bit ridiculous at times, but that's part of the fun. If you want to know what all the hype is about, then give it a try.

DRINKING IN CHIANG MAI: ROOFTOP BARS

MAP P256, P278 & P281

Yayee Rooftop Bar: Owned by Thailand's celebrity sweetheart Ananda Everingham; cocktails by renowned mixologists and sunset views. *5pm-midnight*

MAI The Sky Bar: This trendy, cosmopolitan rooftop bar (the highest in the city) sits atop the Melia Hotel and has a distinct Bangkok vibe. *6pm-midnight*

Hong's Sky Bar: Unrestricted views of Doi Suthep served alongside a menu of exceptionally crafted drinks, snacks and bottle service. *4pm-midnight*

HIDELAND: A Thai–Japanese-style rooftop bar on a low-rise building overlooking Chang Mao Rd. Great for a social media check-in. *5-11.30pm*

TOP EXPERIENCE

Doi Suthep

The mountain of Doi Suthep is most famous for the temple that overlooks the city, glistening atop the skyline like a lantern in the night. But past the temple and out onto the mountain roads behind it lies so much more that often gets overlooked by the regular traveller.

KOBCHAIMA/SHUTTERSTOCK

Wat Phra That Doi Suthep

TOP TIPS

- Hire a *rot daang* for the day and enjoy a hassle-free tour of the mountain.
- Temples and palaces follow strict dress codes; knees and shoulders should be covered at all times.
- Wat Pha Lat (p264) is also on Doi Suthep, accessible by road or via the Monk's Trail (p264).

PRACTICALITIES

- Entrance 50฿
- Arrive early for sunrise views and morning chants.

Wat Phra That Doi Suthep

Not quite at the summit but offering stunning views of the city, Wat Phra That Doi Suthep is one of northern Thailand's most sacred temples. At its base, you can buy alms and take photos for a small fee, while at the top of the 306 steps flanked with *naga* (snake deities), you can meet monks, perform rituals and admire the golden *chedi* that glistens in the warm tropical sunlight.

Bhubing Palace

Just past the temple and nearer to the summit is Bhubing Palace *(50฿)*, which serves as a tranquil retreat for the royal family when visiting the north. The stunning gardens and grounds are home to rare roses, cool-climate flowers and a fountain that dances to soft jazz composed by the late Rama IX.

Khun Chang Khian

Khun Chang Khian is a quaint and quiet Hmong hill-tribe village surrounded by Siamese sakura trees that are famous for their bright-pink flowers, which bloom between December and January. The park and gardens are open year-round, and visitors can opt to stay the night in local homestays, meet villagers, pick strawberries and sample locally grown coffee.

Contemporary Art at its Finest

See the works of Southeast Asia

The **MAIIAM Contemporary Art Museum** *(maiiam.com; adult/child 150฿/free)* is the only standalone collection of Thai and Southeast Asian contemporary art in the country. Featuring both temporary exhibitions and a permanent family collection, it presents a unique assembly of new and contemporary Thai art that stands out against tradition.

Initiated by Jean Michel Beurdeley and his late wife Patsri Bunnag, MAIIAM's shimmering building of glass-and-mosaic cladding was built to share their private collection with the people of Chiang Mai and in memory of Chao Chom Iam, a royal consort to Rama V and direct ancestor of the family.

Throughout the year, the museum mounts a wide range of long-term and temporary exhibits, from visual art and design to fashion, live performance, film screenings, educational programmes, lectures, workshops and, of course, art. The museum also has a small cafe that serves tea, coffee, snacks and cocktails, plus a shop that sells museum merchandise, prints, designer products and rare artist books, including hard-to-find copies and limited editions. The museum is open from 10am to 6pm and is closed Tuesdays.

CHIANG MAI'S BEST GALLERIES

Gallery Seescape: A prominent destination featuring upcycled works by artist Hern Larpjaroensook and other upcoming local talent.

Wattana Art Gallery: Take in the creative moods of local contemporary art, with three floors of gallery space surrounded by thick jungle foliage.

Baan Tuek Art Centre: Free to enter community-forward art space that showcases contemporary exhibitions and screenings.

Dream Space Gallery: Street-art gallery that offers clean walls for artists to let their creative visions flourish – from a spray can.

Jing Jai Gallery: Located within the popular Jing Jai Market are works from emerging contemporary Thai artists that break the mould.

Stroll along Mae Kha Canal

MAP P253

Chiang Mai's reclaimed waterway

Once a written-off canal that became an open sewer, **Khlong Mae Kha** was recently revived through a high-profile city restoration project that has breathed new life into this historic waterway, which once served as a vital artery for the Lanna Kingdom.

Although there's no farmland left for the water to irrigate, the canal is now cleaned, paved and landscaped, and lined with market stalls, hole-in-the-wall eateries and locally owned shophouses. There's a slightly Japanese feel to the design, but the shops along the banks are generally Thai-style, owned and run by residents who have lived on the canal for centuries. Open every day between 3pm and 10pm but significantly busier at weekends, you can walk along the promenade and shop for souvenirs, or admire the community murals while you sip on a beer.

In November, the canal transforms into one of the most atmospheric spots to enjoy the Loy Krathong festival. With floating lanterns, canal-side candles and handmade *krathong*

EATING IN CHIANG MAI: AMERICAN FOOD

MAP P253 & P281

Dinky's BBQ: Texan-owned smoked-BBQ joint serving spicy beans, pulled-pork sandwiches and fall-off-the-bone ribs. *11am-9pm* ฿฿

Duke's (Ping River): Classic American cuisine with portions to match. Think overloaded pizzas, towering burgers, pies and Tex-Mex fare. *10am-10pm* ฿฿

Smash Daddy's Burgers: By far some of the city's best smashed burgers, served generously with calorific shakes and sides. *9.30am-10pm* ฿฿

Butter is Better: The good ole' days of Americana live on at this old-fashioned diner and deli, serving food the way it used to be. *8am-5pm Wed-Mon* ฿฿

(floating offerings) drifting peacefully downstream, it offers a more intimate alternative to the crowds along the river. And, if you're lucky, you may be privy to a performance by Chiang Mai's one and only nose-flute player.

Party at Chiang Mai's Tawandeng

MAP P278

Thai-style country cabaret clubbing

Clubbing in Thailand is a little different to what you'd expect elsewhere. Despite the extensive foreign influence in recent years, clubs still tend to swap the dancefloor for tall standing tables where partygoers can keep their bottles of whisky and mixers, creating cramped but highly social environments.

While Bangkok has adopted a more international approach, Chiang Mai's club scene is still very Thai, making it a great place to see how locals really party. Probably the most unique of the lot is **Tawandang Mahason** *(facebook.com/Tawandangmahasoncm; free; age 20+)*. A chain of clubs found across the country, Chiang Mai's Tawandang is one of the biggest and is like nothing you've ever experienced before.

Dropping you right into the heart of country clubbing culture, electrifying cabaret-style stage performances accompany a generous helping of live Thai country and folk that doesn't stop until the wee hours. The bizarre blend of traditional Thai performance, food served direct to your dancefloor table and distinct nightclub atmosphere promises an unforgettable night out. Get there early to secure a table, as free-standing patrons aren't permitted, and there's no bar service. Once the party gets going, expect revellers to 'cheers' with you endlessly.

More than Shopping

MAP P253

Air-conditioned cathedrals for all

Ask any Thai where they're going this weekend, and they'll likely have a trip to the shopping centre planned. In Thailand, the shopping centre is a modern-day mecca – an almost ritualistic destination where, even if you don't plan on buying anything, the lure of icy air-conditioning and endless cycles of pop-up markets, brand features, variety shows and A-list concerts draw crowds like you've never seen.

Central Festival *(centralchiangmai.com)* is the city's biggest shopping centre and where most of the fun happens. Aside from the shops and restaurants (many of which are excellent, by the way), it's also one of the city's main venues for concerts and events. Stages in the centre of the shopping centre and

LOCAL MUSIC ROCKS!

Supicha Teddaroon, lead singer of **Suthep Band**

As a local independent artist, I have seen myself and others like me struggle to get gigs while cover bands perform every night. That encouraged me to start the Chiangmai Original community in order to give a platform to over 100 local artists that play original music in Chiang Mai. Aside from a network of bars, we are also putting on regular festivals and fringe-style collab events that turn the whole city into a stage. Be sure to see what's happening when you're here, or if you want to listen to some artists before you arrive, here's a few to get you started: Suthep Band (that's mine!), Chiang Mai Blues, FOXY, Echo Resort, Sudsanen Band, SRWKS and Funkster.

EATING IN CHIANG MAI: EARLY BREAKFAST SPOTS

MAP P256, P278 & P281

Jok Somphet: Serves congee, dim sum and rice dishes to order day and night, with a kitchen that never closes. *24hr* ฿

Koay Chup FahThaNee: Although a little nondescript, this roadside shop opens at 7am to serve piping hot *teochew* noodle soup. *7am-3.30pm Tue-Sun* ฿

See You Soon Cafe: Here you can find classic Western breakfasts, fresh coffee, French toast and healthy hydroponic salads. *6.30am-11pm* ฿฿

Me&Bacon Nawarat: Picture-perfect breakfast food that's generous on the eggs, bacon and sauce. There's a good selection of local coffee, too. *8.30am-4pm* ฿฿

NITINUT380/SHUTTERSTOCK

Central Airport Plaza

in the arena outside are host to celebrities, big bands, food festivals and travelling fairs on an almost daily basis.

The sister property, **Central Airport Plaza** *(facebook.com/CentralChiangmaiAirport)* is hot on its heels, but with an older building, it tends to attract a calmer arrangement of events, including book fairs, motor shows and pet expos.

Needless to say, a trip to the shopping centre may not be on your Chiang Mai bucket-list, but when you find out what's on when you're in town, you may just change your mind.

Next-Level Flower Gardens

A park fit for royalty

Seeing nature in the city is a little harder these days, but **Royal Park Rajapruek** *(royalparkrajapruek.org; adult/child 200/100฿)* takes the gold as the best park in the city, especially if you're not quite ready to venture into the jungley void.

Built in 2007 to commemorate the 60th anniversary of the late Rama IX's accession to the throne, the park has the highest number of tropical plants and flowers in one park in all of Southeast Asia, as well as 33 international gardens that show off plants and landscaping from other nations. It's hard

SIAM TULIPS

Each rainy season (from July to October), parks across the country burst into colour with a splattering of *krachiao bua* (Siam tulips) that are striking to see. Although not technically tulips – they're actually more closely related to turmeric and ginger – Royal Park Rajapruek hosts special events to see over 60,000 of the flowers bloom.

Usually happening at around the same time, the legendary King Bhumibol Tulip also makes an appearance. The tulip was cultivated by a Dutch breeder for the late king in 2009 and features a creamy yellow flower that is reminiscent of Thailand's royal colour, yellow, which also happens to be the colour associated with anyone born on a Monday.

DRINKING IN CHIANG MAI: COFFEE

MAP P256 & P278

Roast8ry Coffee Flagship Store: The creative arm of the Roast8ry brand, this spot brews award-winning blends topped with intricate latte art. *8am-5pm*

Ristr8to: Sister brand to Roast8ry and serving the original menu of lattes and espressos that put Chiang Mai on the coffee map. *7.30am-6pm*

Graph: With a number of cafes around the city, you're never far from a locally sourced Graph specialty coffee. *11am-10pm*

Single Origin Store: As the name suggests, baristas serve up single-origin coffee right on the corner of Thapae Gate. *7.30am-9pm*

ANIMAL WELFARE IN THAILAND

Thailand has made progress in recent years to improve the welfare of captive animals. Landmark laws introduced in 2014 and strengthened again in 2018 have helped trigger a long-overdue crackdown on abusive practices, forcing greater accountability among owners and operators. Many sanctuaries, zoos and rescue centres have since upgraded their facilities, invested in better training and adopted more humane approaches to care. Public sentiment has also shifted, with a growing awareness of animal rights and increasing pressure on businesses to act responsibly. There is still some distance to go, but the direction is clearer than ever.

UPPICHAYA/SHUTTERSTOCK

Elephant sculpture, Chiang Mai Flower Festival

to imagine that when it opened, it drew over 20,000 visitors a day – now, you'll likely have most of the park to yourself.

Free shuttle buses loop the main park circuit, but you can also rent bicycles (check they work before you head out) or golf buggies. No doubt the highlight of the park is the Royal Pavilion, a grand temple-like structure dedicated to the Rama dynasty and modelled after Lanna-style Wat Phanthao in town. Be on the lookout for events while you're here, such as the **Chiang Mai Flower Festival** from December to February. While events are infrequent, they can add a bit of extra fun and activity to your visit.

Hidden Tigers, Creeping Trams

Safari-style natural attractions

Chiang Mai Night Safari *(chiangmainightsafari.com; adult/child 1200/600฿)* is one of only three nocturnal zoos in the world, with tours and enclosures that let you get up close and personal with some of the region's most elusive predators. Despite the name, the park is open all day and allows for both day-time and evening tours, which depart every 30 minutes. However, for the full, intended experience, it's best to arrive later in the afternoon, as the animals get more active once the sun starts to set.

EATING IN CHIANG MAI: BAKERIES

MAP P253 & P281

Nana Bakery: French-style boulangerie known for its fresh-baked buttery croissants; serves out of various locations around the city. *7am-8pm* ฿

Dorle: New but garnering a loyal following, the owner experiments with German-style baked goods that are reworked for a Thai palate. *9am-5pm* ฿฿

Forest Bake: There's something quite special about cakes baked in a forest; find them at this greenhouse cafe hidden inside an inner-city jungle. *9am-5pm Thu-Tue* ฿฿

L'Opera: Authentic French-style bakery known for its eclairs, opera cakes and all the usual bready goodness, best served with hot espressos. *7am-7pm* ฿

The main attraction is a tram ride through the enclosures, passing giraffes, zebras, red kangaroos, boars, gorals, racoons and alpacas before ending with a detour to the nocturnal predator zone, where you'll get close to tigers, jaguars, hyenas and other hunters. Other activities include cowboy shows, petting zoos, jaguar trails and a dedicated learning centre that focuses on conservation and education.

The park takes a science-first approach and does a good job of both educating and entertaining, although those who disagree with zoos will likely not have their minds changed by this place, given the fact that it still houses wild animals in relatively small enclosures.

Learn the Art of Thai Massage

MAP P253

Traditions passed down

A good massage is best received, but have you ever thought about stepping into the role of the masseur/masseuse and learning it for yourself? The **Old Medicine Hospital** *(oldmedicine.org; from 2000฿)* runs regular massage-training courses that are carefully crafted to guide students on a journey through traditional massage and northern massage techniques, as well as traditional Thai medicine.

Founded in 1962 by Master Sintorn Chaichakan, the Old Medicine Hospital quickly became a prestigious massage school, known for its northern interpretation of techniques and traditions first shared by gurus at the famous Bangkok temple of massage, Wat Pho (p57). Now in new hands, the 'hospital' is both a treatment and education centre that's unlike anywhere else in the world.

Whether you're a total beginner or looking to deepen your knowledge, sessions here cover everything from the basics to advanced techniques in Thai massage, herbal compress, foot massage and aroma oil massage. Courses range from quick six-hour intros to comprehensive 500-hour residencies, with qualifications spanning local credentials to internationally recognised California certifications.

Taste Chiang Mai's Famous Coffee

MAP P256

World-class, locally sourced coffee

If you're looking to savour the best locally sourced coffee, **Akha Ama Cafe** *(akhaamacoffee.com)* is a city favourite and a pioneer in hill-tribe coffee, with three cafes in Chiang Mai (and one in Japan). More than just a cafe, Akha Ama also

MASTER OF NORTHERN THAI MASSAGE

Master Sintorn Chaichakan is widely regarded as the pioneer of northern Thai massage and a key figure in the Shivagakomarpaj lineage of massage experts. He studied under the renowned masters of Wat Pho before his expertise caught the attention of Rama IX who, in 1957, requested he develop a massage programme for public benefit. Sintorn Chaichakan returned to Chiang Mai in 1962 to open a clinic dedicated to holistic healing and massage tailored to the northern way of life. Risking opposition from his masters, he slowly adapted the traditional Wat Pho massage routine by slowing it down and incorporating local herbs and traditional medicine. Today, his contributions are officially recognised.

EATING IN CHIANG MAI: FINE DINING

MAP P256 & P281

Service 1921: Riverbank restaurant in a former British embassy that's home to refined dining with an eccentric British-intelligence spin. *noon-10pm* ฿฿฿

Le Crystal: Legendary old-school fine-dining restaurant serving delicate French and Asian-fusion fare. *5-10pm Tue-Sun* ฿฿฿

Baan Landai Fine Thai Cuisine: Thai fine-dining with authentic, traditional fare that celebrates local flavours in a relaxing atmosphere. *11am-2.30pm & 5-10pm Tue-Sun* ฿฿

Cuisine de Garden: A changing Nordic-style tasting menu of local ingredients with table-side presentation. *6-10pm Wed-Sun, plus 12.30-2.30pm Fri-Sun* ฿฿฿

CHIANG MAI'S COFFEE STORY

Chiang Mai's love affair with coffee can be traced back to the days of opium, when government and nongovernment organisations looked to replace poppies with something more sustainable (and far less dangerous). Through a royal initiative, a unique arabica strain was developed as an alternative local cash crop, encouraging highland communities to shift towards more secure livelihoods. Four decades later, Chiang Mai's coffee culture is unlike anywhere else in the world, with more coffee shops than 7-Elevens and an enthusiasm that borders on obsession. From tiny street-corner booths where aunties try their best at drip coffee to award-winning latte-art champions and roasters experimenting with fermentation methods.

runs a social enterprise that empowers hill-tribe villages to grow coffee in more sustainable ways. Their dedication to single-source coffee is second to none, and you can even visit their factory in Mae Rim if you have the time.

If you'd rather get a little more hands-on with everything coffee, **PTT Tour** *(ptttour.com; 082 234 5237; adult/child 3800/1900฿)* organise regular hill-tribe coffee tours that 'forget fancy lattes' and reveal the real stories, people and production behind Chiang Mai's world-famous coffee. Tours last the entire day, starting with jungle treks into hill-tribe villages before hearty vegetarian lunches give you the energy to roll up your sleeves and try your hand at coffee-tree planting, plus coffee-bean harvesting, roasting and blending.

The Mesmerising Khantoke Dinner

MAP P253

The city's original Lanna culture show

The **Old Chiang Mai Cultural Centre** *(oldchiangmai.com)* serves up the unique northern tradition of *Khantoke* – a royal dinner and theatre performance that's the first of its kind in Thailand. Stretch out on comfortable floor seating and be served authentic all-you-can-eat northern Thai delights on rattan trays. While you feast, traditional musicians set the stage for an enchanting evening performance of costumed dancers who chant, twirl and contort, leaving you mesmerised as they journey through culture and time.

Expect to see both typical and atypical Thai imagery, from the graceful dance of Fon Ram to the powerful rhythms of the Sabad Chai drum that eventually morph into an unforgettable fire-dance finale. The family-friendly Khantoke dinner lasts two hours and starts at 6.30pm sharp. Choose from regular tickets *(per person 690฿; minimum two people per booking)* or a number of special dinner options, including the **Legacy Premium Set** *(per person 1290฿)* that guarantees front-row seats.

Chiang Mai from the Sky

Follow the wind in a balloon

Balloon Adventure Thailand *(balloonadventurethailand.com)* is northern Thailand's only hot-air-balloon operator, offering unforgettable views of Chiang Mai (and Chiang Rai) from the sky. You can opt for chartered flights *(two people 30,000฿)* or catch the magic during scheduled high-season flights where you share the basket in exchange for more budget-friendly rates. Lift-off is from the clubhouse at **Horizon**

DRINKING IN CHIANG MAI: LGBTIQ+ BARS

MAP P256, P278 & P281

Ram Bar: Chiang Mai's original '*kathoey* cabaret bar' is led by a fun-loving group of LGBTIQ+ owners. Shows start at 8pm every night. *7pm-1am*

Sound Up: The city's only gay nightclub has a laser-lit dance hall spanning multiple floors; it only gets busy after midnight. *11pm-4am*

Blow CNX: A more recent hit on the *kathoey* cabaret scene, Blow draws a younger and more risqué crowd. *6pm-midnight Thu-Tue, shows 10pm Thu-Sat*

Sapphic Riot: A cosy little cocktail bar and community space in the heart of town that's lesbian and queer friendly. *7pm-midnight Tue-Sun*

ATIWAT WITTHAYANURUT/SHUTTERSTOCK

Hot-air balloons, Balloon Adventure Thailand

Village & Resort, where welcome drinks are served and safety briefings completed. Over the course of 45 minutes, you'll gracefully follow the wind, taking in the mesmerising landscapes of northern Thailand before returning to the ground.

Once back on land, you'll enjoy a traditional champagne celebration and savour the thrill of the journey with a take-home flight certificate. Morning schedules begin at 5.30am (you'll be finished by 9am), while sunset schedules often tack on extra activities such as farm tours before the 4.45pm take-off.

Topiary & Ostriches

Manicured gardens and petting zoos

If you're planning on exploring the many parks and gardens that can be found in the north, **Tweechol Botanical Garden** *(tweecholbotanicgarden.com; adult/child 86/43฿)* is an ideal introduction. With just the right balance of garden to attraction, the 115-acre private garden flows between enchanting greenhouse installations, old teak houses turned mini museums and a collection of animal paddocks that let you feed the animals and, if you're lucky, pet them, too.

It's best to rent a bicycle to get around the park or, if you have lots to carry, golf carts plus a driver will cost you 350฿ for 78 minutes. As you make your way through the garden,

KHANTOKE'S ROYAL ORIGINS

Not just something invented for the amusement of tourists, Khantoke is an ancient Lanna tradition that stems from the royal courts of old. Classical dancers once entertained and soothed local royalty while they dined on lavish feasts. Guests would sit on mats or cushions around a pedestal of food called a *Khantoke*, and share curries, sticky rice and delicate bites prepared for special occasions. Over time, Khantoke dinners became a ritual that the king's subjects enjoyed replicating for visitors, eventually evolving into the cultural tradition we see today – a celebration of local customs and Lanna heritage. Today's Khantoke experiences echo that historic warmth, blending communal dining, dance and storytelling.

EATING IN CHIANG MAI: LARB CULTURE

MAP P281

Laap Bunker: This spot is best known for its tiny servings of northern Thai *larb*, allowing you to try different dishes without breaking the bank. *4pm-midnight Tue-Sun* ฿

Laap Lung Noi: Beloved among locals, this hang-out serves classic northern *larb* alongside freshly grilled sticks of boiled eggs, pork and beef. *11.30am-8.30pm* ฿

Withilarb Chareon-muang: Catering to a more modern audience, this spot has a clean yet local feel that sits well with those less-than-iron stomachs. *11am-10pm* ฿

Larb Duang Dee Mee Sook: Rich, meaty buffalo *larb* served both raw and cooked alongside an endless supply of herbs and salad. *11am-10pm* ฿

BEST & WORST MONTHS TO VISIT CHIANG MAI

Chiang Mai's calendar is packed with festivals and events year-round, so there's always something seasonal to enjoy. The cooler Thai winter (October to January) is widely considered the best time to visit, when temperatures drop, skies are clear, and festivals such as Yi Peng, Loy Krathong and the usual New Year celebrations see the city come alive. By February, the heat returns, along with hazardous PM2.5 pollution from the forest fires and slash-and-burn farming that plague the region. Sadly, Chiang Mai is best avoided during this time – until the summer, that is, when the water-soaked Songkran Festival (p281) washes away any fiery sins and rings in another year of good rain and prosperity.

CHETTARIN/SHUTTERSTOCK

Blackitch Artisan Kitchen

find themed zones nestled between perfectly manicured topiary sculptures, *King Kong*-style figures, mythical serpents, tropical greenhouses with hundreds of weird and wonderful species, and landscape-defining ponds and waterfalls.

On the far side, you'll find enclosures with lovingly cared-for bambi deer, plant-hungry ostriches and even a grumpy old camel that may spit at you if you get too close. On the ponds, you can board the paddleboats to share the water with the ducks, while kids can make use of the playgrounds and miniature cottages. The teak-house museum is also surprisingly detailed, with exhibits on the Lanna way of life, Buddhist art and a small collection of archeological finds.

Unusual Fine-Dining at Blackitch

MAP P278

A tasting menu with a twist

Chiang Mai has an impressive spread of fine-dining restaurants, with an unusually different assortment compared to Bangkok. A standout among the crowd is **Blackitch Artisan Kitchen** *(blackitch.com; per person 2000–3000฿)*, which serves a seasonally themed menu packed with rare and unusual local ingredients. The unforgettable and appropriately intimate 10-course dinner draws inspiration from unique Thai and Asian cooking techniques, coupled with the science of food-waste mitigation.

Step into the small shophouse, and you'll pass through a corridor lined with all kinds of pickled mysteries before heading up a tight staircase into the six-table 2nd floor, with an open-plan kitchen tightly squeezed into the corner.

More than food, each visit feels like a performance as the staff follow a choreographed dance of service and food preparation.

Pamper Yourself in an Oasis

MAP P256

Chiang Mai's most famous spa

No trip to Chiang Mai is complete without indulging in a Thai massage or two. While massage shops line almost every street, **Oasis Spa** *(oasisspa.net; from 1500฿)* stands out as one of the city's finest. A step above the rest, it offers premium massages that justify a higher price tag – although still relatively reasonable.

Around for over two decades, the spa first began as the city's first luxury day-spa, blending ancient Lanna-era healing techniques with modern pampering. Today, the therapists are still among the city's most well-trained (with many certified through their royally acclaimed therapist academy), while each tropical spa location (there's two in Chiang Mai, and a few in Bangkok, Pattaya and Phuket) is more beautiful than the last.

The spa menu is geared towards package experiences that range from two to four hours and incorporate local ingredients such as coconut with unusual techniques such as four-hand massages, 24-carat gold masks and Ayurvedic treatments. Booking in advance is required.

OTHER TOP SPAS IN CHIANG MAI

Makkha Health & Spa: Minimalism meets old-world elegance to bring Thai and aromatherapy treatments to the masses.

Fah Lanna Spa: Award-winning garden spa best known for its signature herbal steam rooms, reiki massage packages and soothing royal baths.

Let's Relax Spa: One of the country's best chain-spa brands, with four branches in Chiang Mai: the main one is in the Night Bazaar.

Health Land: A slightly more clinical approach to Thai massage, performed in Japanese-style treatment rooms.

Sense Onsen Suandok Wellness & Spa: A chain of more modern massage spots found across the city.

Spin Clay with the Masters

MAP P253

Artisan ceramics and handmade souvenirs

InClay Studio *(inclaystudio.com; 081 785 1943)*, a homegrown studio that's been around for over 15 years, offers unique insights into pottery and a few easy-to-grasp pottery sessions for those interested in learning the way of the wheel. Owned and run by award-winning artist Jirawong Wongtrangan, the gallery and studio have grown over the years and now occupy a corner of the orchard at his family home.

The two main workshops focus on hand building and spinning. Learn to make your own cup by hand *(1090฿)* or master the art of wheel throwing *(1790฿)* – eventually raising your own creation by the end of the four hours. Finished products will be fired and glazed on your behalf, a process that takes between two and three weeks. If you won't be around to pick them up, postal delivery can be arranged.

Jirawong's ethos is all around sharing expertise, believing strongly in exchanging experiences and developing life-long creative skills that you can take away with you. With this in mind, it's no surprise that he often sets up special classes that dig deeper into specific techniques (such as marbled clay) and even the odd residency programme from time to time.

Even if you don't join his workshop, his personal collections – much of which you can buy and take home to use or give as gifts – are always on display in his studio *(10am-5pm, closed Sun)*.

Shop for Arts, Crafts & Kitsch Creations

A community of living artists

If quirky artisan shops and handmade souvenirs are your thing, then **Baan Kang Wat** *(facebook.com/baankangwat)* has you covered. Located in a student-heavy district near

CHIANG MAI'S HERITAGE MUSEUMS

Lanna Folklife Museum: Housed in a former courthouse in the heart of town, this is a great first-stop for understanding northern Thailand and the unique cultural identity of the Lanna Kingdom *(adult/child 90/40฿)*.

Chiang Mai City Arts & Cultural Centre: Journey through Chiang Mai's history, from its founding to modern times. Bilingual displays tell stories of new and old through art, diorama and multimedia *(adult/child 90/40฿)*.

Chiang Mai Historical Centre: Home to a permanent exhibition of archeological sites and finds, as well as the Feun Ban Yan Wiang public source library *(cmocity.com; adult/child 90/40฿)*.

Wat Umong (p280), this charming community of galleries and shophouses is mostly artist-owned and gives off a strong Hogsmeade vibe, complete with irregular shaped two-to-three storey houses, dead-end walkways, hidden alcoves and a maze of alleys packed with people.

Originally established by students looking to sell their art and teach workshops, it's since transformed into a much larger development while thankfully still retaining its core identity and purpose. Wander through the main entrance, and you'll soon be pleasantly lost. Hours later, you'll find yourself enrolled in a woodcut-print workshop or in the amphitheatre watching a performance, taking notes on how to craft your own Lanna lantern at home.

There's a fair amount of food and drink on offer, too, all equally artisan, but don't expect to find a big meal here. It's more of a snacking vibe as you keep a hand free for bags of trinkets and souvenirs bought along the way. Thankfully, there are some great restaurants nearby if you work up an appetite. And if their regular offerings aren't enough, there's also an overflow market area that fills up most weekends, with Sundays being the busiest day for visitors, and arguably the most fun. Baan Kang is open from 11am to 6pm and is closed Mondays.

Take a Breather at Angkaew Reservoir MAP P253

Tranquil moments in the university

Escaping the buzz of the old city is easy when you have a mountain so near. For many people who live in the city, **Angkaew Reservoir** is the go-to spot for a moment of calm – with students chilling with friends after class, joggers working up a sweat and the odd artist sitting on the verge sketching the sunset.

Located within the main campus of **Chiang Mai University**, you don't need any identification to enter, though some taxis may drop you at the gate, requiring a short walk in.

Early morning and dusk see the most activity, when the reservoir's pathways fill with joggers running the circuit, so keep to the side if you're just strolling. It's really one of the most tranquil and picturesque spots in the inner city, and a great waypoint between town and Doi Suthep (p266).

EATING IN CHIANG MAI: NORTHERN THAI FOOD MAP P253 & P278

Tong Tem Toh: The northern-Thai-style hors d'oeuvre platter is ideal for those unfamiliar with local cuisine, although expect a wait – it's popular. *8am-11pm*

Han Thueng Chiang Mai: One of the city's best places to try authentic northern fare; no excuses are made for its spicy, sweet and salty flavours. *10am-9.30pm*

Huan Soontaree: Riverside local dining set to the tune of famous Lanna folk singer Soontaree Vechanont, who still performs nightly. *4.30-11pm Mon-Sat*

Huan Muan Jai: Home to a menu recommended by Michelin Bib Gourmand; expect hard-to-find traditional dishes and local delicacies. *11am-3pm, 5-9pm Thu-Tue*

NIMMANHAEMIN BAR-HOPPING

By day, Th Nimmanhaemin is best explored armed with a camera and an appetite. By night, lively clubs and bars transform the area.

START	END	LENGTH
Maya Lifestyle Shopping Center	Warm Up Cafe	4.5km; 4hr

Start your pub crawl just before 6pm on the rooftop of **1 Maya Lifestyle Shopping Center** for a sparkling cocktail and the best sunset views of Doi Suthep (p266). Back on ground level, cross the road and sip on a Chinese-brand beer in **2 Think Park** before topping up with wine and cold cuts at **3 One Nimman** as the shopping centre's souvenir markets make way for courtyard bars.

Slip through the side street that connects soi 1 to soi 5 and you'll come across an (easy-to-miss) elevator that's open to the street. Ride it to the top and you'll find **4 Forbidden Bar**, your second cocktail bar of the night.

Once warmed by some sticky-rice-infused cocktails, maintain the momentum by stopping at **5 BRINE** (p264) for fermented drinks and nibbles, then head to the *John Wick*-themed **6 Continental Bar** next door – both rank among the city's most lauded. Time your last sip to a strict 10pm, as you'll want to pop next door to **7 Blow CNX** (p272) to catch the cabaret show (Thu and Sat) that will have you dancing whether you like it or not. Just before midnight, grab a can of IPA from **8 Chiang Mai Craft Beer** (p262) and mooch over to **9 Warm Up Cafe**, Chiang Mai's biggest nightclub,.

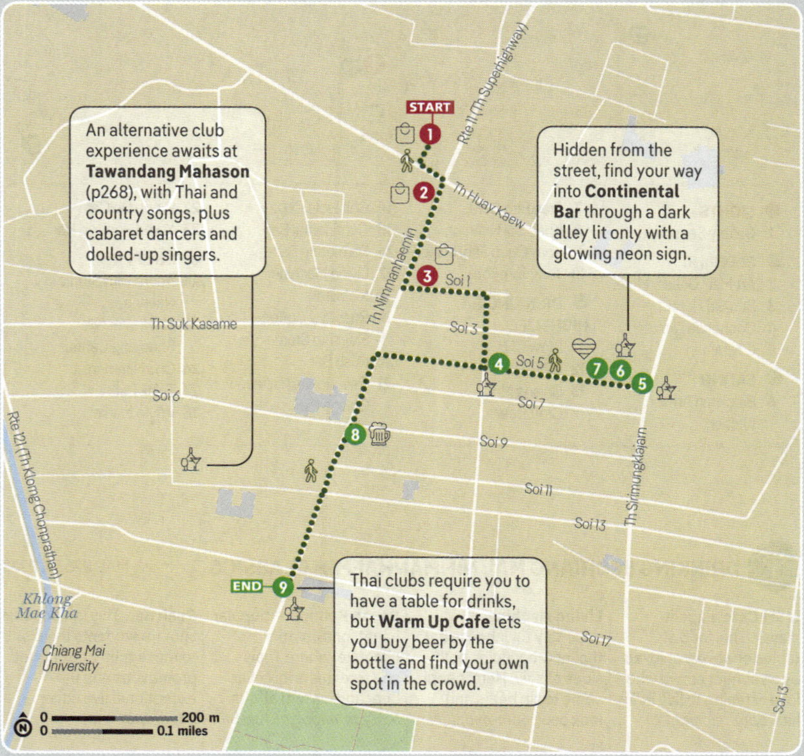

An alternative club experience awaits at **Tawandang Mahason** (p268), with Thai and country songs, plus cabaret dancers and dolled-up singers.

Hidden from the street, find your way into **Continental Bar** through a dark alley lit only with a glowing neon sign.

Thai clubs require you to have a table for drinks, but **Warm Up Cafe** lets you buy beer by the bottle and find your own spot in the crowd.

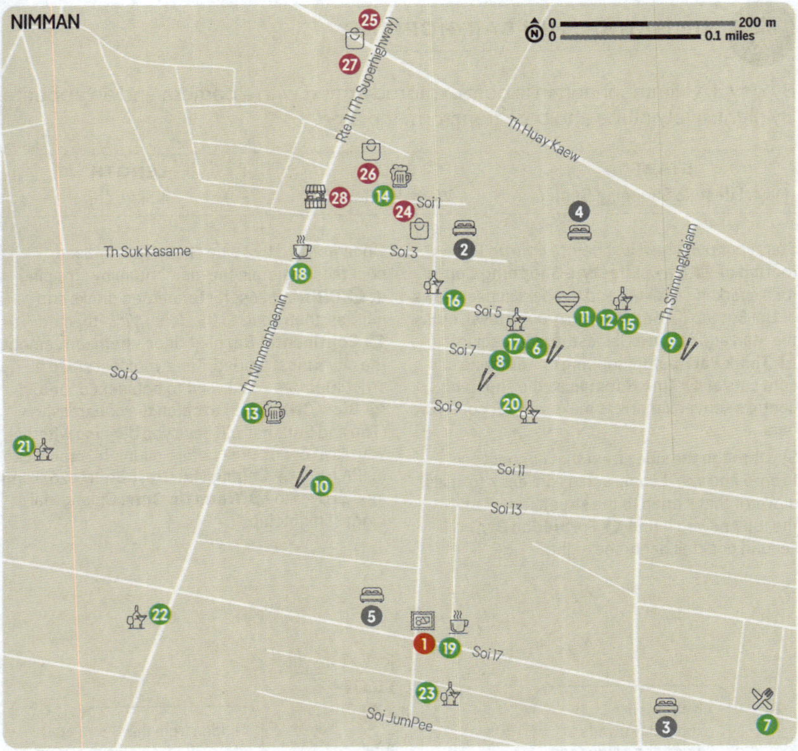

NIMMAN

SIGHTS
1 Gallery Seescape

SLEEPING
2 Art Mai? Gallery Hotel
3 Buri Siri Hotel
4 Cochet de Nimman
5 G Nimman

EATING
6 Blackitch Artisan Kitchen
7 Free Bird Cafe
8 Khao Soi Nimman
9 Koay Chup FahThaNee
10 Tong Tem Toh

DRINKING & NIGHTLIFE
11 Blow CNX
12 BRINE
13 Chiang Mai Craft Beer
14 Chit Hole CNX
15 Continental Bar
16 Forbidden Bar
17 Living Machine
18 Ristr8to
19 Roast8ry Coffee Flagship Store
20 Rush Bar
21 Tawandang Mahason Chiang Mai
22 Warm Up Cafe
23 Yayee Rooftop Bar

SHOPPING
24 Adorn with Studio Naenna
25 Maya Lifestyle Shopping Center
26 One Nimman
27 Think Park
28 White Market

DRINKING IN CHIANG MAI: NIMMANHAEMIN CLASSICS

MAP P253 & P278

LISM Cafe: Expect classic Thai food and tables of whisky enjoyed by a younger crowd who love listening to live indie hits. *5pm-midnight*

Living Machine: A once-tiny townhouse bar that now occupies both sides of soi 7. Here, people come to sip beers and look cool. *6pm-midnight*

Seven Pounds: A popular haunt for a chattier clientele, where Thais and foreigners mix over beer and current affairs. *5.30pm-midnight Tue-Sun*

Rush Bar: This is a popular spot for students thanks to the regular beer-buffet promotions and the exceptional live cover band. *6pm-1am*

The Forgotten City of Wiang Kum Kam

Chiang Mai's own almost-Atlantis

Wiang Kum Kam *(facebook.com/wiangkumkam; free)* is probably Chiang Mai's most forgotten, yet most underrated, ruin. Just a few kilometers south of the old city, it's an ancient capital city of the Lanna Kingdom – the buried predecessor to Chiang Mai. Built by King MEngrai, the city stood for just 10 years before it was abandoned due to repeated flooding. Yet in that short space of time, some magnificent buildings were created, many of which were used for centuries but eventually lost beneath layers of earth. It wasn't until the 1980s that the ruins were rediscovered and preserved as a historic site.

The unassuming entrance suggests an air of abandonment, but meander through the quiet village roads and shaded pathways, and you'll stumble across some incredible temple ruins, defined by crumbling *chedi* and faint inscriptions that hint at the area's past grandeur. Blissfully uncrowded, the best time to visit is when the light sits low on the horizon (morning or evening) and casts long, dramatic shadows from the pillars and structures that remain. Although renting bicycles from the visitor centre is recommended *(20฿)*, we prefer the horse and carriage option *(per tour 200฿)*.

Wat Chedi Liam is a beautifully preserved Burmese-style stupa with a stepped pyramid design that reflects the Hariphunchai style – a tiny but influential Mon kingdom in what is now modern-day Lamphun. The temple is one of just a few that remain active today, with resident monks keeping the 800-year-old site very much alive. Wiang Kum Kam is located down a few windy lanes; most take *rot daang* or taxis here.

Forge Your Own Chiang Mai Silver

MAP P256

Jewellery-making using local materials

Nova Jewelry Collection *(nova-collection.com)* shares the talents of locals with a series of one- to five-day jewellery-making workshops. These English-language classes make use of locally sourced silver and decades of experience, combining traditional jewellery techniques with more modern tools and practices. Classes *(from 3500฿)* run from 10.30am to 4.30pm any day of your choice and cover three specific skillsets – ring making, pendant making and bezel-stone setting, with the last requiring experience in the first two. Bookings require a minimum of two and a maximum of six people, so giving as much advance notice as possible is recommended. Workshop

CHIANG MAI SILVER

Chiang Mai's silver craft dates back over 700 years to the time of the Lanna Kingdom, where it was deemed both a highly respected artisan trade and spiritual art form. The craft flourished when the kingdom settled in Chiang Mai, thanks to its position along key historic trade routes (including an offshoot of the silk road).

Much of the silver tradition stems from ethnic groups who once populated Wua Lai, an area south of the city walls known for its hand-beaten repousse work. Walk down Th Wua Lai and you'll find dozens of silver artisans crafting rings, pendants and amulets to this day. Also keep an eye out for the stunning **Wat Srisuphan**, a temple covered entirely in silverwork.

DRINKING IN CHIANG MAI: TRENDY DJ BARS

MAP P256 & P281

Toys Club: Japanese-style city pop meets vintage videogames and frigid highballs, all enjoyed to the sounds of touring vinyl DJs. *10am-midnight Tue-Sun*

NOISE: Late-night bar/club in the inner city that features mainly house, served to a bobbing crowd of party addicts. *9pm-3am Wed-Sat*

Deaf Shop: Most nights feature sets from DJs, who play a mix of their own music and records that patrons pick from the shop walls. *7.30-midnight Thu-Sat, 2.30-6.30pm Sun*

Sriphum Melodic: Vintage-style decor frames evening sets of DJs and live bands spinning reggae, dancehall and dub, without a cliche in sight. *5pm-midnight*

staff are flexible and can adapt the lesson to match your own designs; they suggest sketching designs before you arrive to give you more time to handle the silver. Theoretically, there's no limit on the sterling silver you use, but at 70฿ a gram (on top of the course fee), it depends how deep your pockets go.

Tunnel under a Temple

MAP P253

Forest Buddhism underground

Chiang Mai has no shortage of ornate temples, but only a few stand out for being the opposite. Alongside Wat Pha Lat (p264), the temple of **Wat Umong Suan Phutthatham** is likely Chiang Mai's most famous forest temple and another construction from the King Mangrai era, dating back some 700 years.

Despite being as old as some ruins, Wat Umong remains a working monastery, with resident monks, meditation sessions and occasional monk chats (although when asked, monks never seem to know exactly when these will happen).

Walk its calm pathways, and you'll soon understand why Wat Umong is so beloved. The temple itself is hidden within a forest and is partially underground, hence its name *umong,* which translates to 'tunnels'. Step closer to the bell-shaped *chedi* and you'll find mysterious brick tunnels that disappear underneath the ground, with tiny candles leaving soot marks on the alcoves that dot the walls. Deeper still, statues of the Buddha dance in the flickering light as devotees leave flowers and unlit incense as offerings.

Out of the tunnels, you'll find a pond that's frequented by hundreds of friendly pigeons, and winding forest walks lined with famous 'talking trees', named for the whimsical Buddhist quotes on life, death and philosophy (in both Thai and English) that are found within their branches. And when you're done walking, you'll find one of Chiang Mai's best kept secrets opposite the entrance – a no-name auntie-run Thai massage shack that delivers some serious shoulder prodding.

Songkran in the City

The best place for a water fight

While every year offers something different, the Thai New Year celebration of **Songkran** (13–15 April) brings a full week of watery fun to Chiang Mai as people symbolically wash themselves anew; it also sees the entire nation descend into a three-plus-day water fight in celebration of said new year.

We think Chiang Mai is the best place to celebrate Songkran, and for good reason. The 1km looped moat sets the stage for

KEEPING THE DINNER EXPERIENCE ALIVE

Lanna Commins, renowned Thai singer and daughter of Soontaree Vechanont

Thailand's old-school restaurants used to feature live music almost everywhere you went. After Covid, a lot of long-standing locations in Chiang Mai closed down, causing the city to lose some of its old world charm and put a lot of musicians out of work. While my mother sings at our restaurant just like the good old days, I tend to spend my time working with local Chiang Mai indie musicians who are now leading a city-wide music revival that adds a new dimension to the local culture I know and love.

EATING IN CHIANG MAI: ALTERNATIVE DINING

MAP P281

Ikigai: Home-cooked farm-to-table Blue Zone cuisine. The 'long lunch' buffet sees individual portions served until you say stop. *5-10pm Tue-Fri, noon-10pm Sat* ฿฿

Aquila: Chef Phubase Chuprakong's table-side steaks are something of legend – they're the best cuts served this side of Argentina. *noon-2.30pm, 5-10pm* ฿฿

Jartisann Cheeserie: One of Chiang Mai's few cheesemakers showcases its creations through platters and gooey baked pastas. *10.30am-8.30pm Tue-Sun* ฿฿

Maadae Slow Fish Kitchen: By-weight servings of grilled-to-order fish caught fresh, plus spicy southern Thai fare. Queues likely. *11am-2pm, 5-9pm* ฿฿

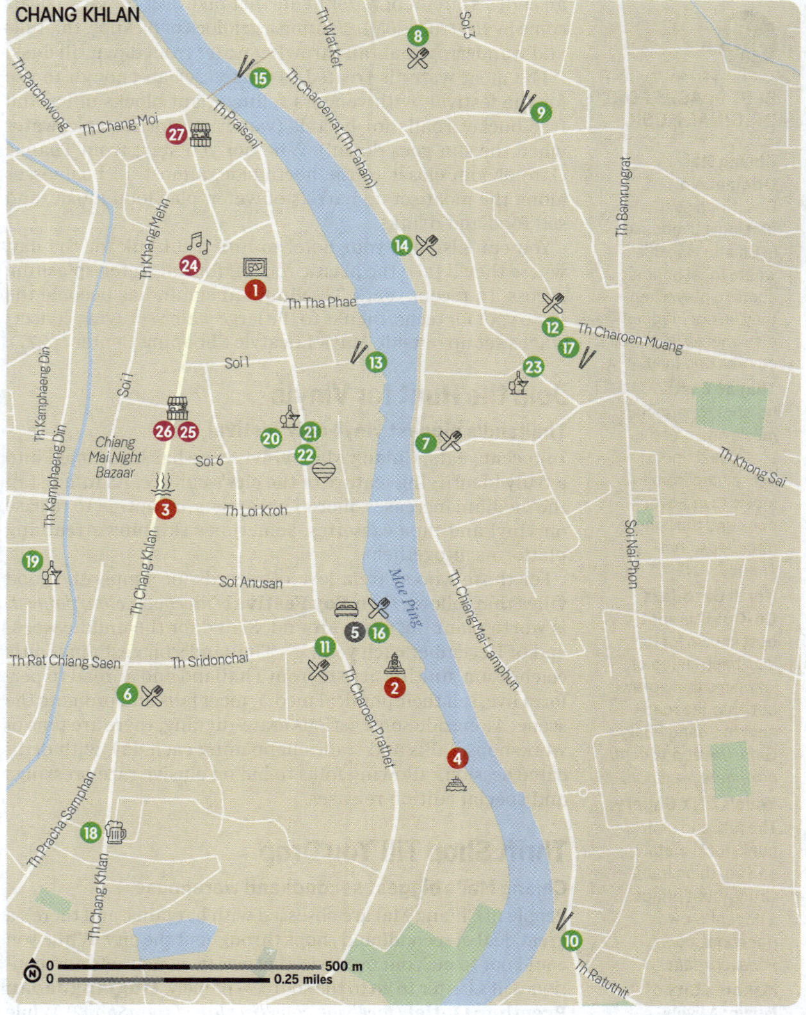

SIGHTS
1 Baan Tuek Art Centre
2 Wat Chai Mongkhon

ACTIVITIES
3 Let's Relax Spa (Chiang Mai Pavilion)
4 Mae Ping River Cruise

SLEEPING
5 Anantara Chiang Mai Resort

EATING
6 Butter is Better
7 Duke's (Ping River)
8 Forest Bake
9 Khao Soi Pa Pai
10 Laap Bunker
11 L'Opera
see 24 Maadae Slow Fish Kitchen
12 Me&Bacon Nawarat
13 River View Bar
14 Riverside Bar & Restaurant
15 Sai Ping Bar & Restaurant
16 Service 1921
17 Withilarb Chareonmuang

DRINKING & NIGHTLIFE
18 Grumpy Old Men
19 Hong's Sky Bar
20 MAI The Sky Bar
21 Noir CMI
22 Ram Bar
23 Toys Club

ENTERTAINMENT
24 Thapae East

SHOPPING
25 Kalare Night Bazaar
26 Night Bazaar
27 Warorot Market

BEST PLACES FOR ORIGINAL MUSIC

Chiang Mai OriginaLive: Described as the first indie livehouse in Chiang Mai, this is where local bands come to play when they've not gigging elsewhere. *(facebook.com/cnx.og.live)*

Thapae East: A hotspot for original music and creative arts, you'll find everything from folk music to indie rock, punk and blues here. *(facebook.com/ThapaeEast)*

North Gate Jazz Co-Op: This spot is best known for its laid-back lineup of jazz jams that sprawl out onto the road next to Chang Puak Gate. *(facebook.com/northgate.jazzcoop)*

Yoda's CNX Gallery: The place to go for punk, rock, metal and anything loud. Grungy, but brings a decent crowd. *(facebook.com/yodascnxgallery)*

Mahoree City of Music: A lively community hub that celebrates northern Thai artists and more creative sounds most nights. *(facebook.com/mahoree.city.of.music)*

an endless circuit of water fights that take over the city. Locals come by the truck-load, creating a gridlock of pickups, tuk-tuks and wandering souls all throwing water from dawn till dusk.

The moat water is treated to make it clean enough to use for the festival, with vendors selling giant blocks of ice and free bucket refills for barrels (watch out for ice-cold water when the sun goes down!). Whether you start from Thapae Gate or join closer to the north side, almost all businesses along the moat set up barrels of water, play loud music, and sell food and drinks.

You can also ask your hotel to hire a tuk-tuk for the day, where they'll take the plastic roof off for full water-splashing access. In recent years, Th Nimmanhaemin has become the go-to spot for teens, thanks to the large water-spraying concert stages set up outside Maya Lifestyle Shopping Center (p277).

Join the Hunt for Vinyls

Thailand's biggest vinyl-only festival

In recent years, Chiang Mai's vinyl scene has blossomed into a truly identifying feature of the city's culture. As interest in the medium increases, more Thai artists are opting to release on vinyl and tape cassettes, sometimes skipping streaming platforms altogether.

For those who share a love of records (or simply the good vibes that follow), then **Poy Festival** *(facebook.com/poyfest)* is worth planning a trip around. Slated for the middle weekend of December each year, it's Thailand's biggest vinyl-only celebration, uniting artists from Thailand and abroad to perform live, sell their physical media, meet fans and promote the scene. Alongside some serious crate-digging, there are tons of workshops, talks and trades happening each day, with dedicated sessions allowing folks to bid on elusive rare pressings and special edition releases.

Thrift Shop Till You Drop

Chiang Mai's biggest secondhand warehouse

People in Chiang Mai are obsessed with bargains, and there's a great deal of secondhand shops throughout the city. While you could opt to pick out overpriced pieces from markets and boutiques, it's better to go to the source – namely, **Hugjang Japan Premium Outlet** *(facebook.com/HugJangJapanShop2)*. While there's a few locations around the city, this one, to the south of the city, is the biggest, sharing a giant warehouse space with **Chiang Mai Second Hand Warehouse Madam Muk**.

Hugjang Japan ships in tonnes of secondhand Japanese clothing, shoes, kitchenware, decor, furniture, trinkets, toys, instruments and artwork every week, and between them, both warehouses serve the city's secondhand industry, with rows upon rows of clothing for sale, sometimes for as little as 10฿ apiece. While some wares are nicely sorted and hung on rails, you'll find that most of it is piled up sufficiently high to get lost inside. There's also a ton of crockery and curious Japanese-style trinkets that you won't find anywhere else.

Beyond Muang Chiang Mai

While based in the city, you can venture into the villages and mountains that surround it, and *still* have time to get back for dinner.

Places

Beyond the bustling streets and ancient temples of Chiang Mai city lies a vast and diverse landscape that captivates the mind and ignites that spirit of adventure. Spanning misty mountains viewed from warm and cosy Japanese-style lodges to serene floating cabins and adventurous jungle-canopy coasters, there's so much on offer just a stone's throw from the city.

The surrounding areas that sprawl out from the city centre offer the perfect opportunity for active day-trips (that keep you grounded in old city hotels by night) and multiday jaunts (that feel more remote than they actually are). Wherever you turn, the warm hospitality of local communities continues to make these areas special for all who visit. The real wonders of Chiang Mai await, beyond the city walls.

GETTING AROUND

Rot daang can be hired to take you to destinations far out of the city for a negotiated price (around 1000฿ to Chiang Dao; 1500฿ to Mae Wang). Ask drivers to wait and pick you up once you're done, or you may get stranded. Other coloured trucks follow routes out of the city centre: white and yellow head northeast to Doi Saket; green heads to Mae Rim and blue heads to Lamphun.

Mae On

TIME FROM CHIANG MAI: 1HR

Stay in Mae Kampong

Mae Kampong is one of Thailand's most beautiful hillside villages, reminiscent of the small towns seen in Japan's Kyoto. With around 400 inhabitants, Mae Kampong is some 1400m above sea level and has become a model example of community tourism in Thailand, with no chain hotels, shops or restaurants. There isn't even a 7-Eleven.

With one main strip and a small waterfall temple in the middle of town (**Wat Khantha Phueksa**), there's little else to do here other than sample the famous *sai oua* (spicy northern Thai sausage sold by **Sai Oua Mae Nim**), sip on a coffee at one of its many cafes – we recommend crossing the mini suspension bridge to **Teddu Coffee** *(facebook.com/Tedducoffee)* and then retreat to your homestay for a peaceful afternoon surrounded by nature.

Getting here is easiest if you have your own car. Otherwise, get a minibus from Warorot Market (p261) for 150฿. Although you can do a day trip, it's better to stay a night or two at one of the many homestays in the village. Rooms range from 400฿ to 3000฿, depending on what facilities and feel you're looking for. As the Japanese vibes haven't been lost on locals, many

RENTING BIKES IN CHIANG MAI

Renting a motorbike in Chiang Mai to explore its outer reaches is both easy and cheap, and for many, it's one of the most convenient ways to experience the city's far-flung temples, mountains and rural villages. However, police in the city are vigilant and will stop and fine any foreigner without a valid Thai or international driving licence, so make sure you're properly covered before setting off. By law, you must also wear a helmet, and checkpoints frequently target those who ignore this rule. When arranging a rental, check the small print carefully and inspect the bike closely, as some hire companies have been known to avoid paying insurance claims or attempt to charge riders for minor scratches that may have already been there.

have opted to follow the trend to create mini East Asian getaways in the clouds.

Visit Muang On cave

Tham Muang On *(30฿)* is one of Chiang Mai's more impressive and underrated natural wonders. Various local legends trace its spiritual significance back centuries, with its vast caverns meandering through limestone hills.

The site has long been a place for locals and monks, and is now happily shared with a fair helping of tourists, too. Getting inside requires a considerable hike up the steps, flanked by *naga* (snake deities), to reach the cave entrance. Step inside, and you're free to wander through its caverns and passageways, with each turn revealing shrines, offerings and remnants of ancient rituals etched into the walls. At its deepest part, a 10m-long reclining Buddha lies in spiritual contemplation, much like the monks and hermits who came here to seek enlightenment decades before. The caves are open from 8am to 5pm.

Doi Saket

TIME FROM CHIANG MAI: **45MIN**

Zipline through the canopy

If you have a head for heights and nerves of steel, then the jungle canopies between Doi Saket and Lampang's Chae Son are where you'll find three of northern Thailand's most competitive zipline operators – each trying to outdo the other with the biggest, fastest and longest rides, and all within shouting distance of one another.

Jungle Flight Chiang Mai *(jungleflightchiangmai.com; 2100–6400฿)* is famous for having the world's longest 'jungle coaster' – a death-defying thrill-ride that flings you around the canopy as you're suspended underneath a single steel track. Their zipline packages offer various combinations of ziplines, coaster rides, abseil points, panoramic views, sky-bridge traversals, lunches, and even a combo cooking school add-on.

Just down the road, **Skyline Jungle Luge** *(skylinejungleluge.com; 2250–2450฿)* does things a little differently. Their signature experience is a 2km self-driving luge track that's more similar to downhill go-carting than alpine tobogganing. This comes on top of standard half- and full-day zipline packages.

KingKong Smile Zipline *(kingkongzipline.com; 1700–2500฿)* rounds out the trio with Asia's longest and highest

EATING IN MAE KAMPONG: HANGOUT RESTAURANTS

Rabiang View: The northernmost spot of the village has beautiful views. You'll find great cake and equally good coffee here. *8am-5pm* ฿฿

MiiPaaAii: A Japanese-themed homestay with stunning valley views from their private bar and BBQ garden that's open to day visitors. *2-6pm* ฿฿

At-Mae-Kampong: Though small, this cosy village restaurant serves delicious food, and the 2nd-floor balcony is perfect for people-watching. *8am-8pm* ฿฿

Noodle Poh Oui Mae Oui: Noodles are the staple here, but the generous owners often share grilled eggs and intestines on sticks with curious patrons. *7am-8pm* ฿

KWANCHAI/SHUTTERSTOCK

Tham Muang On

zipline course, which rockets riders 1200m through the trees at speeds of up to 112km/h.

Ride ATVs through the jungle

For those into adrenaline, **Base ATV** *(facebook.com/thebaseatv; one-/two-hour tours from 1800/2800฿)* offers some exhilarating sightseeing tours from the four wheels of a self-driven all-terrain vehicle (ATV). Guided ATV routes disappear into the jungle pretty much straight out of the gate, following wild and muddy tracks past reservoirs, streams and hidden villages that are rarely seen by tourists.

The two-hour tours include a scenic stop for free coffee and cakes at forest-home cafe **Baan Samadhi**, and a visit to **Doi Saket Hot Springs** *(30฿)*, where you can boil eggs in the spring water and soak your feet in the communal baths. The range of routes and vehicle options (including all-terrain buggies and kid-sized quads), as well as regular special-route collaborations with nearby homestays and boutique hotels, make it easy to turn your thrill ride into a full day-and-night escape.

Hang Dong

TIME FROM CHIANG MAI: **30MIN**

Swim the Grand Canyon

The **Grand Canyon Water Park** *(grandcanyon-waterpark.com; adult/child from 950/750฿)* features dramatic cliffs, inflatable toys and an array of adrenaline-pumping activities. Once an old, abandoned quarry, it was taken over and transformed into what it is today: a massive inflatable obstacle course with kid's splash zones, giant waterslides, ziplines, cliff jumping and wakeboarding.

Lifeguards are plentiful, and they aren't shy to join in the fun. Admission includes life jackets and full access (except for wakeboarding, which costs extra).

SMOKEY SEASON

The weather in the mountains can be cruel. From January to April, a toxic haze of dust arrives, scientifically referred to as PM2.5. This particulate matter – smaller than 2.5nm in width, meaning it can enter the lungs and even cross into the bloodstream – blankets the city and surrounding province as farmers burn fields and forests in preparation for the next growing season. If you visit during this period, it's essential to monitor air quality levels (AirVisual is the app everyone uses) and keep an N95 mask handy for days when the pollution spikes. As the monsoon hits around June or July, the smog eventually dissipates, but dengue fever arrives with the rain, so protect yourself from mosquitoes, which come out in force around dusk, and after heavy showers.

CYCLING IN CHIANG MAI PROVINCE

Although a pedal-powered mountain climb may not be for the faint-hearted, the province's many mountains (and city lanes) make for an exciting playground that's just waiting to be explored on a bicycle. Pro cyclists can contact **Bike Zone Chiang Mai** *(bikezone.co.th)*, the city's leading bike shop, where you can hire a decent road bike and join regular ride-outs on roads and over mountain trails; they can also provide GPX routes on request. For the less serious rider, **NK Bike Rentals** *(from 100฿; 081 671 1330)* and **Chiang Mai Bicycle** *(from 100฿; chiangmaibicycle.com)* both have city and road bikes for hire, perfect for joining one of the monthly **Critical Mass** *(facebook.com/CriticalMassCNX)* social rides around the city.

EDUSMA7256/SHUTTERSTOCK

Grand Canyon Chiangmai

Interestingly, the site is home to another, similarly named attraction, **Grand Canyon Chiangmai** *(097 929 8559; 150฿)*, which offers a tamer collection of kayaking, bamboo rafting and paddleboarding. While clearly positioned to lure visitors from its larger namesake, the affordable entrance fee makes it a fair alternative. It's open from 9am to 7pm.

And if that's not enough to keep you busy, the nearby **Grand Canyon Shooting Range** *(091 830 8388)* lets you lock, load and blow off some steam (literally), with 50-shot shotgun, rifle and handgun courses *(from 1700฿)*. It's open from 10am to 5pm.

Cocoon yourself in tropical steam

In recent years, there has been a boom in spas, saunas and ice baths throughout Chiang Mai, but few offer an experience quite like this one. Hidden in a small oasis outside of town, **Cocoon** *(facebook.com/BambooDomeHome)* brings together the best of open-air sauna experiences in the garden of a peculiar earthen-bamboo house.

More like a home than a spa, a day pass *(300฿)* includes use of the ice baths, herbal steam room and saltwater pool, while an extra 100฿ will give you access to the Finnish-style barrel sauna. The guests who come here are predictably chill, sipping bottles of beer or kombucha as they strike up conversation with others at the pool or in the steam room.

EATING IN HANG DONG: OUR PICKS

Sukhum.hangdong: Snack on oven-fresh bagels, brownies and sandwiches, and sip locally sourced coffee in this natural spot just out of town. *7am-5pm* ฿฿

Cheun Rue Thai Cafe: The Tai Resort's main cafe and eatery serves colourful smoothies, local coffee and a mix of Thai and western favourites. *8am-5pm* ฿

Hom Huan Noodle: A local favourite, with easy noodles and rice dishes served to tables in teak *sah lah* (open pavilions) among the paddy fields. *8.30am-4pm* ฿

Bella Goose Cafe on the Pond: Generous servings of fresh, healthy food and American breakfast classics that are guaranteed to fill you up. *7am-4pm* ฿฿

With food, drinks and the odd yoga class, sound healing session or evening social, you could easily spend a full day here. It opens from noon to 7pm and is closed Mondays. Thankfully, staff come and warn guests when it's near closing time and will arrange taxis and car-shares back into town for those who didn't come with their own wheels.

Visit a living museum

Baan Tawai Woodcarving Village has been a staple on the Chiang Mai tourist trail since the 1950s. Home to generations of master craftsmen and women, it's known far and wide as the place to go for teak carvings, furniture, ceramics and imported antiques.

The village is mostly condensed into one main strip, with rows of shophouses selling everything from cabinets and bed frames to stucco carvings of cats, Buddha heads, pots and even tissue boxes. Strolling around, you'll spot the artisans themselves hard at work, chiseling away at their latest creations and pausing only to greet and beckon to passers by.

Baan Tawai is often described as a living museum – partly for its master woodworkers and craft traditions, and partly because it feels frozen in time; sadly, workshops are slowly closing as the village inevitably ages. While most shops have names in Thai only or don't have any names displayed, a few shops, such as **NK Bantawai** *(nkbantawai.com)* and **Desiam Warehouse** *(089 635 8133)*, stand out for stocking Thailand's largest collections of Burmese, Indian, Chinese and Thai antiques, all of which can be shipped home.

PU SAE YA SAE CEREMONY

Each year in the foothills of Doi Suthep, a buffalo is sacrificed. Some of its flesh is eaten raw by a witch doctor, said to be possessed by the spirits of giants who once feasted on humans here. Although quite graphic, the centuries-old Pu Sae Ya Sae Ceremony holds local cultural significance, with hundreds of people flocking to the event in search of blessings and good tidings for the year ahead. To see for yourself, head to the shrine at **Wat Phra That Doi Kham** in June and ask for details – the dates are often known just a few days or weeks before due to some mysterious Buddhist calculations, making it notoriously difficult to plan for, even for locals.

Mae Rim

TIME FROM CHIANG MAI: **30MIN**

Make paper from elephant poop

If you're feeling green (and don't mind a bit of poo), you can get crafty at **Elephant PooPooPaper Park** *(poopoopaperpark.com; 150฿/under-5s free)* by turning elephant dung into paper.

Perfect for those who aren't squeamish (or kids that just love to go 'ewww'), its equal parts quirky, educational and eco-friendly. The entrance fee gets you access to the open-air museum and hands-on workshops that have you washing fresh poop, making pulp from what's left and turning it into paper using traditional techniques.

The whole thing is pleasantly smell-free and a great way to learn about elephants without exploiting them. Guides walk you through the whole process in English and talk about how sustainable tourism, if done correctly, can benefit elephants.

DRINKING IN CHIANG MAI: COFFEE BEYOND THE CITY

Nermu Coffee: Coffee sourced from nearby villages can be enjoyed in this greenhouse-style hill-tribe home hidden in the mountains. *7am-5pm Tue-Sun*

Summit Coffee: Open early and a popular spot for cyclists, Summit has good coffee and a decent menu of mainly sausage-based dishes. *7.30am-5pm Mon-Sat*

Jungle De Cafe: Sip coffee from a net hammock floating above a waterfall while you contemplate which zipline or canopy walk to do next. *9am-6pm*

Chiang Mai Cream Tea House: Classic English cream teas, sandwiches and coffees by an eccentric Thai auntie with connections to the UK. *12.30-5pm Sep-Apr*

MAE WANG'S UNIQUE GEOLOGY

Mae Wang is one of Chiang Mai's most quietly fascinating districts, shaped as much by geology as by culture. Its most striking feature is Pha Chor, a 30m wall of sculpted sediment that first formed millions of years ago when the Ping River shifted its course, leaving compacted riverbeds that slowly eroded into dramatic pillars. Today, traces of river beds and sedimentary pillars can be found across the region. The valley is also home to long-established Karen communities whose elephant-keeping traditions predate modern tourism, as well as river-fed rice terraces and orchards nourished by seasonal floods. Together, these elements give Mae Wang a character distinct from Chiang Mai's other districts – part geological archive, part cultural crossroads.

There's also a shop filled with dung-made notebooks, cards, stationery and other gifts – great for themed souvenirs with an interesting backstory.

Chill at the Huay Tueng Thao Reservoir

Right on the edge of Muang Chiang Mai, just as Mae Rim begins, you'll find **Huay Tueng Thao Reservoir** *(huay tuengthao.com; 50฿)*, one of the city's favourite Sunday destinations. Lined with floating bamboo-hut restaurants on almost every side, people tend to come here on weekend afternoons with cravings for papaya salad, *tom yum goong* (Thailand's famous spicy soup) and a few too many bottles of ice-cold local beers. Families dine, play in the water and relax until sunset, while more active citizens skip the afternoon lunch and opt for doing cycling circuits around the reservoir or jogging on its many field and forest trails that lead up into the hills of Doi Suthep-Pui (p266).

At the far end of the reservoir, you'll find a peculiar grassy knoll topped with straw statues of King Kong and other oversized animals, as well as a small kiosk that rents out swan paddleboats and floating inner-tube rings. There's also a zipline that crosses the water (although it's not always open), mini-ATV rides for kids and a small sheep enclosure where you can feed the sheep in exchange for a few baht. There's even a single cabin *(1500–2000฿)* on the lakeside that you can rent for the night, although you'll need to book it quite far in advance.

Get here early in the afternoon to secure a floating hut (they fill up fast), and note that the reservoir closes before sunset for safety reasons, so expect to be booted out at 5.30pm sharp.

Explore the Erotic Garden

Despite its remote location, the **Erotic Garden and Teahouse** *(facebook.com/eroticgarden; 300฿)* is anything but shy. Bold and beautiful, this private home turned open-air garden-gallery celebrates themes of sensuality, floral reproduction and the female form. Brainchild of the charmingly zany artist Khun Suwalee, who's always on-site and eager to give a guided tour, the garden ebbs and flows between ceramic structures of naked bodies, suggestively positioned pillars and archways, protruding mounds and towering gold penis statutes – all playfully positioned between orchids, vines and flowering trees.

Tours are giggle-friendly, and the sense of innocent inquisitiveness is hard to shake off; it ends with a serving of herbal teas and homemade cakes under a breezy tree-covered

EATING IN MAE SA VALLEY: OUR PICKS

Ironwood: A picturesque garden cafe serving artful dishes with a modern twist; perfect for a relaxed, scenic meal mid-explore. *9am-5pm* ฿฿

Pa Sri Kitchen: Hidden down a back road off the main drag, find authentic northern Thai cuisine made with fresh, local ingredients. *9am-7pm Thu-Tue* ฿

Roaster Lab: Coffee aficionados will love this spot, known for its specialty brews, the menu of western favourites and the minimalist design. *8.30am-5pm Thu-Tue* ฿

Volks Trattoria: The fresh pasta and extensive wine list makes this boutique hotel eatery stand out against its jungly surroundings. *5-9.30pm* ฿฿

SARAWUT KONGANANTDECH/SHUTTERSTOCK

Huay Tueng Thao Reservoir

verandah. Open-mindedness is key here – far from lewd, it's an artistic (and slightly Buddhist) exploration of fertility, freedom and femininity in its most natural form. Photography is allowed but should be respectful, and children under 12 are not permitted. The gardens are open from 10am to 5pm Thursday through Sunday.

Mae Teng

TIME FROM CHIANG MAI: 1HR

Ascend the 'Sticky Waterfall'

If you've ever dreamed of walking up a gushing waterfall, then now's your chance. **Nam Tok Bua Tong**, nicknamed the 'Sticky Waterfall', allows visitors to defy gravity and climb up its many fast-flowing levels thanks to a rare natural phenomenon. The cartoonish rocks cling to your feet as you step on them due to the calcium and limestone deposits – built up over millennia – creating a porous texture that prevents the slippery stuff (such as algae) from growing.

A collection of ropes and wooden steps helps visitors navigate the three-tiered waterfall, best experienced when starting at the bottom and working your way up. With certain areas feeling more like a water park than a naturally occurring waterfall, it's surprising that this is one of the few national park treasures that is free to enjoy.

After splashing around the waterfall, spread out on the grassy areas at the top and order a small picnic from the cafe before walking it off and visiting the nearby seven-colour spring, **Namphu Chet Si**. Charting a *rot daang* that will wait for your return costs around 1000฿ all-in, but if you make the 60km trip out of Chiang Mai by motorbike, you'll see a lot more on the way.

AN ELEPHANT ACTIVIST

Annie Suphonnaphat Jenselius is founder of **Erawan Elephant Alliance Organization**

I was born on a land where the elephant is a national symbol, and I have always been familiar with these majestic creatures, collaborating with Mae Taeng Elephant Park for nearly a decade. Through this work, I have come to realise the vast complexity and richness of the Thai elephant story – far beyond what is often portrayed. Travellers to Thailand should look under the surface and really understand the true aspects of elephant care, culture and conservation from a truthful and ethical perspective, rather than through a lens that prioritises profit and social clout.

For more on animal welfare in Thailand, see p616.

THE MOUNTAIN'S MILITARY PROTECTION

Much of the forested land around the foothills of Doi Suthep and Mae Rim is under the military control of the Royal Thai Army's 33rd Military Circle. The ownership dates back to long before the mountain became a national park in 1981, designated as such to protect its ancient forests from encroachment and illegal logging during the 20th century, and due to its strategic location. In 2015, a luxury housing project encroached into the park, drawing criticism and protest until it was agreed that the land would be left as was and rewilded. Now, many years later, people in Chiang Mai still bring up the project as a reason to protect the forest, mainly due to its environmental, spiritual and political importance.

Stay overnight on an isolated reservoir

The floating hotels on **Mae Ngat Somboon Chon Dam Reservoir**, found within **Sri Lanna National Park** *(adult/child 100/50฿)*, are becoming a thing of legend. Around for decades, the reservoir is witnessing a resurgence of interest in the wake of pandemic-inspired local tourism. As a result, this idyllic spot just an hour north of the city has become a magical escape where mobile signals disappear and nature consumes.

Mountain Float (p298; *mountainfloatchiangmai.com)* is the reservoir's OG. It transports guests directly to their luxurious floating villas via long-tail boats that glide over the mirror-like lake. While some areas may feel a bit dated, the charm lies in the array of activities. Kayaking, SUP boards, water trampolines, karaoke and private dining options more than make up for its somewhat rougher-than-expected edges. **Velaloy Floating Resort** *(facebook.com/velaloy)* is a slightly newer option that's a close second if the other is booked up. There's certainly a casual approach to water safety here – life jackets are recommended but not enforced – and the deep waters, lack of walkway railings and absence of phone signal require extra caution, especially at night.

Pick tea and drink it, too

Although coffee dominates in Chiang Mai, tea still holds a special place, influenced by Chinese traditions and the forests full of wild tea. And while the real hero is undeniably *cha yen* – the distinctly sweet and luminous orange tea that's unmistakably Thai and served on almost every street corner – the mountainous terrain lends itself to a growing market that's focused on a more refined and delicate tea culture.

For a real forest-to-table tea experience, day trips to **Araksa Tea Garden** *(araksatea.com)* include tea plucking, tea cultivation tours and tea sampling over deliciously light lunches. Their most popular activity is the **Tea Tour** *(650฿; including lunch 1150฿)*, where you can explore the wild tea garden, learn about the growing and processing methods that follow age-old traditions, lend a hand in picking the tea leaves and sample their best harvests, with cups of tea paired with traditional Thai snacks. If you prefer the art of the pour, they also offer workshops on tea blending, pouring and pairing.

EATING IN MAE RIM: BEST SPOTS

Steak of the Day: Fresh market-inspired menus that change daily. In Mae Rim; it's also known as Rimm Phi Romm. *11am-8.30pm Mon-Sat* ฿฿

Bombay Hut: British-Indian food served to a small number of pre-booked customers three times a week. *10am-7pm Fri-Sun* ฿฿

KHAO by Four Seasons: A high-end must for those who can afford it, with local food inspired by the culinary diversity of Thailand. *8am-7pm* ฿฿

Krua Lawng Khao: Northern Thai classics served from a quaint wooden house overlooking paddy fields. *11am-7pm* ฿

And Ann Coffee: A quaint coffee shop in the heart of Mae Rim, among dense trees; serves light bites, cakes and coffee. *9am-4pm Tue-Sun* ฿

Sequ Restaurant: Enjoy freshly cooked Italian-Thai fusion dishes while the kids pet the farm animals next door. *10am-8pm* ฿฿

Rab-a-bit: Good coffee, excellent breakfasts and an all-day Thai menu that strikes the balance between fancy and delicious. *9am-6pm* ฿฿

Ngon Vietnamese: Classic Vietnamese food made for Thai tastes: think lots of herbs and spicy sauce. *6.30am-9.30pm* ฿฿

EXPLORE MAE SA VALLEY

Mae Sa Valley is one of Chiang Mai's most picturesque locations, densely populated with attractions and wild experiences, from grand waterfalls to jungle coasters.

START	END	LENGTH
Mae Rim	Mon Jam	18km; six to eight hours

Begin in the lowlands as you pass through Mae Rim and head into the valley, taking a left onto Route 1096 that follows the Mae Sa river upstream. Stop first at the 1 **Siam Insect Zoo** *(siaminsectzoo.com; adult/child 200/150฿)*, where you can learn about the region's biodiversity and get up-close with Thailand's weirdest creepy crawlies.

Continue up the valley and you'll soon come to 2 **Nam Tok Mae Sa** *(100฿; plus vehicle 30฿)*, a 10-storey waterfall that's one not to miss, especially if you're exploring by motorbike and need to cool off. Keeping things natural, the next stop is the 3 **Queen Sirikit Botanic Gardens** *(qsbg.org; adult/child 100/50฿)*, Thailand's first and most renowned botanical garden, home to a vast collection of plants and rare, indigenous Thai flora. Rides, trails and glasshouses will keep you occupied for hours.

Continue straight before turning onto Route 4051, heading in the direction of the village of Mon Jam. Detour to 4 **Pong Yaeng Jungle Coaster & Zipline** *(053 106 327; per ride 200฿)* on the way. Feel your stomach in your mouth at the bungee-style 'Quick Jump', or reach breakneck speeds along Thailand's only toboggan-style jungle coaster.

End your trip with a sweet, 360-degree sunset view from atop a cabbage-patch garden viewpoint in the village of 5 **Mon Jam** *(facebook .com/monjam.cnx; per garden 30–40฿)*.

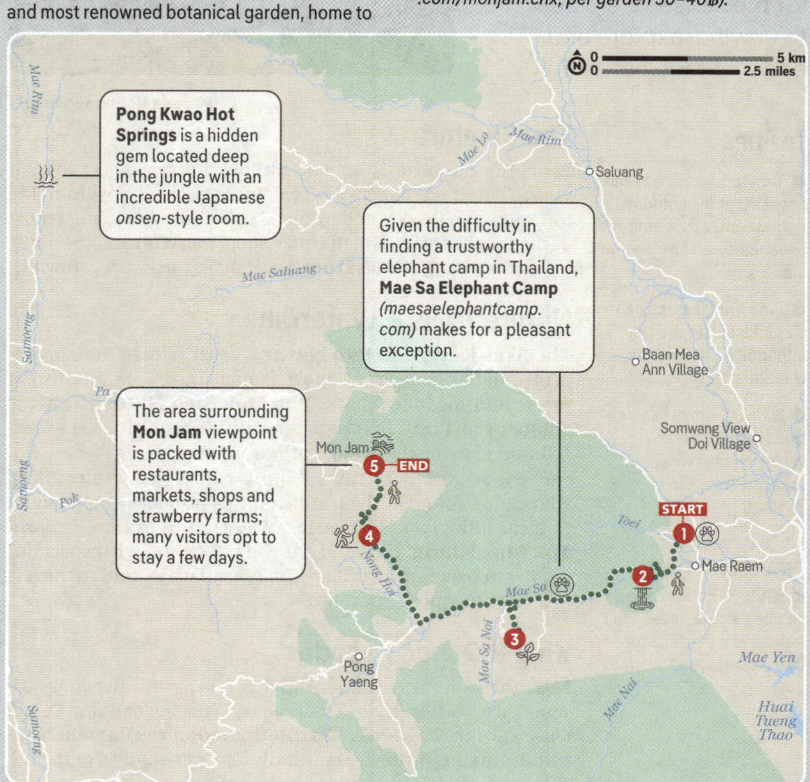

TOP EXPERIENCE

Doi Inthanon

Rising majestically to 2565m above sea level, Doi Inthanon is Thailand's highest peak and a nature-lover's paradise. With cool, crisp air and a diverse array of flora and fauna, its pristine nature trails, waterfalls and hill-tribe villages make for a refreshing paradise. This is Chiang Mai's sanctuary for the senses – a place to unwind, explore and become mesmerised.

ALEXANDRE.ROSA/SHUTTERSTOCK

Pagoda Nopphonphusiri

TOP TIPS

- Temperatures can reach near 0°C at the summit during winter (November to January), so bring warm clothes.
- Free tourist maps can be picked up at the Doi Inthanon National Park Headquarters.
- Native Siamese sakura trees near Siriphum Waterfall blossom pink for a few weeks in late January.

PRACTICALITIES

● 300฿ ● Entrance fee can be used to access the trails and waterfalls for free if used the same day.

The Summit

Reaching the peak is a must, although don't expect a great view. There's no hike up to speak of, as cars drive right to the top, although it's covered by forest and shrouded in mist most of the year. A shrine, small coffee shop, museum and the alluringly mossy **Ang Kha Nature Trail** make the visit worthwhile.

Nature Trails & Waterfalls

The 3km **Kew Mae Pan Nature Trail** *(closed Jun-Oct)* is probably the mountain's most famous, given its mixture of forest and meadow views. **Pha Dok Sieo Nature Trail** is another short trail that passes a stunning multitiered waterfall and ends at the village of Mae Klang Luang, where hot coffee is served. Both trails require guides *(per group 200฿)* who can be found at the trailhead; this provides employment to local hill-tribes. The easiest waterfall to explore is **Nam Tok Mae Klang**, located near the park gate, with space for picnics and swimming. The 40m **Nam Tok Wachirathan** is probably the most impressive.

King & Queen Pagodas

Near the summit, you'll also find two beautiful pagodas surrounded by well-kept gardens. Erected in honour of Rama IX and Queen Sirikit, **Pagoda Noppamethanedon** and **Pagoda Nopphonphusiri** *(100฿)* are culturally and spiritually significant.

Chiang Dao

HIDDEN DESTINATION | FRESH MOUNTAIN AIR | COSY GETAWAY

Chiang Dao is an often overlooked destination that's closer to the city of Chiang Mai than many realise. Towering over villages and valleys, the limestone mountains here are majestic, their sheer cliffs and cloud-brushed ridgelines creating a dramatic backdrop that's visible for miles. At Chiang Dao's heart lies a small but charming town filled with easygoing resorts, independent cafes and fun activities that sit in the shadow of Thailand's third-highest peak.

Beyond these gentle getaways, winding roads disappear into the hills, leading to rustic homestays, forest communities and wild nature trails that feel a world away from big city life. Seek spiritual solace at sacred cave temples; camp atop the precarious peaks of Doi Chiang Dao Luang; or sample unfamiliar delicacies at vibrant hill-tribe markets. Whatever your pace, Chiang Dao promises an authentic, invigorating escape – one that contrasts beautifully with the busy streets of Chiang Mai just an hour south.

TOP TIP

Chiang Dao is a sleepy spot, so pre-arranged transport outside your resort is a must, especially after sunset when the town goes to sleep. Locals are most active in the mornings, with temples, markets and streets buzzing from first light.

Scale the Mighty Mountain

Scale the windy peaks of Doi Luang

From November to January, **Doi Luang Chiang Dao** *(doichiangdaobiosphere.com)* opens to a limited number of hikers who want to scale it. This 230-million-year-old limestone massif is Thailand's third-highest mountain; its dramatic, sheer cliffs and towering presence make it arguably the most impressive.

GETTING THERE & AROUND

Chiang Dao is about two hours north of Chiang Mai along Rte 107. The journey here is especially spectacular, winding between mountains as the road climbs. Private transport is best for getting around, but there are buses *(every 30 min; 40฿)* that travel from the Chang Phueak Bus Terminal in Chiang Mai. Minibuses *(150฿)* also travel the same route, offering faster and more comfortable rides.

The town itself is relatively small. Most hotels and resorts in the area operate pick-up services. If you drive yourself, beware that Mae Mae and the surrounding hillside villages have limited parking.

WILDLIFE SPOTTING

Doi Chiang Dao Luang is famed for its wealth of wildlife hidden among its cliffs and climbs. On your hike, keep one eye on the ground, looking out for ancient sea fossils, and keep the other out ahead to spot rare birds, mammals and plants. Endangered mountain deer known as goral are populous here, often hanging out on the sheer cliffs. In the brush, big-headed turtles and Asian golden cats scour the land for food but often avoid people. The incredibly rare parrot flower can also be seen here – a beautiful psittacine that resembles a flying cockatoo; it's only found in northern Thailand and Myanmar. If you're making this trip without a long-lens camera, be sure to bring a pair of binoculars.

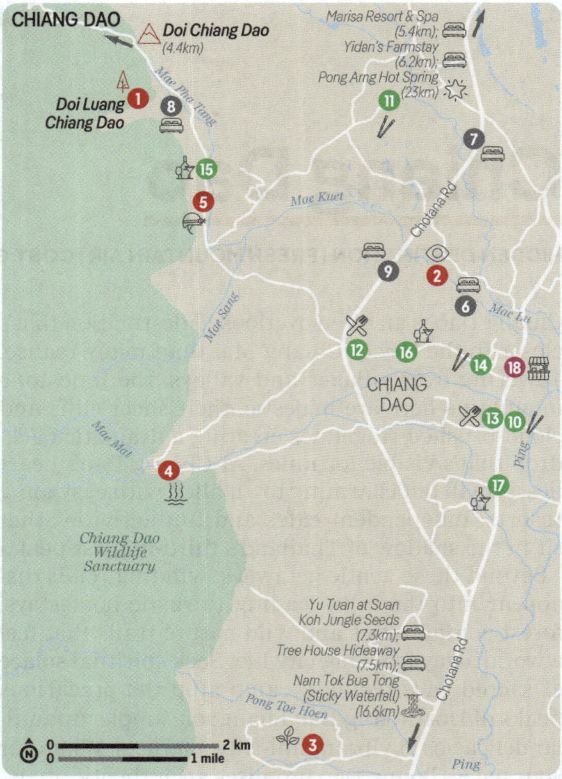

CHIANG DAO

HIGHLIGHTS
1 Doi Luang Chiang Dao

SIGHTS
2 Choeng Doi Distillery
3 Suan Buachompoo

ACTIVITIES
4 Chiang Dao Hot Springs
5 Wat Tham Chiang Dao

SLEEPING
6 Ban Suan Tawan Chiang Dao
7 Campian
8 Chiang Dao Nest
9 MonChomDoi

EATING
10 Khaosoi Pa'toi
11 Marabai Bar & Restaurant
12 Microkosmos Craft Beer & Burger Bar
13 Mountainella Café
14 VELAR

DRINKING & NIGHTLIFE
15 Cave Bar
16 Charoen Bar Whiskey & Cocktails
17 Cojon

SHOPPING
18 Tuesday Market

The mountain is within the Chiang Dao Wildlife Sanctuary, a UNESCO Biosphere Reserve. This means that only a limited number of hikers – 'researchers', as per their official terminology – are allowed to climb it every year. Reservations can be made through the website or via private message on their Facebook page *(facebook.com/welovedoichiangdao)*, and should be made as far in advance as possible. Local hotels and tour operators can also help facilitate – probably the easiest option.

Once signed up, you'll need to arrive in Chiang Dao a day early to pay the fees *(around 1000฿)*, join the safety briefing and do an equipment check (gear rentals available). The hike begins at 8am the following day with a short truck ride to the trailhead, which leads 8km to the 2175m summit. Tents are set up at the top, dinners cooked on camping stoves and sunsets admired.

The next morning, many like to wake up early and catch the sunrise over the epic mountains, with giant shadows and bright reflections darting across the valleys below. Be sure to bring warm clothing, as temperatures regularly drop to near freezing – in itself a rare experience for Thailand.

Make Local Thai Spirits

Private tours of Choeng Doi Distillery

As Chiang Dao's only contemporary micro-brewery, **Choeng Doi Distillery** *(choengdoi.com)* crafts small-batch spirits using only organic, locally sourced rice and sugarcane. Aside from navigating Thailand's strict alcohol-production laws, the two owners have made it their mission to share the process with the world – with no part of their production off-limits, and all experiences absolutely hands-on.

Open by appointment only from October to March, Jeen and Pam lead tours of the distillery, tailoring everything about your visit to align with your interests. Depending on the season, you might find yourself planting rice, harvesting sugarcane, working in the lab to figure out new botanical blends, setting up fermentation tanks, distilling batches or even bottling finished products.

Beyond the distillery, which overlooks Doi Chiang Dao Luang, tours include visits to their private estate gardens (where most of their botanicals are found) as well as curated visits to local bars, restaurants, springs, caves, waterfalls and forest trails. Requests can be made for deeper dives into the Chiang Dao region, including optional forest tours led by a legendary local biologist and natural farmer, trips to **Suan Buachompoo** (Thailand's first certified organic farm for fresh teas and flowers), and a host of other bespoke recommendations for off-the-radar activities, restaurants, bars and homestays rarely seen by the average traveller.

A LOVE FOR LOCAL AGRICULTURE

Jeen Snidvongs, owner and found of **Choeng Doi Distillery**

What originally drew me to Chiang Dao was the quiet revolution in agricultural practice that was happening, led by the new generation of farmers who studied in Bangkok or abroad and returned home to help transform their family land into a place that produces higher quality fruit, vegetables and other agricultural products. With a focus on sustainability, science and marketing, all the while respecting their traditions, the new generation of producers are growing some of the best produce in the whole of Thailand, and they're always keen to chat. I often introduce a few to distillery visitors when the chance presents itself.

DRINKING IN CHIANG DAO: SUNDOWNER SPECIALS

Charoen Bar Whiskey & Cocktails: Quaint Charoen has fruity cocktails (plus a bistro-style Thai food menu). *noon-9pm Thu-Tue*

Marabai Bar & Restaurant: A rustic, relaxed hangout. Decent cocktails and a pool table will have you back for more. *5pm-midnight*

Cave Bar: Even if you don't stay at Chiang Dao Nest, the bar always has a good atmosphere, especially when the owners are around. *5-11.30pm*

Cojon: A cool garden hangout with a camping feel. In the winter months, fires roar and regular band appearances keep it busy. *5pm-midnight*

OFF-ROAD CHIANG DAO

Chiang Dao's backroads are best explored from the seat of an off-road motorbike, especially if you want to reach the remote villages and forested ridgelines that regular vehicles can't access. Several Chiang Mai–based operators offer multiday adventures on enduro motorbikes, following old roads, gravel tracks and rugged mountain trails that wind deep into Chiang Dao and beyond. **Enduro Tours** *(letsridetheworld.com)* and **Siam Enduro** *(siamenduro.com)* both provide fully guided trips, with routes designed for beginners through to seasoned riders. **POP Big Bike Rental** *(popbigbike.com)* also hires out bikes for independent exploration, allowing experienced riders to craft their own journey – just make sure to check insurance details and return the bike without a scratch.

SAIKO3P/SHUTTERSTOCK

Wat Tham Chiang Dao

Hot Springs & Caves

Chiang Dao's natural attractions

Wat Tham Chiang Dao *(40฿, with guide 150฿)* is a vast and eerie cave complex that disappears 12km under the impressive Doi Chiang Dao Luang. Part temple, part natural wonder, there are two main areas: the main cave, which takes about 30 minutes to an hour to explore unguided, and a deeper section that can only be explored with a local guide. The cave has played a part in folklore dating back millennia, with Buddha images and perplexing rock formations alluding to stories of ancient mythical creatures and 1000-year-old hermits.

Pressed tightly against the foothills of the mountain where the Mae Mat and Mae Ka rivers meet are the **Chiang Dao Hot Springs** *(free)*, which offer the most spectacular natural bathing experience in the area. Swap the smell of guano for sulphur at these personal, open-air pools, which can be rented for 50฿ an hour and pair perfectly with an ice-cold beer and sticky rice and chicken. Most of the people you meet here will be chilling at the communal concrete tubs that sit haphazardly on the edge of the stream.

To the north, **Pong Arng Hot Spring** *(100฿)* offers a slightly more communal feel, but it has the advantage of being next door to Nam Tok Sri Sangwan, a lesser known and equally exciting waterfall alternative to Nam Tok Bua Tong (p289) (aka the 'Sticky Waterfall').

EATING IN CHIANG DAO: OUR PICKS

Microkosmos Craft Beer & Burger Bar: Organic burgers and veggie options pair with ice-cold tap and bottled craft beers served all day. *4-11.30pm Wed-Mon* ฿฿

Mountainella Café: Delicious home-baked goods, savoury bites, cakes and cookies; there's also a varied and modern coffee menu. *8am-5pm* ฿฿

VELAR: Japanese–Thai fusion served with helpings of sake. Their hot-pot is so unique, you'll not find anything like it anywhere else. *9am-9pm Fri-Wed* ฿฿

Khaosoi Pa'toi: On the main street but almost hidden from view, you'll find the best chicken, beef and pork *khao soi* in town. *10am-5pm* ฿

Shop the Jungle's Finest Goods

Tuesday morning market

Although locals can pick up fresh produce every day from Chiang Dao's main wet market, it's the **Tuesday Market** (located next to the bus station) that really stands out. Far from touristy, this morning market feels raw and real thanks to its unique array of foraged, hunted and handmade products.

Both city dwellers and hill-tribe people pitch up to sell their forest finds of the week – everything from wild honey collected by hand from the top of 100m-high tualang trees to wild mushrooms, deep-fried bamboo worms, forest chicken, wild boar and even *rang peung* (jungle honeycomb) – replete with fully developed grubs – that's grilled over an open fire before being served in a banana leaf.

Aside from the food, there's also a good selection of handcrafted tools and materials – all with some form of practical application – including rice steamers, medicinal herbs, gardening tools and sun hats. The earlier you go, the better the experience, as produce disappears quickly and by midday, the sun is scorching. For all of the markets in Chiang Mai, this one offers a rare opportunity to meet ethnic Lisu, Hmong, Akha and Yao communities, some still dedicated to wearing their traditional dress. The market is open from 6am to noon.

Sleep by the Fire

Rustic tours in Mae Mae

Tucked away in the hills adjacent to Doi Chiang Dao Luang is a village called Mae Mae, an off-the-beaten-track destination that's home to a number of small homestays offering authentic mountain-life experiences. **Tree House Hideaway** *(treehouseinchiangmai.com)* offers incredible views of the jungle canopy, as well as stays and programmes that immerse you in unspoiled nature. Guests are encouraged to interact with local culture and experience the vast outdoors. Given the mountain location, it also has a number of rafting, zipline and elephant activities at hand that contrast well with the sleepy and peaceful scenes of Mae Mae.

Down in the valley at the bottom of the village is **Yu Tuan at Suan Koh Jungle Seeds** *(091 856 1603; book using a Thai speaker)*, a very local homestay that takes you back to basics. The name Yu Tuan, which translates to 'Go Wild', says it all – no electricity, outdoor toilets and little more than a firepit for evening light. Time passes slowly as you float between river paddling, herb picking and dealing with bugs. At dusk, a tour up to a viewpoint overlooking the far side of Doi Chiang Dao Luang includes curries cooked in bamboo stems and jungle whiskies with friendly villagers who communicate via eager hand gestures and the clink of shot glasses.

WILD HONEY MEAD

Thailand has long been known for its abundance of wild honey, harvested seasonally from wild hives found deep in the jungle by locals who follow traditional, low-impact gathering methods. This rich, floral honey has recently found an unexpected new expression through the **Day Drinkers Collective** *(@daydrinkers.collective)*, a small Chiang Dao–based mead producer. Using age-old fermentation techniques, they transform raw honey, water and yeast into mead, allowing different honey profiles to shape each batch's flavour and aroma. The result is a distinctly northern Thai take on one of the world's oldest alcoholic drinks. While their meadery is open for casual drop-ins, the real story is how Chiang Dao's forest honey has quietly entered Thailand's craft-beverage scene. Their bottles can now be found at selected bars and restaurants across the country.

Places We Love to Stay

฿ Budget ฿฿ Midrange ฿฿฿ Top End

Muang Chiang Mai

Map p256 & p278

Nuan Nil Bed and Breakfast ฿ A perfect spot for any backpacker who wants to be in town but enjoys a clean, good night's sleep. The place is famed for its chilled-out owner who spends his day at the coffee machine.

Libra Guest House ฿ One of the best backpacker guesthouses in the city, with a very friendly and hospitable owner who is always willing to help out. Aircon and fan rooms are inexpensive, and there's a pool in the garden out back.

Buri Siri Hotel ฿฿ Old-style northern-Thai decor with spacious rooms and a ground-floor pool that sometimes hosts events; there's also a co-working cafe on-site. Just next to Th Nimmanhaemin, with great road links to the old city.

Cochet de Nimman ฿฿ Small, beautifully appointed cabins offer quiet serenity in a spot surrounded by trees that were here well before Nimman arrived.

Le Charcoa Hôtel ฿฿ With architecture that looks like it would fit better in a fairytale, this hotel is uniquely charming and looks great in photos. The hotel's fresh-bread breakfasts are a winner, too.

Art Mai? Gallery Hotel ฿฿ Comfortable mid-range hotel in the heart of Nimmanhaemin. Each floor showcases a different art style in both decor and room design, while the lobby and shared spaces have regular exhibitions and events to keep you occupied.

G Nimman ฿฿฿ This pure-white circular-shaped hotel is a contemporary landmark, contrasting with the old shophouse that surrounds it. Rooms – which promise bizarre yet highly Instagrammable stays – open up to a central pool.

Rachamankha Boutique Hotel ฿฿฿ Luxury Lanna-style hotel grounds and rooms, with nightly dance performances at dinner. High prices guarantee the highest quality of northern Thai stays.

Beyond Muang Chiang Mai

Baanpong Lodge ฿฿ A fun, party-vibe spot on the outskirts of the city; it marries natural escapes with a social energy that gravitates around the pool and bar. Suitable for families, but with late-bar parties most weekends.

Tai Resort ฿฿ Located almost opposite the buffalo market (p261), this resort offers quality rooms at reasonable prices and a five-star feel. Complete with on-site cafe, restaurant and landscaped gardens.

Bantunglom Resort ฿฿ Reconnect with nature among working rice paddies. The on-site chef makes fresh pasta every day, and the bay-window bathtubs set the scene.

Nern Jam Sai ฿฿ Spend some time with yourself in this out-of-town teak-house getaway that overlooks forests and river creeks. Slightly Japanese in style, the purpose is escape: staff members keep to themselves and there's nothing but a restaurant on-site.

Mountain Float ฿฿฿ The first impressions are nothing short of magical as you are transported to your very own floating villa by a speedboat that gently glides over a mirror-like reservoir (p290) just north of Chiang Mai.

Mae Sa Valley

Baan Mon Muan ฿฿ Mountain-top lodging in newly built teak cabins that feel older than they are and overlook mountain communities below. Although quiet, the restaurant is exceptional and Michelin-recommended.

Skyview Monjam ฿฿ Among all the glamping spots near Mon Jam, this one stands out as a must for those keen for a view – the bedroom is walled in floor-to-ceiling glass that overlooks the valleys below. Outdoor bathtub and local-luxury amenities included.

Sukantara Cascade Resort ฿฿ Once described as the most beautiful waterfall resort in the world, this stunning spot has a waterfall flowing throughout the property; it's serviced by local Karen staff who are very friendly.

Villa Tammatari ฿฿฿ A beautiful private house that sleeps up to 12 guests, with views overlooking the flower farms of Mae Sa Valley below. Self-catered, but optional extras such as excursions, as well as chefs and masseuses, are easily organised.

Onsen @ Moncham ฿฿฿ For those who like to soak, do it surrounded by forest trees at the province's best Japanese-style *onsen*, found within this luxury resort complex on the top of a mountain.

Chiang Dao

Map p294

Yidan's Farmstay ฿ Described as a 'secret garden' in the hills of Chiang Dao, this is where those with a passion for sustainable living and deep connections come. Lots of activities and a fun combination of Chinese and Thai cultural learning.

Chiang Dao Nest ฿฿ The first resort in Chiang Dao. Old, well-maintained bamboo cottages are scattered amid meticulously tended tropical gardens, shaded by towering yang trees and Doi Luang Chiang Dao.

Ban Suan Tawan Chiang Dao ฿฿ A simple but charming resort set around lakes and gardens. Each room is a standalone wooden prefab cabin with various styles and bed combinations.

Campian ฿฿ A camping-style four-star resort with options of pool villas, forest cabins, gallery housing and honeymoon suites. The central fire pit is where most social activities happen here.

MonChomDoi ฿฿ Your more stereotypical Thai hotel, with stunning views over the town and Doi Luang Chiang Dao beyond. Rooms are spacious and centrally located.

Marisa Resort & Spa ฿฿ Quiet and somewhat basic, the resort aims to be be four star but is maybe a little less. However, that doesn't take away from its beautiful setting, clean rooms and worthwhile on-site spa and activity options.

Mae Wang

Karen Eco Lodge ฿฿ A peaceful private resort that promotes ecotourism through package stays that include elephant experiences, cooking classes and traditional farming.

Raibumrungphol ฿฿ Resort glamping in nature; it's under an hour from the city, with a decent combo of good food, rice paddy-view pools and dome rooms with optional rooftop sofa beds for stargazing.

Chai Lai Orchid ฿฿฿ Nonprofit luxury resort-style mountain retreat that promotes local culture, complete with elephant wake-up calls, balcony banana breakfasts and indigenous cuisine that's fresh and locally sourced.

BESTSINESS/SHUTTERSTOCK

G Nimman, Chiang Mai

Researched by David Eimer

Northeastern Thailand

NATURE, FOOD, HISTORY AND MEKONG SUNSETS

The multicultural northeast is Thailand's most underrated destination, home to the country's least-explored national parks and historical sites, as well as the mighty Mekong River.

Northeastern Thailand – always known as 'Isan' – is bounded by the majestic Mekong in the north and east and is a diverse blend of cultures and communities, yet it's by far the least-visited region of the country. Only around 1% of foreign tourists venture here, ensuring that there's plenty of elbow room in the many national parks and historical sites.

Isan's landscapes are as varied as its people. In the north lies green, fragrant forest punctuated by dramatic peaks that rival anything to be found in northern Thailand. To the east, lush jungle provides cover for meandering streams and arid moonscapes alike. And in the south, the ruins of a former Khmer empire dot the red, sandy soil. Wherever you are, the mix of Thai, Lao, Cambodian and Vietnamese influences make a mark on the region's architecture, language and fiery food.

Isan is also the kingdom's most populous region and its people are the economic backbone of Thailand, with many migrating south for work. Despite that, there's still a distinct divide between the northeast and the rest of the country, and Isan remains both Thailand's best-kept secret and one of its last real frontiers. If you have a desire for authentic experiences, aren't afraid to get off the tourist trail and can live without an umbrella in your drink, this is the place for you.

THANET SAREESRI/SHUTTERSTOCK

THE MAIN AREAS

NAKHON RATCHASIMA CITY (KORAT CITY)
Gateway to Isan and Khao Yai.
p306

KHON KAEN
Isan's liveliest city.
p320

CHIANG KHAN
Festivals and Mekong views.
p326

For places to stay in northeastern Thailand, see p356

SERRA PHOTOGRAPH/SHUTTERSTOCK

Left: Steamed rice rolls; Above: Phra Mahathat Kaen Nakhon (p321), Khon Kaen

UDON THANI
Ancient civilisations and natural splendours. p333

NAKHON PHANOM
Mekong sunsets and Vietnam in Isan. p340

UBON RATCHATHANI
Waterfalls, national parks and riverside beaches. p347

Chiang Khan, p326

It's not as 'undiscovered' as it once was, but this charming Mekong-side town makes a good base to explore the wild, untamed beauty of Loei Province.

Udon Thani, p333

Not as pretty as its regional rivals, but this boomtown is home to some of Isan's finest dining. Nearby Ban Chiang is an archaeological superstar.

Khon Kaen, p320

Isan's unofficial capital and one of Thailand's fastest-growing cities, Khon Kaen is a lively student town with national parks just a couple of hours away.

Nakhon Ratchasima City (Korat City), p306

Known for its distinctive culture and unique cuisine, Korat sits close to wonderful Khao Yai National Park and is easily reached from Bangkok.

Ubon Ratchathani, p347

The gateway to the 'Emerald Triangle', where Thailand meets Laos and Cambodia, Ubon is a laid-back town, while the surrounding countryside is all rivers, forests and waterfalls.

Find Your Way

The northeast covers a big area, but roads are reasonable, trains connect parts of the region and major cities have airports. Sadly, though, it's not possible to cruise the Mekong for any distance.

Nakhon Phanom, p340

Peaceful Nakhon Phanom offers Mekong sunsets, has a palpable Vietnamese influence and is one of Isan's most pleasant towns to kick back in for a few days.

BUS & MINIVAN

Minivans and buses connect all the principal cities and towns. Buses also link Isan to Bangkok and Chiang Mai, as well as to Vientiane, Thakhek, Savannakhet and Pakse in Laos. Slower and less frequent buses and minivans run to local destinations.

CAR & MOTORBIKE

Cars can be rented in many places, although it doesn't cost much more to hire a car and a driver, allowing you to lean back and enjoy the view. Motorbikes are less useful because distances are longer here. We don't recommend driving at night in Isan.

TRAIN

Thailand's Northeastern Line links Bangkok with Isan. There are two branches: one runs to Vientiane in Laos via Nakhon Ratchasima, Khon Kaen and Udon Thani; the other heads to Ubon Ratchathani via Buriram. Trains are a relaxed way to travel, but generally slower than buses.

0 — 100 km
0 — 50 miles

Plan Your Time

Almost all foreign travellers to Isan visit Khao Yai National Park in the south of the region. With more time, head to the sleepy towns of Chiang Khan or Nakhon Phanom for stunning sunsets.

KASBAH/SHUTTERSTOCK

Phanom Rung Historical Park (p318)

If You Only Do One Thing

● Make straight for magnificent **Khao Yai National Park** (p314), where elephants, gibbons, bears and deer roam over 2000 sq km of forest, while yellow-beaked great hornbills soar overhead. Despite Khao Yai's size, this is one of the easiest national parks for independent travellers to access, with plenty of hiking trails, impressive waterfalls and both day and night tours on offer. Tons of accommodation is available both inside and outside the park. Combine your visit with a trip to nearby **Nakhon Ratchasima City** (p306), which makes a fine base for exploring the Khmer ruins of **Phimai** (p311), the architectural inspiration for Cambodia's Angkor Wat, or head east to **Phanom Rung** (p318), another ancient Khmer temple complex, which perches dramatically on the edge of an extinct volcano.

SEASONAL HIGHLIGHTS

December to February is the best time to visit Isan, when temperatures are lower and the landscape is lush. Some national parks close during the June–October rainy season.

JANUARY

Normally the coldest month in Isan, with daytime temperatures occasionally as low as 20°C – distinctly chilly for Thailand. Mountains can be dusted with frost as nighttime temperatures drop towards 0°C at altitude.

FEBRUARY

The best month to visit **Red Lotus Sea** (p336) south of Udon Thani, when the lake is blanketed with fuchsia-coloured water lilies. On Valentine's Day, the lake is absolutely rammed with loved-up couples.

APRIL

Thai New Year, or Songkran, falls mid-month, the biggest party of the year for locals. At **Nong Khai** (p338), the islands in the Mekong host celebrations, as do the riverside beaches of **Ubon Ratchathani** (p347).

A Week to Wander

● After exploring **Khao Yai National Park** (p314), wind your way north, stopping to take in buzzing **Khon Kaen** (p320), Isan's most happening city, and the nearby **Nam Nao National Park** (p323), where spectacular sunrise and sunset views await, alongside elephants and rare birdlife. Then carry on heading north to photogenic **Chiang Khan** (p326), a town of traditional wooden houses surrounded by temple-studded rolling hills and with fine views of Laos on the opposite bank of the Mekong. End your week by tracking the Mekong to **Nong Khai** (p338) and then south to **Udon Thani** (p333), home to some of Isan's best restaurants and just an hour away from the ancient archaeological finds at **Ban Chiang** (p335), perhaps the most important prehistoric site in all Southeast Asia.

More Than a Week

● Spend more time in lovely Loei Province, making sure to hike through the primate-filled forests that lead to the summit of **Phu Kradueng** (p329) for horizon-spanning views. If you're in Loei in June or July, you're in luck because it's the time for **Pee Ta Khon** (p331), Isan's most extraordinary festival. People parade dressed as ghosts and the music and dancing is non-stop for three days as the locals seek to wake the spirits. After all that partying, head east to peaceful **Nakhon Phanom** (p340), where the Mekong sunsets are sublime and some of Isan's most sacred temples sit nearby. Finish up your Isan tour by heading south to **Ubon Ratchathani** (p347), a relaxed riverside city surrounded by waterfalls and national parks.

JUNE

A key month for festivals, the most notable of which is the exuberant **Pee Ta Khon** (p331), a bawdy and bizarre three-day party designed to wake the dead.

OCTOBER

The weird and wonderful **Naga Fireballs** (p339) draw tens of thousands of spectators to watch giant balls of flame shooting up above the Mekong at the time of the full moon.

NOVEMBER

The maple forests of **Phu Kradueng National Park** (p329) explode in a gorgeous riot of red and orange, while water levels are low enough to marvel at **Sam Phan Bok** (p350), the Mekong's largest rock reef.

DECEMBER

Peak time for visiting **Khao Yai National Park** (p314), as it's cooler, the trails are dry and wildlife is out and about. Make sure to book accommodation well in advance, especially for weekends.

Nakhon Ratchasima City (Korat City)

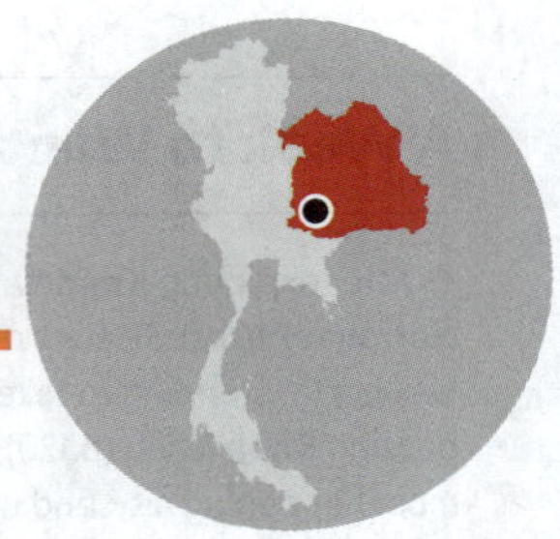

NIGHT MARKETS | FOOD | HISTORY

TOP TIP

Life in Korat seems to revolve around the monument to Thao Suranari (known as 'Ya Mo'), and the markets and restaurants around it. Go see the action in person to get a feel for the city.

Nakhon Ratchasima, still mostly known by its former name of Korat, is something of a marvel: a vibrant provincial city that maintains a unique identity. Indeed, residents of Korat consider themselves separate from not only Isan but other regions of Thailand as well. On weekends, the locals dress up in their best *mudmee* (woven silks) to pay their respects to the statue of 'Ya Mo' ('Grandma Mo'), the 19th-century heroine who saved Korat from an invading Lao army.

Korat's distinct culture extends to the city's architecture – a mix of central Thai and Isan styles – and the local food; Korat puts its own spin on classic Thai dishes like *pat tai* and *som tam*. There's little in the way of standout sights here, but the night markets are great and many travellers pass through, thanks to Korat's proximity to Khao Yai National Park and the ancient Khmer sites of Phimai and Phanom Rung.

Visit Isan's Biggest Night Market

Eat like a local

The king of Korat's many night markets is the vast **Seven Save One Night Market**, 6km southwest of the city centre. It's the largest night market in all Isan; there are even free shuttle buses to move visitors around the different sections. There's a huge array of eats, from specialities like *pat mee Korat* (the local version of *pat tai*) to Isan and Thai classics

GETTING THERE & AROUND

Korat has two bus stations. Terminal 2 has long-distance buses to Bangkok, Chiang Mai, Khon Kaen and Udon Thani, as well as minivans to Phimai, while the much smaller Terminal 1 is for local destinations, including Pak Chong (for Khao Yai National Park). From Korat's railway station, trains run north to Khon Kaen, Udon Thani and Vientiane or south to Pak Chong, Ayuthaya and Bangkok. Motorcycle taxis and tuk-tuks are easy to find in the centre of town or you can use the Grab ridesharing app.

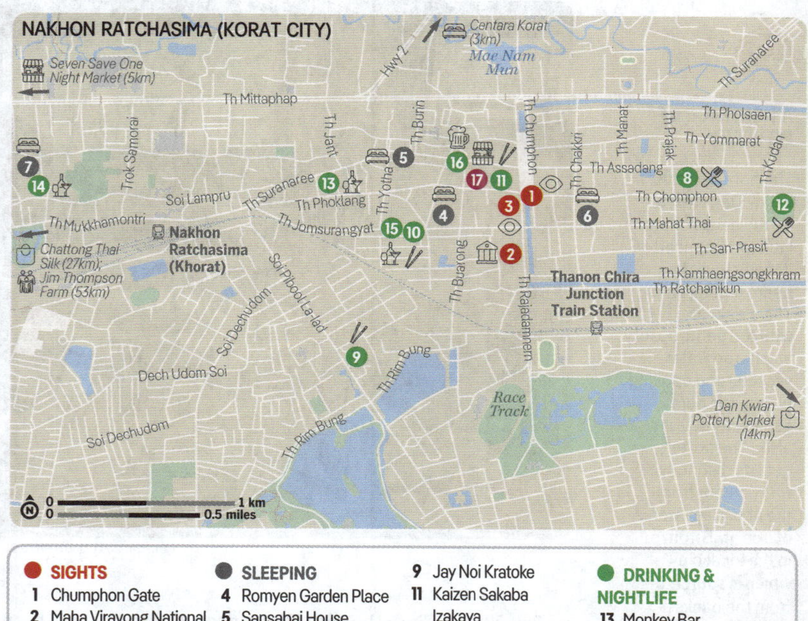

SIGHTS
1 Chumphon Gate
2 Maha Viravong National Museum
3 Ruen Korat (Korat House)
see 1 Thao Suranari Monument

SLEEPING
4 Romyen Garden Place
5 Sansabai House
6 Urban-Bamboo
7 Within-Korat

EATING
8 3rd World Burger
9 Jay Noi Kratoke
11 Kaizen Sakaba Izakaya
11 Kanom Jeen Yai Pow
12 Wat Boon Night Bazaar

DRINKING & NIGHTLIFE
13 Monkey Bar
14 Muu Bar
15 Not Too Bad
16 Some Might Say

SHOPPING
17 Mae Kim Heng Market

and a smattering of Japanese and Korean options. But you can also shop for clothes, animals or amulets, get a haircut or tattoo or just sit at a bar with a beer.

Much more sedate is the **Wat Boon Night Bazaar** in the old town. It's mostly takeaway Thai and Isan food here, but there are a few places to sit and eat. Another good choice is the **Mae Kim Heng Market**, the only one that's also open during the day, when fresh fruit and flowers are on sale. But head to the rear of the market and there's a string of fine food stalls, some of which stay open 24/7.

Weaving a Web

Korat's silk-weaving centre

Pak Thong Chai, about 35km south of Korat, is a hub of the traditional Thai silk-weaving industry and a must-see for fabric aficionados. *Mudmee*, known as ikat in Malaysia and Indonesia, is the art of weaving silk fabrics with intricate patterns using wooden looms. In *mudmee* weaving, a single horizontal thread is responsible for the fabric's patterns. The work is time-consuming and it's a dying tradition, with all the weavers coming from the older generation.

In Pak Thong Chai itself, **Chattong Thai Silk** sells fabric and can direct you to the local weavers. Located 25km south

A HERITAGE OF POTTERY

The pottery made in tiny **Dan Kwian** on the banks of the Mun (pronounced 'Moon') River has been popular with Thais since the 1940s, with the good-quality *ang* (large water vessels) and cooking pots made here especially sought after. The pottery gets its distinctive rusty colour from the abundant stores of iron and bronze in the local clay, which is sourced from the banks of the Mun River. Japanese techniques were subsequently adopted by the villagers to enhance their pottery and more modern kilns with better temperature control are now used. For a close-up look at this pottery – and to pick up a few items yourself – head 20km southeast of Korat to the **Dan Kwian Pottery Market**.

NELLY NAREE/SHUTTERSTOCK

of Pak Thong Chai, the **Jim Thompson Farm** does its best to keep the art alive by showcasing the process of silk weaving from silk worm to the finished product, available at the outlet store in front. While the shop is open year-round, the farm runs tours in December and January only. To see the actual fabric outside those months, head to the nearby village of **Baan Japoh** where the loud clacking of looms staffed by septuagenarians can be heard from houses. Always ask before stepping inside to watch.

It's best to visit the area with your own wheels or a taxi – Pak Thong Chai is very spread out – and come early; most of the weaving is done between 5am and 10am.

Soak Up Some History

Monuments and museums

No trip to Korat is complete without a pilgrimage to the monument of **Thao Suranari**, fondly nicknamed 'Ya Mo' (or 'Grandma Mo'), who is credited with saving the city from the invading army of the King of Vientiane in 1826 by smuggling

EATING IN KORAT: OUR PICKS

Kanom Jeen Yai Pow: Our pick for *kanom jeen*: thin rice noodles with chicken or fish in a luscious, flavoursome sauce. Inside Mae Kim Heng Market. *24hr* B

Jay Noi Kratoke: Their local-style noodles – *pat mee Korat* – are recommended by the likes of the Michelin Guide, but the *som tam* is even better. *8am-9pm* B

3rd World Burger: Long-standing and slightly eccentric place in the south of town with decent burgers and all the trimmings. *noon-8pm Tue-Sun* B

Kaizen Sakaba Izakaya: Japanese food is big in Korat and this surprisingly authentic place is always buzzing with a young crowd. *6pm-midnight Tue-Sun* BB

Silk weaving, Jim Thompson Farm

knives to imprisoned men, who then rose up and repelled the Lao forces. Today, Thao Suranari's statue marks the city centre and inspires hordes of Thais, both locals and visitors, to pay their respects and make wishes daily. An annual festival held in Ya Mo's honour is also celebrated at the end of March.

Just behind her statue, **Chumphon Gate** is the only survivor of Korat's original city gates. Once part of the now long-gone city walls, the gate is the entrance to Korat's old town, where a few wooden houses are still standing. Also nearby is **Ruen Korat**, or Korat House, a picturesque 1905 structure that's a prime example of Korat's unique architectural hybrid of central and Isan styles.

Maha Viravong National Museum (*80฿*) is Korat's most worthwhile exhibition space, housing a small but rather fine collection of Buddhist and Khmer statuary, mostly from the 6th to 13th centuries. The museum is open Wednesday to Sunday and is tucked away in a historic house relocated to a compound that's about 600m south of the Thao Suranari monument.

KORAT SPECIALITIES

Two local dishes to seek out while you're in Korat are *som tam Korat* and *pat mee Korat. Som tam Korat* features the same ingredients as the mild central Thai version of *som tam*, but with the addition of Isan-style fermented fish sauce and, sometimes, field crab. *Pat mee Korat* appears similar to *pat tai* at first glance, but boasts more flavour thanks to the use of Chinese brown-bean sauce *(tao jiew)*. It also comes with a hearty sprinkling of chillies and is made with a local style of soft rice noodles *(mee Korat). Pat mee Korat* is widely available in Nakhon Ratchasima Province but is very rare elsewhere in Thailand.

DRINKING IN KORAT: OUR PICKS

Monkey Bar: Korat's expat hang-out has live sport, pool and darts, puts on bands and offers a menu of Western classics. *10am-midnight*

Some Might Say: One of a growing number of craft-beer bars in Korat – try the local mango ale. Also has a wine list. *6pm-midnight Tue-Sun*

Muu Bar: Low-lit cocktail bar with comfy sofas and decent drinks. It's on the ground floor of the Within-Korat hotel. *5pm-midnight*

Not Too Bad: A cool coffee shop by day and a laid-back bar with gentle live music Thursday to Saturday nights. *7am-5pm Sun-Wed, to midnight Thu-Sat*

Beyond Nakhon Ratchasima City

Places

GETTING AROUND

Khao Yai National Park is easily reached from Korat city or Bangkok, thanks to the train station at nearby Pak Chong. Regular minivans and buses also connect Pak Chong with Korat and Bangkok. From Pak Chong, *songthaew* (pick-up minibuses) make the 30km run to the park entrance, otherwise you can hire a motorbike. Hourly minivans link Korat city with Phimai, but Phanom Rung can only be reached by taxi or with your own wheels.

Thailand's best-known national park and ancient Khmer ruins vie for visitors' attention in this slice of southern Isan.

Nakhon Ratchasima Province, mostly known as Korat just like the provincial capital, belies the popular image of southern Isan as a sun-baked expanse of dust. In fact, rural Korat is surprisingly verdant and acts as the garden of Isan, growing rice, sugar cane and lots of fruit.

For visitors, it's splendid Khao Yai National Park in the far south of the province that is the principal draw: over 2000 sq km of wildlife-packed forest that's easy to access. But Korat and the neighbouring province of Buriram are also home to the superb ancient temple complexes of Phimai and Phanom Rung, which compete with each other as the most significant Khmer ruins in all Thailand.

Wat Pa Lak Roi

TIME FROM NAKHON RATCHASIMA CITY: **40MIN**

Welcome to Buddhist hell

Wat Pa Lak Roi is no place for the faint-hearted. Once you pass through the *Jurassic Park*–style entrance, guarded by giant gorillas and loomed over by a skeletal devil, you enter one of Thailand's weirdest temples. This is a vision of Buddhist hell, where hundreds of colourfully painted statues depict sinners being dismembered, impaled, tortured, torn apart or roasted alive. And that's just the stuff we can write about; some of the tableaux here are far too graphic and/or debauched to describe. Whether it's the school kids strung up for being bad pupils, the alcoholics speared as they fight over bottles of booze or the deviants being literally ploughed in half, the photo opportunities are extraordinary.

Despite the shocking nature of the statues, the temple is a popular spot with locals for weekend family outings, perhaps to give children an early induction into the true

KAIKORO/SHUTTERSTOCK

Phimai Historical Park

meaning of karma. The temple is free to visit (so make a donation for its upkeep) and a taxi from Korat should cost 800฿ return.

Phimai

TIME FROM NAKHON RATCHASIMA CITY: 1HR

Angkor Wat in Isan

Phimai Historical Park *(200฿)*, 60km northeast of Korat, was the architectural inspiration for Angkor Wat in Cambodia and is one of Thailand's most impressive and important surviving Khmer temple complexes. Phimai is much smaller than Angkor, but it's almost as evocative: surrounded by shady trees and a low wall beyond which is the unassuming town of Phimai.

The fact that the ruins sit slap in the centre of Phimai, with small-town life going on all around, makes them not only very accessible, but also brings the buildings alive a little; it's not too hard to imagine how bustling Phimai must have been during its heyday in the 11th, 12th and 13th centuries, when it was one of the Khmer empire's major cities and connected with Angkor via the Ancient Khmer Highway.

There has been a temple here since at least the 8th century, although most of the existing buildings were erected in the late 11th century by Khmer King Jayavarman VI. Despite being built as a Mahayana Buddhist temple, Phimai has carvings that feature many Hindu deities, while many design elements – most notably the main shrine's distinctive *prang* (Khmer-style) tower – were later used at Angkor Wat.

You enter over a cruciform **naga bridge**, which symbolically represents the passage from earth to heaven, and then through **Pratu Chai** (southern gate) of the outer wall, which stretches 565m by 1030m. The orientation to the south (though not due south) is unusual since most Khmer temples face east.

USEFUL ISAN PHRASES

Isan has its own dialect, which is closely related to the Lao language. Here are a few useful phrases to learn.

Sabaidee bor? – How are you?
Pen yang? – What's the matter?
Bor pen yang – No problem.
Saab ee-lee – That's really delicious.
Kop jai lai lai – Thank you very much.
Jao a-yu tao dai? – How old are you?
Jak mong lao? – What time is it?
Pai sai? – Where are you going?
Kao jai bor? – Do you understand?
Maen bor ?– Is that correct?
Koy bor samart gin sin – I don't eat meat.
Sukdee der – Good luck.

BAN PRASAT HOMESTAY

About 20km east of Phimai is Ban Prasat, a farming village that 3000 years ago was home to an early agricultural civilisation whose existence was unearthed in the 1990s, when archaeologists started discovering pottery and metal tools in the area. Today, though, it's almost as well-known for **Ban Prasat Homestay**, an award-winning homestay programme that dates back to 1966 and served as the model for other rural homestay initiatives in Thailand. Visitors are put up in local homes, eat with the families and are shown, or can take part in, farming activities or the making of handicrafts. Some families speak a little English and participating homes have signs outside, although it's best to contact them in advance *(089 581 7870 or via facebook.com/banprasarthomestay).*

It's often written that Phimai was built facing south to align with Angkor, though historians reject this theory since it doesn't face Angkor directly.

A raised passageway, formerly covered by a tiled roof, leads to the inner sanctum and the 28m-tall main shrine built of white sandstone and covered in superb carvings. Inside the adjacent **Prang Brahmathat** is a replica stone sculpture of Angkor King Jayavarman VII, sitting cross-legged and looking very much like a sitting Buddha.

Like all the statuary from Phimai, the original sculpture of King Jayavarman VII is in the **Phimai National Museum** *(virtualmuseum.finearts.go.th),* about 800m north of the ruins. The museum was closed for renovations at the time of writing (it is expected to reopen by summer 2026), but it's well worth a look, housing not just relics from Phimai but artefacts from across Isan.

A giant banyan tree

Just 2km northeast of Phimai Historical Park is **Sai Ngam**, which is both Thailand's oldest and largest banyan tree. The 350-year-old giant is more of a forest than a tree, its interlocking branches and gnarled trunks extending over 3200 sq metres and covering a small island. Paths have been cut through the tangle of branches, although you'll be ducking your head if you're tall, and there are a number of spirit houses dedicated to various tree deities, all of whom are female. Just to the side of the tree is a line of food stalls, with a covered area for eating, which makes a decent lunch stop.

While some visitors regard Sai Ngam as rather spooky and a potential setting for a horror movie (most locals steer clear of the place after dark), many Thais come to Phimai specifically to visit the tree (rather than the historical park) and pay their respects to the resident spirits. That's because banyan trees have special powers in Thai folklore. Blessed with the ability to grow and multiply, stretching its roots deep underground, the banyan tree is considered the 'tree of life' by Thais and is believed to be able to grant occasional wishes.

Phimai makes an easy day trip from Korat: simply catch one of the minivans that run hourly from Korat's Terminal 2 bus station to Phimai's clock tower, a short walk from the historical park. Motorbike taxis wait at the clock tower and will spin you to Sai Ngam and back for 80฿. There are a handful of hotels around town if you fancy experiencing Phimai's sleepy charms for a day or two.

Buriram

TIME FROM NAKHON RATCHASIMA CITY: **2HR**

City of sport

Buriram city, the capital of the eponymous province that lies east of Nakhon Ratchasima, is a mecca for fans of motorsports, thanks to the presence here of the **Chang International Circuit** *(bric.co.th).*

AMNAT30/SHUTTERSTOCK

Sai Ngam

GETTING TO CAMBODIA FROM SURIN

A Thai-Cambodian frontier dispute at the time of writing meant that all border crossings between Thailand and Cambodia were either closed or operating reduced hours. When the borders are fully open, travellers can head to Cambodia from Isan via the Chong Jom–O Smach border crossing in the south of Surin Province.

Not many foreigners cross here, but it's normally hassle-free and once you're in the Cambodian border town of O Smach, buses make the 160km run south to Siem Reap and Angkor Wat. It's not possible to enter Cambodia with an e-visa at this border, but 30-day Cambodian visas are available on arrival for US$30 (you might be asked to pay a few dollars more).

Every March, the Chang International Circuit hosts the **PT Grand Prix of Thailand**, part of the Moto GP World Championship, the motorcycling equivalent of Formula 1. The race is by far the highest-profile sporting event staged in Thailand and is hugely popular: over 200,000 fans descend on Buriram for three days of races and parties. That's perhaps not surprising when you consider that there are over 22 million motorbikes on Thailand's roads. Scoring a ticket for the Grand Prix is the easy bit; hotels book out very early and some people end up commuting from neighbouring provinces. But the track hosts many other motorbike and car races throughout the rest of the year.

Soccer team **Buriram United** *(buriramunited.com)*, the Thai champions at the time of writing and the most supported football team in the country, are another massive source of local pride. Matches at **Chang Arena**, known to diehards as 'Thunder Castle', draw the biggest crowds of any football club in Southeast Asia and attending a game here is a boisterous and fun experience, with the local fans normally very welcoming to foreign visitors.

EATING & DRINKING IN BURIRAM: OUR PICKS

So Krao Walking Street: Buriram's weekend night market has tons of food, as well as places to sit and eat, and live music. *4-9.30pm Sat & Sun* ฿

Kwang Jao: Visit in the morning for crispy pork or bowls of *congee* (Chinese-style rice porridge) and noodles. It's just south of the train station. *7am-3pm* ฿

Tumkratoei: Centrally located place with a nice garden that offers classic Isan dishes, made good and spicy as the locals like. *10.30am-9pm* ฿

ChuomPhon Coffee: Long-standing and old-school breakfast stop; match your coffee with *patongko*: deep-fried dough sticks. Expect a queue. *4-9am*

PLUTONIAN_P/SHUTTERSTOCK

White-handed gibbon

TOP EXPERIENCE

Khao Yai National Park

Khao Yai is Thailand's oldest and most famous national park and the principal reason many foreigners visit Isan. Covering 2168 sq km of wildlife-packed greenery, Khao Yai is one of the largest intact monsoon forests remaining in mainland Asia. The park's proximity to Korat city and Bangkok, as well as long-established tourist infrastructure, make it an easy destination to visit.

DON'T MISS

- Wildlife watching
- Waterfalls
- Hiking trails
- Night safaris
- Viewpoints

Wildlife Watching

Everyone who comes to Khao Yai wants to see some of the estimated 200 wild elephants who roam here and you have a 50% chance of doing so, according to the rangers and tour guides. There are a number of salt licks scattered around the park and the pachyderms often congregate at them, especially early in the morning, around sunset and after dark, which is why staying inside the park and/or joining a night safari are both good options.

PRACTICALITIES

● khaoyainationalpark.com/en ● tickets 400฿ ● 6am-6pm (night safaris excepted)

SOFT_LIGHT/SHUTTERSTOCK

TOURS

Most foreigners join tours of Khao Yai and you'll almost certainly see more wildlife if you do, because the guides are adept at spotting animals and carry telescopes on tripods to zoom in on them. Two long-standing and popular tour companies are **Greenleaf** *(greenleaf tour.com)* and **Bobby's** *(bobbysjungletour khaoyai.com)*. Both follow similar itineraries and charge 1500฿ for a full day tour, including lunch and transport to/from your accommodation.

But there are many other animals to enjoy here apart from elephants. They include sambar deer, who hang out around the visitor centre and camping sites in the early morning, sun and black bears, gaur, barking deer, otters and a variety of lizards, snakes, spiders and scorpions. Most visitors will see and hear white-handed and pileated gibbons, while pigtail macaques are easily visible by the side of roads. Bird-watchers will be in paradise because Khao Yai has almost 300 different avian species, including yellow-beaked great hornbills, who soar overhead in numerous spots, and the Siamese fireback. But you have almost no chance of seeing the handful of Indochinese tigers who survive here, or the more numerous clouded leopards.

Waterfalls

There are a number of waterfalls in and around Khao Yai, but not all are easy to reach. If you're feeling lazy, try little **Nam Tok Kong Kaew**, which is just 150m from the visitor centre, where it's possible to swim outside the June-to-October rainy season. There's also a rope bridge here to take you across the waterfall.

Far more impressive is thundering **Nam Tok Haew Narok**, or 'Hell Gorge Waterfall', which is the largest waterfall in the park. Its three levels combine to form a 150m drop, and it really rocks in the rainy season. It's an easy 800m walk to the top of the first level, which is 50m high, but you are then faced with descending (and subsequently ascending) 199 steep steps to the viewpoint, where you'll be hit by the spray from the falls. It's not possible to swim here and the second and third levels aren't accessible. The waterfall is in the far south of the park, 23km from the visitor centre.

TOP TIPS

- Always wear leech socks during the June–October rainy season. There are fewer leeches at other times of the year but ticks emerge, so leech socks are still useful. All tours provide them.
- Wear a hat, long and light trousers, hiking boots or decent trainers. Always carry water with you.
- The average full day tour involves about 6km of walking with some ascents. Anyone reasonably fit should be able to manage.
- If you have your own transport, or are prepared to hitch around the park, it's possible to visit Khao Yai independently.
- Stop in at the visitor centre: the staff are friendly, knowledgeable and speak English.

EATING

There are restaurants at busy locations inside the park, including the visitor centre, campgrounds and some waterfalls. All close by 6pm, so plan ahead. Outside the park, there are many restaurants along Th Thanarat serving both Thai and Western fare, but you'll need your own wheels to reach them as there are very few Grab drivers in the Khao Yai area.

But the prettiest waterfall in Khao Yai is 25m-high **Nam Tok Haew Suwat**, which scooped a starring role in the 2000 backpackers-in-peril movie *The Beach*, starring Leonardo DiCaprio. It has water year-round (though very little from March to May) and you can walk down to the bottom, but swimming isn't allowed. Haew Suwat can be reached by car or via a couple of hiking trails (closed in the rainy season).

Hiking Trails

Khao Yai means 'Big Mountain', so treks here are no walk in the park if you want to head deep into the forest, which it's only possible to do accompanied by a ranger. Most people stick to the seven defined hiking trails, but even some of those require a ranger as a guide (500฿ to 1000฿, depending on the trail) because so many visitors have got lost in the past and ended up staying overnight with the monkeys.

Trail 1 (1.2km) The Kong Kaew Waterfall Nature Trail is a paved loop starting at the suspension bridge behind the visitor centre. It's not difficult, but it does have some steep spots.

Trail 2 (3km) This easy trail connects Haew Suwat and Pa Kluai Mai waterfalls. Crocodiles are often seen in the river a short way past the latter falls.

Trail 3 (3.3km) This mildly challenging walk to the Nong Phak Chi Observation Tower starts at a small parking area by the Km 33 pillar. This is one of Khao Yai's best wildlife-spotting and bird-watching areas and is used by many tour groups. Combine it with Trail 5 to walk back to the visitor centre.

DARKPUZZLE/SHUTTERSTOCK

Nam Tok Haew Narok (p315)

Trail 4 (2.7km) An easy, relatively little-travelled trail to a viewpoint of the Sai Sorn Reservoir. A ranger guide is required.

Trail 5 (5km) Starting not too far south of the visitor centre, this is a good wildlife-watching trail – you'll almost certainly see gibbons and great hornbills – that ends at the Nong Phak Chi Observation Tower. It makes a good combination with Trail 3.

Trail 6 (8km) The longest marked trail in the park goes from the visitor centre to Haew Suwat waterfall. A ranger guide is mandatory and it's not open in the June–October rainy season. This is the most taxing trail, with a few rough spots and big hills, but it's still not too hard.

Trail 7 (2km) The so-called Thai-American Friendship Trail is a gentle loop around Sai Sorn Reservoir.

Night Safaris

Night safaris are a popular choice because they offer the best chance of seeing elephants, as well as other animals you definitely won't spot during the day, such as civets, porcupines and jackals. If you are lucky enough to glimpse any of the park's big cats, it will be at night.

There's no walking involved in the night safaris. Instead, you travel in open-top trucks mounted with powerful searchlights, which the ranger operator uses to illuminate the forest. There's no guarantee that you'll spot much wildlife; some visitors get to see lots of animals, others don't.

All night safaris are run directly by the park and can be booked at the **visitor centre** for 600฿ per person. Tours leave at 7pm or 8pm and last around an hour. Khao Yai can get cold at night, especially from November to March, so bring warm clothes. One thing to note is that you will also have to pay the rangers to drive you back to your accommodation (500฿ to 1000฿, depending on where your hotel is). Even if you've rented a motorbike, we wouldn't advise riding Khao Yai's unlit roads at night.

Viewpoints

Several viewpoints are scattered around the park. **Nong Phak Chi Observation Tower**, which overlooks a little lake and a salt lick, is one of the best wildlife- and bird-watching sites in the park. Many tours come here. Deep in the southeast of the park are the **Khao Khieaw** and **Pha Diaw Dai** viewpoints. The former is the highest viewpoint in central Thailand and offers great views over the surrounding forest, while Pha Diaw Dai (closed June to September) is popular for catching sunrise and sunset (**Sai Sorn Reservoir** is another good sunset spot). Other worthwhile viewpoints include the **Km.30 Viewpoint** in the north of the park and the **Km.18 Viewpoint** south of Haew Narok waterfall.

SLEEPING

There are a variety of rooms and bungalows (from 800฿) inside the park, which have to be booked via the national parks website *(nps.dnp.go.th)*. These, though, book out months in advance. It's much easier to find a place at one of Khao Yai's two campsites (tent rental is 200฿). These have the added attraction of being popular with some of the wildlife. The downside is that, on weekends especially, you'll be sharing them with local students and schoolkids, so expect some noise. Numerous resorts and hotels sit close to the park or you can stay in Pak Chong, 30km up the road.

AMCHERRY/SHUTTERSTOCK

TOP EXPERIENCE

Phanom Rung Historical Park

Prasat Phanom Rung is the most spectacular Khmer monument in Thailand, crowning the summit of an extinct volcano in the south of Buriram Province. The temple was built between the 10th and 13th centuries to honour the Hindu god Shiva and the setting is simply awesome, with views over the surrounding rice fields and Cambodia's Dangrek Mountains visible in the far distance.

DON'T MISS

- Promenade
- Naga bridges
- Main sanctuary
- Main tower
- Prasat Muang Tam

Promenade

One of the great things about Phanom Rung is that it is rarely crowded, except at festival time, allowing visitors the chance to appreciate the complex in peace and quiet. The first structure you'll encounter is the promenade, one of the complex's most remarkable aspects. It begins on a slope 400m east of the main tower with three earthen terraces. Next comes a cruciform base for what may have been a wooden pavilion. To the right of this is the **Phlab Phla**, a 13th-century pavilion believed to have been used by visiting royalty to change and bathe before religious ceremonies. You then step down

PRACTICALITIES

● 044 666 251 ● tickets 200฿, or 250฿ (combined ticket with Prasat Muang Tam) ● 7am-6pm

to a 160m-long **processional walkway**, flanked by 70 sandstone pillars topped with carved lotus flowers in the early Angkor style.

Naga Bridges

The processional walkway ends at the first and largest of three naga bridges, which date back to the 12th century, flanked by 16 five-headed *naga* (mythical serpents) in the classic Angkor style. As at all Khmer temples, these symbolic 'bridges' represent the passing from the earthly realm to the heavenly. Fifty-two steep sandstone steps lead onto the second and third bridges.

Main Sanctuary

The third naga bridge leads to the main sanctuary, where statues of white stone sit quietly with napping bats on the ceiling as their only companions. On the eastern portico of the **mandapa** (hall in front of the main tower) is a Nataraja (Dancing Shiva) and the well-known Narai Bandthomsindhu lintel, which represent the destruction and rebirth of the universe respectively, while on the southern entrance are the remains of Shiva and Uma riding their bull mount, Nandi.

Main Tower

The main tower has a gallery on each of its four sides, and excellent sculptures of Shiva and Vaishnava deities can be seen in the lintels and pediments over the doorways and in various other key points on the exterior. The central cell of the tower contains a sacred **lingam**, or phallic symbol, representing Shiva's strength. The pipeline that once carried holy water to the lingam is still intact and leads out into the courtyard. Beyond the main tower, two 10th-century **brick sanctuaries** are the oldest buildings here.

Prasat Muang Tam

Located 8km southeast of Phanom Rung is Prasat Muang Tam, or 'lowland castle', a little-seen Khmer temple complex set in a restful park-like enclave in the middle of the village of Khok Meuang. Prasat Muang Tam is even older than Phanom Rung, dating back to late 10th and early 11th centuries, and, like its younger sibling, it's dedicated to Shiva. A combined ticket grants entrance to both temples.

The complex faces east, like most Khmer temples, but has a distinctly unusual layout. Most significantly, the five towers of the central sanctuary are grouped three in front and two in back rather than the expected quincunx cross shape. Prasat Muang Tam is also the only Khmer temple to have four L-shaped ponds at each corner. Just across the road is **Baray Muang Tam**, a Khmer-era reservoir lined on one side by shaded food stalls.

CELEBRATING THE SUNRISE

In the first week of April, the sunrise aligns with the 15 doorways of the central sanctuary of Phanom Rung, triggering an annual festival featuring traditional Thai music, dance, costume, handicrafts and, of course, a lot of food. As Phanom Rung is a Hindu shrine celebrating Shiva, Buddhist elements are less present at this festival, but a fun atmosphere still prevails, especially when night falls.

TOP TIPS

- Arrive early, wear a hat and carry water; it gets very hot here.
- Dress respectfully and choose trainers rather than flip-flops.
- There are food stalls, gift shops, an information centre and a small collection of statuary from the site just before the ticket office.
- Visitors with mobility issues will struggle to get up the site's steep, uneven steps.
- The food stalls by Prasat Muang Tam make a good lunch stop.
- There's no public transport to Phanom Rung. A taxi from Korat city should cost 2500฿ to 3000฿ return, including waiting time.

Khon Kaen

NIGHT MARKETS | TEMPLES | LAKE LIFE

GETTING AROUND

Khon Kaen is one of Isan's best-connected cities. The main bus station, known as Bus Terminal 3, is 8km southwest of the centre and has buses heading across Isan, as well as to Bangkok and Chiang Mai. Khon Kaen's train station is much more central and has trains north to Udon Thani and Vientiane (Laos) and south to Korat and Bangkok. The airport is in the far west of the city and has numerous daily flights to Bangkok.

TOP TIP

Metered taxis and motorcycle taxis are mostly confined to the bus and train stations, the airport and shopping malls. Tuk-tuks cruise the streets, but they have been known to overcharge foreigners. The easiest way to get around is by using the Grab ridesharing app.

Khon Kaen is the unofficial capital of Isan and one of the fastest-growing cities in Thailand. With excellent markets and a thriving handicrafts scene, Khon Kaen offers an urban take on life in the northeast, a glimpse perhaps into Isan's future. The city has a large student population – you'll see them everywhere in their white shirts and black skirts or trousers (the Thai university uniform) – and Khon Kaen's youthful and buzzy vibe comes as a pleasant surprise if you've been spending time in sleepy villages or quiet Mekong-side towns.

But for all of Khon Kaen's shopping malls and new apartment blocks, it's still a traditional Thai town, as evidenced by its many temples and the fact that lovely Bueng Kaen Nakhon, the lake that's the true centre of town, is packed out with locals every night. All of which makes it easy to spend a few days here.

A Panoply of Night Markets

Street eats everywhere

Khon Kaen is blessed with a number of popular night markets in which to mix with the locals, sample delicious and cheap food and shop for local handicrafts. By far the biggest and best of them is **Ton Tann**, which is open every night and has a huge choice of food (and plenty of places to sit and eat), as well as bars and live music. There's also a wide range of clothing in the aptly named 'Fashion Building', and accessories and handicrafts made by local artisans, including traditional fabrics from Chonnabot (p325), a long-established silk-weaving town 55km southwest of Khon Kaen.

Saturday's **Walking Street Night Market** in the centre of town also mixes food, clothes and local handicrafts. Once you've chosen your meal, you can picnic in the adjoining park, where there's normally some form of live music. Also in the city centre is the worthwhile **Ruen Rom Night Market**, which has lots of food stalls and tables to sit at and stays busy until late. Ruen Rom is closed Mondays.

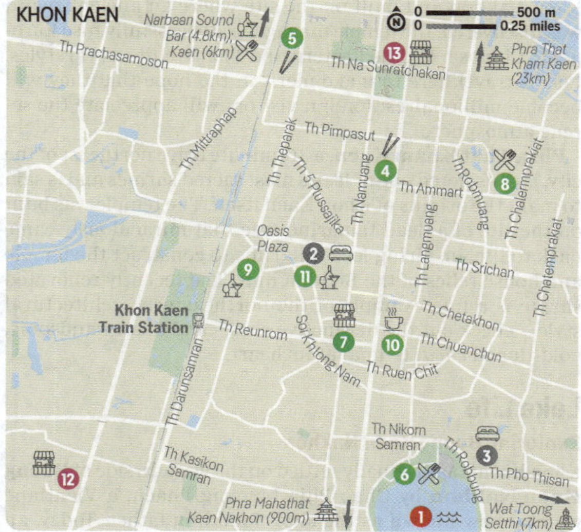

SIGHTS
1 Bueng Kaen Nakhon

SLEEPING
2 Ad Lib Khon Kaen
3 J-Boutique Hotel

EATING
4 Baan Heng
5 Gai Yang Rabeab
6 Rim Bueng Night Market
7 Ruen Rom Night Market
8 Tawanthong Vegetarian Food

DRINKING & NIGHTLIFE
9 Gentle Khon Kaen
10 Neighbour Cafe
11 Smile Bar

SHOPPING
12 Ton Tann Market
13 Walking Street Night Market

Temple Hopping

Making merit in Khon Kaen

Khon Kaen's most impressive temple is **Phra Mahathat Kaen Nakhon**, better known as Wat Nong Wang. The nine-storey stupa soars above the southern end of Bueng Kaen Nakhon and offers panoramic views over the city from its observation deck. It also features enlightening modern murals depicting Isan culture and Khon Kaen's history.

Wat Thung Setthi ('Millionaire's Field Temple') emerges from the dry landscape like a rare desert flower in a setting that brings to mind the Taj Mahal. About 7km east of Bueng

SOM TAM – NOT JUST GREEN PAPAYA

Som tam, the spicy green papaya salad that's an intrinsic part of so many meals in Isan, comes in more than just one version, since it can be made with basically anything, even green bananas. Some of the most common variations found on Isan menus include *tam kow poht*, a salad of corn kernels, usually accompanied by pounded tomatoes and chillies; *tam tang gua*, made with thin slices of cucumber; *tam paa*, or 'jungle *tam*', usually made with rice noodles, papaya strands and snails; and *tam mua*, or 'crazy *tam*', a mix of whatever the chef has at hand, typically including rice noodles, papaya and *moo yaw* (steamed pork sausage).

DRINKING IN KHON KAEN: OUR PICKS

Narbaan Sound Bar: Nightly live music, local and foreign beers and decent Thai food draw a young crowd to this fun and lively spot. *6.30pm-1am*

Gentle Khon Kaen: Stylish speakeasy bar with a proper hidden entrance behind a fake shopfront, creative cocktails and affable bartenders. *7.30am-midnight*

Neighbour Cafe: No wi-fi, and laptops are banned from this quirky, pleasant cafe and bar housed in an attractive wooden house. Thai and Western food too. *8.30am-9pm Tue-Sun*

Smile Bar: Friendly Aussie-run bar with live sport. One of a number of foreigner-orientated bars located near the Pullman Hotel. *2pm-1am*

Kaen Nakhon and built on the site where an ancient sword was discovered, the temple manages to successfully fuse European, Chinese, Middle Eastern and Thai architectural styles. Locals travel here to make merit in the hope that they will become millionaires; foreign visitors will appreciate the serene atmosphere.

Phra That Kham Kaen, a 40-minute drive northeast of the city, is considered one of Isan's most sacred shrines and is said to mark the origins of Khon Kaen itself. The temple was built on the site of a dead tamarind tree that miraculously came back to life, inspiring local pilgrims to construct the temple and house relics of the Buddha in it. The recently renovated shrine is a fine example of the northeastern architectural style – check out the distinctive roof – and has a handsome, gold-tipped *chedi* (stupa) at its heart.

MUST-TRY ISAN DISHES

By now, you should know all about the holy trinity of Isan cuisine: *gai yang* (grilled chicken), *som tam* (spicy papaya salad) and *kow neow* (sticky rice). Here are a few other lesser-known Isan dishes worth trying.

Jaew hon: Also called *'jim jum'*, this Isan-style hotpot sees the diner dipping raw meat and vegetables in a spicy broth for quick cooking.

Meeang plaa pow: Fish grilled over charcoals, stuffed with aromatic herbs, then served alongside lettuce leaves, rice noodles and dipping sauces for easy assemblage of your own 'taco'.

Tom sap: Soup, flavoured with lemongrass and chillies, that packs a big punch and is typically made with pork ribs, though duck, chicken and even beef offal versions exist.

Lake Life

Exploring Bueng Kaen Nakhon

Khon Kaen was originally settled on the western side of **Bueng Kaen Nakhon** by Chao Phia Mueang Phaen, a Vientiane general now known as the city's founding father. Today, an enshrined monument on the lake's grounds is devoted to him, but the 100-hectare lake and park around it is now a gathering place for all of the city's residents.

In the early morning, Khon Kaen's senior citizens flock here to take their daily constitutional along the newish 3km elevated walkway snaking over the lake's waters. But twilight after 5pm is when the park truly comes alive, drawing out the city's surprisingly large population of joggers, who either take advantage of the park's plethora of paths or chat with their friends while stretching in their jogging clothes. Anyone reasonably fit should be able to walk around the lake in a brisk 45 minutes.

Other people come for **Rim Bueng Night Market**, open every day from 4pm to 9pm. The food and clothes stalls stretch around the north and northwest of the lake for quite a way and draw an especially big crowd on weekends. The park offers bicycles for rent; a 4.6km biking path winds around the perimeter of the park. Paddleboats can also be rented for close-up views of the lake's fish and turtles, popular with young children, while Instagram-lovers make a beeline for the park's dinosaur statue.

EATING IN KHON KAEN: OUR PICKS

Gai Yang Rabeab: This humble hot spot is a top pick for *gai yang* and *som tam*. Portions are big, so come hungry or in a couple. *8.30am-3.30pm* ฿

Tawanthong Vegetarian Food: An excellent and cheap semi-open-air vegetarian food court that also does vegan coffee and smoothies. It's a local favourite. *6am-2pm* ฿

Baan Heng: Thai-Chinese dishes, including Hong Kong–style breakfasts, served in a comfortable converted shop house. *6am-9pm* ฿

Kaen: Upmarket but relaxed place in the north of town that puts a creative twist on traditional Isan and central Thai cuisine. *11am-3pm & 5-9pm Wed-Mon* ฿฿฿

Beyond Khon Kaen

One of Isan's most worthwhile national parks and a huge dinosaur graveyard lie to the west of Khon Kaen.

Khon Kaen city might be dynamic, but the forests that lie to the west of it are mostly untouched, unpopulated and wild. This is some of the most incongruously 'Alpine' terrain in Isan, where photogenic pines carpet rolling hills of startling beauty, providing shelter for the animals and birds who live in the little-seen Nam Nao National Park, located on the far western fringe of the northeastern region.

If you're wondering why there are so many dinosaur statues scattered around this part of Isan, a trip to the Phu Wiang National Park will explain all. This is one of the world's biggest repositories of dinosaur fossils and it's also home to the kid-friendly Phu Wiang Dinosaur Museum.

Places

GETTING AROUND

Buses travelling from Khon Kaen to Phitsanulok can drop you at the entrance to Nam Nao National Park, from where it's a 2km walk to the visitor centre. For Phu Wiang National Park, catch a bus to Chom Phae and a taxi from there. But it's more convenient to hire a taxi. Expect to pay 1500฿ return to Phu Wiang from Khon Kaen.

Nam Nao National Park

TIME FROM KHON KAEN: 2½HR

Elephants, birds and forests

Nam Nao National Park *(200฿),* or 'Cold Water National Park', spreads over 960 sq km in the far west of Isan and 99% of that is considered virgin woodlands, home to bamboo groves, hill evergreens, green savannahs, and most famously, miles

WERANUT/SHUTTERSTOCK

Red-headed trogon, Nam Nao National Park

A 100-YEAR-OLD CULINARY TRADITION

Many Thais believe that Khon Kaen Province is home to the tastiest *gai yang* in the country. In particular, the grilled chicken sold at **Khao Suan Kwang** (Deer Park Mountain), 54km north of Khon Kaen city, has acquired near-mythical status. It's a culinary tradition that started over a century ago, when the village hosted a train stop and locals started grilling chicken for hungry passengers. The chicken, which is raised organically in the area, is marinated in 14 sauces and herbs, and grilled over charcoal atop deep-fried garlic before being sprinkled with a copious lashing of black pepper. Thai foodies make the pilgrimage here by car, but the grilled chicken sold at Gai Yang Rabeab (p322) in Khon Kaen city is almost as good.

SITTHIPONG PENGJAN/SHUTTERSTOCK

Tham Pha Hong Viewpoint, Nam Nao National Park

of Instagram-friendly pine forests. Besides its vast network of trees, Nam Nao also hosts a wide range of wildlife and is considered a paradise for bird-watchers – over 350 species live here, including golden-crested mynas, collared owlets, silver pheasants and snowy-browed flycatchers.

But Nam Nao's biggest draw is its mammals. Around 200 elephants roam here and encounters are frequent enough that the park campsite and bungalows are ringed by electric fences to keep them from disturbing your sleep. Gaur and deer are also numerous and similarly gregarious, but the sun bears, golden jackals and gibbons are more elusive, while the clouded leopards are hardly ever seen. Night safaris, either on foot or riding in the back of an open-top truck armed with a searchlight, are available for 80฿ per person, but only if you're staying overnight in the park.

Aside from animals, most people come to Nam Nao for the park's spectacular vistas. The **Tham Pha Hong Viewpoint**, located 10.7km west of the visitor centre, is famous for its sunsets, but **Phu Khor Viewpoint**, 5km west of the visitor centre, is lauded for its views of the 'sea of fog' from December to February, when a mist rolls into the valley. Roughly 15km from the main road at Km 53, **Phu Khum Khao Pinery** is noted for its dense tract of pines. Pick-up trucks run to all the viewpoints: book a seat at the **visitor centre**.

Four marked **hiking trails** (1km, 3km, 4.5km and 5.8km) branch out from beside the visitor centre through a variety of habitats. Anyone reasonably fit should be able to walk them. You'll need to hire a ranger to hike anywhere else in the park. There are also a couple of waterfalls here. The 20m-high **Nam Tok Haew Sai** is the prettiest, offering great swimming 700m from the main road, while **Nam Tok Sai Thong**, 1.5km from the main road, is 30m wide with 4m-high cascades. Both are best seen during the June–October rainy season.

Accommodation at Nam Nao is a reasonable deal, although the cheapest bungalows are old and basic. **Bungalows** need to be booked in advance via the national park website *(dnp.go.th)*; tents for the **campsite** are nearly always available. There's a small shop and a restaurant by the visitor centre, but they close by 7pm and neither sells alcohol. Most people bring their own supplies with them.

Make sure to bring warm clothes with you as well. Nam Nao sits at altitude and temperatures can drop dramatically here, especially from December to February when overnight frosts are not unknown. Leeches can also be a problem in the park, so wear leech socks (available at the visitor centre). Nam Nao is 150km northwest of Khon Kaen and is sometimes closed in June, so check before coming.

Phu Wiang National Park

TIME FROM KHON KAEN: 1½HR

Dinosaur country

Until 1976, no one knew that the Phu Wiang Valley west of Khon Kaen was one of the world's largest dinosaur graveyards. Then a geologist prospecting for uranium stumbled upon the fossilised remains of a previously unknown 15m-high dinosaur, subsequently named *Phuwiangosaurus sirindhornae* in honour of Princess Maha Chakri Sirindhorn, the current king's sister. Now the area, said to have been created by a long-ago asteroid strike, is home to the 380 sq km **Phu Wiang National Park** *(200฿)*, where a number of other new dinosaur species have been unearthed, including *Siamotyrannus isanensis*: carnivorous thunder lizards related to T-rex.

The visitor centre is 7km from the park entrance and from there a 3km **Dinosaur Nature Trail** takes visitors past some of the dinosaur excavation sites and viewpoints. If you're lucky, you might encounter students working at the sites, who'll invite you to join them for a closer look at the fossils. Sites 2 and 3 are particularly interesting because they are where the park's oldest fossils were found: those of *Siamotyrannus isanensis* (dating back 130 million years), providing proof that the tyrannosaurus was originally from Asia.

Be warned, though, that the trail is fairly arduous. The first kilometre is a steep and sweaty climb through deciduous forest to the first viewpoint. The descent is also taxing, especially in the wet, involving a lot of scrambling over rocks and through trees. Take water with you and wear trainers rather than flip-flops.

You can combine a trip here with a visit to the **Phu Wiang Dinosaur Museum** *(60฿)*, which is 4km east of the national park. This is one of Isan's better museums (with good English captions), housing some of the fossils discovered in the national park, reconstructed skeletons and, best of all for kids, life-size moving models of dinos complete with sound effects. The museum is open from 9.30am to 4.30pm Tuesday to Sunday. Both the park and museum are about 90km west of Khon Kaen.

CHONNABOT SILK

The little town of **Chonnabot**, 55km southwest of Khon Kaen, sits at the heart of one of Thailand's most successful silk-weaving regions and is famous for producing top-quality *mudmee*: intricately patterned silk. While Chonnabot fabrics are sold at Khon Kaen's Ton Tann Market (p320), there's a far wider selection on offer in Chonnabot itself and the town is a major silk-shopping destination. Most of the shops can be found on Th Sriboonruang, aka Silk Rd. If you're here in the morning, wander west or north of Silk Rd to watch ageing weaver women working at their looms. A taxi from Khon Kaen to Chonnabot should cost around 1200฿ return, or catch a train or bus to nearby Ban Phai and a taxi from there.

Chiang Khan

MEKONG VIEWS | TRADITIONAL TOWN | RIVERSIDE LIFE

GETTING AROUND

To get to Chiang Khan, hop any bus to Loei city, from where slow *songthaew* (pick-up minibuses) travel the 50km north to Chiang Khan. The town itself is eminently walkable, or take advantage of the free bicycles offered by many guesthouses. Tuk-tuks, known as *samlor* here, can spin you to nearby sights. SAMS Chiangkhan (p356), a guesthouse on Walking Street, rents motorcycles for 250฿ a day if you want to travel further afield.

TOP TIP

Try to avoid Chiang Khan on weekends and public holidays, when it can be absolutely rammed with local visitors. Chiang Khan is less busy during the June–October rainy season. Prices are generally higher here than elsewhere in Isan, thanks to the town's popularity.

Chiang Khan sits on the sandy banks of the Mekong River and is as close as you can get to Laos without actually swimming across. Stunning Mekong views aren't the only reason, though, that Thai visitors in particular flock to this small town in the far north of Loei Province. The town's riverside Walking Street, officially known as Th Chai Khong, is lined with photogenic traditional wooden houses, almost all of which have been converted into guesthouses, restaurants and cute cafes, and come nightfall the street turns into a vast market with food, handicrafts, buskers and artists.

While some people regard Chiang Khan as rather touristy, and it is busy with travellers these days, it's still peaceful during daylight hours and it remains a charming place to kick back for a few days, with many visitors content to find a perch by the Mekong to watch the world go by.

VIP Views Over the Mekong

Surveying a timeless landscape

Make sure to visit **Skywalk Chiang Khan** *(60฿)*, 22km south of town, for awesome views of the Mekong, which reappears here in Thailand after veering off into Laos past Chiang Rai, meeting the Hueang River. *Songthaew* transport visitors from the parking area up the hill to where the skywalk – an open-air glass-floored walkway – juts out over the Mekong from underneath a giant golden Buddha. You then don a pair of shoe covers (to protect the glass) and slither onto the skywalk, either walking confidently or tiptoeing at the edge if you're worried about the glass giving way (it won't).

You're 80m above the ground here, so don't look down if you're scared of heights, and the views are simply sublime, with the wide and fat Mekong sliding past the lush hills of Laos. The skywalk is open 7am to 6pm every day, which unfortunately means that you can't really catch the full majesty of

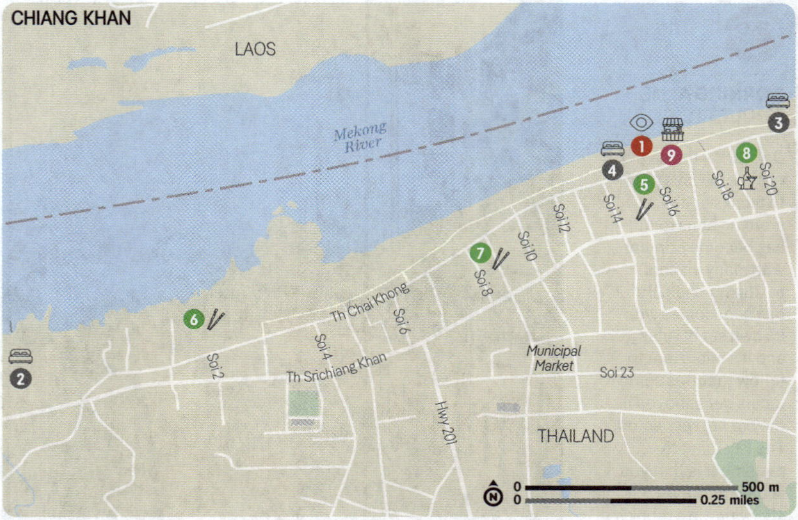

CHIANG KHAN

SIGHTS
1 Chiang Khan Promenade

SLEEPING
2 River Tree Resort
3 SAMS Chiangkhan
4 With a View Hotel @ Chiang Khan

EATING
5 Nung Nung Len Len
6 Smile@Chiang Khan
7 Song Phu Mia

DRINKING & NIGHTLIFE
8 Miss U Bar

SHOPPING
9 Chiang Khan Walking Street

the sunset from here; early morning is best for photography. There's no public transport from Chiang Khan, but guesthouses often organise shared vans here.

Riverside Life

Hanging by the Mekong

Many visitors spend their days taking selfies and waiting for the sunset, before an evening of eating and browsing their way through the stalls of **Walking Street** (from 5pm to 10pm). But there are other things to do, including either walking or cycling the **promenade** that runs alongside the Mekong here.

Early risers will want to catch the daily **morning alms ceremony**, when monks from nearby Wat Si Khun Muang parade

EATING & DRINKING IN CHIANG KHAN: OUR PICKS

Song Phu Mia: Cute noodle shop and cafe on the ground floor of the Husband & Wife Guesthouse. Try the *khao soi*. Also does craft beers. *8am-10pm* ฿

Nung Nung Len Len: Down an alley off Walking Street; look for the white sign with 'Welcome' in red letters. The fish dishes are especially tasty. *4-11pm* ฿฿

Smile@Chiang Khan: Mekong fish specialities, as well as Isan classics, with indoor and outdoor seating by the river. It's a popular sunset dinner spot. *11am-9.30pm* ฿฿

Miss U Bar: Long-standing driftwood bar – a Thai island vibe in Isan – with a sardonic owner, strong cocktails and decent music. *4pm-midnight*

MORNING ALMS ETIQUETTE

Dak baht – the giving of alms (always food) to monks on their morning alms round – has become popular with many visitors to Chiang Khan. But *dak baht* comes with its own set of rules and it's important to follow them, as some locals get annoyed if they're not respected. The key thing to remember is that you should only ever put sticky rice in a monk's bowl (never hand anything to a monk directly). All other foodstuffs should be given to the people who follow close behind the monks for that purpose, or be donated directly to the temple. It's also important to be respectful when taking photos – don't stick your phone or camera in the monks' faces – and give them plenty of space.

NUMPUPHOTO/SHUTTERSTOCK

Mekong promenade (p327)

along Walking Street in their orange robes. This isn't Luang Prabang, though, so don't expect hundreds of them; around 10 monks can normally be seen between 6am and 6.30am.

For a truly close-up view of the Mekong, visit **Kaeng Khut Khu**, a famous bend in the river with a small set of rapids that's 6km east of town (200฿ return in a tuk-tuk). From November to May, lower water levels reveal colourful rocks and, with the hills as the backdrop and a few fisherfolk out on the river, it's a picturesque scene.

It's also possible to hire a boat – 800฿ for 30 minutes – to see both banks of the river and grab some pics mid-Mekong. A few restaurants line the river here serving Mekong-fresh specialities like a spicy soup of *pla nam khong* (freshwater fish) or *goong ten*, aka 'dancing shrimp', where baby shrimp are tossed live in a spicy tart dressing and served under a lid to keep them from escaping.

Beyond Chiang Khan

Natural treasures and supreme views await in Loei Province, as long as you are willing to trek to them.

With some of the most remarkable views in Thailand, dramatically lush Loei Province hosts a wealth of natural beauty and is the epitome of an unspoiled rural idyll. Loei's many national parks mean that much of the landscape is protected, while friendly people make the trip to this remote part of Isan more than worth your while.

Foreign travellers are thin on the ground, but you will see Thai tourists out in the wild enjoying panoramic vistas over the province's many mountains and unusual landscapes. But there are also quirky hilltop temples and opportunities for riverside lounging. Loei offers something for every nature lover willing to put in the time and effort.

Places

GETTING AROUND

Buses from Loei city and Khon Kaen stop at Phu Kradueng town, from where you can take a *songthaew* or taxi to the national park. Dan Sai can also be reached by bus from Loei city. You'll need your own wheels, or to hire a car and driver, to reach Phu Pa Po and Suan Hin Pha Ngam.

Phu Kradueng National Park

TIME FROM CHIANG KHAN: **2HR**

Sky-spanning views and star-gazing

Phu Kradueng National Park *(400฿)*, 130km south of Chiang Khan, is the most popular protected area in Loei Province and its eponymous peak is famous across Thailand. Climbing the mountain and spending the night atop the heart-shaped summit plateau is something of a rite of passage for many students and hikers in the region, who also come to see the wildlife – elephants, Asian jackals, Asiatic black bears, sambar deer, serows, macaques and white-handed gibbons – that inhabit the 348-sq-km park, alongside a wide variety of birds and butterflies.

The park covers a high-altitude plateau cut through with trails and peppered with cliffs and waterfalls. Rising to 1316m, Thailand's second-oldest national park is always cool at its highest reaches (the average year-round temperature is 20°C), where its flora is a mix of pine forest and savannah. November to February is probably the best time to visit, when the trails are dry but the landscape is still lush. The park is closed June to September, to give it a chance to recover from all the visitors.

From the park entrance, it's 500m to the small visitor centre at the base of the mountain, where you should register before starting climbing; also there are a few shops and restaurants. Almost everything else is up top. The main trail scaling Phu

EXPLORING THE NORTHERN MEKONG

Aarya Surindhara, owner of Le Domaine du Mékong and Pak Chom native

Where to drive Hwy 211 from Chiang Khan through Pak Chom to Nong Khai is one of the most scenic routes in Thailand. White beaches emerge along the Mekong here in the November–February cool season, and there are also rocky canyons, rapids, lush islands, inlets and lakes to see.

Where to swim I would focus on the stretch from Chiang Khan to Pak Chom and Sangkhom where there are plenty of islands, inlets and lakes that are formed when the water recedes. Swim where there are visible white beaches and don't swim in the June–October rainy season or when currents are strong. Local fisherfolk are your best guides.

Kradueng is 5.5km in length and takes about three to four hours. It's strenuous (visitors climb 1200m in height), but not too challenging (except when it's wet) since there are steps at most of the steep parts. The hike is quite scenic and there are rest stops with food vendors about every 1km.

Once on top, it's another 3km to the main visitor centre and all the accommodation. The reward for all that walking is sky-spanning views over the entire province and fine stargazing come nightfall. Porters can be hired to carry your gear balanced on bamboo poles for 30฿ per 1kg. For safety reasons you are not allowed to start your hike up the mountain after 2pm; it's best to start climbing in the early morning so you reach the summit for lunchtime.

Phu Kradueng's summit plateau covers an area of 60 sq km, so there are plenty of hiking opportunities once you've ascended. In all, there are 20km of trails here, with the one that passes six waterfalls in a forested valley being the most beautiful, even after November when the water has largely dried up. There are also many clifftop viewpoints, some ideal for sunrise and sunset, scattered around the mountain.

Staying the night at the summit is essential; many people choose to linger for longer. The campsite can accommodate up to 5000 people (the park gets super-busy during holiday periods) and tents can be hired for 200฿, along with sleeping bags, mats and pillows. There are also bungalows, which need to be booked through the national parks website *(dnp.go.th)*, but these are normally reserved a long time in advance. Facilities are reasonable, with cold showers and restrooms, as well as restaurants and food stalls that stay open late into the night.

Phu Pa Po & Suan Hin Pha Ngam

TIME FROM CHIANG KHAN: **2HR**

Mountains and karsts

If you're visiting Loei between June and September when Phu Kradueng is closed for forest recovery, never fear because Loei harbours many other picturesque peaks. **Phu Pa Po**, 50km north of Phu Kradueng and 70km south of Loei city, is known as the 'Mt Fuji of Loei' for its resemblance to Japan's famous mountain. Visitors pay 80฿ per person to travel via *e-tek* (a tractor turned into a truck) to three separate viewpoints, passing avocado, guava and dragon-fruit trees along the way.

The first stop is perfect for a picnic thanks to its pleasant views and convenient gazebo. The second viewpoint further up the hill is the best for sunsets (which typically happen around 6pm, right when the park closes). The final viewpoint involves a 250m climb via steps etched into the earth to the top of the 800m-high peak, yielding panoramic views of Phu Kradueng, Phu Luang and Suan Hin Pha Ngam.

Suan Hin Pha Ngam *(100฿)*, a 15-minute drive from Phu Pa Po, is famous for its limestone karsts, which are said to resemble the 'Stone Forest' found outside Kunming in southwest China. There's a visitor centre, where you can hire a guide, or ride an *e-tek* to **Suan Sawan**, or 'Heavenly Garden', where a

C.APHIRAK/SHUTTERSTOCK

Suan Hin Pha Ngam

ramble of metal walkways clamber up the limestone to the park's highest point, 800m above ground.

Back down at the bottom, you can choose from an array of Thai medicinal teas that promise to cure everything from sore throats to haemorrhoids, or make merit at the shrine dedicated to the local hill spirit (said to be a petite, pale woman), just in case you, like the locals, fear the spirit will follow you home. Next, travel 2km north of Suan Hin Pha Ngam to **Nam Tok Paeng Din**, popular for its gently cascading waterfall. Papaya-salad and noodle vendors at the water's edge make this an ideal spot for lunch.

Dan Sai

TIME FROM CHIANG KHAN: **2HR**

Waking Buddha from the dead

Once a year, the quiet hamlet of **Dan Sai** – literally the 'Left Gate' – crawls with visitors, its streets clogged with traffic and its air punctuated by the distinctive wail of regional *mor lam* tunes played at ear-splitting decibels. Welcome to **Pee Ta Khon**, arguably Isan's most distinctive festival, where participants dress like the spirits who will roam the land for a few days as the much-needed rains arrive.

Typically held over three days in June or July (local spirit mediums decide the date) and also known as the Ghost Festival, Pee Ta Khon focuses on morning merit-making in the temples and merry-making everywhere at night. Temples throb with the sound of live drums and most partygoers, from the village elders to the youngest toddlers, are dressed in rainbow hues, their faces obscured by hand-painted masks and their belts laden with tinkling bells.

BEST OTHER NATIONAL PARKS BEYOND CHIANG KHAN

Phu Ruea National Park: Tabletop mountain famous for its cliff, which resembles the prow of a boat, and its pine forests.

Phu Luang Wildlife Sanctuary: Around 100 elephants inhabit this remote and little-seen park also known for its orchids.

Phuphalom Forest Park: Spanning over 1000km, this park is believed to be home to a mythical *naga*.

Phu Suan Sai National Park: Popular with bird-watchers, it also houses four boulders (*'Hin Si Thit'*) that locals pray to every three years.

Phu Bo Bit Forest Park: Get into shape for the ascent of Phu Kradueng by climbing through the forest here for fine sunset views over Loei city.

PIMALI HOSPITALITY TRAINING CENTER

If you're driving Hwy 211 from Chiang Khan to Nong Khai, you'll pass **Pimali Hospitality Training Center**, near the end of the road on the rural outskirts of Nong Khai. This beautiful hotel with spacious wooden bungalows also serves as a training centre for disadvantaged local youth, some of whom are orphans, who would otherwise find themselves in low-paying jobs in the fields, a factory or in sex work. By gaining experience at Pimali, workers are gaining skills to help them get hospitality jobs, as well as learning English. If you can't stay here to support the scheme, as many longtime travellers to Thailand do, stop in at the highly rated restaurant where ingredients are sourced from Pimali's own garden.

PLOYPEMUK/SHUTTERSTOCK

Pee Ta Khon festival (p331)

The origins of this festival are usually ascribed to the Buddhist scripture *Vessantara Jakata*, which details Buddha embarking on a long journey and then dying in one of his past lives. But there are also strong local folklore elements, and the colourful outfits and raucous music are attempts by festivalgoers to wake the dead; the roaming spirits are evidence of their success.

Pee Ta Khon was once a sedate affair, when participants dressed in outfits of saffron, like monks' robes. The bright colours and sexual innuendo of costumes depicting both male and female genitalia are more recent additions. Celebrations climax on the final day, when a parade with floats held in town ends at **Wat Phon Chai**, where of course, much food and drink is consumed. Wat Phon Chai is also home to the **Pee Ta Khon Museum**, which has a great display of masks and costumes worn during the festival.

Dan Sai is 115km southwest of Chiang Khan. If you haven't got your own transport, it's best reached by bus from Loei city.

Udon Thani

CITY LIFE | PARKS | RESTAURANTS

Big and brash Udon Thani was transformed from a humble small town into one of the northeast's four main cities by the impact of the Vietnam War, which boosted the local economy and brought thousands of US soldiers to this corner of Isan. Today, Udon is a sprawling and bustling commercial centre that's still home to a sizeable community of foreigners.

Udon will never win any prizes for its looks, but it does have three public parks, including excellent Nong Prajak Park, which act as the city's hubs, as well as many night markets and some of the finest restaurants in the region, which are good enough to draw Thais here from across the kingdom. Close to the city, too, are a range of attractive destinations, including the UNESCO World Heritage site of Ban Chiang, a popular lake and Isan's version of Stonehenge: an eye-catching park full of strangely shaped rock formations.

GETTING AROUND

Udon has excellent transport connections. The airport has numerous daily flights to Bangkok, while the railway station in the centre of town has trains north to Vientiane (Laos) and south to Khon Kaen, Korat and Bangkok. The main bus station, also centrally located, has buses and minivans across Isan, as well as to Bangkok. Tuk-tuks are everywhere, although the Grab ridesharing app is generally the easiest and cheapest way to get around the city.

Nong Prajak Park

Udon's beating heart

It's a sign of the times that many of the attractions at Nong Prajak Park have been designed with social media in mind. The lake at the heart of the park, named after city founder Prince Prajak Silapakom, is now recognisable to Thais everywhere, thanks to the family of giant yellow ducks who bob on the water and feature in so many photos (the ducks are brought onshore in stormy weather). Then there's the equally photogenic huge vase in the Ban Chiang style, a large clock made of flowers and an @Udon Thani sign that's lit up at night.

Even without the recent additions, the park is the beating heart of Udon and is always busy in the early morning and late afternoon and evening, with locals taking advantage of the running track, renting bicycles, posing on the water-spanning bridges, joining free aerobics classes or simply promenading. Head to Th Thesa on the east side of the park for food stalls and massage places. Udon's worthwhile **Walking Street market** is held just off Th Thesa on Friday and Saturday evenings.

TOP TIP

Many people who stay in Udon for any length of time rent a motorbike to get around. Happy Motorbike Rental, opposite the Central shopping mall, rents a range of automatic and manual bikes from 200฿ per day.

SIGHTS
1 Nong Bua Park
2 Nong Prajak Park
3 Sanjao Pu-Ya
4 Thai-Chinese Cultural Centre
5 Udon Thani City Museum
6 Wat Phothisomphon

SLEEPING
7 Pakdee House
8 Pannarai Hotel
9 Udon Backpackers
10 VELA Dhi Udon Thani Hotel

EATING
11 Dose Factory
12 Papaya Salad Jay Gai 1
13 Samuay & Sons

SHOPPING
14 Walking Street Market

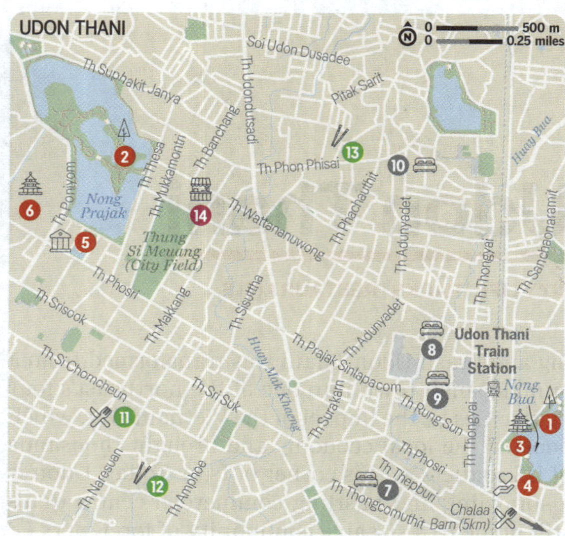

PATTAYA OF THE NORTHEAST

One of the legacies of Udon hosting a US air base during the Vietnam War is its thriving bar scene, said to be Isan's equivalent of Pattaya's infamous nightlife.While there are a few sleazy joints, the majority of the foreigner-orientated bars – clustered on and around Th Sampanthamit in the centre of town close to the main night market – are simply places for foreign residents and visitors to drink, watch live sport and play pool.

Museums, Temples & More Parks

Explore Udon's history

Udon Thani City Museum sits at the south of Nong Prajak Park and is housed in Udon's most distinguished non-religious building: a yellow-walled mansion with a red-tiled roof that was once a school. It offers an engaging ride through the history of Udon from the dinosaurs onwards, but is at its most interesting covering the post-WWII period and Udon's transformation during and after the Vietnam War. Entry is free and the museum is open from 9am to 4pm Tuesday to Sunday.

Just off the southwest corner of Nong Prajak Park is **Wat Phothisomphon**, Udon's most renowned temple, with a 1300-year-old Buddha statue, a popular *naga* shrine and a *chedi* fronted by a grand staircase flanked by two golden dragons. Climb to the second level of the *chedi* for great views of the surrounding city.

Close to the centre of town is **Nong Bua Park**, which has a lake and running and bicycle paths and serves as a hub for Udon's large Thai-Chinese community. Check out **Sanjao Pu-Ya**, a Chinese temple at the southern end of the lake that looks great when lit up at night. Nearby, too, is the **Thai-Chinese Cultural Centre**, which has a gorgeous garden, a tea shop and a museum covering the history of the Chinese community in Udon.

EATING IN UDON THANI: OUR PICKS

Papaya Salad Jay Gai 1: The legendary *som tam paa* (jungle *som tam*) features fermented rice noodles, bamboo shoots, horse tamarind seeds and snails. *8am-4pm* ฿

Chalaa Barn: Flies the flag for Udon Thani cuisine with seasonal variations and delicate flavours. On the outskirts of town, but well worth the trip. *11am-9.30pm* ฿฿

Dose Factory: Popular cafe restaurant with an industrial-design theme, Mediterranean-inspired menu and fine coffee, juices and smoothies. *10am-10pm* ฿฿

Samuay & Sons: Innovative place that relies on purely seasonal and foraged food to give a new twist to classic Isan cuisine. *noon-8.30pm Tue-Sun* ฿฿฿

Beyond Udon Thani

Udon Thani Province hosts an ideal smattering of interesting sights featuring natural beauty and ancient history.

The region around Udon Thani has a bounty of rewarding sights, from a world-renowned museum of a forgotten civilisation to a water-lily-flecked lake and a park full of enigmatic rock formations. Nong Khai in the far north of the region offers a taste of Mekong living, too, as well as being a hub for travellers heading to/from Laos.

Udon Thani Province was only incorporated into the then Siam in the early 19th century and there's always been a significant Lao influence here. The province also played a part in the Vietnam War, with both US forces and Vietnamese nationalists calling the area home at different times.

Places

GETTING AROUND

There are no direct buses from Udon Thani to Ban Chiang, Red Lotus Sea or Phu Phrabat Historical Park, so you're better off hiring a car and driver to reach them rather than relying on a mix of *songthaew*, tuk-tuks or motorcycle taxis from nearby villages and towns. There are hourly minivans (55฿) to Nong Khai from Udon's main bus station from 7am to 6pm.

Ban Chiang

TIME FROM UDON THANI: **50MIN**

Discovering an unknown civilisation

The story of the ascent to global recognition of Ban Chiang has become archaeological legend. It begins with the clumsiness of a Harvard student, who tripped over a tree root in 1966 only to fortuitously discover a half-buried pot from an ancient culture. A mass excavation ensued, uncovering a burial site that is now considered evidence of the most important prehistoric civilisation in Southeast Asia. As such, Ban Chiang became a UNESCO World Heritage site in 1992.

In fact, the very first evidence of this Bronze Age civilisation appeared a few years before 1966, when a Ban Chiang doctor building a new house uncovered a cache of distinctive vases in 1957. What he discovered ultimately turned out to be the location of a 5000-year-old mass burial site. Today, the site, located on the grounds of **Wat Pho Si Nai**, has been given over to the archaeological excavation pit, where visitors can see replicas of a few skeletons and shards of pottery arranged as they would have appeared when first discovered.

These days, all the finds from the Wat Pho Si Nai site, and the other ones that were subsequently uncovered nearby, are housed in the excellent **Ban Chiang National Museum** *(virtualmuseum.finearts.go.th/banchiang, 200฿)*, 1km west of the burial site, which is open 9am to 4pm Wednesday to Sunday and has good English captions. Some of the pottery is simply exquisite, featuring the distinctive red whorls on buff backgrounds that characterise the Ban Chiang style.

BEST BAN CHIANG HANDICRAFTS

Ban Chiang Indigo Dye Weaving Centre: Learn how to weave and dye traditional clothing coloured with indigo dye bearing elaborate designs.

Ban Chiang Pottery & Painting Group: For the artistically inclined (or the curious), this place allows you to throw and paint your own pots.

Sor Hong Daeng Ban Chiang Weaving Group: This women's weaving group mostly makes indigo-dyed cotton fabric, including *mudmee*. Visitors are welcome.

Add-Ann Ban Chiang: Avoid tomb-raiding and come here instead to buy exact replicas of what you've seen at the museum.

Puan Coffee: Cute place in a traditional wooden house with a fine range of locally produced pottery and souvenirs.

Also on display here are stone tools, iron axe-heads, spear-heads, hooks and bronze bracelets, which adorned the arms of the dead, along with jewellery and other artefacts. There are also reproductions of the excavation pit and working atmosphere of the site, as well as fascinating glimpses of what the prehistoric culture might have been like – the discovery of rice fragments indicates that it was a farming civilisation.

Ban Chiang remains a rustic and pleasant small town that's good for a wander once you've finished in the museum. There are still traditional wooden houses here, alongside a number of handicraft outlets and workshops.

Visit the White Lotus Temple

Located 5km north of Ban Chiang, **Wat Santi Wanaram** is a rather extraordinary modernist temple in the shape of a flowering white lotus (hence its nickname, White Lotus Temple). The shrine's design is thought to be unique in Thailand and it sits on an island in an artificial lake, connected to the mainland by a bridge, so that, from a distance, the temple actually seems to be floating on the water. Inside, the temple is decorated with scenes from the life of Buddha and features an ornate, gold-leaf ceiling.

The surrounding grounds are very peaceful and made a good spot for a picnic; there's a restaurant and shop. Also here are some weird animal statues reminiscent of *Wallace and Gromit* characters and a green-tinged pond that's home to crocodiles. We don't know why the crocs are here, but they are very big so don't mess with them. The temple is free to enter and open daily during daylight hours.

Red Lotus Sea

TIME FROM UDON THANI: **50MIN**

A carpet of floating blossoms

Red Lotus Sea, or Talay Bua Dang, is undoubtedly one of the most photographed sites in Isan and gives visitors a taste of Thailand cranked up to 11. This freshwater lake, 40km southeast of Udon Thani, is virtually blanketed with the fuchsia colours of blooming water lilies between October and February, when it becomes one of the most popular destinations in Isan. Visitor numbers peak on Valentine's Day, when the lake is absolutely swarmed with boats carrying loved-up couples eager for bright pink blossoms as the backdrop to their social media.

Sometimes known as Nong Han, and bordering both Nong Han and Kumphawapi districts, the unusual lake is said to have emerged after a king decided to hold a rocket festival to determine who would marry his daughter. Because of the princess's beauty, the competition was fierce – involving various intrigues including murder and black magic – and became so disruptive that *nagas* from a nearby river flooded the area with water, thereby creating the lake.

The blooms start to emerge in late October, with January and February the best months to see them. It's important to get here early – sunrise ideally – both for better photographic conditions and because the flowers start to close up around

BANGPRIKPHOTO/SHUTTERSTOCK

Wat Santi Wanaram

10.30am and are completely closed by noon. You'll also see plenty of birds here, as well as water buffalo grazing at the lake's edge.

Ban Diam is the main access point for the lake. Head to the village pier where boats for hire await. Choose either a small one (300฿ per hour) or a big one for up to 10 people (500฿ per hour) and then set off, with the boat inching through the flowers for some great photo opportunities. Although the blooms are really only a marvel for a couple of months, the lake provides an intriguing glimpse into rural life year-round, with much of the local population in the area dependent on fishing.

Phu Phrabat Historical Park

TIME FROM UDON THANI: **70MIN**

Visit Thailand's Stonehenge

No one really knows the true origins of this mysterious, mystical place peppered with bizarre rock spires, whale-sized boulders and improbably balanced rocks reminiscent of the Stonehenge prehistoric site in the UK. With its beguiling mix of prehistoric art, religious sites, rock formations and hiking trails, **Phu Phrabat Historical Park** *(100฿)* is one of Isan's most compelling sights and experiences.

Some of the rock paintings here are believed to date back as far as 6000 years ago and it was in prehistoric times that many of the rock formations were initially modified for various religious functions. Dvaravati-era *sema* stones – used to demarcate sacred areas in Buddhist temples – presumably from about 1000 to 1200 years ago, are plentiful, and the ground under some rocky overhangs has been painstakingly carved into smooth platforms. The Khmer later added Hindu elements to the site.

Make sure to check out the prehistoric paintings on several rock overhangs, best seen at side-by-side **Tham Wua** and **Tham Khon**, which demonstrate that the area was probably regarded as a holy site 3000 to 4000 years ago. The park's

MULTICULTURAL ISAN

Udon Thani Province stands out even in multicultural Isan for its diverse mix of ethnicities. The majority of the population are Tai-Lao, but there are also significant Vietnamese, Chinese and Khmer communities, as well as smaller numbers of Tai Phuan, Tai Yo and Kuy people. That reflects both how Isan has always been a crossroads of cultures and the region's relatively recent integration into Thailand. These days, many northeastern people no longer stress their Lao or Khmer roots, instead describing themselves as 'Thai-Isan' or '*Khon* Isan', literally 'Isan People'. But even the word 'Isan' is an import, deriving from the Pali term for the northeast, which in turn is derived from a Sanskrit word for one of the many manifestations of the Hindu god Shiva.

THE SHAMAN OF SALA KAEW KU

Luang Pu Boun Leua Sourirat, the creator of Sala Kaew Ku, was a mystic from Laos whose idiosyncratic blend of Buddhism and Hinduism attracted many followers in both Laos and Isan. Luang Pu expressed his beliefs through the hundreds of statues of gods, demons, humans and animals he designed from 1958 onwards. His first 'installation' was Buddha Park, directly opposite Nong Khai on the other side of the Mekong, where over 200 religious-themed statues still draw local and foreign visitors. He began creating new statues in Nong Khai after fleeing Laos ahead of the 1975 communist takeover. Luang Pu died in 1996, but his mummified body is on display at Sala Kaew Ku and his disciples insist that his hair still grows.

KENNAMAE_BKK/SHUTTERSTOCK

Phu Phrabat Historical Park (p337)

highlight is **Hor Nang Usa**, an overturned-boot-shaped outcrop with a shrine built into it. Nearby is **Bo Nang Usa**, an artificial reservoir carved 5m deep into solid rock.

Many of these rock formations are signposted with names that allude to the local legend of Princess Nang Usa, who was forced to live here by her overprotective father until she escaped to marry her suitor. A climb beyond the rock formations to **Pha Sadej** ends with views that can stretch all the way to Laos on a really clear day.

A web of trails meanders past the many sites and you can see them all in a leisurely two hours, but some people spend a lot more time here. South of the entrance is **Wat Phra Phutthabat Bua Bok**, with its namesake Lao-style *chedi* covering a Buddha footprint.

Phu Phrabat is 70km northwest of Udon Thani and open daily from 8.30am to 4.30pm.

Nong Khai

TIME FROM UDON THANI: 1HR

Border-town life

Nong Khai, 55km north of Udon Thani, has been a hit with travellers for years. It sits right by the Mekong just 20km south of the Lao capital Vientiane, but its popularity isn't just due to its proximity to Laos. Many visitors are seduced by the dreamy pink sunsets and the languid pace of life here and end up staying for longer than they originally intended.

There are also a few worthwhile sights to keep you occupied. The bizarre religious sculptures at **Sala Kaew Ku** *(40฿)*, about 5km east of central Nong Khai, are one of Isan's more enigmatic attractions: a wonderful smorgasbord of photogenic cement statues of Buddha, Shiva, Vishnu and other deities. Some of the statues are over 20m high and all reflect their late creator's unique synthesis of Buddhist and Hindu philosophy.

Bicycles can be rented at the eastern end of Nong Khai's **Walking Street**, allowing visitors to pedal alongside the Mekong. The Saturday **night market** on Walking Street is always lively and fun, too. Alternatively, dive into nearby **Tha Sadet**, a long-standing border-town market where goods from China, Laos and Vietnam are on sale alongside local toys, handicrafts, food and lots of clothes. Finally, the **Isaan Rum Distillery**, 12km south of town, offers tours of its organic rum-making process and tastings for 120฿ per person and also has a pleasant lakeside restaurant.

The mysterious Naga Fireballs

The one time of year when Nong Khai becomes busy with visitors is during October at the end of Buddhist Lent, when tens of thousands of locals line the banks of the Mekong to catch the phenomenon known as the **Naga Fireballs**. These balls of red flame – some as big as basketballs – appear to rise out of the river and shoot up into the sky, sometimes as high as 200m above the Mekong.

But who exactly is behind the fireballs is a mystery worthy of Agatha Christie. Some theorise that the fireballs are the result of swamp-gas explosions with a great sense of timing; others say Laotian soldiers are firing flares into the sky to trick gullible Thais. Then there's the original explanation: that the fireballs were congratulations to the Buddha from the *nagas*, the mythical serpents who live in the Mekong. The *nagas*, a common motif in temples throughout Isan, are considered Buddha's main protectors. A **statue** of his chief protector, the seven-headed Mucalinda, stands on Nong Khai's Walking Street and is a key gathering point for fireball watching.

What is certain is that the phenomenon has been happening for a long time – the fireballs were known as 'ghost lights' back in the 1980s – and they've also been spotted along other stretches of the Mekong. These days, though, Nong Khai is fireball central and their appearance triggers one of Isan's major festivals, known as **Bang Fai Phaya Nak**, with the party ballooning from the first full moon after Buddhist Lent into a weeklong celebration, replete with rowing contests, dance performances and, of course, lots of food and drink. The climax of the festival is a parade of boats along the Mekong, followed by a light and sound show. Whether the fireballs are actually naturally occurring or something cooked up by local tourism officials now seems like a moot point; it's best just to give yourself up to the festivities.

GETTING TO LAOS FROM NONG KHAI

The **Nong Khai–Vientiane border crossing** is one of Thailand's busiest frontiers, enabling travellers to move between Isan and the Lao capital, either by road or train. If you already have a Lao visa, hop on one of the four daily buses (55฿) that travel between Nong Khai's bus station and Vientiane's Talat Sao bus terminal (there's also a daily bus to Vang Vieng).

If you don't have a Lao visa (US$35 to US$42 or 1500฿ at the border), take a tuk-tuk (80฿) to the Thai-Lao Friendship Bridge, where buses (20฿) run you across to the Lao side. Once through immigration, buses or taxis can transport you to Vientiane. Alternatively, jump on a train at Nong Khai's railway station; visas are issued when you arrive at Vientiane's Khamsavath Station.

EATING IN NONG KHAI: OUR PICKS

Macky's Riverside Kitchen: Mekong-side traveller hangout serving some of the best Western food in Isan – try the fish and chips – as well as Thai classics. *7am-9pm* ฿

Daeng Namnuang: Famous Vietnamese restaurant on Walking Street that's both good value and good quality. Popular with the locals. *9am-8pm* ฿

Nanping Sun Vegetarian Restaurant: Solid all-vegan hole-in-the-wall Thai place that's busiest in the morning. Choose from the daily buffet or menu. *7am-7.30pm* ฿

River Chill: Relaxed riverside restaurant with Mekong fish specialities, beer and cocktails, a rooftop for sunset views and live music. *3pm-midnight* ฿฿

Nakhon Phanom

MEKONG VIEWS | VIETNAMESE CULTURE | HISTORY

GETTING AROUND

The airport is 17km west of town and has daily flights to Bangkok. Nakhon Phanom's bus station is centrally located with connections across Isan, including with Udon Thani, Ubon Ratchathani, Khon Kaen and Nong Khai, as well as Bangkok. There are also four buses a day to Thakhek in Laos. Tuk-tuks and motorcycle taxis prowl the streets, but the Grab ridesharing app is a more convenient way of getting around if you haven't hired a bicycle.

TOP TIP

Nakhon Phanom is perhaps Isan's most cycle-friendly city, so do take advantage of the 13km bicycle path along the Mekong here. Bikes can be hired at a number of places around town, while many hotels also offer them.

Nakhon Phanom is one of Isan's most pleasant stops; a city by the Mekong that feels like a small town. Life here is focused on the riverfront – the weekend Walking Street Market stretches along the Mekong and is one of the best in the northeast. Nakhon Phanom means 'City of Mountains', but in fact the undulating karst peaks all lie across the river in central Laos, so you'll be admiring rather than climbing them. The views are great, though, especially during a hazy sunrise.

Temples here have their own distinct style, a reflection of Nakhon Phanom's long and rich history, which dates back to the 12th century. Formerly a key city in Laos' Lan Xang empire, Nakhon Phanom was also once under Khmer control. These days it's much better known for its Vietnamese connections, with Ho Chi Minh, the father of modern Vietnam, a former resident and many ethnic Vietnamese living here.

Vietnam in Isan

On the trail of Uncle Ho

Nakhon Phanom's connections with Vietnam go back to 1928, when a then-unknown Vietnamese revolutionary moved to the village of **Ban Na Chok**, 3km west of Nakhon Phanom. He would later become famous as Ho Chi Minh, or Uncle Ho, the man who led Vietnam to independence from France and who was president of North Vietnam when it battled US-backed South Vietnam during the Vietnam War (or the American War if you're Vietnamese).

Uncle Ho departed Nakhon Phanom in 1930 (having also spent time in Udon Thani). For the next 50-odd years, his presence in the kingdom was not fondly remembered by the Thai authorities. That's because, firstly, his campaign against the French empire in Indochina prompted the arrival of an estimated 70,000 Vietnamese refugees to Nakhon Phanom from the late 1940s on. Then, in the 1960s, Ho's war against

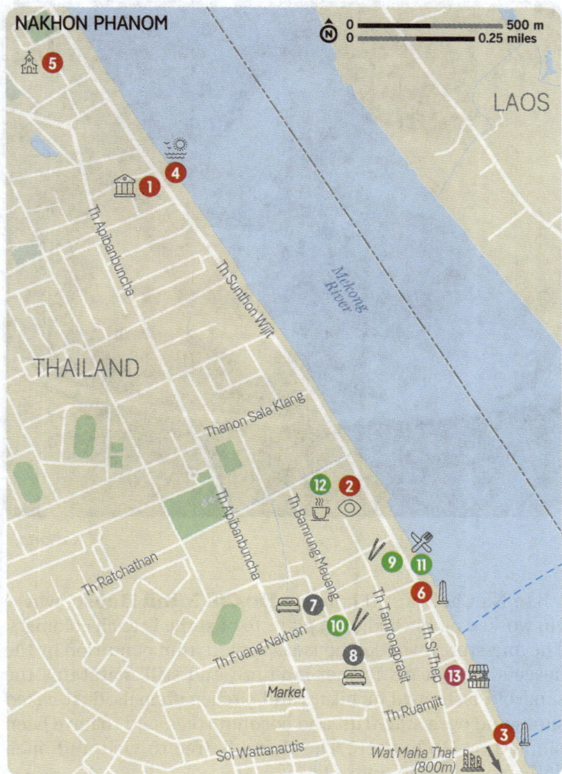

SIGHTS
1 Former Governor's Residence Museum
2 Former Nakhon Phanom Courthouse
3 Naga Statue
4 Si Khotrabun Golden Sand Beach
5 St Anne's Cathedral
6 Vietnamese Memorial Clock Tower

SLEEPING
7 Porpiang Hotel
8 Windsor Hotel

EATING
9 Susura
10 Vietnamese Kitchen
11 Walking Street Market

DRINKING & NIGHTLIFE
12 Termsuk Coffee House

SHOPPING
13 Indochina Market

South Vietnam and the US inspired local revolutionaries to turn Nakhon Phanom Province into a hotbed of communist resistance to the Thai government, despite the fact that Nakhon Phanom also hosted a US military base (now the airport) during the same period.

But time is the great healer and Uncle Ho's sojourn in Nakhon Phanom is now celebrated by both Thailand and Vietnam as a symbol of the friendship between the two countries, while the once-unwelcome Vietnamese refugees have been fully integrated into local life.

EATING & DRINKING IN NAKHON PHANOM: OUR PICKS

Vietnamese Kitchen: One of Nakhon Phanom's most authentic (and busy) Vietnamese eateries has tasty and reasonably priced dishes. *7am-9pm* ฿

Susura: It's not just Thai-Vietnamese in Nakhon Phanom; this fun place offers fine Thai-Japanese dishes, like *khao soi* ramen or *pad krapao tonkatsu*. *11am-9pm* ฿

Walking Street Market: Weekend night market by the Mekong offers Thai and Vietnamese choices. There's a nice riverside dining area. *5-10pm Fri-Sun* ฿

Termsuk Coffee House: This stylish spot has an attractive garden and a good range of coffee, cakes and pastries. There's also fast wi-fi. *8am-5pm Mon-Sat*

THAI-VIETNAMESE CUISINE

Thai dishes with a strong Vietnamese influence can be found all over Isan. Perhaps the most popular of these is *kai kata*, or 'egg in a pan', said to have been invented by the Vietnamese when US soldiers requested American-style breakfasts. The egg is typically baked with minced pork or *moo yaw* on top, with a sweet bun on the side. Another dish, *goo ay jap yoo an,* is a Vietnamese take on Chinese rice noodles, featuring thick, sticky strands in a pork broth. This being Thailand, it's served with added chilli powder. Visitors will also encounter *khao ji,* a local version of the famous Vietnamese banh mi baguette sandwich that's also a staple across the Mekong in Laos.

VACHIRA P/SHUTTERSTOCK

Kai kata

Ban Na Chok is still home to **Ho Chi Minh House**, where Ho worked on his fledgling plans to oust the French colonists. The one-storey wooden house is kept in mint condition by the descendants of his former landlord and still maintains the same old-fashioned furniture and kitchen utensils, dust-caked shoes and even star-fruit and coconut trees said to have been planted by Ho himself. The house is free to visit and open daily from 8am to 6pm.

Vietnam's government later deemed the house wasn't a grand enough memorial to their founding father's time in Thailand and so paid for the **Ho Chi Minh Museum** (opened in 2014), 500m down the road from his former home. There are some photos on display here, but it's really more of a shrine than a museum. Thai visitors, though, enjoy the opportunity to take photos dressed up in the traditional Vietnamese clothes that can be rented here. The museum is free and open 8am to 6pm Monday to Saturday.

Tuk-tuk drivers will spin you to Ban Na Chok and back for 300฿ including waiting time, but it's also easy to cycle here.

CYCLING NAKHON PHANOM'S RIVERFRONT

Pedal by the Mekong and discover some of Nakhon Phanom's most distinctive sights. You could also walk this route.

START	END	LENGTH
Thoet Phrakiat Park	St Anne's Cathedral	6km; two hours

Start at ❶ **Thoet Phrakiat Park**, which sits right by the Mekong and offers splendid views of the mountains across the river in Laos. From there pedal north to ❷ **Wat Maha That**, which has a fine white and gold Lao-style *chedi* and dates back to the 12th century and Nakhon Phanom's founding. Carry on a little further up the riverfront to the ❸ **Naga Statue**, Nakhon Phanom's most photographed monument, a huge seven-headed *naga* that spouts water and which Thais make offerings to.

Your next stop is the ❹ **Indochina Market**, where a variety of Lao and Chinese goods mingle with local products. Just up the road is the ❺ **Vietnamese Memorial Clock Tower**, built in 1960 as a gift from the Vietnamese residents of Nakhon Phanom. It looks best when lit up at night.

Now cycle along Walking Street until you come to the ❻ **Former Nakhon Phanom Courthouse**, a 1918 building revealing a French architectural influence that clearly jumped the Mekong from Laos. Further up the road, the ❼ **Former Governor's Residence Museum** is a colonial-style yellow and green mansion that's housed visiting Thai royalty. Locals believe it is haunted.

End your tour at ❽ **St Anne's Cathedral**, a handsome twin-steepled structure with stained-glass windows that caters to the local Catholic community, who are mostly ethnic Vietnamese.

Si Khotrabun Golden Sand Beach The Mekong's water levels drop between February and May, revealing this sandy beach opposite the Former Governor's Residence Museum.

Nong Saeng Park This park is just past St Anne's Cathedral and has its own shady bicycle path surrounding an artificial lake.

Beyond Nakhon Phanom

Places

Two of Isan's most sacred and mystical temples lie beyond Nakhon Phanom, as well as sandstone cliffs featuring extraordinary rock formations.

North of Nakhon Phanom you enter a jungly region punctuated by rocky outcrops that jut dramatically into the sky. Little-visited Bueng Kan Province seems almost feral compared to the lush rolling landscapes of the provinces to the east, its peaks like stones welded together into fantastic shapes and the foliage a haven for snakes.

But if you make the effort, you'll discover a wondrous temple that clings precariously to the side of a mountain and a former hermits' enclave that's fast becoming one of Isan's go-to destinations. For a complete contrast, head south of Nakhon Phanom to join the pilgrims making their way to That Phanom, home to the holiest temple in all Isan.

GETTING AROUND

All buses or minivans heading south from Nakhon Phanom pass through That Phanom, or you can catch a slow *songthaew*. A taxi from Nakhon Phanom will cost 1000฿ return. You'll need your own transport to reach Phu Sing Hin Sam Wan and Wat Phu Tok in Bueng Kan Province; hiring a car and driver for the day is the best option.

That Phanom

TIME FROM NAKHON PHANOM: **50MIN**

Isan's most sacred shrine

Wat Phra That Phanom is regarded as both the northeast's holiest shrine and a potent symbol of Isan identity. Dominated by a colossal *chedi* that's 53.6m high, with a 16kg solid-gold umbrella laden with precious gems adding 4m more height, the temple is a major pilgrimage stop for devout Thai and Lao people, who come to pray to the relics of Buddha believed to be enshrined here.

Local legend has it that the temple was originally erected in 535 BCE, after Buddha told his disciple Mahakasyapa that he wanted one of his chest bones to be interred here in order for Buddhism to survive. In fact, the temple likely dates back to the 9th century CE, and has been rebuilt a number of times.

The temple sits at the heart of the peaceful Mekong town of That Phanom, 55km south of Nakhon Phanom, and is the focus of a lively annual **festival** held in either January or February. At any time of the year, the surrounding food and handicraft stalls are always busy.

Wat Phu Thok

VESPA_FOTO/SHUTTERSTOCK

Wat Phu Thok

TIME FROM NAKHON PHANOM: 2¼HR

Magical mountainside temple

A key piece of advice given to meditation newbies at Thai retreats is to stay firmly in the present by analysing every step and acknowledging every emotion. This teaching comes in handy, along with the virtue of perseverance, when climbing the rickety staircases and walkways at Wat Phu Thok, also known as 'Lonely Mountain'. It's one of Isan's true wonders: a unique temple that clings to the side of a giant sandstone outcrop, 359m above the ground.

The precarious paths lead past the shrines and monks' huts scattered around the mountain on cliffs and in caves, and provide fabulous, if stomach-dropping, views over the surrounding countryside. A final scramble up roots and rocks takes you to the forest on the summit, which is considered the seventh level. Be aware that poisonous snakes slither around this level – signs in Thai warn of this – and that visitors with mobility issues will struggle from levels 5 and 6 onwards. If you don't like heights, you may want to skip Wat Phu Thok altogether.

Wat Phu Thok was the brainchild of revered monk Luang Pu Juan, who conceived a temple on seven levels depicting the seven stages of Buddhist meditation. Luang Pu Juan died in a plane crash in 1980 while en route to Bangkok for the Queen's birthday celebrations, but not before seeing the temple finished. Wat Phu Thok is now one of Thailand's principal meditation retreats and the resident monks work assiduously to maintain the grounds and make sure that all the wooden staircases and walkways are safe. But, in all honesty, some of them don't feel very secure.

If you're fit and ready to hustle, you can get up and down the various levels in a sweaty hour or so, but it's far better to take your time and savour the quiet and the views. The temple is 150km northwest of Nakhon Phanom and only really accessible by taxi or your own wheels.

ISAN'S FOREST TEMPLES

Wat Phu Tok is a prime example of the forest temples that Isan is known for. These shrines, normally located in isolated mountainous areas or national parks, form a distinct tradition within Thai Buddhism, emphasising meditation, monastic discipline, a rigorous practise of Buddhism and living in harmony with nature.

Isan is the birthplace of the Thai forest tradition, which began in the early 20th century when legendary monk Luang Pu Mun started going on remote retreats. His disciples established many of Isan's most prominent *wat pa*, or 'forest temples', such as **Wat Pa Phu Pang** in Ubon Ratchathani Province. There are also many newer ones, such as Wat Phu Thok and **Wat Pa Phu Kon**, a spectacular mountaintop shrine in Udon Thani Province.

GETTING TO LAOS FROM MUKDAHAN

While foreigners can cross to Laos from Nakhon Phanom, the **Mukdahan–Savannakhet border crossing**, 100km south of Nakhon Phanom, is far more popular with Western travellers, not least because Savannakhet has direct buses to Vietnam. At least six daily buses (40฿) make the journey from Mukdahan's bus station to Savannakhet's bus terminal. Lao visas can be obtained at the border (US$35 to US$42 or 1500฿) and this is a hassle-free, if busy, place to cross; expect the whole process to take two hours. Savannakhet is an increasingly popular destination in its own right, thanks to its night market by the Mekong and French-era architecture, but it also has an airport, plus buses to Vientiane and Hanoi in Vietnam.

9ROBOT/SHUTTERSTOCK

Three Whales Rock, Phu Sing Hin Sam Wan

Phu Sing Hin Sam Wan

TIME FROM NAKHON PHANOM: 2½HR

Stunning views and sandstone cliffs

Phu Sing Hin Sam Wan *(100฿)*, in the north of Bueng Kan Province, was once a destination for monks seeking complete isolation to meditate. Now the cliffs (sometimes referred to as Three Whales Rock) in Bueng Kan Province have morphed into one of Isan's newest and most in-demand tourist destinations, thanks to the array of photogenic animal-shaped rock formations here and a series of vantage points offering stunning views of the countryside below and the Mekong snaking away in the far distance.

At the visitor centre, *songthaew* await to transport visitors to the various viewing points. Most people pay 500฿ to tour the five main sites, but you can pay more if you want to visit further ones. There's also the option of hiring a drone operator (700฿ to 1000฿) to capture aerial pics of you posing on the cliffs (most of the online photos of Three Whales Rock are drone shots). Many local visitors do this, and the buzzing of drones hovering overhead can be a bit annoying if you just want to contemplate the landscape in silence.

The first stop is a **temple** carved into the sandstone at which locals pray to a golden Buddha. After that comes the main attraction: **Three Whales Rock**, where three sandstone cliffs next to each other are said to resemble a family of whales – mum, dad and baby whale – 'swimming' together. Only the mum and dad cliffs are accessible. Be warned that the cliffs are slippery, with sheer drops off either side – there are no guard rails – so watch your step.

Close by, the **Hermit Cave Viewpoint** gives visitors a chance to create their own 'flying' photo shoots, complete with witches' brooms. At the **Elephant Rock**, which actually does look like an elephant, a copse of bamboo trees hides shy bluebirds, while the **Lion's Head Gate** bookends another popular view towards the far-off Mekong.

Phu Sing Hin Sam Wan is open daily from 5am to 5pm. A return taxi from/to Nakhon Phanom will cost 2500฿.

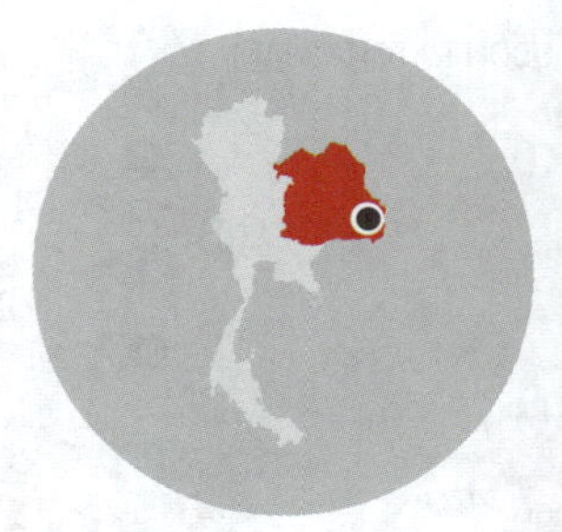

Ubon Ratchathani

RIVERSIDE BEACHES | MUSIC | FOOD SCENE

Ubon Ratchathani is the most laid-back of Isan's four major cities, its citizens always eager to flock to the riverside beaches to make merry. Like many of Isan's cities, Ubon boomed on the back of the Vietnam War and now has a big student population, but it still feels like a provincial town, with almost everything in easy reach of the centre. Head south of there and the neighbourhoods seem more village-like than urban.

Yet there's a flourishing food scene here, some of the best handicrafts in Isan and plenty of bars and music venues. There are also parks and temples to wander, while Ubon makes an ideal base for exploring the natural splendours that lie to the east and north of the city. Ubon flies under the traveller radar and not many foreigners pass through, but those that do generally enjoy themselves.

GETTING AROUND

Ubon's airport is 2km from the city centre and has daily flights to Bangkok. The bus station is 6km north of the centre. There are frequent connections across Isan, as well as to Bangkok and Chiang Mai. Two buses a day run to Pakse in Laos. Ubon's train station is 5km south of the centre and the final stop on the eastern branch of Thailand's Northeastern Line. There are six daily trains to Bangkok via Korat. The Grab ridesharing app is the best way to hop around town.

Discover the Heart of Ubon

Explore Thung Si Mueang

Ubon's principal park and the heart of the city is **Thung Si Mueang**. It's distinguished from its counterparts elsewhere in Isan by the moat that runs round it. There are also plenty of shady areas and most of Ubon's major sights sit close by.

The impressive golden **City Pillar Shrine** is just south of the park and draws locals to make merit in the hope of having their wishes of riches granted. The shrine is only a few steps from the **Ubon Ratchathani National Museum** *(120฿)*, housed

DRINKING IN UBON RATCHATHANI: OUR PICKS

Wrong Way Cafe: Ubon's favourite foreigner hangout has friendly staff and regulars, live sport and a menu of Western classics. *4pm-midnight Fri-Wed*

LIFE Roaster: Top coffee stop with a flavourful Thai and Ethiopian beans. It's in a converted wooden house and also does pastries and cakes. *7.30am-4.30pm*

Barn: A coffee shop by day and a cosy cocktail bar by night. There are other Thai-style bars nearby. *9am-midnight Tue-Sun*

Ubon Tap Taste House: Centrally located craft-beer pub with local and imported brews. Gets busy later in the evening and sometimes has live music. *5pm-midnight Wed-Mon*

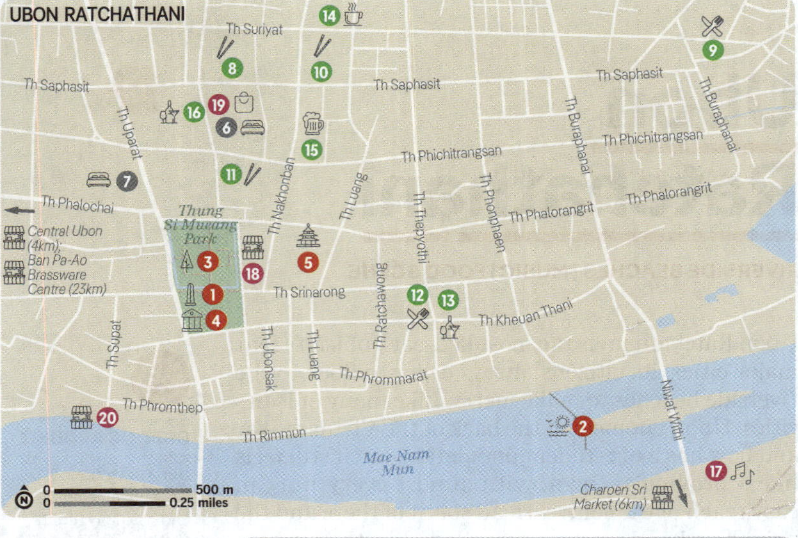

SIGHTS
1 City Pillar Shrine
2 Hat Wat Tai
3 Thung Si Mueang
4 Ubon Ratchathani National Museum
5 Wat Thung Si Mueang

SLEEPING
6 Phadaeng Hotel
7 YUU Hotel & Café

EATING
8 Indochine
9 Outside Inn
10 Porntip Gai Yang Wat Jaeng
11 Sam Chai Cafe
12 Utthayan Bunniyom

DRINKING & NIGHTLIFE
13 Barn
14 LIFE Roaster
15 Ubon Tap Taste House
16 Wrong Way Cafe

ENTERTAINMENT
17 Chom Jan Bar & Restaurant

SHOPPING
18 Night Market
19 Punchard
20 Riverside Walking Street

TRADITIONAL ISAN INSTRUMENTS

Mor lam bands normally have five or six musicians, as well as singers, playing traditional instruments. The *kaen*, most associated with *mor lam*, is a mouth organ made of bamboo that produces a high-pitched, harmonica-like sound. The *pi*, not to be confused with the guitar-like *phin*, is a type of oboe, while the *khoey* is a form of flute. The *saw duang* is a kind of two-stringed fiddle, while the *saw u* resembles a banjo. Keeping the tempo are the cymbal-like *sing*, the *kap*, a wooden clapper, and various drums known as *kong*.

in an attractive 1918 building that was once the provincial government headquarters. The museum offers insights into local history and culture and has some impressive pottery and statuary. It's open 9am to 4pm Wednesday to Sunday. A **night market** gets going at 4.30pm every day almost next door to the museum.

Just to the east of Thung Si Mueang is atmospheric **Wat Thung Si Mueang**. Built during the reign of Rama III, it's known for its Tripitaka Library, set in an ancient wooden house on stilts over a lake to protect the books from termites.

Hit the Beach

Riverside life in Ubon

Ubon Ratchathani might be land-locked but there are a few beaches here. That's because, as a city sporting two rivers, the definition of a beach in Ubon is basically any stretch of sand next to water. Remember, too, that in Thailand the locals don't go to the beach to sunbathe or swim, but primarily to eat and party, with just a little bit of splashing around to cool off.

This explains a place like **Hat Khu Duea**, 9km west of the city centre, where the sandy banks of the Mun River have been taken over by restaurants, whose floating cabanas for dining extend out over the water, linked by wooden walkways. All serve essentially the same thing: dancing shrimp, or live baby shrimp in a spicy dressing, and grilled snakehead fish, both perfect with an ice-cold beer.

Meanwhile, **Hat Wat Tai** doesn't exist for most of the year. But if you time your visit from December to May, a beach appears around the rim of a small island in the middle of the Mun River, close to the centre of town. Currently, the only way to set foot on the island is by walking halfway along the bridge above the island and taking the stairs down to it. When the beach does manifest, restaurants set up and it's a lively scene, especially on weekends.

Slave to the Rhythm

Isan country music

Isan country music is, lyrically, just like country music everywhere: songs about unfaithful lovers, working in the fields and homesick rural folk adrift in big cities. But the music, known as *mor lam* and *luk thung*, is entirely unique to Isan and has long formed the soundtrack to life here, whether blasting out of a pick-up truck or from speakers set up on one of Ubon's beaches.

The two genres are often confused with each other. *Mor lam*, literally 'doctor of dance', has centuries-old roots derived from Lao culture and is sung in a rap-like, percussive delivery accompanied by the *kaen*, a bamboo reed instrument, and the *phin*, a two- to four-string guitar. Meanwhile, *luk thung*, or 'child of the fields', is more plaintive and reminiscent of American country music, but incorporates many other influences including Afro-Cuban music and Japanese *enka*.

Tawandang Ubon Ratchathani, 6km northwest of the centre, is by far the most prominent music venue in Ubon, featuring both *mor lam* and *luk thung* shows with traditional dancing. Don't bother showing up until 9pm to 10pm; you'll almost certainly be the only foreigner present. Another popular venue for *luk thung* is **Chom Jan Bar & Restaurant** on the southern banks of the Mun River opposite the island that's home to Hat Wat Thai. Any big temple celebration or festival, like the That Phanom Festival (p344) in Nakhon Phanom, will also feature *mor lam* bands.

BEST SHOPPING

Punchard: Quality Isan handicrafts, silks and local fabrics, many featuring new designs allied to traditional methods. *9.30am-5.30pm Thu-Tue*

Riverside Walking Street: Not just eats, but a decent range of clothing, handicrafts and souvenirs right by the Mun River. *5-10pm Fri-Sun*

Central Ubon: Ubon's premier shopping mall has clothes and phone shops, a food court, cinema, supermarket and glorious air-con to escape the heat. *10am-9pm*

Ban Pa-Ao Brassware Centre: This village 23km northwest of the centre is known for its silk weaving and unique brass handicrafts; you can watch them being made and buy some at reasonable prices. *9am-5pm*

Charoen Sri Market: If you're craving market action, head to this photogenic place in the south of Ubon with tons of food, flowers and clothes. *3am-8pm*

EATING IN UBON RATCHATHANI: OUR PICKS

Indochine: Renowned Thai-Vietnamese restaurant with authentic flavours, indoor and outdoor eating areas and surprisingly reasonable prices. *9am-8pm* ฿

Porntip Gai Yang Wat Jaeng: Ubon's premier purveyor of grilled chicken, *som tam* and other classic Isan dishes. There's air-con in the back. *8am-5pm Thu-Tue* ฿

Sam Chai Cafe: Thai-Vietnamese-style breakfasts – noodle dishes and *khao ji* – but they also do their own take on an American breakfast. *5.30am-1.30pm* ฿

Utthayan Bunniyom: Super-cheap vegetarian Thai place run by volunteers from a Buddhist religious group. Most of the food is gone by 11am. *6am-2pm* ฿

Beyond Ubon Ratchathani

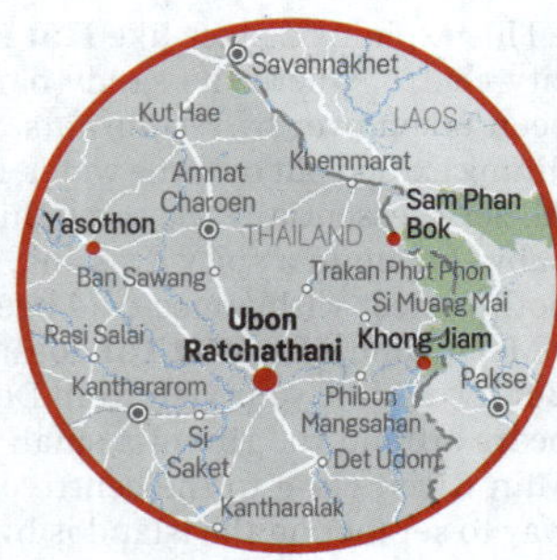

GETTING AROUND

Minivans run hourly from Ubon's bus station to Chong Mek via Khong Jiam, the jumping-off point for Pha Taem National Park and where the Mekong meets the Mun River. A return taxi to the park from Khong Jiam should be 800฿. For Yasothon and the rocket festival, hourly buses run from Ubon's bus station. You'll need to arrange your own transport to Sam Phan Bok. A return taxi from Ubon will cost 2500฿.

Waterfalls and rivers dominate the landscape outside Ubon Ratchathani, while there are awesome sunrises and prehistoric paintings to marvel at.

The region east of Ubon Ratchathani is known as the 'Emerald Triangle', where Thailand, Laos and Cambodia converge. As the name suggests, the countryside is wonderfully lush during and after the June–October rainy season, when the many waterfalls in the national parks really gush and the rivers rise and carve through the sandstone rocks to create reefs and alien-like moonscapes.

But there's still plenty do if you're here in the February–May dry season, including heading north to participate in Isan's most famous festival, hiking to the prehistoric paintings at Pha Taem National Park, where you can also catch the first sunrise in Thailand, and goggling at bi-coloured rivers and Mekong-side temples.

Sam Phan Bok

TIME FROM UBON RATCHATHANI: **2HR**

Thailand's Grand Canyon

Sam Phan Bok (loosely translated as '3000 holes') is probably the most popular attraction outside Ubon Ratchathani for Thai travellers. The site is the biggest rock reef along the Mekong and was formed by centuries of river waters shaping the soft sandstone rocks, which transform into the 'land of 3000 lakes' after the June–October monsoons have soaked the landscape without completely immersing it, typically from November to May. From June till October, the rocks and holes are mostly completely submerged and there's nothing to see.

It's fun to pretend you are walking on the moon while wandering randomly among the sandstone craters, and the photo opportunities are superb (night photography here is awesome). Thai visitors, though, have developed their own map of must-see sights that every traveller to Sam Phan Bok should visit for posting social-media selfies.

The most famous of these is the so-called **Grand Canyon**, a thick rift of rock resembling its namesake in the US (only

APIGUIDE/SHUTTERSTOCK

Sam Phan Bok

much smaller) and bordering a stream that is navigable by boat when the waters are high enough. The mauve-ish layers of stone also beckon to bouldering enthusiasts with their unusual shapes and obvious abundance of places to climb.

Another popular attraction is the **Mickey Mouse Hole**, three circles connected to resemble the iconic Disney mascot. Although there are several places that could pass as Mickey Mouse, there is only one true one, usually only found when bringing along a guide who can lead you to the correct location and take your photo once you've found it.

Other much-photographed sites include the **Challenging Hole**, so named because you can leap from one side to the next and the **Fireplace Hole**, set in a wall of stone. Then there's the **Elephant Trunk Bridge**, jutting out over a pool of water, the **Star Bridge**, a doughnut of rock inside which you can repose next to a reflecting pool, and the **Love Hole**, a deep pool of water flanked by similar-looking promontories.

Clambering to all these sites in the middle of the day isn't advised because it gets super-hot here. The best time for visiting is either sunrise at around 6am to 6.30am (which requires a seriously early start if you're coming from Ubon) or in the late afternoon at around 4pm, which is when most locals turn up. The light for photos is much better at these times, too. Make sure to bring water and a hat and wear hiking boots or trainers rather than flip-flops.

The area is free to visit, but many people hire a pick-up truck and driver to transport them around the various sites for 200฿ per person (although it is possible to walk to them). Freelance guides, who are often just local kids, are also available. Their fee is up to you; 100฿ to 200฿ is normally fine. Boat trips are also available (from 500฿).

Sam Phan Bok is 120km northeast of Ubon and right on the border with Laos. You'll need a car or taxi to get here.

WHY I LOVE UBON RATCHATHANI

David Eimer, Lonely Planet writer

Ubon Ratchathani might be the most underrated province in all Isan. I love the old-school seaside vibe of the riverside beaches in Ubon itself, and the restaurants are great, but it's what lies beyond the capital that makes the province so special. Waterfalls and rivers are everywhere and the sunrise views at Pha Taem National Park or Sam Phan Bok are simply supreme. Then there's the sheer timelessness of the countryside: the rice fields and grazing water buffalo that transport you back to the Thailand of old. Best of all is that Ubon Ratchathani sees few foreign visitors and the sights are so unspoiled. There's nowhere better to get off the tourist trail than here.

GETTING TO LAOS FROM CHONG MEK

The **Chong Mek–Vang Tao border crossing**, 33km south of Khong Jiam, funnels travellers on the overland Southeast Asia route to Pakse in southern Laos, from where it's another three hours south to the frontier with Cambodia. This is the only Thailand–Laos land-border crossing, so you don't get to cross the Mekong here.

Minivans from Ubon Ratchathani or Khong Jiam drop passengers close to the border post in Chong Mek, from where it's a five-minute walk to the Lao side (Lao visas are available for US$35 to US$42 or 1500฿). There's plenty of onward transport to Pakse. It's easier, though, to catch one of the two daily buses (9.30am and 3pm, 200฿) that run directly from Ubon Ratchathani's bus station to Pakse's main bus terminal.

Khong Jiam

TIME FROM UBON RATCHATHANI: **80MIN**

Where two rivers meet

The bucolic riverside town of Khong Jiam, 80km east of Ubon Ratchathani and sometimes spelled 'Khong Chiam', sits on a picturesque peninsula and is famous as the place where the mud-brown Mekong River meets the blue-green Mun River. The waters do not mix, creating a clear demarcation between the two rivers that's visible from the walkway behind pretty **Wat Khong Jiam**. The phenomenon is best seen from December to May, when the difference in colour between the two rivers is really stark.

The boats that usually ferry locals to and from Laos can be persuaded to take passengers up close to the bi-coloured waters for 800฿. Outside of the June–October rainy season, when currents are very strong, you can also negotiate a fishing trip here.

But Khong Jiam offers more than just bi-coloured waters. **Wat Tham Khuha Sawan** sits just above the town and the views across the Mekong to Laos from atop the bell tower are tremendous. This is one of the most-visited temples in the province; check out the stunning all-white *boht* (ordination hall), the beautiful nine-pointed *chedi* and one of the biggest gongs in Thailand (decorated with the flags of the members of ASEAN; the Association of Southeast Asian Nations).

An even more-photographed temple is **Wat Sirindhorn Wararam**, 25km south of Khong Jiam. Thanks to judiciously applied paint containing phosphorus, parts of the temple absorb enough sunlight during the day to emit an eerie glow at night, typically around 6pm to 6.30pm. Try not to use your flash while queuing with the hordes of locals who turn up to capture it.

End your tour of Khong Jiam at charming **Tohsang Cotton Village**, a couple of kilometres east of town, which demonstrates the labour-intensive process of making traditional cotton textiles, from weaving to indigo dyeing. People come from across Thailand to purchase the clothing made here and, for 300฿, visitors can participate in an indigo-dyeing workshop themselves. There's also a great coffee shop.

Yasothon

TIME FROM UBON RATCHATHANI: **2HR**

Celebrate Isan's most famous festival

Isan's rocket festivals are the wildest of the region's parties and the celebration staged in Yasothon, 100km northwest of Ubon Ratchathani, is the most raucous and famous of them all. Known as **Bun Bang Fai**, the rocket festivals erupt at the end of the hot season in May and June. They see locals drinking, dancing and tempting fate by firing homemade rockets into the sky, as a reminder to the ancient gods of rain, Phaya Taen, and rice, Phra Mae Phosop, to send enough rainfall for an abundant harvest.

SIRIRACH SAMATH/SHUTTERSTOCK

Wat Sirindhorn Wararam, Khong Jiam

Legends behind Bun Bang Fai vary, but most involve a conflict between Phaya Khan Khak, the 'Toad King' (some say this is one of the Buddha's pre-enlightenment lives), and Phaya Taen, who either withheld or forgot to send the rains for many years, resulting in widespread death down on earth. After they stopped fighting, Phaya Taen promised to send the rains every year.

Almost every village in Isan launches at least a couple of rockets, but it's Yasothon that hosts the biggest party, which is now heavily promoted by the Thai tourism authorities. The event normally takes place on the second weekend in May, with parades of floats, dancers and musicians on Saturday and rocket launches on Sunday. The nights are given over to drinking, eating and dancing to the music that blasts out from the different stages, everything from traditional Isan country music to EDM.

Individual villages in the area spend months organising costumes and music, rehearsing the dancers and building the rockets, which usually feature a *naga* head at their tip. Traditionally the rockets were made of bamboo stuffed with gunpowder, but PVC pipes are mostly used now. The largest rockets can be 3m long and hold 120kg of gunpowder. Mix that with all the alcohol being consumed and you have a recipe for danger. Accidents, some fatal, do happen, so keep your wits about you and don't take your safety cues from the locals.

ISAN'S CULTURAL DEBT TO LAOS

Much of what makes Isan such a culturally distinct region has its origins across the Mekong in Laos. This includes some of the most prominent festivals, like Bun Bang Fai, which are celebrated equally vigorously in Laos. Then there's language: the Isan dialect spoken by almost all locals is very close to Lao. Indeed, apart from slang expressions, the only real difference is that Isan is written in the Thai alphabet rather than the Lao one.

Many Isan dishes that are considered quintessentially Thai are also Lao in origin, such as the *som tam* and *larb* salads, although the Isan versions are much spicier, while sticky rice as an accompaniment to every meal is also a Lao tradition.

WUT.ANUNAI/SHUTTERSTOCK

Nam Tok Soi Sawan

TOP EXPERIENCE

Pha Taem National Park

Pha Taem National Park is awesome but relatively little-visited, a consequence perhaps of its former reputation among locals as the 'mountain of death'. That changed once prehistoric paintings were discovered here in 1981 and Pha Taem is now also known for its wonderful waterfalls and as the home of Thailand's first sunrise, thanks to the country's easternmost point being located here.

DON'T MISS

- Prehistoric paintings
- Waterfalls
- Sunrises
- Rock formations
- Wildflowers

Prehistoric Paintings

Pha Taem's ancient rock paintings, thought to be 3000 to 4000 years old, are etched on the face of **Pha Taem Cliff** below the **visitor centre**. A tree-shaded 3.6km walking trail leads past four groups of paintings before looping back to the visitor centre. Anyone reasonably fit and mobile should be able to manage the trail, but it does get slippery in places.

The first group of paintings is the clearest, depicting fish traps, elephants and giant catfish, but the second group is just as evocative, if smaller and more faint. The third group

PRACTICALITIES

● 045 252581 ● tickets 200฿ ● 5am-6pm

is especially interesting as the paintings illustrate an agricultural lifestyle, including a human figure chasing a deer. The fourth group are more indistinct and lie at the top of the cliff along a very narrow path with a sheer drop on one side. Take extreme care if you visit them.

Waterfalls

Pha Taem's most photographed waterfall is the unusual **Nam Tok Saeng Chan**, which features a long stream of water tumbling into a pool via a natural hole cut in a limestone ledge. Locals believe Saeng Chan is best seen when the moon is waxing, hence it's known as the 'moonlight' waterfall, but it's actually at its best when it's raining. Around 3km north of Saeng Chan is **Nam Tok Thung Na Mueang**, a wide and 25m-high cascade.

Pretty **Nam Tok Soi Sawan** is surrounded by forest and sports 25m-high cascades that resemble a necklace. It's fine to swim here. On the way to Soi Sawan, **Pha Sok** has a natural pool described as 'nature's Jacuzzi'; it can be accessed with the park rangers from October onwards. The waterfalls flow from June to December and all are at least 30 minutes' drive from the visitor centre.

Sunrises

There are brilliant views of the Mekong and Laos at a number of places in the park, including from Pha Taem Cliff close to the visitor centre, but it's sunrises that Pha Taem is most famous for. Thai travellers flock here to catch Thailand's first sunrise from **Pha Chana Dai Cliff**, which marks the easternmost point of the kingdom. The viewpoint is in the remote north of the park and you'll need a decent vehicle, ideally a 4WD, to reach it via the rough access road. The views of the Mekong are amazing at any time of the day but, if you can't be here for dawn, the sunrise at Pha Taem Cliff is only a minute or so behind.

Rock Formations

The most interesting rock formation in the park is the row of mushroom-like rocks known as **Sao Chaliang**. Said to have been created after an ocean dried up, the mushroom 'caps' are festooned with embedded shells, while the 'stems' were shaped by a mix of water and wind.

Wildflowers

Some 40 species of wildflowers, including insect-eating ones, burst into delightful bloom in December and January, transforming the rocky landscape into superbly photogenic fields of purple, yellow and red. The meadows are 1km east of the park campsite.

SLEEPING & EATING

The only place to stay inside the park is the campsite 2km north of the visitor centre, close to Sao Chaliang. Tents and camping gear can be hired and there are bathrooms. There's a cafe next to the visitor centre and a few simple restaurants close to the park entrance. Alternatively, there are plentiful accommodation and eating options in Khong Jiam, 22km south of Pha Taem.

TOP TIPS

- Wear a hat and hiking boots or good trainers, and carry water.
- Visitors with mobility issues will struggle to reach many of the sights in the park.
- The waterfalls can't be accessed from the visitor centre. You find them via other park entrances, so you'll need transport. The visitor centre provides a map.
- If you're camping, bring your own supplies of food and drink.
- There's no public transport to the park. Either catch a minivan from Ubon to Khong Jiam and then a taxi to the park (800B return), or a return taxi directly to the park from Ubon (2000B).

Places We Love to Stay

฿ Budget ฿฿ Midrange ฿฿฿ Top End

Nakhon Ratchasima City (Korat City) Map p307

Sansabai House ฿ Long-standing budget option with clean and comfortable, if old-fashioned, rooms in the centre of town.

Within-Korat ฿฿ This laid-back hotel is the most distinctive and stylish in Korat, with artful decor, comfy beds and a couple of communal areas.

Urban-Bamboo ฿฿ A welcoming boutique place that's almost budget in price. Modern, well-kept rooms and a downstairs restaurant. Some English is spoken.

Romyen Garden Place ฿฿ Rooms are big and have balconies at this veteran place that looks its age now. There's a small pool and gym and the location is central.

Centara Korat ฿฿฿ Korat's top digs are a little out of the way, but the rooms are predictably plush and there's a rooftop pool, gym and restaurants.

Buriram

Qoo Hotel ฿฿ Modern, well set-up rooms in a central location close to restaurants, shops and the bus and train stations.

Hotel Agnes ฿฿ Newish hotel with comfortable, if sterile, rooms and a rooftop bar. It's walking distance to the night market and bus station.

Khao Yai National Park

More Than Sleep Hostel ฿ Pak Chong's best hostel lacks character but has big and airy dorms. Bicycles and motorbikes can be hired and tours arranged.

Pak Chong Center Poshtel ฿฿ Decent-sized rooms in a distinctive bamboo and metal structure across the road from Pak Chong's night market.

Hotel des Artists ฿฿฿ Serene, tastefully decorated hotel close to the park entrance. There are great mountain views, but rooms are compact.

Ozone Hotel ฿฿฿ This resort is surrounded by nature and is walking distance to the park entrance. Rooms are big and bright and the swimming pool is great.

Khon Kaen Map p321

Baan Hall Hostel ฿ There are no dorms at this friendly place, but the rooms are cheap and clean. There's a downstairs cafe and communal area.

J-Boutique Hotel ฿฿ Sparkling bright rooms with balconies at this Japanese-themed newcomer close to Bueng Kaen Nakhon. Offers free bikes.

Mai Thai Guesthouse ฿฿ Veteran guesthouse with a well-deserved good reputation. It's a little out of the way in the west of town.

Ad Lib Khon Kaen ฿฿฿ Sleek and smart hotel that draws the fashionable crowd with a cool cafe, rooftop restaurant and a nice pool.

Chiang Khan Map p327

With a View Hotel @Chiang Khan ฿฿ Riverside place that's budget by Chiang Khan standards. Small rooms in a traditional wooden house, the best with balconies.

SAMS Chiangkhan ฿฿ A modern building at the eastern end of Walking Street; rooms are big, if functional (some have Mekong views). Rents motorbikes.

River Tree Resort ฿฿฿ Just west of Walking Street, this recently renovated resort has fine rooms overlooking the Mekong, a big pool and decent service.

Chiang Khan River Mountain Resort ฿฿฿ Relatively upmarket hotel providing prime Mekong views in a peaceful setting on the edge of town. Good for families.

Dan Sai

Phupiang Pho Da Arte Resort ฿฿ A Pee Ta Khon festival–themed hotel with charming, colourful rooms and a good cafe.

PhuNaCome Resort ฿฿฿ Massive rooms with balconies and good views in a faded but comfortable setting. It's on the eastern edge of town.

Udon Thani Map p334

Udon Backpackers ฿ Veteran hostel with an industrial-chic design theme, decent dorms and a cool cafe. It was undergoing a refit when we visited.

Pakdee House ฿ Quiet and clean budget option 1.5km south of the city centre. The no-frills rooms come with small balconies and are well maintained.

Pannarai Hotel ฿฿ Sizeable rooms are fraying around the edges, but the location is perfect: close to the Central shopping mall, bus station and bars and restaurants.

VELA Dhi Udon Thani Hotel ฿฿฿ There's a vague 1960s space-age theme at this hushed upmarket choice. Pleasant, modern and large all-white rooms and a pool and gym.

Nong Khai

Mut Mee Garden Guesthouse ฿ Old-school traveller hangout with a variety of rooms set around a leafy garden. Helpful staff and right by the Mekong.

Amanta Hotel ฿฿฿ Slick upmarket choice with large and contemporary rooms. No pool but the rooftop restaurant/bar has fine Mekong views.

Nakhon Phanom

Map p341

Windsor Hotel ฿ It's been around a while, but the functional rooms here come with balconies and it's walking distance to the Mekong and everything you need.

Porpiang Hotel ฿฿ Amiable midranger on a quiet street that's just a short walk from the Mekong. Compact, modern rooms, and bicycles can be hired.

River Hotel ฿฿฿ This is Nakhon Phanom's top choice, although it's inconveniently located 3km south of Walking Street. The mountain and Mekong views are great.

Ubon Ratchathani

Map p348

Phadaeng Hotel ฿ Friendly veteran with large, old-fashioned rooms and lots of quirky art on display. The location is ideal and staff are pleasant.

Outside Inn ฿ Big and plain rooms are set around a pleasant garden at this homely guesthouse. The restaurant serves the best Western food in Ubon.

YUU Hotel & Café ฿฿ Newly renovated in an attractive, if slightly eccentric, style, with decent rooms that have big balconies and a good attached cafe/restaurant.

Centara Ubon Ratchathani ฿฿฿ Ubon's high-end option is on the western side of town; it's convenient for shopping malls but not much else.

Khong Jiam

Baan Kiengtawan ฿฿ Well-kept rooms and villas in a quiet but convenient location. It's walking distance to the river and they can arrange transport to Pha Taem National Park.

Tohsang Heritage Khongjiam ฿฿฿ Super rooms, although not all have been upgraded, at this posh riverside resort with a great pool and splendid vistas.

Yasothon

Big Elephant Hotel ฿ Plain rooms, and there are no pachyderms here, but it's close to the bus station and restaurants.

U-Sabai Villa ฿฿ A bright and clean place that's probably the best midrange option. It's 2km north of the old town.

KITTIPONG CHARAROJ/SHUTTERSTOCK

Centara Korat, Korat City

For places to stay in Ko Chang and the eastern seaboard, see p408

RUSLAN KERIMOV/SHUTTERSTOCK

Above: Ko Chang (p364); Right: Underwater World Pattaya (p403)

Researched by Austin Bush

Ko Chang & the Eastern Seaboard

BEAUTIFUL BEACHES AND NATURE NEAR BANGKOK

While the southern region of Thailand is most popular for a beach vacation, the eastern sea coast also has some sandy corners for you to explore.

If you're visiting Thailand for only a short time and don't have the time to fly down south but still feel like a beach getaway, the Gulf of Thailand has got you covered. The region is particularly popular with Thai travellers since it's within driving distance of Bangkok, so it's easy for families to pop over to Ko Chang for a quick beach vacation, or for a big group of friends to cross over to Ko Samet for a weekend of partying before going back to work on Monday.

But convenience isn't the only draw. Those with more time could spend weeks hopping between Ko Chang, Ko Kut, Ko Mak and the uninhabited islands that form the archipelago. The eastern seaboard is also replete with little-visited, often stuck-in-time towns and villages that warrant overnight stays, as well as wetlands and mangrove forests that can be explored in the form of day trips. This corner of Thailand is also an underrated food destination, home to some of the country's highest-quality fruit and seafood, and in Chanthaburi and Trat provinces, a distinct and delicious regional cuisine – all factors that may compel you to postpone that trip down south.

Simply put, the eastern region is perfect to explore if you're after an easy, but also low-key, unflashy and less-explored Thailand destination.

PANWASIN SEEMALA/SHUTTERSTOCK

THE MAIN AREAS

KO CHANG & TRAT PROVINCE
Home to Ko Chang but also so much more. p364

CHANTHABURI PROVINCE
Ancient neighbourhoods and delicious fruit. p378

RAYONG PROVINCE
Ko Samet or mainland fun. p390

CHONBURI PROVINCE
More to offer than just Pattaya. p397

Chonburi Province, p397
Only an hour's drive from Bangkok and you're right on the beach. If your time is limited and you need a quick beach getaway, make it this one.

Rayong Province, p390
Ko Samet draws everyone here, but don't just stop there – the mainland offers both fresh fruit and fun day trips.

Find Your Way

Ideally, it'd be best to have a car to travel around in this part of Thailand but going car-free isn't the end of the world. There are plenty of car- or bike-rental shops and public transport at these destinations.

Chanthaburi Province, p378

Don't make beaches your top priority in this coastal destination – go there for gem markets, fruit and delicious eastern cuisine.

Ko Chang & Trat Province, p364

The third-largest island in Thailand offers both jungle life and civilisation in one easy-to-access package.

TRAIN

Unfortunately, the State Railway of Thailand doesn't head to the heart of this region, connecting Bangkok only with Chachoengsao and Sa Kaew, two destinations tangentially linked to the eastern seaboard.

BUS & VAN

Bangkok's Ekkamai Bus Terminal is the city's main terminal for public transportation to/from the eastern seaboard, and offers a variety of minivans or buses heading in this direction.

AIR

The region's main airport is in Trat, which operates flights to/from Bangkok. There's also U-Tapao Rayong–Pattaya International Airport – but located less than two hours from Suvarnabhumi International Airport and largely operating international flights, it's not much help for domestic travel.

Plan Your Time

The good thing about this part of Thailand is that there are destinations for however much time you have, from a one-meal beach getaway to a weeklong island-hopping trip.

DELTAOFF/SHUTTERSTOCK

Hat Bang Bao (p373), Ko Kut

If You Have Only One Day

- With only one day to spend, spend it in **Bang Saen** (p400). It may not be the sexiest beach in Thailand but it's the closest to the capital, and a charming throwback to the type of beach getaways that used to be standard among Thais. In recent years, Bang Saen has been creeping in an upscale direction, and now there's a handful of cool restaurants and cafes along its 2.5km-long sandy beach. As such, it makes a perfect lunch or dinner getaway out of Bangkok – and you can jump on one of those banana-boat rides, too.

SEASONAL HIGHLIGHTS

Fruit season coincides with low (monsoon) season, when most places close. The eastern region has activities at different times.

JANUARY & FEBRUARY

It's still high season, but compared to Christmas it's better timing to avoid big crowds.

MARCH

The temperature starts to rise. It's a summer holiday for Thai schools so you may see a lot of families.

APRIL

This is the hottest month in Thailand, but it comes with the biggest water-fight festival, **Songkran Festival** (p35).

A Weekend Road Trip

- If you have a couple of nights, hire some wheels and head to **Chanthaburi Province** (p378). It's a four-hour drive from Bangkok, but you'll be rewarded with some of Thailand's best fruit and seafood, a provincial capital with heaps of charm, mangrove forests, and beautiful and little-visited beaches in the Gulf of Thailand, none of which require a flight or ferry transfer.

- And if you've set your sights even further, Chanthaburi is the natural gateway to **Sa Kaew Province** (p388), where you can visit one of the region's biggest markets, the Khmer-era ruins at Prasat Sdok Kok Thom, or even cross the border to Cambodia in a long weekend.

A Week of Island Living

- If you have a week and are serious about beaches, make it to these three islands – Ko Chang, Ko Kut and Ko Mak – in Trat Province.

- We recommend you start at **Ko Kut** (p372), take in all the nature and spend three days walking around barefoot, before moving to the even smaller island, **Ko Mak** (p374). Spend another three days on Ko Mak and really give your body that break it needs, before moving on to **Ko Chang** (p364) for some civilisation. Here you can readjust to people and 7-Elevens again on your last night before heading back to Bangkok.

MAY & JUNE
Some days are rainy, some are just bright and hot. Beaches are doable but people are starting to pack up to leave.

JULY & AUGUST
Avoid the islands if possible. Head over to Chanthaburi or Rayong for their fruit season instead.

SEPTEMBER & OCTOBER
Rain dies down and humidity starts dropping; people start to travel again.

NOVEMBER & DECEMBER
Thailand has the most tourists flying in, so wherever you go, you'll run into a crowd.

Ko Chang & Trat Province

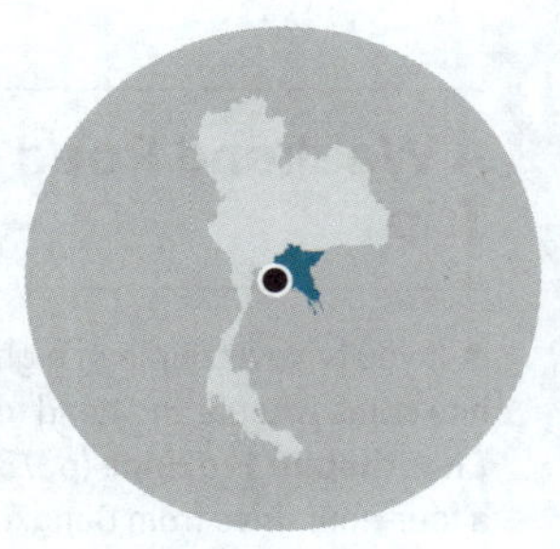

ISLANDS | SEAFOOD | DIVING

GETTING AROUND

Trat is home to the region's only airport, with flights to/from Bangkok.

Bangkok's Ekkamai Bus Terminal (the city's main terminal for public transportation to/from Thailand's eastern region) has frequent buses and minivans to various points in Trat.

The main ferry terminals in Trat are in Ao Thammachat and Laem Sok; numerous buses and minivans from Ekkamai Bus Terminal will take you directly to these piers (there are also direct buses to/from Suvarnabhumi International Airport). Otherwise, within Trat Province, public transportation isn't great and you'll probably need to hire a car or motorcycle to get to some of the more remote destinations.

Trat is in the easternmost part of Thailand, on the border with Cambodia, and is probably best known as the place to catch a ferry to Ko Chang, Ko Mak or Ko Kut. However, Trat has more to offer than just a pier. The provincial capital, also called Trat, has a rich cultural heritage and an underappreciated old-world charm. And the greater province is where you'll find villages that are home to diverse ethnic communities, an extensive coastline, mangrove forests, 'landless' floating villages and, yes, let's not forget those amazing islands. Ko Chang is the third-largest island in Thailand, with a variety of vibes, activities and crowds. Sweet little Ko Mak measures just 16 sq km and doesn't have any speeding traffic, wall-to-wall development, noisy beer bars or crowded beaches. And Ko Kut, also widely called Ko Kood, is often feted as the perfect Thai island.

Party Time

MAP P366

Bar-hopping on Ko Chang's west coast

If you arrive at Ko Chang's pier and turn right, you'll be faced with hotels, 7-Elevens across the road from each other (or next to each other) and many more restaurants than your stomach could handle in your entire trip. This, for better or worse, is Ko Chang's buzzy west coast, and it's worth a stay – or at least a visit – especially if you're looking for some action.

The last thing you'll be at **Lonely Beach** is companionless, as this is Ko Chang's backpacker enclave and the liveliest place to be after dark – until at least 3am. Here, vodka buckets are passed around and the speakers get turned up at the area's legendary bars such as **Himmel Bar** and **Ting Tong**. The beach has pebbles at the southern end and towards Bailan Bay but there's a decent sandy strip to the north. Its original, long-forgotten name is Hat Tha Nam.

AVTK/SHUTTERSTOCK

Lonely Beach

GETTING TO KO CHANG

The airport in Trat has daily flights to/from Bangkok. The main ferry crossing to Ko Chang is called Ao Thammachat, and is at Laem Ngop, in Trat Province, approximately a six-hour bus ride from Bangkok's Ekkamai Bus Terminal (there are also direct buses to/from Suvarnabhumi International Airport). Ferries, which depart approximately every 30 minutes from 6.30am to 6.30pm, take 30 minutes and can accommodate cars and buses.

Active Family Time

MAP P366

Hit the beach – with the kids

Ko Chang's west coast is also a clever option for families, offering both approachable beach areas and kid-friendly active pursuits.

Hat Kaibae is a lively beach zone, but not in a way that will deter families and couples. A slim strip of sand unfurls around an island-dotted bay that's removed from the worst of the package-tourist scene but still has plenty of bars and restaurants along the main road. There is kayaking to the outlying island of Ko Man Nai and low tide provides hours of beachcombing.

A brief spin north, **Ao Khlong Prao** is a pretty sweep of sand pinned between hulking mountainous headlands and bisected by two estuaries. A highlight is the canal lined with stilt shophouses and some of the island's better restaurants and guesthouses. At low tide, beachcombers stroll the rippled sand eyeing the critters left naked by the receding water. Sprawling luxury resorts dominate here and the primary pastime is sunbathing by the pool, as high tide gobbles up much of the beach. Alternatively, **SUP Station Koh Chang** *(facebook.com/supstationkohchang)*, based here, hires stand-up paddleboards for 500฿ for one hour or 800฿ for two hours.

TOP TIP

If you do have your own wheels, the ferry at Ao Thammachat can accommodate vehicles, making it easier to get around Ko Chang.

EATING ON KO CHANG: LOCAL EATS

MAP P366

Zong Zi Pad Pad: Upscale-feeling place near Ao Khlong Prao that serves, almost exclusively, cuisine from Trat Province. *11am-8pm Fri-Wed* ฿฿

Ban Ta Klua: A short menu at this charming, canal-side restaurant at Ao Khlong Prao spans dishes specific to Thailand's eastern region. *11am-10pm* ฿฿

Jae Eaw: Cheerful, brightly lit, Thai-style seafood place near Ao Khlong Prao. *10am-10pm* ฿฿

J Mam Seafood: Also near Ao Khlong Prao, one side here is a seafood retailer, another is a restaurant. The seafood is fresh from the retailer. *10am-9pm* ฿฿

KO CHANG
42
Hat Chang Noi Peninsula
Ao Sapparot
Ao Khlong Son
39
Suan Luang (Thai Navy)
Sai Thong
Ban Khlong Son
20
Tha Dan Kao
Ban Dan Mai
Khao Chom Prasart
5
Ban Than Mayom
11
Khlong Mayom
22
Laem Chaichet
See Ban Khlong Prao
Khlong Prao
10
Ban Khlong Phrao
Ao Khlong Prao
Ko Chang
Ao Nam Khun
Ao Salak Kok
13
32
2
Ban Salak Kok
24
Khao Salak Phet
GULF OF THAILAND
9
8
40
Ban Salak Phet
30
12
4
Ao Salak Phet
Ban Bailan
27
Ko Maphrao Nai
Ban Jekbae
Ruang Tan
Ban Bang Bao
3
7
16
Ao Bang Bao
Ko Maphrao Nok
29
Laem Bang Bao
Ko Lao Ya Nai
0
5 km
0
2.5 miles
Ko Khlum

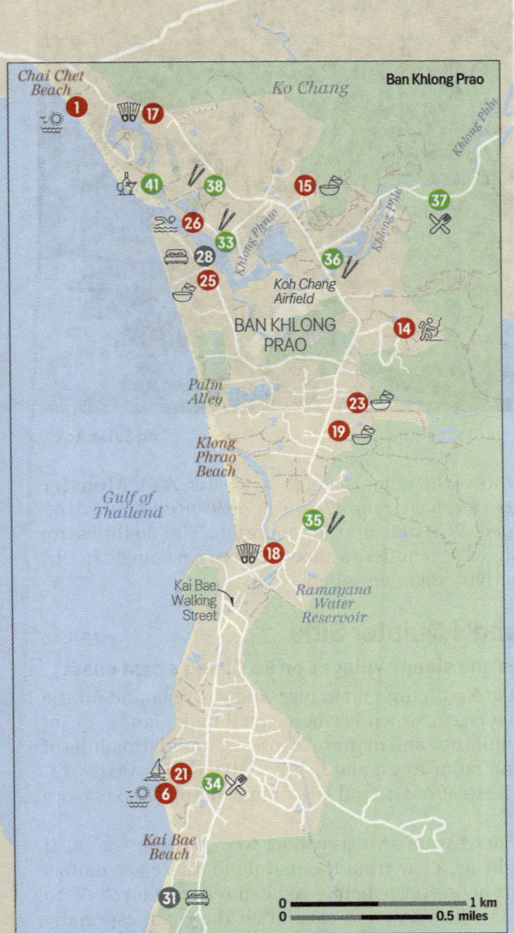

SIGHTS
1 Ao Khlong Prao
2 Ao Salak Kok
3 Ban Bang Bao
4 Ban Salak Phet
5 Durian Plantation Je Na Ko Chang
6 Hat Kaibae
7 Hat Khlong Kloi
8 Lonely Beach
9 Nam Tok Khiri Phet
10 Nam Tok Khlong Plu
11 Nam Tok Than Mayom
12 Red Bridge
13 Salak Khok Mangrove Forest

ACTIVITIES
14 ATV Monster Adventure
15 Ban Suan Thai Cooking Class
16 BB Divers
17 Chang Diving
18 Dolphin Divers
19 Kati Culinary
20 Koh Chang Animal Project
21 N. Kai Bae Speed Boat
22 Nam Thai Cooking School
23 Napalai Thai Cuisine School
24 Salak Khok Boat Tour
25 Santhiya Tree Koh Chang Resort
see 7 SUP Adventure Asia Paddle Boarding
26 SUP Station Koh Chang
see 3 Thai Ocean Academy
27 Tree Top Adventure Park

SLEEPING
28 Baan Rim Nam
29 Bhuvarin Resort
30 Mangrove Hideaway
31 Sea Escape Ko Chang
32 Spa Koh Chang Resort

EATING
33 Ban Ta Klua
34 El Barrio
35 J Mam Seafood
36 Jae Eaw
37 Metzgerei Baum
see 18 Sale e Pepe
38 Zong Zi Pad Pad

DRINKING & NIGHTLIFE
see 40 Himmel Bar
39 Shambhala
40 Ting Tong
41 Vanilla Sky

TRANSPORT
42 Ao Thammachat Ferry Pier

THAI COOKING CLASSES ON KO CHANG

Kati Culinary: Recommended hands-on cooking classes complete with recipe books.
Napalai Thai Cuisine School: The morning class is separated into seven categories: soup, stir-fry, salad, curry paste, curry, appetiser and dessert.
Nam Thai Cooking School: Classes take from four hours minimum duration, and you'll make around six dishes per course. Healthy recipe courses also available.
Ban Suan Thai Cooking Class: This outfit lets you choose your own three dishes and one curry out of 27 dishes. Classes last about three hours. *bansuancooking.com*
Santhiya Tree Koh Chang Resort: This resort offers a cooking class that spans four dishes every Tuesday, Thursday and Saturday. *santhiya.com*

SURAPONG BUACHAROEN/SHUTTERSTOCK

Ao Salak Kok

And for those who've had enough salt water, **ATV Monster Adventure** *(facebook.com/ATVmosteradventurebynara)* offers a guided ATV tour up the mountain. The facilities are safe and aimed at families to allow them to participate in this extreme activity together, safely.

The Island's Quieter Side

MAP P366

Mangroves and sleepy villages on Ko Chang's east coast

Take a left at Ko Chang's main pier, and you're bound for the island's east coast, which is where you'll find a landscape of rural communities and mangrove forests, undulating hills of coconut and palm trees, and fishing villages. It's vastly different to the west coast, and is a wonderful place to explore for a half-day.

You will need your own transport to explore this area. If you didn't bring a car from the mainland, there are motorbike rental shops everywhere – you can rent one for 200฿ to 300฿ per day. Be very, very careful on the road, especially after it has been raining. There are no barriers to stop you from going over the cliff on most parts, and the roads here are very hilly and winding.

The dense tangle of **Salak Khok Mangrove Forest** at **Ao Salak Kok** is protected by a group of fisherfolk who recognise its ecological importance. Mangroves are the ocean's nurseries, fostering the next generation of marine species, as well as resident birds and crustaceans, and this bay is now Ko Chang's prime ecotourism site. Villagers operate an award-winning programme to preserve the environment and traditional way of life. **Salak Khok Boat Tour** *(087 748 9497)* offers a wooden-boat tour year-round. For 800฿, the boat (powered by human energy; can take up to four people) will take you around the bay for 40 minutes to see the mangrove forest, but not out to sea. It's open daily 8am to 4pm, but call first to see if the weather and water conditions are good enough to go out.

Further south, **Ban Salak Phet** is a sleepy community full of stilt houses and fishing boats, a charming Buddhist temple and yawning dogs who stretch out on the roadside. Follow signs to the **Red Bridge**, a 520m-long elevated walkway that spans a mangrove forest before culminating in a panoramic view of Salak Phet Bay.

'TIS THE SEASON

Be aware that many of the attractions on Ko Chang are seasonal, sometimes only running during the high season, from approximately October to February. If you visit outside of these months, you can expect fewer visitors, but don't expect all businesses (including restaurants) to be operating. Even the ferries between Ko Chang, Ko Mak and Ko Kut have reduced schedules during the low season, crossing only a handful of times per day. You've been warned.

Family-Friendly Beach Fun

MAP P366

An active, wholesome stay on Ko Chang's south

Ko Chang's far-southern end offers some quiet, low-key attractions for a family looking for a base or a day trip.

Located at the island's far-southern tip, **Hat Khlong Kloi** is a narrow sandy beach away from the package-tour scene. Though on the tourist map, it still has a hidden-away feel. There are all the requisite amenities (beer, food, fruit, massage) and a few guesthouses. **SUP Adventure Asia Paddle Boarding**, located on the beach, offers both rental and courses for stand-up paddleboarding – a great excuse to head down if you're not already staying here. Not far away, **Tree Top Adventure Park** *(treetopadventurepark.com; from 700฿)*, offers an ecofriendly jungle adventure course with zipline circuits for children to play in and tire themselves out for the day. It's only open during the high season, from October to February.

Nearby, at the former fishing community of **Ban Bang Bao**, built in the traditional fashion of interconnected piers, the villagers have handed in their nets to instead rent out portions of their homes to souvenir shops and restaurants. The long pier is great for a wander, a shopping excursion or a meal. It's also the jumping-off point for boats to Ko Mak and Ko Kut.

Critter Care

Help abandoned animals while on Ko Chang

At the nonprofit centre **Koh Chang Animal Project** *(kohchang animalproject.org ; 089 042 2347)*, abused, injured or abandoned animals receive medical care and refuge. It also provides general veterinarian services and spaying and neutering. Volunteers and donations are welcome. Travelling vets and vet nurses often drop by, while non-vets help with numerous odd jobs. It's best to call ahead. Most *sorng taa ou* (passenger pick-up truck) drivers know how to get here;

EATING ON KO CHANG: FOREIGN CUISINE & FRUIT

MAP P366

Sale e Pepe: Near Ao Khlong Prao, this place does the best pizzas on the island. *noon-10pm Thu-Tue* ฿฿

El Barrio: Tired of Thai? Consider the only place on Ko Chang serving authentic Mexican food. Located near Hat Kai Ba. Closed in monsoon season. *5-10pm* ฿฿

Metzgerei Baum: On the road that leads to Nam Tok Khlong Plu is this German restaurant. Weisswurst and other sausages are made in-house. *11am-5pm Tue-Sat* ฿

Durian Plantation Je Na Ko Chang: Grab durian right from the farm. Call and check in advance that the fruit is in season during your visit: 082 448 7386. ฿฿

NATIONAL PARK FEES

Mu Koh Chang National Park is a land and marine national park that covers the entire archipelago and protects much of the inland part of Ko Chang as well. Conservation efforts are a bit haphazard, but you will be required to pay the national park entrance fee (usually 200฿) when visiting the island's more famous waterfalls. Keep your ticket, as admission at one waterfall allows same-day entry to others on the island. If you arrived via car or motorcycle, at some places you'll also be asked to pay a parking fee in addition to the national park entrance fee.

TUTAE/SHUTTERSTOCK

Nam Tok Khlong Plu

tell them you are going to 'Ban Lisa' (Lisa's House), east of Khlong Son.

Splash Zone

MAP P366

Chasing waterfalls in Ko Chang's interior

If it's nature you came for, you're in luck. Ko Chang is home to three visit-worthy waterfalls, each of which is a great place to spend a half-day walking, lazing riverside and swimming. In general, the waterfalls are at their most impressive during the rainy season (from approximately May to October), but high water and slippery rocks can also make them more difficult to approach. You'll need your own wheels (or will need to charter a *sorng taa ou*) to visit them.

Nam Tok Than Mayom *(200฿)* is a series of three waterfalls along the stream of Khlong Mayom. At press time, the bridge that crosses the stream was being renovated, which meant that reaching the topmost waterfall involved crossing a stream via clinging to a rope, perhaps an obstacle for some visitors. The view from the top is superb and nearby there are inscribed stones bearing the initials of Rama V, Rama VI and Rama VII.

DRINKING ON KO CHANG: OUR PICKS

MAP P366

Shambhala: Perched at the northern end of the island, this poolside bar has a magnificent outlook across a green lawn to a secluded golden sweep of beach. *noon-9.30pm*

Vanilla Sky: Delightfully scruffy beach bar at Ao Khlong Prao. There are more sophisticated places nearby, if that's what you're looking for. *11am-8pm*

Himmel Bar (p364): This is Lonely Beach's most legendary bar; come for cocktails, themed parties, a light show and DJ sets. *7pm-5am*

Ting Tong (p364): Things can get raucous at this longstanding backpacker bar on Lonely Beach that, in theory at least, is open 24 hours. *5pm-4am*

The island's biggest and most impressive waterfall, **Nam Tok Khlong Plu** *(200฿)*, is a three-tiered cascade with a pool where you can swim. It's easily accessible from Khlong Prao: head 1.5km off the main road, pay the park entrance fee, then head on up a 600m jungle path.

Nam Tok Khiri Phet is a small waterfall, 2km from Ban Salak Phet. It's a slightly challenging 15-minute walk from the road and rewards you with a small, deep plunge pool. It is usually less crowded than many of the larger falls and is easily reached if you are in the neighbourhood of Ao Salak Phet.

Blow Some Bubbles

MAP P366

Learn to dive on Ko Chang

Ko Chang may not be as popular as Ko Tao when it comes to diving, but it's a good place to start for beginners, or those intrigued by this underwater activity. The ocean does get quite rough out on the Gulf of Thailand during monsoon season so try to plan your diving trip for the high season only.

Based at Bang Bao, **BB Divers** *(bbdivers.com)* is a well-run diving school and tour operation with branches in Hat Sai Khao and a dive centre on the island's south tip, as well as an outpost on Ko Kut. It offers both scuba diving and freediving lessons (high season only).

Chang Diving *(changdiving.com)* is a professional diving set-up at Ban Khlong Prao offering a good range of excursions and courses. A PADI beginner's scuba-diving course starts at 14,490฿ per person.

With over 18 years of experience, **Dolphin Divers** *(scubadivingkohchang.com)* is based out of Hat Khlong Prao. The discovery course for scuba diving starts at 11,000฿. A day-trip tour that includes two dives starts at 3500฿.

At **Thai Ocean Academy** *(thaioceanacademy.com)*, based out of Bang Bao, a four-day beginner course for RAID scuba diving starts at 14,900฿, and a three-day advanced course starts at 18,500฿.

A must-see dive spot in this region is the sunken **HTMS Chang** – the largest shipwreck in Thailand. Experienced wreck divers can explore cargo holds at depths of 27m to 29m.

Desert Island Fantasy

MAP P366

Explore uninhabited islands near Ko Chang

Just off Ko Chang's west coast are a handful of small islets that make an excellent half- or full-day snorkelling and swimming trip. These can be accessed via group-tour excursions or you can charter a boat with an outfit such as **N. Kai Bae Speed Boat** *(081 982 9870)*. A full-day tour of these islands costs 12,000฿. For this price, you'll leave the shore at 9am and be back at 4pm. Lunch and snacks are all included on board. A half-day (1pm to 4pm) is 6000฿. Group-tour boats only operate during the high season, so if you ever find yourself on Ko Chang during monsoon season and want to do an ocean tour, a private boat is your only option.

I AM KOH CHANG

This website *(iamkochang.com)* is hands down the best source of information on Ko Chang. The site was created by the British-Thai owners of Baan Rim Nam (p408), a guesthouse operating on Ao Khlong Prao since the early 2000s, and spans everything from beach primers to restaurant recommendations. It's also an excellent resource for active pursuits on the island, which can range from planning a jungle hike to details on how to visit an abandoned resort in the area, as well as a few suggestions for volunteer opportunities on Ko Chang.

Hat Khlong Chao

TOP EXPERIENCE

Ko Kut

For those seeking untouched nature and an escape from everyday life (your phone won't even have reception in most parts), Ko Kut is your answer. On top of powder-white beaches, you can trek through lush tropical jungles filled with butterflies on your way to a waterfall, or stay in one of Thailand's most luxurious resorts.

DON'T MISS

- Hat Bang Bao
- Ban Ao Yai
- Nam Tok Khlong Chao
- Hat Khlong Chao
- Ao Yai Kee

Beautiful Beaches

White-sand beaches with gorgeous aquamarine waters lie along the western and southern sides of Ko Kut, some occupied by a single resort but accessible to all.

In the island's far north is **Ao Yai Kee**, a bay with a beach stretching approximately 500m. The beach area has beautiful white sand and coconut trees as a backdrop.

Hat Khlong Chao is one of the most popular, must-visit beaches on Ko Kut. Despite being popular, it's still very peaceful and comes with a sandy beach and clear turquoise water, nestled amid coconut trees.

PRACTICALITIES

● departure point for ferries: Laem Sok ● one-way boat tickets from 600฿ ● low season: early June to late September

Our fave beach on the island is the semi-concealed **Hat Bang Bao**, a graceful bay ringed by rocks and palm trees, with several photogenic piers.

Hat Khlong Hin, in the island's south, takes the form of a small cove with a shallow but fine-sand beach and a border of rocks. It's reached by a bumpy dirt path, which means it sees fewer visitors.

And **Ao Phrao** is considered the last bay of the island and has its longest beach. It also has a lot of shade and it's a good spot for water activities along the entire bay.

Floating Villages

On the far-eastern side of the island, **Ban Ao Yai** is the island's largest stilt fishing village; the houses are arranged in the sea, with elevated platforms connecting them. It's worth a visit for the view and to have lunch at one of the seafood restaurants, such as **Noochy Seafood**.

Ban Ao Salad, the island's main ferry pier, used to be a notorious hideout for pirates who raided the surrounding waters. Nowadays, it's an elevated fishing community where you'll find shrimp, clams, crabs and fish for purchase.

Ao Phrao is also home to a tiny floating village, where you'll encounter locals going about their daily routines.

Waterfalls

Nam Tok Khlong Chao is a medium-sized waterfall where the water flows down a 10m-high rocky cliff into a wide and deep pool. You can take a dip in the pool to cool down after trekking through the tropical jungle, with butterflies to keep you company. During the rainy season, when the water level is high, reaching the falls is done by gripping ropes on slippery rocks, an excursion that may not be appropriate for everybody.

Nam Tok Khlong Yai Kee is a secluded waterfall nestled amid trees and rocks, a short walk from the parking area. It's a refreshing spot for swimming, with a picturesque pool beneath the falls with harmless small fish that nibble the skin off your feet.

Diving & Snorkelling

Diving is possible in the waters just off Ko Kut. During the monsoon season, from approximately May to October, operators focus on the island's eastern shore, while during the rest of the year diving is done on the opposite side. Some outfits offer excursions to Koh Rang Marine Park, a protected area where more fish and sealife can be spotted. Operators on Ko Kut include **BB Divers** *(bbdivers.com)*, **Koh Kood Divers** *(kohkooddivers.com)* and **Paradise Divers** *(kohkood-paradisedivers.com)*.

CONTESTED TERRITORY

At 25km long and 12km wide, Ko Kut (also known as Ko Kood) is Thailand's fourth-largest island. It's also Thailand's easternmost island, and in recent years Cambodia has laid claims to the island, citing a 1907 treaty between Siam and France.

TOP TIPS

- Visit during monsoon season to feel like the only person on the island, perfect for some quiet time. But be aware that many businesses close.
- Scooters for rent are easy to find and the best way to get around. They cost around 300฿ for 24 hours.
- *Sorng taa ou* are another way to get around, though make sure you hold onto the rail tight.
- Your ferry ticket typically includes resort pickup.

GETTING AROUND ON KO CHANG

Ko Chang is accessed by ferries that can carry vehicles, so most Bangkokians prefer to just take their own car across to the island. There are plenty of motorbike- or car-rental shops on the island, if you have decided not to drive there.

When you get off the ferry at the pier, there will be *sorng taa ou* waiting to pick you up and drop you off at the hotel. Prices depend on how many passengers there are and how far you're going, but you can expect to pay around 60฿ to 200฿.

FOKKE BAARSSEN/SHUTTERSTOCK

Cinnamon Scenic Boardwalk

Dock Destination

MAP P377

Tread Ko Mak's unique piers

On **Ko Mak**, piers are more than for just docking boats. **Cinnamon Scenic Boardwalk** *(50฿)* is a Ko Mak landmark. This wooden bridge extends into the sea and when you walk to the end and turn around, you'll get the full view of Ko Mak. It is about 500m long, making it the longest pier on the island. Along the way, there are platforms extending into the sea where you can lie down, relax and listen to the sound of the waves.

And forget about your typical beach clubs, located on the beach; **Blue Pearl Bar** *(200฿)* is on a pier in the middle of the sea and is abundant with marine life. The crystal-clear water allows you to see all the colourful fish and other sea creatures while you sip a cocktail. This is a popular spot on Ko Mak for watching the sunset. Admission, which is generally only collected during the high season, includes a drink.

EATING & DRINKING ON KO KUT & KO MAK: OUR PICKS

Ko Mak Seafood: With a big overwater deck, Ko Mak Seafood is considered one of the best places in the archipelago for seafood. *10.30am-8.30pm* ฿฿

Ra Beang Mai: Enjoy Thai flavours at this family-run restaurant overlooking one of Ko Kut's canals. Closed outside of high season. *11am-9pm Tue-Thu* ฿฿

Food Art Hut: Ko Mak's cosy go-to for Western-style coffee drinks, smoothies, bowls, baked goods and other similarly light, healthy meals. *8am-9pm* ฿

Hidden Gem by Monkey Bar: On Ko Kut's Hat Bang Bao. A toes-in-the-sand experience overlooking one of the island's handsomest bays. *1-11pm*

Artsy Island

Take in outsider art – or dance – on Ko Mak

Ko Mak's wildest attraction is undoubtedly the **Ko Magic Arts Garden**. This fantastical, sometimes creepy, semi-erotic-leaning assemblage of cement statues in the jungle was created by a former rubber tapper from Myanmar who went by the name Somchai. He lived on site, creating anatomically explicit women and monkeys out of concrete until his death in 2023. On Google Maps, it's listed as The Kingdom of Somchai's Affection; keep your eyes peeled for a tiny roadside sign.

Ko Mak is usually peaceful, offering a perfect chance to just chill by the beach. However (for now), a couple of festivals bring live DJs to the island. **Thaibreak Festival** *(thaibreak.net)* is in summer (March to April) and **Fly to the Moon** *(flytothemoonfestival.com)* is a New Year's Eve music festival.

Abandoned Resorts & Island Deer

MAP P377

Explore the smaller islands near Ko Mak

Ko Mak is probably the most convenient jumping-off point for the archipelago's small islands.

Ko Kham is reached by taking a kayak across from Ao Son Yai; that's the closest point, about 1km away. If you're not up for kayaking, you can hire a boat by contacting any resort in the Ao Son Yai area. Ko Kham's claims to fame are its pristine white-sand beach, waters so clear that you can see to impressive depths, and a creepy abandoned resort.

Ko Kradat is another tiny island close to Ko Mak that you can get to in five minutes by long-tail boat. The main highlight here is the herd of hundreds of deer that inhabit the island, earning it the nickname 'Safari in the Sea'. There's a tractor service to take you around the island to see the deer in their natural habitat.

Not too far from Ko Kradat is another island, accessible by walking across the sea during low tide. Known as **Ko Khai Hua Roh**, this island is home to a single tree, which at press time was allegedly suffering from an excess of social media attention.

The smallest inhabited island in the archipelago is **Ko Wai**. Despite its size, it's endowed with gin-clear waters, excellent coral reefs for snorkelling, and a handsome view across to Ko Chang. If you stay overnight, expect to share the bulk of your afternoons with day-trippers and enjoy the remainder of your time in peace. Note that most accommodation on Ko Wai closes from May to September, when seas are rough, flooding is common, and power is rationed and intermittent (except at the resorts). Outside of this time, and with advance notice, boats that link Ko Chang with Ko Mak and Ko Kut can make a stop at Ko Wai.

GETTING TO KO KUT & KO MAK

Laem Sok, in Trat Province, is the jumping-off point for ferries to Ko Kut and Ko Mak. From Bangkok, buses from Bangkok's Ekkamai Bus Terminal head directly to the pier; or you may need need to get a bus to Trat, then take a minivan or *sorng taa ou* to the pier, around 50km away.

A variety of companies – Koh Kood Express, KohKood Princess, Boonsiri Ferry, Seudamgo – link the smaller islands with the mainland and Ko Chang via speedboats, with more frequent departures during the high season (from October to May).

GETTING TO CAMBODIA FROM THAILAND

Ban Hat Lek/Cham Yeam is a permanent border crossing between Thailand and Cambodia. It's open daily 6am to 10pm. Stock up on US dollars before crossing.

A tourist visa costs around US$30. You may be asked for 1500฿ (about US$45) or US$30 plus a 100฿ to 300฿ fee. Cambodian e-visas are not accepted at this border crossing.

A tuk-tuk to Koh Kong will cost US$5. From Ko Kong, there are minivans to Phnom Penh, Kampot and Sihanoukville. A taxi should cost US$3 per person and a driver will wait until there are four passengers.

Urban Escape

MAP P377

Explore Trat's former market streets

Trat's eponymous provincial capital is often neglected by those heading to the islands. But it's worth an overnight stay, in particular to explore its charming streets on foot.

The **Trat City Museum** *(20฿)* is an old wooden building, built during the reign of King Rama V. Exhibitions are divided into six sections and showcase the province's rich history in all its dimensions from prehistoric times to the present. In particular, there's a focus on Trat's former role as an important place of commerce going back to the late 18th century, elements of which can still be seen today, just a few streets away.

The former **Talat Rim Khlong** ('Canal-Side Market') extends along today's Th Thana Charoen, which runs along the Bang Phra Canal. An elevated path runs beside the canal in parts, and a few old buildings still remain. The parallel street, Th Lak Muang, was formerly known as **Talat Yai** ('Large Market'), and specialised in bulk goods, in particular the province's spices. The street is home to a handful of shophouses that blend Western and Asian styles, as well as **Residence Kampot**, a former French residence. It's at its liveliest on Saturday afternoons, when it hosts a market. At its western end the street terminates at Th Chai Mongkhon, formerly known as **Talat Khwang** ('Cross Market'), once another busy place of commerce.

Three Cultures

MAP P377

Get into local lifestyles at a homestay in Ban Nam Chiao

Ban Nam Chiao is a village in rural Trat Province that's home to three communities: Thai, Chinese and most notably, Muslim. The latter forms the longest-standing Muslim community in the province, and the village's **Algrubar Mosque** is thought to be more than 200 years old. The village straddles both sides of Mae Nam Chiao, and it's home to a Chinese shrine and a Buddhist temple, as well as the so-called 'Bridge to Test Your Willingness' – a high, arched wooden bridge crossing the river that's said to test one's fear of heights.

In recent years, the community has opened its doors to outsiders in the form of a **homestay** *(061 660 0955; 089 244 6702)*. Visitors can stay with one of three different families, and the fee of 1690฿ includes meals and a boat excursion to replant mangrove forests and witness the local craft of weaving traditional hats.

EATING IN TRAT PROVINCE: OUR PICKS

MAP P377

Pu Noodle Shop Sukhumwit: This Trat restaurant is known for noodle soup loaded with different types of seafood, like fat mantis shrimp. *8am-3pm* ฿

Kiew Nong Bua: Longstanding destination in 'downtown' Trat for Chinese-style noodle dishes; don't miss the eponymous wontons. *6am-9pm* ฿

Khanom Thai Pa Nom: A respected vendor of Thai-style sweets – including some region-specific options – in Trat. *10am-5pm* ฿

Cherry-Anne Seafood Restaurant: Recommended seafood shack at the edge of the sea in rural Trat, where crab and mantis shrimp are menu headliners. *10am-8pm* ฿฿

Architecture Expedition

MAP P377

Visit a classic Bangkok-style temple in Trat

The oldest Buddhist temple in the region, **Wat Bupharam** makes for a worthwhile side trip from Trat. It was built around 1652, although most of the structures that can be seen today likely date from the 18th century. Although it's located more than 300km from the country's capital, it's considered a fine example of Bangkok-style architecture. The ordination hall, which holds a reclining Buddha statue, is fronted with bits of Chinese porcelain, a technique used on a larger scale at Bangkok's Wat Pho and Wat Arun. The interiors of the other structures are home to rustic wall paintings with Chinese influences, and even the monks' quarters are from the early Bangkok era. There's a museum, but you'll have to ask someone to open it for you. It's located 3km west of Trat.

SIGHTS
1 Ban Nam Chiao
2 Trat City Museum
3 Wat Bupharam

SLEEPING
4 Ban Nam Chiao Homestay

EATING
5 Cherry-Anne Seafood Restaurant
6 Khanom Thai Pa Nom
7 Kiew Nong Bua
8 Pu Noodle Shop Sukhumwit

TRANSPORT
9 Ao Thammachat Ferry Pier
10 Laem Sok Ferry Pier
11 Trat Airport

TRAT'S MUSLIMS

Trat Province is home to a small but visible Muslim community. Known colloquially in Thai as Khaek Jaam (or Chams, in English), they belong to an Austronesian ethnic group who are thought to be some of the first inhabitants of coastal Cambodia and Vietnam. The Chams adopted Islam around the 11th century, and in the 18th and 19th centuries they fled from current-day Vietnam and Cambodia to Thailand to escape war. Today, their ancestors can still be found in Ban Nam Chiao, in Trat, which is home to two mosques, and Ban Yai Mom, a coastal village south of Trat's provincial capital.

Chanthaburi Province

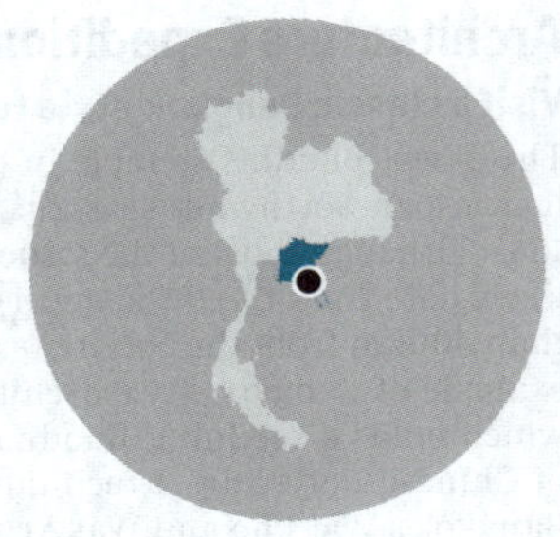

FRUIT | HISTORY | FLOATING VILLAGES

GETTING AROUND

From Bangkok, there are relatively frequent buses and minivans connecting Ekkamai Bus Terminal and various points in Chanthaburi Province. The nearest airport is in Trat.

As Chanthaburi Province isn't quite on the main tourism trail, public transport is lacking. If you plan to do a lot of exploring, a hired car or motorcycle is obligatory.

The centre of the provincial capital, also called Chanthaburi, is small enough to navigate on foot.

TOP TIP

If you're new to Thai fruit, you can visit one of Chanthaburi's many fruit farms (p381) where they let you try all the types of fruit available and pay as you go. This way you can taste everything at once and decide on your favourites.

Chanthaburi Province may not be a popular or a well-known destination but it definitely has a lot to offer. Most Thais would know the provincial capital of the same name as Thailand's gem city – gem trading is a big deal here, and the surrounding countryside was once home to many mines. Today, those same soils provide Thailand with some of the country's highest-quality fruit, from the infamously pungent durian, to rambutan, mangosteen and many more. Chanthaburi Province is also home to a unique, delicious, herb-forward cuisine as well as some little-visited and beautiful beaches. Yet unlike its more popular neighbour, Rayong, Chanthaburi has a more provincial, laid-back vibe. While there aren't many tourists around yet, they're not a rare sight either – and since Chanthaburi hasn't been overtaken by mass tourism, you'll find the locals are extra friendly and welcoming.

A Shiny, Sparkling Visit

MAP P379 & p380

Engage with Chanthaburi's legacy of gemstones

For generations, Chanthaburi has been the epicentre of Thailand's gem business. Locals will tell you that gems are not as easy to find on the ground nowadays but Chanthaburi remains the gem city: the skills still remain. Families still import gems from overseas, put them through various processes until they become shiny jewellery, and trade or sell them.

The futuristic-looking **Chanthaburi Gem & Jewellery Centre** should be the first stop you make if you would like to learn more about the city's legacy of gemstones. It's free to visit and opens daily from 9am to 5pm. On the 2nd floor, there's a museum dedicated to everything you need to know about the gem industry of Chanthaburi, from all the various different gem types and processes from mining to heating up the raw stones to turn them into shiny gems, to shaping them up. Once you've walked through the museum and learned about

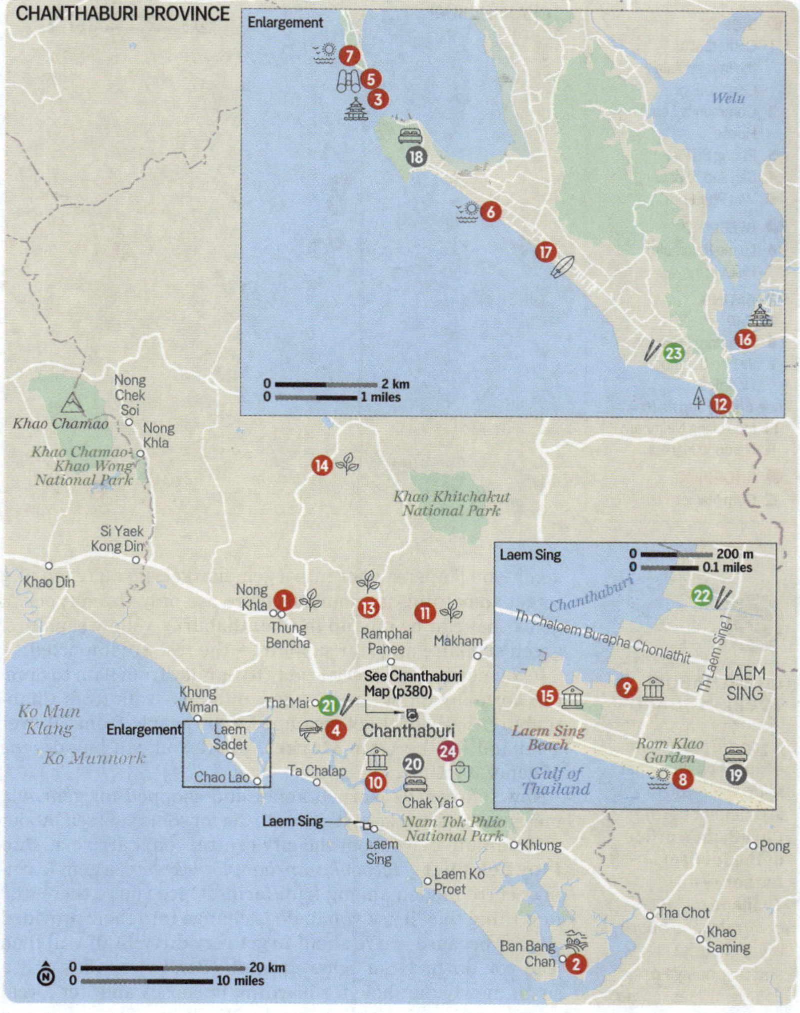

SIGHTS
1 Baan Suan Ratchanat
2 Ban Bang Chan
3 Ban Hua Laem Pagoda
4 Bao Ploy Lek Phet
5 Chedi Klang Nam Viewpoint
6 Hat Chao Lao
7 Hat Khung Wiman
8 Hat Laem Sing
9 Khuk Khi Kai
10 King Taksin the Great Shipyard
11 KP Garden
12 Pink Coast
13 Rinradee Orchard
14 Suan Pho Ruay Organic Orchard
15 Tuek Daeng
16 Wat Pak Nam Khaem Nu

ACTIVITIES
17 Chanthaburi Surf Tribe

SLEEPING
see 2 Ban Bang Chan Homestay
18 El Vaso Resort
19 Laem Sing Natural Beach Resort
20 Tum Baan Suan

EATING
see 20 Khrua Bua Khao
21 Kuaytiaw Muu Liang Phraya Trang
22 Ruean Rim Nam Seafood
23 Yai Tu Seafood

SHOPPING
24 Bean to Bar

SIGHTS
1 Cathedral of the Immaculate Conception
2 Community Learning House
3 Phong Sri Pier
4 San Jao Talat Lang
5 Wat Phai Lom

SLEEPING
6 Luang Rajamaitri Historic Inn

EATING
7 CAP
8 Chantorn Pochana
9 Je Eed Seafood Noodles
see 6 Kuay Jap Pa Mai
10 Muu Liang Nirimnam
11 Namphu Market

SHOPPING
12 Gem Market

CHANTHABURI TOURISM BOARD

If you are looking for suggestions for what to do while you're in Chanthaburi, the **Chanthaburi office of the Tourism Authority of Thailand** *(facebook.com/tatchanthaburi)* is very helpful and responsive on Facebook Messenger. You can message them with any questions you have and they will usually respond within a few minutes with some great local recommendations. *(tatchan@tat.or.th; 663 948 0220).*

gems, you'll open a door into a gem market. If you're looking to get something for yourself, there are only three types of gems that can be dug up in Chanthaburi – yellow sapphire, green sapphire and star sapphire – the rest are imported.

If you need more, every Friday to Sunday from 9am to 6pm, the normally quiet streets a few minutes' walk from Chanthaburi's cathedral get swamped with people from all over Thailand for the **Gem Market**, where you can buy dozens of gems at a time.

Now that you've learned about and shopped for gems via museums and markets, it's time to dig for some yourself. About a 30-minute drive from the city centre, you'll arrive at **Bao Ploy Lek Phet** *(facebook.com/baoploylekphet)*, a gem learning centre hidden among fruit farms. Once you're there, the first thing they'll ask you to do is change into their provided clothes because you're about to get very dirty. Staff will then lead you down 4–5m below ground – don't worry, it's only a small, newly dug hole for learning purposes and not a real mine, so it's safe to climb down. You'll be given tools and then you can dig and take some of the soil back up to ground level, before being led to the cleaning area where you'll use the watering hose and your hand to try to find gems in the soil. You pay 500฿ for this workshop and you can take home whatever gems you find. They will also provide you with some snacks, drinks and a souvenir – a gem based on your birthday (for example, if you were born on a Monday, you'll get yellow sapphire). Be sure to arrange your visit in advance.

YUT CHANTHABURI/SHUTTERSTOCK

Gem Market

Sweet Fruity Frenzy

Gorge on fruit in Chanthaburi

Chanthaburi is arguably Thailand's most prolific fruit producer, and if you visit around May, when the annual fruit festival happens, to June, when the season winds down, you're in luck. Indeed, fruit tourism is now a thing in this part of Thailand, and several orchards have opened their doors to tourists, some offering all-you-can-eat fruit buffets for a flat fee, others weighing and selling high-quality fruit.

The most common types of fruit in Chanthaburi include **durian** (p384), a gold mine for the locals; the price for 1kg of the already-peeled fruit goes as high as 1300฿ or even more in some cases. Some people find it unbearable, others can't get enough, and pretty much all hotels across Thailand and the Skytrains in Bangkok have banned people from bringing them in. The smell is something, but the taste is something else. There are also so many different varieties to explore with

HOLY CHANTHABURI

Chanthaburi's location next door to French Indochina resulted in a unique cultural legacy: Catholicism. In 1893 the French took control of Chanthaburi's port, handing it back in 1905 only after Siam relinquished territorial claims in Cambodia. Work on Chanthaburi's Cathedral of the Immaculate Conception (p383), still Thailand's largest Catholic church, was commenced by French missionaries during this window. And from the 19th century all the way to the 1970s, persecution of Catholics in Vietnam led to a constant stream of refugees; today an estimated 1% of Chanthaburi is Catholic, and the province has its own diocese.

EATING IN CHANTHABURI: OUR PICKS

MAP P380

Chantorn Pochana: Charmingly old-school restaurant specialising in Chanthaburi's famously herbaceous, fragrant fare. Also a culinary-leaning souvenir stop. *10am-8pm* ฿

Chui Restaurant: Located south of the city centre is this slightly more upscale, seafood-forward take on local dishes. *11am-10pm* ฿฿

Je Eed Seafood Noodles: The speciality here is noodles that feature all kinds of seafood caught in Chanthaburi, especially mantis shrimp. *9am-4pm* ฿

Muu Liang Nirimnam: Get a bowl of *muu liang*, Chanthaburi's signature noodle soup, at this longstanding place in Chanthaboon Waterfront Community. *9am-2pm Tue-Sun* ฿

CALAMANSI EVERYWHERE

A unique sight in Chanthaburi is people using calamansi, known locally as *som mapiit* or *som jiit*. It looks like a small lime but has an orange-hued interior and a flavour that's just a bit sweeter than that of the typical lime. Instead of orange juice or lemonade, you might see locals squeezing glasses of fresh *som mapiit* juice (it's delicious with soda water and a bit of honey). And because they're tart, it's also common to see calamansi served with dishes for squeezing instead of limes, something you won't normally see anywhere else in Thailand.

different sweetness and texture. Durian is available from approximately May to July.

Once you peel the thick purple skin off a **mangosteen**, you expose the sweet and refreshing, juicy white pieces. Many hotels ban them due to the purple goo that can stain bedclothes. It doesn't stink like durian but you have to watch out for the pips that could slide down your throat. Available from March to June.

The red, hairy **rambutan** is one of the fruits that most Thais grew up eating and will have formed some of their very first memories. It's also served in the form of *loy kaew,* a dessert that consists of the fruit in sugar syrup, topped with crushed ice. Available from May to June.

You may have seen **longan** in neighbouring countries to Thailand or even in Bali, but guaranteed they are nothing like the Chanthaburi longan, which is bigger and crispier. This fruit is super sweet and fragrant and available between July to August.

Compared to other fruits in the eastern region that have made it to the mainstream, you'll find that **longkong** is not as well known although it's just as juicy and sweet. Watch out for the sticky resin from the peels that, even though harmless, might require you to wash your hands with soap a few times afterwards. Available from May to July.

Just like durian or rambutan, on the outside, **sala** doesn't look very appealing at all; some people call it the snake fruit because of the texture of the peel. This is the least sweet fruit in our list, but the slightly sour flavour gives it a unique and refreshing character. Like rambutan, this is a common fruit used to make *loy kaew*. Available from May to November.

If all this appeals, make a point of visiting during May, when the annual **Chanthaburi Fruit Festival** is held. There's a particular emphasis on durian, and events include fruit-carving demonstrations, fruit competitions and a parade with fruit-bedecked floats.

No Land, No Problem

MAP P379

Live the life aquatic at Ban Bang Chan

Ban Bang Chan, in Chanthaburi's southeastern corner, is known as Chanthaburi's Moo Baan Rai Phaen Din, or 'Landless Village'. It's an entire community built on stilts above water, complete with Chinese and Buddhist temples, and a health centre, yet for nearly two centuries it has been totally disconnected from the rest of the province by road. Overnight homestays allow visitors an insight into this unique way of life.

There are 13 different homestays on Ban Bang Chan; do some research to see which is best for you. A typical outfit such as **Ban Bang Chan Homestay** *(banbangchan-homestay.com)* includes boat transportation from Khlung District, meals and excursions for 1600฿ per person. The excursions in this case are ostensibly to witness the area's brahminy kites (p385), but are more raucous than you might expect with floating water slides and pumping music.

EXPLORE CHANTHABURI'S RIVERSIDE COMMUNITY

Alongside the banks of Mae Nam Chanthaburi, Chanthaburi's Chanthaboon Waterfront Community is one of the region's most well-preserved urban areas.

START	END	LENGTH
Luang Rajamaitri Historic Inn	Wat Phai Lom	2km; two hours

1 **Luang Rajamaitri Historic Inn** is a good starting point to explore the city's charming, ancient Chanthaboon Waterfront Community. Like the inn, many of the area's old structures have been turned into cafes, souvenir shops and hotels. Continue south along Th Sukhaphiban and you'll pass notable buildings and Chinese shrines; some of these are linked to signs with QR codes that provide historical and architectural information. At the street's southern end, you'll reach 2 **Community Learning House**, the place to pause and dig into the neighbourhood's history and unique architecture.

Cross the Chanthaburi River and make a stop at the 3 **Cathedral of the Immaculate Conception**, Thailand's largest cathedral. It started as a modest chapel in 1711 and since then has been renovated several times. The upstairs hosts a gallery (don't forget to check the opening times before visiting), and the statue of the Virgin Mary at the front is decorated with more than 200,000 sapphires.

Head south to your last stop, 4 **Wat Phai Lom**. This Buddhist temple is believed to have been built in the early 18th century when Ayuthaya was the capital city of Thailand, as proven by the murals in one of the older buildings. Here, you'll also find the biggest reclining Buddha in Thailand's eastern region at almost 55m long.

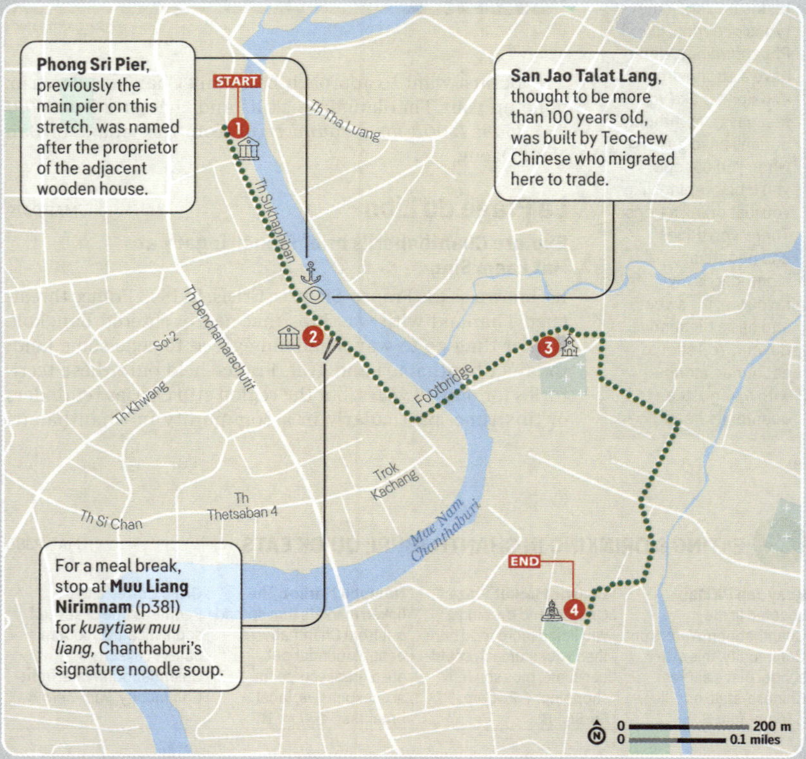

Phong Sri Pier, previously the main pier on this stretch, was named after the proprietor of the adjacent wooden house.

San Jao Talat Lang, thought to be more than 100 years old, was built by Teochew Chinese who migrated here to trade.

For a meal break, stop at **Muu Liang Nirimnam** (p381) for *kuaytiaw muu liang*, Chanthaburi's signature noodle soup.

CHANTHABURI'S DURIAN

Ratchanat (Eed) Kitjagan is the second-generation owner of Baan Suan Ratchanat), a durian farm in rural Chanthaburi.

The durian in Chanthaburi is good because of the soil. It's dry, which makes the flesh dry – durian shouldn't have stringy flesh, it should be smooth, and a durian with dry flesh tastes better. Some types of durian, like Phuangmanee, don't have a strong aroma and don't make you feel gassy. Monthong durians have gas; when you eat one, you'll be burping, like you just drank a Pepsi! There's positives and negatives. Monthong is my favourite; it's sweet and has a distinctive flavour. You should eat durian along with mangosteen to counter its heat!

M3NIZZ/SHUTTERSTOCK

If you just want to approach Ban Bang Chan as a day trip, hone up your Thai language skills and charter a **boat** *(091 655 3668; 1200฿ for a round trip)* from the village of Ban Nam Daeng.

La Plage du Lion

MAP P379

Explore Chanthaburi's brief French legacy at Hat Laem Sing

It's known as the Franco-Siamese Crisis. In 1893 France threatened Thailand with warships that nearly entered Bangkok. Rather than go to war, Thailand agreed to cede some land: today's Chanthaburi and Trat. France held onto these territories for only 10 years, but the region still carries reminders of this time, particularly in a community in Chanthaburi

EATING & DRINKING IN CHANTHABURI: QUICK EATS

MAP P380

Kuay Jap Pa Mai: Located in the Chanthaboon Waterfront Community, this old-school place serves Chinese-style noodles. *7.30am-3pm* ฿

Centric Market Plaza: On weekend evenings, you'll find more food here than your stomach could consume, plus souvenir shopping. *4-9.30pm Fri-Sun* ฿

Namphu Market: The linked markets that spread out from Chanthaburi's central roundabout are a great source for an inexpensive, local breakfast. *4-10am* ฿

CAP: 'Coffee and People' is one of several sophisticated, modern cafes in the city's Chanthaboon Waterfront Community. *9am-6pm* ฿

Hat Laem Sing

Province's far south, an area that makes for a historical half-day excursion, if you have your own wheels.

Today, most locals know **Hat Laem Sing** ('Lion Beach Peninsula') as a strip of sand backed by food stalls and restaurants – it's a handsome beach worth visiting for a swim and a meal. But head inland and you'll encounter **Tuek Daeng** or the 'Red Building', built in 1893 as headquarters for the French incursion. The space was later a nursing home and a library, but today it's empty. A short walk away is **Khuk Khi Kai**, literally 'Chicken Shit Prison'. Built by the French around the same time as a prison for troublesome Thais who objected to their rule, the name comes from the fact that the ceiling was allegedly comprised of chicken pens.

BRAHMINY KITE

The brahminy kite, known in Thai as *insii daeng* ('red eagle') and sometimes in English as the red-backed sea-eagle, has become something of a tourist draw in Chanthaburi and Trat. The handsome bird has rusty brown plumage and a white head and breast, and lives on the coast and in inland wetlands, where it's primarily a scavenger, feeding on dead fish and other animals. You can join excursions to see the brahminy kite in Ban Bang Chan, in Chanthaburi, and Pak Nam Prasae, in Rayong, among many other places.

EATING IN CHANTHABURI PROVINCE: FRUIT FARMS

MAP P379

Baan Suan Ratchanat: This second-generation durian farmer northwest of Chanthaburi hosts visitors from mid-April until the fruit's gone (June). *facebook.com/baansuanratchanat*

Rinradee Orchard: A B&B right in the middle of an orchard with a fruit buffet deal around every June. *rinradee.com*

Suan Pho Ruay Organic Orchard: Established in 1961 and now certified organic, this farm is open to visitors year-round. *facebook.com/richdadfarm*

KP Garden: In addition to fruit, this farm also offers fruit-based snacks – if you're intimidated by durian, the crispy durian chips are a good place to start. *facebook.com/KPgarden*

LOCAL INGREDIENTS

Bai Chamuang: Forget the region's gemstones, this tart leaf with no colloquial English name is a 'gem' for your palate. Famously used in pork curry.

Krawan: Camphor root is a herb commonly grown in this part of Thailand. The aroma reminds us of a Chinese medicine shop (in a good way), and it has a light crunchy texture.

Phrik Thai: Chanthaburi's pepper – used in its fresh green state or dried – is famous across the country.

Kapi: Just like durian, you either hate shrimp paste – actually made from krill – or you love it.

Kang: While shrimp and prawns are consumed regularly everywhere in Thailand, it's rare to see mantis shrimp. In Chanthaburi (and Trat), this sea creature is on the menu just about everywhere.

GOWITHSTOCK/SHUTTERSTOCK

Pink Coast

Hang Ten

MAP P379

Dip into Chanthaburi's burgeoning surf scene

West of Chanthaburi is a wide peninsula that's home to **Hat Chao Lao**, a long, wide beach that also has waves big enough for surfing. The best months to surf in Chanthaburi are from May until October, and the best people to contact are the folks behind **Chanthaburi Surf Tribe** *(facebook.com/chanthaburisurftribe)*. They're working hard to make the scene happen, and even throw an annual surf and skate festival around June. These days they've expanded their operations to include a bar, and they also offer SUP rental and lessons outside of the surf season.

Pink Rocks & Tiled Temples

MAP P379

Explore the Hat Chao Lao peninsula

If surfing's not your thing, the area surrounding Hat Chao Lao has some low-key attractions that are worth exploring for a half-day or via a hired motorcycle or car. At the peninsula's northern tip, seemingly floating in the middle of the sea, you'll see **Ban Hua Laem Pagoda**. Head over to the **Chedi Klang Nam Viewpoint** for a more dramatic perspective of this unique spot. Just north is **Hat Khung Wiman**, a nice narrow beach with a pleasant westerly outlook. The road through the village continues south to various viewpoints on a nearby promontory, then loops round to a fishing village on the bay side; there are good places to snack on simple seafood here.

At the peninsula's southern end is the so-called **Pink Coast** *(400฿)*, a protected area known for its red, pink and brown-red stones. The stones can be seen near the parking lot, or there's a 500m nature trail that spans more viewpoints and an even larger assemblage of coloured rocks.

And just across the water is **Wat Pak Nam Khaem Nu**, a Buddhist temple located by the seaside. Sea breeze and saltwater were damaging the exterior of the temple, so locals decided to coat it with ceramic tiles, following ancient style where two colours are used – in this case, blue and white – making it look unlike any other Buddhist temple in the country.

From Bean to Bar

MAP P379

Savour Chanthaburi's chocolate

Chanthaburi is one of a handful of places in Thailand where cacao is grown. **Bean to Bar** *(beantobarchan.com)*, a small cultivator just outside Chanthaburi, is taking this several steps further and is roasting cacao seeds to produce award-winning chocolate, as well as other cacao-derived products.

The small farm, located 10km southeast of Chanthaburi, is home to around 30 cacao trees, whose fruit and seeds make their way into a variety of items: chocolate chips, cacao nibs, cacao fruit juice, chocolate bars, roasted cacao seeds and more. These, as well as a menu of chocolate drinks, can be purchased at the small cafe. The owner, who goes by Jeena, tells us that Chanthaburi's chocolate is known for its fruity, less bitter flavour profile. If it's available, she can provide a taste of fresh cacao fruit; with advance notice, she can also organise private courses in cacao cultivation and chocolate production.

Water World

MAP P379

Learn about Chanthaburi's seafaring legacy

South of Chanthaburi, where the eponymous river meets the sea, is the **King Taksin the Great Shipyard**, an archaeological site that makes for a pleasant, rural half-day excursion if you have a car or motorcycle.

The shipyard is the place where, in 1767, King Taksin assembled troops and allegedly built 100 warships that allowed him to liberate his kingdom from the Burmese. The remains of some of these boats were found in 1980 by Thailand's Underwater Archaeology Division. Parts of this discovery, still underwater, can be seen today in the compound. An adjacent museum documents the excavation process and provides background information on shipbuilding during this era in Thailand. In another building, visitors can explore a life-size model junk, and the compound is also home to a decommissioned contemporary battleship.

CHOCOLATE FROM CHANTHABURI

Kad Kokoa: Offers four single-origin locations: Chanthaburi, Chiang Mai, Chumpon and Prachuab Kirikhan. *kadkokoa.co*

PRIDI Cacaofevier: The project was started by three chefs who wanted to find a great local alternative to imported chocolate. *(pridicacaofevier.com)*

Shabar: Handcrafted micro-batch chocolate and other products like chocolate milk, or cookies. *facebook.com/shabarchocolate*

Bean to Bar: Produces a variety of cacao-derived products, from cacao fruit juice to chocolate bars. *beantobarchan.com*

Paradai: This Thai brand has made award-winning bars using cacao from Chanthaburi. *facebook.com/Paradai.Chocolate*

EATING IN CHANTHABURI PROVINCE: OUR PICKS

MAP P379

Khrua Bua Khao: South of Chanthaburi in charming Nong Bua, this casual restaurant specialises in region-specific dishes. *10am-3.30pm Wed-Sun* ฿

Kuaytiaw Muu Liang Phraya Trang: Rustic place, east of Chanthaburi in Tha Mai. Worth the trip for *kuaytiaw muu liang*, pork and rice noodles in herb broth. *9am-3pm* ฿

Ruean Rim Nam Seafood: When locals in Chanthaburi want crab, they head to this restaurant near Hat Laem Sing. *8.30am-9.30pm* ฿฿

Yai Tu Seafood: A recognised destination for seafood on Hat Chao Lao; as with much of the region, there's an emphasis on mantis shrimp and crabs. *9am-9pm* ฿

Beyond Chanthaburi Province

Chanthaburi shares a border with Sa Kaew Province, a rural area home to an important border crossing with Cambodia, as well as Khmer empire ruins that are worth a visit.

GETTING AROUND

From Bangkok, there are frequent buses and minivans connecting Ekkamai Bus Terminal and the border crossing at Aranyaprathet.

Sa Kaew and Aranyaprathet are also the only places in the greater eastern seaboard region that can be accessed by train.

The nearest airport is in Trat.

As Sa Kaew Province isn't quite on the main tourism trail, public transport is lacking, and if you plan to do a lot of exploring, a hired car or motorcycle is obligatory.

Sa Kaew is best known as a border crossing point to Cambodia, and for its border market – the region's largest place of commerce – but there's more to this sleepy province than meets the eye. The border market is a fun place to vicariously visit Cambodia via window-shopping, chatting with Cambodian vendors or eating a Cambodian meal. Prasat Sdok Kok Thom, the area's largest Khmer temple complex, is a fun place to travel back in time. And bordering Isan, Thailand's northeast region, Sa Kaew is also a great place to dip your toes in the country's rural heartland.

Sa Kaew Province

TIME FROM CHANTHABURI: **3HR**

Market day

The border town of **Aranyaprathet**, in Sa Kaew Province, can appear to be one large market. In fact, it's several markets stitched together to form a mega-market. Known in Thai as **Talat Rong Kluea**, it's the largest place of commerce in the eastern region, and takes the form of dozens and dozens of stalls selling cheap clothing and housewares, and it's worth a morning stroll.

The market is so large that there's a station that hires golf carts to the more ambitious shoppers. Many of the vendors here are Cambodian, who cross on a daily basis to sell items. This also means that it's possible have a Cambodian-style meal without crossing the border.

When we visited, a diplomatic spat between Thailand and Cambodia meant that the border was closed and the market was downright dead, an occasional occurrence.

Palace of reeds

Sa Kaew Province is home to a handful of Khmer-era ruins, the most accessible and largest of which is **Prasat Sdok Kok Thom**. It's located around 40km northwest of the border market at Aranyaprathet, and is worth a half-day excursion if you have your own transport.

KOBCHAIMA/SHUTTERSTOCK

Prasat Sdok Kok Thom

GETTING TO CAMBODIA FROM THAILAND

Poipet/Aranyaprathet is a permanent border crossing between Thailand and Cambodia. It's open daily 6am to 10pm.

Located 148km west of Siem Reap, this is a busy border. Cambodian e-visas are valid here, otherwise, a tourist visa costs around US$30. You may be asked for 1500฿ (about US$45) or US$30 plus a 100฿ to 300฿ fee.

It's worth noting that Poipet is a notorious hotbed of scammers so keep your guard up. Avoid any offers of free transportation, which is almost certainly a precursor to a scam that typically involves taking tourists to a fake border crossing terminal where a large fee is demanded for visas.

A visit starts with the excellent museum, which provides the context and history of the temple complex, as well as that of the Khmer empire and other similar structures in Thailand.

The temple complex itself, which was dedicated to the god Shiva, was built around the 11th century and is located on one of the two major roads that formerly connected Angkor Wat with current-day Thailand. A French explorer found the ruins in 1901, but they weren't properly renovated by Thai authorities until the '90s. An important discovery was an inscription stone with Sanskrit and Khmer writings, which provided scholars with valuable insights into the history of the Khmer empire. Nearly as impressive as the temple complex is the adjacent *baray*, or pond, a land feature that the ancient Khmers used to control flooding.

Bountiful butterflies

Pang Sida National Park straddles both Sa Kaew and Prachinburi provinces. The richness of the ecosystem supports wildlife such as elephants, gibbons, deer, wild boar and more. But the main attraction here is butterflies. From June to July, more than 350 species of butterfly gather here, as do aficionados for an annual butterfly-watching festival. Take a walk to the Phong Tiam area, about 1km from the park headquarters, then to the Hin Daad lawn, where park rangers will guide you to the best spots to see the butterflies. There's a waterfall in this area too, Nam Tok Pang Sida.

EATING IN SA KAEW PROVINCE: OUR PICKS

Yay Tem: This massive, popular, bar-feeling place in Sa Kaew specialises in Vietnamese food. *10.30am-midnight* ฿

Je Ngek: Located between Sa Kaew and Aranyaprathet, this roadside restaurant serves Vietnamese dishes. *8.30am-7pm* ฿

YaiTaam VietNam Food: Yet another place for Vietnamese food in Sa Kaew Province, this time in Aranyaprathet. Try *naem nueang*, something of a DIY spring roll. *7.30am-7pm* ฿

Talat Rong Klua: Aranyaprathet's border market has Cambodian-style baguette sandwiches, noodle dishes and other breakfast and lunch dishes. *7am-5pm* ฿

Rayong Province

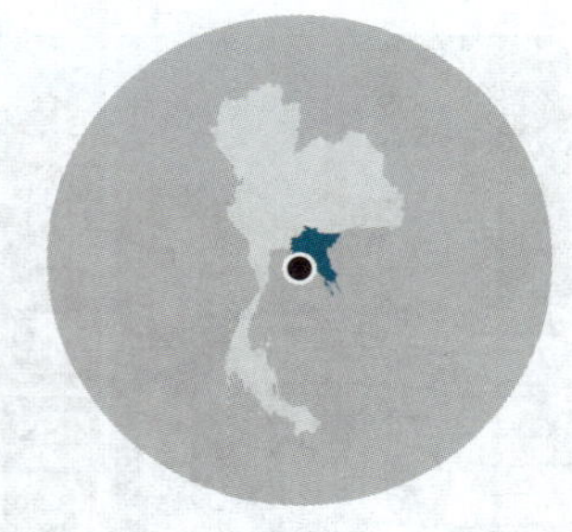

TINY ISLANDS | HISTORY | NATURE

GETTING AROUND

From Bangkok, there are frequent buses and minivans connecting Ekkamai Bus Terminal and various points in Rayong Province.

Within Rayong, there are *sorng taa ous*) and Grab is also available, but a rental car will give you much more freedom. Motorbike taxis can be seen everywhere, or you can rent one for around 300฿ per day.

TOP TIP

During monsoon season, you might not be able to find any boats out to Ko Samet and other islands as the sea currents could be rough. Check beforehand.

For many people, Rayong means Ko Samet, regarding the province as little more than an access point for a weekend getaway from Bangkok. However, Rayong has a lot more to offer than its headlining island. Ko Samet is just one of several tiny, white, visit-worthy sand islets in this slice of the Gulf of Thailand. Heading inland, the province is home to some stunning natural areas, and Rayong is one of the top durian-producing provinces in Thailand, and hosts an annual fruit festival from around the end of April until May. The provincial capital of the same name also conceals a charmingly stuck-in-time neighbourhood that's worth a stop or even an overnight stay. And all that coastline also means that Rayong's seafood scene is top-notch.

White Sands & Fire Shows

Everyone has fun on Ko Samet

Ko Samet offers white sandy shores, cosy coves and aquamarine waters that attract ferry-loads of Bangkokians looking for a short getaway. For years the island was the stomping ground of Thai university students and later Bangkok's LGBTIQ+ crowd. These days you'll find foreign backpackers, middle-class Thais and tourists from Asian countries in the mix, all drawn in by the island's legendarily fine, white sands and the fact that Ko Samet is one of the easiest island escapes from Bangkok.

Ko Samet is technically a national park, part of **Khao Laem Ya/Mu Ko Samet National Park**, yet despite being the closest big island to Bangkok, it's also surprisingly underdeveloped, with a thick jungle interior. Apart from its natural beauty, Ko Samet is also known for its vibrant nightlife. The island's northern beaches come alive after sunset, with beach bars and restaurants offering live music, nightly fire shows and lively parties. The main beaches in this part of the island are Hat Sai Kaew, Ao Phai, Ao Prao and Ao Tubtim.

Heading south on Ko Samet, the beaches get smaller, quieter and arguably more beautiful. Ao Lung Dam has a wooden pier that stretches out into the ocean. It's north of Ao Wai, another beautiful, quiet beach. This is where you go to escape the crowds.

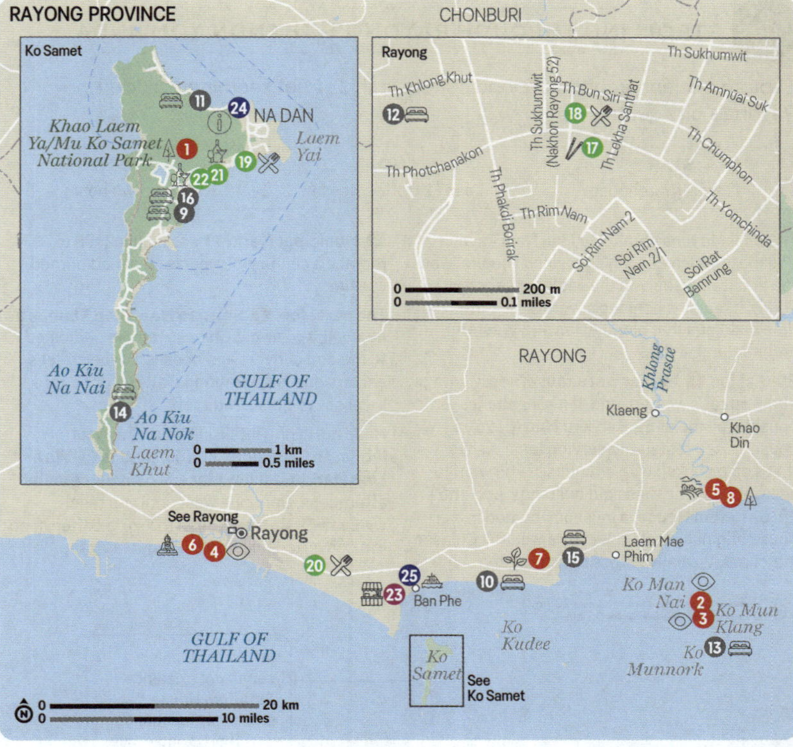

● **SIGHTS**
1 Khao Laem Ya/Mu Ko Samet National Park
2 Ko Man Nai
3 Ko Mun Klang
4 Laem Charoen
5 Pak Nam Prasae
6 Phra Chedi Klang Nam (Samut Chedi)
7 Rayong Botanic Garden
8 Thung Prong Thong

● **SLEEPING**
9 Ao Nuan Bungalows
10 Baan Phe Cabana Resort
11 Baan Ploy Sea
12 Caza VI Serviced Apartment
13 Ko Munnork Private Island Resort
see 5 Ma hah Samut
14 Paradee Resort
15 Ryad Rayong
16 Tubtim Resort

● **EATING**
see 11 Baan Ploy Sea
17 Ban Kru Muu
see 5 Je Nong Zab Ver
see 23 Kang Ban Phe Noodles
see 5 Krua Ya Chim
18 Laan Ek Coffee House
see 23 Paa Jew Ho Mok
19 Ploy Talay
20 Taphong Fruit Market
see 16 Tubtim Beach

● **DRINKING & NIGHTLIFE**
21 Gecko Bar
22 Silversand Bar

● **SHOPPING**
23 Ban Phe Fresh Market

● **INFORMATION**
24 National Parks Main Office

● **TRANSPORT**
25 Ban Phe Pier

A GIANT WELCOME

As you pull into Ko Samet's pier, the first thing you'll see is a giant cement butt. The imposing golden statue of a female giant at Na Dan pier is impossible to miss, and is an allusion to Ko Samet's most famous son, poet Sunthorn Phu. In his epic *Phra Aphai Mani*, a prince is exiled to an undersea kingdom ruled by the lovesick female giant. A mermaid helps the prince escape to Ko Samet, where he defeats the giant by playing a magical flute.

STROLLING THROUGH RAYONG'S THANON YOMJINDA

Explore ancient architecture and culture in this street seemingly hidden in Rayong's city centre.

START	END	LENGTH
Former Warehouse	Laan Ek Coffee House	1.5 km; two hours

Th Yomjinda runs parallel to Mae Nam Rayong, and the street in Rayong's provincial capital was the first trading hub on the eastern seaboard. Today, it remains home to several stuck-in-time buildings that blend Asian and Western architectural styles.

Start at the 1 **former warehouse**, now a garage, at the street's western end. If it's mealtime, consider a stop at 2 **Ban Kru Muu** (p396), a house-based restaurant serving local dishes that's also packed with antiques. If you want to see what's inside these old buildings, pop into 3 **Satudom House**, a museum located in a house originally built in 1919 by a wealthy Chinese merchant. Virtually across the street, the 4 **Municipal Market 1** was built in 1998 to replace a century-old market that had burned in a fire.

The next stop, 5 **San Jao Mae Thap Thim**, is a nearly 150-year-old Chinese temple dedicated to the god of rivers and oceans. At the street's eastern end is 6 **Rayong Gallery**, good for a local souvenir or handicraft.

Head north on Th Taksin Maharat and turn left on Th Chumporn; on your right is 7 **Wat Lum Market**, a lively place of commerce in the afternoons. Continue west until you reach 8 **Laan Ek Coffee House** (p396), a coffee shop in a converted building, and your last stop.

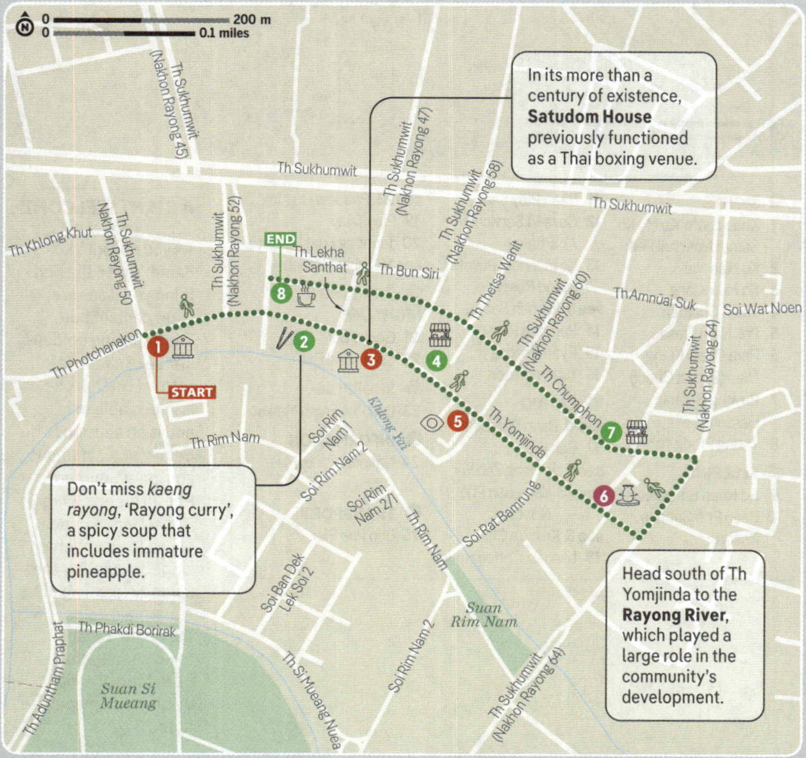

In its more than a century of existence, **Satudom House** previously functioned as a Thai boxing venue.

Don't miss *kaeng rayong*, 'Rayong curry', a spicy soup that includes immature pineapple.

Head south of Th Yomjinda to the **Rayong River**, which played a large role in the community's development.

Market Heaven

Indulge in some of Thailand's best fruit and seafood

Rayong Province is known for its fruit production. One of the largest producers of durian, it's also the place to gorge on fresh pineapple, mango, rambutan and more. Between May and June, Ko Samet–bound Thais stop at **Taphong Fruit Market**, around 12km west of Ban Phe, where in season you can find durian, mangosteen and other top-shelf fruit at bottom-shelf prices.

Then there's the seafood. Rayong sits on the coast of the Gulf of Thailand, so it's guaranteed that you'll never run out of affordable, fresh seafood to eat. The massive **Ban Phe Fresh Market** is a seafood hub for the province, offering seafood straight from the sea, as well as items such as dried squid, shrimp paste, fish sauce and other items for prices that are very reasonable compared to Ko Samet. If you're looking to buy some fresh seafood to bring back and cook at your accommodation, this is where to shop.

An Island to Yourself

Stay on Ko Munnork Private Island

Ko Munnork is a private island and has only one resort you can book: **Ko Munnork Private Island Resort** *(munnorkprivateisland.com)*. The rooms are all full-board and include ferry transport. To visit this island, you have to book directly with the resort.

There isn't much to do, as you might have guessed. The island is so small you could walk around it and the resort has made a path for you to explore. Your phone will most likely not get any reception and wi-fi only works in the lobby. They turn off electricity during the day from 9am to 1pm to save power, and so you could go out and snorkel, read by the beach, swim or kayak.

Rooms offer both garden and ocean views, and are all separated in their own little beach villas. There's a swimming pool on the property. You can pre-order food in advance if you'd like anything special, such as a particular seafood dish, and they will prepare it for you per your request.

The island is very well preserved and most of it is still covered in dense forest with a beautiful white-sand beach. If you're looking for a retreat getaway close to Bangkok, it can't get any quieter and more private than this.

HOW TO GET TO KO SAMET

To get from Bangkok to Ko Samet, there are frequent buses leaving from Ekkamai Bus Terminal to the multiple piers at Ban Phe, in Rayong. There are two types of boat that take you to Ko Samet. The big wooden fishing boat will set you back around 120฿ and takes about 30 minutes. The speedboat takes 15 minutes and costs around 300฿. Both run from 9am to 5pm. Once you arrive on the island, there will be *sorng taa ou* shuttles ready to take you to your destination.

Some of the more remote resorts on the island's southern end can arrange for direct speedboats.

EATING IN BAN PHE & KO SAMET: OUR PICKS

Baan Ploy Sea: Regional Thai dishes in a dining room on Ko Samet's north shore that almost feels like a temple. *11am-10pm* ฿฿

Taphong Fruit Market: Obligatory stop for Bangkok people going home from Ko Samet. Durian, rambutan, santol and more, just off the highway. *5am-7pm* ฿

Kang Ban Phe Noodles: Near the piers at Ban Phe is this popular place serving indulgent bowls of Thai-style noodles topped with mantis shrimp. *9am-5pm* ฿

Paa Jew Ho Mok: A native of Phuket is doing her island's take on *hor mok*, steamed curries loaded with fish and herbs. In Ban Phe. *6am-4.30pm* ฿

NATIONAL PARK FEE

Ko Samet is part of the Khao Laem Ya/ Mu Ko Samet National Park (p390) and charges all visitors an entrance fee (adult/ child 200/100฿) upon arrival. If you live and work in Thailand and can prove it, you pay only 40฿, the price Thai people pay. The fee is collected at the **National Parks Main Office**, at Na Dan pier. Hold on to your ticket for later inspections. There's another park office at Ao Wong Deuan, and rangers elsewhere will charge you the fee if you arrive by speedboat.

KARNJ AYU/SHUTTERSTOCK

Baby turtles, Ko Man Nai

Pirate for a Day

Explore Ko Samet's neighbouring islands

Around Ko Samet are other small islands where you snorkel and swim: Ko Ta Lu, Ko Ku Dee, Ko Kham, Ko Kruay and Ko Tham Kangkao. Many companies offer a one-day tour that takes in all five islands. Outfits such as **Dome Travel** *(facebook .com/dometravelrayong)* offer tours for around 800฿ per person. The commute is via a speedboat. For this price you'll get snacks, fruits, water, lunchbox, snorkelling gear, a life vest and an anti-motion-sickness pill. You'll also see other tiny islands along the way that have beautiful coral reefs. This part of the eastern seaboard is unexplored, so the natural surroundings are very well preserved.

A Refuge for Sea Turtles

Visit the Marine Research Centre on Ko Man Nai

The tiny island of **Ko Man Nai**, one of a chain of three islands east of Ko Samet, has become famous for the **Marine & Coastal Resources Research & Development Centre, Eastern Gulf of Thailand**, a centre whose work encompasses turtle breeding, incubation and conservation efforts, focusing on olive ridley, hawksbill and green turtles.

It also offers some breathtaking and unspoiled nature. Its secluded, serene beaches provide a tranquil escape, making it an ideal getaway for those seeking relaxation and rejuvenation. It is worth considering Ko Man Nai if you're planning a trip to Rayong because not only is it beautiful, the work they do to give back and preserve the ocean and marine life is really worth supporting.

Next door is **Ko Mun Klang**, a small island about 10 minutes from Ko Man Nai. It has clean sandy beaches and the sand varies between coarse orange and fine white sand. The highlight is its privacy, allowing tourists to get close to nature. Activities include swimming, snorkelling to see coral reefs, and walking around the island. There is an area that resembles a small lagoon – a sandy slope connects the island to a group of rocks in the sea. When the tide goes down, you can see the sandy slope emerge, similar to a lagoon. It is a beautiful viewpoint.

Access to Ko Man Nai and Ko Mun Klang is via the pier at Ao Makhampom, around 30km east of Ban Phe, in Klaeng District. If you have the budget and speak Thai, you can arrange for one of the fishermen there to take you to the island. Otherwise, you'll need to go with an outfit such as **Phupa Tour** *(phupatour.com)*, also based in the village. They run day-long excursions to Ko Man Nai, as well as to Ko Mun Klang and Ko Ta Lu, that include snorkelling stops and lunch. Book in advance.

FISH SAUCE

The Gulf of Thailand, in particular Rayong Province, is Thailand's largest producer of fish sauce. To make this product, Japanese and Indian anchovies are combined with salt and left in vats for a year or longer. The liquid that results is strained and bottled, sometimes combined with a bit of sugar, in a product known as Grade A fish sauce. A high-quality fish sauce is fragrant rather than fishy, amber-coloured and pleasantly salty and savoury. Lesser-quality fish sauce is made by combining the fish with salt one more time and supplementing this 'second pressing' with seasonings or colourants.

Water World

Mangroves and antiquated charm in Pak Nam Prasae

Pak Nam Prasae is an ancient riverside community in Rayong Province's southeastern corner that has enough draws for a day trip or overnight stay if you have your own wheels.

The old city centre was built along where Nam Prasae empties into the Gulf of Thailand, and is a densely populated village and trading hub for seafood where many of the houses are on stilts. In recent years, the village has generated a low-key buzz among domestic tourists, and its main road is home to a handful of cafes, restaurants, homestays and hotels, and even some street art. Just south of the village, there's a large fishing port, which is also home to the **HTMS Prasae Memorial**, an old royal battleship decommissioned from service during the Korean War that can be visited.

Just as many visitors are drawn to the area's mangrove forests, located just east of the village. A community-based tourism project here conducts boat tours into the forests (200B for up to four people). Tours take about a half-hour, and include stops for spotting brahminy kites near the coasts, trees loaded with hundreds of squawking fruit bats and the highlight, **Thung Prong Thong** (called Golden Meadow in English), an almost valley-like field of mangroves with yellow leaves (it can also be reached on foot via an elevated walkway). It's a lot of fun, and your money goes directly to the community.

EATING & DRINKING ON KO SAMET: OUR PICKS

Tubtim Beach: Linked to the resort of the same name, this is where Thais eat on Ko Samet; you can't go wrong with papaya salad and grilled chicken. *9am-11pm* B

Ploy Talay: This massive restaurant hosts the island's most extravagant fire show, which kicks off every night at 8pm. *7am-10pm* B

Silversand Bar: Ko Samet's clubbiest bar is LGBTIQ+-friendly and has generous happy hours. *11am-midnight*

Gecko Bar: It's hard to miss this rambling, semi-open-air, graffiti-splattered monument to Day-Glo located just east of Ao Phai. *3pm-2am*

PHAK KRACHAP

Restaurants around Pak Nam Prasae, such as Je Nong Zab Ver and Krua Ya Chim, serve a peppery, green vegetable called *phak krachap* that's not found elsewhere in the country. Known in English as rough cocklebur, the immature sprouts of the plant are fried with oyster sauce or added to soups such as *kaeng som*, central Thailand's 'sour' soup. Mature *phak krachap* plants, seeds and seedlings, on the other hand, should not be consumed in large quantities because they contain the extremely toxic chemical carboxyatractyloside as well as at least four other toxins.

From Mangrove to Sea

Witness every side of Laem Charoen

Laem Charoen is a peninsula that juts eastward on Rayong's coast, a finger of land that forms a barrier seemingly protecting the mainland from the ocean. The peninsula is home to a beach worth visiting, and also conceals another worthwhile attraction, both of which make for a nature-focused half-day outing for those who have a motorcycle or car.

Laem Charoen's south coast is known in English as **Moonlight Beach** because of the half moon-like barriers constructed in a line of rocks to prevent erosion from the waves along the coast. There's plenty of food along the beach and people love to take out mats and do a beach picnic at sunset. The sand gets finer, as do the restaurants and hotels, on the peninsula's eastern end.

If you head inland, approximately in the middle of the peninsula, you'll come to the point where Mae Nam Rayong spills into the Gulf of Thailand, creating a mangrove forest. Rayong's **Urban Forest Project** takes the form of around 3km of elevated walkways that slice through this scenic, marshy area. There are bridges and a viewing platform, the latter providing views all the way to the ocean. The path also crosses **Phra Chedi Klang Nam (Samut Chedi)**, a pagoda built in 1873 for sailors, the site of a traditional ceremony in November.

Paddle Power

Get active at Rayong Botanic Garden

If lazing on a beach doesn't do it for you, consider a visit to **Rayong Botanic Garden**. It's a research and collection centre for plants in the eastern region that also doubles as an excellent base for a half-day active excursion. The garden takes the form of a series of wetland islands, through which one can paddle a kayak (100฿ per hour) to explore ponds studded with lotus flowers. Trails also allow for cycling (50฿ per hour) or walking, although some of the garden's bridges were temporarily closed when we visited. Helpful signs indicate local birds and plants, and there are food and drink stalls in the parking lot. We recommend visiting in the late afternoon when the sun is not too bright.

It's located around 30km south of Rayong, and you'll need a motorcycle or car to reach it.

EATING & DRINKING IN RAYONG PROVINCE: OUR PICKS

Ban Kru Muu: Part restaurant, part museum. Enjoy delicious, old-timey local dishes surrounded by likewise bric-a-brac. *5-8.30pm* ฿

Je Nong Zab Ver: Riverside restaurant in Pak Nam Prasae has a mix of seafood and local dishes, including those with *phak krachap. 10am-8pm Tue-Sun* ฿

Krua Ya Chim: Simple-looking seafood restaurant in Pak Nam Prasae with a grandma cooking her own recipes with locally sourced seafood. *3-9pm* ฿

Laan Ek Coffee House: Rayong Cafe decorated in vintage style, set in a 100-plus-years-old Sino-Portuguese-style building. *9am-6pm* ฿

Chonburi Province

BEACHES | FAMILY ESCAPES | HISTORY

For many Thais growing up in the central region, Chonburi Province was their first ever beach experience. That's probably because it's located a mere 80km southeast of Bangkok, making it easily accessible from the capital city. Although Pattaya is the region's most famous – or perhaps most infamous – beachy area, Chonburi is also home to many other more low-key, sandy destinations such as Ang Sila, Bang Saen, Hat Jomtien and Si Racha. And while there are undoubtedly fancier beach destinations in Thailand these days, Chonburi still remains a favourite getaway for those who don't want to board a plane, as it's the site of Wing Khwai, an annual buffalo-racing contest. The province is also home to lots of worthwhile inland attractions that range in scope from natural to artificial, and in recent decades a thriving industrial sector has brought Japanese people – as well as their culture and food – to the region.

GETTING AROUND

Chonburi's big-hitter destinations are well connected to Bangkok. There's no train line in this part of the country; instead you'll find buses and minivans at Ekkamai Bus Terminal located next to Ekkamai BTS Skytrain station as well Suvarnabhumi International Airport.

Within Chonburi Province, it gets a bit more complicated. If you're staying in and around Pattaya, taxis and Grab are plentiful and convenient. Otherwise, for more obscure destinations – particularly those found inland – it's much more convenient to hire a car.

Five Days of Peace & Music

Tap into your bohemian side at the Wonderfruit festival

Despite its name and the culinary proclivities of its host country, **Wonderfruit** *(wonderfruit.co)* is not a food festival. Rather, it's Thailand's Burning Man – of sorts.

A decade old at this point, Wonderfruit is ostensibly a music festival, but the five-day event also spans art and wellness activities, as well as talks and workshops on subjects often having to do with sustainability (and yes, this is Thailand so there is food). In previous years, musical guests have ranged from domestic acts to De La Soul, and the event has pulled as many as 30,000 attendees.

The event is held every mid-December at Siam Country Club, just east of Pattaya. 'Boutique Camping' accommodation is available on site, as well as options for attendees to stay in tents, but note that outside accommodation can be tough to come by.

TOP TIP

Because of their proximity to Bangkok, Chonburi's beaches can get packed during the weekends. Opt for a weekday for a quieter vibe.

CHONBURI PROVINCE
0 10 km
0 5 miles
Chonburi
Meng Hui Cemetery
Pa Chumchon Ban Wang Tako
Ban Bueng
Ban Nong Chak
See Chonburi
Bang Saen
Khlong Bang Prong
Nong Nam Khiao
Bang Phra
Bang Phra Reservoir
Khao Chalat
Khlong Chon Prathan
Navy Agriculture Project
See Si Racha
Si Racha
Khao Phut Khodom
Ko Si Chang
Ko Sichang
Nong Kho
Laem Chabang
Huay Saphan Reservoir
Nong Klang Dong
Huay Khun Chit
Khao Mai Kaeo
See Pattaya
Na Kluea
Pattaya
Pa Chumchon Ban Huai Yai Muk
Map Prachan
Khao Phai
Huay Chak Nok
Huay Yai
Khlong Yai
Khlong Yai Chi
Khlong Sak Chao Dieo
Ko Luam
Ko Phai
Ko Lan
Khao Yai
Khao Reda
Na Chom Thian
Gulf of Thailand
Ban Amphoe Reservoir
Khlong Bang Phai
Khao Nang Yong
Khao Huai Mahaat
Khlong Huai Yai
Huay Tu Reservoir
Ban Chang
Sattahip Naval Base
Khao Mon
Phoot Anan
U-Tapao International Airport
Khlong Thai Wa
Nong Takhian
Sattahip
Maha Chetsada Chao Camp, Marine Division
Ko Phra Noi
Ko Tao Mo
Ko I Lao
Fleet Operations Center and Chuk Samet Pier
Chong Samaesan
Ko Raet
Ko Kham
Ko Samae San
Ko Chan
Ko Chuang
Si Racha
Stilt Houses
Night Square
Th Si Racha Nakorn
Th Thetsaban 1
Th Thetsaban 3
Th Surasak 1
Th Sukhumvit
0 500 m
0 0.25 miles
26
19
5
18
34
10
2
11
15
33
31
30
25
16
32
8
9

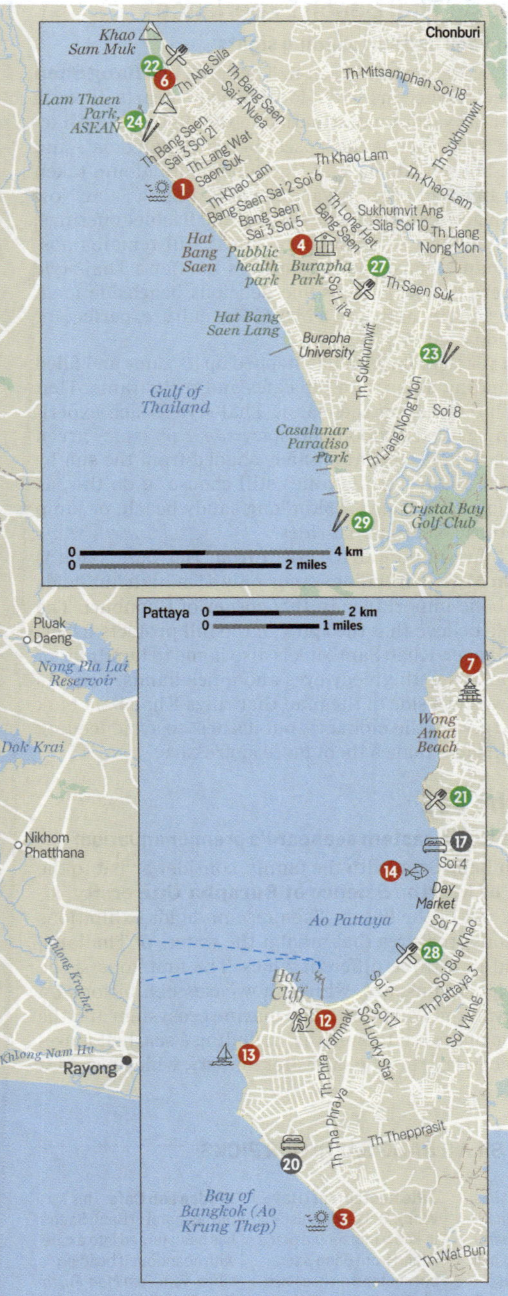

SIGHTS
1 Bang Saen
2 Big Bee Farm Pattaya
3 Hat Jomtien
4 Institute of Marine Science of Burapha University
5 Khao Kheow Open Zoo
6 Khao Sam Muk
7 Sanctuary of Truth
8 Sriracha Shinto Shrine
9 Thai Island & Sea Natural History Museum
10 Wat Khao Tabaek

ACTIVITIES
11 ATV & Buggy Adventures
12 Easycart.net Go-Karting
13 Royal Varuna Yacht Club
14 Squid Cafe Pattaya Tako Trip
15 Underwater World Pattaya

SLEEPING
16 Hotel Kuretakeso Sriracha
17 Mercure Pattaya Ocean Resort
18 Novotel Ko Si Chang
19 Pagoda Hill Cafe & Resort
20 Rabbit Resort

EATING
21 Caravan
22 Hidden Lab Cafe
23 J Ple Restaurant (Hat Won)
24 Khrua Kang Wan
25 Kitaro Sushi
26 Nai Aun
27 Nong Mon Market
28 Saravanaa Bhavan
29 Seafood Club Bangsaen
30 Shishitei
31 Shochu Donya

DRINKING & NIGHTLIFE
32 Rat Fink

ENTERTAINMENT
33 Wonderfruit

SHOPPING
34 J-Park

AVOID TIGER TOURS

Don't pay for tours or services that will let you take photos while cuddling tigers. These tigers are forcibly removed from their natural habitat, separated from their mothers at a young age and subjected to cruel training methods that involve physical abuse. The intention is to break their spirit and force them into submission, enabling tourists to interact with them. The tiger tourism industry in Thailand is largely unregulated, making it difficult to ensure the wellbeing and proper treatment of the animals (p616). By participating in tiger tours, tourists unknowingly contribute to the illegal wildlife trade. The demand for tiger interactions fuels a market that perpetuates the capture and illegal trade of these endangered animals. As much as you'd like a photo with a tiger, avoid at all costs.

The Classic Thai Beach Experience

Visit Bang Saen and surrounding sights

It may not be the sexiest beach in Thailand, but **Bang Saen** holds a special place in a lot of local people's hearts. It was a popular family vacation destination in the 1990s – most likely because Bang Saen is the closest beach to Bangkok – and most Thai households have at least one photo album taken on a film camera of a family vacation at Hat Bang Saen. Now that other places can boast more lavish and flashier offerings, Bang Saen has lost its popularity. But it still remains nostalgic for many Thais, and it continues to offer a Thai-style beach experience – namely some delicious beachside food, family-fun activity and even a bit of local culture, perfect for an afternoon excursion.

In recent years, Bang Saen has stepped up its game and filled the surrounding areas with hip cafes and restaurants. That said, it still delivers on the classic Thai-style beach experience: eating grilled seafood and spicy *som tam* (spicy green papaya salad) in deck chairs, safely shaded from the sun by an umbrella. Many Thai families still choose to do this, as well as enjoy Bang Saen's 2.5km-long sandy beach, or jump on one of those banana-boat rides.

Around a five-minute drive north from Hat Bang Saen is **Khao Sam Muk**, a hill that stands only 45m high but holds great symbolic importance in this corner of Chonburi. The local people believe that the spirit of the hill protects fisherfolk from danger. Khao Sam Muk is also home to hundreds of rhesus monkeys with greedy eyes and quick hands. Vendors along the western side of the road that rings Khao Sam Muk sell fruit to give to the monkeys, but it's best to avoid feeding them, as this just makes them more aggressive.

Under the Sea

Pay a visit to the eastern seaboard's premier aquarium

If you're in Bang Saen with the family, consider a visit to the **Institute of Marine Science of Burapha University**, located just east of the beach. The museum holds exhibitions about various creatures that inhabit the waters of Thailand, categorised into three different zones. The first zone is the marine science museum, which showcases exhibitions on the underwater marine world, the marine ecosystem and the importance of the sea to humans, including a seashell museum. The second part is the saltwater nursery, which provides

EATING & DRINKING IN ANG SILA & BANG SAEN: OUR PICKS

Nai Aun: This place in Ang Sila serves a wide variety of neatly presented, tasty noodle and seafood dishes; don't miss the deep-fried sea bass. *9am-5pm* ฿

Nong Mon Market: East of Bang Saen, this market is known for *khao laam*, sticky rice, coconut milk, sugar and red beans cooked in a bamboo tube. *6am-8pm* ฿

J Ple Restaurant (Hat Won): Only locals used to know this simple place inland from Bang Saen, but seafood dishes have made it popular. *8am-5pm Tue-Sun* ฿

Hidden Lab Cafe: This former hotel in Bang Saen has been turned into a cafe with abandoned building vibes. *9am-7pm Mon-Fri, to 8pm Sat & Sun* ฿

ANIRUT THAILAND/SHUTTERSTOCK

Bang Saen

information about the various sea animals in the Thai ocean. There is an underwater fish-feeding show and you can also feed the fish in the pond yourself. There's also a Touch Pool where you can interact with the sea creatures. Finally, the third section is the underwater-world learning centre, which is divided into 11 zones and showcases marine species. The highlight is the underwater tunnel that stretches up to 37m, taking you into the underwater world to see the marine animals in the deep sea, including the Atolla jellyfish.

Welcome to Little Osaka

A taste of Japan in Si Racha

The coastal town of **Si Racha** still retains elements of a provincial Thai fishing port. But one influence is even stronger these days: that of the city's large Japanese community.

This slice of Thailand's eastern seaboard is home to a string of factories and industrial estates, many of which are owned and run by Japanese people. As a result, Si Racha is thought to be home to as many as 10,000 Japanese residents, having led to the town's nickname, 'Little Osaka'.

Today, Si Racha is the only town in Thailand where the sign on the local government building is also written in Japanese. There's a Japanese school, and the **Sriracha Shinto Shrine** is the first-ever Japanese shrine in Thailand. If it's your first time at a Shinto shrine, posted in front is a helpful step-by-step on

A SAUCE BY ANY OTHER NAME

If Si Racha rings a bell, it's because it's thought to be the origin of what was, for a moment at least, one of the world's buzziest condiments. The city is allegedly where the mild, subtly sweet, smooth chilli sauce that Thais pair with omelettes was invented, perhaps inspired by similar Cantonese-style sauces. Fast-forward a few generations, and 'Si Racha sauce' became the go-to term in Thai for a variety of similar products. In 1980 a Vietnamese immigrant to the US started to sell a spicier, tarter take on the sauce, calling it Huy Fong Sriracha. The product, with its iconic cock logo and green-capped bottle, took off during the 2010s, and today is far better known than the version that inspired it.

EATING & DRINKING IN SI RACHA: OUR PICKS

Shochu Donya: Dine with Si Racha's Japanese community at this Japanese-run restaurant. Don't miss the *hambāgu* platter. *5-11.30pm Tue-Sat, 9am-11.30pm Sun* ฿฿

Kitaro Sushi: Open since 2005, Si Racha's longstanding sushi house offers bright lights and tasty sushi and sashimi made to order. *5pm-1am* ฿฿

Shishitei: Premium *sukiyaki* and *shabu-shabu* (two types of DIY soup) in central Si Racha. *11.30am-1.30pm Mon-Fri, to 10pm Sat & Sun* ฿฿

Rat Fink: Old-timey American-themed *izakaya* that serves snacks, with a friendly, English-speaking owner. *5pm-1am* ฿

CHONBURI'S ISLANDS

Ko Lan: Just 15 minutes via speedboat from Bali Hai Pier in Pattaya, the island has crystal-clear water and several beaches.

Ko Phai: This beautiful, tiny island is perfect for a day trip to kayak, snorkel, dive or swim in its clear waters. Take a speedboat from Pattaya's Bali Hai Pier.

Ko Klung Badan: Just south of Ko Phai, this uninhabited island is a popular destination for snorkelling day tours.

Ko Samae San: This small island off the southern tip of Chonburi Province is part of a conservation project. To visit, go to the ticket counter at the **Thai Island & Sea Natural History Museum** in Samae, in Sattahip.

Ko Kham: A small island right next to Ko Samae San, Ko Kham is rich in natural resources.

AJAYTVM/SHUTTERSTOCK

Sanctuary of Truth

how to pay respect. Our hotel in Si Racha even had an *onsen* (bathhouse), a *yukata* (traditional Japanese dress) room and a 'Golf Simulation Room'.

For casual visitors, Si Racha's centre is positively packed with sushi restaurants and *izakayas* (casual Japanese-style bars) – as well as massage parlours and hostess bars that cater to Japanese men. And a short drive east of town is **J-Park**, a three-storey mall with Japanese restaurants, Japanese stationery stores and even a store selling secondhand designer handbags from Japan.

Where Spirituality Meets Fun

Make merit and adventure at Wat Khao Tabaek

Wat Khao Tabaek *(watkhaotabagsriracha.com; 8am-5pm)* is in inland rural Chonburi, a half-hour east of Si Racha. At first glance, it looks like a typical Thai Buddhist temple, but a closer look reveals a tourism destination that intertwines religion, spirituality and fun in a way that's uniquely Thai. If you have your own wheels, it makes for a fun half-day inland adventure.

Upon arriving at the temple, follow the lead of local visitors and buy a ribbon, which you can tie to a bridge to ensure merit, long-lasting love or both. Follow this bridge up a steep set of stairs (or a winding road) to the temple's highlight: a 226m-long glass skywalk (40฿) that will make your knees weak. Only 100 people are allowed on at a time, and the bridge connects the hilltop with an immense reclining Buddha statue. Your effort grants views of the countryside all the way to the Gulf of Thailand, and is an insight into the type of tourism that Thais love.

Thailand's Sagrada Família

See Pattaya's Sanctuary of Truth

Boldly jutting into the Gulf of Thailand just north of Pattaya is the **Sanctuary of Truth** *(adult/child 500-700/350฿)*. Made entirely of intricately carved wood (without any metal nails) and commanding a celestial view of the ocean, the space is best described as a visionary environment: simultaneously an art installation, religious shrine and cultural monument. Constructed in four wings dedicated to Thai, Khmer, Chinese and Indian religious iconography, its architecture and setting are impressive.

The ornate temple-like complex was conceived by Lek Viriyaphant, a wealthy Thai person who spent his fortune on this and other heritage projects (such as Ancient City near Bangkok, p133) that revived and preserved ancient building techniques and architecture in danger of extinction – in this case hand-hewn woodworking skills. Every part of the 105m-tall building is covered with wood carvings of Hindu and Buddhist gods and goddesses – an artistic consolidation of centuries of religious myths under one unifying roof. The structure has been under construction since 1981 and still isn't finished – not unlike a certain basilica in Barcelona. As such, visitors are required to wear hard hats, and it's possible to observe artisans at work.

Tours in multiple languages are led through the building approximately every 30 minutes. The sanctuary is 1km down Soi 12 off Th Naklua, about 3km from the centre of Pattaya.

RED LIGHT CITY

No other Thai city has a reputation like that of **Pattaya**. Ever since the first US servicemen started arriving in the 1960s for some R&R during the Vietnam War, hedonism has been a permanent guest. Beer bars, go-go clubs and massage parlours are omnipresent, with thousands of sex workers operating in the city. In recent years, as middle-class Thais have increasingly flocked to one of Bangkok's easiest outlets to the ocean, the city's reputation has softened. Yet Walking Street, the infamous epicentre of Pattaya's expansive red light district, remains as raunchy as ever, and although it can't be described as unsafe, it isn't exactly family-friendly.

From Nightlife to Family Life

See the family-friendly side of Pattaya

Pattaya is arguably the home of Thailand's most infamous red-light district. But because of its relative proximity to Bangkok, the influx of domestic tourists has meant that in recent years, the seaside resort town now offers a diverse, fun menu of family-friendly activities as well.

If your kids love animals, consider a visit to **Underwater World Pattaya** *(underwaterworldpattaya.com; adult/child 550/320฿)*. The city's only proper aquarium is home to more than 5000 species of sea animals. It hosts a large acrylic tunnel spanning over 100m and you can have a 180-degree view of the underwater world as if you were diving deep under the sea. **Big Bee Farm Pattaya** *(bigbeefarm.com)* offers a different type of animal experience. Here you can taste honey from various different types of flowers, and the farm also features a bee museum where you can learn about the life of bees and their benefit to our world. On top of that, there's a cafe serving all kinds of honey-related stuff, or shop for bee-related products such as beeswax aromatic candles.

For older kids, you can't go wrong with **ATV & Buggy Adventures** *(atvtourspattaya.com; from 2990฿)*, an off-road

EATING & DRINKING IN CHONBURI PROVINCE: OUR PICKS

Caravan: Russians have brought their food to Pattaya. This place unites cuisines from Mother Russia as well as those from former Soviet regions. *11am-11pm* ฿฿

Saravanaa Bhavan: Pattaya's main drag is home to dozens of Indian restaurants. This chain specialises in southern Indian vegetarian. *9.30am-12.30am* ฿

Seafood Club Bangsaen: Grab some seafood for dinner at this beachside cafe and restaurant in Bang Saen. *11.30am-11pm Mon-Fri, 10am-11pm Sat & Sun* ฿฿

Khrua Kang Wan: This Bang Saen restaurant has served quality seafood for more than 10 years. *11am-9pm Sun-Thu, to 9.30pm Fri & Sat* ฿฿

MOO DENG

Think back in time to the heady days of 2024, and if there's one notable news item from that year, we'd like to think it was Moo Deng. If you were living under a rock, Moo Deng ('Bouncy Pork' in Thai) is the pygmy hippopotamus born that year at **Khao Kheow Open Zoo** in Chonburi Province. Within months, the almost impossibly cute, chubby, naughty little hippo went viral, drawing attention that ranged from unruly visitors to a parody on *Saturday Night Live*.

These days, Moo Deng can still be found at Khao Kheow Open Zoo, although the crowds have diminished, possibly because she's a bit older now. On the day we visited the zoo, Moo Deng slept while a scant handful of visitors took photos. Such is the life cycle of a celebrity.

MR.NOTE19/SHUTTERSTOCK

Easycart.net Go-Karting

safari with ATVs, buggies or Enduro bikes; be prepared to get dirty. If mud isn't your thing, **Easycart.net Go-Karting** *(easycart.net; from adult/child 699/499฿)* is one of the longest go-kart tracks in Asia at 800m. It's safe and suitable for anyone of any age, with two types of driver qualifications and two tracks to make sure that everyone can drive around together harmoniously.

If you want to get out on the water, consider a visit to the **Royal Varuna Yacht Club** *(varuna.org)*. It's the only yacht club in Thailand offering short-term youth lessons in small sailboats. Alternatively, **Squid Cafe Pattaya Tako Trip** *(takotrip.com; 400฿)* is the city's first squid-fishing cafe on a floating platform. This place provides speedboat transfers to and from the shore, and the platform is pretty safe and stable, reducing the chances of motion sickness. They only accept 200 customers per day, so make sure you book in advance with them directly.

A Quiet Getaway at Hat Jomtien

This part of Pattaya is worth it

Thai people who wish to escape city life and avoid the crowds of tourists and adult entertainment just 4km north in Pattaya choose to stay in Hat Jomtien.

Compared to Hat Pattaya, Hat Jomtien offers fewer nighttime entertainment options, making it suitable for those who enjoy a quieter atmosphere. The beach stretches for 6km and is accompanied by leafy road along its entirety, as well as beach chairs and food stalls so you can enjoy the ocean without going hungry, ever. For water-sports enthusiasts, this beach offers various activities including banana-boat rides, jet skiing, windsurfing, sailing and parasailing. And for landlubbers, there are restaurants, tour companies and other tourist services, making it suitable for those who enjoy a quieter atmosphere without being too isolated.

Beyond Chonburi Province

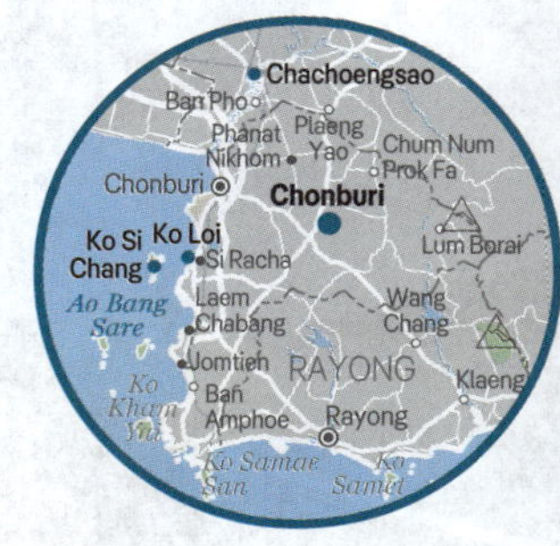

Chachoengsao Province feels rural and stuck-in-time, which is exactly what makes it so charming.

If Pattaya is a bit too much for you, next door is the provincial-feeling town of Chachoengsao. The provincial capital's nickname is Paet Riw, which literally means 'Eight Streaks', a reference to the generous number of cuts that could be made to the particularly large local snakehead fish found in Mae Nam Pakong before they were dried in the sun – an indicator of the semi-rural vibe here.

Although not quite worth an overnight stay, Chachoengsao is worth a half-day trip, especially on a weekend when the excellent Banmai Market is running. If you don't have time to head to Ayuthaya or elsewhere in Thailand's central region, Chachoengsao provides a taste of a typical, old-school, central-Thailand riverside town, complete with a famous temple and a mix of Thai and Chinese cultures.

Places

GETTING AROUND

Frequent buses and minivans run between Bangkok and Chachoengsao. The city is also connected to Bangkok via train. But if you want the freedom to explore sights outside of the city centre, such as Banmai Market, the best option is to rent a car.

Chachoengsao

TIME FROM BANGKOK: **2HR**

Market village

Your best strategy is to hit Chachoengsao on a weekend when you can visit the excellent **Banmai Market**. Also known as Talat 100 Pi, the '100 Years Market', it's considered a living museum. The market takes place in a series of old wooden buildings straddling Mae Nam Pakong, some seemingly on the verge of falling into the river. They're linked by elevated pathways, and on weekends locals sell a mix of food and drinks, handicrafts and souvenirs. Even if you're not shopping, the old-time, riverside atmosphere is like time travel. Banmai Market is located around 4km northeast of Wat Sothon, a long walk or an easy hop in a motorcycle or rental car.

A sacred visit

Wat Sothon Wararam Worawihan is a beautiful temple next to Mae Nam Bang Pakong, the river that runs through Chachoengsao. Built during the late Ayuthaya period, it houses the sacred Buddha statue Luang Phor Phutthasothon, considered the guardian deity of the city. According to a story told generation after generation, the statue floated along Mae Nam Bang Pakong and came to rest at the current location of the temple.

ESPA_FOTO/SHUTTERSTOCK

Ko Sichang Pier

TOP EXPERIENCE

Ko Loi & Ko Sichang

If you seek an underrated, less-crowded destination with elements of Thai history, these islands just off Si Racha are for you. Ko Loi, attached to the city by a bridge, is home to a Chinese and Buddhist temple, while Ko Sichang, a short ferry ride away, has a rustic fishing village and a former royal palace compound.

DON'T MISS

- Wat Asdang
- Ko Loi
- Asdang Bridge
- Hat Tham Phang
- Chong Khao Khat

Ko Loi

Attached to the Si Racha via an 800m road, rocky island Ko Loi is the ferry point for Ko Si Chang and is home to an ornate Thai-Chinese temple and a viewing area for impressive sunsets. It also has a public park, a sea-turtle sanctuary, a Chinese pavilion and a temple, **Wat Ko Loy**, located on a small hill on the island. The temple is home to Luang Pho Tan Chai, a highly revered monk to whom people often come to pay their respects. There are elevated viewpoints where you can see the entire island from up high.

PRACTICALITIES

- Ko Loi: 10-minute walk from the roundabout on Jerm Jom Rd
- Ko Sichang: boats from Ko Loi (60฿; 40 minutes; 6am-6pm)

Ko Sichang Pier

Ko Sichang is home to a rustic pier where colourful fishing ships dock. On land, old wooden houses and the fact that no cars are allowed on the island lend an old-school fishing village vibe.

Phra Chudadhuj Palace

Ko Sichang is home to a former royal compound that makes for a wonderful wander. Work on Phra Chudadhuj Palace kicked off in 1889 as a summer residence for King Chulalongkorn (Rama V) and the royal family. Construction stopped in 1893 when French soldiers landed on Ko Sichang. The soldiers soon left, but in 1900 Rama V ordered that some of the buildings be relocated. Those that remain today have a beautiful blend of Thai and Western architectural styles, and the greater compound is home to ponds, gardens and pavilions for visitors to explore.

Just north, the compound's iconic element is the **Asdang Bridge**, a long white wooden pier stretching out into the sea. **Vadhana Mansion**, located just south of the pier, showcases Ko Sichang during the reign of Rama V in the form of old paintings, photographs and European-style sculptures.

It was Rama V's idea to build **Wat Asdang** in 1892, located a brief walk south of the pier. Unlike any typical temple that you have seen around Thailand, its pagoda is in Gothic style. The doors and windows come with stained glass, adorned with pointed arches and decorated with intricate patterns. Walk inside to see all of the Gothic details and then go through the back door to the outside and you'll find a Buddha statue sitting peacefully in the back garden.

Chong Khao Khat

This is a cliff located at the back of Ko Sichang. If viewed from a distance, it has a cleft, therefore locals refer to it as Chong Khao Khat, or the 'Cliff Gap'. This cliff gap makes a uniquely good sunset-catching spot with a bridge that stretches along the cliff, perfect for taking a walk in the cool sea breeze.

Hat Tham Phang

Hat Tham Phang is considered the only beach on Ko Sichang where you can jump in and swim, as other beaches could be too steep or rocky. It is the longest beach on the island, offering plenty of space for sunbathing and relaxing with food stalls selling fresh juice or seafood, and beach beds are available.

ACCOMMODATION

There's one big chain hotel here – the four-star Novotel, sitting over a cliff with a pool and spa. Other options range from family-run homestays to three-star resorts. For a quieter vibe, Ko Kham Yai is a smaller island at the front with homestays in its fishing village, a five-minute boat ride away.

TOP TIPS

- The island is bigger than you might think, so consider hiring a motorcycle from the main pier.
- On the island, they still use the old-school tuk-tuk known locally as *skylab*.
- The teakwood structure that once formed part of Phra Chudhadhuj Palace was demolished and reassembled as the Vimanmek Mansion in Bangkok.
- There's an incinerator for municipal waste on the island (unfortunately) and on some days, depending on the wind, you might be able to smell it.

Places We Love to Stay

฿ Budget ฿฿ Midrange ฿฿฿ Top End

Ko Chang

Map p366

Baan Rim Nam ฿฿ Spacious, exceedingly well-run rooms over a mangrove-lined river estuary near Hat Khlong Prao.

Spa Koh Chang Resort ฿฿ It doesn't get any more luxurious and comfortable than this on this side of the island.

Bhuvarin Resort ฿฿ Sprawling resort located on the very deep end of Ko Chang up on the hilly cliff, so you get the best views.

Sea Escape Ko Chang ฿฿ Tidy, cottage-like bungalows only a few steps away from Ko Chang's Kai Bae Beach.

Mangrove Hideaway ฿฿ Fronting a mangrove forest on Ko Chang's far southeastern corner, this environmentally friendly guesthouse feels hidden.

Ko Kut & Ko Mak

Bann Makok ฿฿ Tucked into the mangroves on Ko Kut, this place resembles a traditional raised fishing village. Closed during the monsoon season.

Siam Beach Resort ฿฿ Simple, old-school bungalows on prime real estate overlooking one of Ko Kut's prettiest bays.

Seavana Beach Resort ฿฿ Stylish wine-coloured buildings overlook a garden, coconut palms and white sand at this top-drawer set-up near Ko Mak's northern pier.

Koh Mak Cococape Resort ฿฿ Attractive, earthy-feeling rooms and bungalows on a jungly, isolated cape on Ko Mak.

Koh Kood Resort ฿฿ Family-run for nearly 20 years, this resort on the eponymous island tumbles down a jungly hillside overlooking Hat Bang Bao.

Big Easy ฿฿ Distinctly un-flashy but cosy wooden bungalows on a quiet stretch of beach on Ko Mak's western end.

Kiri Private Reserve ฿฿฿ The most luxurious place to stay on Ko Kut, if not the entire eastern seaboard, with arrivals via private flights.

Tinkerbell Resort ฿฿฿ Absolute beach frontage at the southern end of Khlong Chao makes this resort hard to ignore.

Trat Province

Map p377

Klongyai Center ฿ Tidy, modern rooms in Khlong Yai, 15km north of the border crossing with Cambodia.

BaanRimNam Resort ฿฿ Handsome, spacious, well-maintained rooms in a two-storey building overlooking Trat's canal.

Rimklong Boutique Hotel ฿฿ Stay in one of Trat's charming heritage buildings. The owner here is friendly and helpful.

Banpu Resort Trat ฿฿฿ A convocation of contemporary-feeling above-water villas at the edge of a mangrove forest in rural Trat.

Ban Nam Chiao Homestay (p376) ฿฿฿ Get into the local lifestyle via a stay with a family in this canal-side village. Rates include meals and activities.

Chanthaburi Province

Map p379 & p380

El Vaso Resort ฿฿ Architecturally striking villas located north of Hat Chao Lao.

Laem Sing Natural Beach Resort ฿฿ Tidy, modern-feeling bungalows near the beach at Hat Laem Sing.

Tum Baan Suan ฿฿ Bright bungalows surrounding a garden a few clicks south of Chanthaburi. The friendly owner here speaks some English.

Ban Bang Chan Homestay (p382) ฿฿ Stay with a local family in this floating village in rural Chanthaburi Province. The fee includes boat transfer and meals.

Luang Rajamaitri Historic Inn (p383) ฿฿฿ Stay in a historic building in Chanthaburi's old town at this boutique hotel on the river with 10 unique rooms.

Rimnam Klangchan ฿฿฿ This business-leaning hotel right on the river in Chanthaburi manages to retain a homey feel.

Sa Kaew Province

River Resort & Spa ฿ Pet-friendly hotel in Sa Kaew that boasts both a lotus pond and swimming pool.

Baan Anong Hotel ฿ Vast, capable, clean rooms in a two-storey building only a few kilometres west of the border crossing in Aranyaprathet.

Rayong Province

Map p391

Caza V1 Serviced Apartment ฿ Cosy, colourful, cheap and located mere steps from Rayong's charming Th Yomjinda.

Tubtim Resort ฿฿ With the eponymous bay at its feet and a solid restaurant, this un-flashy, longstanding operation on Ko Samet is a favourite of repeat visitors to the island.

Ma hah Samut ฿฿ A charming old wooden house by the river in Pak Nam Prasae has been turned into a small hotel. River view rooms boast lots of light, a duplex setup, and the promised vistas.

Baan Ploy Sea ฿฿ Attractively weathered wood structure peering over Ko Samet's northern coast. Attached to one of the island's better restaurants.

Baan Phe Cabana Resort ฿฿ Expansive resort east of Ban Phe that's pleasantly surrounded by both garden and sea.

Ao Nuan Bungalows ฿฿ Simple fan-cooled affairs with shared cold-water bathroom and romantic air-conditioned retreats on a quiet cove on Ko Samet.

Ko Munnork Private Island Resort (p393) ฿฿฿ The only place to stay on tiny Ko Mun Nork. Rooms are all full-board and include ferry transport.

Ryad Rayong ฿฿฿ A Moroccan-style boutique resort (it's a thing) in eastern Rayong with a pool surrounded by a garden.

Paradee Resort ฿฿฿ The poolside villas here are nestled in a private cove on Ko Samet's southern end. Access is via private speedboat.

Chonburi Province

Map p398

Hotel Kuretakeso Sriracha ฿฿ You will feel like you've been teleported to Japan at this Si Racha hotel that boasts an in-house *onsen*, hi-tech toilets and a *yukata* room.

Pagoda Hill Cafe & Resort ฿฿ If you want to be close to nature and stay somewhere secluded and quiet, this resort spans a mere four rooms near the Khao Kheow Open Zoo.

Mercure Pattaya Ocean Resort ฿฿ A location a short walk from the beach and a pool with waterslide make this a great choice for families in Pattaya.

Rabbit Resort ฿฿ Stunning, stylish and secluded bungalows and villas on Hat Jomtien. A family-friendly pool makes this a good place to take the clan.

Novotel Ko Si Chang ฿฿ An expansive resort, ranging from rooms to bungalows, that's the nicest place to stay on tiny Ko Si Chang.

Chachoengsao

Oui J'aime ฿฿ This contemporary-feeling city hotel is decorated in loft industrial style via metalwork.

Ruen Lampoo Resort ฿฿ A homestay resort located on the banks of Mae Nam Pakong south of Chachoengsao, appealingly surrounded by mangroves.

KITTI GAYSORN/SHUTTERSTOCK

Koh Mak Cococape Resort

For places to stay in Hua Hin and the upper gulf, see p449

Above: Hat Thung Wua Laen (p447); Right: Prachuap Khiri Khan (p434)

Researched by Chawadee Nualkhair

Hua Hin & the Upper Gulf

BEACHES, MOUNTAINS, FORESTS AND CULTURE

The upper gulf has everything you could hope for in Thailand, all in one relatively compact space.

A few hours' drive from the capital, the upper gulf is mainly known for Hua Hin, a typical weekend and summer retreat for holidaying Bangkokians. But there is much more to this region than beach resorts. Phetchaburi, recently named a UNESCO Creative City of Gastronomy, is rediscovering itself amid its markets, storefronts and walkways, where graffiti depicting people and animals who live in the neighbourhood is as lovingly maintained as the city's monuments, temples and eateries. Prachuap Khiri Khan, where roving macaques haunt the streets in search of a stray snack, holds its own quiet charm, ringed by three picturesque bays and crowned by the spires of its most famous temple. Further down the gulf, Chumphon, the 'gateway to the South', exists in contradiction between its old-timey historical town centre and the jungle-clad mountains and beaches that line it, a push-and-pull between city and nature. And Hua Hin – not just a weekend getaway for Bangkok yuppies – hides its own secrets, neighbourhoods where monks visit at dawn to receive offerings of freshly steamed Chinese buns and sticky skewers of sweet pork.

Between them lie swaths of lush greenery, much of it national park land, home to millions of animals like elephants, leopards, bears, birds and monkeys, not to mention unique trees, plants and flowers.

AMNAT30/SHUTTERSTOCK

THE MAIN AREAS

PHETCHABURI
Rich in culture and edible history. p414

HUA HIN
A traditional seaside haven for families. p421

PRACHUAP KHIRI KHAN PROVINCE
A treasure trove for nature lovers. p434

CHUMPHON PROVINCE
Empty beaches and full bellies. p444

Find Your Way

Whether you're based in Hua Hin or Prachuap Khiri Khan, you'll find plenty to occupy you from sandy white beaches and tranquil waves to arduous hikes and playful animals.

Phetchaburi, p414

Frequently overlooked in favour of its neighbours, this town is a good base for exploring the region's northern mountains, forests and beaches.

Hua Hin, p421

The traditional summer retreat of the Thai aristocracy enjoys a wealth of entertainment options, plus a supremely soft, wide beach.

Prachuap Khiri Khan Province, p434

Its capital is a sleepy town with fishing boats dotting the bay.

Chumphon Province, p444

More than a transit hub, this overlooked destination has great beaches, islands and national parks.

MOTORBIKE & CAR

Motorbike rentals start around 200฿ per day; car rentals start around 1200฿ per day. While pricier than public transport, they do reach remote places outside of the bus network and are more convenient.

TRAIN

Train travel is a bargain around Hua Hin and the upper gulf. The Southern Line railway runs south from Bangkok to the border of Malaysia, with stops at Hua Hin and most of the towns in the region.

EM7/SHUTTERSTOCK

Hat Hua Hin (p421)

Plan Your Time

Use Hua Hin or Prachuap Khiri Khan as your jumping-off point for day trips to the national parks; return to the city in the evening for street food at the night markets or seaside dining.

A Weekend Away

- If you're here on a weekend, head to **Hat Hua Hin** (p421) to soak up the sun. Spend the evening trawling artisan stalls at **Cicada Market** (p427) before having an open-air feast at **Tamarind Market** (p428). Next day, head to **Khao Sam Roi Yot National Park** (p430) and hike to **Phraya Nakhon Cave** (p430), before lazing on the beach at **Ao Manao** (p441).

Five Upper Gulf Days

- Stop off in Phetchaburi to visit the **Phra Nakhon Khiri Historical Park** (p414). The second day, enjoy sun and seafood on **Hat Hua Hin** (p421). Next, spend a morning at **Ao Manao** (p441) before touring **Kuiburi National Park** (p431). Spend a day at **Wildlife Friends Foundation** (p419) before renting a bike for a ride around **Pranburi Beach** (p435) on your last day.

SEASONAL HIGHLIGHTS

JANUARY
January is peak season in Hua Hin: the weather is dry and pleasant, though hotels and resorts are more expensive.

APRIL
Thai New Year/ Songkran celebrations, hot days and humid evenings: make sure to pack accordingly.

JUNE
June ushers in the rainy season, although there are still plenty of sun-filled days.

NOVEMBER
Rainy season is over and the weather is dry and sunny again. It's the start of peak tourist season.

Phetchaburi

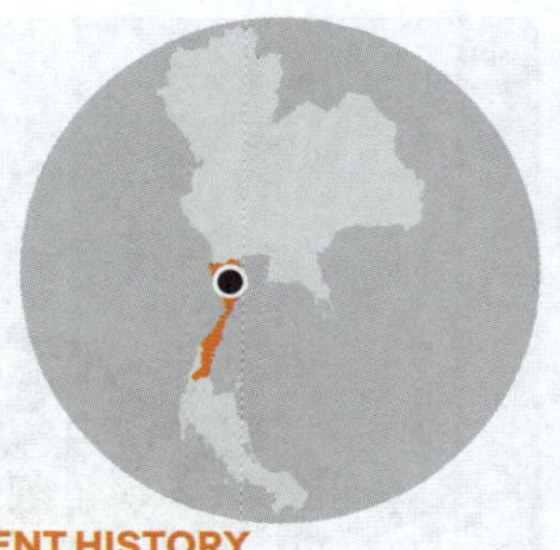

UNIQUE CUISINE | CHARMING WALKWAYS | ANCIENT HISTORY

GETTING AROUND

Phetchaburi is about two hours from Bangkok by car, which explains why minivans are the most popular way to get here. They leave daily from the Southern and Mor Chit bus terminals in Bangkok from 6am to 7pm. Otherwise, take the frequent train from Bangkok to Phetchaburi's Railway Station for 50฿ to 950฿.

In Phetchaburi proper, getting around is easy; most of the town centre is navigable on foot, and everything else is reachable by taxi or ride app. Getting to Hua Hin and Cha-am is also easy via minivans and air-conditioned buses.

Only around two hours south of Bangkok with traffic, the 'Diamond City' – Phetchaburi's literal translation – is often overlooked, treated as a place for a restroom stop or lunch break before moving on to more exciting pastures further south. That is a shame, since Phetchaburi possesses all the qualities many travellers look for in Thailand: interesting history, beautiful buildings, a charming city centre, friendly people and, of course, great food.

People from Phetchaburi like to say that those who live here don't need to travel anywhere else in Thailand, since Phetchaburi has it all: forest, beach, river and mountains. They are also proud of the town's rich history as a royal fort in the Sukhothai and Ayuthaya eras. Today, visitors to Phetchaburi are greeted with a tranquil town next to a clear green river, overseen by the spires of a white palace in the distant mountains. Further afield are sparkling, empty beaches and the dramatic mountainscape of Kaeng Krachan.

History Lessons

Phetchaburi's most famous landmark

For those interested in architecture or Thai history, a visit to **Phra Nakhon Khiri Historical Park** *(150฿)* is a must. Known locally as Khao Wang (Palace Hill), the park has a commanding position over three separate hilltops with panoramic views overlooking the city of Phetchaburi and the countryside.

Built under the royal command of Rama IV and completed in 1860, Phra Nakhon Khiri was originally a summer palace for both Rama IV and Rama V. Visitors will find temples, palaces and royal halls throughout the compound. From the main palace, follow the cobblestone paths to the three separate summits, each adorned with a stupa. **Phra That Chom Phet** is 40m high and located on the central summit. It's possible to climb through the stupa's interior up to its waist. The

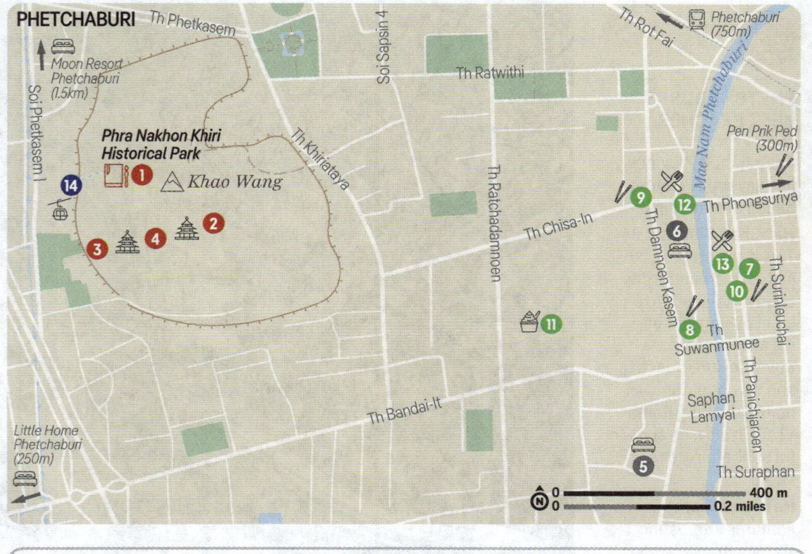

HIGHLIGHTS
1 Phra Nakhon Khiri Historical Park

SIGHTS
2 Phra Prang Daeng
3 Phra That Chom Phet
4 Wat Phra Kaew Noi

SLEEPING
5 Banthai Guest House
6 White Monkey Guesthouse

EATING
7 Khao Chae Mae Aon
8 Mae Lamiad
9 Mae Phad Pat Thai
10 Nam Than Tanote Mojito
11 Nok Noi Dessert
12 Rabieng Rimnam
13 Rim Nam Market

TRANSPORT
14 Phra Nakhon Khiri Historical Park Western Entrance

western summit is the site of **Wat Phra Kaew Noi** (Little Wat Phra Kaew), which was built in the style of the Temple of the Emerald Buddha in Bangkok's Grand Palace. **Phra Prang Daeng**, a stupa with Khmer-influenced designs, rounds out the summits. There is also an observatory here that was a favourite with Rama IV, who was an avid astronomer. The part of the palace on the western summit is a **national museum** (open 8.30am to 4.30pm).

If you don't want to tackle climbing the hill at the eastern entrance, there's a cable car at the **western entrance**, although it does close periodically for maintenance. This is a big place; be prepared to walk to reach the main pagoda and other viewpoints.

TOP TIP

Phetchaburi is the fifth Thai province to earn UNESCO's Creative City of Gastronomy designation, and for good reason. If you're looking for a one-stop shop for Phetchaburi cuisine, go to **Rim Nam Market** in the morning and take in the graffiti along Soi Rim Nam.

Eat Something Unique

Discover why Phetchaburi's cuisine is famous

UNESCO awarded Phetchaburi 'Creative City of Gastronomy' status a few years ago, but as the accolade arrived around the time of the COVID epidemic, its reception was muted. This means that many visitors – including Thais – have yet to discover the genuine pleasure of tucking into a local meal

PHETCHABURI'S BEST BEACHES

Phetchaburi Province has several excellent beach destinations.

Hat Chao Samran: This is the closest, just 15km from the city centre. Adjacent to a local fishing village, it's also known as Royal Leisure Beach and was popular during the King Rama VI era. It's a nice spot for sunbathing or a stroll.

Hat Puek Tian: Features interesting statues from a famous Thai epic, including a giant ogre rising from the waves and a demure flutist sitting on the rocks. It's 20km southeast of Phetchaburi city; you'll need private transport to get here.

Hat Cha-am: A long, clean stretch of sand 44km southeast of Phetchaburi city, with a variety of water sports and seafood restaurants.

TBBSTUDIO/SHUTTERSTOCK

from the 'town of three flavours': sour from its juicy limes, sweet from its excellent palm sugar and salty from its superior salt flakes.

A fusion of central Thai and Chinese elements, what sets Phetchaburi apart is influence from the Mon community, thought to have been Southeast Asia's earliest inhabitants. Originally from southern China, they are believed to have set up a fortress in Phetchaburi as early as the 8th century. One dish that is attributed to the Mons is *khao chae*, or 'summertime rice', a chilled rice porridge with perfumed water. Although *khao chae* is served throughout central Thailand today during the summer months (March to April), Phetchaburi serves it all year long at **Khao Chae Mae Aon** *(089 410 1969; per bowl 100฿)* on Soi Rim Nam, cementing its status as a local culinary treasure.

EATING AROUND PHETCHABURI PROVINCE: OUR PICKS

Pa Yunh: Possibly Phetchaburi's most well-regarded restaurant, serving a wide range of good Thai dishes. *11am-9pm* ฿฿

Pae Yuan: Not to be confused with Pa Yunh, this restaurant is almost as popular and is good with the deep-fryer. *10am-9.30pm* ฿

Mae Lukchan Bangtabun: Really good Central Thai seafood like Thai mackerel simmered in curry *'chu chee'*-style. *8.30am-9pm* ฿฿

Krua Bangtabun: Fresh Thai seafood and eye-wateringly spicy jungle curries. *10am-6pm Tue-Sun* ฿฿

Phra Nakhon Khiri Historical Park (p414)

THE SPECIAL FOOD OF PHETCHABURI

Adam Gottschalk is the presenter of OTR Food & History on Youtube. *@otr.offtherails*

There's no reason I can think of why Phetchaburi doesn't have the same hordes of visitors as Chiang Mai, but while the oversight is a travesty, it does mean you'll have some of the best food in Thailand all to yourself. The cuisine is an off-the-wall mishmash of three different groups. There's the ancient Mon, who lend their *khao chae*, or rice soaked in scented candle-water; a holiday delicacy everywhere else, street food in Phetchaburi. There are the Thai-Chinese fishermen, who've turned the town into a paradise for seafood. And there are the Siamese, who make the local toddy palm into an incredible curry.

Not surprisingly given the abundance of toddy palm sugar here, toddy palm curry is also a local delicacy. This sweet, salty and spicy melange can be found at **Rabieng Rimnam** *(facebook.com/rabiengrimnampetchburi; per person 300฿)*, in a charming old house with rooms for rent, and **Palmyra Kitchen Tanote** *(facebook.com/tanotekitchen; per person around 200฿)*, which also serves another local favourite, deep-fried papaya fritters.

Phetchaburi also churns out delicious desserts daily. The most famous dessert here is *ka nom mor gaang*, a baked coconut custard said to be of Portuguese origin, and *ka nom than*, or toddy palm cakes, like steamed cupcakes made with rice flour and topped with fresh coconut flesh. For a taste of these favourites, try Phetchaburi's most famous sweets shop, **Nok Noi Dessert** *(081 434 9627; dessert under 100฿)*.

EATING IN PHETCHABURI: SNACKS

Mae Lamiad: Specialising in *kanom mor gang* (curry pot sweets), a coconut custard snack topped with deep-fried shallots. *8am-5pm* ฿

Pen Prik Ped: A long-running pork-noodle-soup shop, popular for the extra-spicy zing of its noodles. *9.30am-3pm Wed-Mon* ฿

Nam Than Tanote Mojito: It's not alcoholic, but this mix of soda water, local limes, palm sugar and salt flakes is refreshing. On Riverside Walk. *9am-3pm* ฿

Mae Phad Pat Thai: A local institution dishing out *pat tai*, a dish many believe was invented in the 1940s to 'Thai-ify' Chinese noodles. *4-11pm* ฿

Beyond Phetchaburi

Explore a truly underrated part of Thailand, rich in verdant countryside and wild animals

Places

GETTING AROUND

What this area has in wildlife, it lacks in public transport. The best way to travel beyond Phetchaburi's city centre is by renting a car (check online travel sites, but expect prices to start from 600฿ per day) or using a ride app like Grab or Bolt.

Outside Phetchaburi town is a vast expanse of national park, where nature lovers can camp, hike and swim to their heart's content. At Kaeng Krachan National Park you can pitch tents at the many campsites, and equipment can be rented at good prices. Even if you decide to visit for a day, you will find plenty of trails, caves and waterfalls to occupy you, where fish can be found kissing your toes in shallow pools and the water is blessedly cool. Who knows? You might even see an elephant in the wild. A little further beyond the park, one of Thailand's best wildlife refuges awaits, with an adjacent lodge in case you want to get to know the animals better.

Kaeng Krachan National Park

TIME FROM PHETCHABURI: **30MIN**

Camp among the animals

Thailand's biggest national park, **Kaeng Krachan** *(thainationalparks.com/kaeng-krachan-national-park; adult 300฿)* is famous for the plethora of animals that live here, from leopards and elephants to hornbills and king cobras. Nature lovers typically set up camp in one of two sites: **Ban Krang Campsite** (good for birdwatching and close to caves) or **Phanoen Thung Campsite** (popular for beautiful vistas like the 'sea of mist' during the cool season of December to January). Ban Krang is the easier to get to, reachable by regular car, while Phanoen Thung can only be reached via vehicles with 4WD. Visitors can get rides to both campsites from headquarters (round trip to Ban Krang is per person 1400฿, to Phanoen Thung 2500฿); camping gear can be rented from headquarters (two-person tent 150฿), with sleeping bags and pillows costing 10฿ to 30฿ each. Visitors with their own camping equipment pay 30฿ per person to use the camping ground. Both campsites host restrooms and restaurants, but on weekdays when it's not crowded they close, so you might want to bring your own food. The park is open 8am to 4.30pm. From Phetchaburi, Kaeng Krachan town is accessible by minivan, after which you must take a taxi to park headquarters.

SUTIPONG/SHUTTERSTOCK

Camping, Kaeng Krachan National Park

WHAT TO BRING CAMPING

Of course, experienced campers know well to bring tents, sleeping bags, something with which to make a fire, and a little shovel. But Thailand has a few other considerations that campers may not have to worry about in other countries. Insect repellent is extremely important, and the stronger, the better (that means DEET if you can stand it). During rainy season, special leg coverings that close around the ankle may be necessary to ward off leeches. Modest – but breathable – clothing that covers the shoulders and shins will be needed if you plan to visit any temples. And finally, a first-aid kit that includes activated charcoal or Pepto-Bismol (a Thai alternative is the 'Flying Rabbit' brand) will ease worries about possible stomach troubles.

Cavort with carp

Probably Kaeng Krachan's most famous waterfall, **Nam Tok Pala-U** *(adult 300฿)* is a stunner. It boasts 16 tiers of clear emerald water and is accessible on foot. Visitors are free to swim in the ponds with carp and hike along the edges with butterflies. Even better, the road to the waterfall from **Huad Sai Village** is known to be home to many elephants, so you could get a good view of some pachyderms on your way to and from your swim. The waterfall has its own entrance into the park on the far-southern end and is a little over an hour's drive from Hua Hin (you can take a taxi or *songthaew* from Hua Hin's bus terminal). Open 8.30am to 4.30pm.

Wildlife Friends Foundation

TIME FROM PHETCHABURI: **33MIN**

Making friends with monkeys

In operation on the fringes of Kaeng Krachan for 24 years, the **Wildlife Friends Foundation Thailand** *(wfft.org; full-day tour with lunch adult/child 1600/1100฿, half-day 1100/700฿)* is Thailand's biggest wildlife rescue centre, caring for more than 800 animals spanning 65 different species and blanketing

EATING & DRINKING NEAR KAENG KRACHAN

Camper Coffee & Chill Cafe: A charming outdoor spot a few minutes' south of Rte 3499, featuring coffee, Thai food and live music. *8am-5pm* ฿

Hidden Vibe Cafe: On the southern edge of Kaeng Krachan Reservoir, this swish-looking coffee bar enjoys a lovely view. *8am-6pm Sun-Fri, 7.30am-8pm Sat* ฿

Smith Cafe: Set in a pretty garden on Rte 2062, this full-service restaurant serves spicy stir-fries, papaya salads and cold beer. *9am-9pm* ฿

Kenaray's Kitchen: A cosy cafe in a stylish farmstay features a menu of Thai-Italian-American favourites and pet toucans. *10am-8pm Fri-Wed* ฿

GETTING CLOSER TO THE ANIMALS

Home to over 800 animals (and climbing), the Wildlife Friends Foundation Thailand is always in need of volunteers, hosting up to 75 at any one time. If you have some time on your hands and feel like immersing yourself in the important work at the WFFT, you can choose to help out at either the Wildlife Rescue Center (home to over 600 gibbons, macaques, bears and birds, to name a few), the Elephant Refuge (where over 20 elephants reside), the Wildlife Hospital (for qualified vets and vet students) and the PAT-Welfare Clinic (WFFT's latest venture, it offers neutering and vaccination services to stray dogs and cats and is located between Cha-am and Hua Hin). Best of all, you can volunteer at all of them if possible!

PONGPOL TEINPOTHONG/SHUTTERSTOCK

Rescued elephant, Wildlife Friends Foundation Thailand (p419)

over 90 hectares. With the help of up to 75 volunteers, 130 full-time employees from the nearby village and four full-time veterinarians, WFFT rescues animals on a regular basis, with the ultimate view of releasing them back into the wild. However, many of the animals – rescued from zoos, private homes, circuses and temples, where they were dumped – have sustained brain damage, severe bodily injuries or were captured too young to learn any real-life skills, making them lifelong residents of the foundation. The tour, which can take two hours to the whole day, takes you to many of the animals' enclosures with an English-language tour guide, making this as ethical a 'zoo' as you'll probably find. After lunch, full-day tour guests get to visit the Tiger Rescue Centre and Elephant Refuge, where you can greet a few of the elephants and feed them. Unlike many other rescue foundations, WFFT has a strict no-breeding rule, as the animals are ultimately meant to be repatriated. Although they prefer you to book online, you can arrive at the **I-Love-Phants Lodge** (on-site at WFFT) and join as a walk-in if there is space; same goes for staying there. Even if there's no space, having lunch overlooking the elephant enclosure as the gibbons sing is a fun experience in itself. If you don't have wheels, you can request WFFT pick you up where you are staying at an extra cost.

EATING NEAR WFFT: OUR PICKS

Chomview Seafood: A restaurant overlooking the beach in nearby Cha-am, recommended for its seafood. *10am-10pm* BB

Chom Talay Restaurant: A Thai seafood restaurant next to the ocean with reasonable prices. *11am-10pm* BB

Krua Khun Lek: Well-made, well-priced Thai food with live music in the evenings. *11.30am-9pm Wed-Mon* B

Chomtan Phetchaburi: Open-air Thai cuisine such as jungle curry, stuffed omelettes and stir-fried fish with green peppercorns. *10.30am-10pm Wed-Mon* B

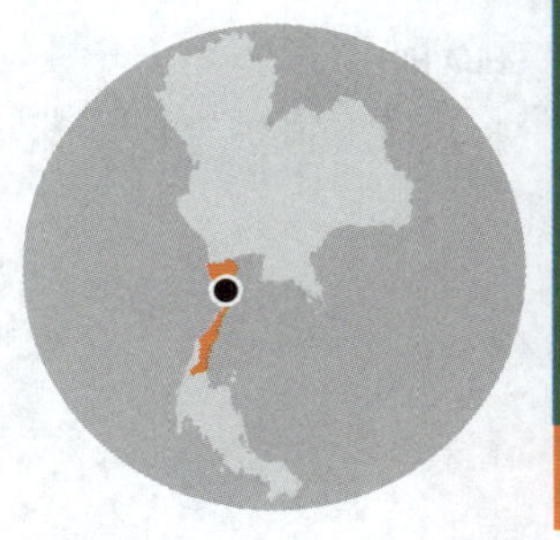

Hua Hin

SOFT BEACHES | FAMILY FUN | WATER SPORTS

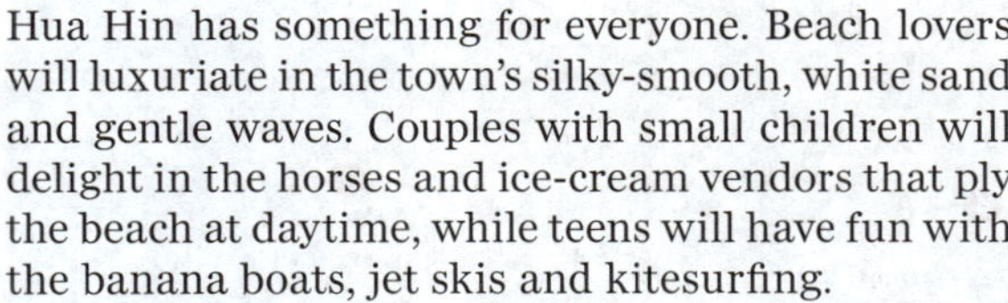

Hua Hin has something for everyone. Beach lovers will luxuriate in the town's silky-smooth, white sand and gentle waves. Couples with small children will delight in the horses and ice-cream vendors that ply the beach at daytime, while teens will have fun with the banana boats, jet skis and kitesurfing.

But there's more to Hua Hin than just fun in the sun. Beyond the main stretch of beach, Europeans have carved out mini-communities for themselves, making charcuterie and selling their own cuisines. Beyond the main drag of luxury hotels is a town where the locals actually congregate, sipping old-fashioned Thai coffee in the mornings and conversing over plates of freshly steamed dumplings. Unlike seaside rival Pattaya, Hua Hin faces east, meaning the sun hits the town early in the morning. That means Hua Hin is for early risers, a haven for lovers of small pleasures as well as of glam eateries.

TOP TIP

Hang out in the Khao Takiab (also known as 'Monkey Mountain') neighbourhood. The accompanying Khao Takiab Beach is as broad and soft as Hua Hin's and includes all the Hua Hin amenities without the crowds. This also means you avoid the traffic of Hua Hin's main thoroughfare, Th Phetkasem.

Life's a Beach

Spend time at Hua Hin's epicentre

As much as people like to bemoan the crowds (still paltry when compared to Florida or France or even Pattaya), few beaches in Thailand are as broad, soft and accommodating as 8km-long **Hat Hua Hin**. By day, horses roam the sands with their jockeys, looking for children to take on short rides; rented jet

GETTING AROUND

Hua Hin's main market area is full of transport options, from *songthaew* to tuk-tuks to motorcycle taxis. Here, the *songthaew* serves as a kind of bus, and there is a green line (plying the route between Khao Takiab and the airport) and a red line (serving the city centre). There are no official stops for the *songthaew*, so you are expected to 'call' the *songthaew* as you would a taxi. If the colour of the line is not clear on the side of the truck, simply tell drivers your destination and they will tell you if they stop there or not. The price will be 10฿ to 15฿, depending on what time it is.

HUA HIN

Boat Noodle Mr Kra (1.5km); After Morning Cafe (2.5km)
Baan Itsara (250m); Kuang Seng Noodies by Tata (1.5km)
0 500 m
0 0.25 miles
Tha Thiap Reua Pramong
Gulf of Thailand
Th Phetkasem
Soi 53
Th Naebkehardt
Th Chomsin (Soi 55)
Soi 70
Soi Ruampow
Th Naresdamri
Soi Selekam
Th Sasong
Soi Bintabaht
Th Amnuaysin (Soi Hua Hin 74)
Soi Hua Hin 59
Soi Kanjanomai
Soi Hua Hin 74/2
Th Damnoen Kasem
Soi 63
Hat Hua Hin
Train Station
Royal Hua Hin Golf Course
Soi 78
Th Liap Thang Rot Fai
Th Phetkasem
The Place Skatepark & Event Space (1km)

Soi 88
Soi 88
Soi 94

HIGHLIGHTS
1 Hat Hua Hin

ACTIVITIES
2 Efoil Thailand
3 Hua Hin Fishing Pier
see 2 KBA Kitesurfing School
4 Royal Hua Hin Golf Course
5 Surfspot Hua Hin

EATING
6 Brasserie de Paris Hua Hin
7 Dorfstadl Restaurant & Bar
8 Koti
9 Nai Hoi Fish Wonton Shop
10 Ogen
11 Saphan Pla Night Market

DRINKING
12 Le Pub Hua Hin
13 Monsoon Valley Wine Bar
14 Pakkati Coffee Studio
15 Velo Cafe

SHOPPING
16 Hua Hin Night Market

skis churn circles in the water; banana boats speed past with screaming teens in tow; and kitesurfers dot the skies from November to April. At night, karaoke crooning can be heard from the occasional seaside restaurant and the waters light up with fluorescent green-tipped ships, fishing for squid attracted to the colour. For some people in search of real peace and quiet, this may seem like a bit too much activity. But for others in search of beachy fun (and things to do as a family) relatively close to Bangkok, there are few places around that beat Hua Hin.

At the crack of dawn (around 6am), monks start strolling the beach, granting blessings to people who offer them food to make merit. If you are so inclined, you can make an offering too, as long as it's in a portable bag – Buddhism dictates that monks can't be picky about what food they are given. Women must make sure not to touch the monks but only the offering bowl. You can then receive a blessing from the monk, which is received with your hands in a *wai* (palms-together Thai greeting) and your head bowed.

A number of kitesurfing (and kiteboarding) schools operate on the beach, including **KBA Kitesurfing School** *(facebook.com/kitethailand; 1hr lesson 2200฿)*, which is open year-round, **Surfspot Hua Hin** *(surfspotthailand.com; 6hr class 7900฿)* and **Efoil Thailand** *(efoilthailand.com; 1hr 3500฿)*, which focuses on a sailing/surfing hybrid called windfoiling. All rent out equipment if you are more experienced.

DIY kind of people can rent their own jet skis (30 minutes around 700฿) on the beach or take a banana-boat ride (15 minutes for up to five people 500฿). As for horse rides, they can cost from 400฿ for 20 minutes up to 1000฿ for an hour, but photos will cost 50฿ extra per person.

WHY DO BANGKOKIANS COME HERE?

Hua Hin has a long history with the royal family, with Rama VI and Rama VII having both built summer palaces here in the 1920s. This tradition of spending part of the year in Hua Hin continued with Rama IX, who spent much of his time at Klai Kangwon ('Far from Worries') Palace. To mark the special relationship Hua Hin enjoys with the royal family, **Rajabhakti Park** south of Hua Hin boasts the statues of seven Thai kings who played pivotal roles in Thai history. As a result of the royal family's long history in Hua Hin, many Thais have sought to summer in the seaside town as well, and the tradition (to some extent) has continued to this day.

Hit the Fairways in the Upper 'Golf'

Twelve courses to choose from

Believe it or not, golf – once considered the purview of the baby boomer – is growing, with the number of people playing globally rising by 34% over the past seven years, according to the Royal & Ancient Golf Club of St Andrews. These numbers don't even include the United States, where golf participation has risen 38% compared to pre-pandemic levels, the National Golf Foundation says.

All of which is to say, you or someone you know already plays golf, or is considering picking it up. Where better than Hua Hin, which abounds in golf courses in every possible direction?

DRINKING IN HUA HIN: COFFEE

Pakkati Coffee Studio: A tranquil spot in a quiet part of town serving excellent coffee. *7.55am-5.05pm*

Collins Coffee Bar: Another charming, out-of-the-way spot owned by a Melbourne native. *8am-4pm*

After Morning Cafe: Besides coffee, this one also dishes out good pastries, making it popular with French expats. *8am-6pm Sat & Sun*

Velo Cafe: Coffee in an open, airy space near Hua Hin Fishing Pier, this spot is convenient for refreshments after a long walk. *7.30am-4.30pm*

HUA HIN FESTIVALS

Hua Hin Jazz Festival: Held in June, live jazz downtown on two separate stages draws thousands of guests.

Centara World Masters Golf Championship: Hosting 400 golfers from 30 countries at Asia's biggest golf tournament, also in June.

Hua Hin Food Festival: Held in early December, this event showcases local cuisine for four days at the Royal Queen Park.

Songkhran: Many locals flee Hua Hin during April because the town becomes inundated with Bangkokians. During Songkhran (13 to 15 April), the streets are alive with water fights and partying.

New Year's: Sit on the sand for fireworks at midnight, and add to the air pollution by warbling karaoke by the beach.

MAI GROVES/SHUTTERSTOCK

Black Mountain Golf Club

Officially, Hua Hin has 12 golf courses, but if you include areas within an hour's drive, you get exponentially more. Regardless of how wide or narrow your scope, all would generally agree that frequent PGA stop **Black Mountain Golf Club** *(blackmountaingolfclub.com; per person around 4690฿)* is among the best – not just in the area, but in Thailand. There are practice greens to try out putts, a good pro shop and even a spa to ease your sunburned limbs.

Also popular with local golfers is **Pineapple Valley Golf Club** *(pineapplevalleygolfclub.com; per person 2995฿)*, designed by the country's top golf-course architect, Pirapon Namatra, spread out over a hill with panoramic views of the Gulf of Thailand. But if you want to play 18 holes on a little slice of local history, go to the **Royal Hua Hin Golf Course** *(royalhuahingolfcourse.com; per person 2250฿)*, Thailand's oldest international-standard 18-hole golf course. Built in 1924 for British railway workers and Thai aristocracy with homes in the area, the course may get muddy at times, but it is still a draw due to its historical significance. Rates do not include golf-cart rental, compulsory caddy fee, caddy tip and follower fee.

EATING IN HUA HIN: THAI FOOD

Let's Sea: Part of a hotel, it's popular mostly for its decor and people-watching opportunities. *7am-10pm* ฿฿฿

Tanya's: A popular restaurant known for its Central Thai cuisine, with three seatings a day. *1-2.30pm, 5-6.30pm & 7-8.30pm* ฿฿

Khao Soi: For whatever reason, there is a northern Thai curried noodle restaurant in Hua Hin, and it's popular. *11am-9pm Tue-Sun* ฿

Koti: In the centre of town, popular mostly for the fact that it's been here forever. *noon-midnight* ฿฿

Splashing Out

Jump into a water park

In keeping with Hua Hin's long-time reputation as a family destination, a couple of water parks have sprouted up in the area boasting special features of their own. The self-proclaimed 'number one water park in Hua Hin' is **Vana Nava** (*vananavahuahin.com; adult/child from 1200/890฿*), which bills itself as a 'water jungle'. Instead of vine-strewn trees and wild animals, you get more than 20 slides and rides, a 'Lost World' mini-park with resident T-rex, and a hot-spring oasis. The park boasts Thailand's largest water slide, the Abyss, and the country's first anti-gravity tube-slide, the Aqualoop. There's also an aquatic obstacle course (the Aquacourse, of course) and what it says is Asia's first virtual-reality slide, enabling you to don VR glasses to experience a 'Snow World', a 'Galaxy Voyage' or a 'Mysterious Jungle'. To go along with the 'jungle' theme, the park has also brought over more than 200,000 kinds of plants from other parts of Thailand to encourage the 'tropical' feel of the place.

But this dizzying array of activities does not make up Hua Hin's only water-park option. There's also **Black Mountain Water Park** (*adult/child 900/450฿*). Not only is it a less aggressively priced option, but it also sports a gentler, more chill vibe and just happens to be close to Black Mountain's golf course, enabling a parent to have a fun day out on the links while the children are entertained elsewhere. This park has nine different slides, a wave pool, and a 'Wakeboard Zone' lagoon for water sports like cable skiing and wakeboarding.

OTHER PLACES TO TAKE THE KIDS

It's possible, as difficult as it may be to imagine, that your child can get tired of hanging out on the beach. If that does happen, some other options for entertainment include **Hua Hin Skate Park**, the first skate park of its kind in Hua Hin and founded by actor Lek Patravadi Mejudhon (of *White Lotus* fame). Inside the park are two skate bows, a quarter pipe, mini ramp, manual pad and fun box, and for the parents who don't know what any of that is, there is also a cafe. Open 8am to 6pm, it's also open to rollerbladers and entry is free with registration.

Further north is **The Place Skatepark & Event Space**, an indoor spot for skateboarders wary of getting sunburned. Open 9am to 11pm.

Do Beaches the Thai Way

Stuff your face with Thai seafood

Thais are not the type to lie out in the sun all day, soaking up the rays. In the middle of the day, they are more likely to be found scowling in the shade of a tree under a big hat, or happily munching on seafood under a fan – the whole reason why Thais go to the beach in the first place. Because of this, Hua Hin is fairly bursting with seafood spots of differing quality, popularity and reputation.

Among the most beloved is **Raan Aharn Go Mark** (*facebook.com/komarkhuahin; mains around 300฿*), which isn't even by the beach. It's on the far side of a busy highway, with a strip-mall feel. In spite of that, it's perpetually packed, with diners vying for plates of stir-fried crabmeat with holy basil,

DRINKING IN HUA HIN: OUR PICKS

Sky Hua Hin: Situated in the nearby Holiday Inn, this rooftop bar is popular for its incredible views and generous drinks. *5pm-midnight*

Lost & Found Hua Hin: A fun space modelled after a well-loved fraternity house with good service, decent food, cocktails and music. *5-11.30pm*

Bunker Bar: A cheap and cheerful outdoor spot by the sea, this bare-bones establishment is basically a couple of chairs with booze. *1-9pm Thu-Tue*

Le Pub Hua Hin: A British-style pub, but open air and with decent food. *1pm-1am Mon-Sat, noon-midnight Sun*

A COMMUNITY OF FOODIES

Hua Hin doesn't just harbour fresh Thai seafood. There is a smattering of Europeans making and selling items that remind them of home, like **Baan Fostier**, run by a Swiss man and his Thai wife who make their own salami, saucisson, coppa and pâté out of local animals. A similar undertaking is **La Charcuterie Française**, where a French couple make ham, paté, rillette, and even venison sausage under strict French hygiene conditions (HAACP). As for locally made cheese, Italian-owned **Del Casaro** makes its own mozzarella, burrata, scamorza, mascarpone and ricotta from local milk. Finally, **Monsoon Valley Vineyard** produces award-winning wines and runs tours of its beautiful vineyard daily (book ahead on the website).

TOT NKTD/SHUTTERSTOCK

Fishing, Hua Hin

Chinese-style soft oyster omelettes, and fresh clams stir-fried in chilli jam. A more picturesque restaurant is the seaside **Baan Itsara** *(facebook.com/itsarahuahin; mains around 250฿)*, a longstanding player in Hua Hin serving simply grilled white tiger prawns and your choice of whole fish either steamed in soy sauce or fried under a mountain of crispy garlic.

Madame Green Seafood *(mains 250฿)* on Hat Khao Takiab is a big local name, but long-time Hua Hin-ers say a better nearby option may be **Aowtakiab Seafood Hua Hin** *(aowtakiabseafood.com; mains around 300฿)*, where you can choose a type of seafood to be prepared in a multitude of ways: in a soup, in a curry, stir-fried, steamed, deep-fried, you get the picture. Finally, there is **Sopa Seafood** *(081 880 7112; mains around 250฿)*, another local favourite in spite of its charmless location. Even then, its sour curry with holy basil leaves and sun-dried squid are superb.

Gone Fishing

Hua Hin's most under-the-radar pastime

It might be surprising to hear that Hua Hin is one of Thailand's most popular fishing spots. Relatively gentle waves and an abundance of beaches, combined with an ample supply of pomfret, Thai seabass (aka barramundi) and mullet, lure

DRINKING IN HUA HIN: WINE

Monsoon Valley Wine Bar: Run out of the local gourmet Villa Market, so you can do your shopping and sipping in one place. *9.30am-6.30pm*

Taboo Tapas Wine & Lounge: A stylish Spanish-style wine bar with good tapas as well as Thai and international faves. *noon-11pm Wed-Mon*

Wine Bubble & Berry: Good selection of reds, whites and bubblies with knowledgeable staff and chilled-out vibes. *11am-10pm*

Malo Cafe & Bar: A cosy, warm spot with beautiful interiors, exemplary service and the occasional wine tasting event. *5pm-midnight Fri & Sat, to 1am Sun*

thousands of dedicated fishers each year to pit their skills against the local schools.

Hua Hin Fishing Pier *(thailand-huahin.com/huahin-fishing-pier)*, situated right in the heart of town, is the traditional centre of fishing in Hua Hin, and fishers can still be found there with rods in hand, testing the (admittedly now crowded) waters. They can also be hired to guide you on your fishing journeys, either on the pier, or by boat; squid boats can also be rented to take you on their nightly rounds (ask about rates and times beforehand). But longtime fishermen will say this pier is over-commercialised and direct you to **Khao Takiab Pier**, which is far less crowded and set at the foot of a nearby mountain on which a pretty temple sits. If you are willing to brave the monkeys, the temple offers a great view of Hua Hin proper.

If you are less experienced, you may want to start out at **Hua Hin Fishing Lodge** *(huahinfishing.com; adult/child fishing rods included 1900/950฿)*, where 44 kinds of fish are kept in freshwater ponds, making them easier to hook. Those serious about learning can stay on the premises in one of three bungalows, and a playground is on site for young children, as is a restaurant.

If a couple of freshwater ponds seems too 'small fry' for you, check out **Jurassic Mountain Resort & Fishing Park** *(jurassicfishingthailand.com; day package with rods, bait & meal 7700฿)*, set further north in Cha-am. Promising four-star facilities and world-class sportfishing, Jurassic stocks native carp, redtail catfish and alligator gaur, as well as an 181kg giant arapaima that has yet to be apprehended.

Markets Ahoy

Shop under the stars

As with all Thai towns popular with Thais themselves, Hua Hin is chock-a-block with markets, especially on weekends. The most popular weekend market is **Cicada Market** *(cicadamarket.com)*, which provides a treasure trove of local artisanal clothing, jewellery and bags to buy alongside hand-painted fans, fabric-flower hair accessories, sculptures made out of discarded car parts, and perfume sachets. Your shopping spree will be accompanied by the soothing sounds of various live bands playing jazz, pop and even a traditional Thai-modern music hybrid. There are shadow-puppet shows, an entire section dedicated to local art, and enough Hua Hin-themed T-shirts to outfit an American football team (defence

HOW TO FISH IN HUA HIN

Tammatep Sudasna na Ayudhya is a fisher and occasional fishing-tour guide. *facebook.com/Tammatep*

I've been fishing here for 18 years. I like to fish right on Hua Hin Beach. No one's fishing on the beach but me. It's 10 times harder than on a boat.

When it's sunny the fishing is better, fish can see the bait. After a rain, it's murkier water. Fish can't see as much, and the freshwater drives the fish away. To be successful, you need patience and consistency. You have to cast at the same spot a lot. You have to act like you're bait fish and keep casting and casting.

If you're new at fishing, just ask a lot of people.

EATING IN HUA HIN: WESTERN FOOD

Ogen: Great Middle Eastern food with a good range of dishes for vegetarians, like hummus, Israeli salad and falafel. *noon-11pm* ฿฿

Dorfstadl Restaurant & Bar: Specialising in Bavarian food and good German beers. *3pm-midnight Tue-Sun* ฿฿

Brasserie de Paris Hua Hin: Central beachside spot recommended for its steaks, especially its grass-fed Chateaubriand for two. *noon-10pm* ฿฿฿

Trattoria by Andreas: This super-popular Italian spot is flooded with Bangkokians (reserve on weekends) and is close to Cicada Market. *noon-2pm & 5-10pm* ฿฿฿

WHAT'S WITH ALL THE EYE GRAFFITI?

If you spend any time in the town centre – or even as far south as Prachuap Khiri Khan or as north as Cha-am – you might spy some eye-related graffiti on the sides of buildings or even on pedestrian crossings. This graffiti, and the question of whether it constitutes valued creative expression or not, is currently at the centre of a local controversy. Following complaints from some locals, authorities have fined the artist (who goes by the name of 'Joe') thousands of baht and ordered him to scrub the graffiti from the areas under dispute. However, others see the art as charming and a valuable expression of artistic merit. Take a walk through town to decide which side of the debate you fall on.

2P2PLAY/SHUTTERSTOCK

Hua Hin Night Market

and offence). And this being Hua Hin, there's a section devoted solely to golf. There is a food court here, as well as clean bathrooms, and just across the road (Hua Hin Soi 23) there is a market dedicated solely to food, **Tamarind Market** *(facebook.com/tamarindmarkethuahin)*, which is open 4pm to 11pm Friday to Sunday.

If you want to go somewhere a bit closer to the centre of town, there's **Hua Hin Night Market** on Hua Hin Soi 72, the OG when it comes to Hua Hin's nighttime shopping destinations. Although its allure has waned a bit after the introduction of rivals like the Cicada Market, it's still well attended, with an entire street closed off to traffic to allow vendors to display their wares. There's also a good number of street-food vendors, particularly of grilled seafood. It's open nightly from 5pm to midnight.

Finally, right on Hua Hin's fishing pier stands the **Saphan Pla Night Market** *(facebook.com/saphanplahuahin)*, which takes place Friday to Sunday between 5pm and 10pm. The focal point here, not surprisingly, is the fresh seafood, although non-seafood options like barbecue and burgers are also available. Live music also plays here, adding to the breezy, relaxed ambience.

EATING IN HUA HIN: NOODLES

Boat Noodle Mr Kra: Traditional Ayuthaya-style boat noodles with small portions (order two or three in one go). *8am-4pm* ฿

Little Duck Restaurant: In spite of the name, the signature noodles here include duck and pork. *10am-9pm Wed-Mon* ฿

Nai Hoi Fish Wonton Shop: A longstanding local favourite specialising in handmade fish dumplings. *10am-3pm* ฿

Kuang Seng Noodles by Tata: Noodle soups centred on delicious braised chicken. *9am-4pm Thu-Tue* ฿

A WALKING BREAKFAST THROUGH THE MARKET

Be a super multi-tasker and explore Hua Hin's morning market while breakfasting at the same time.

START	END	LENGTH
Chatchai Market	Jek Pia	Around 1km; 15 minutes

Go down Th Dechanuchit to the 1 **Chatchai Market** entrance on your right; it will be marked by a *ta ko* (coconut custard on sago and taro) stall. If you have a sweet tooth, this particular vendor is excellent, so you can grab a container and munch along the way; if not, continue on by the various snack aisles until you hit 2 **Pailin's Sticky Rice**, distinguished by its big bunch of faux-mangoes by the sign. You can grab a pre-packaged mango sticky rice set or continue through the veg section and then the fish section before turning right at the edge of the market.

Continue on into the prepared food stalls, past the mobile *khao gaang* (rice curry) vendor to the 3 **Chatchai Market exit**, which will deposit you out onto the street. Turn right towards Th Phetkasem and cross it, ducking into Hua Hin 57 (Th Dechanuchit).

On your right, past Koti restaurant, you'll find 4 **Somchai Patonggo**, where a vendor deep-fries Chinese-style crullers out of freshly rolled dough. Grab a bag and head on over to 5 **Jek Pia**. Surrounding this restaurant are a group of mobile vendors. Among the most popular is the *jok* (Chinese-style rice congee) vendor. You can eat your bowl at a table at Jek Pia, where you should order a Thai-style coffee.

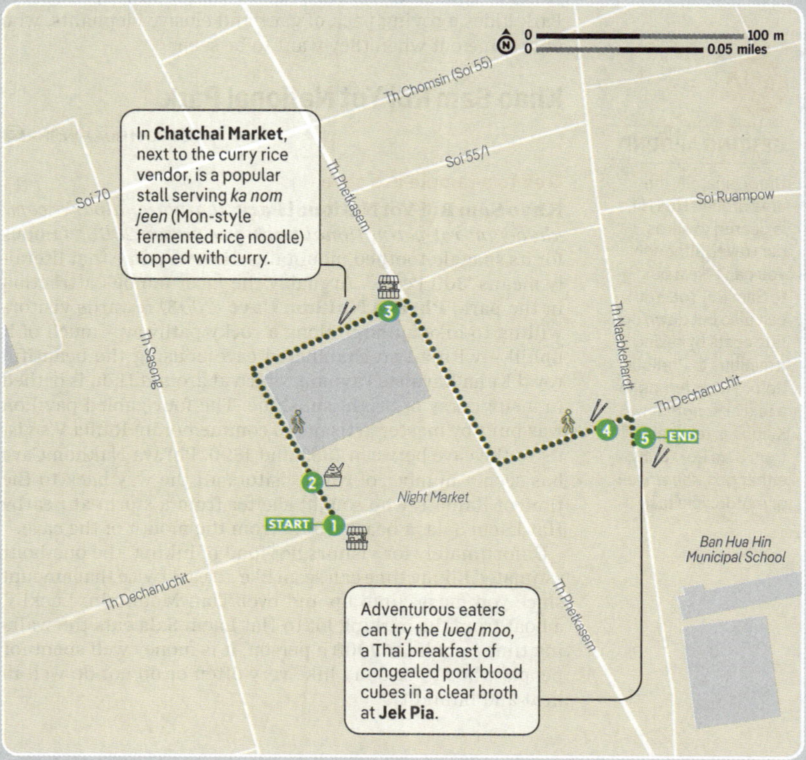

In **Chatchai Market**, next to the curry rice vendor, is a popular stall serving *ka nom jeen* (Mon-style fermented rice noodle) topped with curry.

Adventurous eaters can try the *lued moo*, a Thai breakfast of congealed pork blood cubes in a clear broth at **Jek Pia**.

Beyond Hua Hin

A wealth of mountains, caves and canals that go largely unexplored and wildlife that is largely unvisited.

Places

GETTING AROUND

Unfortunately, the area around Hua Hin is geared towards car travel, although you can take a bus to Sam Roi Yot. You can also cut down on ride costs by taking a minibus to Pranburi before transferring to a taxi or *songthaew*. Kuiburi is reachable from Sam Roi Yot by either taxi, *songthaew* or motorcycle taxi.

Because Hua Hin's beaches are so great, it's hard to tear yourself away from the silky sands, sunscreen and piña coladas to lace on a pair of hiking boots and work up a different kind of sweat. But for a certain type of traveller, the region just outside of Hua Hin is a trekking paradise: jammed full of jagged ridges and dark, mysterious caves with the occasional canal alongside which dancing crabs cavort. That's Sam Roi Yot National Park, which resembles a crown of peaks surrounding a valley of aquaculture farms; just beyond it, Kuiburi National Park hides a roving pack of gaur and elusive elephants, who only come out when they want to be seen.

Khao Sam Roi Yot National Park

TIME FROM HUA HIN: **1HR**

Trek to a temple in a cave

Khao Sam Roi Yot National Park (*thainationalparks.com/khao-sam-roi-yot-national-park; per person 200฿*), famous for its snaggle-toothed mountains, bears a name that literally means '300 Peaks'. Arguably the most famous attraction in the park, **Phraya Nakhon Cave** *(200฿)* rewards visitors willing to hike an hour along a rocky pathway – much of it uphill – with a two-chambered cave housing the beautiful royal Kuha Karuhas Pavilion, which at around 11am is bathed in a single ray of bright sunshine. The four-gabled pavilion was built by master artisans to commemorate Rama V's visits to the cave between 1863 and 1890. Phraya Nakhon Cave has seen a number of royal visitors all the way back to the time of Rama I, who sought shelter from a storm at nearby Hat Laem Sala, a beach 400m from the mouth of the cave.

Unfortunately for visitors not fond of hiking, the one-hour estimated hiking time can seem like at least twice that amount since you must climb up and over Tian Mountain. Luckily, a boat from the parking lot to Hat Laem Sala cuts the walking time in half. At 200฿ a person, it is money well spent for people who either don't hike very often or do not do well in heat and humidity.

PARILOV/SHUTTERSTOCK

Phraya Nakhon Cave, Khao Sam Roi Yot National Park

Whiz along Khao Daeng Canal

If scrambling over rocks for two hours is not your cup of tea, you can opt for a leisurely long-tail boat ride along **Khao Daeng Canal** *(visitsamroiyot.com/khao-daeng-canal; per person 200฿, plus boat max 6 passengers 500฿)*. The roughly one-hour ride takes you past numerous mangroves and some of the park's most interesting limestone rock formations – besides Khao Daeng (or 'Red Mountain', named for its red face), there's 'Little Crocodile' (resembling a small crocodile standing up) and 'the Eight Elders' (eight standing rocks grouped together). Birdwatchers can see egrets fishing for food and *plaa theen*, which translates to 'footed fish'. These fish propel themselves by their forefins along the wet sand, making for interesting watching if you are so inclined. At the end of the ride, you will pass a fishing village and see how the local fisherfolk live before reaching where the canal meets the ocean and heading back to the pier.

Kuiburi National Park

TIME FROM HUA HIN: 1½HR

Chase after elephants

If you love elephants and wish to see one in the wild, **Kuiburi National Park** *(thainationalparks.com/kui-buri-national-park; adult/child 200/100฿)* is your best bet, with rangers estimating a 95% success rate. The park is home to 22 known

MORE ABOUT SAM ROI YOT

Thailand's first 'marine' (coastal) park, Khao Sam Roi Yot is a beautiful detour in an area known more for its beaches than its mountains. This park has it all: caves, limestone karsts, mangroves, forests and beaches, much relatively underexplored. Established as a national park in 1966, Sam Roi Yot holds important archaeological artefacts, such as prehistoric cave paintings that date back 3000 years. These include paintings of hunting scenes, drawings of humans wearing accessories, and even a child's skeleton from the Ice Age. The park also holds a special place in Thai history, as it is the location where Rama IV – an avid astronomer – hosted European guests during a solar eclipse.

EATING IN SAM ROI YOT: OUR PICKS

Yoksod Seafood: On the way to Phraya Nakhon Cave is this delicious seafood spot. The steamed blue crabs are recommended. *10am-6pm* ฿฿

Tam Sai Seafood: Great seafood dishes, including a nice crab curry and a salad with shrimp, cashews and deep-fried shallots. *10am-6pm Thu-Tue* ฿฿

Krua Khun Joie: Aquafarms cluster at the foot of the Sam Roi Yot mountains. This restaurant takes advantage of its proximity to seafood. *9am-7pm* ฿

Jim Dang: Good basic Thai seafood like stir-fried squid with garlic and fried rice with crab. *9am-8pm* ฿฿

BEST TOUR OPERATORS IN THE AREA

If you'd like to arrange your own tour instead of relying on Kuiburi National Park, check out **Siri Safari Kuiburi Tour**. This operator also offers tours to Phraya Nakhon Cave, a nearby lotus pond hosting more than 300 species of birds, and local temples. Another option is **Ton Ton Travel**, a wildlife-focused local travel agency. It also guides visitors through Khao Yai, Kaeng Krachan and Huai Kha Khaeng Wildlife Sanctuary (p165) in central Thailand. Finally, **Ken Diamond Tour** is based in Hua Hin. This small Thai/German agency takes customers to Khao Sam Roi Yot National Park and a tour of the Wildlife Friends Foundation for rescued animals (p419), with a particular focus on Prachuap Khiri Khan and Hua Hin.

elephant families (over 300 elephants in total), which have the run of over 900 sq metres of forestland in which to munch vegetation to their hearts' content. Unfortunately (or fortunately, depending on how you look at it), the animals are wild, so a sighting cannot be guaranteed; parts of the park remain closed to the public.

Besides elephants, Kuiburi shelters the biggest population of gaur (wild cattle species) in Thailand, at an estimated 100 and counting. These can be spied easily all over the park, some quite close to the forest roads. Other, less easily spotted mammals include gibbons, deer, jackals and even rumours of tigers and leopards, though these are very rarely spotted (no pun intended). There are also over 260 species of birds, including a wealth of hornbills, partridges and crested firebacks, and around 60 known reptiles species like pit vipers and roughneck monitors.

Visitors can arrive by car to the **Huai Luek Ranger Station**, 16km north of the park headquarters, on their own, but they must then hire a safari pick-up with a guide (850฿ for one pick-up holding a maximum of six people). These guides, all armed with walkie-talkies, patrol the grounds on the hunt for elephants, and once one is spotted, they will all rush to the spot in the hopes of catching them – much like paparazzi rushing to photograph a celebrity in LA. Unfortunately, there is little wildlife to be spotted at the visitor centre beyond some birds and an alarmingly large spider, and the park headquarters are not recommended for visiting at all.

The park recommends that visitors arrive by 3pm to allow time to find a guide. Viewing hours are 2pm to 6pm, but the national-parks website advises booking a tour in advance, or with a tour operator in Hua Hin or Pranburi.

Cha-am

TIME FROM HUA HIN: **40MIN**

Bake on a quiet beach

Technically in Phetchaburi Province, Cha-am embraces a rural feel despite its close proximity (26km) to Hua Hin. It's particularly popular among couples looking for a romantic getaway, travellers in search of tranquillity and families who are eager for a hassle-free holiday with sand as far as the eye can see. Originally a fishing village, Cha-am is famous for fresh seafood; stop at the local restaurants to enjoy the catch of the day.

EATING IN HUA HIN: VEGETARIAN

Veggie Tales Cafe: Popular for its vegetarian takes on Thai dishes like *pat tai* and crispy 'pork'. *10am-7.50pm Thu-Mon* ฿

Green Dining Vegan and Vegetarian: Well-priced traditional dishes like *dom yam* soup and spicy bamboo shoot salad. *10am-6pm Mon-Sat* ฿

Hua Hin Vegan Cafe: A more swish cafe setting for Western vegan dishes, raw juices and smoothies. *10am-10pm* ฿฿

3 Monkeys Restaurant: Not solely plant-based, but it does have a vegetarian and vegan section to its menu. *11am-11pm Wed-Mon* ฿฿

SIRICHAI PUANGSUWAN/SHUTTERSTOCK

Hat Cha-am

The main attraction in town is **Hat Cha-am**, a long stretch of casuarina-lined sand and an ideal beach for families and independent travellers. It's free of beach vendors; activities here include swimming, sunbathing, jet skiing and banana-boat rides. Although the sea can appear murky, the beach is shaded by trees and there are plenty of umbrellas to retreat to during the hottest hours of the day, making the beach a nice alternative to the hotel swimming pool.

Even on busy weekends, the atmosphere is remarkably laid-back, and the beach is within walking distance of many restaurants and small Thai-style shops. Away from the beach, there are mangrove forests to explore, bicycling trips to take and even horse riding. With plentiful beachfront accommodation available at prices that won't drain the bank account, Cha-am is an excellent alternative to staying in Hua Hin.

Phetkasem Hwy runs through Cha-am's busy town centre, which is about 1km away from the beach via Th Narathip. This is where you'll find banks, the fresh market, the train station and most bus stops. There are plenty of ATMs and a few extended-hours exchange booths along Th Ruamjit.

CHA-AM FOREST PARK

Located 20km north of Hua Hin and established in 1992, Cha-am Forest Park is a verdant natural park brimming with flora and fauna. Once called Khao Nang Phanturat Forest Park, this protected patch of land is believed to be the setting for the Thai folktale *Sang Thong*, in which a prince (Sang Thong himself) is somehow born from a conch shell to a beautiful queen. Alas, he is banished by an evil stepmother and must disguise his beauty behind a hideous mask, only to return to reclaim his troubled kingdom after finding and marrying his princess. You will not find Prince Sang Thong here today, but you will find white-handed gibbons and long-toed geckos in 336 hectares of beautiful greenery.

EATING IN CHA-AM: OUR PICKS

Village Restaurant & Bar: Modest restaurant serving excellent Thai cuisine, fresh seafood and coffee, wine and spirits. *10.30am-10pm* ฿฿

Auntie Paew's Kitchen @Pana's Bar: Popular with locals, this beachside spot serves good (and well-priced) Thai seafood. *11am-9pm Wed-Mon* ฿

LoveBread Cha-am: Serving Thai and Western brunch favourites to a packed house on most days. Book ahead on Sundays. *8am-6pm* ฿฿

Dee Beach Cafe: A cute seaside place serving pasta, steak and fried rice. *10am-9pm Thu-Tue* ฿

Prachuap Khiri Khan Province

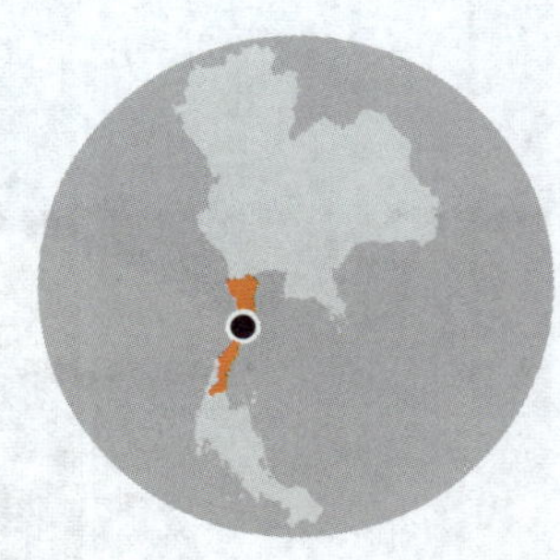

PEACE & QUIET | OCEAN WAVES | FORESTED MOUNTAINS

TOP TIP

If you don't fancy zipping all over the province for outdoor activities, you can choose Pak Nam Pran, centred on Pranburi Beach, as your home base. The town is popular with artists and Bangkok expats and has the feel of a beachy bohemian village.

A scenic fishing port with a sweeping turquoise bay dotted with limestone outcrops, the provincial capital of Prachuap Khiri Khan is an unexpected delight. Charming and relaxed, the town provides a great escape from the crowds, just 100km south of Hua Hin. 'Prachuap' (as the locals call it) does not see much tourism and consequently offers a glimpse into the 'real' Thailand, where locals are going about their daily lives. There is plenty to explore, including dense mountainous areas, a few islands and quiet beaches.

Prachuap Khiri Khan is home to a Royal Air Force base and was an invasion point for Japanese troops during WWII. The town is close to a number of national parks, and features the spectacular coastline of the Gulf of Thailand. Because of this, the province is also a hub for all manner of outdoorsy types with ample opportunities for kitesurfing, biking, caving and fishing.

Athletic Pursuits

Thailand's kitesurfing and cycling hub

The term 'hidden gem' is horribly overused, so let's just say Prachuap Khiri Khan is an 'unexpected treasure', especially for nature enthusiasts. About 1300 sq km of the province is given over to national parks, making overdevelopment an

GETTING AROUND

There is not much in terms of mass transit here, so you are mainly left to your own devices. It's a popular hub for mountain bikers, so there are plenty of bicycle-rental shops (around 50฿ per day) as well as rental shops for motorcycles (around 1200฿ per week) along the waterfront. If you are only zipping around town, *rot kuang kang* (motorcycles with seats in a sidecar) and *songthaew* can be found, especially at the waterfront.

Kitesurfers, Hat Pranburi

impossibility (for now). Because of that, Prachuap's hills are generously chequered with trails for hiking and bicycling, and its beaches – far less crowded than those of its sister Hua Hin to the north – are wide and uncluttered enough to make kitesurfing a pleasure.

The most popular beach for kitesurfing is probably **Hat Pranburi**, which stretches for 7km and is largely absent of people when the sun is at its brightest (most of the day). Named after the town behind it, 'Pranburi' can roughly be translated to 'city of wind', an apt moniker for this tranquil slice of coastline. During the cool season (November to January), burly winds buffet the area, making it more suitable for experienced windsurfers, but February to June sees gentler breezes and is considered an ideal time for beginners. A number of businesses cater to budding windsurfers (and its more challenging offshoot, wingfoiling), but the most established is **Yoda Kiteschool** *(087 017 6428)*, which rents out equipment and gives lessons.

When it comes to cycling, paths line most beaches and, as many roads are not that busy, make cycling almost anywhere in the province easy. One of the more unexpected drawcards for local cyclists is **Fort Thanarat**, an army camp open to the public. Here, a relatively easy and pleasant 15km cycling trail runs along Pranburi River towards Myanmar, making for a diverting few hours of exploration. The fort also offers rock climbing, a 50m pool, a driving range and an 18-hole golf course (per person 800฿; call ahead to reserve).

TAKE A HIKE

If you don't like to cycle and don't fancy kitesurfing, don't despair: Prachuap has you covered even if all you want to do is walk. Trails in Pranburi Forest Park and Khao Sam Roi Yot National Park can be made even more accessible with the help of a trusty tour operator like Ken Diamond Tour (p432), which offers a seven-hour experience through Pranburi Forest Park that includes pick-up and drop-off (provided you're in Hua Hin, Cha-am, Pak Nam Pran or Nong Kae) and another walk through Khao Sam Roi Yot National Park that includes a long-tail boat ride and guided tour to Phraya Nakhon Cave.

EATING IN PRACHUAP KHIRI KHAN: OUR PICKS

Talay Rab Lom Restaurant: Good Thai food in Prachuap Khiri Khan town. Try the *pad cha*, or stir-fry with ginger and green peppercorns. *10am-9pm* ฿฿

Krua Ban Pa: Well-regarded Thai seafood like southern Thai-style sour curry with fish eggs in a no-frills setting in Pak Nam Pran. *10am-9pm Thu-Tue* ฿฿

Sit-Ney: A popular lunch spot serving Thai favourites like fried rice and *pad se-ew*, a popular rice noodle dish stir-fried with soy sauce. *7am-3pm Tue-Sun* ฿

Krua Hua Ban: Reasonably priced open-air Thai seafood – try out the shrimp dishes in particular. *9am-8pm Thu-Tue* ฿฿

PRACHUAP KHIRI KHAN PROVINCE
HIGHLIGHTS
1 Hat Pranburi
2 Nam Tok Huai Yang National Park
SIGHTS
3 Ao Bo Thong Lang
4 Ao Manao
5 Ban Krut
6 Bang Saphan Yai
7 Beach Behind Khao Kalok
8 Fort Thanarat
9 Hat Ban Krut
10 Ko Ku Ram
11 Ko Nom Sao
12 Ko Rawing
13 Ko Sang
14 Ko Sing
15 Ko Thalu
16 Nam Tok Huai Yang
17 Nam Tok Khao Lan
18 Nam Tok Kha-on
19 Pak Nam Pran
20 Pranburi Forest Park
21 Sam Roi Yot Beach
22 Tham Khan Kradai
23 Thap Sakae
24 Wat Ao Noi
25 Wat Khao Chong Krajok
26 Wat Tham Khiri Wong
27 Wat Thang Sai
28 Wing 5 Airbase
ACTIVITIES
29 Adventure Cycling Thailand
30 Ken Diamond Tour
31 Yoda Kiteschool
SLEEPING
32 Jungle Cafe & Guesthouse
33 Nam Talay Resort
34 Pranberry Earth
Pak Nam Pran
Pran Buri Forest Park
Pran Buri
Pak Nam Pran
Beach Rd
Hat Pranburi
Soi 29
Thao Kosa Forest Park
Gulf of Thailand
0 500 m
Kaeng Krachan National Park
Phra Nakhon Khiri Historical Park (57km)
Nong Phlap
Huay Mongkhon
Hua Hin
Thap Thai
Khao Takiab
Khao Tao
Pa La-U
Khao Yai
Mae Nam Pranburi
Pranburi Dam
Mae Nam Pran Buri
Khao Noi
Pranburi
See Pak Nam Pran
Huai Tahd Phraek Sai
Sila Lot
THAILAND
Dolphin Bay
Sami Roi Yot
Kuiburi National Park
Bang Rong Jai
Ban Rai Mai
Bang Pu
Ko Sattakut
Khao Sam Roi Yot National Park
Ban Somron
Ban Khao Daeng
Yang Chum
MYANMAR (BURMA)
Kuiburi
Huay Baunok
Ao Khan Kradai
Ao Noi
Nikhom
Ao Noi
See Prachuap Khiri Khan
Theinkun Chaung
Dan Singkhon
Khlong Wan
Ko Aen

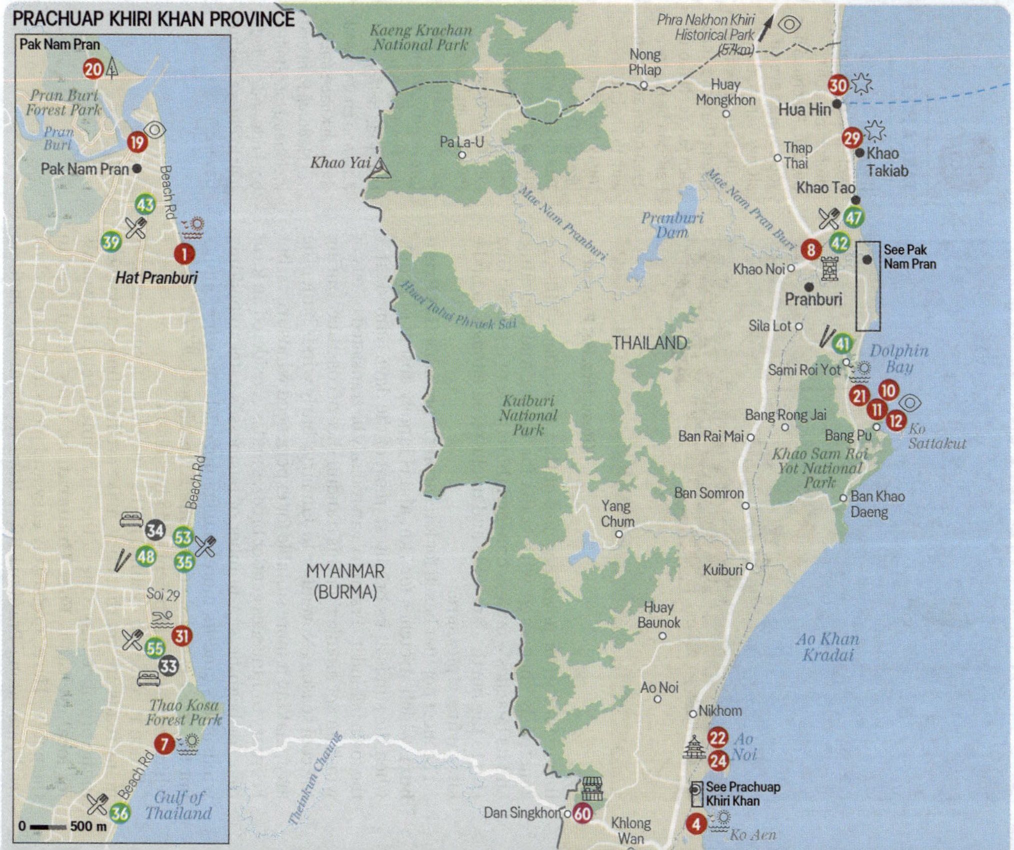

EATING
35 Aleenta Restaurant
36 Baan Pal Coffee
37 Bayern Himmel
38 Boobun
39 Brown Brew & Bistro
40 Cafe Wien Bangsaphan
41 Chicken and Bee
42 Forget Me Not Cafe & Farm
43 Hitch & Round Cafe and Space
44 I Ta Lay
45 JanRam
46 Jimpizza
47 Juergen's Corner Cafe & Restaurant
48 Krua Ban Pa
49 Krua Ban Suan
50 Krua Hua Ban
51 Le Panorama
52 Li's Restaurant
53 Pranberry
54 Raan Aharn Chan Super
55 Schnitzelwirten
56 Sit-Ney
57 Talay Rab Lom Restaurant

DRINKING & NIGHTLIFE
58 Cro-magnon

SHOPPING
59 Ban Krut Morning Market
60 Burmese Border Market
61 Saturday Market

TRANSPORT
62 Ban Pak Khlong Pier

WHY ARE MANGROVES IMPORTANT?

Prachuap Khiri Khan hosts nearly 810 hectares of mangrove forest, which comprise trees or shrubs that grow in brackish water along the coast, adapting to tolerate more salt than most plants. Their adaptability also makes them good at taking in carbon dioxide, thereby mitigating the effects of climate change.

Because mosquitoes love to breed among the mangroves, people have come to regard these tropical coastal swamp areas as a nuisance, but they actually play important roles in fighting erosion and keeping the shoreline intact. They can guard against errant waves or even tsunamis by acting as natural barriers to the water. Better yet, they are home to a wide range of marine animals, from fish and shellfish to birds and lizards.

Going Green

Immerse yourself in Prachuap's unique scenery

With its undulating mountains thickly furred by greenery and a shoreline latticed by mangroves, Prachuap gives visitors a peep into a unique part of Thailand. There are elephants, bats, wild peacocks and more than a few monkeys living among a smattering of sparkling blue bays, sandy beaches, and limestone karsts hollowed out by caves. Little wonder, then, that nature aficionados flock to this part of the country to spend as many as six months exploring the hills and hollows of the region.

Of course, with an abundance of mountains come many waterfalls. That's why water-loving Thais go to **Nam Tok Huai Yang National Park** *(thainationalparks.com/huai-yang-waterfall-national-park)*, named for its main attraction, the seven-tiered **Nam Tok Huai Yang**. Five of its tiers are accessible via trails, but you must hire a park ranger (around 300฿ for a few hours) to reach the last two tiers, which will involve some rock climbing. **Nam Tok Khao Lan**, which features a 50m-high waterfall, is best visited during the rainy season (June to October), when you can swim in a pool on the top level. Meanwhile, **Nam Tok Kha-on** boasts nine tiers and is located 44km south of the park's main visitor centre.

The province is also home to 283 hectares of mangrove forest, essential for hosting a number of animal species. In the border region between Prachuap and Hua Hin lies **Pranburi Forest Park** *(thainationalparks.com/pran-buri-forest-park)*, known for its winding 1km boardwalk over mangrove forest. Originally a series of shrimp farms, the park was established in 1982 to protect the ecosystem, which forms the natural habitats of crabs, mudskippers and over 110 types of birds. Although most of the park is given over to research, visitors can also take long-tail boats along the park's canals during high tide periods (500฿ for groups of up to eight people) if walking isn't their forte.

Making Merit

Temples, two ways

Obviously, Prachuap Khiri Khan has its share of beautiful and interesting temples, a few of which are made infinitely more exciting with the addition of wild monkeys. Around 8km north of Prachuap's city centre sits **Wat Ao Noi**, named after one of Prachuap's three bays. Nestled into the foot of the hill,

EATING IN PAK NAM PRAN: WESTERN FOOD

Pranberry: Specialising in Italian food, this spot next to Hat Pranburi is part of the popular 'Pranberry' hospitality group. *11am-2pm & 5-10pm Wed-Mon* ฿฿

Schnitzelwirten: German food is surprisingly popular in Thailand, which explains the largely Thai clientele at this cosy spot. *10am-10pm Tue-Sun* ฿฿

Aleenta Restaurant: A mix of modern Thai and international cuisines, this hotel restaurant also offers a seaside afternoon tea and good vegan options. *11am-10pm* ฿฿

Juergen's Corner Cafe & Restaurant: A comfortable open-air spot with pizza, pork chops and German apple cake. *11am-9pm* ฿฿

STROLL PRACHUAP KHIRI KHAN TOWN

Take in the best sights of Prachap Khiri Khan town, the provincial capital.

START	END	LENGTH
Prachuap Khiri Khan Train Station	Ao Manao	3.6km; one hour

Start your walking adventure at ❶ **Prachuap Khiri Khan Train Station**. The pretty wooden station is painted red and beige and makes for a great photo-op. From the train station, walk 200m east along ❷ **Thanon Kong Kiat**. While Prachuap Khiri Khan is a sleepy place, the restaurants and shops along Th Kong Kiat are always bustling. Continue walking down to the ❸ **pier**, and enjoy the paved promenade of Ao Prachuap. This gracefully curving bay and oceanfront promenade is punctuated by dramatic headlands at both ends and is the town's crowning feature. The sunrise here is superb. Backtrack to Th Sala Cheep and turn right to find the ❹ **Prachuap Khiri Khan City Pillar Shrine**. The shrine's architecture is reminiscent of the Khmer (Cambodian) style. Th Sala Cheep runs the length of the town; from the City Pillar Shrine, follow the signs along the road heading south to the university. You'll pass a variety of street vendors, charming coffee shops, a few seafood restaurants and plenty of local Thai eateries. There is also a pharmacy on this road and a modern convenience store. After grabbing a bite to eat or something to drink, make your way to ❺ **Wing 5 Airbase** (p441). Just beyond the entrance on the left, you need to sign in, so bring your passport with you. From here, you can flag down a motorbike taxi or tuk-tuk, or tackle the long walk to reach ❻ **Ao Manao** (p441).

The north side of Th Kong Kiat holds the **Prachuap Khiri Khan Night Market** every night.

If you have time, check out **Thanon Sala Cheep**, perpendicular to Th Kong Kiat, for a little local flavour.

You might also find some friendly lemurs at **Ao Manao** during your time there.

MONKEY BUSINESS

Scattered throughout the province of Prachuap Khiri Khan and close to many of the tourist attractions live various species of monkeys. While their curious faces may be cute to look at, macaque monkeys in particular can be quite aggressive, and know no shame or fear. Do not feed or provoke them, or you risk getting bitten. It's not just food they're after – plastic bags and camera bags are also targets. This is the same type of monkey that you'll encounter when visiting Phra Nakhon Khiri Historical Park in Phetchaburi. The other monkeys in the province are dusky leaf monkeys, which are more docile and completely adorable.

RATTANAPATPHOTO/SHUTTERSTOCK

Stairs to Wat Khao Chong Krajok

this temple links Ao Noi with the adjacent bay of Ao Khan Kradai. Wat Ao Noi's most distinguishing feature is its beautifully wrought chapel, built entirely of teak wood, without the use of nails. Enclosed inside are murals showing Buddha's life story. Behind Wat Ao Noi, on the hill facing Ao Noi, you can find **Tham Khan Kradai**, also known as the 'Cave of the Reclining Buddha' and believed to have once served as shelter for sailors caught in storms. It's accessible via a fairly imposing staircase that passes a hall covered mostly in oyster shells. Inside the big cave at the top, you will find two reclining Buddha figures in two separate chambers, one of which is estimated to be over 300 years old.

Arguably the most famous of Prachuap Khiri Khan's temples is **Wat Khao Chong Krajok**, which perches on top of Khao Chong Krajok (literally 'Mirror Gap Hill') at the end of 396 steps (Prachuap's religious community appears to be very fit). While the temple does house replicas of Buddha's footprint and the Great Relic Pagoda, the real draw may be the incredible panoramic views from the top of the hill, 245m above sea level. This is why this temple is most popular during sunrise and sunset, when the landscape is either bathed in the dawn light or in a dusky violet hue right before the sun disappears below the horizon.

But about those monkeys. Make sure not to bring food with you on the climb up, or a surprisingly belligerent gang of macaques will not hesitate to harass you for it. If you are nervous about the climb, bring a stick to wave around as a scare tactic.

EATING & DRINKING IN PRACHUAP KHIRI KHAN DISTRICT

Brown Brew & Bistro: A stylish, modern eatery in Pak Nam Pran, this brick-clad cafe ensures that sweets lovers will be in heaven. *9am-9pm Wed-Mon* BB

Chicken and Bee: This place in Sam Roi Yot District harbours a small but delicious menu as well as handmade items to take home. *10am-5.30pm Thu-Tue* BB

Hitch & Round Cafe and Space: Good coffee and bread in Pak Nam Pran. Adjoining bookshop, gallery space and vinyl store. *7.30am-5pm Wed-Mon* BB

Forget Me Not Cafe & Farm: Yet another cute farm-themed cafe in Prachuap Khiri Khan with beautiful surroundings. *8am-5pm Wed-Mon* B

It's in the Water

Exploring Prachuap's beaches

Prachuap is most known as the 'town of three bays': Ao Manao, Ao Noi and Ao Prachuap. While Ao Noi is famed for Wat Ao Noi (p438) and Ao Prachuap is known for its wide promenade and close-up views of the mountains of Khao Ta Mong Lai Forest Park, the crowning glory of the province (when it comes to beaches, that is) is surely **Ao Manao**. Rather unusually, it can be found within the **Wing 5 Airbase**, which means that you might have to sign in at the entrance with a military officer (bring your passport just in case). Even then, Ao Manao is exceptionally popular for its crystal-clear water and long stretch of soft sand wedged between two picturesque mountains. You'll find beach chairs, umbrellas and inner tubes, as well as a scattering of Thai and seafood restaurants. There is also a WWII monument to honour the heroes who defended Ao Manao from the Japanese, and a corresponding museum only open on holidays and weekends.

Further north is Hat Pranburi (p435), which in recent years has seen the beginnings of a boom in hipster eateries and hotels. Nearby are roads a-plenty for cyclists winding past pineapple plantations and into thickly forested hillsides, among trees nurturing wild peacocks and blue-tailed bee-eaters.

South of Hat Pranburi lies a beach simply known as the '**Beach Behind Khao Kalok**'. It's notable for its colourful fishing village, which resembles a parking lot for fishing boats during low tide. Further down from that is the beach widely known as 'Dolphin Bay' for the longstanding resort that anchors it; officially it is called **Sam Roi Yot Beach** after the national park behind it. Here, you can rent kayaks on the waterfront (per hour 50฿, two-person kayak 100฿) or hire a boat (starting from 1200฿ for up to six people) to explore the tiny islands in the bay: **Ko Ku Ram**, **Ko Nom Sao** and **Ko Rawing**.

Discover an Overlooked Beach Town

Take a trip back in time to the Thai seashore

Thais often speak longingly of coastal towns from 50 years ago, when all there was to entertain you were a couple of resorts, a handful of decent restaurants, a wide stretch of soft sand and, of course, the ocean waves. Travellers in search of that coastal town from long ago will find it in **Ban Krut**, 1¾ hours south of Prachuap Khiri Khan town on the Gulf of Thailand. Ban Krut is ripe for the picking by a wider audience

THE LEGEND OF KO NOM SAO

Ko Nom Sao, which roughly translates to 'Young Woman's Breast Island', is the site of a tragic local love story. Because of her beauty, a young woman named Yomdoy was expected to marry into wealth and status; her father hoped for an alliance with a Chinese ruler, but her mother wanted a union with a Phetchaburi prince. Somewhat illogically, the father grew so incensed with the conflict that he tore Yomdoy's body apart, with half forming Ko Nom Sao and the other half travelling all the way to Chanthaburi in eastern Thailand. Today, some Thais believe a goddess spirit protects the island, and young women travel to a shrine there to offer bras as offerings to gain the goddess's blessing.

EATING IN PRACHUAP KHIRI KHAN TOWN: SWEETS

Boobun: Delicious bread and teas popular with the locals, plus a second floor with a serene ocean view. *8.30am-4.30pm Sat-Thu* ฿฿

Baan Pal Coffee: Popular for its freshly squeezed fruit smoothies and sweet *roti* (flatbread) in condensed milk or chocolate. *8am-5pm* ฿

JanRam: Located in Prachuap Khiri Khan's night market, this dessert spot specialises in ice cream and egg custard. *10.30am-8pm Tue-Sun* ฿

Cro-magnon: Good coffee, lava cake and pandan coconut custard toast in comfortable, contemporary surroundings. *9.15am-8.30pm* ฿

CELEBRATING A GOLDEN JUBILEE

When 1996 rolled around, Thailand launched into a series of major celebrations to celebrate Rama IX's Golden Jubilee, marking the 50th year of his reign and making Rama IX Thailand's longest-reigning monarch. Celebrations included a rare Royal Barges Procession on the Chao Phraya River, the minting of commemorative coins and banknotes, and the construction of culturally significant buildings all over the kingdom. One of these buildings was **Wat Thang Sai**, a Buddhist temple constructed in 1996 in the shadow of Phra Mahathat Chedi Phakdi Praka. The temple is impressive, with nine pagodas that sit on top of Thong Chai mountain overlooking Ban Krut Beach. The temple grounds have beautiful gardens and a few fearsome-looking statues.

after becoming in recent years a favoured destination for Thai families sick of fighting for hotel rooms and restaurant tables in more well-known towns like Hua Hin.

The best feature of Ban Krut is, of course, the expansive and relatively empty **Hat Ban Krut**, practically abandoned by midday because of the sun. The gentle waves make paddling by the shore easy for even the most inexperienced swimmer. If you prefer to explore, bikes can be rented from most of the hotels beachside for around 100฿ per day. If you prefer hassle-free rentals or are a dedicated biker, contact a tour operator like **Adventure Cycling Thailand** *(adventurecyclingthailand.com)*, based in Hua Hin.

A sleepy town like Ban Krut is perfect for exploring via scooter or motorbike, which can be rented with help from your hotel. If you have no particular plan, driving down the coast is a good place to start. Driving south from Hat Ban Krut to **Ao Bo Thong Lang** is a scenic 25-minute jaunt, and all along the beachside road you'll see locals drying fish in the sun. Pass a small fishing community and a tiny temple before arriving at the bay. Stop here to take photos, go for a swim or just relax.

Heading north, you can follow the coast to **Wat Tham Khiri Wong**, a cave temple with a few monks living on site and worth a stop if you are passing by. From here, continue onto the town of **Thap Sakae**, where there are a few local shops, cafes and a daily local market. The network of roads and dirt tracks jutting out from the coconut groves are worth exploring.

Trawl Ban Krut's Markets

Photo opportunities (and bargains) at local markets

Visitors to Thailand cannot live on sunbathing alone (although some may try). A ready diversion in Ban Krut are its surprisingly numerous markets. Fresh ingredients, ready-made dishes, clothing, fun souvenirs and even furniture can be found at these markets if you have the patience to explore. Better yet, dedicated shop-o-phobes will get to experience the day-to-day rhythms of coastal village life.

The **Ban Krut Morning Market**, open daily 6am to 8am in front of the train station, is a prime place for good people-watching, since this is where locals congregate for their basic kitchen needs. If you are here on a Saturday, the twilight **Saturday Market** *(bankrutguide.com)*, held in a large field near the railway crossing between 5pm and 7pm, gives off a festive atmosphere with prepared dishes like grilled chicken and sticky rice, plus clothing for eagle-eyed clotheshorses.

EATING IN BAN KRUT: OUR PICKS

Li's Restaurant: Spicy Thai food featuring fresh seafood and a wide selection of homemade fruit smoothies. *10am-9pm* ฿฿

Krua Ban Suan: A cute open-air spot with a solid Thai menu including crispy pork and stuffed omelettes. *10am-8.30pm Wed-Mon* ฿฿

Jimpizza: A simple beachside stall specialising in pizza made from fresh dough. Unique options include the San Marco, with egg and chorizo. *4-8pm* ฿

Bayern Himmel: An open-air Bavarian place close to the beach with food that is praised by actual Germans. *noon-7pm Fri-Wed* ฿฿

SPBSHUTTER/SHUTTERSTOCK

Textiles, Burmese Border Market

BEST THINGS TO BUY AT THE BURMESE BORDER MARKET

Gemstones: An eye-opening range of gems, jewellery and crystals are available for sale here, although shoppers must be careful not to get scammed.

Textiles: Traditional sarong-like Burmese *longyi*, often patterned in colourful designs, also make nice souvenirs.

Thanaka: The traditional Burmese 'sunscreen', made from ground bark, can be spied on cheeks throughout the country, with its distinctive white hue.

Carved woodware: If your customs officers aren't too strict, you can also find wooden trays and bowls to take home, along with carved utensils and decorative items.

Orchids: Flower lovers will have a field day here.

Finally, the **Burmese Border Market** (aka Dan Singkhon Market), around 40 minutes away by car, has recently been re-opened on weekends and features Burmese vendors who cross into Thailand to sell everything from produce to furniture. Although Thai vendors can venture over into Myanmar, it's not advisable for regular travellers to go there at this time.

Go Island-Hopping off Bang Saphan Yai

Get your doctorate in beach bumming

Twenty-five minutes south of Ban Krut, you'll find the tiny town of Bang Saphan Yai, mostly known as a launching pad from where you can swim, snorkel and fish at a handful of small islands. The three most famous are **Ko Thalu**, known for its three white-sand beaches; **Ko Sang**, rich in coral and a draw for snorkellers; and adjacent to it, **Ko Sing**, shaped like a lion's head and popular for fishing. On the east side of Ko Thalu is a coral graveyard with a variety of dead species, including flower corals.

From **Ban Pak Khlong pier**, you can take a boat to the most popular island, Ko Thalu, in the morning and return in the afternoon, but you can also negotiate with the captain to tour all three islands. Boats usually seat up to 10 and cost around 4500฿ for a three-hour trip.

EATING IN BANG SAPHAN YAI: OUR PICKS

I Ta Lay: Considered the best restaurant in town, this seaside spot serves good Thai food, especially sour curry *(gang som)*. *noon-10pm Mon-Sat* ฿฿

Raan Aharn Chan Super: A reasonable beachfront restaurant specialising in one-dish favourites like fried rice. *10am-9.30pm* ฿

Le Panorama: Part of the Coral Hotel resort, this restaurant serves European food as well as Thai food. *7am-2pm & 7-10pm* ฿฿

Cafe Wien Bangsaphan: Somehow, there's an Austrian restaurant here with sausages and *kaiserschmarm* (sweet pancake). *10am-8pm* ฿฿

Chumphon Province

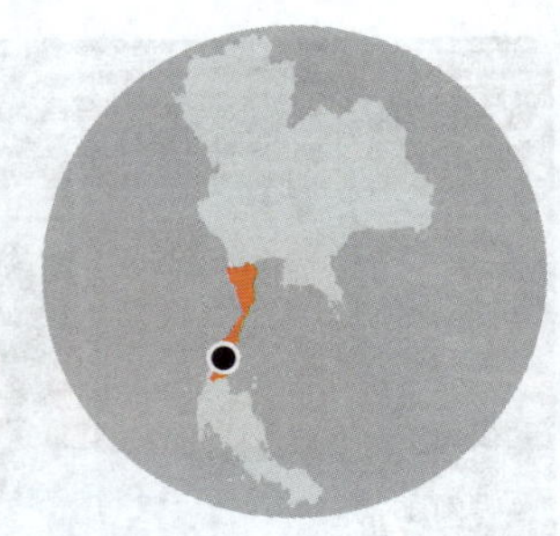

BEACHES | WILDLIFE | FRESH SEAFOOD

GETTING AROUND

Chumphon lacks a mass-transit system, instead relying on cars, motorcycles and motorcycle taxis to get around. Daily rentals for motorcycles should run between 200฿ and 300฿, while car rentals start from 1000฿ per day. Motorcycle taxis are easy to flag and should start from around 30฿.

TOP TIP

Although Chumphon is frequently used as a mere launching pad for onward travel to the islands, take a breather here for at least a night and explore the natural sights around the area – the beaches here are usually free of crowds, even on weekends.

Known as the 'Gateway to the South', Chumphon manages to combine a southern Thai feel – palm trees, glittering blue water, miles of sandy beaches – with a sleepy village vibe that is more evocative of the area to its north. Although it lacks the infrastructure of towns like Hua Hin or even Phetchaburi, it makes up for it in natural beauty and abundant wildlife... not to mention more than 220km of coastline, much of it more beautiful than its better-known neighbours. Bracketed by the Andaman Sea and the Gulf of Thailand, Chumphon is an obvious fit for beachcombers; providing 70% of Thailand's fish alongside Surat Thani and Prachuap Khiri Khan, Chumphon is also a no-brainer destination for seafood lovers. It's the kind of place for people seeking a peaceful, unpretentious tropical getaway, with a focus on sunbathing, punctuated by the occasional sightseeing stop, market ramble and open-air seafood feast.

Snorkel Mu Ko Chumphon National Park

A treasure trove of natural beauty

With over 40 islands, most of which are relatively untouristed, **Mu Ko Chumphon National Park** *(200฿)* is probably the biggest draw of the region, especially for divers. Although part of it is on the mainland, the park still enjoys beautiful coral, protected beaches and a wealth of fish that include clownfish, parrotfish and the occasional whale shark. It makes the trek here more than worth it, and visitors can even stay overnight if they find it difficult to tear themselves away.

There are a number of tour operators that ply these waters, but Mu Ko park itself can arrange trips for you at the entrance, especially if you are part of a larger group of five to 10 people. For 3500฿ per day, they will take you to four islands – **Ko Lung Ga**, **Ko La Wa, Ko Lak Rad** and **Ko Mattra** – with the option of staying overnight at **Ko Gula** for an extra charge. These islands are known for the clearest water of the national park.

HIGHLIGHTS
1 Mu Ko Chumphon National Park

SIGHTS
2 Coconut Island
3 Deer Island
4 Hat Pharadonphap
5 Hat Sairee
6 Hat Thung Wua Laen
7 Khao Dinsor
8 Klong Tha Charakhe

ACTIVITIES
9 Siam Cat Charter Tours

SLEEPING
10 At Night
11 Chumphon Cabana Resort
12 Maliblues Bed & Dinner

EATING
13 Fai-Deang Restaurant
14 Green Kitchen Restaurant
15 Guaythiew Nuea Nai Dum
16 Hor Chia Dim Sum
17 Jay Muay Kaeng Som Noodles
18 Old Time Cafe
19 Raan Aharn Krua PS Vegan
20 Take a Seat
21 Thien Chai
22 To the Moon
23 Yai Puad
24 Yim Shop Vegetarian

SHOPPING
25 Chumphon Night Market

INFORMATION
26 Chumphon Provincial Hall

TRANSPORT
27 Pontaweesin Pier

MANGROVE FORESTS

Mu Ko Chumphon National Park isn't simply about the islands. There are also mangrove forests on the mainland, which can be explored via a series of wooden walkways built up over the marshland. Even if you are not a mangrove aficionado, you can enjoy the quiet of the forest, punctuated by the occasional popping sound from imploding cavitation bubbles in the mud made by snapping shrimp. A wooden suspension bridge crosses **Klong Tha Charakhe** (Crocodile Pier Canal), which was once full of saltwater crocodiles but is now (perhaps blessedly) empty. At the edge of one of the walkways is Khlong Tha Charoek fishing community, roughly 1km from the bridge.

JESSE33/SHUTTERSTOCK

Ko Thalu

You can also contact **Siam Cat Charter Tours** *(siamcat-chartertours.com; adult/child 1500/800฿)* for one-day trips to four islands, and unlike the national-park tours, these include breakfast and lunch. Besides the aforementioned islands (available on even days), Siam Cat can also take you to **Ko Ngam Noi**, **Ko Ngam Yai**, **Ko Ga Loke** and **Ko Thalu** (on odd days). These islands are known for the collection of hard and soft corals along their shores as well as for having the highest density of black coral of anywhere in Thailand.

Alternatively, if you are just a couple or solo, you can arrange your own snorkelling trip at **Pontaweesin Pier** in Tha Yang District, which should cost you no more than 1200฿ per day.

Become a Beach Bum

Sampling Chumphon's beaches

Chumphon does foster a wide variety of terrain from dense jungle to rocky hillside to swampy mangrove, but let's face it: most people come here for the beaches, and don't want to stray that far from them. Luckily for them, Chumphon

EATING IN CHUMPHON TOWN: STREET FOOD

Hor Chia Dim Sum: In southern Thailand, dim sum is a popular streetside breakfast, served with an especially spicy dipping sauce. *6am-8.30pm* ฿฿

Guaythiew Nuea Nai Dum: Straightforward soup noodles made with beef close to the train station. *7am-3pm* ฿

Thien Chai: Known for its delicious *khao man gai* (Hainanese-style chicken rice), this humble street stall draws patrons from all over town. *8am-4pm* ฿

Fai-Deang Restaurant: Chinese-style stir-fried specialties, good enough to satisfy any Chinese auntie and uncle. *3pm-2am* ฿

is home to many popular beaches (not including the ones on Mu Ko National Park's many islands), each with its own particular vibe.

Probably the most popular Chumphon beach is **Hat Thung Wua Laen** (Cattle Farm Beach). Crowds come here for the wide stretches of relatively clean sand, gentle waves and leaning palm trees, which provide much-needed shade in the daytime. Another bonus to this beach is that it is amply served by eating establishments, including Chumphon Cabana (p449; *chumphoncabana.net*) and Maliblues Bed & Dinner (p449), which also encompasses an art gallery and hosts live music after 7.30pm.

Another crowd pleaser is **Hat Sairee**, named for its long, crescent shape. Although it can appear fairly deserted during the off-season, it is popular with Thais at peak times (around dusk) for the sheer variety of seafood eateries lining the beach (the entire reason Thai people go to the beach). Many Thais also go to see the shrine dedicated to the Prince of Chumphon, and to clamber over the decommissioned navy ship next to the shrine. You can also hire a boat from Hat Sairee to visit **Coconut Island**, which sits in the water like a ball dropped from the edge of the crescent. Because protected birds live there, you must get permission from **Chumphon Provincial Hall** one week in advance, or simply sail around it.

To truly enjoy a mostly empty beach, go to less-known **Hat Pharadonphap**, rimmed by coconut trees and seafood shacks, or the 5km stretch of white sand that is **Hat Tham Thong-Bang Boet**, framed by limestone peaks and pine trees.

Get Close with Local Wildlife

Walk circles around Deer Island

One of Chumphon's quirkiest attractions has to be **Deer Island**, a part of **Nong Yai Park** and reachable via a wooden suspension bridge that is arguably the biggest draw in the area. Known as **Mai Kiam Bridge**, the suspension bridge wows and occasionally frightens aunties who cling to the sides as it wobbles above the water, leading onto a viewpoint with an up-close-and-personal look at Chumphon's Javan rusa deer population. You can stop and feed the deer with the bananas for sale, available alongside fish food for whatever lurks beneath the surface of the murky water. If you decide to walk your way around the wetlands, it will amount to around 2km and take you a little over 30 minutes. You will pass an 'activity pavilion' (possibly an attempt at an upstart market but now

WHO IS THE PRINCE OF CHUMPHON?

Visitors to any of Chumphon's well-known sights are likely to encounter the framed photograph of a smiling young man in military uniform on the wall. This is Prince Abhakara Kiartivongse, also known as the 'Prince of Chumphon' and the founder of the Thai navy. The 28th child of Rama V and a Britannia Royal Naval College graduate, he subsequently served in the navy for Great Britain before the birth of the Royal Siamese Navy in 1900. There are more than 200 shrines dedicated to the prince in Chumphon because he spent time there while trying to recover from a long illness. He passed away in 1923 at the age of 42 after a bout of influenza.

EATING IN CHUMPHON PROVINCE: VEGETARIAN FOOD

Take a Seat: On the outskirts of Chumphon town and set next to a beach sits this homey cafe with vegan pizza and chow mein. *7am-8pm Thu-Tue* ฿

Green Kitchen Restaurant: Chumphon town restaurant offering a separate vegetarian and vegan menu. *9am-8.30pm* ฿฿

Raan Aharn Krua PS Vegan: Vegan versions of Thai standards like *dom yam* noodles in Chumphon town. *6.30am-1.30pm Tue-Thu & Sat* ฿

Yim Shop Vegetarian: Come to this Chumphon town spot for basic Thai vegetarian fare at good prices. *7am-1pm* ฿

BUY BY NIGHT AT CHUMPHON NIGHT MARKET

No Thai town is really a Thai town without its own dedicated night market, and Chumphon is no different. Besides the requisite street-food offerings (think oyster omelettes, pizza and noodles), there is also clothing, bags and random tchotchkes with which to delight your friends back home. Best of all, this market is patronised mostly by locals, lending visitors a great snapshot of Chumphon life. On weekends, the market expands to in front of City Hall. Open daily 6pm to 11pm along Th Krommuang east of the train station.

TAL KONGKIAT/SHUTTERSTOCK

Buzzard, Khao Dinsor

empty, save for a working bathroom) and realise that this project – part of the 'Monkey Cheeks' reservoir, born after the 1989 typhoon – entertained far bigger ambitions than its current scope suggests.

But deer aren't the only animals drawing nature lovers to Chumphon. **Khao Dinsor**, also known as 'Eagle Cliff', offers a plethora of birdwatching activities for the diehard birder, with Chinese goshawks, Japanese sparrowhawks, black bazas, shikras and buzzards occasionally circling the skies overhead. Many of these birds – called 'raptors' by birders – are most often seen from August to November while on their southward migration. Even better, the profusion of flowers lures a veritable armada of absurdly large butterflies that flit inches from your face with little fear.

EATING IN CHUMPHON TOWN: OUR PICKS

Jay Muay Kaeng Som Noodles: Offering a wide range of dishes from fish porridge to stir-fried noodles in soy sauce. *10am-11pm* B

Old Time Cafe: Comfortable setting for Thai food like fried rice, as well as Western faves like chicken wings and burgers. *4-11pm Mon-Fri, from 11am Sat & Sun* BB

Yai Puad: Solid southern Thai dishes like sour curry, fried eggs with local *'miang'* leaves and salt-fried fish in an open-air setting. *11am-5pm Thu-Tue* BB

To the Moon: A festive beach restaurant that is a surefire crowd pleaser, with strong cocktails and Thai food under the stars. *9.30pm-midnight* BB

Places We Love to Stay

฿ Budget ฿฿ Midrange ฿฿฿ Top End

Phetchaburi

Map p415

Little Home Phetchaburi ฿ Comfortable rooms with en suite bathrooms, balconies with mountain or city views, and an excellent location.

Banthai Guest House ฿ Super-reasonable air-conditioned rooms with either private or shared bathrooms in a wooden house surrounded by nature.

White Monkey Guesthouse ฿฿ A three-minute walk from town with air-conditioning, private bathrooms, free wi-fi and parking, and a shared kitchen, garden and lounge.

Moon Resort Phetchaburi ฿฿ Less than 1km from downtown Phetchaburi, this charming hotel boasts garden views, outdoor fireplace and seating area as well as the usual amenities.

Kaeng Krachan

Baan Maka Nature Lodge ฿฿ Set in a garden within 5km from Kaeng Krachan, air-conditioned rooms with private bathrooms in idyllic surroundings.

Nana Resort Kaengkrachan ฿฿฿ With a swimming pool, coffee shop and in-house masseuses, you may never have to leave this place, but if you do, you are well situated to explore Kaeng Krachan's mountains and waterfalls.

Hua Hin

Nicha Suite Hua Hin ฿ A surprisingly reasonable hotel with modern rooms decorated with carved wooden accents and bright colours. Located close to town.

Luna Hut Resort ฿฿ A cute spot in a garden near the beach with balconies overlooking the garden or mountain, a swimming pool and free parking. Only a few steps from Hat Khao Takiab.

A Villa Hua Hin Hotel ฿฿ Close to town with everything you'd expect, including breakfast and an in-house restaurant.

Peri Hua Hin ฿฿฿ A pretty property close to a prime Hat Hua Hin location built to resemble a fishing village, but with a 27m swimming pool.

Cha-am

OYO 394 Nana Beach Cha-am ฿ A great location with all the expected amenities like free wi-fi, a 24-hour front desk and free parking.

SP Park Hotel ฿฿ Air-conditioned rooms with balconies and bathrooms, with a saltwater swimming pool and garden and mountain views, close to Cha-am train station.

Prachuap Khiri Khan Province

Map p436

Jungle Cafe & Guesthouse ฿ Super-reasonable beachfront hotel with sea views, free wi-fi and air-conditioning. Shared bathrooms.

Nam Talay Resort ฿฿ Only a few steps from Khao Kalok and Hat Pranburi, this reasonably priced hotel is perfect for lovers of hiking, cycling and kitesurfing.

Pranberry Earth ฿฿฿ Pricey but charming small hotel in Pak Nam Pran with spacious rooms, sprawling garden and in-house cafe. A tiny studio sleeping four and tiny 'bug' room sleeping two are also available.

Ban Krut

Baan Grood Arcadia Resort & Spa ฿฿ An expansive property looking out onto Hat Ban Krut set in a well-manicured garden. Comfortable, spacious rooms with a swimming pool and snack bar can be expected, as well as a good breakfast.

Ban Krut Resort ฿฿ Very reasonable prices for comfortable rooms, beach views and free bicycles to explore the area.

Chumphon Province

Map p445

At Night ฿ Close to Chumphon town's train station, a playfully decorated space in walking distance of almost everything.

Chumphon Cabana Resort ฿฿฿ This longstanding resort on the southern edge of Had Thung Wua Laen boasts spacious rooms and an excellent restaurant, as well as a massage parlour on the grounds.

Maliblues Bed & Dinner ฿฿฿ Just north of Chumphon Cabana, extremely stylish rooms with everything you would ever need, including hot tub.

LEMARET PIERRICK/SHUTTERSTOCK

For places to stay in Ko Samui and the lower gulf, see p504

Above: Hat Lamai (p463); Right: Ang Thong Marine National Park (p467)

THE MAIN AREAS

KO SAMUI
Modern amenities and island life. **p456**

KO PHA-NGAN
Hidden bays beyond the Full Moon Party madness. **p469**

KO TAO
Diving and making new friends. **p478**

Researched by Choltanutkun Tun-atiruj

Ko Samui & the Lower Gulf

BEACH PARTIES, WELLNESS AND SOUTHERN FLAVOURS

Thailand's lower gulf blends luxe island escapes with off-the-radar gems, where hammock naps and jungle hikes await the curious.

Sapphire-blue waters, powder-soft sands and lush jungles form the rich tapestry of Thailand's lower gulf. At its heart sits Ko Samui, the country's second-largest island, where palm-fringed beaches with rickety huts and coconut shakes once drew backpackers. Today, Samui blends luxury resorts, hip beach clubs and wellness retreats without losing the laid-back spirit that made it famous.

Neighbouring Ko Pha-Ngan still hums to the rhythms of island life. By day, travellers rise early for sunrise yoga and vegan brunches; by night, they dance barefoot on Hat Rin's sands beneath the full moon. Quieter northern and eastern shores reveal family-friendly beaches and hidden coves. Just to the north, little Ko Tao has earned its reputation as Southeast Asia's diving epicentre, with technicolour reefs, towering granite pinnacles and a growing rock-climbing scene. After dark, backpackers swap stories at glowing beach bars.

Back on the mainland south of Surat Thani, Ao Khanom remains blissfully under visited. Here, pink dolphins glide past empty beaches while caves, waterfalls and small fishing villages wait inland, offering a glimpse of traditional Thai life far from the crowds. Head deeper south and you'll find a cute mountainous town, Phatthalung, where every scooter ride becomes a jungle food trip with plenty of unique dishes you won't find anywhere else. Hat Yai remains one of the most developed cities in this part of Thailand, but if you keep going south, Songkhla Old Town awaits to show you its artsy side.

TZIDO SUN/SHUTTERSTOCK

AO KHANOM
Pink dolphins, quiet beaches and untrodden paths. p485

PHATTHALUNG PROVINCE
Mountains, traditional villages and so much food. p494

SONGKHLA PROVINCE
A growing southern art community. p498

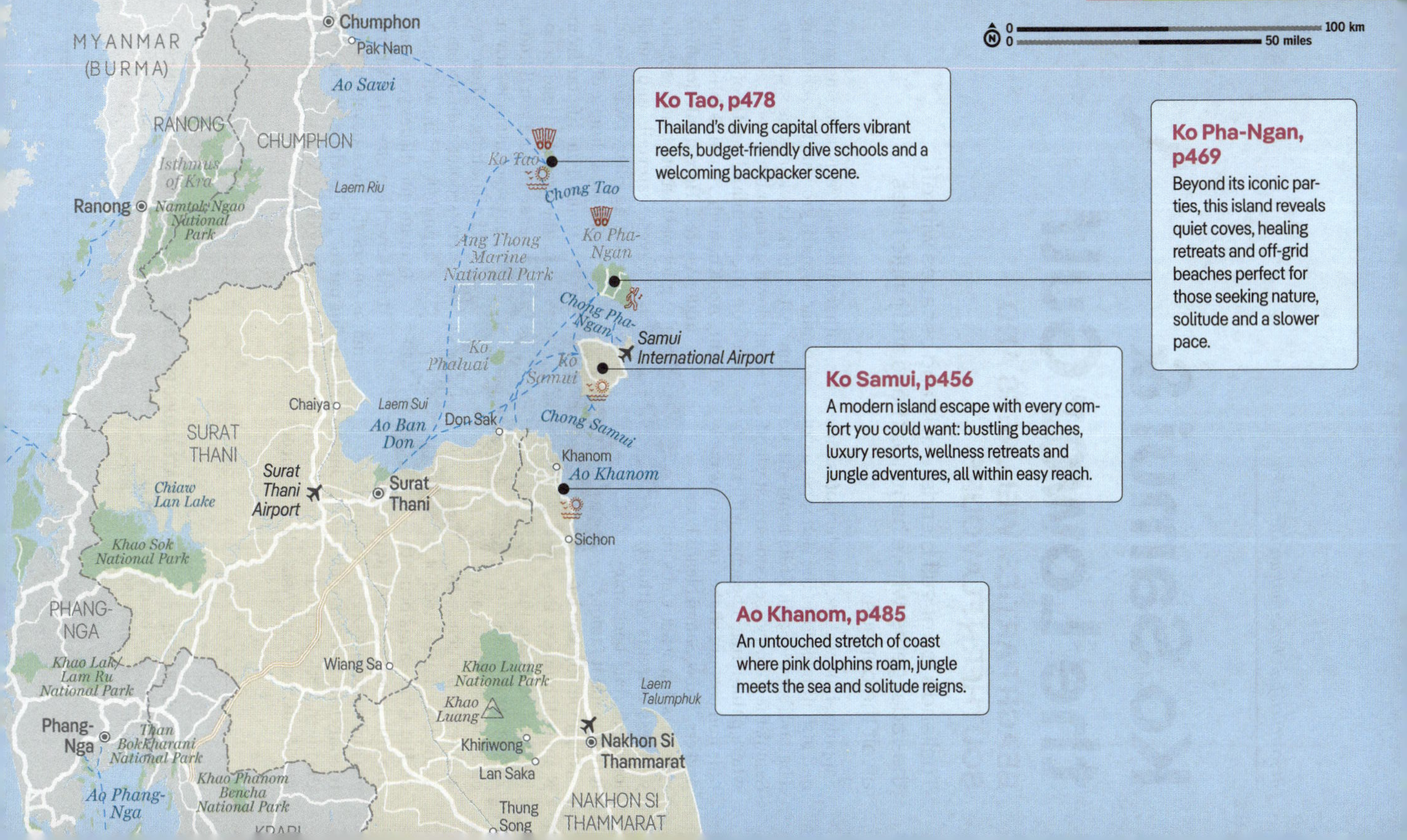
Ko Tao, p478
Thailand's diving capital offers vibrant reefs, budget-friendly dive schools and a welcoming backpacker scene.
Ko Pha-Ngan, p469
Beyond its iconic parties, this island reveals quiet coves, healing retreats and off-grid beaches perfect for those seeking nature, solitude and a slower pace.
Ko Samui, p456
A modern island escape with every comfort you could want: bustling beaches, luxury resorts, wellness retreats and jungle adventures, all within easy reach.
Ao Khanom, p485
An untouched stretch of coast where pink dolphins roam, jungle meets the sea and solitude reigns.
0 100 km
0 50 miles
MYANMAR (BURMA)
Chumphon
Pak Nam
Ao Sawi
RANONG
CHUMPHON
Isthmus of Kra
Laem Riu
Ranong
Namtok Ngao National Park
Ko Tao
Chong Tao
Ko Pha-Ngan
Ang Thong Marine National Park
Chong Pha-Ngan
Samui International Airport
Ko Phaluai
Ko Samui
Chaiya
Laem Sui
Ao Ban Don
Don Sak
Chong Samui
SURAT THANI
Khanom
Ao Khanom
Surat Thani Airport
Surat Thani
Chiaw Lan Lake
Sichon
Khao Sok National Park
PHANG-NGA
Khao Lak/Lam Ru National Park
Wiang Sa
Khao Luang National Park
Khao Luang
Laem Talumphuk
Phang-Nga
Than Bokkharani National Park
Khiriwong
Nakhon Si Thammarat
Khao Phanom Bencha National Park
Lan Saka
Ao Phang-Nga
Thung Song
NAKHON SI THAMMARAT

Phatthalung Province, p494
Thailand's often overlooked and skipped destination, perfect for those seeking the unbeaten path.

Songkhla Province, p498
A southern city where street art, cafe culture and creative energy meet heritage temples and lake-front sunsets.

BOAT
The best way to jump from place to place, whether between islands or from an island back to the mainland or even in some cases, like on Ko Pha-Ngan, to reach a secluded beach without a sweaty jungle trek.

TRAIN
Southern Thailand is long and narrow and trains run its length, which means they're a very convenient (and cheap) way to see the whole region.

MOTORBIKE & SCOOTER
Some destinations can be remote, so catching public transport might not be feasible. Renting a motorbike and riding it yourself may be the best solution for travellers.

Find Your Way

Thailand's lower gulf is a treasure trove of islands and coastal towns. From developed Ko Samui to laid-back Ko Pha-Ngan and Ko Tao and less-visited mainland gems, these destinations let you explore at your own pace.

Plan Your Time

The only downside to island-hopping the lower gulf is deciding how to fit it all in. Factor in ferry connections and flight or train schedules. The good news? Distances are short and there are plenty of transport options.

TANIA.TOLPYGINA/SHUTTERSTOCK

Nam Tok Na Muang 2 (p461)

A Perfect Samui Day

- Start your morning with sunrise at **Hat Chaweng Noi** (p462), where the sand is soft and the vibe is calm before the crowds arrive. Grab a beachside coffee or smoothie bowl at a trendy cafe, then head north to the iconic Big Buddha at **Wat Phra Yai** (p466)for a dose of culture and breathtaking views without having to trek. By late morning, head inland to **Nam Tok Na Muang** (p461) for a refreshing dip in a jungle waterfall.

- After lunch at one of the local seafood restaurants, spend the afternoon on **Nam Tok Na Muang** (p461) or if you're feeling like something more exciting, why not head south to the **La Rhumerie De Koh Samui** (p464), a local rum distillery. As the sun sets, head over to Fisherman's Village Night Market where you can find food and toast the day with cocktails.

SEASONAL HIGHLIGHTS

No matter when you visit, there's always something happening – from diving and beach parties to local food markets and traditional temple celebrations.

DECEMBER

This is the peak of the dry season, with warm, sunny days, calm seas and minimal rainfall. It's the most popular time for tourists, especially families and couples, who want to experience the best of Ko Samui's beaches and outdoor activities.

MARCH

While still warm, this period sees slightly higher temperatures and more humidity. It's a good time to visit if you want to avoid the peak-season crowds and potentially find better deals on accommodation.

APRIL

This is the hottest month of the year in Thailand, and it can also be very humid. Songkran, or Thai New Year, brings island-wide water fights mid-month. Summer storms are uncommon but can happen.

Five Days on Ko Tao

- It takes one full night to travel to Ko Tao from Bangkok via an overnight bus and a morning ferry, so once you arrive on the island, you might want to take it easy on the first day. Start with a chill day just reading on **Ao Leuk** (p479) then grab dinner at **Fizz Beach Lounge** (p483), where you can catch a fire show. Sign up for a diving course for the next day and spend the next few days getting your open-water certificate.

- After that, dedicate a day to diving at **Sail Rock** (p476) or scooter to hidden coves like **Ao Tanote** (p479). Wind down with yoga, kayaking or a beach massage, then hit a jungle party.

- On your last day, brunch at a cafe and toast your trip with a barbecue at one of the restaurants on **Hat Sairee** (p478) – the best beach to catch a sunset.

A Week in the Lower Gulf

- Start your adventure with two or three nights on Ko Samui. Spend lazy mornings on **Hat Mae Nam** (p465) or **Hat Lamai** (p463), then explore island highlights like **Wat Phra Yai** (p466) – go early to have the temple to yourself. Leave a day for a boat trip to **Ang Thong Marine National Park** (p467).

- Next, ferry to Ko Pha-Ngan. Begin with sunrise yoga and vegan brunch in **Hat Srithanu** (p473), then wander beaches like **Thong Nai Pan Noi** (p477). If your timing is right, join the infamous **Full Moon Party** (p472).

- Finally, head to Ko Tao for a dive course. Snorkel **Shark Bay** (p483) or hike to **John Suwan Viewpoint** (p483). Got extra time? Detour to **Ao Khanom** (p485) and try to catch sight of pink dolphins.

MAY

The heat diminishes but the humidity remains, and there might be slightly more rain than April but it'd hardly be noticeable.

JUNE

Start of the rainy season but you're still likely to get beautiful weather most days with occasional downpours. Waterfalls and greenery are at their most vibrant.

JULY

Diving and snorkelling off **Ko Tao** (p480) is best in July and August when the visibility is superb: up to 30m. The area could be filled with European visitors on their summer holiday, so book ahead.

OCTOBER

Monsoon season sees heavy rain and storms. Ferries are sometimes disrupted, and many dive schools close for the season. But the pros? There are fewer tourists, and flights and accommodation is cheaper.

Ko Samui

BEACHES | WELLNESS | CONVENIENCE

GETTING AROUND

Samui's main road loops around the island, hugging the coastline. A motorcycle or scooter is the cheapest and easiest way to get around as you may find that the ride-hailing app Grab is twice or triple the price of Bangkok. To rent one, prices start at 200฿ per day and could be more during high season. Note that there are a lot of accidents and police checkpoints (where you could get fined from 500฿ to 2000฿), so wear a helmet and watch your speed.

TOP TIP

If you use a ferry or catamaran service by Lompraya, it offers a shuttle van service to drop you off or pick you up at the hotel for 150฿. This is the cheapest transfer option available if you are a solo traveller.

Ko Samui is Thailand's second-largest island, after Phuket in the east, and draws nearly three million visitors each year. Fringed by white-sand beaches and emerald waters, it's big enough to have everything, and travellers can find it at their own pace, whether they're searching for beach parties or seclusion.

Hat Chaweng and Hat Lamai, along the east and southeast coasts, are the busiest and most developed beaches, known for their vibrant atmosphere and abundant facilities. Quieter alternatives include Hat Mae Nam in the north, Ao Phang Ka in the southwest, and Hat Lipa Noi and Hat Nathon on the west coast – all offering some peace, with glorious sunsets away from the crowds.

Until the 1970s, Ko Samui was little known outside the region. Today, development has transformed much of the coastline, though the island's interior remains largely jungle, with waterfalls, coconut plantations and occasional monkeys. Offshore, just a boat ride away, you'll find the uninhabited islands of Ang Thong Marine National Park.

Wellness & Retreats

MAP P457 & P458

Find your balance on Ko Samui

Beyond its beaches and nightlife, Ko Samui has become one of Thailand's most established hubs for wellness, meditation and restorative retreats.

Dipabhavan Meditation Center *(dipabhavan.org)* is set on a quiet forested hillside with glimpses of the sea. Retreats typically run for several days and follow a simple, structured schedule of seated and walking meditation, dhamma talks and light communal chores. Accommodation is basic and meals are simple vegetarian fare eaten in silence. The absence of phones and outside distractions helps visitors settle into the rhythm of practice. Fees are donation-based.

Continued on p460

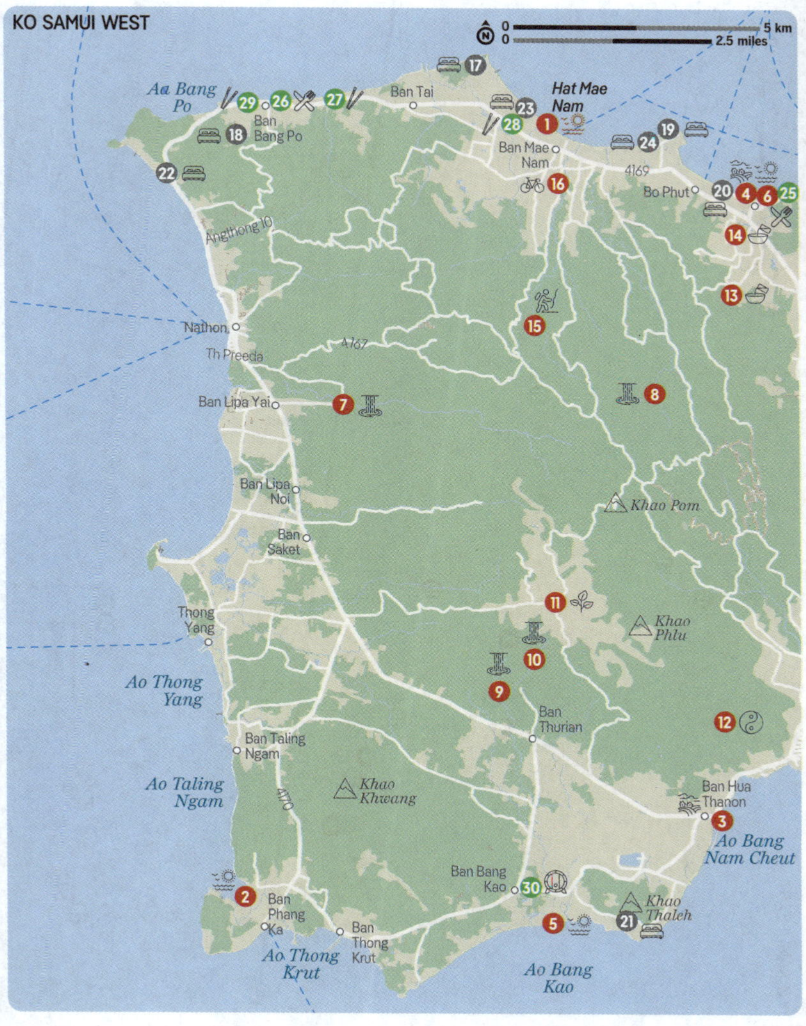

HIGHLIGHTS
1 Hat Mae Nam

SIGHTS
2 Ao Phang Ka
3 Ban Hua Thanon
4 Fisherman's Village
5 Hat Bang Kao
6 Hat Bo Phut
7 Nam Tok Hin Lad
8 Nam Tok Khun Si
9 Nam Tok Na Muang 1
10 Nam Tok Na Muang 2
11 Secret Buddha Garden

ACTIVITIES
12 Dipabhavan Meditation Center
13 Jungle Kitchen
14 Smiley Cook Thai
15 Tree Bridge Zipline
16 X-Quad

SLEEPING
17 Belmond Napasai
18 Code Samui Hotel
19 Escape Beach Resort
see 4 Hacienda
20 Hansar Samui Resort
21 Kamalaya Wellness Sanctuary
22 Mud
23 Shangrila Bungalow
24 Treehouse Silent Beach
see 19 W Koh Samui

EATING
25 2 Fishes on the Beach
26 Bang Por Seafood
27 Chan Hom
see 4 Fisherman's Village Night Market
28 Ran Lan Saka
29 Thai Mama Home Cooking
see 15 Tree Bridge Coffee

DRINKING & NIGHTLIFE
see 20 Easy on Tams
30 La Rhumerie De Koh Samui
see 19 Woobar

KO SAMUI EAST

HIGHLIGHTS

1 Hat Chaweng
2 Hat Lamai

SIGHTS

3 Crystal Bay
4 Hat Bang Rak
5 Hat Chaweng Noi
6 Wat Phra Yai
7 Wat Plai Laem

ACTIVITIES

8 100 Degrees East
9 Elite Gym & Fitness
10 Go Samui Cook
11 Independence Yacht Charter
12 iSUP Samui
13 Koh Fit
14 Lamai Fitness
15 Tamarind Springs
16 Thai Culinary Class by the Beach at Melati Resort & Spa
17 Ultra Bodies Gym

SLEEPING

18 79 Beach Club & Resort
19 B House Samui
20 Baan Haad Ngam Boutique Resort & Villas
21 Baan Samui Resort
22 Jungle Club
23 Kimpton Kitalay Samui
24 Library Hotel
25 Lub d
26 Vikasa Yoga

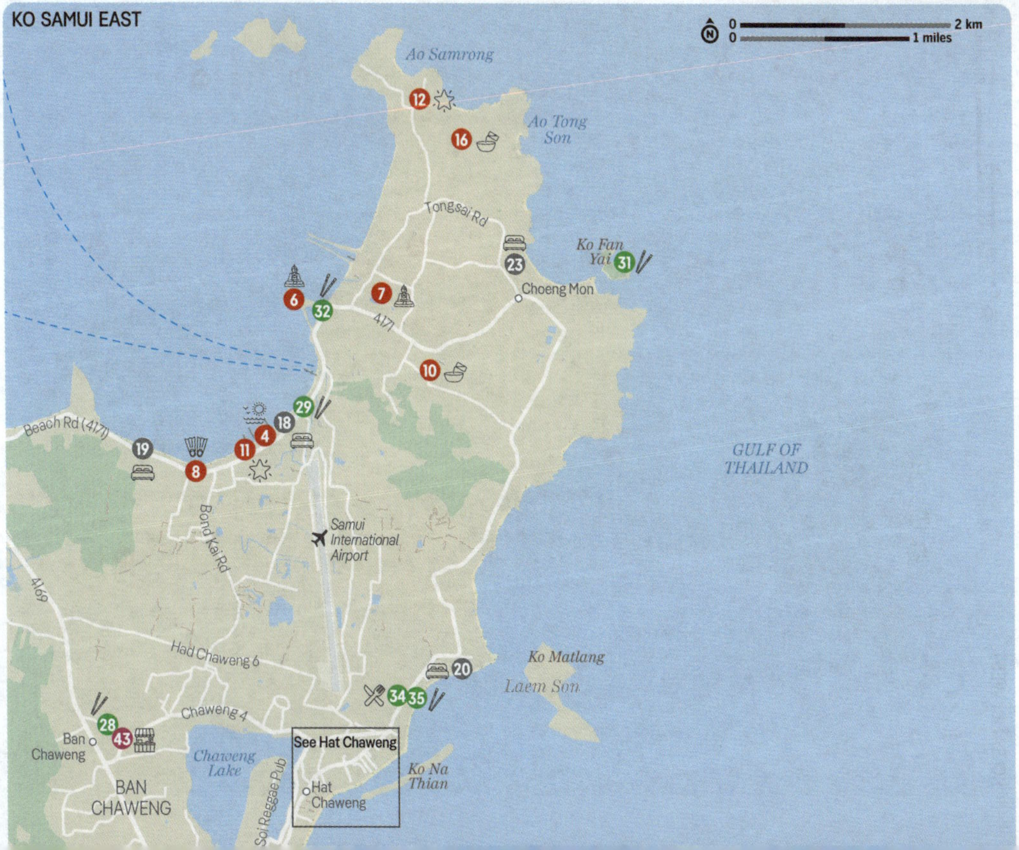

EATING
27 Dara Serene
28 Kapi Sator
29 Khao Hom
30 Khaw Glong Thai
31 Long Dtal Restaurant
32 Pa Taew Thai Buffet
33 Phensiri
34 Sexy Fish
35 Tent
see 19 Tito's Bitchin' Burritos

DRINKING & NIGHTLIFE
see 18 79 Beach Club & Resort
see 19 Bar Bohem
36 Cabanas Beach Club
37 Chalay Rock Bar
38 Crystal Bay Beach Club
39 House of Suzy
40 Powder Room
41 Pride Bar Samui
42 Tikibox

SHOPPING
43 Si Khao Night Market

BEST KO SAMUI COOKING CLASSES

Smiley Cook Thai: Operating since 2012, this farm-to-table experience teaches sustainable Thai cooking, from harvesting organic herbs to making curries and sipping herbal drinks.

Go Samui Cook: A family-run class led by Samui native Geng. Kids are welcome to join, colour and cook alongside parents in this laid-back kitchen.

Thai Culinary Class by the Beach at Melati Resort & Spa: Held by the beach at a five-star resort, this intimate class (maximum four guests) includes premium ingredients and a recipe-filled USB.

Jungle Kitchen: Evening-only classes using traditional, electricity-free methods. Prepare a full Thai dinner by candlelight, surrounded by jungle sounds.

FIVETONINE/SHUTTERSTOCK

Kamalaya Wellness Sanctuary

Continued from p456

On the island's south coast, **Kamalaya Wellness Sanctuary** *(kamalaya.com; villa not incl wellness programmes from 17,000฿)* is a long-running favourite for travellers seeking a more comprehensive wellness programme. Built around a cave once used by Buddhist monks, the resort blends tropical landscaping with quiet pathways. Stays range from short programmes to multi-week plans for stress management, detox or recovery, supported by naturopaths and experienced therapists. Meals lean towards wholefood cuisine, and guests typically spend their days moving between consultations, treatments and slow time by the pool.

Perched on a cliff between Chaweng and Lamai, **Vikasa Yoga** *(vikasa.com; rooms from 5775฿)* appeals to travellers looking for a more sociable, yoga-centred experience. The property's open-air *sah lah* (often spelt *sala*) catch steady sea breezes, and classes run throughout the day, ranging from gentle flow to more athletic sequences. Many guests share long communal meals at the organic buffet, while day visitors can drop in for classes (from around 600฿). Accommodation spans simple hillside rooms to more comfortable ocean-view bungalows, all connected by steep paths.

For spa, **Tamarind Springs** *(tamarindsprings.com; 4hr spa package from 5500฿)* offers one of Samui's most atmospheric

EATING ON THE NORTH COAST: OUR PICKS

MAP P457 & P458

Tree Bridge Coffee (p465): Traverse a rope bridge to a treehouse-like cafe with sea views and eight short ziplines ideal for children or nervous types. *9am-6pm* ฿

Thai Mama Home Cooking: Homestyle Thai dishes served fresh in a friendly, laid-back setting. *10am-9pm* ฿

2 Fishes on the Beach: Italian-inspired seafood and steak served beachfront at sunset in a refined atmosphere. *5-10.30pm* ฿฿

Tito's Bitchin' Burritos: Flavour-packed Mexican burritos served casually with vibrant vibes and friendly service. *noon-10pm Sun-Fri* ฿฿

day experiences. Hidden amid dense jungle near Lamai, the spa is centred around natural granite boulders, herbal steam caves and outdoor plunge pools. Visits typically begin with a self-guided circuit of steam and cooling pools before moving to an open-air massage *sah lah*. Treatments draw on Thai massage traditions, and the overall experience is more nature-based than luxury-focused.

Hikes & Waterfalls

MAP P457

Jungle trails and waterfalls

If partying isn't on your agenda, Ko Samui offers plenty of peaceful escapes for travellers keen to explore the island's natural side, with a handful of accessible jungle trails and waterfalls that make rewarding day trips.

The two Nam Tok Na Muang falls, 12km inland from Nathon, are the island's best known. **Na Muang 1** is an easy, signposted walk to a 20m cascade with a natural pool suitable for swimming; parking is free, though small stalls line the approach. A steeper, sometimes slippery trail continues to **Na Muang 2**, a taller fall set deeper in the forest, with viewpoints along the way that reward the climb.

Near Nathon, **Nam Tok Hin Lad** is reached by a 2km shaded trail through bamboo groves and dense jungle. The path follows the river and ends at a quiet pool that's good for cooling off. The trail can be muddy after rain, and there are no facilities beyond a small temple at the trailhead, so bring water and snacks.

Further inland above Maenam, **Nam Tok Khun Si** sits among durian orchards and is best in the rainy season when water flow is strongest. A short, uneven track leads to several small tiers with swim-friendly pools. The surrounding viewpoint over Samui's central hills makes it a good stop for travellers exploring the interior by scooter or car.

High in the central highlands, the **Secret Buddha Garden** (also known as Tarnim Magic Garden) blends small cascades with moss-covered statues and shaded stone paths. There's a modest entrance fee of 100฿, and the steep access road requires confident driving, but the cool forest setting and sculpted terraces make it one of the island's more atmospheric inland spots.

Trails across the island's central hills are generally unmarked and can be slippery, especially after rain. Good footwear, water and a basic map or GPS are essential for those planning to explore deeper into the forest.

SOUVENIR GUIDE

Ko Samui offers a range of authentic souvenirs that capture its laid-back charm. Since it's known to be the coconut island, locally made coconut products are a must – think coconut oil, soaps and handcrafted coconut bowls, all perfect for bringing a piece of Samui home. Handwoven textiles and Thai silk scarves showcase traditional craftsmanship and make elegant gifts. Markets and boutiques in Fisherman's Village (p465) and Hat Chaweng (p462) are ideal spots to hunt for handmade jewellery, wooden carvings and ceramics. For foodies, locally produced dried fruits, spicy chilli pastes and fragrant Thai herbs offer a taste of Samui's culinary heritage. For a different kind of souvenir, the island also has many decent tattoo shops.

EATING ON KO SAMUI: SOUTHERN THAI FOOD

MAP P457 & P458

Chan Hom: A Michelin Bib Gourmand beachfront gem offering fresh southern Thai seafood. *11am-8pm* ฿

Pa Taew Thai Buffet: Authentic southern *ka nom jeen* (fermented rice noodles in curry) with other ready-made southern curries served on rice. *5am-3.30pm* ฿

Bang Por Seafood: Serves fresh southern Thai seafood dishes where you can dine while dipping your toes in the sand. *10am-10pm* ฿

Kapi Sator: A Michelin Bib Gourmand spot serving bold southern Thai flavours with fresh local seafood. *10am-10pm* ฿฿

KOH SAMUI'S CANINE SANCTUARY

Established in 2016 by Russian veterinarian Dr Elena Kireeva and her partner Stefan Koenig, **Pariah Dog Foundation** is a compassionate nonprofit dedicated to rescuing and rehabilitating stray dogs on Ko Samui. The foundation provides shelter, medical care and food to these animals, many of whom have been abandoned or neglected. A significant aspect of their mission includes sterilisation programmes aimed at controlling the stray-dog population on the island. The foundation operates solely on donations and the support of volunteers, relying on the generosity of the global community to continue its life-saving work. Visitors are welcome to meet the dogs and learn more about the foundation's efforts.

NETFALLS REMY MUSSER/SHUTTERSTOCK

Hat Chaweng

Hang at Hat Chaweng

MAP P458

Ko Samui's busiest beach

Hat Chaweng is Ko Samui's most famous and developed beach, stretching for about 7km along the island's east coast. It's the busiest stretch of sand on Samui, but the size of the bay means different areas have their own atmosphere. The northern end is rockier and generally quieter, attracting couples and families who prefer fewer crowds. The central section is the most commercial, lined with beach bars, restaurants, sunloungers and vendors selling everything from fruit to sarongs. At the far southern end, **Hat Chaweng Noi** is a smaller, more sheltered bay with a calmer vibe and several midrange and upscale resorts.

Chaweng, along with Hat Lamai to the south, is the heart of Samui's tourism infrastructure. The lanes and roads behind the beach are a dense grid of shops, massage parlours, tour agencies, souvenir stands and nightlife venues. Accommodation here covers all budgets, from simple hostels and guesthouses to high-end boutique hotels and luxury resorts. Several beachfront places turn into party hubs after dark, with DJs, fire-dancing shows and bars staying open into the early hours with little chance of an early night for anyone

EATING ON KO SAMUI: SOUTHERN THAI FOOD

MAP P457 & P458

Phensiri: Sustainable southern Thai cuisine using garden-fresh, seasonal island-grown produce. Bold flavours. *noon-10pm* ฿฿

Long Dtai Restaurant: Clifftop southern Thai seafood with panoramic bay-view dining. *5-11pm Thu-Tue* ฿฿฿

Khao Hom: Century-old family recipes, fiery southern curries and standout mango sticky rice. *10am-9pm* ฿

Ran Lan Saka: Food YouTuber Mark Wiens called it 'probably my favourite meal' – authentic southern Thai rice-and-curry. *5am-2pm Mon-Sat* ฿

staying nearby, so it's worth checking other locations carefully if you value sleep.

While the commercial sprawl can feel overwhelming, the beach itself is still one of the island's highlights. A sweeping curve of fine white sand backed by palms and dotted with granite outcrops, it delivers classic tropical scenery with easy access to amenities. It's a convenient base for travellers who want dining, shopping and nightlife within walking distance.

The sea off Chaweng is clearer and more swimmable than many other parts of Samui, but waves and rip currents can be stronger here, particularly during the monsoon season from November to February. The calmest conditions are usually from July to October, when the water is flatter and more suitable for swimming. Always check local flags and warnings before going in.

Chaweng is well suited to travellers who enjoy an active beach holiday with plenty of options for eating, drinking and entertainment. Those seeking a quieter atmosphere will find more laid-back stretches of sand at Chaweng Noi or on other parts of the coast.

SAMUI IN THE RAINY SEASON

While pretty much the rest of the country experiences the monsoon season from around mid-May until mid-October, Ko Samui gets the rain from September to November, bringing lush greenery and fewer tourists. Unlike the heavy monsoon storms of other Thai regions, Samui's rain usually comes in short, intense bursts, often in the late afternoon or evening, leaving plenty of sunshine for beach time and exploration. The island's tropical forests and waterfalls are at their most vibrant, perfect for hikes and nature lovers. Accommodation and flight prices dip during this quieter period, making it an attractive time for budget travellers. However, some sea activities may be limited due to rougher waters.

Chill at Lamai & South Coast

MAP P457 & P458

The more laid-back and rustic side of the island

The southeast and south coasts of Ko Samui wind around a series of bays, coves and rocky headlands, offering a mix of busy beaches and quiet stretches of sand that become increasingly secluded the further south you travel. Having your own transport is almost essential in this part of the island, as public-transport options are limited and distances between beaches can be considerable.

Hat Lamai is the main beach along this coast and the second most popular on Samui after Hat Chaweng. While it doesn't have quite the same sweep of dazzling sand, it remains an attractive and spacious beach, with shallow water that makes it especially good for swimming in the central section. The heart of Lamai is lined with resorts, restaurants, massage shops and bars catering to a broad mix of visitors. The northern and southern ends of Lamai are quieter and more relaxed, where the sand gives way to rocky patches and fewer crowds. It's common to see driftwood and other debris washed up here due to the tides, though most beachfront hotels clean their sections daily.

One of the highlights of this stretch of coast is **Crystal Bay**, also called Silver Beach. Tucked between Lamai and Chaweng Noi,

EATING IN HAT CHAWENG: OUR PICKS

MAP P458

Dara Serene: Known for its lobster dishes and seafood platters. *11am-11pm* ฿฿

Tent: Serving contemporary Thai cuisine where you can dine while sitting in beanbags on the beach. *7am-11pm* ฿฿

Khaw Glong Thai: Offers traditional Thai dishes with customisable spice levels. *1-10pm* ฿

Sexy Fish: An elevated seafood restaurant with a fine-dining vibe. *3-10pm* ฿฿฿

SUSTAINABLE RUM DISTILLERY

David Giallorenzo, owner of La Rhumerie De Koh Samui

What's something most visitors get wrong or miss about Ko Samui?

South Samui for sure and they miss the last authentic area in Ko Samui.

How has Ko Samui changed over the past few years?

Many projects, many new foreign investors and new residents. All prices increase strongly for investment and for tourists on holiday trips. More people, more buildings, more business, more traffic jams...

How can visitors support the island sustainably?

Same as they do at home. All choices they make must integrate sustainability approaches. The main concern about this point is more about government infrastructure investment for sustainability, and they are huge to support the growth strategy of the island.

SERGII FIGURNYI/SHUTTERSTOCK

Crystal Bay (p463)

this small cove has clear turquoise water, powdery sand and excellent conditions for snorkelling along the rocks at either end. A handful of small resorts and beach restaurants give it a relaxed atmosphere without feeling overdeveloped.

Further south, the road skirts **Ban Hua Thanon**, a working fishing village and home to Samui's long-established Muslim community. The area has little in the way of tourist facilities but is known for its fresh market, a colourful mosque and several good-value halal restaurants.

From here, the coastal road twists through a landscape of coconut plantations, small villages and quiet bays. This is one of the best parts of the island to explore by motorcycle or scooter, as the traffic eases and the scenery becomes more rural. Accommodation is limited, so it's worth booking ahead if you plan to stay overnight.

On the southern coast, **La Rhumerie De Koh Samui** *(fb.com/larhumeriedesamui)* in Ban Bang Kao is a French-run distillery producing craft rums from local sugarcane. Visitors can tour the production area and sample different rums at the tasting bar set in a shady garden of tall palms. **Hat Bang Kao** itself is a long, rocky beach good for walking and collecting shells, though swimming is limited by shallow water and coral.

At the far southwest tip of the island lies **Ao Phang Ka**, a peaceful cove known for scenic sunsets and calm views

DRINKING IN CHAWENG: OUR PICKS

MAP P458

Tikibox: Serves really creative and good-quality rum-based tiki cocktails. *2pm-2am* BB

Cabanas Beach Club: Stylish beachfront day-to-night club with pools, DJs and gourmet food stations. *7am-midnight* BBB

Powder Room: Speakeasy cocktail lounge mixing nu-disco beats with inventive drinks and retro charm. *6pm-midnight Mon-Sat* BB

Pride Bar Samui: Inclusive LGBTIQ+ lounge with cocktails, karaoke, cabaret and games. *6pm-2am* BB

across the bay. The sand here is soft, but the sea remains shallow and rocky, making it better for paddling and relaxation than swimming.

This part of Samui feels quieter and less polished than the busier area in the east, rewarding those who take the time to explore with unhurried coastal scenery, friendly villages and a glimpse of the island's slower pace of life.

Dodge the Crowds on the North Coast

MAP P457

Family-friendly spots with safe-to-swim beaches

Hat Mae Nam is the main beach along the north coast and remains one of Samui's most attractive stretches of sand. It's a long, wide crescent with calm water, fine for swimming and generally free of jet skis, making it a good choice for families with young children. Small restaurants and cafes sit just behind the beach, many offering shaded seating and simple Thai dishes, while the main road provides a broader range of dining and shopping options. For sweeping views over the bay and out to Ko Pha-Ngan, head up to the **Mae Nam Viewpoint** on the road towards Hat Nathon; the steep track is walkable, though most visitors arrive by scooter.

East of Mae Nam, the laid-back area around Baan Tai offers a quieter, narrower stretch of sand backed by coconut palms and low-key bungalow resorts, ideal for travellers seeking a slow pace without the crowds.

Markets & the Northwest Coast

MAP P457 & P458

Explore local food and shop for souvenirs

Fisherman's Village in Bo Phut has become one of Samui's most popular destinations in recent years. The narrow main street, lined with preserved Chinese-style shophouses, has been converted into boutique hotels, souvenir shops, cocktail bars and restaurants serving everything from fresh Thai seafood to European bistro fare. Many places have open-front seating with views of the bay, and the atmosphere shifts from relaxed in the daytime to lively after sunset. The popular **night market**, held on Monday, Wednesday, Friday and Saturday, draws big crowds for its street-food stalls, grilled seafood skewers, handmade crafts, live music and cocktails mixed from colourful cart bars. It can be extremely busy in the high season, so arrive early if you plan to eat, wander or shop.

For a more local, low-key alternative market, **Si Khao Night Market** – a 20-minute scooter ride inland – offers cheaper

KO SAMUI TOURS

X-Quad: Follow jungle tracks through mountain adventures on an ATV or a buggy. *xquad-samui.com*

Independence Yacht Charter: Cruise around with a private yacht experience, with custom routes. *independence-yacht-charter.com*

Tree Bridge Zipline: Fly over treetops on a nine-cable zipline course and explore the island's lush interior on elevated walkways. *treebridgezipline.com*

100 Degrees East: Join one of Samui's top dive operators for small-group snorkelling trips to offshore reefs and islands. *100degreeseast.com*

iSUP Samui: Paddle from Choeng Mon or Bangrak as the sun dips over the bay, guided by experienced stand-up paddleboard (SUP) instructors. *isupsamui.com*

DRINKING IN LAMAI & ON THE SOUTH COAST: OUR PICKS

MAP P457 & p458

House of Suzy: Charming dim-sum and Chinese-inspired cocktails in heritage shophouse. *6pm-midnight Mon-Sat* BB

Chalay Rock Bar: Rustic cliff-side reggae bar perched on Lamai's Hin Ta rocks. *10am-8pm Tue-Sun* B

Crystal Bay Beach Club: Relaxed beachfront spot serving seafood, pizzas and cocktails, with live DJs. *8am-10pm* BB

La Rhumerie De Koh Samui: Sustainable local rum distillery with a bar and restaurant. *11am-9pm Tue-Sun* BB

BEST KO SAMUI GYMS

Lamai Fitness: Offers fitness, weight-loss, and detox packages for all levels, ideal for visitors seeking a structured wellness reset.

Elite Gym & Fitness: A Chaweng standout with modern equipment, air conditioning, and group classes in a more upscale and professional setting.

Koh Fit: A big centre featuring a full gym, pool, boot camps, and an onsen spa for post-workout recovery, and a cafe serving healthy food.

Ultra Bodies Gym: Offers quality weight-training machines, free weights, Smith racks, and cardio gear – a solid value for travellers.

food, fewer tourists and the feel of a more everyday Thai night market.

Just beyond Fisherman's Village, **Hat Bo Phut** curves around the northeast coast for a couple of kilometres. The sand here is more golden and coarse compared with Chaweng, and while the water can be murkier, the beach remains pleasant for long walks and quiet sunbathing. The western end is more peaceful, backed by small resorts and swaying palms, and the gentle slope of the shoreline makes it a good spot to linger at sunset or watch fishing boats head out in the early evening.

Connect with Yourself on the Northeast Coast

MAP P458

Popular temples and easy access to offshore adventures

Around the headland, **Hat Bang Rak** – also known as Big Buddha Beach – takes its name from the prominent golden statue at **Wat Phra Yai**, which rises 12m above the temple grounds and is visible from much of Samui's northeast coast. Early mornings are the best time to visit: the temple is quiet, the light is soft, and you'll have a better chance of photographing the Buddha without tourists in the frame. The surrounding complex includes small shrines, viewpoints and stalls selling amulets and iced drinks, and the elevated walkway provides sweeping views over the bay towards Ko Pha-Ngan. Bang Rak also makes a practical base for diving and snorkelling trips, as Samui's most established dive operator, 100 Degrees East (p465), has its office here. Its boat departs from the nearby pier, offering small-group trips to local reefs and islands such as Ko Tao and the Ang Thong archipelago.

Just a short distance away, **Wat Plai Laem** showcases Samui's most striking Buddhist artwork: a vivid, 18-armed statue of Guan Yin, the Chinese Goddess of Compassion, set on a platform in the middle of an ornamental lake. The statue's bright colours and intricate detailing make it one of the island's most photogenic sights, especially in the late afternoon when the light reflects off the water. Visitors can wander the surrounding walkways, feed the fish, or step inside the nearby *viharn* (assembly hall) to see murals depicting scenes from Chinese and Thai Buddhist traditions. Despite its popularity, the temple complex often feels calm and spacious, making it a worthwhile stop even if you're simply passing through the area.

DRINKING ON THE NORTH COAST: OUR PICKS

MAP P457 & P458

Bar Bohem: Hidden cocktail bar owned and run by an ex Iron Balls gin guy who moved from Bangkok. *7pm-2am* BB

79 Beach Club & Resort: Affordable beach club with good house music and a really big pool overlooking the ocean. *11am-10pm* BB

Easy on Tam's: Late-night dancing spot, playing remixes of popular sing-alongs. *5pm-2am* BB

Woobar: Located inside W Koh Samui, it offers panorama views of the ocean and great service. *noon-midnight* BB

Beyond Ko Samui

Explore Ang Thong's untouched islands and discover Surat Thani's vibrant markets and authentic southern Thai life.

A short boat ride west of Ko Samui lies Ang Thong Marine National Park, a dreamy group of jungle-clad islands ringed by emerald seas. Explore limestone caves, hike to panoramic viewpoints, paddle into hidden lagoons or snorkel off deserted beaches – Ang Thong is a must for nature lovers. Back on the mainland, Surat Thani, often overlooked by travellers, makes for a rewarding detour. As the main ferry hub to Samui, it's easy to dismiss, but linger and you'll discover buzzing street-food stalls, a colourful night market and a low-key riverside vibe. There are a few floating markets – a local favourite, packed with snacks, crafts and plenty of authentic southern Thai flavours.

Ang Thong Marine National Park

TIME FROM KO SAMUI: **45MIN FROM BANGRAK PIER**

Untouched nature and mini island-hopping

Scattered like emerald jewels across the Gulf of Thailand, Ang Thong Marine National Park is a breathtaking group of 42 uninhabited islands cloaked in dense jungle, ringed by sheer limestone cliffs and surrounded by sapphire-blue seas. Officially protected since 1980, the park remains one of the most pristine natural attractions in southern Thailand. Accessible only by licensed tour operators from Ko Samui, Ko Pha-Ngan or Ko Tao, Ang Thong is a favourite for kayaking

GETTING AROUND

To reach Ang Thong Marine National Park from Ko Samui, most travellers join an organised day trip with a licensed tour operator. Tours typically depart from Nathon Pier or Bangrak Pier in Bo Phut by speedboat or slow boat, depending on the operator. Prices start around 1500฿ to 2500฿ per person, usually including snorkelling gear, lunch, park fees and hotel transfers. Advance booking is recommended, especially during peak season, as daily visitor numbers are limited to protect the park's ecosystem.

To reach Surat Thani from Ko Samui, the easiest way is via Lomprayah's high-speed catamaran from Nathon Pier to Donsak Pier on the mainland. From there, Lomprayah offers shuttle services to Surat Thani town, airport, train station or bus terminal.

THINK TWICE ABOUT KO MAT SUM

Also known as Pig Island, Ko Mat Sum has shot to Instagram fame for its sunbathing pigs – but don't expect a hidden paradise. The pigs live out in the open (not very hygienic), and the island's tiny beach is often packed with day-trippers snapping selfies. Tours usually bundle Ko Mat Sum with Ko Taen, another nearby island with mediocre snorkelling and little else to offer. While the novelty of pigs on a tropical beach might sound fun, the reality feels more like a tourist trap, with noise, queues and little space to unwind. If you're after a genuine island experience, your money is better spent elsewhere, ideally on a destination that values conservation and atmosphere over gimmicks.

through arched rock corridors or limestone overhang tunnels, snorkelling off hidden beaches and hiking jungle trails to panoramic viewpoints.

The park famously inspired Alex Garland's cult novel *The Beach*, though the film was shot elsewhere. Among the highlights is **Ko Mae Ko**, home to the spectacular **Emerald Lake** (Thale Nai) – a saltwater lagoon cradled inside a collapsed sinkhole, reachable via a steep 20-minute climb with sweeping views at the top. On **Ko Wua Ta Lap**, where you'll find the park's ranger station and main base, there are basic bungalows, a campsite and a short but challenging trail up to a lookout point that rewards with one of Thailand's finest vistas. While amenities are minimal, staying overnight lets you experience the islands without the daytime tour crowds. Visitor numbers are capped to protect the fragile ecosystem, so book ahead.

Surat Thani

TIME FROM KO SAMUI: **45MIN**

Experience untouristed southern Thai village life

Often bypassed by travellers, Surat Thani is more than just a gateway town. Direct flights from Bangkok to Ko Samui can be expensive. If you have time, flying into Surat Thani and making the overland journey to the islands could not only save you money, but also reward you with a taste of southern Thai life along the way.

Perched on the banks of the Tapi River, this busy provincial town hums with street markets, friendly locals and a gritty charm that's a world away from the tourist beaches. The weekend-only **Ban Don** and **Pracha Rat** floating markets offer a glimpse of traditional river life, with long-tail boats brimming with snacks, fruit, seafood and handmade crafts. Strolling the bustling night markets, you'll find southern Thai favourites like fiery curries, grilled river prawns, and *ka nom jeen* noodles served with rich coconut-based sauces.

Though it's known mainly as a transport hub, Surat Thani makes a good base for exploring before you cross over to island life. The vibe is laid-back, the prices are friendly and the experience feels refreshingly untouristed – a rewarding detour for curious travellers.

EATING IN SURAT THANI: OUR PICKS

Keo Pla: A Bib Gourmand noodle shop since 1959, serving rich fish dumpling broth with herbal aromatics and generous portions. *8am-1.30pm* ฿

Day & Night of Suratthani: Stylish spot walking distance from the river with Thai-fusion dishes, craft cocktails and industrial-chic interiors. *11am-midnight* ฿฿

Sum Gradang Nga: Local favourite for southern Thai food. Expect fiery curries, crispy fish and fragrant rice in a laid-back, family-run setting. *11am-10pm* ฿

Lucky Restaurant: Hearty Thai-Chinese stir-fries and seafood soups in a casual atmosphere. Quick service, generous portions, wallet-friendly prices. *10am-8pm* ฿฿

Ko Pha-Ngan

BEACHES | BALANCE | BEATS

Travellers discovered Ko Pha-Ngan in the late 1970s, when the locals fished and farmed, accommodation consisted of bamboo beach huts and nightlife meant sitting around a fire on the beach. Those days are long gone, but the bohemian spirit lives on. Famous for its Full Moon Party, Ko Pha-Ngan has outgrown its reputation as just a party island. Yes, Hat Rin still hosts beach raves, but beyond the glow paint and buckets lies a wonderful island that rewards deeper exploration.

The island's north and east coasts are home to secluded bays, coral reefs and dense jungle meeting the sea. In the centre, forested hills and waterfalls provide hiking routes and viewpoints, while the west coast is a magnet for the wellness crowd – think yoga *sah lahs*, plant-based cafes and holistic healing retreats.

Ko Pha-Ngan has struck a balance few islands can: it's as easy to find all-night beats as it is sunrise meditation.

GETTING AROUND

Most travel is by scooter, with rental prices starting around 200฿ to 250฿ per day. The island's interior is mountainous and unpaved in places, so stick to the coastal roads unless you're an experienced rider. *Songthaew* (shared pick-up trucks) connect popular spots, especially around Full Moon dates, but service can be irregular elsewhere.

Beaches & Beats

All about the parties

Hat Rin is Ko Pha-Ngan's best-known destination, infamous and iconic in equal measure. It's home to **Hat Rin Nok** (aka Sunrise Beach), a glorious arc of fine white sand that might well be the island's most beautiful beach – when it's not packed with thousands of ravers. For most of the month, it's surprisingly serene: you'll find long-tail boats gently bobbing offshore, a few sunbathers scattered across the sand, and beach bars playing chillout music as the sun rises or sets.

Every month the beach hosts the Full Moon Party (p472), but the area is about more than this. Beyond the crowds and chaos, Hat Rin has surprising variety. On the peninsula's far side lies **Hat Sareekantang** (aka Leela Beach), a quiet curve of white sand backed by swaying palms and midrange resorts – perfect for recovering in peace.

Continued on p472

TOP TIP

Looking for something quieter than Full Moon but still vibey? Check out the Half Moon and Jungle Experience parties held inland – smaller, more local, and often with better music.

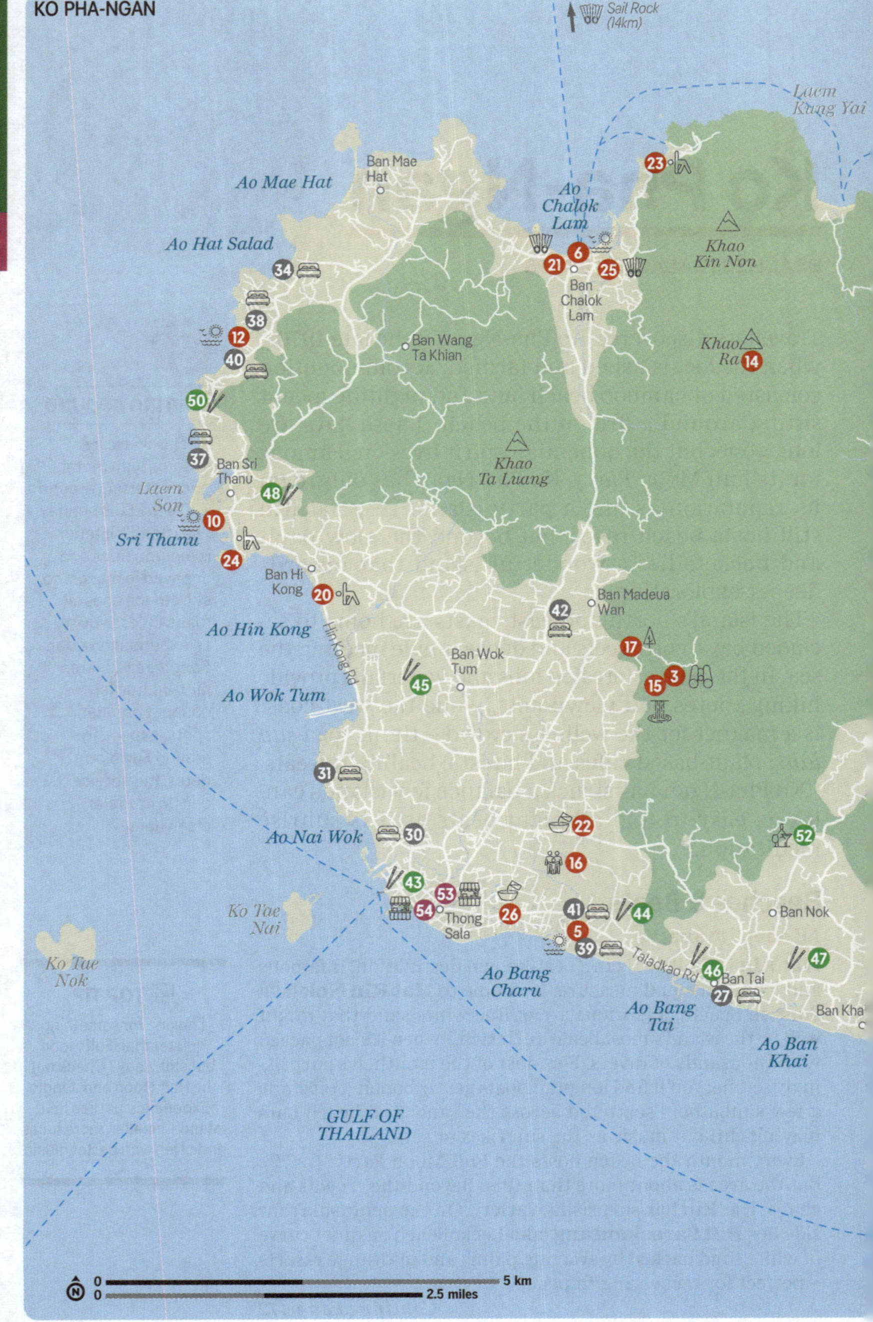
KO PHA-NGAN
Sail Rock (14km)
Laem Kung Yai
Ban Mae Hat
Ao Mae Hat
Ao Chalok Lam
Ban Chalok Lam
Khao Kin Non
Ao Hat Salad
Ban Wang Ta Khian
Khao Ra
Khao Ta Luang
Ban Sri Thanu
Laem Son
Sri Thanu
Ban Hi Kong
Ban Madeua Wan
Ao Hin Kong
Hin Kong Rd
Ban Wok Tum
Ao Wok Tum
Ao Nai Wok
Ko Tae Nai
Ko Tae Nok
Thong Sala
Ao Bang Charu
Taladkao Rd
Ban Nok
Ban Tai
Ao Bang Tai
Ban Khai
Ao Ban Khai
GULF OF THAILAND
0 5 km
0 2.5 miles

HIGHLIGHTS
1 Full Moon Party
2 Hat Rin Nok

SIGHTS
3 Domsila Viewpoint
4 Hat Ban Kai
5 Hat Ban Tai
6 Hat Chaloklum
7 Hat Khontee
8 Hat Rin Nai
9 Hat Sareekantang
10 Hat Srithanu
11 Hat Than Sadet
12 Hat Yao
13 Hat Yuan
14 Khao Ra
15 Nam Tok Phaeng Noi
see 16 Organic Raw Honey Shop and Products
16 Raitiaviset Organic Farm
17 Than Sadet-Ko Pha-Ngan Sok National Park
18 Thong Nai Pan Noi
19 Thong Nai Pan Yai

ACTIVITIES
20 Ananda Yoga
21 Apnea
see 12 Haad Yao Divers
22 Muai's Thai Traditional Cooking Academy
23 Ocean Experience
24 Orion Healing
25 Sail Rock Divers
26 The Phangan Thai Cooking Class

SLEEPING
27 Divine Comedie
28 Havana Beach Resort
29 Hideout Hostel
30 Jungle Vibes
31 Kupu Kupu Phangan Beach Villas & Spa by l'Occitane
32 Longtail Beach Resort
33 Mai Pen Rai
34 Salad Hut
35 Sanctuary
see 9 Sarikantang Resort & Spa
36 Sea Breeze Resort
37 Seetanu Bungalows
38 Shiralea Backpackers Resort
39 Tiki Beach
see 1 Tommy Resort
40 TropiCoco Beach Resort
41 Wanderlust Hostel
42 Wonderland Healing Center

EATING
43 Auntie's Restaurant
44 Coconut Home
45 Dear Phangan
46 Fisherman's Restaurant & Bar
47 Nong View Restaurant
48 Pum Pui Restaurant
49 Rasta Baby
50 Wave Sunset Restaurant and Bar

DRINKING & NIGHTLIFE
51 Eden Garden
52 Oxa Party

SHOPPING
53 Thong Sala Local Market
54 Thong Sala Walking Street

THE ISLAND'S WET-SEASON REALITY

Ko Pha-Ngan's wet season, roughly October to December, brings dramatic shifts that shape how you explore the island. Beaches often have stronger currents and reduced visibility, making snorkelling less rewarding and swimming riskier on exposed coasts. Heavy rain can churn up sediment, leaving the water noticeably murkier than in peak season. Long-tail services to remote east-coast bays, including Haad Yuan and Haad Tien, may be cancelled when the seas get rough (and they often are). Inland, the island is at its most vibrant, with waterfalls flowing and jungle trails lush and shaded, but paths become slippery and steep sections tricky, so care and sturdy footwear are essential.

Continued from p469

There's also **Hat Rin Nai** (Sunset Beach), which has a decent view at dusk but isn't great for swimming.

Hat Rin town, separates the beaches, but it only takes 10 minutes to walk from one side of the peninsula to the other. The town is compact and walkable, filled with tattoo studios, cafes, souvenir shops and travel agencies. It's an ideal base if you want to experience both the high-octane energy of the Full Moon Party and the calm charm of Ko Pha-Ngan's quieter east coast – with long-tail boats ready to whisk you to hidden bays like Hat Than Sadet and Hat Yuan (p477).

For a more low-key but equally fun night, check out alternative events like the Half Moon Festival in the jungle north of Ban Tai, or the Black Moon Culture and Shiva Moon parties, which focus more on underground beats and local crowds.

Full Moon Madness

Explore what draws travellers from all over the world

The **Full Moon Party** at Hat Rin Nok is Ko Pha-Ngan's most infamous export – a wild, beachside blowout that has reached near-mythic status along Southeast Asia's backpacker trail. Legend has it the first bash was a casual send-off at Paradise Bungalows in the late 1980s. Now? Anywhere from 5000 to 30,000 partygoers descend on the island each month, their bodies glowing with UV paint and minds set on one thing: dancing till dawn.

By 10pm, crowds surge past the entrance gate (200฿; wristband included) and spill onto Hat Rin Nok (p469), aka Sunrise Beach. Bars blast duelling soundtracks ranging from EDM and house to hip-hop, trance and drum'n'bass. There's no central stage – just a chaotic, sand-slicked strip of sound and lights. Fire performers twirl flaming batons. Buckets of alcohol – vodka, gin, rum or whisky mixed with Coke or Red Bull – line the beach. Drunken dares turn into games of petrol-drenched fire-rope jumping, equal parts thrill and hazard. Pace yourself and avoid anything stronger than a Red Bull mixer; shady vendors and scams do exist. Scams might include vendors reporting sales of drugs to the police and the buyer faced with paying a big fine or jail.

Some claim the Full Moon has lost its edge, but there's no denying its spectacle. Despite the thousands of intoxicated bodies crammed together, the vibe is surprisingly chill and incidents are rare. Still, if crowds aren't your thing, it's worth exploring the island's lesser-known alternatives.

EATING ON KO PHA-NGAN: OUR PICKS

Pum Pui Restaurant: A long-running favourite for homestyle Thai food with bold southern flavours. *1-4.30pm & 6-10.30pm* ฿฿

Fisherman's Restaurant & Bar: Beachfront seafood with a rustic-luxe vibe; sunset tables are worth booking ahead. *1-10pm Mon-Fri, 5-10pm Sat & Sun* ฿฿

Auntie's Restaurant: A humble, market-style kitchen serving classic southern Thai. *1-9.30pm* ฿

Nong View Restaurant: A very local, family-run Thai eatery known for fresh seafood, spicy southern dishes and generous portions. *10am-10pm* ฿฿

OLEGD/SHUTTERSTOCK

Full Moon Party

The **Half Moon Festival**, held inland in a jungle clearing near Ban Tai, delivers pro lighting and big-name DJs – though ticket prices can sting. More underground still are the guerrilla-style raves advertised through flyers or on *phanganist.com*, including those at the legendary **Eden Garden**, perched on the remote east coast and reachable only by longtail or rough forest track.

Party season means a surge in demand – Hat Rin gets booked out fast, so book in advance. But there's no real need to stay here if you're only here for the Full Moon Party, as many hostels across the island offer shuttles or boats to and from the action.

And if you're around during the party 'off-weeks' (usually just before or after the full moon), don't fret – **Oxa Party** has become the island's go-to for high-quality sound systems, artfully curated house and techno lineups, and intimate jungle-meets-beach vibes. With its relaxed crowd and late-night dancing under the palms, it's the kind of party the Full Moon used to be.

OM, SHANTI & SUNRISE JAMS

Long before Full Mooners descended, Ko Pha-Ngan drew a slower tribe: yogis, healers and seekers chasing stillness (or starlit drum circles). The east coast is the island's spiritual heartland: the **Sanctuary** has led the wellness charge for decades, with yoga, detox, ecstatic dance and open-mic nights under the palms. On the opposite coast, **Hat Srithanu** is a full-blown conscious-living enclave, home to vegan cafes, breathwork sessions, cacao ceremonies and tantra schools. It's common to see handpan sound baths or reiki shares advertised on roadside chalkboards. Whether you're here to align your chakras or just sip kombucha while journalling at sunrise, Ko Pha-Ngan offers a haven for the spiritually curious and the barefoot bohemian alike.

South Coast Slow Days

Calm sunsets and laid-back beaches

The south coast of Ko Pha-Ngan unfolds in a string of tranquil bays and jungle-backed beaches, offering a more relaxed vibe than the island's busier centres.

The quieter sands of **Hat Ban Kai** and **Hat Ban Tai** feel unhurried, with long stretches of coconut-fringed shore framed by views of Ko Samui across the water. While the shallow sea here isn't ideal for swimming, the coast is perfect for slow mornings, beach walks and sunset-watching. Behind the beach, you'll find a dispersed community of long-stayers, family-run cafes and casual bars, creating a friendly, lived-in feel without the intensity of the party scene. Many travellers settle in for weeks, drawn by the relaxed pace and accessible

ISLAND SHOPPING FINDS

Ko Pha-Ngan's shopping scene goes beyond neon tank tops and Full Moon merch. In Srithanu, browse handmade jewellery crafted from shells, crystals and silver by local artisans, or pick up natural body products and organic teas at wellness-minded boutiques. Over in Hat Rin, markets offer upcycled sarongs, hand-painted tees, and beachwear stitched by resident tailors. Thong Sala Walking Street Market (especially lively on Saturdays) is a great spot for ecofriendly souvenirs, coconut bowls and batik prints. For something truly unique, look out for island-made essential oils and incense blends. Supporting these small makers is not only a more mindful way to shop – it's also how to bring home a little Pha-Ngan magic.

ALIONABIRUKOVA/SHUTTERSTOCK

Hat Chaloklum

wellness options like beachfront yoga sessions or Thai massage huts tucked under the palms.

Further inland, the main roads pass small neighbourhoods with local shops, simple houses and family-run eateries. This part of the island is less built-up, and it's one of the easiest areas to explore independently thanks to its flat terrain and well-paved roads. Scooter rental is widely available across the south coast, and bicycles are also an option for short, relaxed rides.

Thong Sala: Ko Pha-Ngan's Main Town

Markets, food and everyday island life

Thong Sala, the island's largest town and ferry port, has grown into a busy mini-hub where travellers come for errands but stay for the atmosphere.

Thong Sala Local Market is the heart of it all: a lively sprawl of grills, noodle stalls, curry pots and dessert carts that begins to warm up before sunset. It's one of the best places to sample southern Thai flavours cheaply, from chilli-spiked seafood to sweet *roti*. The market opens from 11am to 5pm, except Saturdays when it's 5pm to 10pm.

Just a short walk away, the **Saturday Walking Street Market** (5pm to 10pm) transforms the main road into a night-time bazaar of handicrafts, live music and local snacks. The crowd is a mix of residents, long-term expats and visitors, giving the whole area a communal feel.

Thong Sala is also home to two of Ko Pha-Ngan's most popular cooking schools. **Muai's Thai Traditional Cooking Academy** *(fb.com/muaicookingacademykohphangan; 1600-1800฿)* teaches classic dishes in an intimate garden setting, while **Phangan Thai Cooking Class** *(087 278 8898;*

1500-1800฿), run by warm and charismatic Chef Oy, guides students through market shopping before a hands-on cooking session. Both offer a deeper connection to the island's food culture than the average tourist experience.

Hiking into Ko Pha-Ngan's Interior

Leave the beaches behind for waterfalls

Ko Pha-Ngan's interior is a world of dense forest, running water and birdsong.

For a rewarding half-day adventure, tackle the Nam Tok Phaeng–Domsila Viewpoint hike, which leads to one of the island's highest peaks. It begins inside **Than Sadet-Ko Pha-Ngan Sok National Park**. The trail winds past **Nam Tok Phaeng Noi** flowing strongest in the wet season, before climbing steadily to **Domsila Viewpoint**. From the top, the island spreads out beneath you in a patchwork of forested hills and distant bays.

Khao Ra is Ko Pha-Ngan's longest and most demanding marked hike, leading to the island's highest summit at around 627m. The route takes about 1½ hours each way and follows a steady jungle ascent, passing a stream and the island's main reservoir before climbing into thicker forest. The final section is steeper, with a few short scrambles over rocks and roots. At the top, a clearing offers wide views across the island's northern coast, including Hat Chaloklum, while a large boulder on the eastern side provides an additional vantage point for those confident on uneven terrain.

Wellness & Healing in Srithanu

Spiritual recharge and quiet community

Wellness is the west's real signature. The village of Srithanu has evolved into the island's spiritual heart, drawing in a barefoot, holistic crowd with its daily offerings of health-focused activities. Long-running centres such as **Orion Healing** *(orionhealing.com; from 2200฿)* set the tone: think beachfront yoga pavilions, plant-based cafes, herbal steams and therapists offering everything from breathwork to Thai massage that combines yoga-like stretches.

Another standout space is **Wonderland Healing Center** *(wonderlandhc.com; dorm bed per night 2000฿)*, set in a leafy pocket near the inland lagoon. It feels almost like a retreat village: open-air *sah lah*, herbal steam rooms, a vegan cafe and schedules packed with yin, kundalini and sound-healing sessions.

DETOX DIARIES

Ko Pha-Ngan is famous for its spiritual side – and nowhere is that more evident than in its detox scene. Think week-long juice cleanses, daily colonics, silent fasting retreats, and herbal steam saunas tucked deep in the jungle. Some spots, like Orion Healing and **Ananda Yoga**, are well regarded for blending science with spirituality. Some can veer into culty territory, with questionable claims and hefty price tags. If you're curious, start light: a one-day juice cleanse, a sunset herbal sauna session, or a gentle yoga and clean-eating combo. It's easy to get swept up, but don't feel bad for craving a mango sticky rice afterwards.

EATING ON KO PHA-NGAN: OUR PICKS

Rasta Baby: Restaurant with a bar serving good Thai and Western dishes. *11am-midnight* ฿

Coconut Home: Laid-back local place on the beachfront offering simple Thai dishes. *9am-9pm* ฿

Dear Phangan: Michelin Bib–recognised local restaurant serving seafood dishes with a modern and luxury touch. *6-10pm* ฿฿฿

Wave Sunset Restaurant and Bar: Breezy beachfront on the cliff – a perfect spot to catch a sunset. *9.30am-10pm* ฿฿

CONSCIOUS KO PHA-NGAN

On Ko Pha-Ngan, reef restoration projects near Chaloklum, beach cleanups led by locals, and initiatives to become a 'Green Island' reflect a growing commitment to conservation. **Raitiaviset Organic Farm** supports the island's self-sufficiency with sustainable produce. Next to it, there's also **Organic Raw Honey Shop and Products**. Centres like **Ocean Experience** pair eco-tourism with community wellness. Wonderland Healing Center (p475) offers community-based vegan retreats and steam saunas. So choose reusable over plastic, join a tide-clean clinic, or simply spend a few evenings at socially aware cafes and beachfront businesses. You're not just visiting the island: you're helping to preserve it.

MIKE UNDERWATER/SHUTTERSTOCK

Snorkelling & Diving

Calm coast for rewarding underwater exploration

Hat Yao anchors the coastline with a long, gently curving beach and one of Ko Pha-Ngan's healthiest fringing reefs. Slip into the water from the soft sand and you'll be swimming above coral gardens within minutes with shafts of sunlight cutting through clear, shallow water. Several operators, including **Haad Yao Divers** *(haadyaodivers.com; beginner dive course 9800฿)*, run beginner-friendly courses and shore dives, making it an easy place to try scuba for the first time.

Hat Chaloklum doubles as the island's northern dive hub, with easy access to **Sail Rock**, a sheer, chimney-like pinnacle rising from deep water 14km offshore and widely considered the Gulf of Thailand's top dive site. Whale shark sightings are a real possibility here, and operators such as **Sail Rock Divers** *(sailrockdiversresort.com; dive 2200-3100฿)* run well-organised trips with small groups and experienced guides who know the site's currents and contours intimately. For those drawn to breath-hold diving, **Apnea** *(apneakohphangan.com; dive 2000-3000฿)* remains the village's benchmark for free-diving, offering structured depth training in calm, sheltered conditions that drop off quickly into deeper blue – ideal for practising equalisation and steady descents.

East Coast Beach-Hopping

Wild, mostly roadless and just isolated enough

Curling north of Hat Rin, Ko Pha-Ngan's east coast is a chain of jungle-backed coves where steep green hills drop to white-sand beaches accessible mainly by long-tail boat. The lack of roads keeps the atmosphere blissfully low-key; days slip by

Whale shark, Sail Rock

to the sound of surf and cicadas, making this coastline ideal for families and anyone seeking quiet.

Hiring a long-tail boat from Hat Rin Nok (full circuit around 3000฿) is the easiest way to explore. The first stop is **Hat Khontee**, a tiny pocket of pale, powdery sand wedged between boulders and dense jungle. With no road access and only a couple of low-key places to eat, it feels secluded even in high season. Waves can be livelier here, especially on windy days, but the cove's natural enclosure keeps the water swimmable when conditions are fair.

A short ride north lies **Hat Yuan**, a deep, sheltered bay with coarse golden sand, calm swimming, and palms leaning towards clear turquoise water. When the light is right, you can see reef patches under the surface, and the beach has just enough small cafes for a cold drink between swims.

Much further along, **H`at Than Sadet** offers a different mood altogether, a narrow strip of soft, white sand framed by a freshwater river and a wooden bridge. The beach is swimmable when seas are calm, though currents can strengthen during the wet season. At night, bioluminescent plankton sometimes sparkle in the shallows, giving the place a slightly magical, castaway feel.

The journey continues to the twin bays of **Hat Thong Nai Pan Noi** and **Hat Thong Nai Pan Yai**, the most developed and accessible beaches on this coast. Noi is the more refined sweep: fine ivory sand, gentle waves, sunloungers, a scattering of chic bars, and the island's most polished resorts. The water stays shallow for metres, making it excellent for children and relaxed swims. Yai, just over the headland, is broader and more easygoing, with a long, bright-white shoreline, casual eateries and a mellow, village-like feel. Both are rare on the east coast for having restaurants, small shops, and easy access to kayaks and SUPs.

BOAT SKILLS 101

Long-tail boats are your ticket to Ko Pha-Ngan's remote corners – think Hat Khuat, Hat Yuan or the dramatic coves near Hat Than Sadet. Expect to pay around 3000฿ to 3500฿ for a full-day east-coast tour (up to six hours). Always confirm whether the price includes fuel, return fare and wait time. Departures from Hat Rin, Chaloklum and Thong Nai Pan are most common, but small bays may have boatmen too. Mornings (before 11am) offer calm seas. Use apps like Tides Near Me to avoid grounding or awkward beach landings. Bring waterproof bags, beach towels, reef-safe sunscreen and snorkel gear. Some boatmen offer masks, but not always.

Ko Tao

DIVING | NATURE | PEOPLE

GETTING AROUND

Ko Tao is so small that public transport barely exists here. Almost everyone gets around on a motorcycle or scooter. To rent one, prices start at 200฿ per day. Different shops ask for different forms of deposit, ranging from no deposit to 4000฿ to 7000฿, to leaving your passport – go with whatever you're comfortable with, there are plenty of options. However, despite a lot of steep routes, the island overall is very walkable.

The smallest of the Samui, Pha-Ngan, Tao trio, Ko Tao may only take 15 minutes to cross by scooter, but it's packed with a big personality. Long hailed as Thailand's scuba-diving capital, Ko Tao draws ocean lovers from around the world keen to earn their open-water certification.

Beyond its underwater offerings, Ko Tao is gaining a name as a rock-climbing and bouldering destination, with granite crags and sea cliffs offering climbs for all levels. Hikers can test their legs on steep jungle trails that connect beaches and viewpoints, though even a casual stroll can feel like a mini trek in this terrain. The island is also ringed with soft-sand beaches perfect for a nap, a snorkel or a lazy afternoon read.

Despite its size, Ko Tao boasts a buzzing nightlife, from beach bars and pub crawls to hidden jungle parties. The island's especially welcoming to solo travellers, thanks to its tight-knit community vibe and the ease of meeting new people over shared dives, hostel dinners or happy-hour cocktails.

TOP TIP

For those looking for an affordable private, personalised free-diving experience with just y ou and one instructor, contact Instagram: *@freedivewiththomas*. This operator will meet with you and curate a programme suitable for your needs (4000฿).

Sunsets & Nightlife

Relaxing evenings and after-dark parties

Ko Tao's main hub is **Hat Sairee**, a lively 3km stretch of west-coast sand just north of Mae Hat. It's the island's most developed beach, home to dive shops, bars, restaurants, resorts and travel agencies – a one-stop zone for both daytime adventures and nightlife. Most visitors base themselves here for the unbeatable mix of scenery and social buzz.

The northern end is quietest, with a coral reef just 30m offshore that's ideal for snorkelling. The central section turns into party central after dark, while the southern tip is lined with laid-back resorts. No matter where you are, sunsets here are stunning.

Nearby, **Ban Mae Hat** is also busy because it's Ko Tao's port, with all ferries departing and arriving here. As such, it lacks the charm of Hat Sairee, and its sandy beach, which is split in two by the ferry piers, has too many boats nearby to be swimmable. But it's fine for sunset viewing. Mae Hat, too, is a working village with a proper market, and so it feels more vibrant than other spots on Ko Tao.

On top of all the beach clubs with live DJs almost daily and vibrant restaurants with upbeat atmospheres, Ko Tao also hosts a few big parties every few days. There's the **Secret Party Koh Tao** with two stages, several DJs, shows and performances, with bodypainting and a food market. Another one is the **Escobar** jungle party with five stages playing different kinds of music. Or for something smaller, located on a quiet beach that requires a bit of trekking, go for **Leo Beach Music Festival**.

Hidden Bays

Explore east-coast beaches

Drive east from Hat Sairee and you'll find yourself zigzagging through Ko Tao's steep, jungle-covered interior, where winding roads cut sharply through the hills before descending to the island's secluded eastern bays. Though this side feels far removed from the island's buzz, it's no more than a 10- to 15-minute ride between the coasts.

This is Ko Tao at its most tranquil – less developed, more rugged and with some of the island's best snorkelling. Families and nature lovers especially appreciate the quiet, shallow beaches framed by boulders and coral reefs just offshore. Resorts here are mostly midrange, and each bay feels like its own little world.

Two standout beaches are **Ao Tanote** and **Ao Leuk**, both with white sand and snorkelling with colourful fish and baby blacktip sharks. The waters are calm and clear, ideal for swims. Next to Ao Leuk, adventurous travellers can hike down to Baan Nam Cha, a secret teahouse with live-in artists. The climb is steep but rewarding, with workshops in painting and sea-glass jewellery, usually costing no more than 400฿.

Hikers will also find trails that criss-cross the island, connecting east and west in short but sweaty bursts. Routes between Ao Tanote, **Hat Laem Thian** and Hat Sairee take you through lush hills and past hidden viewpoints – just bring plenty of water and good footwear.

SUSTAINABLE KO TAO

Jantra 'JJ' Samphanphae moved to Ko Tao in 2016 to run Dearly Hostel (p505). Many visitors may miss Ko Tao's dedicated community striving to protect the ocean and promote sustainable living. They also overlook why it's expensive: limited resources, reliance on rainwater and imported fuel, and rising housing demand all drive prices up. The island's natural beauty depends on constant, often invisible, local efforts. Koh Tao hosts several annual events. The biggest is **Spotlight** in May or June, which promotes sustainable tourism. Other events include **Koh Tao Fishing Game**, **Swim for Sharks** and **World Ocean Day**. While here, minimise waste, especially single-use items. Respect marine life. Never take shells or coral. Local dive teams lead monthly beach cleanups you can join.

EATING & DRINKING ON KO TAO: CAFES WITH BEACH VIEWS

Baan Nam Cha: This place requires strong calves to get to, but the east-coast views and the vibe are worth it. *8am-6pm* ฿

Koppee: A peaceful and calm beach club on the south coast with a small swimming pool and good fries. *9am-10pm* ฿฿

Coconut Monkey: Sits right on Ao Mae, and you will be able to find the best kombucha here for only 50฿. *8am-5pm* ฿

Caffeine Dealer Hinwong Bay: A wooden shack that sits on the sand, offering many varieties of coffee bean. *8am-4pm* ฿

Diving Schools on Ko Tao

Ko Tao is one of the world's top and most affordable diving destinations, home to granite pinnacles, coral reefs, WWII wrecks and over 85 dive schools. It's perfect for beginners, with warm, clear waters and sheltered bays ideal for learning. Free-diving schools also exist, though they're less common. Snorkellers can join dive boats or explore east-coast reefs independently. Whether you're a seasoned diver or a curious first-timer, Ko Tao offers easy access to Thailand's vibrant underwater world.

Where to learn how to dive...

Black Turtle This top-tier PADI 5 Star Career Development Centre offers comprehensive courses, from Open Water and specialties (Night Diver, Nitrox) to Divemaster and Instructor internships, with a strong focus on buoyancy skills. Its marine conservation efforts include hands-on coral-reef ecology courses, covering reef health, species identification, and restoration techniques, taught by PADI-qualified marine scientists (prices starting at 6000฿).

Blue Chitta Blue Chitta offers free diving and yoga retreats by the sea. Its signature three-day immersive retreat Freediver Level 1 course (13,000฿) includes theory, water training and certification, meditation and breathing classes, yoga classes, an ice-bath workshop and accommodation for three nights with one meal per day plus community dinner. Blue Chitta promises eco-minded training in small, supportive groups (four people on average).

IMONE TOGNON/SHUTTERSTOCK

Go Diving This boutique free-diving centre offers everything from two-hour pool taster sessions to full Level 2 certification (dives to 30m across three days). Its popular SSI Level 1 course runs over two days, including theory, pool training and open-water dives (7900฿). Trips include coral-reef exploration, Sail Rock and Chumphon Pinnacle, with all gear included, safety-trained instructors, and small groups (maximum four students). Perfect for beginners and breath-hold buffs wanting an almost-private experience with an eco-focus.

New Heaven Dive School New Heaven Dive School is one of Ko Tao's most established eco-dive centres, offering small-group SSI and PADI courses for all levels. Its standout is the Reef Conservation Program, which ranges from one day to four weeks to eight- to 12-week internships (15,000฿ to 75,000฿), where divers get hands-on experience in coral restoration, sea-turtle monitoring and marine ecology. This is the spot for those seeking expert instruction with a focus on ocean conservation.

Tech Diving Thailand This diving centre stands out for offering specialised training rarely found on the island. It runs cavern, intro-cave and full-cave training, plus trimix tech dives to 100m+, using top-tier gear, nitrox and trimix blend stations (100,000฿). Small groups benefit from expert instructors, while expeditions include liveaboard wrecks, mainland cave mapping and underwater research missions. It caters to serious divers looking to go beyond the recreational norm.

FROM LEFT: IMONE TOGNON/SHUTTERSTOCK, ISRA.HONG/SHUTTERSTOCK

HTMS Sattakut

HOW TO

When to go Diving is possible year-round, but March to September offers the calmest seas and best visibility. Whale shark sightings peak in April and May, while October to November can be choppy with reduced visibility.

Book ahead Popular dive schools fill up fast, especially for certification courses. Reserve your spot early – many offer discounts for online booking or package deals with accommodation.

Before you go Avoid alcohol the night before and eat a light breakfast. Stay hydrated, bring reef-safe sunscreen and don't fly within 18 hours after diving to avoid decompression sickness.

Budget Intro dives start at around 2500฿, while full Open Water courses cost 9000฿ to 12,000฿. Most prices include gear, certification fees and boat trips. Plan for extra if you want video footage or specialty dives.

Top Dive Sites

The best dive sites around Ko Tao lie at offshore pinnacles within 20km of the island. These underwater formations are home to vibrant coral, swirling schools of fish and the occasional megafauna sighting. **Chumphon Pinnacle** is the standout: a submerged mountain carpeted in anemones and frequented by giant trevally, tuna and grey reef sharks – with lucky divers spotting whale sharks in season.

Closer to the island, **Green Rock** is a popular playground of caverns, caves and narrow swim-throughs best suited to those with a few dives under their belt. For beginners, **Japanese Gardens** and **Mango Bay** offer calm conditions and colourful coral in shallow water – perfect for Open Water students or snorkellers. **Twins**, just off the northwest coast, is a reliable favourite, often visited by moray eels, blue-spotted rays and green turtles.

Further afield, **Sail Rock** (p476) draws divers hoping for whale shark encounters and features an iconic vertical swim-through known as 'the chimney'. **Southwest Pinnacle** offers deeper dives among giant groupers and barracuda. Ko Tao also caters to niche interests with wreck dives, including **HTMS Sattakut**, and even cave diving for the trained and curious.

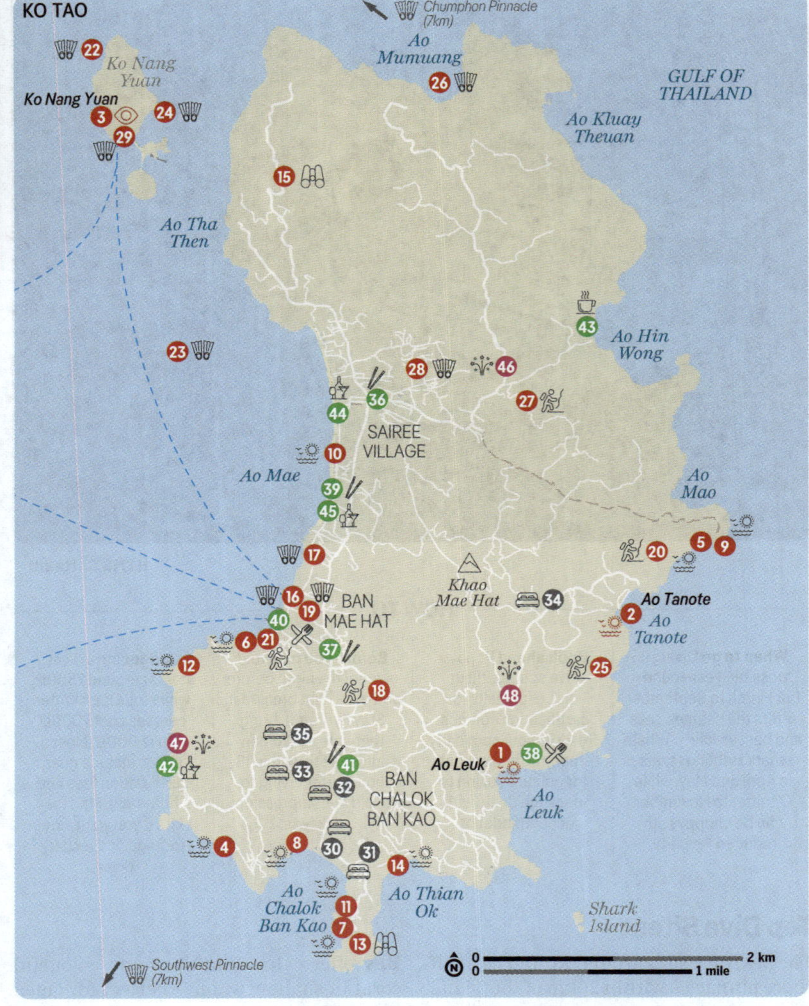

Ko Tao's Beaches & Best Views

Coves, views and secret snorkelling spots

South of Mae Hat, Ko Tao slows its pace. The beach bars fade, replaced by hillside resorts and a quieter, more laid-back vibe. This area's main hub is **Hat Chalok Ban Kao**, a scenic, curve-shaped bay flanked by boulders. The beach here is shallow and calm, and at low tide a sandbar appears - ideal for wading and sunbathing.

Just west lies **Ao June Juea**, a quiet cove with soft white sand and decent snorkelling. It's easy to reach by scooter – no trekking required. Head east instead and you'll find **Hat Taa Toh**, a narrow beach with a walkway leading to **Freedom**

HIGHLIGHTS
1 Ao Leuk
2 Ao Tanote
3 Ko Nang Yuan

SIGHTS
4 Ao June Juea
5 Ao Laem Thien
6 Ban Mae Hat
7 Freedom Beach
8 Hat Chalok Ban Kao
9 Hat Laem Thian
10 Hat Sairee
11 Hat Taa Toh
12 Jansom Bay
13 John Suwan Viewpoint
14 Shark Bay
15 Top Point

ACTIVITIES
16 Black Turtle
17 Blue Chitta
18 Bunker
19 Go Diving
20 Golden View
21 Goodtime Adventures
22 Green Rock Dive Site
23 HTMS Sattakut
24 Japanese Gardens Dive Site
25 Lang Khai
26 Mango Bay
27 Mek's Mountain
see 30 New Heaven Dive School
28 Tech Diving Thailand
29 Twins Pinnacle

SLEEPING
30 Bubble Bungalow
31 Chintakiri Resort
32 Dearly Koh Tao Hostel
33 Deisha View Jungle Hostel
34 Tanote Good View
35 Wonderland Jungle Hostel Koh Tao

EATING
36 995 Roasted Duck
37 Aunt Miau Curry Rice
38 Baan Nam Cha
39 Chef Table by Mama
40 Coconut Monkey
see 30 Koppee
41 Tra Kul Kao's Kitchen

DRINKING & NIGHTLIFE
42 Banana Rock
43 Caffeine Dealer Hinwong Bay
44 Fizz Beach Club
see 19 Islander Hostel
45 Maya Beach Club

ENTERTAINMENT
46 Escobar
47 Leo Beach Music Festival
48 Secret Party Koh Tao

Beach. Both beaches sit on private land and typically charge an entrance fee (50฿ to 100฿), though early risers often slip in before staff arrive – and get the whole beach to themselves.

From Freedom Beach, a short but steep trail climbs to **John Suwan Viewpoint** *(50฿)*, from which there are sweeping views over the southern coastline. For a more rugged adventure and fewer crowds, try the tougher trail to **Top Point**, where you'll be rewarded with vistas over the island's north.

Just across the headland from Freedom Beach is **Shark Bay** *(100฿)*, where lucky snorkellers may spot blacktip reef sharks or sea turtles cruising the shallows.

Rock Climbing & Bouldering

Ko Tao's granite playground is a climber's dream

Ko Tao is fast becoming one of Thailand's premier rock-climbing destinations. The island's 200-million-year-old granite landscape offers everything from coastal crags to inland walls, with routes for total beginners through to seasoned climbers. Many travellers pair diving days with a morning climb or squeeze in a quick bouldering session between beach naps.

ECO DOGS & BEACH CLEANUPS

Ko Tao may look spotless, but ocean-bound plastic still washes ashore and a pair of golden retrievers, Money and Fanta, are on the case. Trained by local boatman Uncle Chai, these eco-dogs dive into shallow water and scamper along the beach to collect rubbish. If you'd rather get hands-on yourself, join the island's weekly beach and reef cleanups. Coordinated by Koh Tao Clean-Up, sessions rotate beaches, reefs and roadsides – check islandtravelkohtao.com/koh-tao-eco/koh-tao-clean-up for details. All gear is provided, and tours often finish with a swim. It's fun, social and far more memorable than just swimming – because you're giving back to Ko Tao's marine paradise.

DRINKING ON KO TAO: BEST BARS

Fizz Beach Lounge (p455): Sink into a beanbag right on the beach and sip a cocktail as the sun goes down. *4pm-1am* ฿฿

Banana Rock: A bit of a trek to get here, but you'll have an quiet beach to yourself as you lounge in the wooden house. *4pm-2am* ฿

Maya Beach Club: If you love deep house with a live DJ, this is your spot. It sits right on Hat Sairee on the west coast. *noon-9pm* ฿

Islander Hostel: Technically a hostel, but it has a BBQ and a live band every Thursday and Sunday, with beer pong on Friday. *8am-11.30pm* ฿

REACHING THE ISLETS

Just a 15-minute long-tail from Ko Tao, Ko Nang Yuan is one of the best spots in the lower gulf for easy-access snorkelling. To reach the islets from Ko Tao, the easiest option is a long-tail boat from Hat Sairee. These traditional boats operate daily and cost around 350฿ to 450฿ per person for a round trip, depending on the season and group size. The ride takes about 15 minutes, offering scenic views along the way. Be sure to agree on the return time with your boat operator before departing.

One of the most scenic spots is **Jansom Bay**, just south of Mae Hat, where you can scale seaside boulders in the cool morning shade and snorkel in the bay's clear waters afterward. Inland, **Mek's Mountain** is the go-to beginner zone, while the east coast is home to more challenging routes at **Golden View**, **Ao Laem Thien** and **Lang Khai**. The latter, along with Ao Leuk (p479), is also popular for bouldering – free climbs up small rock formations.

Goodtime Adventures, based in Hat Sairee, is the island's original climbing operator, offering everything from half-day intros to a more advanced route. For indoor options, check out the **Bunker**, Ko Tao's only climbing gym (open daily from 9am to 8pm).

Snorkelling Trio

Think coral reefs, panoramic views and secret bays

Once you've had your fill of Ko Tao's dive sites, jungle trails and golden beaches, there's still more to uncover just offshore. The surrounding waters are home to **Ko Nang Yuan** – a stunning trio of islets linked by a sandbar – and a scattering of reef-fringed bays and snorkelling spots perfect for a day trip. The snorkelling here is superb: expect coral gardens, parrotfish and the occasional blacktip reef shark cruising the shallows.

Though privately owned, the island is open to visitors (entry fee 250฿), with a small restaurant and designated swim zones to help protect the reef. To avoid the crowds, arrive early via long-tail boat from Mae Hat or Hat Sairee. Boats leave regularly and can be arranged through any local agency or directly with beach boatmen.

You can jump straight in from the main beach or swim around to the Japanese Gardens (p481) on the eastern side, a calm, shallow reef teeming with technicolour fish. Bring your own mask and snorkel or rent gear from the beachside shop, but leave the fins behind, as they're banned to help protect the fragile coral. Shaded picnic areas and a restaurant make it easy to linger, and most tour boats don't head back until mid- or late afternoon. Time it right and you'll have the late-day light all to yourself.

A 15-minute walk uphill leads to Ko Nang Yuan's iconic **viewpoint**, where you can take in the panoramic stretch of white sand linking the three islands – best seen at low tide. Don't forget water and good shoes; the path is short but steep and rocky.

EATING ON KO TAO: BEST RESTAURANTS

Chef Table by Mama: Southern cuisine served in the style of a laid-back cook's table, like eating dinner cooked by a friend's mum. *6-10pm* ฿฿฿

995 Roasted Duck: Thai-Chinese flavours at this popular veteran, which specialises in all things roast duck. *9am-3.30pm & 5.30-9pm* ฿

Aunt Miau Curry Rice: Praised and frequented by locals, this place has several already-cooked southern Thai dishes for you to add to your rice. *7am-7pm* ฿

Tra Kul Kao's Kitchen: Clean, comfortable, affordable and serving Thai food that isn't adapted to tourist taste buds. *10am-9pm* ฿

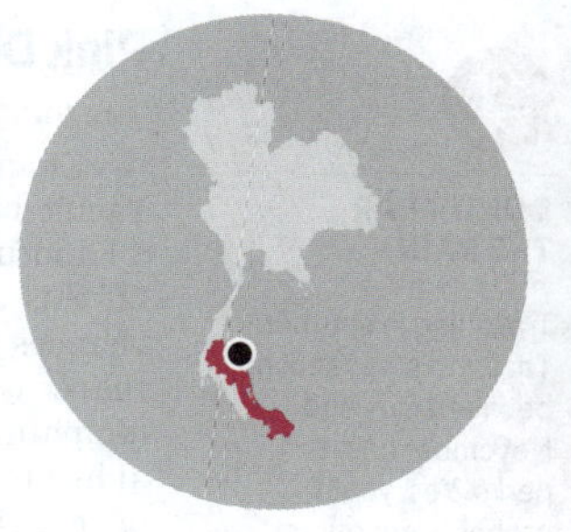

Ao Khanom

DOLPHINS | SOLITUDE | JUNGLE

Mostly off the radar for foreign travellers, Ao Khanom is a rare find: a serene string of palm-fringed beaches on the east coast of Nakhon Si Thammarat Province that still feels untouched. The white-sand coastline faces the Gulf of Thailand, offering sunrise views, emerald waters and an absence of the usual crowds, beach vendors or thumping nightlife. Jet skis are banned to protect the area's star attractions: the rare and endangered pink dolphins that sometimes swim close to shore. This is a place for slow travel. Just a few hours from Surat Thani or Nakhon Si Thammarat city centre by car, Ao Khanom offers a refreshing alternative to the gulf's more built-up islands. With sleepy fishing villages, cave-studded hills and jungles backing the coast, Ao Khanom is as close as it gets to Thailand's beach towns of old, before the influx of mass tourism.

TOP TIP

If you're catching a minivan or bus from Surat Thani or Nakhon Si Thammarat, be sure to specify Hat Nai Plao or Ao Khanom Beach as your drop-off. Khanom town is inland and not on the beach – about 5km away. For a smoother experience, pre-arrange a pickup through your accommodation.

GETTING AROUND

Ao Khanom has no public transport to speak of, so your best bet is to rent a scooter or car if you want to explore the area freely. Many local places to stay can arrange rentals (from 250฿ per day for scooters) or provide transfers to town or beaches. The main road hugs the coastline and connects all the major beaches, waterfalls and viewpoints. Taxis and private transfers are available through resorts, but are relatively expensive. Khanom is also a great place for cycling if you don't mind a few hills. The coastal road is mostly paved and lightly trafficked.

DON'T FEAR THE RAIN

Travelling in southern Thailand's wet season between May and November has its perks. Yes, you'll probably encounter rain, often in short, dramatic bursts during the afternoon or evening, but skies tend to clear quickly, leaving behind fresh air and lush, glistening landscapes. The waterfalls are at their most powerful during this time, and the forests are vibrant with orchids, birdsong and mist. Accommodation is easier to find, prices are lower and popular spots like Ao Khanom's beaches remain blissfully uncrowded, as this is considered the low season in Thailand. Just pack light rain gear, waterproof your daypack and embrace a slower pace. If you're lucky, you'll have jungle trails and empty shores all to yourself.

Pink Dolphins & Island-Hopping

The multicolours of the ocean

Ao Khanom's claim to fame is its population of pink Indo-Pacific humpback dolphins, a rare subspecies found only in a handful of places in Asia. Around 50 to 60 individuals live off this coast, and while sightings aren't guaranteed, your chances are good, especially from November to March when the sea is calmest. These dolphins, known locally as *'pla-loma'* (dolphin), are born grey and turn pink with age. The unusual hue is not due to diet, as many believe, but rather a result of scar tissue and blood vessel visibility beneath their skin, often caused by play-fighting between males.

You can book dolphin-watching tours through most resorts or operators like **Khanom Tour Thailand**, which runs daily long-tail boat trips. Tours often depart from Ban Laem Prathap pier and head towards the small islands of Ko Tha Rai and Ko Noi and the surrounding marine area, where the dolphins are most active in early mornings. These trips typically last half a day or a full day.

Most boat tours include a stop at Pancake Rock, or Khao Hin Phap Pha, on **Ko Tha Rai**, where sedimentary cliffs have eroded into peculiar layers that resemble a stack of pancakes. Another common destination is **Ko Noi**, an uninhabited island with a freshwater pool in its interior and pristine snorkelling conditions just offshore. Some tours provide basic snorkel gear and refreshments.

For land-based dolphin watching, head to Laem Prathap viewpoint just off the peak of **Hat Laem Prathap**, where binoculars come in handy. Mornings are best, especially after dawn, when the light hits the water and dolphins sometimes surface close to shore.

Ao Khanom takes its conservation efforts seriously: boat operators are instructed not to chase or surround the dolphins, and jet skis are banned throughout the bay to reduce noise pollution.

Wild Beaches & Hidden Nature

Jungle-backed sand, waterfalls and caves

Ao Khanom's 15km coastline is a patchwork of palm-fringed beaches, coconut groves and quiet coves. During the week, it's not uncommon to have entire stretches of sand to yourself. The beaches remain relatively undeveloped, and in some areas the jungle reaches right down to the sand. There are no loud

DRINKING COFFEE IN KHANOM: BEST CAFES

Khanom Espresso: Bright and busy coffee shop a couple of streets back from Hat Na Dan. *8am-5pm Mon-Fri, to 5.30pm Sat & Sun* ฿

Near Me Home Cafe: A cute little coffee shop set inside a cosy home full of plants and natural light. *8am-5pm* ฿

Rimlay Cafe & Bar: Located right on the beach where you can lounge around for hours: go for the day-time coffee, stay for the sunset drinks. *8.30am-9pm* ฿

Frankie's Cafe: Great spot for a coffee break or breakfast. Has a nice, shaded 2nd-floor terrace that looks out on a garden. *8am-4pm Wed-Mon* ฿฿

SIGHTS
1 Hat Khanom
2 Hat Na Dan
3 Hat Nai Plao
4 Hat Thong Yi
5 Nam Tok Hin Lat
6 Nam Tok Samet Chun
7 Wat Kradang Nga

SLEEPING
8 Hallo Villa
9 Khanom Beach Resort and Spa
10 Khanom Hill Resort
11 Le Petit Saint Tropez
12 Margarita Beach

EATING
13 Ao Khanom Seafood
14 Bai Chaplu Restaurant
15 Beach Mountain Club
16 CC Beach Bar & Restaurant
17 Lost and Found Bar & Grill
18 Nong Sao's Kitchen Restaurant
see 18 Santorini Restaurant

DRINKING & NIGHTLIFE
19 Frankie's Cafe
20 Khanom Espresso
21 Near Me Home Cafe
22 Rimlay Cafe & Bar

SHOPPING
23 Saturday Evening Market

MOTORCYCLE TIPS

In Ao Khanom and much of the lower gulf, renting a scooter is often the most practical way to get around, especially with limited public transport. Helmets are mandatory by law – fines range from ฿500 to ฿2000 – and essential for safety. Inexperienced riders should take extra caution on winding or poorly maintained roads, and comprehensive travel insurance is highly recommended.

Although most rental shops won't ask for it, you're legally required to hold an international driving permit when riding a motorcycle in Thailand. Without one, you may face fines if stopped by police and risk complications with insurance in the event of an accident. Always ride defensively and within your limits.

SUCHART BOONYAVECH/SHUTTERSTOCK

Hat Na Dan

beach clubs or rows of umbrellas; instead, you'll find wooden shacks, long-tail boats pulled up under casuarina trees, and the occasional hammock strung between two palms.

Start your beach tour at **Hat Kho Khao**, a long, crescent-shaped bay northwest of the main town. It's one of the area's best beaches for swimming, with fine sand and a gentle slope into clear, calm waters. Just south, **Hat Khanom** is even quieter, backed by cliffs and dense jungle. In the early mornings, you may spot local monks walking the beach for alms.

The heart of the area is **Hat Na Dan**, a dazzling 9km expanse of soft white sand that stretches along the central coast. This beach is wide and flat, great for running or walking at low tide. Some simple beach bars and older resorts dot the area, most with restaurants and relaxed vibes. A bit further south is **Hat Nai Plao**, the main tourist beach, with the highest concentration of accommodation options. Resorts here range from budget bungalows to boutique hotels with pools and sea views.

EATING IN AO KHANOM: OUR PICKS

Ao Khanom Seafood: Restaurant in a vast wooden barn overlooking Hat Nai Plao. Every consumable seafood option. *10am-10pm* ฿฿

CC Beach Bar & Restaurant: The restaurant/bar here is as lovely as it gets in Ao Khanom. Thai and Western classics. *11am-midnight* ฿฿

Lost and Found Bar & Grill: Dimly lit backyard dining serving steak and BBQ alongside Thai classics like spicy glass-noodle salad. *4pm-midnight Thu-Tue* ฿฿

Klang Aow Seafood & Resort: Rustic, beachfront spot serving fresh seafood in an open-air setting. Great for long lunches or sunset dinners. *10am-10pm* ฿฿

If you want true solitude, continue south to **Hat Thong Yi**, a secluded bay just around the headland. With no development and few visitors, it feels like your own private hideaway. The surrounding forest is thick and home to hornbills, macaques and monitor lizards.

A scenic road runs parallel to the coast from Laem Prathap in the north to Hat Thong Yi in the south, with several elevated viewpoints along the way. Stop at one of the wooden platforms to soak up panoramic views of the coastline – particularly beautiful at sunrise or on misty mornings.

For something more spiritual, visit **Wat Kradang Nga**, a small hilltop temple with sweeping views and a peaceful atmosphere. It's often overlooked by visitors but provides a serene stop between beach hops.

Slow Days in the Village

Market and amenities in Khanom town

The area's main inland centre is **Khanom town**, a sleepy, sun-drenched village with a few banks, convenience stores and local restaurants. There's a small **Saturday Evening Market** near the municipal office with street food, handmade crafts and live local music. It's one of the best places to try Khanom's signature dish: *khao yam*, a southern-style rice salad with dried shrimp, shredded coconut and herbal leaves.

Waterfalls & Caves

Scenic nature and topography

Inland from the coast, the area's limestone hills are home to caves, streams and waterfalls. **Nam Tok Samet Chun**, 5km inland from Hat Nai Plao, is the most impressive waterfall in the area. There's a large aqua-blue pool here that sits at the foot of a series of falls, cascading down a hillside creating smaller, equally beautiful, clear pools just begging to be swum in. **Khao Wang Thong Cave**, about 15km from the beach, is the most extensive cave system in the area, featuring giant stalactites, echoing chambers and bat colonies. You can enter alone, but a local guide is recommended – guides provide torches and share stories about the cave's history and formations.

Nearer the coast, **Nam Tok Hin Lat** provides short, rewarding hikes with small pools for cooling off. These are best visited in the rainy season, though it's slippery after heavy rains.

A NEW ERA FOR NAKHON

Phurinat Siwamok, Nakhon Si Thammarat (p490) native born and raised, now Samui resident.

How much has Nakhon changed?

Both a lot and very little. The city's main roads look much the same as they did 20 years ago, but new routes, cafes, gyms and malls have sprung up as the city expands.

What are the must-visit places?

Wat Phra Mahathat Woramahawihan remains the spiritual centrepiece. For nature, head to Khao Sien, Lansaka for misty views, Sichon-Khanom for dolphins and seafood, and Ai Khiao Waterfall or Kiriwong, known for fresh air, long streams and cycling through a community rooted in nature.

How is the city evolving today?

Post-COVID, many young people returned home, creating homestays and cafes in historic spaces, reviving a quiet city with contemporary charm.

EATING IN AO KHANOM: OUR PICKS

Santorini Restaurant: Seafood spot inside Santorini Resort with breezy views. Thai and Western faves with a few Italian-inspired touches. *8am-8pm* BB

Beach Mountain Club: Beachfront hangout with beanbags, DJs and a post-sunset crowd. Thai comfort food, seafood and cocktails. *8am-9pm* BB

Nong Sao's Kitchen Restaurant: Small roadside eatery dishing up honest, home-style Thai food with a southern kick. Popular with locals. *9am-9pm* B

Bai Chaplu Restaurant: Bold flavours near the Khanom coast. Fiery curries, fresh grilled seafood and noodle soups. *10am-8pm Fri-Wed* BB

Beyond Ao Khanom

Visitors who travel inland from Ao Khanom are rewarded with a wildlife-packed national park, temples and traditional Thai towns.

Places

GETTING AROUND

Ao Khanom is a 1½-hour drive from Surat Thani Airport or a one-hour drive from Nakhon Si Thammarat Airport. From either airport, private transfers, taxis or minivans can be arranged to Khanom town or your resort. If coming from Ko Samui, you can take a ferry to Donsak Pier, then a taxi or minivan (about 45 minutes) to Ao Khanom. Some ferry operators offer combo tickets including hotel drop-off. Most places can help arrange dolphin tours, scooter rentals or airport transfers.

Venture inland from Ao Khanom to discover a different side of southern Thailand. While Ao Khanom's coastline charms with its beaches and pink dolphins, the inland stretch of Nakhon Si Thammarat Province offers a deeper dive into history, culture and nature – and is refreshingly free of crowds.

Nakhon Si Thammarat is a lively and authentic Thai town that rarely features on the international tourist trail. Once a powerful trading port in the Srivijaya Empire, the city has deep roots and a proud identity. Today, its standout attraction is Wat Phra Mahathat Woramahawihan, southern Thailand's most revered Buddhist temple. Wander the city's night markets and you'll likely be the only foreigner – a rare treat in Thailand these days.

Roughly 30km west of Nakhon Si Thammarat, Khao Luang National Park beckons nature lovers with misty peaks, gushing waterfalls and dense evergreen forest. The park is home to hundreds of orchid species, rare animals and excellent hiking trails.

Nakhon Si Thammarat

TIME FROM AO KHANOM: 2HR

An ancient city and its temple

Often shortened to just 'Nakhon', Nakhon Si Thammarat is one of Thailand's oldest cities. Sitting 85km south of Ao Khanom, the city is packed with significant history, tracing its roots back over a thousand years to the Srivijaya Empire. The legacy of this once-mighty kingdom remains visible today in the form of grand temples, crumbling fortifications and the pride of its people.

The city's main artery, Th Ratchadamnoen, is lined with streetlamps topped with golden sculptures of the 12 animals of the Thai zodiac – each one representing a satellite state that once paid tribute to the ancient Nakhon Kingdom. It's a small but striking reminder that Nakhon was once the religious and administrative heart of peninsular Siam.

Another testament to the city's former importance is its spiritual centrepiece, **Wat Phra Mahathat Woramahawihan**, a sprawling temple complex anchored by a 77m *chedi* (stupa),

AFTER6PM/SHUTTERSTOCK

Wat Phra Mahathat Woramahawihan

its whitewashed body topped with a gleaming gold spire. This stupa is believed to enshrine a relic of the Buddha – a claim that draws devoted pilgrims from across Thailand and beyond. Encircling the *chedi* are rows of miniature stupas, each representing a noble family or province that once paid homage to Nakhon. Wander further to discover the *viharn tapen noi*, an intimate sanctuary believed to be one of the oldest surviving structures on site, as well as several small museums within the temple complex that house Lanna-style Buddha statues, votive tablets and centuries-old manuscripts.

After your temple visit, stroll a few minutes west to see the **ancient city walls**, made of red laterite and dating back to the 13th century.

Museum double-act

Near the old city centre you'll find **Nakhon Si Thammarat National Museum**. This museum is an excellent primer on the region's layered history, with exhibits spanning prehistoric tools, Dvaravati-period Buddha images, Srivijayan stone lintels and centuries-old ceramics. Many artefacts were unearthed locally, providing insight into Nakhon's enduring status as a crossroads of cultures and ideas.

A short walk to the northeast brings you to the charming **Suchart Subsin Shadow Puppet Museum**, set in a traditional southern Thai wooden home. This small but engaging museum displays hand-crafted *nang da lung* puppets used in traditional shadow theatre – an art form rooted in Nakhon culture. Time your visit right and you might catch a live performance (100฿), complete with live narration and southern Thai folk music.

To market, to market

Come evening, Nakhon's cosmopolitan spirit emerges at its bustling night markets. The most popular is the **Tharian Night**

A SPIRITUAL STOP IN NAKHON

Located in Sichon, just south of Ao Khanom, **Wat Chedi** – better known as Wat Ai Khai – has become one of southern Thailand's most popular pilgrimage sites. Thai visitors flock here to pay respects to Ai Khai, the spirit of a young novice monk believed to grant wishes, particularly for success in business, luck and lotteries. The temple grounds are lively with offerings of rooster statues, fireworks and incense, all given in gratitude for answered prayers. While relatively unknown to foreign travellers, the temple offers a fascinating glimpse into modern Thai spiritual life. Visitors are welcome – just dress modestly and observe the reverent atmosphere that surrounds this unique and deeply local site.

WHAT TO PACK FOR KHAO LUANG

A trek up Khao Luang, southern Thailand's highest peak, is a rewarding but rugged adventure, and being well prepared makes all the difference. Trails can be muddy and steep, so sturdy hiking shoes and leech socks are essential. Bring a lightweight rain jacket, especially during the wet season, and warm layers for chilly nights at the summit camp (temperatures can dip below 10°C). You'll need your own sleeping bag, torch and refillable water bottles – water purification tablets or a filter are highly recommended, too. Treks must be arranged in advance through park rangers, who will guide you and help coordinate meals. Also, always make sure to leave no trace and bring back whatever you take up there.

Market near the train station, where locals queue for smoky grilled chicken, stir-fried noodles and southern-style curries rich in turmeric and lemongrass. Look out for *kow mok gai*, a chicken biryani or a *mataba roti* stuffed with curried meat or vegetables – echoes of Nakhon's past as a vibrant trading post along the Indian Ocean routes.

Khao Luang National Park

TIME FROM AO KHANOM: **2HR**

Wildlife and waterfalls in the deep south

Just northwest of Nakhon Si Thammarat, **Khao Luang National Park** *(fb.com/klnp009)* is a lush, mountainous sanctuary that protects some of the richest biodiversity in southern Thailand. At its heart towers Khao Luang, the region's highest peak at 1780m. The park lies about 105km southwest of Ao Khanom, and is a magnet for nature lovers, waterfall chasers, birdwatchers and intrepid hikers keen to conquer its jungle trails.

The park's thick evergreen forest, dotted with giant bamboo groves and moss-covered trees, supports a wealth of flora and fauna unique to the southern peninsula. With over 300 species of orchids, including rare varieties that bloom only at higher altitudes, the area transforms into a riot of colour during the rainy season. The park is also a hotspot for birdwatching, particularly during the migratory months from October to March, with hornbills, pittas, broadbills and rare babblers flitting among the canopy.

Wildlife thrives here too, although many of the larger animals remain deep inside the park. Malayan tapirs, pig-tailed macaques, dusky langurs and the goat-like Sumatran serow can be seen along less-trafficked trails, while deep in the park's heart roam clouded leopards, panthers and – very occasionally – tigers. Park rangers report that while tiger sightings are exceedingly rare today, signs of their presence (tracks, scat) have been recorded in the most remote areas.

Most visitors, though, are drawn by the park's waterfalls, particularly the multi-tiered marvel **Nam Tok Karom**, located just a short stroll from the visitor centre and park headquarters. This 19-level cascade tumbles dramatically through dense forest, forming emerald pools ideal for a refreshing dip. Another easy-to-reach gem is **Nam Tok Tha Pae**, a quieter alternative framed by mossy rocks and thick foliage. Several caves are also tucked into the park's limestone ridges.

Accommodation within the park includes basic bungalows near the visitor centre (book ahead in peak season) and designated camping grounds with toilet and shower facilities. There's also a restaurant at the headquarters serving simple Thai dishes, open during daylight hours.

Summiting Khao Luang

For serious hikers, summiting **Khao Luang** is the park's ultimate adventure. This two-day trek is demanding, and must be done with licensed park rangers (arranged in advance

NUT IN-ORN/SHUTTERSTOCK ©
Khao Luang National Park

through the headquarters). The trail typically starts at Ban Kiriwong, a mountain-fringed village known for its ecotourism initiatives and fruit orchards. From there, hikers ascend through thick jungle, often slick with mist and leeches, crossing rivers and scrambling over roots and rocks as the terrain becomes steeper.

Overnight is spent at a camping area near the summit, where temperatures can drop sharply, especially between November and February. The summit itself is a rugged plateau with jaw-dropping panoramic views. Hikers are rewarded with a profound sense of solitude, the scent of wild orchids, and the haunting calls of gibbons echoing across the slopes.

Trekkers must be in good physical condition, bring their own sleeping bags and warm clothes, and carry in (and out) their supplies. Food can be arranged with guides ahead of time. The park limits group sizes and monitors weather closely, so check in advance during the rainy season, when trails may be closed for safety.

Ban Kiriwong

TIME FROM AO KHANOM: **2HR**

Soak in the village vibes

Nestled in a mountain valley at the edge of Khao Luang National Park, Ban Kiriwong is often hailed as Thailand's most environmentally friendly village. Surrounded by rivers, fruit orchards and misty peaks, it's a serene base for slow travel and eco-conscious experiences. Visitors can cycle through the village, learn to dye cloth using natural colours from local plants, or join a homestay for a taste of southern Thai hospitality. The area is also famed for its seasonal fruit – especially durian and mangosteen – which you can sample fresh from the orchard. With crisp mountain air, friendly locals and easy access to nature, Ban Kiriwong is a quiet gem well worth the detour.

RESPECTFUL TRAVEL IN MUSLIM COMMUNITIES

Many coastal villages in southern Thailand, including parts of Ao Khanom, are predominantly Muslim, with strong community traditions and a slower, more conservative pace. Visitors are warmly welcomed, but a little cultural sensitivity goes a long way. Dress modestly, especially in quieter areas. Women should cover shoulders and knees, and both men and women should avoid revealing swimwear away from the beach. Remove shoes before entering homes or mosques, and ask permission before photographing people or religious buildings. During Ramadan, be mindful of eating or drinking in public during daylight hours. A respectful approach not only shows good manners, it often opens doors to richer local interactions.

Phatthalung Province

NATURE | CULTURE | SLOW LIVING

GETTING AROUND

While the city centre is cute, compact and walkable, renting a motorbike or car gives you the most freedom to explore the wider province at your own pace, especially rural landscapes.

TOP TIP

Travel back to Bangkok by booking a private 1st-class sleeper on the southern rail line. These carriages come with exclusive bathrooms, showers to which only 1st-class passengers have access, and a vintage-style restaurant carriage. The 14-hour journey costs about twice as much as flying (which takes just an hour), but it offers an unforgettable experience.

Set against a backdrop of misty mountains and vast wetlands, the southern province of Phatthalung is often overshadowed by its beachier neighbours. However, this inland gem charms with its stunning nature, traditional crafts, amazing food and deep cultural roots.

Thale Noi, the province's star wetland reserve, best explored by long-tail boat at sunrise, offers plenty to birdwatchers and photographers. Away from the water, Phatthalung's shadow-puppet tradition, *nang da lung*, keeps the province's artistic spirit alive. On top of that, Phatthalung is recognised by UNESCO as the birthplace for *nora*, a southern Thai traditional dance drama. Phatthalung city, the provincial capital, offers a quiet charm: think old markets, slow cafes or morning merit-making at temples with locals.

For those seeking nature and culture without the crowds, Phatthalung invites you to slow down, look closer and linger.

Art, Cultures & Markets

Exploring a cradle of southern Thai culture

In this southern province age-old performing arts and handmade crafts still thrive. At the **Shadow Puppet Gallery** *(fb.com/nangtalunggallery; free)*, travellers can learn about one of southern Thailand's most iconic art forms, *nang da lung*, which sees intricate leather puppets used in shadow plays that blend folklore, humour and social commentary. The gallery offers live demonstrations and showcases puppets crafted by hand. Workshops on making the *nang talung* characters are also available if booked in advance.

The roots of *nora*, Phatthalung's UNESCO-listed dance drama, also run deep here. The elaborate costumes, high-pitched vocals and powerful movements of *nora* performances remain a living tradition at temple fairs and local festivals. Visit **Wat Tha Khae** to see the place where it all started; the temple has a school that teaches the next generation *nora*.

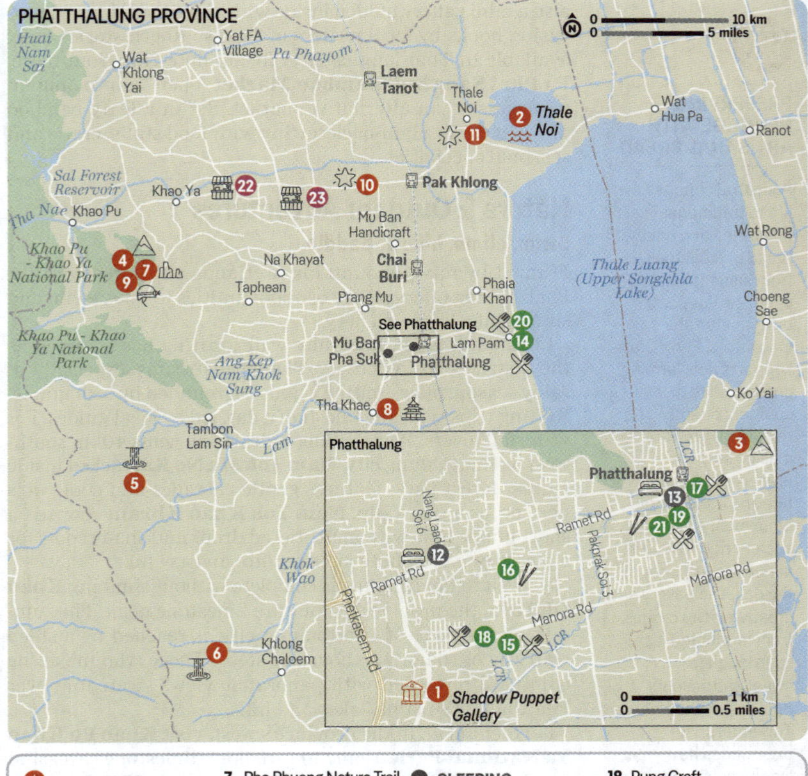

HIGHLIGHTS
1 Shadow Puppet Gallery
2 Thale Noi

SIGHTS
3 Khao Ok Talu
4 Khao Pu Khao Ya National Park
5 Nam Tok Khao Khram
6 Nam Tok Ma No Ra
7 Pha Phueng Nature Trail
8 Wat Tha Khae

ACTIVITIES
9 Matcha Cave
10 Napokae Learning Centre
11 Ren Ta On Eco Printing & Natural Tie Dye

SLEEPING
12 Dusit Princess
13 Merdelong Hotel

EATING
14 Kanam Coffee
15 Kris Home Project
16 Na Rong Khanom Jeen Phatthalung
17 Porktail Noodles By Kosak First Branch
18 Pung Craft
19 Roof 6/6 Bar & Bistro
20 Suni Mueang Trang
21 Tom Bak Kut Teh

SHOPPING
22 Lad Tainod's Green Market
23 Pa Phai Sang Suk Bamboo Market

Beyond performing arts, a 30-minute motorcycle ride north of the city centre, **Ren Ta On Eco Printing & Natural Tie Dye** *(fb.com/chomsaangaey; 890฿)* typifies Phatthalung's love for nature and craft. Using leaves, bark and flowers, this small studio creates earthy, hand-dyed fabrics through sustainable processes. Workshops offer travellers a chance to try their hands at eco-printing.

On Sundays Phatthalung's markets give a taste of local life. A 30-minute motorcycle ride northwest of the city centre, you'll find **Lad Tainod's Green Market** *(fb.com/tainodgreenmarket)*, which springs to life on Sundays (8am to 5pm) with fresh produce, organic goods and handmade products sourced from nearby farms and communities. There's also a mini gallery hidden inside with a 'Writer's House' showcasing books by local writers of Thai southern stories (only available in Thai language). A five-minute ride from there, **Pa Phai Sang Suk Bamboo Market** (open 7am to 5pm on weekends) is an alternative market. Set in a leafy bamboo grove, it offers a laid-back setting with food stalls, crafts and seasonal specialties.

PRESERVING HERITAGE WITH ARTISANAL BREAD

Pung Craft brings new life to traditional Thai rice by making unique bread and pastries from ancient local rice varieties. Founded by agricultural innovators, Pung Craft supports rice-farming communities by sourcing directly from local growers, making sure to preserve heirloom rice and agricultural biodiversity, as ancient rice varieties are becoming rarer by the day. The bakery's creative menu ranges from fermented-rice sourdough to sweet and savoury rice-based pastries. This enterprise exemplifies how small-scale food innovation can drive both cultural preservation and rural economic empowerment.

Nature & Outdoor Adventures

Swim, climb, hike or paddle

Framed by misty mountains, wetlands and forested hills, Phatthalung offers plenty of opportunities to hike, swim and simply take in the scenery.

In Amphoe Kong Ra, white-water rafting has emerged as the district's go-to activity. The local streams, especially in rainy season, offer exciting rapids surrounded by lush jungle. Rafting trips typically take half a day, led by local guides. For waterfall lovers, Phatthalung hides a few gems 40km southwest of Phatthalung city. **Nam Tok Ma No Ra**, tucked inside a quiet forest park, features gentle cascades and cool pools perfect for a quick dip. **Nam Tok Khao Khram** rewards a short jungle hike with multi-tiered drops and shady spots for a picnic or a rest. Both sites require an easy hike.

No visit to Phatthalung is complete without climbing **Khao Ok Talu**, the province's signature limestone peak. The summit, on the edge of Phatthalung city, is reached by a steep stairway of roughly a thousand steps. Those who make the climb are rewarded with panoramic views stretching over Phatthalung's plains, lakes and hills.

Further afield, in the province's west, visit **Khao Pu Khao Ya National Park**. Home to rare flora, limestone caves and jungle-clad trails, the park's highlights include **Matcha Cave**, known for its tranquil chambers; and there are several waterfalls in the surroundings. The park's viewpoints, especially Bee-Hive Cliff (access via **Pha Phueng Nature Trail**), located about 250m from the tourist centre, provide sweeping vistas over the forest canopy.

Wetlands Wonder

Visit buffalo and birds at Thale Noi

Phatthalung's most iconic natural wonder is **Thale Noi** – a vast freshwater wetland where lotus fields, buffalo herds and rare migratory birds create a picture-perfect scene at dawn.

EATING IN PHATTHALUNG CITY: OUR PICKS

Kris Home Project: Pairing modern coffee orders with Chinese fried dough. *8am-3pm Mon & Wed-Fri, 9am-4pm Sat & Sun* ฿

Suni Mueang Trang: Located east of the city on Thale Noi. Serves Thai southern dishes using locally sourced fresh seafood. *9am-8pm* ฿

Roof 6/6 Bar & Bistro: A big food menu and 360-degree views of the whole town with Khao Ok Talu as a backdrop. *7am-midnight* ฿฿

Pung Craft: A cafe that innovatively revives ancient Thai rice through breads, supporting local farmers. *8am-5pm Thu-Tue* ฿

Buffalo, Thale Noi

Sunrise boat tours glide through the misty waters. Tours are especially popular from December to April when birdlife is most abundant. The area also supports traditional fishing villages and local craft communities, giving visitors a chance to experience life on the lake.

For a hands-on encounter with Phatthalung's agrarian heritage, drive 15 minutes east of Thale Noi to the **Napokae Learning Centre** *(fb.com/napokae)*. This community-run project (closed Tuesday) teaches traditional rice farming, buffalo care and ecofriendly living. Travellers can join farm activities, walk among the rice paddies or simply relax in the rural setting.

PHATTHALUNG: INSIDE STORY

Thanawut Poadoon is a Phatthalung-born surgical assistant.

Has Phattalung changed?
Phatthalung is a city rich in nature. Back in the day, there were only forests and mountains. Now, some areas have been developed, but it's still quite small and maintains a low-key, simple lifestyle.

What do visitors often get wrong about Phatthalung?
That the province only has forests and mountains to offer. It has so much more to offer, like all the local food that you won't find anywhere else.

How can visitors support Phatthalung?
Help preserve nature and the environment, and reduce the use of plastic waste. Learn about Phatthalung's local culture such as the origin of the *nora* dance performance.

EATING IN PHATTHALUNG CITY: OUR PICKS

Tom Bak Kut Teh: Come to this city-centre breakfast spot for a taste of the Chinese side of a southern Thai town serving hot soup and dim sum. *5.40am-noon* ฿

Porktail Noodles By Kosak First Branch: Porktail noodles are a signature dish in Phatthalung. Try them at least once while you're here. *8am-3.30pm* ฿

Kanam Coffee: Only a 15-minute motorbike ride from the city, come here for coffee and Thai dessert surrounded by rice paddies and ponds. *9am-7.30pm* ฿

Na Rong Khanom Jeen Phatthalung: Crab curry and other coconut-milk curries plus fried chicken with shallots and fresh veg. *6am-noon Wed-Mon* ฿

Songkhla Province

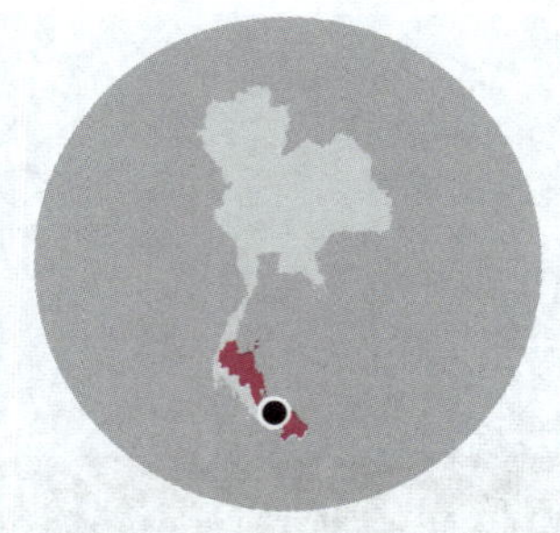

HERITAGE | ART | LAKE LIFE

GETTING AROUND

Songkhla is compact enough to explore on foot or by tuk-tuk. *Songthaew* also run regular routes around town and to nearby beaches. Getting around the city and the nearby beach is convenient thanks to the Grab ride-hailing app, while frequent minibuses and taxis make the short 30km hop south to Hat Yai quick and easy.

Located in the province of the same name, the historic port town of Songkhla offers a laid-back slice of southern Thailand with a strong local identity. It's known for its peaceful Old Town quarter, where colourful Sino-Portuguese shophouses line quiet streets dotted with temples, street art and cosy cafes. Stroll along the waterfront promenade at Samila Beach, home to the famous Golden Mermaid statue, or explore the fishing villages and street markets serving fresh seafood. Songkhla's small-town charm blends Thai, Chinese and Malay influences, giving it a character distinct from more touristed southern destinations. It's a great stop for history buffs, foodies and anyone seeking a cultural detour far from the party islands. The province's other main town, bustling Hat Yai, is within easy reach, just 30km south.

Songkhla Old Town

Heritage streets, waterfront charm and art

Once an area bustling with global trade, Songkhla is now a sleepy port city perched between Songkhla Lake and the sea. Dating back to the 10th century, Songkhla's predecessors thrived on Chinese commerce. By the 17th century, the Sultanate of Singora – founded by Muslim rulers – had turned this coastal outpost into a strategic trading post for the Ayuthaya Kingdom, the British East India Company and the Dutch. Today, Songkhla retains its historic charm as one of southern Thailand's best-preserved heritage towns.

The Old Town, with its narrow streets and colourful Sino-Portuguese shophouses, is a delight to explore on foot. Many old wooden homes have been repurposed into cosy cafes, family-run eateries, indie galleries and boutique shops. The vibe is low-key, but stay a while and you'll notice the town's quiet pride in its multicultural past. Key stops include **Hub Ho Hin** *(fb.com/HarbourHubhoehin; free)*, a former rice mill turned cultural space, popular with locals for dance performances and home to a small but engaging local history exhibit. Another stop is **a.e.y.space** *(aeyspace.com; free)*, an art space that

TOP TIP

Base yourself in Old Town if you want to soak up Songkhla's creative, local vibe – it's packed with street art, galleries and traditional cafes.

showcases exhibitions and hosts artists in residence, helping shape Songkhla Old Town into an artsy hub.

Don't miss the **Songkhla National Museum** *(fb.com/songkhlanationalmuseum; 150฿)*. Housed in a grand Chinese mansion built in 1878, it showcases everything from ancient bronzes to historic maps, photos and weaponry. Opposite, you'll spot remnants of the old city walls, where weekend night markets spring to life with snacks, souvenirs and a relaxed community buzz. If you're up for some activity, rent a bicycle (per hour 50฿) or join a boat or kayak trip across Songkhla Lake with **Songkhla Station** *(fb.com/sstation2017)*, a local cafe and tour organiser housed in a lovingly restored Chinese shopfront.

Remains of the Sultanate

A forgotten kingdom across the lake

Venture just north to **Singha Nakhon**, where remnants of the old Sultanate of Singora linger in quiet villages and overgrown hilltops. To get here, cross Songkhla Lake via the Tinsulanonda Bridge, a scenic 6km causeway linking the peninsula to the mainland; *songthaew* and taxis make the short 15-minute drive from Old Town. History buffs can seek out the atmospheric **Sultan Sulaiman Shah and Family's Cemetery**, shaded beneath two intertwined trees, just 5km from the bridge. Further along the eastern shore, the **Singora Fort 8** ruins stand sentry over the Gulf of Thailand – a windswept spot and one of the best places in the area for sunset views.

Quiet Sands of the Northern Coast

Beach escapes close to Old Town

When the heat of the day kicks in, head to the nearby coast. **Hat Samila**, walking distance from the Old Town, is known for its **golden mermaid statue** and easy swimming. For something calmer, slip north to **Hat Muang Ngam**, around 7km from Old Town. Use ride-hailing app Grab or *songthaew* to make the short hop along the coastal road, delivering you to a long sweep of soft sand with gentle waves and a decidedly local feel with barely a crowd in sight, perfect for making an easy half-day trip from Old Town.

Cosmopolitan Hat Yai

Street food and city life in a cultural crossroad

Seen as southern Thailand's most cosmopolitan city, Hat Yai hums with a lively mix of Thai, Chinese and Malay influences. Though often overlooked by international tourists, it's a favourite getaway for Malaysian and Chinese visitors, drawn by its buzzing markets, eclectic street eats and low-key city vibe. Hat Yai isn't a place of grand monuments; it's a city best explored through its vibrant street life, bustling night bazaars and hawker stalls dishing out southern Thai favourites.

The action centres on **Kim Yong Market**, a hive of fresh produce, local snacks, dried fruits and cheap electronics. Come evening, **Greenway Night Market** *(fb.com/greenwaymarket)* and the **ASEAN Night Bazaar** *(fb.com/hatyainightmarket)*

GRANDPA NEVER DRUNK ALONE

Tucked just off Nakhon Rd in Songkhla Old Town, **Grandpa Never Drunk Alone** *(fb.com/grandpa263)* is a laid-back dive-bar cafe that doubles as a creative hub for the city's youth. Founded by two locals seeking a space to express themselves, this intimate venue blends evening cocktails, daytime coffee, live DJs, art and conversation – all under softly lit, mannequin-decorated walls. Guests range from tattooed young people to surfers grabbing boards from the rack at dusk. The vibe is inclusive and spirited. Drop in for handcrafted cocktails or creamy affogato made with local ice cream.

CRAFTING A CREATIVE FUTURE FOR OLD TOWN

Pakorn 'Aey' Rujiravilai is a Songkhla-based designer who opened a.e.y.space (p498).

What is a.e.y.space? It's a nonprofit project I co-founded 13 years ago. Songkhla Old Town is very small and the new generation often prefer to move to bigger cities, so this town was left with mostly old people. I opened this space to bring the younger generation back a little, to create something in their hometown.

Are there local events travellers should know about? There's a **Pakk Taii Design Week** around the end of August until early September each year, which transforms Songkhla into a gallery-hopping journey. There's also a traditional **Lak Phra** (dragging Buddha statue) festival around the end of September or early October where decorated boats or carts carry Buddha statues.

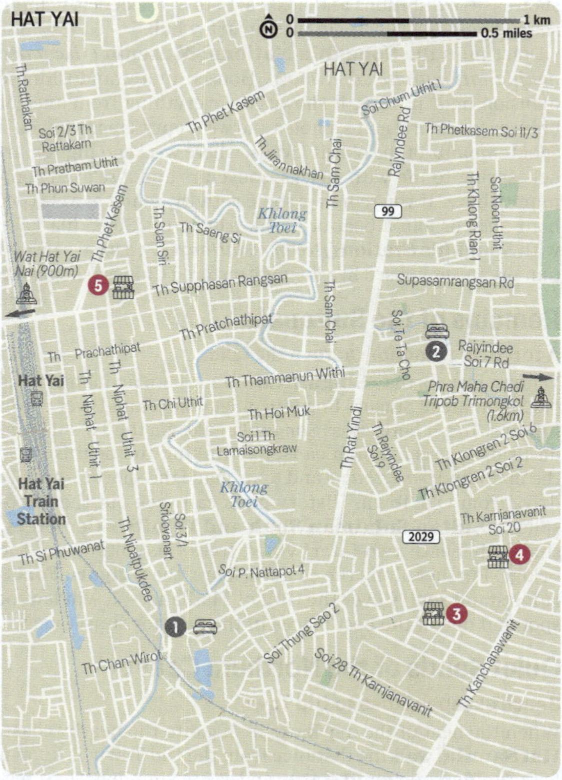

HAT YAI

SLEEPING
1 Goodnight Poshtel
2 Modern Budget Hotel

SHOPPING
3 ASEAN Night Bazaar
4 Greenway Night Market
5 Kim Yong Market

take over, dishing out sizzling southern-style grilled seafood, bold curries and coconut desserts, alongside racks of bargain clothes and souvenirs. Street food is king here, with dishes like *ka nom jeen* and *Hokkien mee*.

Hat Yai lacks classic tourist attractions, but sights like the shimmering **Phra Maha Chedi Tripob Trimongkol** (the Stainless Steel Pagoda) and the giant reclining Buddha at **Wat Hat Yai Nai** add cultural flair.

Beyond Songkhla

Discover a side of Thailand few tourists see, where cultures from across Asia converge in a complex, layered past.

Places

Southern Thailand's Deep South – particularly the provinces of Pattani, Yala and Narathiwat – offers a strikingly different experience from the beach-hopping norm. Tucked along the Malaysian border, these provinces are steeped in history, rich in diversity, and shaped by centuries of trade, migration and religion. Long overlooked by mainstream tourism due to decades of conflict, this region is slowly gaining attention for its cultural resilience, culinary identity and fascinating stories. Expect vibrant markets, centuries-old mosques, intricate local crafts and a food culture unlike anywhere else in Thailand. This part of Thailand is rewarding for travellers willing to venture further into this rarely explored corner. Here, every encounter reveals traditions preserved through community and determination.

Pattani

TIME FROM SONGKHLA: **2HR** 

Thailand's Deep South

The Deep South has long been a melting pot of influences – Malay, Chinese, Thai, Arab, Indian and European – making it one of the most culturally layered regions in Thailand. Trade routes that once linked Siam to the British and Dutch East India Companies also brought Chinese immigrants from Fujian and Hainan, many of whom settled in port cities like Songkhla and Pattani. These early traders built elaborate

GETTING AROUND

The easiest gateway into Thailand's Deep South is Hat Yai, which has frequent flights from Bangkok and Kuala Lumpur, as well as train and bus connections from major southern cities. From Hat Yai, it's a one- to three-hour journey by road to Pattani, Yala or Narathiwat. Minivans run regularly from Hat Yai's two main bus terminals, or you can hire a private car and driver.

While travel is possible, the region has experienced ongoing political unrest and armed conflict, particularly in rural areas. Independent travel is not advised at night, and it's essential to stay updated on local security conditions. Check travel advisories from your government and consult local sources before visiting. If you go, go respectfully – this is a place of deep cultural pride and resilience.

HANDICRAFTS OF THE BORDER PROVINCES

Southern Thailand's border provinces are home to intricate handicrafts that reflect centuries of cultural exchange between Thai, Malay and Islamic traditions. In Narathiwat, look for handmade batik – fabric dyed in bold, floral patterns – created by local women's cooperatives. Pattani is known for its delicate *ko lae* boat models, which are hand-carved and painted in vibrant colours, echoing the real-life fishing vessels along the coast. In Yala, you'll find traditional woven textiles with the gold thread used in ceremonial dress. Don't miss Songkhla lace *(kho mae)*, a rare local technique passed down through generations. These crafts not only make beautiful souvenirs but also support community livelihoods.

shrines and shophouses in the Sino-Portuguese style, many of which still line the historic quarters today.

In Pattani, two significant houses of worship sit almost side by side, encapsulating the region's dual spiritual heritage. The **Krue Sae Mosque** (Masjid Kerisik), believed to be over 500 years old, is built in red brick with Gothic-style arches – a rare fusion in Thai architecture. A few hundred metres away lies the **Chao Mae Lim Ko Niao Shrine**, dedicated to a Chinese goddess. Legend has it that Lim Ko Niao hanged herself from a cashew tree when her brother, who had converted to Islam and married a local princess, refused to return to China with her. That tree still stands where the shrine is today.

For religion, the Deep South is majority Malay-Muslim, a group whose roots stretch back to the ancient Sultanate of Pattani. Since the 16th century, this Islamic kingdom thrived as a trading hub until it was gradually annexed by the Thai state. To this day, the region retains a distinct identity – one reflected in its cuisine, customs and language. You'll hear Bahasa Melayu as often as Thai, see hijabs in every village and find centuries-old mosques anchoring the community. Food here also speaks of deep cultural roots. Southern Malay dishes, such as beef rendang, *massaman* curry, and *roti* served with curry, showcase a heavier use of spices than their central Thai counterparts.

While rich in heritage, the Deep South has also endured decades of conflict and a fraught struggle for autonomy. Since the early 2000s, the provinces of Pattani, Yala and Narathiwat have witnessed recurring unrest. The causes of the conflict are complex. Profound grievances run deeper than politics. This remains one of Southeast Asia's longest running low-intensity conflicts. Yet even amid disruption, everyday life continues. Markets still operate, children attend school, mosques still call to prayer.

Betong

TIME FROM SONGKHLA: **4HR**

Inside Betong's long history

Nestled in the mountainous folds of Yala Province near the Malaysian border, Betong is Thailand's southernmost town – and one of its most culturally distinct. Surrounded by the misty Titiwangsa Range, this remote borderland feels more like a hill station than a tropical Thai settlement, with cool mountain air, winding switchback roads and foggy vistas that draw domestic travellers searching for calm, cooler climes and a taste of something different from the beach-heavy south.

Betong's population is a microcosm of the Deep South's multicultural identity. Thai Buddhists, Malay Muslims and Chinese descendants live side by side, shaping a local culture where temple bells, mosque loudspeakers, and the clatter of Chinese teahouses exist in effortless harmony. This cultural mix is visible at every turn. Walk through Betong's compact centre and you'll pass gold-lettered Chinese shophouses, halal food stalls grilling satay and making *roti* on hot iron plates,

SAKCARED/SHUTTERSTOCK

Piyamit Tunnel entrance

roadside shrines glowing red with incense, and local monks collecting alms at dawn.

Betong's history is often associated with the **Piyamit Tunnel**, a 1km-long underground complex built in the 1970s by members of the Malayan Communist Party who had retreated into the border forests. The 1km-long tunnel, designed as a hidden base and living quarters, is now one of Betong's most visited historical sites.

Despite its remote location, Betong has a certain kitschy charm that endears it to visitors. In the centre stands a **massive red postbox** – once promoted as the tallest in Thailand – a symbol that has become both a quirky photo spot and a nostalgic reminder of Betong's connection to the outside world. A 30-minute drive from there will take you to **Betong Winter Flower Garden**, featuring seasonal blooms, colourful installations, and viewpoints overlooking terraced hills. While not exactly a natural wonder, it adds to the town's unexpected mix of homespun attractions and scenic mountain appeal.

Another popular spot is the **Skywalk Aiyerweng** *(200฿)*, a glass walkway above the sea of mist that blankets the valley most mornings from November to February. The journey there, along winding mountain roads dotted with small villages and rubber plantations, is as memorable as the view itself.

Cross-border trade and tourism with Malaysia have brought some economic uplift in recent years. Malaysian travellers cross over for weekend breaks, food trips and the cooler air, giving Betong's small hotels, markets and teahouses steady business. Yet even with this influx, the town hasn't transformed into a tourism machine. Betong remains grounded, shaped more by local rhythms than by visitor expectations.

GETTING TO MALAYSIA FROM SUNGAI KOLOK

The border crossing at Sungai Kolok-Rantau Panjang is one of the most direct land routes between Thailand and Malaysia. From Sungai Kolok town, it's a short walk or tuk-tuk ride to the Thai immigration checkpoint. After crossing the Golok River bridge, you'll reach Rantau Panjang in Malaysia's Kelantan state. Buses and taxis connect to Kota Bharu (about 45 minutes away) and beyond.

Note: this area is part of Thailand's conflict-affected Deep South. While the border remains open and is commonly used by locals, independent travellers should exercise caution. Avoid crossing at night, check the latest travel advisories, and be respectful of security procedures on both sides. A valid passport and entry stamp are required.

Places We Love to Stay

฿ Budget ฿฿ Midrange ฿฿฿ Top End

Ko Samui

Map p457 & 458

Hat Chaweng

Lub d ฿฿ An upmarket and social hostel featuring decent dorms, two pools and a beachfront location.

Jungle Club ฿฿ Supreme views from this popular place perched atop a very steep hill. Great pool and restaurant.

Baan Haad Ngam Boutique Resort & Villas ฿฿ Comfortable rooms and villas in a neatly landscaped garden at the quiet northern end of Chaweng.

Baan Samui Resort ฿฿ Spacious, wood-floored rooms and beachside restaurant and pool set on a pretty stretch of Chaweng.

Library Hotel ฿฿฿ Huge, minimalist, light-filled rooms at this swanky boutique option with an on-site library and excellent restaurant.

Mae Nam & the North Coast

Treehouse Silent Beach ฿ Compact bungalows set around a garden at this excellent budget choice. Beachfront restaurant.

Escape Beach Resort ฿ A rare beachfront midrange option in this part of Samui. Comfortable rooms and a pool.

Shangrila Bungalow ฿฿ Old-fashioned bungalows, but they're on a lovely, quiet stretch of Hat Mae Nam.

W Koh Samui ฿฿฿ Ultra-luxury resort with private pool villas, cutting-edge design and panoramic ocean views, plus a signature spa and renowned dining experiences.

Belmond Napasai ฿฿฿ Smart seafront villas set in manicured grounds. Yoga, tennis and windsurfing are available.

Code Samui Hotel ฿฿฿ Contemporary hillside suites with sweeping sea views, kitchenettes and a sleek infinity pool, ideal for long stays and style-conscious travellers.

Bo Phut & the Northeast

79 Beach Club & Resort ฿฿ A chic beachfront resort with a lively beach club and a huge pool right by the sea serving great pizza and cocktails.

B House Samui ฿฿ A boutique-style hotel featuring bright, airy rooms that sit right on the beach, with a pool area and a secret cocktail bar.

Hacienda ฿฿ Boutique guesthouse in Fisherman's Village has lovely, bright rooms, sea views and a cute rooftop pool.

Hansar Samui Resort ฿฿฿ Upmarket option in Fisherman's Village. It has a super pool, gym and spa.

Kimpton Kitalay Samui ฿฿฿ Modern beachfront retreat blending comfort and convenience, perfect for younger travellers with style.

Nathon & the West

Mud ฿฿ Comfortable and big bungalows above a cove north of Nathon. Good restaurant.

Ko Pha-Ngan

Map p470

Hideout Hostel ฿ Hat Rin's best hostel. Comfortable dorms with bathrooms, big communal areas and a pleasant vibe.

Jungle Vibes ฿ Mellow hostel set in a garden of tamarind trees on the outskirts of Thong Sala.

Wanderlust Hostel ฿ Thong Sala's party hostel. Beds are lumpy, but there's a pool and sauna.

Tiki Beach ฿ Friendly resort in Hat Ban Tai with beachfront rooms, garden bungalows, a restaurant and pool. Daily activities.

Shiralea Backpackers Resort ฿ Bathrooms could be better, but dorms are fine. Big communal area, pool and gym. A 20-minute walk from Salad beach.

Seetanu Bungalows ฿ Mix of budget (fan-only) and midrange bungalows on a nice stretch of west-coast beach. Popular with families.

Mai Pen Rai ฿ Spacious but simple fan-only bungalows steps from Hat Than Sadat. Good restaurant.

Divine Comedie ฿฿ Quirky bungalows with a vague Art Deco feel. Beachfront pool. Five-minute walk from Ban Tai Pier.

Salad Hut ฿฿ Beachfront place with 14 well-appointed wooden bungalows at tranquil Hat Salad. Good pool and restaurant.

TropiCoco Beach Resort ฿฿ Sparkly, attractive rooms in a prime spot on pretty Hat Yao. Decent family option.

Tommy Resort ฿฿ Beachfront place with tidy poolside bungalows and a busy bar adjacent to the Full Moon madness.

Sea Breeze Resort ฿฿ Sprawling collection of well-maintained rooms on a hillside overlooking Hat Sareekantang.

Longtail Beach Resort ฿฿ Family-friendly place on Thong Nai Pan Yai with cute, compact bungalows around a pool.

Havana Beach Resort ฿฿ Solid midrange option on Thong Nai Pan Yai. Sizeable rooms with balconies and a good pool.

Sarikantang Resort & Spa ฿฿฿ Smart cabins set among swaying palms on one of Hat Rin's finest stretches of sand.

Kupu Kupu Phangan Beach Villas & Spa by l'Occitane ฿฿฿ Sophisticated beachfront resort with huge bungalows, plunge pools and a rated spa. Southwest coast.

Ko Tao

Map p482

Deisha View Jungle Hostel ฿ Awesome sea views, but getting here involves climbing a lot of steps.

Bubble Bungalow ฿ Tidy and reasonably priced bungalows, both air-con and fan, with balconies overlooking Chalok Ban Kao.

Tanote Good View ฿ Rustic hillside hotel a short bike ride from Ao Tanote, with stunning sunrise views and basic amenities.

Dearly Koh Tao Hostel ฿฿ Upmarket and well-maintained hostel spread over three buildings. Decent dorms and a pool where you can take your diving course.

Chintakiri Resort ฿฿ Well set-up rooms, great views, but a lot of stairs.

Wonderland Jungle Hostel Koh Tao ฿฿ Laid-back hostel surrounded by lush jungle, offering cosy dorms, private rooms, a social vibe and yoga classes, just a short ride from the beach.

Ao Khanom

Hallo Villa ฿ Big bungalows and a pool set in a leafy compound; walking distance from Hat Khanom.

Margarita Beach ฿฿ Eight bamboo bungalows with balconies strewn around a beachfront garden at Hat Khanom.

Le Petit Saint Tropez ฿฿ Well-maintained, stylish rooms set around a pool, just back from Hat Nadan. Top-notch restaurant.

Khanom Hill Resort ฿฿฿ Slick operation on a nice slice of Hat Nai Plao. Two pools and a popular restaurant.

Khanom Beach Resort and Spa ฿฿฿ Ao Khanom's posh option has its own strip of private beach in the middle of Hat Nadan.

Phatthalung

Map p495

Merdelong Hotel ฿ Modern budget hotel in the heart of Phatthalung: easy access to local markets and attractions.

Dusit Princess ฿฿ Upscale hotel with contemporary rooms, an outdoor pool, fitness centre and excellent dining, offering comfort in the city centre close to city sights.

Songkhla Province

Map p500

Goodnight Poshtel ฿ Trendy Hat Yai hostel featuring sleek dorms and private rooms, a shared kitchen and social spaces, perfect for budget travellers who appreciate design.

Modern Budget Hotel ฿ Simple, contemporary rooms in Hat Yai, with essential amenities, friendly service and a convenient location for exploring Songkhla's attractions on a budget.

Songkhla Tae Raek Antique Hotel ฿฿ Charming heritage stay in a restored shophouse, set amid Songkhla Old Town's vibrant streets.

Kleun Ngam ฿฿ Stylish boutique guesthouse with bright, airy rooms and an on-site cafe, steps from the Songkhla Old Town waterfront.

MARGARITA YOUNG/SHUTTERSTOCK

Belmond Napasai, Mae Nam

Researched by Philipp Meier

Phuket & the Andaman Coast

THAILAND FOR BEACH LOVERS

Jungle-covered islands, heavenly beaches, a people rightly proud of their Peranakan heritage and superb adventures – find this plus food and coffee to write home about.

With its white powdery beaches, limestone rocks jutting hundreds of metres out of emerald water, and islets blanketed by jungle, the Andaman Coast delivers on the promise of travel brochures. Phuket Island is known for exuberant nightlife, glitzy coastal resorts and a cosmopolitan mix of cultures.

To the north of Thailand's largest island, Phang-Nga brings a lot to the table, too – from viewpoints and movie locations to world-class dive sites and gushing waterfalls. Hippie enclaves, bubbling hot springs and natural wonders await in Ranong further north.

To the south are isles galore; you can go island-hopping down to the Malaysian border. The beaches get prettier the further south you go, particularly in the Malacca Strait, where the water is as clear as gin. The currents running down to Singapore, around the corner to Tioman Island and back to Satun, cleanse the ocean. The water is always fresh.

South of Krabi karst peaks march through the region like trampling mammoths, and north of the Muslim enclave of Satun lies an often-neglected gem: Trang. A city and a province, Trang offers very different big-city experiences. After sampling an airy sponge cake, you can venture into a network of caves. To give you a teaser, lying flat on a boat centimetres from a ceiling that resembles the spine of a dragon is likely Thailand's most thrilling adventure.

MIRELLE/SHUTTERSTOCK

THE MAIN AREAS

PHUKET
Nightlife, history, spas and culture. **p514**

RANONG
Islands and natural wonders. **p532**

PHANG-NGA PROVINCE
Diving, beaches and a bay. **p537**

For places to stay in Phuket and the Andaman Coast, see p586

FOKKE BAARSSEN/SHUTTERSTOCK

Left: Hat Tonsai (p562); Above: Hat Surin (p513)

KRABI PROVINCE
Beaches, islands and limestone scenery. **p549**

TRANG PROVINCE
Food, caves and pretty waterfalls. **p569**

SATUN PROVINCE
Coffee and paradisal islands. **p577**

Find Your Way

Thailand's west coast stretches along the Andaman Sea with some 740km of stunning coastline and countless islands. Save for a few uninhabited islets and remote villages, the coast is connected by boat, bus and minivan.

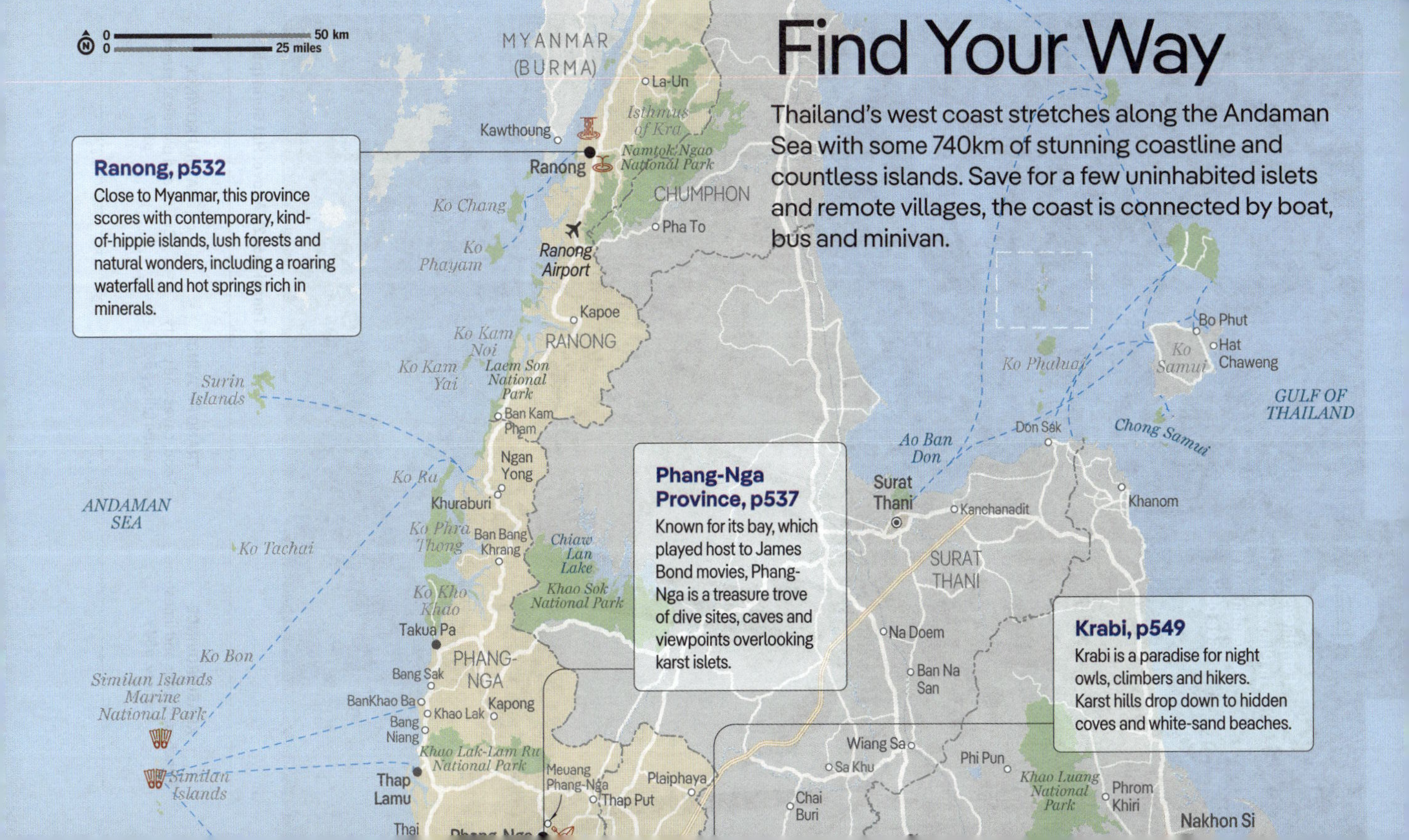
0 50 km
0 25 miles
MYANMAR (BURMA)
La-Un
Isthmus of Kra
Kawthoung
Ranong
Namtok Ngao National Park
CHUMPHON
Pha To
Ko Chang
Ko Phayam
Ranong Airport
Kapoe
Ko Kam Noi
RANONG
Ko Kam Yai
Laem Son National Park
Surin Islands
Ban Kam Pham
Ngan Yong
Ko Ra
Khuraburi
ANDAMAN SEA
Ko Phra Thong
Ban Bang Khrang
Chiaw Lan Lake
Ko Tachai
Ko Kho Khao
Khao Sok National Park
Takua Pa
Ko Bon
PHANG-NGA
Similan Islands Marine National Park
Bang Sak
BanKhao Ba
Khao Lak
Kapong
Bang Niang
Khao Lak-Lam Ru National Park
Similan Islands
Thap Lamu
Meuang Phang-Nga
Thap Put
Plaiphaya
Thai
Ko Phaluai
Bo Phut
Hat Chaweng
Ko Samui
GULF OF THAILAND
Don Sak
Chong Samui
Ao Ban Don
Surat Thani
Kanchanadit
Khanom
SURAT THANI
Na Doem
Ban Na San
Wiang Sa
Sa Khu
Chai Buri
Phi Pun
Khao Luang National Park
Phrom Khiri
Nakhon Si

Ranong, p532
Close to Myanmar, this province scores with contemporary, kind-of-hippie islands, lush forests and natural wonders, including a roaring waterfall and hot springs rich in minerals.

Phang-Nga Province, p537
Known for its bay, which played host to James Bond movies, Phang-Nga is a treasure trove of dive sites, caves and viewpoints overlooking karst islets.

Krabi, p549
Krabi is a paradise for night owls, climbers and hikers. Karst hills drop down to hidden coves and white-sand beaches.

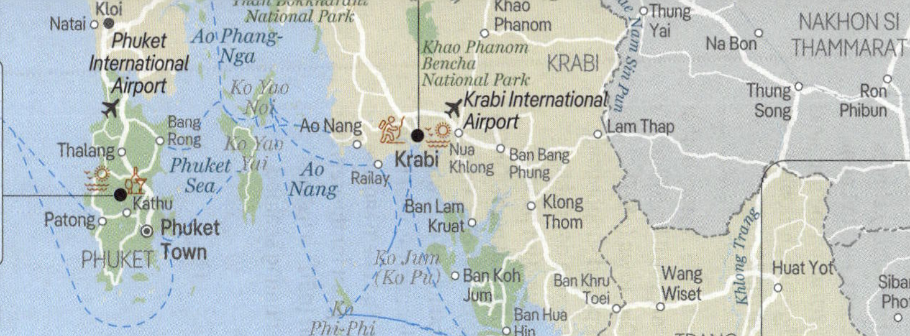

Phuket, p514

Come here for an intoxicating mishmash of Thai, Chinese, Muslim and European cultures, glitzy coastal resorts, powdery beaches and bars to paint the town red.

Trang Province, p569

Food to gorge on, hot springs, caves and fast-moving waterfalls gushing into a series of rock pools – you'd not forgive yourself for skipping this province.

Satun Province, p577

Satun has a smidge of nightlife, possibly Thailand's tastiest coffee and a UNESCO geopark – and tropical islands with crystal waters just offshore.

FROM PHUKET AIRPORT

The Smart Bus (domestic terminal) takes you to Phuket Town and Phuket's west-coast beaches. The Airport Bus to Phuket's Bus Terminal 1 waits outside the international terminal. Khao Lak is an hour's drive, Krabi a two-hour taxi. Car rentals are available.

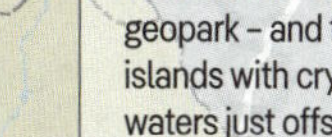

BUS, BOAT & MINIVAN

Start long-distance bus travel to provinces further afield from Phuket's two bus terminals or opposite Highway Police Station, 9km from Phuket Airport. Use ferries or speedboats to Krabi from Phuket's Tha Rassada or Bang Rong. Coaches and minivans run regularly from Krabi International Airport. Visit *busonlineticket.co.th* for good deals.

MOTORCYCLE

Widely available for rent. Make sure you wear a helmet and have an international driver's licence and accident insurance. Checkpoints are everywhere. Beware dogs and humans crossing the road unexpectedly.

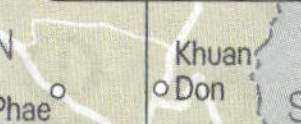
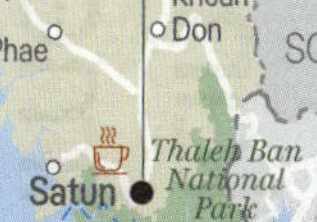

Plan Your Time

Fun in the sun awaits both inland and offshore, but it takes a while to see Phuket and much of the Andaman Coast. Pick a city or region and save some me-time for the beach.

DARI POOMIPAT/SHUTTERSTOCK

Similan Islands (p547)

Pressed for Time

- Should time not be in your favour, choose **Phuket** (p514). A weekend fling with Thailand's most popular island is enough to lounge on the powdery shores of its west coast, hike to **Laem Krating** (p520) when the sun sinks orange and go beach clubbing at **Cape Panwa** (p524).

- If you're a foodie, history buff or coffee person, you'll love Phuket's illustrious **Old Town** (p527), where repurposed shophouses nod to the bygone days of tin barons. Jockeying for position and beautifully lit at night, **On On Hotel** (p586) is one of the most prominent buildings in town. With this movie location as your base, it isn't far to Tha Laem Hin, the jumping-off point for the nearby **Ko Coconut** (p512), a fishers' island with floating seafood restaurants.

SEASONAL HIGHLIGHTS

The Andaman Coast is hottest from January to mid-April. The May to October low season brings rain, fewer crowds and better prices.

JANUARY

Yes, prices may be heavy on your pocket from late November to January, but you can look forward to sun-kissed shores and a very calm Andaman Sea – perfect conditions for water sports and outdoor adventures.

FEBRUARY

February to mid-March are the driest, with daytime highs of 36°C (95°F). The 15-day **Chinese New Year** festival happens across the region. Dates of the lunar new year vary. Check online.

APRIL

The hottest month sees little rain – particularly the first half of the month, which is arguably the best time to go island-hopping.

Five Days to Travel Around

- Three days exploring Phang-Nga Province will not get you bored. Settle in **Khao Lak** (p539) and relax on its wide-open beaches. This quiet town on mainland Thailand has beer bars, international restaurants and tourist attractions like the **Tsunami Boat 813** (p539).

- Alternatively, **Ao Phang-Nga** (p541) will let you follow in the footsteps of James Bond. You can also observe the bay's sea of limestone rocks from Samet Nangshe, a viewpoint known locally as **Ao Tho Li**. A day trip from Khao Lak are the **Similan Islands** (p547). On this archipelago with low-lying rock formations, you'll meet friendly turtles and walk on sand as soft as memory foam. Worth tons of phone storage before returning to earth back home is **Takua Pa Old Town** (p544).

A Week or More in Paradise

- Kick off in **Khao Sok National Park** (p545). After a day on the park's Halong Bay–like Chiaw Lan Lake, hop on a bus bound for the town of **Krabi** (p549), where you can hit the **night market** (p551). Nearby Ao Nang makes a great base for day trips to **Hat Railay** (p560), **Sa Kaew Pool** (p555) or **Dragon Crest** (p556), with cosy evenings at hookah bars.

- After sleeping in, find yourself a room in **Trang** (p569) and get ready for the thrill of your life: nearly grazing the upper wall of **Tham Le Khao Kob** (p575).

- With wiggle room in your schedule, you should have time for swimming the crystal waters of **Ko Lipe** (p582), or a final day in Satun's La-Ngu area, where **Kopi Naka** (p578) serves syrupy *caffe boran*.

MAY
The start of the shoulder season is hit or miss, weather-wise. Rain and the sun peeping sheepishly through clouds take turns this month. This transitional period comes with wallet-friendlier rates and thinning crowds.

JUNE
June is slightly drier than May, yet showers occur frequently. Rural parts may be difficult to reach when dirt roads are muddy. Daytime temperatures still average at 32°C. Roadside stalls sell sweet, crunchy pineapples.

SEPTEMBER
Heavy rains lash the Andaman Coast now that the powerful monsoon brings moist warm air from the Indian Ocean. On the bright side, windsurfing may be fun and prices plummet. Humidity is also low.

OCTOBER
A continuation of September, but splashes of sunshine await in the second half, usually the beginning of the **Vegetarian Festival** (p523), celebrated in Phuket, Phang-Nga and Trang. Daytime highs average at 27°C.

Phuket's Beaches & Islands

With over 40 powdery beaches, each with its own identity, Phuket has much to offer sun-seekers. Some are quiet swaths of sand between jungly hills; others are palm-fringed coves popular with snorkellers. Seafood lovers or people burnt out on city life find peace on offshore islands draped in rainforest. Whether you need a grouper on a plate or a wild half moon of sand to refresh your mind, a vibrant coral reef is only a long-tail boat ride away.

Where to go if you love...

Seclusion

Ko Lon Slap-bang in the middle of Phuket's Ao Chalong, this criminally underrated island has a teal sea and blissfully uncluttered, palm-lined beaches, with homestays as alternatives to camping. Locals make a living from fishing, ecotourism and farming. What makes this island great is everything it lacks. There's no 7-Eleven or road, just walking paths and inland hills sloping to a handful of beaches.

Hat Laem Singh Between Hat Surin and Kamala, Hat Laem Singh is known for its viewpoint overlooking a Caribbean-like shore. Those who actually visit the beach are rewarded with castaway vibes and a stretch of sand beneath coco palms that lean towards the Andaman Sea. A small eatery named View Point Restaurant has opened on the rocks that frame the tropical cove.

Hat Freedom Brilliant white sand and clear, turquoise water characterise this paradisal beach between jungle-covered hills near Hat Patong. Ironically called Freedom Beach long before the island was littered with weed shops, it's now a chill spot shrouded in cannabis clouds, with food and drinks available at the cafe.

Seafood

Ko Coconut This 4.19-sq-km fishers' islet off Phuket's east coast is home to a Muslim community, who live off harvesting coconuts, tapping rubber and fishing, as they have for ages. A few five-star resorts woo tourists in hidden corners, while ramshackle bungalows on stilts dot hamlets. As you'd expect, there's seafood galore – served in floating restaurants off the west-coast pier.

Hat Banana Coconut trees are the backdrop to the blinding white sand and amazonite water of this popular beach. It takes its name from Westerners who mistook *gruay* for *gluay* (banana), after Thais had called it Hat Hin Gruay, or Funnel Rock Beach. Coarse-grained in the north, the sand is flour-like in the south. You won't find any bananas here, but fresh seafood from fishermen is available.

Snorkelling, diving & surfing

Ko Raya Also spelt Ko Racha, Ko Raya's twin islands have coral-white sand and a reef in turquoise water clearer than a swimming pool, making them a diver and snorkeller favourite. Busy in daylight and peaceful at night, Ko Raya Yai has a few hotels, bars and restaurants.

Hat Kata Visit Hat Kata and its golden sand to surf gentle waves ideal for newbies. Depending on the season, kitesurfing is also a popular activity off the Phuket beaches of Nai Yang, Chalong Bay and Hat Rawai.

NOS SEASTAR/SHUTTERSTOCK

Ko Raya (p512)

HOW TO

When to go Visit the beaches early in the morning to avoid the crowds. Ko Coconut can get busy at the weekend when Thais come to eat.

Snorkelling gear Many long-tail boats in Patong and Hat Rawai have snorkelling gear. Bring snorkels and masks to Hat Banana, Ko Coconut and particularly Ko Lon.

Money There are no ATMs at Hat Banana, Hat Freedom and Hat Laem Singh. While you can find some nearby, there aren't any on Ko Lon.

Need to know Ko Lon has no convenience stores, and there's only a cafe at Hat Freedom.

Practical Information

Hat Laem Singh, Hat Freedom and Hat Banana are accessible by scooter, though long-tail boats are more convenient. Hat Freedom is only a 10 minute-ride from Patong, but hiking down the steep track to the beach takes 25 minutes. Also, you'll have to pay 100฿ for 'trespassing'. Getting to Hat Laem Singh is less of a hassle, but it's still a 15-minute walk along the coastline. Using the path that starts at the southern end of Hat Surin near Tukta Food & Drink, you're obliged to stop at View Point Restaurant overlooking Hat Laem Singh. The restaurateur built the path. Hat Banana is accessible from a paved road between Hat Nai Ton and Trisara Villas, but parking spaces are limited. Ko Coconut sits off Phuket's Tha Laem Hin. Water taxis take you to that pier, but scooters are cheaper. You can rent them in Phuket for 250฿ to 300฿ per day, park it at Tha Laem Hin and hop on a public shuttle boat. Motorcycle taxis take you around Ko Coconut. To get to Ko Lon or Ko Raya, hop on a boat at Hat Rawai or Ao Chalong. Speedboats take 40 minutes to Ko Raya; long-tail boats are slower. Ko Raya Yai has coral reefs; Ko Raya Noi's deep dive sites are more suitable for experienced divers. A luxury hotel on Ko Raya Yai named the Racha has a PADI five-star dive centre on the island, while Phuket-based companies offer half-day trips, generally cheaper.

Phuket

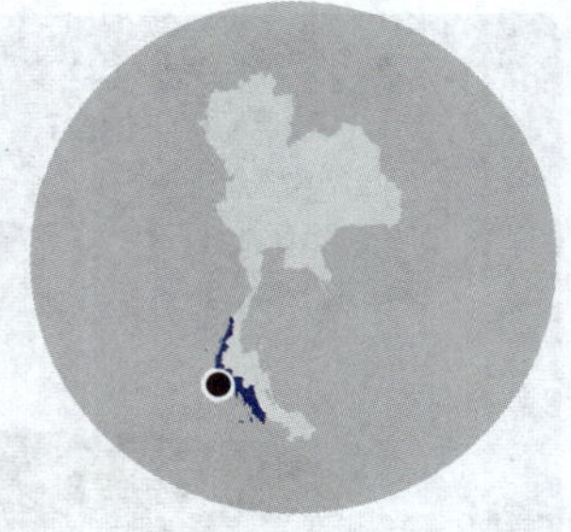

BEACHES | HISTORY & CULTURE | NIGHTLIFE

TOP TIP

Pick your favourite beach and use that as your base to discover the rest of Phuket. To see the real Phuket, head inland or explore the east coast.

Phuket is no longer an impregnable jungle full of wild animals. But there's more to this fascinating island than palm-fringed coves, feathery cabaret shows with sparkling sequins, and Sino-European mansions telling the story of tin barons.

Recognised by UNESCO as a City of Gastronomy, Phuket Town is worth visiting for its decades-old noodle joints run by locals with Thai, Chinese Peranakan ancestral roots. Tour the whole island, and you'll notice Phuket's multicultural jumble in the mosques, temples, churches and shrines derived from trading and tin mining.

Rubber was introduced when tin prices plummeted, and the first backpackers arrived in the 1970s. Originally a form of escape for the tin-mine workers, Phuket's nightlife has lived to tell the tale, while community-based tourism has emerged for those keen to gain local perspective. Whatever you're after, Phuket is an idyllic island, town and province suited to all budgets.

GETTING AROUND

Phuket doesn't have the best public transport, and the 543-sq-km island isn't particularly suited to walking, save for the island's enchanting Old Town.

The Smart Bus (100฿) operates from the domestic terminal every 30 to 60 minutes until midnight. An airport bus (120฿) to Phuket Town runs from the international terminal. While airport taxis come with a tourist premium, minivans to west-coast beaches cost around 180฿.

Tuk-tuks aren't cheap; even for short distances expect to pay 200฿. They're popular, however, with young travellers keen for a night on the town. You can find scooter rental shops around every corner, but note that you need an international driver's licence, and that dogs and humans cross roads unexpectedly. If you aren't pressed for time, hop on the old blue bus from Phuket Town to Patong. The best way to criss-cross Phuket is by Bolt, an Uber-like app.

Phuket's First 'Red-Hair Mansion' MAP P518

Write your own history

One of the best-preserved Sino-Portuguese buildings in Phuket, **Chinpracha House** *(facebook.com/ChinPrachaHouse Museum; adult/child 150/50฿; 9am-4.30pm)* reveals the Chinese-Malaysian, Dutch and British influences that shaped the architectural landscape in Old Phuket Town.

Built by businessman and philanthropist Pra Pitak Chinpracha in 1903, the ornate mansion was Phuket's first Ang Mor Lao, or Red-Hair Mansion. It takes its name from the Europeans who came to Southeast Asia during the tin-mining boom between the late 19th and early 20th centuries.

Exploring the manor, you can spend an hour or two taking in Victorian furniture, Italian ceramic tile floors, rare Chinese decorations and Greco-Roman columns, while learning about this turbulent period of Phuket's history. Ask for Khun Tiw ('Deeoo') to delve deep into Phuket's Thai, Chinese, Peranakan culture. He's the owner of Chinpracha House and provides a wealth of information. You'll find his local history museum on Th Krabi on the fringes of the Old Town.

Discover Phuket's Peaceful Side MAP P516

Unwind at Saphan Hin Park

Repose on one of the copper benches that line the deserted seaside walkway, enjoying views of Ko Sireh, the scent of pines and the caress of a warm breeze. Three kilometres southeast of Phuket Old Town, this spot in **Saphan Hin Park** (open 6am to 10pm) is most peaceful in the morning, when picnicking crowds have yet to appear on the expansive lawn.

The ultra-mellow seafront park has several pavilions at which to sit and gather your thoughts in the shade. By late afternoon, when the sunlight drizzles over the park like honey, people grab a spot on the grass right next to **Kio Thian Keng Shrine**, where the Annual Vegetarian Festival culminates with a grand finale. The scent of barbecue chicken wafts on the evening breeze and the atmosphere becomes lively.

Walking and watching locals roll out their beach mats while kids fly kites can be a cathartic experience.

Walk Among Adorable Pachyderms MAP P516

Spend a morning with elephants

Strolling along a 600m-long canopy walkway, you hear a roar not unlike that of a tiger. As you get closer, you see a pachyderm almost tearing down a jackfruit tree below you, while another elephant seems to be mimicking the cackling sound of a monkey. Don't worry; it's just Kannika. Aged 42, she's demonstrating that she's the leader of the 25 elephants at **Phuket Elephant Sanctuary** *(phuketelephantsanctuary.org; adult/child 1900/950฿; 9am-5pm).*

Today a major tourist draw, elephants are rooted in Thai history. Back then, riding the gentle giants was a safe way to travel, as tigers would attack horses but not elephants. Today,

WHERE THE TERM 'SINO-PORTUGUESE' COMES FROM

Chanachon 'Tiw' Tandavanitj, owner of Chinpracha House and Museum. *@prachakt*

A term first coined by a Thai some 30 to 40 years ago, Phuket gave the Portuguese credit for being the first Europeans on the island. *Sino-colonial?* the locals asked themselves. No, this couldn't be a suitable term because Phuket had never been colonised. *Chinese-Malaysian?* they wondered. Clearly not. For fear of people thinking it was part of Malaysia rather than Thailand, Phuketians didn't even want to say their island was influenced by Malaysia. And yet it was. What you can see in Phuket looks extremely similar to Georgetown in Malaysia. I recommend wandering around Th Thalang, Th Krabi, Th Phang-Nga and Th Dibuk.

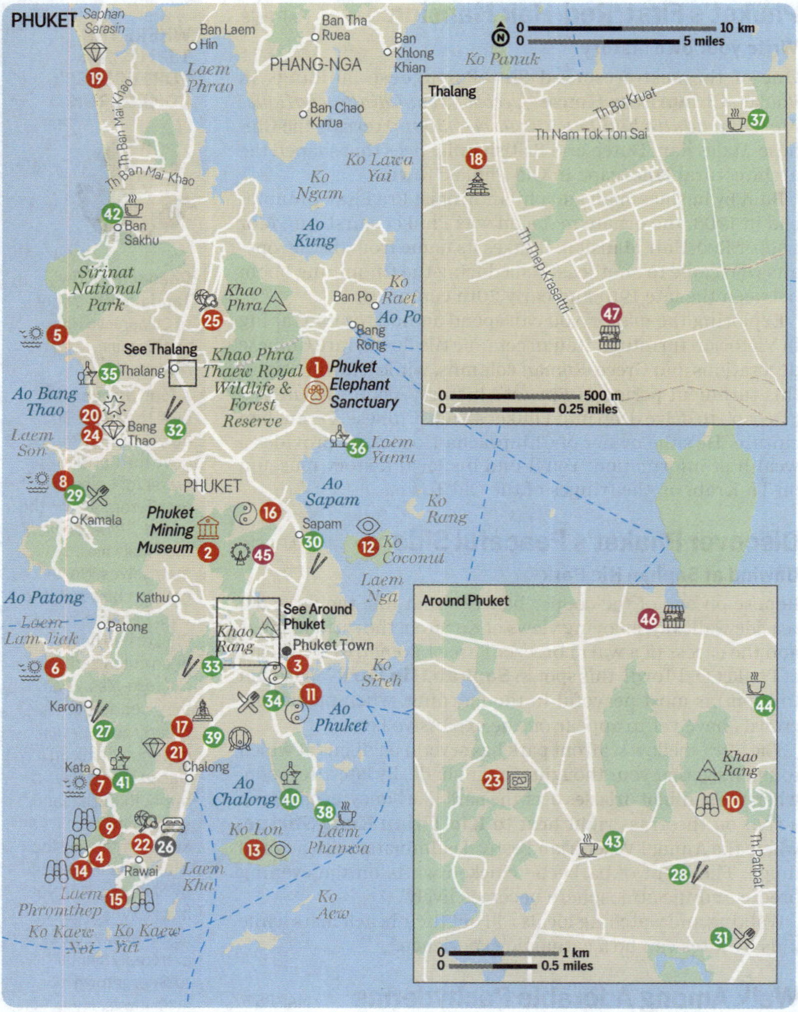

DRINKING IN PHUKET OLD TOWN: CRAFT COFFEE SHOPS

MAP P516 & P518

Shelter Coffee: Now located on Th Vichitsongkram, this spot offers tasty drip coffee roasted by the owner. *8am-4pm Thu-Tue*

Campus Coffee Roasters: More than a specialty coffee shop, Campus Coffee is also an excellent bakery with irresistible brownies. *8am-6pm*

Dou Brew Coffee & Craft: This cafe is a lovely addition to historic Soi Romanee. Try the nutty, chocolatey 'dirty coffee'. *8am-6pm Mon-Fri, to 7pm Sat & Sun*

Daily Dose Phuket Old Town: Get your daily dose of fruits and vitamins at this coffee shop planted in the heart of the Old Town. *7am-9pm*

HIGHLIGHTS
1 Phuket Elephant Sanctuary
2 Phuket Mining Museum

SIGHTS
3 Bang Niew Shrine
4 Black Rock
5 Hat Banana
6 Hat Freedom
7 Hat Kata
8 Hat Laem Singh
9 Karon Viewpoint
10 Khao Rang Viewpoint
11 Kio Thian Keng Shrine
12 Ko Coconut
13 Ko Lon
14 Laem Krating
15 Laem Phromthep
16 Sam Pai Kong Shrine
see 11 Saphan Hin Park
17 Wat Chalong
18 Wat Phra Nang Sang

ACTIVITIES
19 Anantara Mai Khao Phuket Villas
20 Bang Tao Community-Based Tourism
21 Holistic Harmony
22 Jungala Phuket
see 26 Mangosteen Ayurveda & Wellness
23 Phuket Painting Class
24 Sole Mio Phuket
25 Thanyapura Sports & Health Resort

SLEEPING
26 Space House Hotel Phuket

EATING
see 39 Bucha Gallery and Restaurant
27 Dinner in the Sky Phuket
28 Heng Heng Dim Sum
29 Jaras Restaurant
30 Mee Sapam
31 O-Oh Farm Suanluang
32 Sansan Kitchen Halal Breakfast
33 Three Monkeys Restaurant
34 Vegan Phuket

DRINKING & NIGHTLIFE
35 Alto Italian Restaurant & Cocktail Bar
36 Aqua Bar
see 38 Baba Nest Phuket
37 Bloom Espresso
see 1 Booktree Library & Cafe
38 Cafe Kantary
39 Distillery Phuket
40 Flamingo Beach Club
41 Moon Terrace Lounge Kata Rooftop Restaurant
42 Sea Calm Cafe
43 Shelter Coffee
44 Witthaya Home Brewing

ENTERTAINMENT
45 Siam Niramit Phuket

SHOPPING
46 Da Laht Chillva
47 Da Laht Ruam Jai

SOI ROMANEE'S SHRINE

A shrine dedicated to Phuket's Vegetarian Festival was formerly situated on Soi Romanee (p527) in the heart of Phuket Old Town. However, Thais of Hokkien-Chinese descent, to whom Vegetarian Festival is an intensely sacred custom, looked on the Soi Romanee shrine with disfavour. That's because in the early 20th century, sex workers waited for tin-mine labourers in this side street, and commercial sex contravened Taoist principles. The Soi Romanee Shrine, built around 125 years ago, eventually burnt down. Today, the red-green-yellow Jui Tui Shrine (p519) complex in a new Phuket Town location has replaced the Soi Romanee shrine, though many of the strict Taoist devotees refuse to acknowledge the former shrine in the first place.

most of Thailand's 3800 captive elephants are still separated from their babies, isolated and beaten with bull-hooks to make them dance for people's entertainment. Phuket Elephant Sanctuary is fully ethical and part of the Save Elephant Foundation. It's the final home for sick, injured or elderly animals who've been circus elephants or spent most of their lives in the logging industry.

The expansive grounds at the sanctuary allow elephants to roam, bathe, forage and socialise in a natural habitat. During a 90-minute walk preceded by an educational video, you can enjoy riding-free and bathing-free interactions as a guide fills you in on the elephants' stories. No hair on an elephant's back, for instance, means it has been ridden, and the lack of hair can lead to skin infections. It's humid and elephant poo smells like horse manure, but watching them blow air from

EATING IN PHUKET OLD TOWN: DIM SUM RESTAURANTS

MAP P516 & P518

Boonrat Dim Sum: Roll out of bed; this local eatery's pork wraps and dumplings shaped into flowers are worth getting up for. *5.30-10.30am* ฿

Chuan Heang Branch 1: A dim sum restaurant with an open kitchen, fast service, pork dumplings and Chinese paper lanterns. *6-11.30am* ฿

Cafe DimSum Phuket: Thai cuisine, steaks, northern Thai meals and Italian dishes, and dim sum served lovingly in bamboo baskets. *6.30am-5pm* ฿

Heng Heng Dim Sum: This restaurant is often crowded – and for good reason. It serves reasonably priced vegetable salads, soups and dim sum. *6am-1pm* ฿

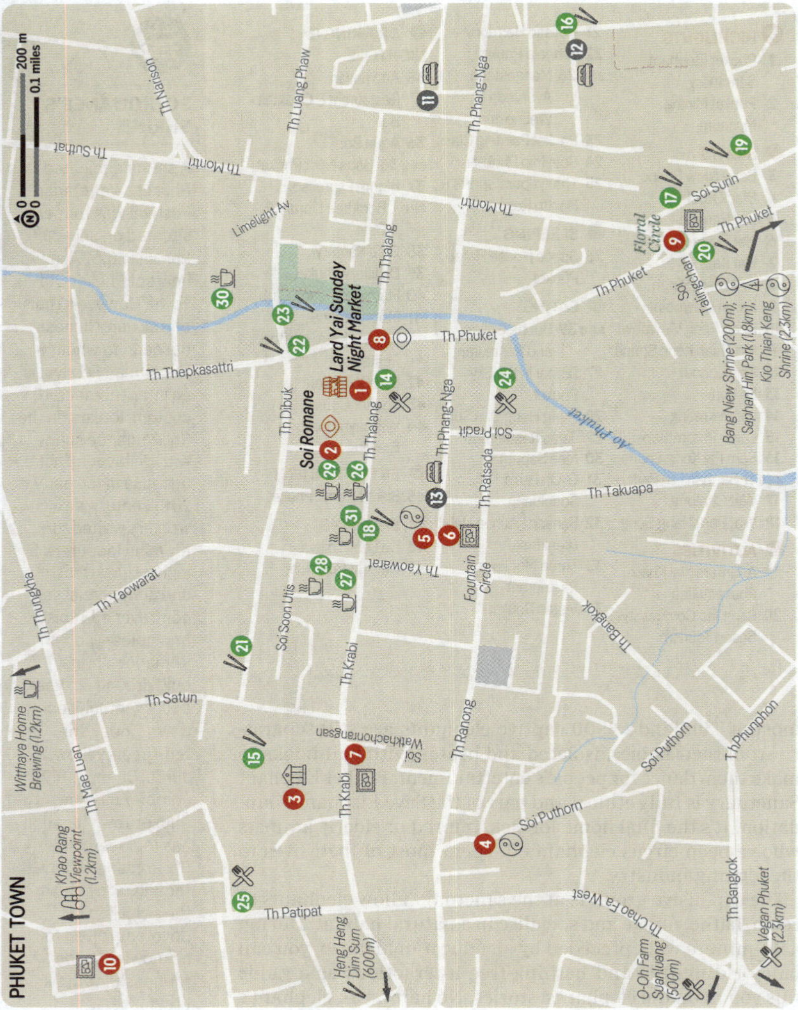

PHUKET TOWN

EATING IN PHUKET TOWN: SINO-PORTUGUESE RESTAURANTS

MAP P518

One Chun: This Old Town restaurant takes its name from the owner being born on a Monday. Try a cooling Phuket dessert here. *10am-10pm* BB

Blue Elephant: This splurge-worthy Michelin-starred restaurant serves Peranakan meals like *moo hong* (Thai pork belly stew). *11.30am-10pm* BBB

Raya Restaurant: Another Michelin-starred restaurant in Old Town, Raya has tasty yellow crab curry and Phuket desserts like *oh aew*, a jelly-based treat. *10am-10pm* BB

Tu Kab Khao: Sino-European both inside and out, this restaurant on Th Phang-Nga offers affordable Phuket meals and pan-Asian cuisine. *11am-9pm* BB

HIGHLIGHTS
1 Lard Yai Sunday Night Market
2 Soi Romanee

SIGHTS
3 Chinpracha House
4 Jui Tui Shrine
5 San Chao Saengtham
6 SiTao Studio Art Cafe
7 Someday Cafe Phuket
8 Th Thalang

ACTIVITIES
9 Art Studio Green Grey
10 Bless Art Gallery
see 10 I-Mon Art Gallery
see 8 Phuket Food Tours
see 9 Xin Massage

SLEEPING
11 Blu Monkey Hub & Hotel Phuket
12 Green Dreams Guesthouse
13 Memory at On On Hotel

EATING
14 Aroon
15 Blue Elephant
16 Boonrat Dim Sum
17 Cafe DimSum Phuket
18 China Inn Garden Restaurant
19 Chuan Heang Branch 1
see 18 Kopitiam by Wilai
see 9 Mee Kola
20 Mee Ton Poe Phuket Town
21 NumNum Old Town Cafe & Restaurant
22 One Chun
23 Raya Restaurant
see 6 Tu Kab Khao
24 Vegan Table
25 Vegetarian Restaurant Nong J

DRINKING & NIGHTLIFE
26 Bookhemian
27 Campus Coffee Roasters
28 Daily Dose Phuket Old Town
29 Dou Brew Coffee & Craft
30 Refresh Cafe
31 Thalang 31

their trunks and letting them nab bananas from your hands is quite an experience. Suitable for all ages, the half-day programme includes iced sodas and snacks plus a free T-shirt.

Behind-the-Scenes Look at Distillery Phuket

MAP P516

Sip your way through crafted tipples

Get the inside scoop on distilling spirits and enjoy a good mouthful of Chalong Bay Rum. **Distillery Phuket** *(thedistilleryphuket.com; 11am-10pm)* offers tours around the establishment, including lunch and discovery visits where you can sample rum, gin or vodka. Laughs are guaranteed! There's no need to worry about the environment – the distillery uses sustainable production methods and pure sugarcane, and a guide fills you in on its history. If you're into strong drinks, you'll love the two-hour rum cocktail workshop (1290฿), which you can book on the distillery's website. The workshop includes a guided tour of the premises, guidance on how to craft cocktails as well as a tasting session, where you can swirl award-winning tipple around your mouth as though it were creamy chocolate.

MUST-SEE TEMPLES & SHRINES

Sam Pai Kong Shrine: Also called Bang Koo Shrine, home to the mythological Monkey God, this Ko Kaeo shrine comes alive during Phuket's Vegetarian Festival.

Wat Phra Nang Sang: Murals of Thalang's history and the legend of a city ruler's wife accused of infidelity.

Jui Tui Shrine: A red-green-yellow shrine in the heart of chaos during the annual Vegetarian Festival.

Bang Niew Shrine: This Old Town shrine hosts the annual 'Blade Ladder' event, where Taoist devotees climb a ladder with razor-sharp blades – barefoot!

San Chao Saengtham: Also named Shrine of Serene Light, this ancient shrine built by a Chinese family has murals and a beautiful garden.

DRINKING IN PHUKET: PHOTOGENIC CAFES

MAP P516 & P518

Refresh Cafe: Set in a bamboo hut roofed with the leaves of nipa palms, this quirky cafe has a pool to dip your toes in. *10am-6pm*

Sea Calm Cafe: The mill-style building is designed to follow the owner's vision of a cosy atmosphere that channels vintage British themes. *9am-7pm*

Thalang 31: Paper lanterns, marble-topped teak tables, stools centred around a neon-lit bar. *10am-10pm Mon-Wed, from 11am Thu-Sat, from 1pm Sun*

Bookhemian: With murals, books and a selection of outstanding drinks, this Old Town cafe caters to bookworms and coffee lovers alike. *10am-8pm*

STAGGERING VIEWPOINTS IN PHUKET

Karon Viewpoint: Halfway between Hat Kata Noi and Nai Harn, this lookout offers bird's-eye views of three crescent beaches.

Laem Krating: Possibly the best spot to watch the sunset on the island, this place offers unbroken sea views.

Laem Phromthep: The most popular sunset viewpoint in Phuket looks out over Ko Man and attracts up to 3000 people per day.

Khao Rang Viewpoint: Home to monkeys, this hilltop viewpoint overlooks Phuket Town – best visited after dark when the cityscape is aglow.

Black Rock: This jaw-dropping viewpoint looks out over Windmill Viewpoint, Ko Man and Ko Bon, and requires only an easy 20-minute walk.

CYSUN/SHUTTERSTOCK

Wat Chalong

Uncover a Magical Secret

MAP P516

Visit Wat Chalong

Imagine you've fled into a temple to escape the raiding Ang-Yi soldiers and Chinese tin-mine labourers. They're members of a Chinese secret society, who are burning and looting the city of Phuket in a dispute over better working conditions – or land title deeds, depending on the source you consult. This was the reality for Phuket's villagers in 1876. But luck and an enigmatic monk was on their side. When Ang-Yi troops advanced near **Wat Chalong** *(wat-chalong-phuket.com; 8am-5pm)* in Phuket's Tambol Chalong, a monk named Luang Por Cham created a magic cloth. Lore has it that the cloth, worn as a turban, protected people against spears, knives and bullets as if by magic. Ironically, it wasn't just denizens of Phuket who later revered the monk. Surviving Ang-Yi members who'd lost the battle also honoured his gilded statue and life-sized wax figure. Today, you can join locals who believe miracles still happen at the temple. They pray and donate lotus and sweet-scented jasmine garlands, burst firecrackers and bow to pay their respects to Luang Por Cham. Besides, a 60m-high *chedi* houses a splinter of Buddha's bone on the top floor. Complete with murals of Buddha's life and a terrace overlooking the temple grounds, Phuket's largest and most visited temple is well worth a visit. Located between central Phuket Town and attractions like Hat Rawai and Laem Phromthep, Chalong is the gateway to the southernmost tip of the island.

EATING IN PHUKET: POPULAR RESTAURANTS

MAP P516 & P518

Sansan Kitchen Halal Breakfast: This restaurant gives dim sum its own spin, with pork-free shrimp dumplings and *ka nom jeen*. *6.30am-noon Tue-Sun* ฿

Aroon: Adds flavourful curry to what would otherwise be a flaky pancake eaten as a Thai dessert. *6am-4.30pm Mon-Sat* ฿

Mee Sapam: Established in 1952, this noodle restaurant serves *sapam* (village) twists on Hokkien noodles, including briny *hoy kratib* clams. *9am-5.30pm* ฿

Jaras Restaurant: A Hat Kamala restaurant that serves mouthwatering seafood, from lobster meals to blue crab curries. *noon-9.30pm* ฿฿฿

Sample Southern Flavours

MAP P518

A chef's tour

Peep inside the kitchen and ignore your hunger pangs for just a bit – you're about to get the inside scoop on cooking Hokkien noodles. A local banters and introduces the chef, who's stirring yellow noodles in a wok. Southern Thai meals you won't find elsewhere in the kingdom also sizzle at other restaurants you'll visit on a Southern Flavours tour with **Phuket Food Tours** *(achefstour.com; 2000฿)*. Make sure you arrive with an empty stomach because you'll be diving headfirst into Phuket's local food scene, which is based on ethnic diversity. The four-hour food tour from 3pm to 7pm showcases the secrets behind the island's gazillions of tastes, including eateries in back alleys of the Old Town that only travellers in the know have heard about. Look forward to tucking into spiced chicken curry puffs or leaf-wrapped *miang kham* bites. You also get to know the tamarind tang of southern *gaeng som*, a sour fish soup. Capped at eight guests, it's a tour of superlatives.

Step Back in Time in Bang Tao

MAP P516

Dive into community-based tourism

Look beyond high-end bars and swanky beach resorts to Bang Tao, a self-sufficient Muslim-Thai community that still depends on fishing and agriculture. During a tour with Sonthaya 'Tiki' Kongthip, head of the Bang Tao community, you can explore the neighbourhood on a 150cc tricycle, visit an organic farm or learn how to rustle up stir-fries and curries. The **half-day tour** *(062 228 7896; 800฿)* starts on Hat Bang Tao, where you watch fishermen unload white snappers, fresh barracudas and glittering butterfish. The guys here don't belong to any sea gypsy tribe, even though the *chao leh*, or people of the sea, have lived on Phuket shores for generations. While these Bang Tao community members have adopted techniques like spearfishing, they usually fish with nets that hang vertically in the water and drift with the current. Continuing the bumpy tour in the back of Tiki's tricycle, you might see smiling Thai kids on the way to a rubber plantation. Lab, an 85-year-old man of the 8000-member community, has tapped rubber since he was 10, and he's still going strong. Tell him to slant a cut and watch as a milky, odourless liquid oozes out of the tree, dripping into a cup. After visiting an organic farm, you can end the tour on Hat Bang Tao, eating fish you bought earlier while listening to the waves washing ashore.

COMMUNITY-BASED TOURISM

Sonthaya 'Tiki' Kongthip, tour guide and head of Phuket's Bang Tao community. Locals started promoting Phuket when cheap plastic heralded the tin's demise. The first backpackers came in the 1970s. Fifteen years ago, everyone liked Ko Phi-Phi. Now people are visiting Phuket's villages – for talking, learning and having an experience. With CBT, you can share money with local people, who also like to have a good experience with tourists. Meet fishermen and rubber-plantation workers, or take a cooking class to have fun. You can also go hiking and spot red jungle crabs on your way to PhuView viewpoint. Founded by the Tourism Authority of Thailand in 2012, Bang Tao community-based tourism saves 10% of the tourist spend to help members in need.

EATING IN PHUKET TOWN: POPULAR LOCAL RESTAURANTS

MAP P518

Kopitiam by Wilai: A restaurant in the heart of Old Town offering iced butterfly-pea drinks, stir-fries and southern Thai meals. *11am-8pm Mon-Sat* ฿฿

China Inn Garden Restaurant: Notable for its red facade, Chinese door wings and handicraft shop. *10.30am-6pm Wed, Thu & Sat, to 8pm Fri, to 7pm Sun* ฿

Mee Kola: Furnished with plastic chairs and red paper lanterns, this eatery specialises in Hokkien noodles cooked on a charcoal stove. *11am-8pm Tue-Sun* ฿

Mee Ton Poe Phuket Town: Overlooking Surin Circle Clock Tower. Serves Hokkien noodles with flash-fried noodles and a woodfire aroma. *9.30am-6.30pm* ฿

VISIT THALANG LIKE A LOCAL

Enjoy Amphoe Thalang like a local with this walking tour through cafes, shrines and street-food sanctuaries.

START	END	LENGTH
Bloom Espresso	Wat Phra Nang Sang	2.4km; two hours

Discover Tambol Thep Krasatti with this Thalang walking tour, setting out early in the morning at 1 **Bloom Espresso** (p524). Husband-wife duo Maen and Phrae run this cafe hidden on Th Thonsai Waterfall, serving smash burgers and chocolatey dark-roast Arabica coffee from Chiang Rai. Then, stop down the road at the conspicuously yellow 2 **San Chao Namtok Ton Sai**, a sacred shrine guarded by Na Ja, the Chinese patron god of children. Feeling a surge of energy after visiting one of the many shrines in Phuket – an island with more shrines than temples – swing into 3 **Th Ao Ek Vanit** and follow the locals. Nurses slam the doors of their cars, construction workers walk past as smoke billows from charcoal stoves, and mums, with kids wedged between them, park their scooters amid the chaos. On this 350m-long strip with some 20 pedlars, you can stock up on sticky calorie bombs wrapped in banana leaves before slurping a mango shake at 4 **Malay Tea** after the right bend. Then, cool off at the air-conditioned 5 **Lotus Thalang** mall and visit 6 **Da Laht Ruam Jai** in front of Lotus. At this market, held Tuesday, Thursday and Sunday evenings, you can fuel up for crossing the bridge that straddles the congested Th Thepkrasattri. End at 7 **Wat Phra Nang Sang**, which translates as 'temple built by a lady', and admire murals of Thalang's history.

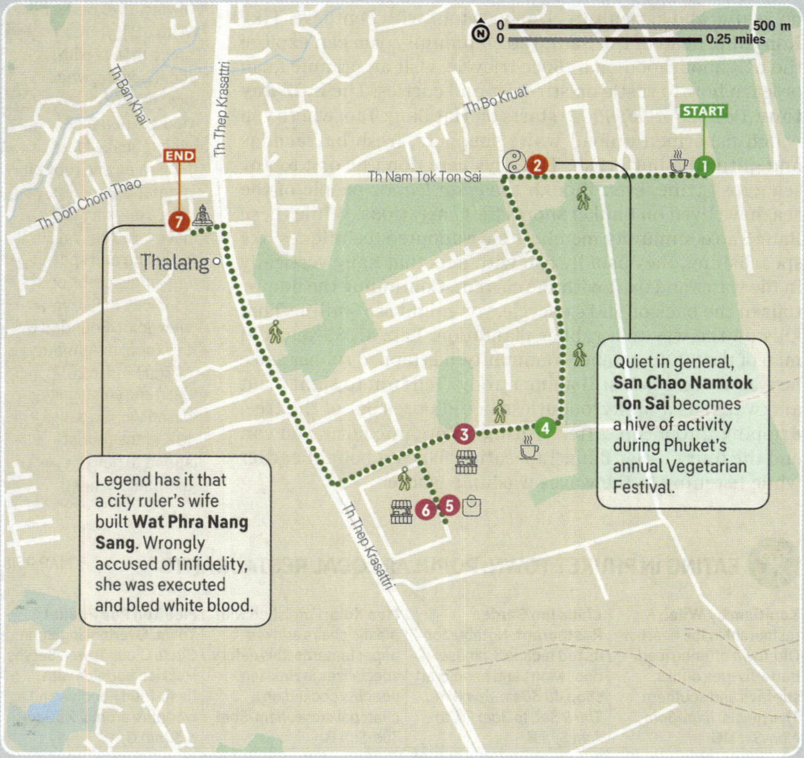

0 500 m
0 0.25 miles
Th Ban Khai
Th Thep Krasattri
Th Bo Kruat
START
END
Th Nam Tok Ton Sai
Th Don Chom Thao
Thalang
Th Thep Krasattri

Quiet in general, **San Chao Namtok Ton Sai** becomes a hive of activity during Phuket's annual Vegetarian Festival.

Legend has it that a city ruler's wife built **Wat Phra Nang Sang**. Wrongly accused of infidelity, she was executed and bled white blood.

Hit Phuket's Night Markets

MAP P516 & P518

Eat fresh, low-priced Phuketian food

Stroll along white marquee tents, and you'll catch the tantalising scents of sticky calorie bombs on the evening breeze. People aren't jostling you; there's enough space and vendors selling golden tuna spring rolls and sticky rice in bamboo tubes live up to the meaning of **Da Laht Ruam Jai**, or 'market of the joined hearts'. Open each Tuesday, Thursday and Sunday from 4.30pm to 9pm in front of Thalang's Lotus mall, this market is a quieter alternative to Phuket's big hitters in and around the Old Town. To get here, you can hop on the **Smart Bus** *(phuketsmartbus.com; 100฿)* at one of Phuket's west-coast beaches and get off at Ban Khian, which is a 15-minute walk from the market.

A must-do for many, however, is the **Lard Yai Sunday Night Market** *(tourismthailand.org/Shop/phuket-walking-street; 4-11pm Sun)* in the centre of Phuket Old Town. Beautifully lit, the historic shophouses that frame **Th Thalang** add visual appeal to this vibrant walking street, where culinary wonders meet local crafts. Wandering aimlessly, you can dig into meats grilled on skewers, only to be greeted by local sweets like *ka nom beu ang*, a crispy pancake with coconut cream and sweet shredded coconut. Apart from food, the stalls offer a splendid variety of handicrafts and clothes, while live music and manora dance shows add cultural appeal. Getting here can be wallet-friendly too. Convenient and dirt-cheap at 50฿, the old **blue bus** *(phuket101.net/phuket-blue-bus)* operates between Patong's Jungceylon shopping mall and Phuket Town.

You can also find a festive atmosphere at **Da Laht Chillva**, a colourful shipping-container market in Phuket Town, close to Central shopping mall. To get to this arty market popular with the younger crowd, you can ride the blue bus to Old Town and then flag down a motorcycle taxi. Open from Monday to Saturday from 5pm to 11pm, Chillva has many fashion and souvenir stalls, as well as street food and live music, of course.

Embrace Your Inner Artist

MAP P518

Pottery-making at Green Grey

Wedge, roll out, sculpt and kiln some clay – your noodle bowl or cup of joe back home is only a workshop away. Kru Wut, the artist behind **Art Studio Green Grey** *(adult/child per hr 500/300฿; 10am-5pm)*, has studied and worked in ceramics for over 20 years. In a two- or three-hour workshop, he

PHUKET'S VEGETARIAN FESTIVAL

Every autumn, Taoists flock to Phuket Town to take part in the Vegetarian Festival. The festival honours the Nine Emperor Gods who emerged 400 years ago. But locals worship thousands of others who are the product of 3000 years of history, including musicians, doctors, businessmen and soldiers. That's why you see musical instruments and war-like objects during the processions thrust through cheeks of devotees. It's not for the faint of heart. Yet walking barefoot on burning coals or climbing ladders with razor-sharp blades is a fascinating spectacle. This festival celebrates spiritual cleansing, good karma and health through deprivation, self-mutilation and fire, all representing the dichotomy between opposing forces embraced by Taoism. See *tourismthailand.org* for details.

EATING IN PHUKET: TRENDY RESTAURANTS

MAP P516 & P518

Three Monkeys Restaurant: This thatched-hut restaurant overlooking the jungle focuses on quality, with a menu that tours the globe. *10am-1am* ฿฿

Dinner in the Sky Phuket: Duck breast topped with miso carrot puree and cranberry sauce is a culinary delight, but in the sky? Out of this world. *10am-10pm* ฿฿฿

Bucha Gallery and Restaurant: Gold tones, reflecting floors, lit walls mimicking shadow puppetry, and delicious food. *11am-10pm Tue-Sun* ฿฿

NumNum Old Town Cafe & Restaurant: Turkish *raki* and Thai staples, including *dom yam gung*, await at this Old Town restaurant. *10am-10pm* ฿฿

COOL ART WORKSHOPS IN PHUKET

Phuket Painting Class: Offers art classes for all levels, teaching oil painting on canvas and watercolour painting.

SiTao Studio Art Cafe: Throw clay on the wheel and paint your heart out at this art cafe offering ceramic pottery and canvas painting.

I-Mon Art Gallery: Two-storey gallery offering hand-carved wood ink art and linocut printmaking workshops.

Bless Art Gallery: Located close to Rang Hill, this art school for kids and adults offers watercolour painting and acrylic painting on canvas.

Someday Cafe Phuket: Decorate cookies, make jewellery and more. Caffeine and creativity are the driving forces at this art cafe.

walks you through ceramic-shaping techniques like sculpting, while ideas and designs are left to the power of your imagination. So unleash your inner artist and hone your creativity; the sky is the limit. Showing you how to roll out clay for varying items, he also elaborates on firing and resulting colour palettes. With all that squeezing, squashing, kneading and glazing, kids have as much fun as adults. The first hour is for sculpting and designing your piece, and the second is for painting and the finishing touches. Depending on the complexity of your design, a third hour may be required. To make a booking, call or text Wut on Whatsapp (065 516 4565) or message him on Facebook. Note that you can't take your creation home right away. It must be kilned twice; it can be shipped worldwide in a fortnight.

Sunset Cocktails & Fire Shows

MAP P516

Go beach clubbing at Flamingo

Fire artists spin burning ropes in a daredevil show that bristles with high-temperature intensity, while pumping beats in time with the performance turn up the heat, doused only by the waves washing ashore. Fiery excitement awaits at **Flamingo Beach Club** *(bandaragroup.com/bandara-beach-phuket/flamingo; free entry; 10am-10pm)* on Saturday evenings at 7.30pm, provided it doesn't rain. Either way, you can swing a leg as a DJ spins tunes on Saturdays. The beach club is snuggled into Ao Yon near Cape Panwa, and has more than a fire show to make you ooh and aah. From hemp ropes and bamboo-woven lanterns to Burmese ironwood tables and cushioned rattan chairs, Flamingo's design values are eye-popping. You could easily spend the whole day at this cosy beach club. Happy hours are from 4.30pm to 6.30pm. To soak up the swanky lounge vibe – epitomised by Manu Chao's 'Me Gustas Tu' – slump into a beanbag that swallows you up, and sip a mojito while the coco palms keep swaying unperturbed.

Reconnect at Jungala Phuket

MAP P516

Meditation and holistic healing

You're lying on your back. A towel covers your eyes as a therapist is coming closer, gently striking a Himalayan singing bowl. As if that didn't deepen relaxation, the sound healer tilts an ocean drum. Tiny beads cascade down its surface, mimicking rushing waves that hush as they meet the sand before retracting back into the ocean. Besides sound baths,

DRINKING IN PHUKET: QUIRKY CAFES

MAP P516

Booktree Library & Cafe: Thousands of books, swing chairs and fruits in your morning brew – this cafe is super-peaceful. *8am-5pm*

Bloom Espresso: A cosy, open-sided cafe that serves smash burgers and dark roast Arabica coffee from Chiang Rai. *7.30am-5pm Sun-Fri*

Witthaya Home Brewing: Wooden benches inside a family home, an in-house guitar and chocolatey dark roast coffee. *8am-5pm*

Cafe Kantary: Sea views and a glass-enclosed porch, plus irresistible brownies and Vietnamese drip coffee made at your table. *8am-11pm*

NIRAD/SHUTTERSTOCK

Phuket-style Hokkien noodles

greenery-surrounded **Jungala Phuket** *(jungalaphuket.com; 550-1900฿)* offers yoga classes, chakra awareness meditation and other powerful therapies to promote healing and relaxation. Sound bath meditation classes are on Tuesdays and Fridays from 5.30pm to 6.30pm. Bookings are only required for private 60-minute sessions. Hop on the Smart Bus to reach this Rawai-based studio. It's open daily.

A Magical Evening Show

MAP P516

Siam Niramit Phuket

Yawning, a young man scoops out water from a river, pouring it over himself as a rooster crows in the background. His father guides a buffalo, which ploughs a muddy rice field, and a woman wearing a wraparound skirt pops out of nowhere. Hold it right there. Have you stepped into a time machine? This is a traditional country scene from Thailand in the 1900s. Transporting you there – immersing you so deeply you feel as though you're in the scene – is the intention of the organisers of **Siam Niramit Phuket** *(siamniramitphuket.com; adult/child 1800/1600฿; 5.30-10.30pm)*. Packed with elements of surprise, Siam Niramit Phuket uses a 300-cubic-metre water tank and pumping systems to make a river materialise on stage. Likewise, to make angels fly gracefully across the stage,

PHUKET'S LOCAL MEALS

Unknown in most regions of Thailand, uniquely Phuketian food is based on ethnic diversity, offering an intriguing mix of cuisines that capture the island's tin-mining history. Thai people and Chinese Peranakans love chewy Hokkien noodles and dim sum – scrumptious, bite-sized morsels of fried or steamed pork dumplings. Muslims go for *rodee*, which are pancakes that come in a mouthwatering variety of sweet tastes. Those who hail from the south of Thailand swear by sour fish soups and crispy rice salads packed with savoury flavours. Arguably the most Phuketian dessert is *oh aew*, a jelly-based treat with shaved ice flavoured with sugar syrup and topped with sugar corn, red beans and perfectly sized watermelon balls.

EATING IN PHUKET OLD TOWN: VEGAN FOOD

MAP P516 & P518

Vegetarian Restaurant Nong J: A vegan restaurant dishing up curries, soups and spicy salads at reasonable prices. *9am-9pm Mon-Sat* ฿

Vegan Table: Meals at this top vegan restaurant include homemade falafels with hummus and freshly baked pita bread. *noon-10pm* ฿฿

Vegan Phuket: Serves plant-based meat, curries and coconut soups. You can eat your food on the terrace and catch some rays. *10.30am-8pm Thu-Tue* ฿฿

O-Oh Farm Suanluang: Near King Rama IX Park, this spot offers vegan options, including avocado tomato toast and healthy salads. *7am-9pm* ฿฿

HOLISTIC MEDICINE CLINICS

Mangosteen Ayurveda & Wellness: Overlooking Ko Bon, this resort boasts an in-house Ayurvedic doctor, yoga, detox options and wellness escapes.

Thanyapura Sports & Health Resort: Thanyapura has a health centre with packages like active detox. A doctor can customise alternative medicines.

Holistic Harmony: This aptly named health centre offers a range of therapies, from hypnotherapy and chakra balancing to osteopathy.

Anantara Mai Khao Phuket Villas: This five-star haven has a spa offering chakra crystal balancing; vitamin and mineral IV drips are available at the clinic.

Sole Mio Phuket: Treatments from redcord suspension therapy to weight management. On Hat Bang Tao.

FSENDEK/SHUTTERSTOCK

Siam Niramit Phuket (p525)

backstage crew members operate a pulley system. Lightning, smoke, thunder and rain are an explosion of special effects as actors retrace the history of Siam, including Thai mythology, Buddhist heaven and hell, the rise and fall of kingdoms, and Thai festivals like Songkran and Loy Krathong. Thai boxing fights are staged with punches, axe-like knees and ultrafast kicks. Performers also play music, picking someone from the audience who ends up playing a clapper-like instrument on the 70m-long, 5000-sq-metre stage. Don't even try to shoot photographs during the 80-minute, wheelchair-accessible show, or laser beams instantly target your phone. Included in the ticket is a pre-show at the 100-year-old on-site Thai village, where you can tuck into northern Thai meals or watch *nang da lung* (shadow puppetry). Shadow puppets are set against a screen, accompanied by traditional Thai music and the voice of a performer who spins yarns, sings and laughs. Positive vibes are palpable throughout the premises, not least because of transgender people clad in feather boas. You can add buffet dinner (400฿) and even hotel pick-up (350฿) to your booking, because getting to Th Ratchakan Thi 9 without a scooter or car is virtually impossible. Visit and you'll be enthralled for hours.

DRINKING IN PHUKET: SWANKY BARS

MAP P516

Baba Nest: Situated at Cape Panwa, this bar is so popular you can only snag a seat if you email *fb@sripanwa.com* a month in advance. *5-8pm*

Moon Terrace Lounge Kata Rooftop Restaurant: Part of Metadee Concept Hotel, this rooftop bar has international and local meals. *5.30-11pm*

Aqua Bar: Natural stone and hints of Art Deco characterise this stylish poolside bar inside Como Point Yamu. Cocktails, smoothies and juices available. *9am-11pm*

Alto Italian Restaurant & Cocktail Bar: Alto serves Italian delicacies like meat balls potato salad with pesto. *6-10pm*

ROAM THE STREETS OF THE OLD TOWN

Discover the iconic shophouses of Phuket and glimpse the bygone days of tin barons on this Old Town walking tour.

START	END	LENGTH
cnr Th Thalang & Th Thepkasattri	On On Hotel	1.13km; 2½ hours

Dive into a bounty of colours on a sunny morning in the Old Town, the home of tin tycoons in the early 20th century. The area abounds with bewitching row houses repurposed as bars, cafes, galleries and souvenir shops. Set out from the Th Thalang-Thep Krasattri intersection and fuel up with a flaky pancake at 1 **Aroon Restaurant** (p520), locally known as the *Rodee* King. Snap away as you wander westward on Th Thalang, lined with purple, barbie-pink and pastel-green shophouses. Then swing into 2 **Soi Romanee** on your right, once a street where sex workers waited for tin labourers. Today, with its rose-coloured buildings and countless cafes, the street is a popular photo spot. At 3 **Rush Coffee**, roasting professional Parinya 'Tong' Yanpisitkul serves nitro cold brew on tap like beer. Around the corner is 4 **Wat Mongkhon Nimit**, its golden roof glinting in the sun. Just as eye-popping are the 5 **murals of King Bhumibol** further west on Th Dibuk. The 'Sino-Portugueseness' of a striking turquoise building jumps out at you at the 6 **Th Yaowarat-Dibuk junction**. Also conspicuous are the slogans on paint rollers at 7 **Mr Zen Art Studio**. Pause for an aromatherapy reward at 8 **Xin Massage** or make a beeline for 9 **Memory at On On Hotel** (p586) on Th Phangnga. Far from the shabby hostel where DiCaprio starred in *The Beach*, it's now a sight to behold.

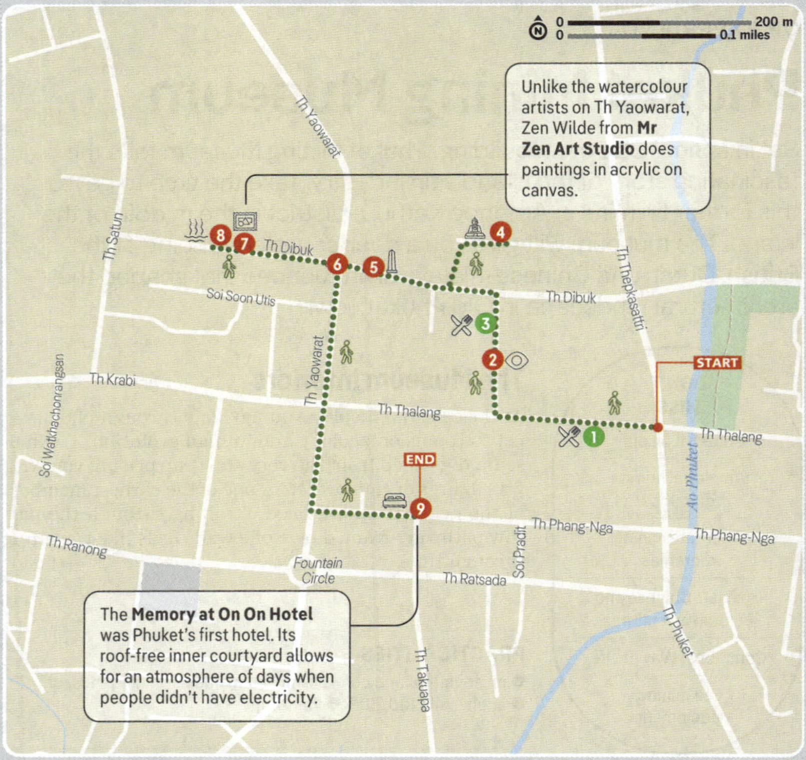

KITTICHAI CHUMANEE/SHUTTERSTOCK

TOP EXPERIENCE

Phuket Mining Museum

Set in a Sino-European building, Phuket Mining Museum tells the fascinating story of the island's tin industry. Take the time to get to this former tin mine in Amphoe Kathu, a district in the middle of the island. The museum will give you a deeper understanding of the British, Dutch and Chinese-Malaysian influences that shaped the architectural landscape in Old Phuket Town.

DON'T MISS

- Celestial display
- Ancestral human dioramas
- Alternate mining dioramas
- Hokkien-Chinese and Peranakan cultures
- Communal Way of Life
- Old mining equipment

The Museum Interiors

At the celestial display, you navigate through planets to get to rooms on geology and human evolution. The museum digs deep from the very start, surprising you with wax figures of *Homo habilis,* one of the earliest members of the genus *Homo*. Indeed, strolling through the narrow pathways framed by stone walls feels like travelling through time.

PRACTICALITIES

- museumthailand.com/en/museum/Phuket-Mining-Museum_2
- adult/child 100/50฿ • 9am-4pm

Further models, which look deceptively real, await at exhibits chock-full of information on mining techniques, including drifting, ground sluicing, open-cut mining, hydraulic mining or open-pit mining techniques like gravel pumping, where mines use bulldozers or explosives. These quirky exhibits are as fun as they are educational. Interesting audio and visual presentations hide at every corner. A dredge-mining operation is staged with bucket ladder dredges, which could dig up ore-containing underwater soil before spouting it down into a drop chute.

The staggering mix of archaeology, machinery and technology continues in the mineral dressing room, where cassiterite, a source of tin, is informatively on show. After working your way through a series of rooms, cross the jetty and get swallowed by the hull of a sailing ship. As you set foot in the next section, Chinese culture gradually unfolds.

A Legacy That Lives On

The demand for tin skyrocketed in the early 20th century, with the realisation that no one could win wars with only weapons. Discovering that cans allowed food to be stored for months, Europeans eagerly wanted tin, kicking off the heyday of the 'black gold'. Tin mining required huge labour forces. Five hundred people who would dig and carry had to be employed in a single tin mine, and few Thai workers were available because King Rama V had abolished slavery. Hence, they needed people from southeast China. Drawn by the tin fever, these Hokkien-Chinese, originally from Fujian, flocked to Phuket to escape China's civil war.

Through their involvement in the tin industry, Phuket's first Chinese immigrants who'd relocated from Singapore, Penang and Malacca became incredibly wealthy. These immigrants, who'd been in Phuket much longer, owned rather than worked in the mines.

Lots of the affluent Chinese immigrants married local women, paving the way for a mixed-blood Peranakan ethnicity. Also called Baba Nyonya, these affluent, Phuket-born people looked down on Chinese workers who arrived in droves from China's southeastern coast. Unlike the Phuket Babas, the mine workers escaped their harsh realities by resorting to gambling, hanging out in opium dens and meeting sex workers.

Gambling and opium smoking come to life in the museum's Communal Way of Life section, where figures of opium addicts on beds taking deep pulls at pipes will catch your eye. This section also tells the story of tin barons and showcases arched windows, paper lanterns, swing doors as well as marble-topped teak tables and dark chocolate-coloured furniture in typically Victorian style.

Another nook of the museum beautifully portrays the enjoyment that ethnic Chinese took in playing the game of Sam-kok.

A SIGHT FOR SORE EYES

Visually appealing both inside and out, the museum spans a whopping 400 *rai* (640,000 sq metres) and comprises several themed sections. Starting with ancient photographs, minerals and money, the connected galleries lead to zones that detail the mining process from ore to ingot. A reminder of the wealth that resulted from tin mining, the most intriguing area dives into Peranakan and Hokkien-Chinese culture.

TOP TIPS

- Allow three hours for marvelling at the museum's top sights.
- Visitors should bring their own water, as there are no restaurants inside the museum.
- Check out the Communal Way of Life section: it introduces visitors to the fascinating world of multicultural interior styles and immigration to Phuket.
- Study the picture archives and models in colourful Peranakan clothes – you'll recognise the Dutch influence in the white shirts.

CYCLE TOUR

Pedalling Ko Yao Noi

In-the-know cyclists ride around Ko Yao Noi, a peaceful island near Phuket. The inland is bedecked with millions of hectares of deep green woodland. Along its coastal road, you'll find little more than mangroves interspersed with fishing hamlets on stilts, plus a few beaches washed by the green-tinted water of Ao Phang-Nga. Rent a bicycle at Tha Manoh pier or join a one-day cycling tour *(feelphuket.com)*.

1 Tha Manoh

After a 45-minute boat ride aboard a longtail and endless views of the limestone rocks that dot the sea, kick off your cycling adventure at Tha Manoh, Ko Yao Noi's southwestern pier. Pick a bicycle and set off on your own, or meet Feel Phuket's guide, who will brief you about the day ahead.

The Cycle: Ride straight before turning left after Sabai Reggae Bar. Head north towards the village of Ko Yao Noi.

2 Ko Yao Noi Village

Get off your bike and enter Ko Yao Noi village. Get the flavour of local life before climbing back on your bicycle. Cycle past open-sided *rodee* restaurants serving halal meals and sweet banana pancakes. A fruit and vegetable market bustles during the day, beckoning with lychee-like longan.

The Cycle: Scoot north then veer off the main road and ride through rice paddies.

ADAM HOGLUND/SHUTTERSTOCK

3 Rong na Cafe & Restaurant

Stop for a fresh coconut at this airy brick-style cafe and restaurant surrounded by a garden sprawling with lush vegetation. Beyond the farm cafe is a patchwork of rice fields that glisten in the late-morning sun, wrapped in a verdant hug of the surrounding hillscapes. The scenery is particularly photogenic from July to December, when everything is green. After enjoying the gentle breeze and fuelling up with yet another refreshing sip of coconut juice, get back on your bike.

The Cycle: Pedal for about 2km along the narrow coastal road.

4 Ban An Pao

Stop in the village of Ban An Pao and gain perspective on life. Here locals living in ramshackle huts on stilts make a living from fishing and rice farming, unfazed by 21st-century conveniences.

The Cycle: Double back south then head east across the island to Hat Tha Khao.

5 Takao Beach Bar

After riding roughly 14km in the morning, pause for lunch at this beach bar on Hat Tha Khao. Eat classic fried rice with chicken, slurp a watermelon shake or quaff a Thai mojito or two. Depending on the tide, take a dip in the bath-warm sea or grab a beach chair. Karst islets off the coast are scattered like corals on the sea floor.

The Cycle: Cycle 5km southward along a gentle, paved route.

6 Hat Pasai

Looking out over karst islets and Krabi beyond, the next stop is a gently sloping stretch of sand fringed by palms, entirely free of sun loungers and beach vendors. End with Thai food and creature comforts at the southern end of the beach. *Sawadee krap!* Cycle west to return to Tha Manoh.

Ranong

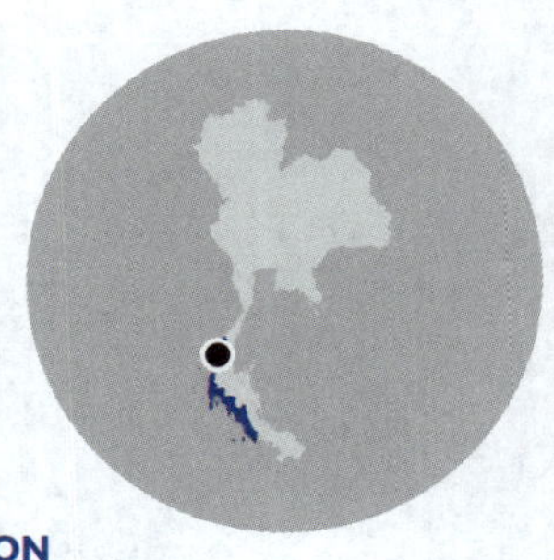

NATURAL WONDERS | HIPPIE ISLANDS | SECLUSION

TOP TIP

If you have a scooter in Ranong, and are looking to travel to Ko Phayam, you can have the scooter transported via slow boat from Tha Thai Kak (200฿). You can then join your scooter in Ko Phayam via a tuk-tuk ride (50฿) to Tha Ranong and a speedboat to the island (350฿).

With its proximity to Myanmar's far-southern tip and the Kawthoung–Ranong sea crossing, it's little surprise that in Ranong city you see so many Burmese people, easily recognised by the Thanaka powder on their cheeks. The northernmost province on the Andaman Coast, Ranong also attracts a growing number of travellers who've heard of the nouveau hippie islands of Ko Phayam and Ko Chang. Both a province and a city, Ranong is the least populated and wettest region of Thailand. Its rainy season can last up to eight months, but that's precisely why Ranong's scenery is awash with lush forests and misty mountaintops. Street markets in the provincial capital are engines of local economic growth, while hot springs and spectacular waterfalls create a paradise for nature lovers. Complete with Sino-European buildings that nod to the bygone days of tin barons, the port town of Ranong is a city worth plotting on your itinerary.

GETTING AROUND

You can drive a car or ride a scooter from Phang-Nga to Ranong, but be aware that a 100km section of Motorway 4 doesn't have street lights. Boats cross from Kawthoung (Myanmar) to Tha Saphan Plaa at Pak Nam's Ranong Fishery Port Office. A shared ride in a long-tail boat costs 100฿. The boat captain will show you to the immigration post on either side of the Kra Buri Estuary – make sure you have a visa. Ranong's bus station, off Rte 4, is 2km southeast of downtown. Rent push bikes in downtown Ranong or cover it on foot. The region's main sights are spread out, so hail a cab or flag down a *songthaew* if rental scooters and cars aren't your preference. The shared pick-up taxis run all day and charge 10฿ for short rides and 20฿ for longer rides.

HIGHLIGHTS
1 Nam Tok Ngao
2 Taryn Hot Springs

SIGHTS
3 Khao Fa Chi Viewpoint
4 Khao Kho Ma Viewpoint
5 Ko Kam
6 Phu Khao Ya
7 Ranong Lighthouse
8 Wat Sai Daeng

SLEEPING
9 A Day Inn Ranong Hostel
10 Sook Hotel
11 Yes No Hotel

DRINKING & NIGHTLIFE
12 12 Cafe Bakery
13 Gachu cashew&cafe
14 Piti Poolside by Phutararesort
15 Pon's Place

TRANSPORT
16 Bus Terminal
17 Tha Ranong
18 Tha Saphan Plaa

The Natural Wonders of Ranong

Soak in hot springs

Rich in minerals like sodium, calcium, potassium and bicarbonate, **Taryn Hot Springs** *(facebook.com/tarynhotsprings; 150฿; 7am-8pm)* are excellent pain and stress relievers. The 43°C pool isn't the hottest in the area, some 8km south of Ranong town, but low-key Taryn corner offers some serious relaxation and is just a 10-minute *songthaew* or scooter ride from the town. On site are four hot outdoor pools with roofs. You can also find three cooler ones, which are still over 30°C. Families can splash about in the lap pool. There's a changing room plus a cafe serving food and drinks from noon. The entrance fee includes a swimsuit, towel and locker, and you can nab biscuits or help yourself at the water dispenser.

Nine kilometres south on Motorway 4 is another regional highlight: **Nam Tok Ngao** *(portal.dnp.go.th; adult/child/car/motorcycle 100/50/30/20฿)*. This tiered waterfall gushes down a 300m-high wall of rock, feeding shallow, milky-grey pools. The best spot for a cooling respite is the run-off near

MOST SCENIC SPOTS AROUND RANONG

Ranong Lighthouse: Attractive pier with a scenic lighthouse and views of Myanmar beyond the Kra Buri River.

Khao Fa Chi Viewpoint: Rambling vistas of Thailand, Myanmar and the river separating the two countries await.

Ko Kam: A white, casuarina-lined beach and emerald water, plus a viewpoint from which to survey this beauty.

Khao Kho Ma Viewpoint: A lookout near the Myanmar border with a campground, nature trail and hotel all on site.

Wat Sai Daeng: This hillside temple has murals that depict the Buddha's life. The exterior is reminiscent of tiered Shan-Burmese style.

MR_GATEWAY/SHUTTERSTOCK

Phu Khao Ya

the base – accessible via a paved, 500m-long path with 113 steps and tourist information signs on flora and fauna. As well as a viewpoint overlooking Ranong, there's a welfare shop, guesthouse and helipad, should you want to splash out. The best way to get here is by rented motorbike, because the shared pick-up taxis drop you off on Motorway 4, several hundred metres from the ticket booth.

Have a Peaceful Picnic

Climb for views

You'd think picnicking is all about food. Far from it! Well, not here. Located some 8.5km south of Ranong city, the peaceful grass hill of **Phu Khao Ya** *(077 502775; free; 5am-6pm)* is about jaw-dropping views. Look towards the east, and you can see the sheer size of Nam Tok Ngao, which is 500m above sea level. The picnic spot at the end of the road that branches off Rte 4 is surrounded by grass. Brown from November to April and deep green in the wet season from May to October, the hill changes its colours with the seasons. Rent a car or scooter in Ranong to get here. Phu Khao Ya isn't well signposted, but travelling from Nam Tok Ngao turn left at the crab statue. Bring what you need; there are no facilities.

DRINKING IN RANONG: CAFES

Pon's Place: Delicious baguettes, mocha cakes, dim sum as well as smoothies, teas and iced Chang beer at this hole-in-the-wall cafe. *7.30am-8pm*

Gachu cashew&cafe: Coffee shop that specialises in pastries, Thai staples and cashew smoothies with oat milk. *8am-5pm Mon-Fri, from 9am Sat & Sun*

Piti Poolside by Phutararesort: Part of Phutara Resort Ranong. Has confectionary, amazing bean juice and a La Marzocco coffee machine. *9am-9pm*

12 Cafe Bakery: Waffles, quality coffee and decor like a cool old Vespa scooter. This modern take on coffee and tea invites you to linger. *8.30am-6pm*

Beyond Ranong

Ko Phayam and Ko Chang are two hippie islands with easygoing vibes and quiet beaches backed by bamboo bungalows.

Secluded slices of sand flanked by beach huts and casuarinas, lanes flanked by rubber trees and squillions of hippie joints – welcome to Ko Phayam, Thailand's last island paradise. Sure, the island facing Myanmar is no longer a secret, but its old-style ethos remains. Back-to-basics travellers are fine being partly off the electricity grid and taking cold showers. There are no convenience stores with ding-dong doorbells and coconut trees are higher than buildings. Ko Phayam's residents, some of who are Moken people, live cheek by jowl with hornbills, monkeys and sea eagles. If that sounds remote, wait till you see neighbouring Ko Chang, a mellow-life island for rough-sleeping visitors.

GETTING AROUND

Speedboats from Tha Ranong (p532) whisk you off to Tha Ko Phayam in 45 minutes. Slow boats departing from Ranong's Tha Tai Kak take two hours. With barely 2m-wide lanes, Ko Phayam is car-free. You can rent a scooter. Walking distances are long; motorcycle taxis cost 60฿ to 80฿. Long-tail boats bound for Ko Chang depart from Tha Tai Kak in the high season. Only the 9.30am boat departs Ranong in low season, when it's best to check *ranongferry.com*.

Ko Phayam & Ko Chang

TIME FROM RANONG: **45MIN TO KO PHAYAM**

Beach-hopping in hippie havens

It's not simply white sand-beaches that Ko Phayam and Ko Chang bring to the table. The appeal of the islands' unspoilt half moons of sand resides in their castaway feel. Hidden away in a cove south of Ao Yai on Kho Phayam, **Hat Palm** is one of the area's best-kept secrets. Rocky at low tide, the beach, with its light-brown sand and a coral reef, is all yours more often than not – except for long-tailed macaques and Palm Beach Restaurant, which offers Thai food and ice-cold Chang and Leo. To get to this former pirate cove fringed by more coastal trees than palms, head for **Ao Ko-Kyu** but continue straight when you see the last 100m of the sandy road leading up to Ao Ko-Kyu's parking spot. At low tide, you can ride almost onto Hat Palm. Ao Ko-Kyu is another rocky cove. Pull

DRINKING IN KO PHAYAM: CAFES

T-Rex: Situated close to the pier, this cafe serves muesli and hot and iced coffee as well as pancakes and Thai staples. *8am-5pm*

Fan's Homemade: With cappuccinos, crunchy rice paper rolls and views of the pier, this cosy cafe makes you feel at home. *7.30am-5.30pm*

Coffee and Resort: Served lovingly on bamboo trays, the coffee tastes particularly nice in this garden setting, and three-fold cushions invite you to linger. *8am-9pm*

Japanese Bakery: From sourdough salmon sandwiches to moka pot coffee, this reasonably priced cafe is worth a visit. *8am-5pm Mon-Sat*

ATTRACTIONS ON KO CHANG

Wat Phra Yai Luang Pho Thamchai: Climb the stairs framed by *naga* snakes to reach a golden Buddha in a lotus-shaped structure overlooking an unnamed beach.

Moken People Village: Tucked away on the northeastern tip of Ko Chang, this village is home to Moken who live in stilted shacks.

Rubber Tree Forests: Neatly aligned rubber trees stretching away as far as the eye can see – a rarity elsewhere; not in Ko Chang.

Tha Ko Chang: The island's northeastern jetty is popular with fishermen casting their lines, dreaming of another catch.

Ao Ta Daeng: Snuggled into Ao Deng, bungalows on stilts above giant boulders and amazing sunsets are worth a photo or two.

LIGHTRECORDS/SHUTTERSTOCK

Ko Phayam (p535)

up and walk down the 101, moss-covered steps to reach the end of the world. Home to hornbills circling in cobalt skies, the coarse-grained beach has no facilities except the hilltop restaurant open in high season. There's hardly a soul in sight at **Ao Kwangpeeb**, a crescent, light-coloured beach with clear water in the north of Phayam, accessible via a sketchy track.

Offering ultimate peace and quiet, Ko Chang's **Ao Yai** is a 30-minute speedboat ride and 15-minute motorcycle-taxi ride from Phayam. Mineral-flecked and stretching for kilometres, it has only a few shacks and funky beach bars, plus a community spirit that's preserved by law.

Live by Thailand's sabai sabai motto

Ko Phayam's **Sabai Sabai Bungalows** *(sabai-bungalows.com)* is all about, you guessed it: *sabai sabai*, or being relaxed and easygoing. Whether you chill in the cushion-filled lounge or sway in a hanging canvas bed – relaxation is high at this hammock heaven run by a Thai woman and her English husband. But that's not to say you need to wait all day for a nightcap in the lounge, lit by paraffin lamps. You can also salute the sun early in the morning and do yoga. Whatever you prefer, don't miss the lively three-hour cooking class (1000฿) from 11am to 2pm. The class (maximum seven people) is available to guests and includes buying ingredients at a local market. The Sabai Sabai employee conducting the class, Wan, tells stories as he shows you the ropes. Whether you prefer the creamy, herbs-based coconut chicken soup or the spicy, holy basil chicken stir-fry, Wan encourages people to judge the food by taste, so that they can develop a repertoire of both recipes and skills.

DRINKING ON KHO PHAYAM: BARS

Hippie Bar: A maze of bamboo poles, treehouses and driftwood, this pirate-style construction is a reggae fortress with chill vibes. *10.30am-1am*

Gecko Bar: With its swings, low-slung tables and colourful plastic chairs on the sands of Ao Yai, this rustic bar is a relaxed hang-out. *7am-midnight*

Kitchen Table: Tiramisu, lasagne and homemade fettuccine pasta with sun-dried tomatoes – this place is all about Italian food. Happy hours too. *5-10pm*

Bubble Bar: Located on Ao Yai in the shade of casuarinas, this laid-back surfer bar serves wine, cocktails and Italian spirits like Amaretto. *9am-9pm*

Phang-Nga Province

BEACHES | NATURAL WONDERS | SECLUSION

With clusters of surreal islands, national parks chock-full of caves and waterfalls, and viewpoints overlooking karst islets, Phang-Nga Province is a paradise for nature lovers. But it hasn't always been a haven of tranquillity. In the 19th century, Phang-Nga experienced a trade boom when Hokkien-Chinese flocked to the province, drawn by its tin reserves. It has also endured conflicts, notably the Siamese-Burmese war, which saw people flee Phuket. These turbulent periods played key roles in birthing Phang-Nga's present-day multicultural jumble.

Legend has it Phang-Nga takes its name from Phu-Nga (coastal forest), its earlier Malay name. There is still rainforest throughout the province, and this draws travellers, as do top dive sites and snorkelling spots around the Similan and Surin Islands. Phang-Nga is quieter than Phuket, even if it was Ao Phang-Nga that played host to two James Bond movies. Bordering Phang-Nga province, Khao Sok has a jungle older than the Amazon and a lake surrounded by limestone rocks that jut hundreds of metres out of emerald water. In short, it's a cracker of a region worth several days.

Note: both the provincial capital and the province itself go by the name Phang-Nga.

TOP TIP

Visit Phang-Nga town, a lovely multicultural, cafe-dotted town where people don't honk. It's also the provincial capital and a convenient base for visits to Ao Phang-Nga, Ko Hong and the islands of Ko Yao Yai and Ko Yao Noi. Tours are bookable in town.

GETTING AROUND

Phuket International Airport is the closest in the region, while Khao Lak is an hour's drive from Phang-Nga town. A taxi ride to the town costs 1700฿ to 2100฿ from Khao Lak, and 1400฿ to 1800฿ from Phuket Airport. Minivans from Phuket Airport cost 400฿ and take you to Khao Lak in 70 minutes. Buses run from Phuket's Bus Terminal 1 and Bus Terminal 2, stopping at Phang-Nga Bus Station. You can rent a car at Phuket Airport and in Khao Lak. Rental scooters are a convenient way to get around, but wear a helmet and bring an international driver's licence – and bear in mind that roads can have potholes, even motorways. Phang-Nga town and parts of Khao Lak are walkable, but generally distances are long. Ao Phang-Nga is well serviced by long-tail boats. While you can get a private boat at Tha Surakul in Takua Thung – 2000฿ to 2500฿ per day – most people book a package tour for 1400฿ to 2900฿, promoted by virtually any hotel within a 150km radius.

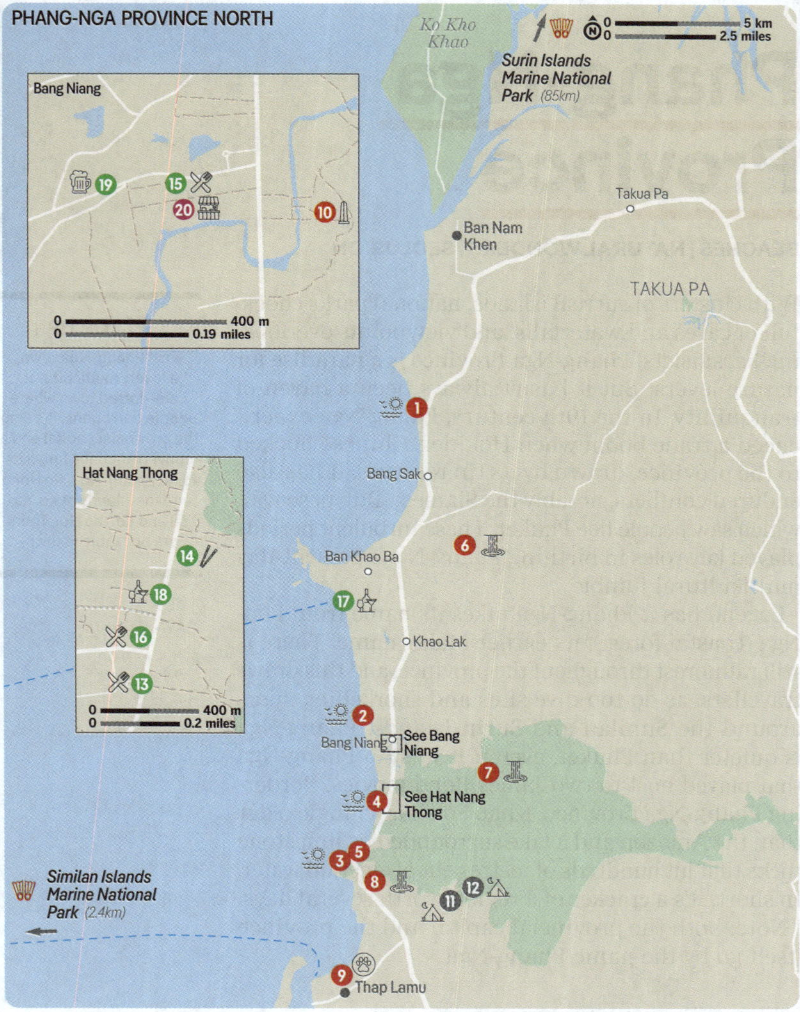

PHANG-NGA PROVINCE NORTH

Ko Kho Khao
Surin Islands Marine National Park (85km)
0 5 km
0 2.5 miles
Takua Pa
Ban Nam Khen
TAKUA PA
Bang Sak
Ban Khao Ba
Khao Lak
Bang Niang
See Bang Niang
See Hat Nang Thong
Thap Lamu
Similan Islands Marine National Park (2.4km)

Bang Niang
0 400 m
0 0.19 miles

Hat Nang Thong
0 400 m
0 0.2 miles

SIGHTS
1 Hat Bang Sak
2 Hat Khuek Khak
3 Hat Lek
4 Hat Nang Thong
5 Khao Lak/Lam Ru National Park
6 Nam Tok Sai Rung
7 Nam Tok Ton Chong Fa
8 Nam Tok Ton Pling
9 Sea Turtle Conservation Centre
10 Tsunami Boat 813

ACTIVITIES
see 11 Khao Lak Andaman ATV Bamboo Rafting

SLEEPING
11 Suanmak Camping
12 Tai Yai Camping

EATING
13 Cappadocia Turkish Restaurant
14 KhaoLak Phu View
15 Let's Eat
16 Little Italy

DRINKING & NIGHTLIFE
see 15 Gecko Bar
17 Memories Beach Bar
18 Monkey Bar
19 Moose's Pub

SHOPPING
20 Da Lant Bang Niang

Sand Between Your Toes in Khao Lak MAP P538

Visit remote beaches

A coastal town in Phang-Nga Province, Khao Lak is situated some 60km north of Phuket's Sarasin Bridge. One reason to visit is to witness the the green-tinted water slide and slosh between the jagged rocks that frame the beautiful cove of **Hat Lek**. Hidden behind the jungle near **Khao Lak-Lam Ru National Park Office** *(portal.dnp.go.th; adult/child 200/100฿; 8.30am-4.30pm)*, this small sandy beach with its tree-suspended swing is a peaceful place you might have all to yourself.

Facility-wise, there's a kiosk selling nibbles and drinks but no alcohol and no ice cream. Still, there are showers, toilets and two ways to get down to Hat Lek. On the hilltop opposite San Chao Pho Khao Lak, a shrine guarded by rooster statues, there's the national-park entrance. If you can't be bothered to scramble on all fours, don't start trekking here.

Some 500m further south on Rte 4 along a downhill curve, there's a small parking area near a hut, where an easily negotiable path begins. The 10-minute hike to the small sandy beach is a walk in the park in comparison. As an aside, the entry fee includes access to Nam Tok Ton Chong Fa (p541) further north.

A five-minute drive down the hill from San Chao Pho Khao Lak sits **Hat Nang Thong**. At this gently sloping beach safe for swimming and snorkelling, you can be at one with nature. Home to ghost crabs, lizards, birds and snakes that you're unlikely to see, this wide-open coastal area is great for beach walks, more so once the sun dips below the horizon. In the morning, though, there's barely any space to spread your towel – not because of crowds but because of high tide. Should you feel like a drink, you can find a few beach resorts here.

Likewise, **Hat Khuek Khak**, just north of Hat Bang Niang across Khuek Khak estuary, is almost deserted. Golden and coarse-grained, it lacks the sparkle of Ko Similan's powdery beaches, but it's empty no matter the tide, making it good for jogging. Restaurants with menus that tour the globe are behind the casuarina-lined beach.

Peaceful **Hat Bang Sak** has almost white sand and is situated in Amphoe Takua Pa. Wear water shoes as protection against shells, corals and rocks, and accept that there are sea lice and jellyfish. The three restaurants dishing up fresh seafood along the shore make up for any difficulties.

ATTRACTIONS AROUND KHAO LAK

Sea Turtle Conservation Centre: Green turtles of all sizes live or grow here before being released into the sea.

Da Laht Bang Niang: This market just off Rte 4 has everything you could possibly need – from quick bites and souvenirs to dry bags.

Tsunami Boat 813: Swept inland over 2km, this police boat was found right here.

Nam Tok Sai Rung: Best visited in the rainy season, this waterfall feeds a pool that's fine for a dip.

Ko Kho Khao: A quick long-tail boat ride from Tha Ban Nam Khem, this peaceful islet has quiet beaches stretching for kilometres.

EATING IN KHAO LAK: RESTAURANTS MAP P538

KhaoLak Phu View: Offering a free shuttle, this hilltop spot overlooking both jungle and sea serves *massaman* soups and *pat tai*. *10am-10pm* ฿

Little Italy: With pizzas, pastas and homemade mushroom ravioli, this place is an Italian heaven. Meat lovers can feast on Australian Angus sirloin. *11am-8pm* ฿฿

Let's Eat: Besides chicken schnitzel, the Hungarian owner offers authentic pork goulash with mashed potato. Near Da Laht Bang Niang. *5-10pm Mon-Sat* ฿฿

Cappadocia Turkish Restaurant: Dine on Turkish flatbread with marinated chicken topped with mozzarella, onions, tomato and capsicum. *11am-11pm* ฿฿

SIGHTS
1 Ao Tho Li Viewpoint
2 James Bond Island
3 Ko Panyi
4 Nam Tok Lampi
5 Nam Tok Ton Phrai
6 Wat Tham Tapan

ACTIVITIES
7 Tham Lot
8 Tham Phanak
9 Tham Phung Chang

DRINKING & NIGHTLIFE
10 2495 Coffee Wangmorkaeng
11 Baan Suan Gong
12 Makalong Cafe
13 Umber Coffee

TRANSPORT
14 Bus Station
15 Tha Surakul

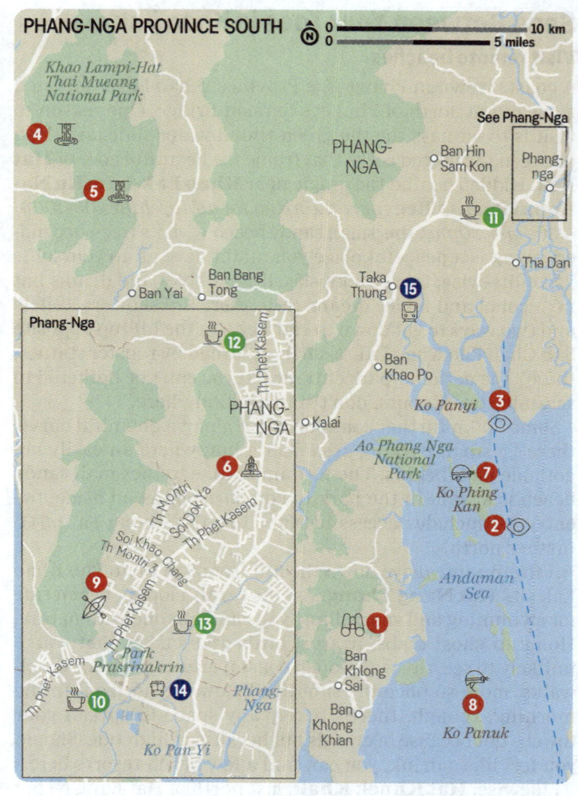

Camping in Khao Lak

MAP P538

Recharge your batteries

A 20-minute scooter ride from Bang La On township – Khao Lak stretches from Lam Kaen to Ban Nam Khem – **Suanmak Camping** *(089 725 4646)* offers plenty of relaxation on weekdays (it can get loud at the weekend, when Thais come to party). Enjoy morning walks along the banks of the Lam Ru Yai stream, lounge in hammocks for hours or kayak up and down the stream. The stream is fine for a dip, though beware the bamboo rafts glide down it. Needless to say, pythons, green

DRINKING IN KHAO LAK: BARS

MAP P538

Gecko Bar: Popular with expats and tourists, this relaxed Bang Niang bar is about meeting people while playing games like foosball or pool. *5pm-3am*

Memories Beach Bar: Between waves, chill and eat at this cool Hat Khuek Khak beach bar, where surfboards grace the wall. *9am-11pm*

Monkey Bar: Situated on Th Phet Kasem, this neon-lit bar is a good place to sip cocktails and to enjoy live music and happy hours. *3pm-1am*

Moose's Pub: The brick wall, lighting and chatty atmosphere make this pub ideal for a casual night out, with bottled beers and Guinness on tap. *4pm-1am*

vipers and mangrove snakes are around, but they're usually coiled up on a tree during daytime. Wake up to birdsong in the morning in one of the tents and bamboo bungalows that are available for rent. If you don't ride a scooter, *songthaew* and taxis run out here. Pitching your own tent in the shelter of a bamboo pavilion costs 150฿ per night. Calling might not be the best idea unless you speak Thai, but you'll find a way to communicate once you rock up. Prices are in the hundreds; the atmosphere is in the millions.

Other notable camping operators include **Tai Yai Camping**, a family-friendly campsite with rooms and tents with pillows, blankets and sleeping mats, run by a mother and daughter duo. **Khao Lak Andaman ATV Bamboo Rafting** is peaceful in the morning when the birds sing; the campsite comes alive when the ATVs roar around the area.

James Bond & Beyond Tour

MAP P540

Follow 007

You might have seen it in a travel brochure: the rocky pinnacle of Ko Tapu where Roger Moore and the baddie duelled in 1974's *The Man with the Golden Gun*. Beyond this iconic movie location are caves, viewpoints and islands worth your time.

Phuket-based **Siam Adventure World** *(siamadventureworld.com; adult/child 3900/2450฿)* runs daily speedboat tours to James Bond Island and popular attractions further afield.

The tour operator collects you from any hotel in Phuket or Khao Lak. The tour starts early in the morning at low tide when **Tham Phanak** – south of James Bond Island – is walkable. Home to hawks, monkeys, birds, reptiles and monitor lizards, this cave opens to a hidden lagoon with marshy terrain. How mangroves inside the lagoon defy the ocean at high tide is one of nature's secrets.

From Tham Phanak, you make the short hop by speedboat to the nooks and crannies of **James Bond Island**, the lair of the Bond villain. From here, before the late-morning sun gets too hot, you can enjoy the panoramic sea vistas of Ao Phang-Nga. After a 45-minute pause on the island, the tour heads to **Ao Tho Li Viewpoint** *(facebook.com/LohLiViewPoint)*, better known as Samet Nanghse, which looks out over the sea of karst islets.

After a short boat journey to the north, you'll arrive at the caves of **Tham Lot**, where a villager paddles you through caverns and tangled mangroves. Fast forward to nearby **Ko Panyi**, a Muslim island with a floating football pitch that former sea gypsies from Java call home, and you'll be tucking into stir-fries and curries. After lunch, there's time to stock up on T-shirts and elephant pants. The last stop on the tour is **Ko Naka**. Catch some rays on this beautiful white-sand island and swim in the turquoise water before the speedboat takes you back to **Royal Phuket Marina**.

Note that all the islands this experience describes are in the **Ao Phang-Nga National Park**. Kayaking tours around the islands in the national park are very popular.

WATERFALLS AROUND KHAO LAK

Nam Tok Ton Pling: Hiding on the fringes of Khao Lak, this pretty, one-level waterfall feeds a milky-green pool that's fine for a dip.

Nam Tok Ton Chong Fa: A four-tier waterfall with gushing cascades and pools with fish nibbling dead skin offer a cooling respite.

Nam Tok Sai Rung: Complete with a pool and streamside cafe, this rocky cascade runs through the jungle some 15km from Khao Lak town.

Nam Tok Lampi: These multi-tier falls are popular with families because of the plunge pool a few minutes' walk from the parking area.

Nam Tok Ton Phrai: There's no internet connection here - just peace interrupted by the raw power of water cascading down rocks.

OTHER PHANG-NGA ATTRACTIONS

Ao Tho Li Viewpoint: A scenic lookout with a cafe and rentable tents on site – within a stone's throw from Ao Phang-Nga.

Phang-Nga Elephant Park: This elephant sanctuary, 21km southeast of Phang-Nga town, offers jungle walks and feeding and bathing with the gentle giants.

Khao Lak-Lam Ru National Park: This national park, with viewpoints and waterfalls, slopes from jungle-clad mountains down to Khao Lak's beaches.

Wat Tham Tapan: A Phang-Nga town temple with staggering views, Buddhist sculptures portraying hell, plus a dragon's mouth opening to a sinkhole.

Tham Phung Chang: Glide on a bamboo raft and wade through narrow passages of this cave on the outskirts of Phang-Nga town.

RUNGSILP SASITORN/SHUTTERSTOCK

Ko Phra Thong

Kayak through mangrove forests

Phang-Nga has surprises up its sleeve. Ko Phra Thong, Thailand's fifth-largest island, hides north of Khao Lak, some 30km as the crow flies.

Reach the island via long-tail boat from **Tha Saphan Pla** or the boat launch at **Bang Daet**, 5km from Khuraburi town amid mangrove canals. One-way deals are 1500฿ for the 75-minute trip – call your resort. Once on the island, scooters cost 300฿ and bicycles 100฿ per day. Note that the 2m-wide lanes may be flooded in the rainy season.

The island's name derives from a legend of a golden Buddha statue buried by pirates. The statue has yet to be found, but golden hues are present in the beaches and Phra Thong's savannah in March – nature's replica of Africa without the lions. White sand dazzles on open grasslands too hot for snakes. It's a nature-lover's paradise, complete with gnarly cajeput trees, nesting turtles and cackling hornbills.

DRINKING IN PHANG-NGA TOWN: COFFEE SHOPS

MAP P540

Makalong Cafe: Mocha and machine coffee, vintage radios, old coffee ads and tiny stools – this small-town cafe is popular for good reason. *7.30am-5.30pm*

2495 Coffee Wangmorkaeng: This artist-owned cafe bristles with character, from the paintings to the coffee roaster. *8am-5pm Wed-Mon*

Umber Coffee: Emphasising quality over decor, this cafe boasts fanciful house blends with caramel and chocolate notes. *7.30am-4.30pm*

Baan Suan Gong: From fruity americanos to wicker baskets and plants, this cafe on the southern fringes of Phang-Nga embodies local flair. *9.30am-6.30pm*

Ko Phra Thong

Zoom in on Google Maps and you'll find that Ko Phra Thong has gazillions of tributaries shaped exactly like the cajeput trees that grow on the island's savannah. And that means kayakers are spoilt for choice when picking a fun route. If you're a guest of **Horizon Eco Resort** *(horizonecoresort.com)*, you can rent a kayak for free. The **Moken Eco Village** *(mokenecovillage.com)* and **Baba Ecolodge Resort** *(babaecolodge.com)* also have kayaks for their guests. So venture out on your own at high tide when it's easier to get into canals. While paddling and gliding into the *klorng* (canals) between Moken and Baba, you'll probably hear the loud cackling of an oriental pied hornbill before you spot this fascinating bird and its helmet. The mangrove channel is also home to brazen macaques. Don't kayak into the channel that separates Ko Phra Thong from Ko Ra, the island immediately to its north; the currents in the channel are unpredictable. However, paddling out to Ko Rang Nok and Ko Pho Ta just off the coast of Moken Village is safe. Here you can glide above corals between the two islands. Enjoy!

WHAT TO DO IN KO PHRA THONG

Birdwatching: At Hornbill Hill, you can watch both hornbills and sea eagles circling in cobalt skies.

Visit the Moken Eco Village: There's something beautiful about the sea gypsies here. Despite leading settled lives, the Moken still regard turtles to be imaginary relatives.

Venture into the mangroves: Home to long-tailed macaques, birds and mangrove snakes, Ko Phra Thong's mangrove channels are a haven for kayakers.

Enjoy beach time: On the island's west coast, spread your towel on the deserted gold-sand beach near Horizon Eco Resort.

Discover the savannah: Explore the grasslands on foot, by scooter or jeep – the play of colours varying seasonally is a visual delight.

EATING IN KO PHRA THONG: OUR PICKS

Aromdee Homestay: Without regular opening hours, it's essential to make a reservation at this seafood restaurant on a pine-fringed beach. *open on demand* ฿

Horizon Eco Resort: In the island's northwest, this rustic beach restaurant at this eco-resort is popular with locals and tourists alike. *7.30am-8pm* ฿฿

Baba Ecolodge Restaurant and Bar: Apart from a few Western meals, this restaurant serves tasty seasonal Thai food. *7-11am & noon-9pm* ฿฿

Mr Chuoi's: Serving Thai staples, beers and cocktails in his bamboo and driftwood bar, Chuoi loves to tell stories about island life. *8am-10pm* ฿

EXPLORE TAKUA PA OLD TOWN ON FOOT

Wander the historic streets of Takua Pa Old Town – the spitting image of Phuket's old city, but with fewer crowds.

START	END	LENGTH
Takua Pa Old Town Wall	Guan Yin Shrine	1.2km; two hours

Takua Pa Old Town seems straight out of a nostalgic documentary thanks to the Hokkien-Chinese immigrants who stayed beyond the tin-mining boom of the early 20th century. Start this walk at 1 **Takua Pa Old Town Wall**, a battle camp 100 years ago. Worth a few pictures, this brick-free mortar wall is over 0.5m thick and 3.8m high. Walk west and visit 2 **Sin Chai Tueng Shrine**. Built in 1912, it's home to Taoist deities like Na Ja, patron god of children. Then turn left into Walking St. Allow a little time for taking in the sheer beauty of the townscape, which comprises terraced houses with arcades. The colourful murals along 3 **Thanon Klun Kaeo** and 4 **Walking Street** vividly recount the town's story from the spice trade and the golden years of tin mining to today's Thai and Chinese Peranakan community heritage. Head south to where smoke from incense rises above a Guan Yu statue at 5 **Kopi Kuapa** cafe, whose 100-year-old building has many chill nooks. The outdoor timber benches backdropped by street art and crumbling brick are perfect for devouring chewy, bite-sized Peranakan sweets while sipping aromatic *caffe boran*. Keep going south to an 6 **unnamed painting studio**, where you'll see flowers painted on trays that hang on the wall, visible from the road. End the walk at 7 **Guan Yin Shrine**, which is dedicated to the goddess of mercy.

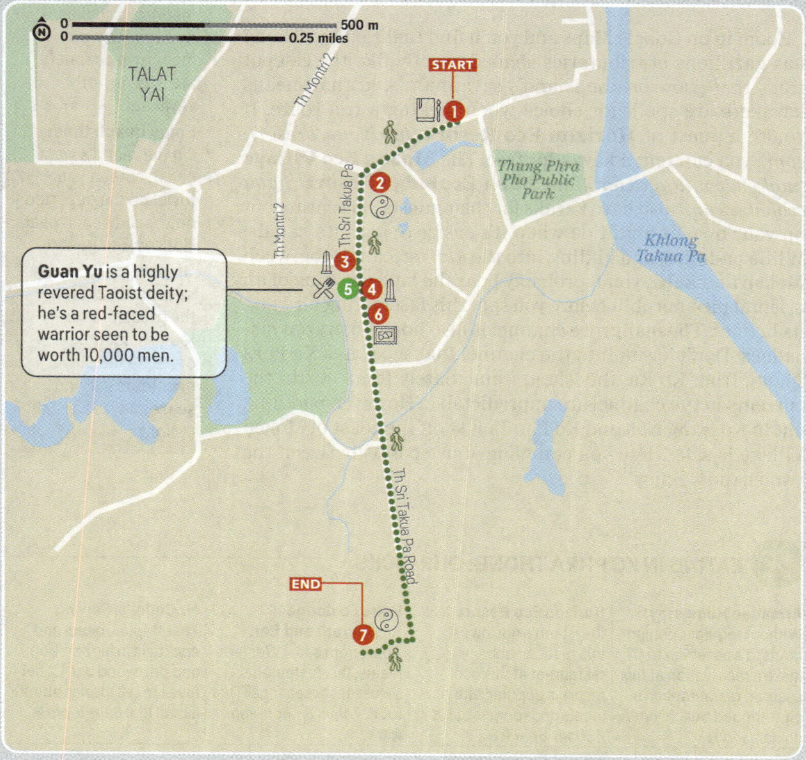

0 500 m
0 0.25 miles
TALAT YAI
Th Montri 2
START
Thung Phra Pho Public Park
Th Sri Takua Pa
Khlong Takua Pa
Th Sri Takua Pa Road
END

Guan Yu is a highly revered Taoist deity; he's a red-faced warrior seen to be worth 10,000 men.

Beyond Phang-Nga Province

Haven for nature lovers: hop between offshore islands and the tranquil Khao Sok National Park.

The year 1976 was critical in Khao Sok's story. Had it not been for communist insurgency groups who set up a stronghold in Khao Sok's jungle, the rainforest, chock-full of endangered wildlife and plant species, would probably have been deforested. But young fighters kept the army and loggers at bay. In 1980 the Thai government established Khao Sok National Park and banned logging in the region. Spanning 739 sq km, the national park sits in Surat Thani Province.

As part of a strategy intended to neutralise the threat posed by communists, Thai authorities reclaimed isolated areas and built a dam in the national park. This gave locals a future.

Today, visitors can discover Khao Sok's tremendous biodiversity. Framing the emerald Chiaw Lan Lake and its floating bungalows, camel-shaped limestone giants also beckon to travellers near and far.

Places

GETTING AROUND

Getting to Khao Sok National Park is easy. Minivans and coaches from Phuket, Krabi and Khao Lak run several times a day. Expect to pay about 320฿ one way. By hopping on a minibus in Khao Lak, you can get to Khao Sok in 70 minutes (or two hours if you take the bus).

Khao Sok National Park

TIME FROM PHANG-NGA TOWN: **1HR 15MIN**

An Adventure Like No Other

Shivers run down your spine as twigs snap and strides approach in a pitch-black rainforest. But for the glimmer of light from the dying campfire, you wouldn't see your hands in front of your face. The candles went out earlier and your guide is snoring peacefully in his hammock. Not for the faint of heart, an overnight jungle tour in Khao Sok National Park takes you well off the trodden path into a forest formerly riddled with gangsters. Today, the rainforest is a respite for tourists who don't mind roughing it.

In business since 2000, the most experienced person in the area is **Khai** *(facebook.com/wassana.maewl; 2500฿)*, who was the first man to guide tours in Khao Sok's jungle. He knows how to start a fire in the rain – crucial because that repels wild animals.

Tours set off in the morning from Khao Sok's **park headquarters** at the end of Khao Sok village, which was once known as *ban sop* (village of the dead). The name derived

BEST KHAO SOK TOUR OPERATORS

Khao Lak Land Discovery: Khao Lak–based operator focused on quality, including insurance, air-conditioned shuttles and multilingual guides.

Khao Sok Tigerman Tours: Offers night safaris and day tours at reasonable prices.

Khao Sok Natureskills Tour: Jungle tours featuring scorpions, frogs and lizards.

Khao Sok Private Tours: Overnight tours and bamboo cooking off the beaten track.

Khao Sok Traveling Tour and Travel: Focusing on Chiaw Lan Lake tours, this operation knows the best viewpoints and waterfalls.

BZ TRAVEL/SHUTTERSTOCK

Chiaw Lan Lake

from a deadly epidemic that swept through the area in 1944, and from its former inhabitants: members of the Thai mafia. They operated from this secluded outpost of the kingdom's communist insurgency back in the 1970s and early '80s. In fact, had it not been for young communist fighters who set up a stronghold in the jungle, keeping both the Thai army and loggers at bay, Khao Sok's flora and fauna would not be what it is today.

You learn all this while trekking deeper into the rainforest with Khai, who hacks a path through the greenery with a machete. During the tour, you may hear happy gibbons in the trees and you'll encounter the refreshing pool of Than Sawan, a 9m-high waterfall that gushes down over rocks. Fast forward to the evening, and Khai serves dinner in bamboo tubes cut in half.

The national park was established in 1980, and logging was banned in this vast region, 33% larger than Phuket. In 1982 the government built Rajjaprabha Dam, in the process creating the huge 165-sq-km **Chiaw Lan Lake**. Today, you can stay at the dam overnight, bathing in emerald water in front of floating bungalows that shake when someone walks past. They're bookable as part of a tour (2500฿ to 15,000฿) at Wassana camp and **Khai Jungle Experience**, steps from Khao Sok National Park headquarters, and at Tha Chiaw Lan, a one-hour taxi ride east of Khao Sok bus stop.

EATING IN KHAO SOK: OUR PICKS

Khao Sok Sunlight: Healthy and spicy salads, rambling vistas of the karst region and hills covered with rubber tree forests. *9am-11.30pm* ฿

Khaosok Rambo Restaurant: Reasonably priced curries and *pat tai* in a bamboo hut plus spontaneous on-site parties. *9am-midnight* ฿

Khao Sok Eagle: An eatery with a chilled-out atmosphere, stir-fries, curries, northeastern Thai favourites and Western culinary delights. *10am-11pm* ฿

Khaosok Mysterious Restaurant and Camp: This camp serves bowls of shrimp porridge to your hammock next to a bubbling brook. *7am-9pm Tue-Sun, from 2pm Mon* ฿

TOP EXPERIENCE

Similan Islands

A symphony of jungle-clad rock formations that make a dramatic backdrop against the Andaman Sea, the Similan Islands were created millions of years ago by a flurry of volcanic anger and the ensuing erosion. Due to soft white coral sand and aquamarine water teeming with marine life, the granite islands have become a diving and snorkelling favourite.

Sail Rock

PHUKET TRAVEL STORE/SHUTTERSTOCK

Snorkel with Curious Turtles

Overtourism is a problem, but the green turtles don't care. One of four species in the Similan Islands, these jumbo-sized turtles move their flippers in a bird-like movement then glide towards you with the elegance of a swan, unperturbed by countless human legs. Forgot your underwater camera? Don't worry; the bath-warm sea is so clear you can photograph them from the boat. Back on land, you can sink your toes into fine white sand, most of which is actually parrotfish poop – heaps of tiny, excreted coral pieces washed ashore. During this one-hour stop on a speedboat trip from Phuket or Khao Lak, you have time for the easy five-minute walk to **Sail Rock**, which looks out over Donald Duck Bay framed by piles of rocks.

Experience the Fascinating Underwater World

One of National Geographic's 'Top 10 dive destinations' worldwide, the nine-island archipelago – technically 11 because two islands were later added to the 140-sq-km national park – offers more than 200 species of hard corals alone. It's a diver's paradise with coral reefs and slopes, boulder swim-throughs and underwater gorges, plus giant trevally, manta rays and whale sharks for the lucky.

TOP TIPS

- For a quieter atmosphere, walk through Island No 4 to Ao Honeymoon in the east.
- Conquer the steep, 20-minute jungle trek to the **Ko Miang** viewpoint overlooking Ao Honeymoon.
- Book a dive safari to see the best dive sites and snorkelling spots.

PRACTICALITIES

- thailand.prd.go.th
- national park fee adult/child 500/300฿ (overnight stays are banned)
- open 15 October to 15 May

TOP EXPERIENCE

Surin Islands

Often compared with the Similan Islands, the Surin Islands have white sand too, if less powdery, and they also score with colourful coral gardens and a laid-back atmosphere. In fact, you can find the kingdom's most impressive range of corals in the Surin Islands. From pink and turquoise formations to plate corals and corals shaped like phonographs, this is a snorkeller's heaven.

PHUKETIAN.S/SHUTTERSTOCK

TOP TIPS

- Take a selfie at Chicken Rock, the icon of the Surin Islands, and walk around Ao Chong Khad's peninsula towards the jetty.
- Look up into the trees at Ao Chong Khad to spot flying lemurs.
- Check out the pineapple-shaped corals at Ao Sapparot.

PRACTICALITIES

- dnp.go.th; 025 620 7603 or 076 472 14547
- national park fee adult/child 500/300฿
- open 15 October to 15 May

Get Your Underwater Camera Ready

Extensive coral reefs fringe the coastline of this five-island archipelago. See triggerfish in the east – where coral-covered slopes provide shelter from the open sea – find Nemo hanging out in sea anemones and spot hawksbill turtles.

Fins and snorkelling goggles are usually provided by tour operators. You can also find reefs in the west, but those are steeper and more suitable for diving. Would you rather swim in these gin-clear waters? Jump off the boat and watch the bubbles rise.

A one-day trip from Phuket or Khao Lak typically includes a stop at **Ban Moken** on Ko Surin Tai, where sea gypsies lead semi-settled lives in bamboo huts on stilts, selling bracelets or bags made from recycled plastic.

To fly a drone, get permission from **Surin Islands Marine National Park Office** in advance. The headquarters on Ao Chang Khad on southwest Ko Surin Neua will refer you to the visitor centre at **Tha Khuraburi** and vice versa, so planning ahead pays. Bungalows and tents are available, but you need to contact the national park authorities in advance.

Meanwhile, imagine what it's like to sip coffee at a bar overhanging the sea, metres above the waves washing ashore.

Krabi Province

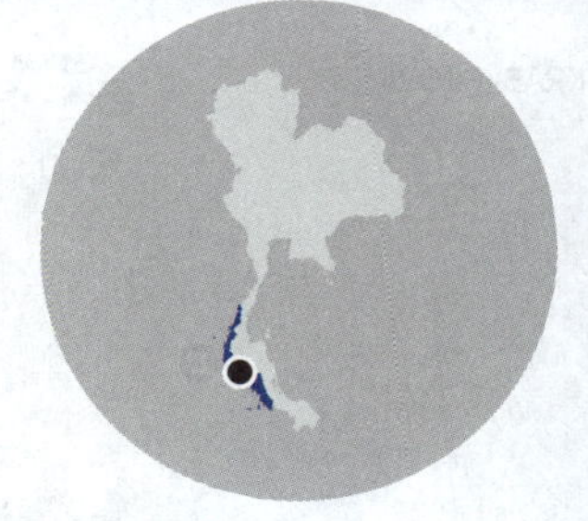

KARST LANDSCAPES | BEACHES | ADVENTURE SPORTS

Formed by the same tectonic smash-up as the Himalayas, Krabi is characterised by towering karst peaks and patches of untamed jungle. Discovered in the depths of Krabi's caves, archaeological finds such as stone axes show that humans pottered around already in prehistoric times. Recorded history dates back to 1200 CE, when Krabi was part of the Nakhon Si Thammarat kingdom. Krabi town, the provincial capital, only gained city status after the emergence of larger societies.

Beautifully golden, onion-domed mosques arrived with Muslim merchants. Backpackers appeared in Krabi in the late 20th century, years after Phuketians had started to promote their island in the 1970s.

Today, Krabi is loved for its beaches, dive sites and rock walls that want to be climbed. Busy in the high season, Krabi is noticeably quieter than Phuket in the low season, offering an idyllic hideaway with plenty of tourist attractions.

TOP TIP

Stay in busy Ao Nang near Hat Railay and plan three days on the mainland, including Krabi town. Riding a scooter is a joy, but keep an eye out for snakes when you ride through villages off the main streets.

BEST SIGHTS IN & AROUND KRABI TOWN

Mangrove Forest: In the middle of Khlong Prasong, home to monkeys, birds and snakes.

Mud Crabs Sculpture: Blending well with the two limestone rocks that frame Pak Nam River; a great spot for a selfie.

Krabi Watch Tower: In Krabi Urban Forest, with 80 steps offering panoramic views of Pak Nam River.

Km 0 – Krabi Nok Awk: Tiny but meaningful, the eagle monument marks the starting point for Krabi city walking tours.

Din Daeng Doi: This viewpoint 20km from town in Tambol Nong Thale is a great sunset spot.

GETTING AROUND

You can easily cover Krabi town on foot. To get beyond the provincial capital, you'll want to use local pick-up minibuses, flag down a taxi or motorcycle taxi or rent a scooter. Krabi International Airport is 14km northeast of the city. Car rentals are available at the airport, as are shared minivans and taxis to Krabi town, which cost 400฿ to 500฿. The Krabi Airport Bus costs 80฿ to 200฿, depending on whether you're headed for Krabi Bus Station, Krabi town or the beaches of Ao Nang and Klong Muang.

Ferries, speedboats and long-tail boats service mainland Krabi with routes to islands in the region. Boats to Hat Railay East and Ko Phi-Phi operate from Tha Khlong Jilad. Krabi Bus Terminal sits 5km north of central Krabi town. Travel agencies run daily minivan tours to other destinations in southern Thailand.

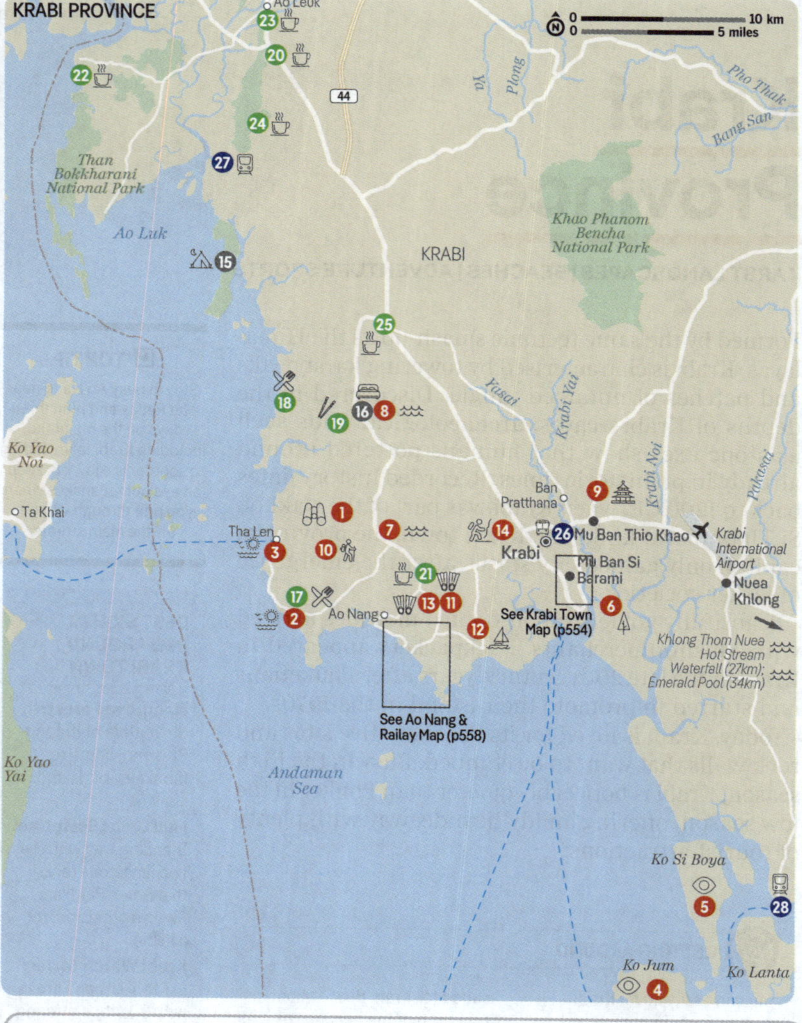

SIGHTS
1 Din Daeng Doi
2 Hat Klong Muang
3 Hat Tubkaek
4 Ko Jum
5 Ko Si Boya
6 Mangrove Forest
7 Mirror Lake
8 Sa Kaew
9 Wat Tham Seua

ACTIVITIES
10 Dragon Crest
11 Kon-Tiki Krabi Scuba Diving & Snorkeling Center
12 Krabi Sunset Cruises
13 Scuba Expert/Krabi
14 Thai'd Up Adventures

SLEEPING
15 Ao Makaren
16 Blu Monkey Pooltara Krabi Hotel

EATING
17 Dragon View Bar & Restaurant
18 Khaothong Hill
19 Kuan Nom Saow Restaurant

DRINKING & NIGHTLIFE
20 149 Cafe Krabi
21 23 Roasters Cafe Krabi
22 Ao Luek Ocean View
23 Chali S Cafe
24 Khunnai Cafe in the Forrest
25 Kope-O

TRANSPORT
26 Krabi Bus Terminal
27 Tha Bakan
28 Tha Laem Kruat

Hit the Krabi Town Night Market

MAP P554

Eat, shop and wonder

Heavy-metal music coming from a stall of a 30-something Thai lady, the scent of homemade essential oils, and watercolour paintings that make you feel Hat Railay's soft white sand – you don't know where to look.

Fret not. The Krabi Town Night Market is a good place to find your feet. Open from Friday to Sunday from 4pm to 10pm, this market in downtown Krabi is more than a flea market. Stir-fried noodles sizzle right in front of you, the air is filled with tantalising aromas of sticky calorie bombs, and meats come in a mouthwatering variety of strongly flavoured tastes. And rather than secondhand souvenirs, you can find quality items such as solid trays and accessories made with rattan and seashells instead of plastic.

On-site concerts add to the lively atmosphere of this market, which is popular with young Thais and travellers alike. Row upon row of marquee tents make you wonder how its vendors can handle the chaos, but the friendly vibe among sellers is palpable.

As you wander through the market alleys, munching on banana-coconut *rodee* (sweet pan-fried flatbread), you get an overview of what Thailand's markets have to offer: food and drink, clothes and handicrafts, as well as entertainment and lovely people who know how to tickle your taste buds.

Awestruck at Khao Khanab Nam

MAP P554

Explore caves with archaeological finds

A 4m-long human skeleton alongside the bones of a big horned snake is not a common sight in Thailand – but this is art. Welcome to **Khao Khanab Nam** *(tourismthailand.org/Attraction/khao-khanap-nam-2)*, a spellbinding three-cave complex situated near Krabi town on the eastern side of Pak Nam River.

Cave walls covered in oxidised copper greet you on arrival. Less than a minute from the pier, you can climb the ladder to the first cave and watch bats hunting insects in erratic movements. The real attraction awaits in the second cave next door, accessible via a 57-step stairway entry. What you see inside, according to a tourist attraction sign, is a giant skeleton of a human-like creature, which supposedly fought a gigantic serpent.

Continued on p555

THAILAND'S FIRE SHOWS

Inspired by old tribal rituals, fire jugglers in Thailand first appeared on the island of Ko Pha-Ngan in the 1980s during one of the original Full Moon parties. Today, fire art is ubiquitous in Thailand. Fire shows are popular on beaches and islands of the Andaman Coast as well as in the Gulf of Thailand. Fire artists show up at dusk to dazzle onlookers with intoxicating performances, typically set to the sound of pumping techno music. Setting the night ablaze, these dancers spin, twirl, twist and dip. Some may even do backflips – anything goes. They also use props that add to the appeal, including poi, chains, burning ropes and sticks drenched in fuel, ignited on both ends for a show that bristles with high-temperature intensity.

EATING IN KRABI TOWN: RESTAURANTS

MAP P554

River Restaurant and Bar: Off Chao Fah Park, this floating restaurant serves stir-fries and fresh red snapper in coconut curry. *11.30am-midnight* ฿฿

Aftersun Music Bar & Social Club: Thai folk songs are played live here. It's a great place to have a beer and devour crispy pork jowl. *6pm-midnight* ฿฿

Homlinda Restaurant: Well-priced *ka nom jeen* (fermented rice noodles) and healthy salads are served here near Krabi watch tower. *11am-9pm* ฿

Max Cafe & Restaurant: Harlequin floors add ambience to this pretty cafe near the mangrove walkway. Try *dom yam* rice with shrimp. *9am-10pm* ฿

HELP ME PICK:

Krabi's Beaches & Islands

With its talcum-white coves and camel-shaped karst peaks jutting out of green water, Ao Nang is a bay of ravishing beauty. The Andaman Sea off the mainland of Krabi Province is studded with some 200 islets. Most are uninhabited, but away-from-it-all bungalows exist on islands that have yet to see their heyday. Massage parlours and hookah bars beckon in Ao Nang town and other shore-hugging resort towns. Well serviced by speedboats, ferries and long-tail boats, these slices of Thailand are within reach.

Where to go if you love...

Seclusion

Ko Jum With murky seas and sand that leans towards coarse-grained, Ko Jum lacks the sparkle of Ao Nang's powdery beaches. But the island northwest of Ko Lanta feels quiet, even if it's no longer a secret. Mosques sit side by side with fishing settlements, while rustic beach bars and resorts serve food and drinks.

Ko Si Boya If it's peace and quiet you're after, then Ko Si Boya is the spot to hit. This island just north of Ko Jum doesn't dazzle with beaches either, but total seclusion makes it a winner. There are more villagers than visitors, and residents are outnumbered by cows. Does that smell of adventure?

Impressive scenery

Hat Railay (p560) Caves and bays with white, flour-like sand framed by giant karst formations make this beach area the earth's most beautiful peninsula. Like Ao Nang town itself, it boasts countless climbing schools, dive centres and luxury resorts. Still, it's retained a castaway feel.

Hat Tonsai Bordering Hat Railay West, Hat Tonsai offers the best of both worlds: limestone rocks suitable for climbing and emerald water, but also a few bars and resorts, plus a slightly more laid-back feel than Hat Railay.

Creature comforts

Hat Ao Nang Besides massage parlours, night markets, luxury resorts and clubs and hookah bars, Ao Nang town has everything you may possibly need. A mini-version of Phuket, it's the centre of the action; people almost forget its beach. Scooters are widely available for rent and tuk-tuks ply the streets for those keen to embark on inland adventures.

Hat Noppharat Thara There's less boat traffic here than at neighbouring Hat Ao Nang, and fewer people visit, even in the high season. Still, you can find everything, from restaurants and resorts to a night market and a gently sloping stretch of sand that's perfect for beach walks or jogging.

Hat Klong Muang A quieter alternative to Ao Nang, this casuarina-lined beach has crystalline water, silky sand and bars, cafes and five-star resorts.

Hat Tubkaek Shells and pebbles also form part of this beach 13km northwest of Hat Noppharat Thara. It's backdropped by swanky resorts near Dragon Crest nature trail.

SERGII FIGURNYI/SHUTTERSTOCK

Hat Ao Nang

HOW TO

Money There are no ATMs in Ko Si Boya; Ko Jum only has a place for withdrawing cash at a minimart, so bring enough baht.

Transport Ko Jum has no public transport bar a few motorcycle taxis, much less Ko Si Boya. Ko Jum has scooter rentals. Cover Railay on foot. Ao Nang beaches have everything.

Need to know Ko Si Boya has no pharmacies and eateries, besides ordinary noodle shops. There are more amenities in Ko Jum.

When to go Crowds are thin and rooms are cheaper from May to October. Sunshine? Hit or miss.

Guides & Other Nuts & Bolts

Exploring Krabi independently gives you freedom, but a guide can converse with locals on your behalf and fill you in on local history. Licensed guides can be arranged through tourHQ.com. Alternatively, rock up to tour agencies along Ao Nang's main strip or hop on a long-tail boat.

You can also hire a driver for the day. A return trip on a red four-wheeled mini-truck costs 1200฿ in a 25km radius around Ao Nang town centre. A return trip including four stops in the area sets you back 1500฿.

Hiring a scooter is convenient, but you need an international driver's licence, and U-turns are unpredictable. Also, red-white stripes on a curb mean you mustn't park or you may find your motorbike locked.

Getting to Ko Jum is child's play. Hop on a shared minivan at Krabi airport, ride a scooter or jump on a dirt-cheap *songthaew* (50฿ to 100฿) in Ao Nang town. Ferries and long-tail boats run from **Tha Laem Kruat** several times a day until 6pm, and are cheaper than those from Krabi town. The easiest way to Ko Si Boya is by long-tail boat from Ko Jum.

ACTIVITIES IN KRABI PROVINCE

Emerald Pool: A never-never land of pleasure, this turquoise mineral pool embedded in the forest is popular for its beauty.

Wat Tham Seua (Tiger Cave Temple): Face the 1237 steps to this temple perched atop a cave network and be rewarded with mind-blowing views of Krabi.

Khlong Thom Nuea Hot Stream Waterfall: Pools, a waterfall and hot stream offering various levels of heat – this national park is perfect for a relaxing soak.

Thai'd Up Adventures: Help! You fly through the jungle, strapped into a harness hanging from a pulley, some 60m above the ground.

Krabi River Walkway: Dotted with landmarks and benches to rest on, this promenade in Krabi town is great for a walk.

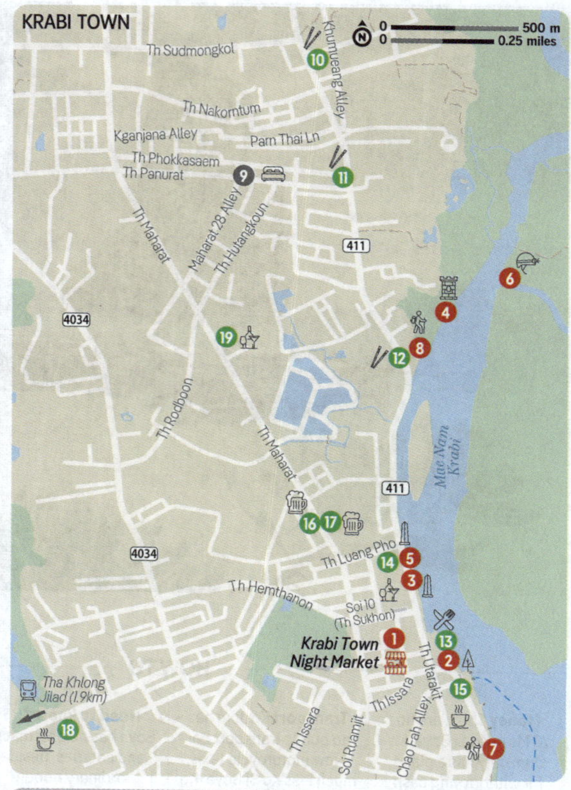

HIGHLIGHTS
1 Krabi Town Night Market

SIGHTS
2 Chao Fah Park
3 Km 0 – Krabi Nok Awk
4 Krabi Watch Tower
5 Mud Crabs Sculpture

ACTIVITIES
6 Khao Khanab Nam
7 Krabi River Walkway
8 Krabi Urban Forest Walkway

SLEEPING
9 Play Poshtel Krabi

EATING
10 Aftersun Music Bar & Social Club
11 Homlinda Restaurant
12 Max Cafe & Restaurant
13 River Restaurant and Bar

DRINKING & NIGHTLIFE
14 A Friendly Bar and Cafe
15 Easy Cafe by Relax Coffee
16 Factory Beer Garden
17 Hangout
18 Jon Cafe Krabi
19 Raruen Krabi Bistro and Bar

DRINKING IN KRABI TOWN: BARS

MAP P554

Factory Beer Garden: Chips and chicken wings, live music and tapped Leo all add to the atmosphere at this lively restaurant. *6pm-1am* ฿

Hangout: Popular with locals and live bands alike, this bar has delicious salmon salad, best washed down with craft beers like Duvel. *7pm-1am* ฿

Raruen Krabi Bistro and Bar: From curries and vegetable salads to single-malt scotch – quality is high at this bistro bar in a garden setting. *5pm-midnight* ฿฿

A Friendly Bar and Cafe: This cocktail bar is the place to watch the world go by. Sip a glass of wine or try vodka lime and soda. *1pm-1am* ฿

Continued from p551

Actually, the skeleton is part of an art exhibition – but, as a local put it, open your heart. As well as stalactites and stalagmites, you can also find prehistoric stone artefacts and cave wall paintings in the hot, humid caves.

Home to chirping and squeaking bats, the tiny third cave opens to a peaceful river view. Entry is free but you need to pay 100฿ to 200฿ for the long-tail boat ride across the river, either from the jetty where the Krabi Urban Forest Walkway (p557) ends (these aren't registered tourist boats, though people still use them), or from **Chao Fah Park**. There, long-tail boat captains tout half-day tours (500฿), which include stops in tangled mangroves and lunch at a restaurant on the river.

Jump into Sa Kaew Pool

MAP P550

Discover a deep, crystal-clear pool

'Still waters run deep', the proverb goes, and it couldn't be truer at **Sa Kaew** *(100฿)*, which translates as 'pool as clear as glass'. Almost as turquoise as glacial ice, the clear, still pool – 21km northwest of Krabi town – looks shallow but is known as the deepest freshwater basin in Southeast Asia. A local cave diver named Sayan Pecharat has confirmed it has a 240m-deep, submerged cave.

There's no need to worry, though. Apart from tiny fish nibbling at dry dead skin on your feet, there are no dubious creatures in the water. You can use the rope tied around a tree and make a splash as you jump into the invigorating water Tarzan style.

The entry fee is reasonable given you get a bottle of water, free parking and a headlamp. The latter could prove useful if you dare to venture into one of the on-site caves. While you don't need a guide to do it – the cave behind the pool is only about 100m long – the gentle wind you may feel isn't a breeze; that's a bat flashing past you.

Get Away from It All

MAP P550

Camp at Ao Makaren

Enjoy camping? **Ao Makaren** *(Makaren Bay Farm Village Krabi; facebook.com/Aomuongbeachboutiquecamp; 081 444 7753)*, a remote campsite in Ao Luek, 31km northwest of Krabi town, is the place for you. Enjoy castaway vibes and a few lonely coconut trees leaning towards the Andaman Sea. There's total silence apart from the exotic boop-boop-boops of crow

KRABI'S SECRET BAY

Anantra 'Togh' Butman, Thai actor and owner of Ao Makaren aka Makaren Bay Farm Village Krabi. *facebook.com/togh.anantra*

Camping is increasingly popular due to people wanting to preserve nature. We sell nature and relaxation. My concept is only one travel group at a time – or two if the first group don't mind. Apart from camping, kayaking and recharging your batteries, here in Ao Luek you can go fishing on long-tail boats, catch fish and shrimp, and get an idea of fishers' lifestyles. In our farm village, you can learn about palm cultivation, solar-powered electricity and groundwater pumping. Ko Hong is a regional highlight, but you need to arrive at 7am if you want to have the beach to yourself.

DRINKING IN KRABI PROVINCE: CRAFT COFFEE

MAP P550 & P554

Kope-O: Sip robusta coffee with chocolatey and floral notes while lounging in a hammock. These coffee roasters near Cafe Amazon know their craft. *7am-5pm*

Jon Cafe Krabi: Krabi town cafe with vintage decor and a garden setting, beautifully presented cakes and aesthetic latte art. *10.30am-4pm Mon-Fri*

Easy Cafe by Relax Coffee: A roofed outdoor and an air-con indoor section, this chill Krabi town cafe serves Thai highland coffee. *7.30am-4.30pm Tue-Sun*

23 Roasters Cafe Krabi: Dark roast coffee, seasonal blends plus vintage coffee equipment, and local flair win you over at this Ao Nang cafe. *8.15am-5.30pm*

KRABI TOWN HISTORY

The 150 near-vertical islets in Krabi Province were once part of the Nakhon Si Thammarat kingdom. In 1782, when modern Bangkok was founded, elephants roamed the area. This prompted the governor of Nakhon Si Thammarat, a province of the Siamese kingdom at the time, to set up an elephant *kraal* (a fenced enclosure where wild elephants were tamed) and guarantee a regular supply of the pachyderms for the larger towns. This paved the way for the development of larger communities, one of which was called Pakasai. In 1872 King Rama V elevated it from sub-county to town status, dubbing it Krabi. Legend has it the name derives from two swords that villagers unearthed by chance.

FOKKE BAARSSEN/SHUTTERSTOCK

Dragon Crest

pheasants, or the chugging sounds of a long-tail boat in the distance.

While this hidden bay framed by palm plantations and towering karst peaks is a 45-minute long-tail boat ride from Ko Hong (p564), it feels like a world away. That's partly because it's only accessible by boat from **Tha Bakan** in Amphoe Ao Luek. It's also because Anantra 'Togh', the Thai owner of this campsite, allows only one travel group at a time – maximum 40 people.

Bamboo huts provide shelter and food when the stomach grumbles, and two dogs are here 'for security'. Alcohol isn't allowed. Togh says his farm village is for learning, kayaking – and relaxing. There's a hammock to do just that, and chairs are provided so you can sit beneath a starlit sky and listen to the waves washing ashore.

If you bring a two-person tent, one night is 100฿ (500฿ if you rent one). Togh can also hook you up with a fisherman for the round trip on a rickety long-tail boat (per boat 1000฿) for a maximum of four people.

Beat the Dragon

MAP P550

Lace up your hiking shoes

Spread your arms atop Dragon Crest, 560m above sea level, and enjoy rambling vistas. One of the best photo spots in the region, the mountain of , also known as **Dragon Crest** *(portal.*

DRINKING IN AO LUEK: CAFES

MAP P550

149 Cafe Krabi: Tasty matcha latte, machine-brewed coffee and cranberry-topped choc-chip cookies at this cafe on Th Phet Kasem. *8am-4pm Tue-Sun*

Chali S Cafe: This cosy cafe near limestone giants trumps with superlatives, from coffee and latte art to healthy salads. *8am-7pm Mon-Fri, from 7.30am Sat, 9am-7.30pm Sun*

Ao Luek Ocean View: This hillside cafe overlooking the ocean dotted with limestone rocks is a peaceful place to sip a cup of joe. *9.30am-7.30pm*

Khunnai Cafe in the Forrest: Yummy passionfruit shakes and orange coffees, attention to detail and food in wicker baskets at this rustic cafe. *8.30am-5pm*

dnp.go.th; adult/child 200/100฿; 8am-2pm), is a crazily steep climb through dense rainforest that eventually opens up to the surrounding karst region and the Andaman Sea beyond.

The trail of almost 4km is a struggle; you've got to climb a squillion stairs and over snake-shaped roots and fallen tree trunks. Ginger-coloured trees you can't find in your local park await in the Auburn Zone, the first window into this otherworldly land.

Bring at least two litres of water. The entrance to the nature trail right after Amari Vogue Krabi Hotel is less than a 30-minute scooter ride from Ao Nang. You'll need to check in and out, giving them your name and phone number. Due to safety concerns, the crest's popular rock outcrop with its drop below is no longer open for Insta shots.

After some two hours of hard work, you're rewarded with cool mountain air and summit views.

Step into Another World

MAP P554

Visit Krabi Urban Forest Walkway

Deafening cicadas welcome you on the concrete bridge that cuts through Krabi town's mangroves in a zigzag. A long-tailed macaque turns its head as you approach, while the maze of roots resembles slithering snakes. Speaking of which, this urban forest is home to mangrove snakes, pit vipers and monocled cobras.

With the **Krabi Urban Forest Walkway** missing parts of its handrail and twigs cracking only metres away, you're actually closer to nature than you think. But it's safe. After all, no one knows their hometown better than the local joggers who use the 526m-long bridge in the evenings.

The path is a world away from the city centre, even if it's within walking distance. You can smell wet earth. Pigeons coo and kingfishers hide in the white, black, red and orange mangroves – identifiable by their roots. Red mangroves are closest to the water, featuring prop roots that have earned them the nickname of walking trees.

Bring a water bottle, as there is no kiosk. Instead, there's a **watch tower** with 80 steps. Offering panoramic views, it stands some 20m tall, looking out over the cityscape and the Krabi River framed by two giant limestone rocks.

There's also a visitor centre, but it's closed in the low season, plus a jetty at the end of the walkway. The long-tail boats that ply between the river anks are not official tourist boats.

POPULAR DIVE CENTRES IN AO NANG

Fast Manta Diving Krabi: This top dive centre in the heart of Ao Nang offers PADI courses, including free diving.

Scuba Expert/Krabi: The fun guides of this dive centre near Tetris Hotel know where to find colourful nudibranch or banded sea snakes.

Dive Ao Nang: This five-star PADI dive centre offers diving at affordable rates, including extra services like hotel pick-up and on-board nibbles.

Sea Gypsy Divers: Passionate about diving, the instructors of this great dive centre dive around Ko Phi-Phi with certified divers.

Kon-Tiki Krabi Scuba Diving & Snorkeling Center: This dive centre is patient when it comes to refreshers and can visit dive sites even when long-tail boats stay ashore.

EATING IN KRABI PROVINCE: RESTAURANTS WITH VIEWS

MAP P550 & P554

Into the Forest: A two-storey cafe with delicious pastries and Brazilian robusta coffee – served in the cradle of nature 20 minutes from Ao Nang. *9am-6pm* ฿

Kuan Nom Saow Restaurant: Serving *massaman*, this popular Khao Thong restaurant overlooks palms, shrubs and rubber trees. *6.30am-7pm* ฿

Khaothong Hill: This hilltop restaurant near Ao Thalane has karst-islet views, confectionary and chocolatey *mochaccino*. *11am-8pm* ฿฿

Dragon View Bar & Restaurant: Designed with bamboo and fisher nets, this spot near Hat Klong Muang has seafood, wine and sea views. *11am-8.30pm* ฿฿

AO NANG & RAILAY

0 500 m
0 0.25 miles

Kon-Tiki Krabi Scuba Diving & Snorkeling Center (1.2km)
Scuba Expert/ Krabi (1.2km)
Krabi Sunset Cruises (2.2km)
See Ao Nang Beach
Ao Nang
Soi Sunset
ANDAMAN SEA
Railay Highlands
Hat Railay West
RAILAY
Walking St
Hat Railay East
Happy Island
Ko Rung Nok
Sa Phra Nang
Laem Phra Nang

Ao Nang Beach
0 200 m
0 0.1 miles

EATING IN AO NANG: OUR PICKS

MAP P558

Kodam Kitchen: Book a table at this roofed, open-sided restaurant just off the main strip of Ao Nang. The affordable Thai cuisine is amazing. *11am-10.30pm* ฿

Cafe 8.98: Skip your hotel breakfast and make a beeline for this quiet cafe. Both Western meals and Thai dishes are available. *7am-11pm* ฿

Jungle Kitchen: This family-run restaurant in a bamboo setting has an open kitchen and serves fresh prawns and grilled pork. *11am-3pm & 5-10pm Mon-Sat* ฿

Burger Daddy: Crave-worthy burgers are not the only treat at Burger Daddy; you can also tuck into chicken wings and crispy salami-topped pizzas. *11am-11.30pm* ฿฿

HIGHLIGHTS
1 Hat Railay East
2 Hat Railay West

SIGHTS
3 Dao Art Gallery
4 East Railay Viewpoint
5 Hat Ao Nang
6 Hat Noppharat Thara
7 Hat Phra Nang
8 Hat Railay
9 Hat Tonsai

ACTIVITIES
10 Dive Ao Nang
11 Fast Manta Diving Krabi
12 Fire Wall
13 Monkey Trail
14 Sea Gypsy Divers
15 Tham Princess

SLEEPING
16 Chill Out Bar & Bungalow

EATING
17 Burger Daddy
18 Cafe 8.98
19 Into the Forest
20 Jungle Kitchen
21 Kodam Kitchen

DRINKING & NIGHTLIFE
22 Boogie Bar
see 20 Chilling Bar
23 Mr Long Bar
24 Tribe Beach Bar

ENTERTAINMENT
25 Blue Dragon Cabaret Show

SHOPPING
26 Landmark Night Market

Using them is banned. But many people use them anyway because they're cheaper than those at Chao Fah Park (p555).

Ao Nang's Highlights in One Cruise

MAP P550

Enjoy a Krabi sunset cruise

Set sail on a Chinese junk and snap away. Climb the mast, take pictures from the bow and get your tan on the top deck. A four-island **sunset cocktail cruise** *(krabisunsetcruises.com; adult/child 3500/2500฿; 1-8pm)* is riddled with highlights. Kicking off at 1pm, you meet your guides and the crew in a remote bay, which sets the stage for a laid-back afternoon.

Originally a merchant ship, the junk is more than 100 years old. It's wheelchair-accessible and has plenty of space to lounge, sit in the shade or get roasted in the sun as you glide smoothly over the waves. The crew serve drinks right away.

At the islands of Chicken, Ko Si, Ko Wa Sam and Ko Poda, you can jump into bath-warm waters and snorkel the underwater paradise. If the views and cocktails don't get the better of you while you kick back on a three-fold cushion, you can grab a stand-up paddleboard or kayak and paddle to the beach.

The cruise continues to less-known spots before heading back to the Railay Peninsula. A Thai buffet-style dinner is ready just after sunset. This smashing tour ends with a stop at Hat Phra Nang (p561), where you can jump into the sea, making the dark water glow as you stir bioluminescent plankton.

ATTRACTIONS IN & AROUND AO NANG

Monkey Trail: Climb the wooden steps through the jungle; you're almost guaranteed to meet long-tailed macaques. The sea views are worth it.

Mirror Lake Krabi: Kayak this crystal lake to enjoy views of limestone rocks and a taste of the jungle. It's 11km north of Ao Nang.

Dao Art Gallery: Beautifully neon-lit, Dao's art gallery is an explosion of colours that border on abstract art.

Blue Dragon Cabaret Show: Pink, glittery, lip-syncing transgender people and playful humour make for good laughs. The show is suitable for kids.

Landmark Night Market: A 20-minute walk along the promenade, Landmark bustles off Hat Ao Nang, with live music, fire spinners and food vendors.

DRINKING IN AO NANG: OUR PICKS

MAP P558

Mr Long Bar: Great for post-dinner drinks, this laid-back bar on the beach road has a casual Rastafarian vibe and live music later in the night. *4pm-1am*

Tribe Beach Bar: A bistro by day, this beach bar morphs into a cocktail bar come nightfall; also offers live DJs and a cool atmosphere. *8am-1am*

Boogie Bar: Don't let the name fool you: this chill bar has happy people, live pop, indie and rock music, and mojitos worth trying. *3pm-1.30am*

Chilling Bar: A fun place to watch football, play pool or just pop in and imbibe – located on the main strip. *11am-3am Tue-Sun, from 2pm Mon*

ALEXANDRE ROSA/SHUTTERSTOCK

Longboats, Hat Railay West

TOP EXPERIENCE

Hat Railay

Krabi's fairy-tale limestone formations come to a dramatic climax at Railay (also spelt Rai Leh), the ultimate Andaman gym for rock-climbing fanatics. Monkeys frolic alongside climbers on the gorgeous crags, while down below some of the prettiest beaches in all of Thailand are backed by proper jungle, just a 20-minute long-tail boat ride from Hat Ao Nang.

DON'T MISS

- Hat Railay West
- East Hat Railay Viewpoint
- Hat Phra Nang
- Hat Railay East
- Hat Tonsai
- Railay Walking Street
- Tham Princess

Getting a Tan

Hat Railay is a fixture on the tourist circuit. While it isn't a filming location in itself, it looks like a scene from the 2000 adventure drama film *The Beach*. Think long-tail boats anchored at the water's edge, emerald waves rolling gently up the sand and a hippie enclave under the watch of giant, stalagmite-shaped limestone rocks.

PRACTICALITIES

● facebook.com/hatnoppharatthara.nationalpark ● open 24hr

It's easy to understand Hat Railay's attraction. Here on soft sands cradled by steepling cliffs, you can truly recharge your batteries. Spread your towel at the northern or southern end of the beach, where there are fewer people and your swims in the crystalline water are less likely to be interrupted by long-tail boats as they chug in and out of the bay. The western part of the peninsula is most suitable for swimming.

Kayaks are available for rent. Secured on the shore, they're waiting as if to remind you to paddle around the corner and check out **Hat Phra Nang** and the maze of stalactites and stalagmites at **Tham Princess**.

Diving

Hat Railay West has seen the biggest development, with luxury resorts and restaurants dishing up stir-fries and curries. Dive centres have also found their way to Railay, even though most dive sites are a 30-minute boat ride off the coast. You can hop on a rickety long-tail boat or a larger boat in the high season. Dive the region's waters to see colourful nudibranch, the fascinating Kuhl's stingray as well as soft corals that look like bunches of flowers.

The nearby islands offer easy diving with swim-throughs, caves and maximum depths of 20m. if you're an experienced diver keen for deeper adventures, join a tour to the King Cruiser Wreck, which sits at 32m some 15km west of Ko Phi-Phi.

Climbing

Cross the Railay Walking Street to enter the realm of climbers. The high wall at the southern end of the beach is where many climbing schools head to help beginners find their feet. For better rock quality, skip the main crags and look for out-of-the-way walls like **Fire Wall** on Hat Tonsai, which is cut off from the mainland. Note that up on these giants, it's hellishly hot.

You'll also sweat buckets if you brave the tough but fun climb to **East Railay Viewpoint**, which overlooks Railay's palm-covered headland and the vast karst region beyond. To get up here through mud, roots and stones, you need to be a sure-footed traveller. Leave the flip-flops in your room; massage parlours offer aromatherapy rewards on return.

Start from the southern end of **Hat Railay East** and climb the first cliff on your left on the path towards Hat Phra Nang. It leads to a lagoon and a hilltop, where you need to turn left. Bring water, bug spray and a camera with enough memory space for at least a thousand pictures.

MUST-KNOW FACTS

The area is split up into three parts: Hat Railay West, Hat Railay East and Hat Phra Nang. Climbers head east for the rocky wall that almost begs to be climbed. Beach lovers are happiest on Hat Railay West, where they can swim and work on their tan. The spiritually minded visit Hat Phra Nang, home to a cave shrine that local sailors worship.

TOP TIPS

- Unlike Tham Diamond at Hat Railay West, Tham Princess is free. Visit the cave in the morning or late afternoon for fewer crowds.
- Stay away from the monkeys and keep food and drinks hidden in your backpack. Foods with strong smells may attract cheeky macaques, even if out of sight.
- Join a night snorkelling tour. Watch the sea glow as you stir bioluminescent plankton. You might feel like Leonardo DiCaprio in the film *The Beach*.
- Hop on a shared long-tail boat taxi from Ao Nang and pay only 100฿.

Krabi Islands

Set sail for the karst islands off Krabi Province, an aquamarine heaven studded with coral reefs.

Places

The ocean off Krabi is dotted with rocky outcrops – some are almost haloed by white-sand beaches. With craggy cliffs that plunge dramatically into deep, green-tinted water, Ko Phi-Phi's Pileh Lagoon is worth a day trip. Night owls and those after a tan are happiest in Ko Phi-Phi Don. Once inhabited by Malay sea gypsies, from whom come the words *don* for mountain and *leh* for moon, Ko Phi-Phi Leh gained international fame when *The Beach* launched a thousand fantasies of Thailand.

Situated in Ao Phang-Nga, Ko Yao Yai and Ko Yao Noi are quieter. Ko Lanta has a relaxed vibe and historic town that attract people from all walks of life.

Ko Phi-Phi

TIME FROM KRABI TOWN: 1½HR 

Beach-hop Phi-Phi's beaches and nearby islands

A casuarina-lined curve of fine, sugar-white sand, **Bamboo Island** is a 45-minute long-tail boat ride from Ko Phi-Phi Don. There's little to do besides chilling in the shade, but that's the point. Be cautious if you go swimming in the turquoise water; stingrays sometimes bury themselves. There's a cafe but no accommodation for overnight stays. However, tour operators in Ko Phi-Phi Don are a dime a dozen, as are private long-tail boats (four hours 3500฿, extra adult/child 500/250฿) at Tha Tonsai and online (longtailboatphiphi.com).

Ko Yung (Mosquito Island) also has a white-sand beach popular with day-tripping sun-worshippers.

You'll also want to check out Ko Phi-Phi Leh's sublime **Ao Maya** *(four hours 3000฿)*. While swimming is no longer

GETTING AROUND

The only way to Phi-Phi, Yao Yai and Yao Noi is by boat. Minivans take you to Ko Lanta via the car ferry from a Krabi pier misleadingly called Tha Hua Hin, next to Pimalay Jetty. The ferry runs hourly from 5am to midnight. Foreigners pay a 50฿ fee per person for taking the car ferry, plus an additional 5฿ for a scooter and a few baht more for a car. Motorcycle taxis and scooter rental are available on Lanta. On Ko Phi-Phi, use long-tail boats or walk.

STOCK PHOTOS 2000/SHUTTERSTOCK

Ko Phi-Phi Don

allowed, sinking your toes in the white, powdery sand and looking at the clear, karst-studded water is priceless.

On Ko Phi-Phi Don, **Hat Nui** is accessible by boat or kayak. It lacks facilities but is a great snorkelling spot and quieter than **Hat Tonsai**. A reef and creature comforts await at **Hat Long**, a serene stretch of white sand facing Phi-Phi Leh. It's serviced by boat taxis from Tha Tonsai (100฿).

Enjoy bird's-eye views of Phi-Phi

Spread your arms on the hilltop overlooking the dozens of limestone giants that frame the twin beaches of Ko Phi-Phi Don. The Phi-Phi Islands have not one, not two but three viewpoints – each with varying difficulty levels.

Considered by many to be the best of the three, **Viewpoint 2** is the one you must visit or else you haven't been to the Phi-Phi Islands. It doesn't come without a price, though. Firstly, the commercialised **Viewpoint 1** charges a 50฿ entrance fee, and you have to pass it to get to the second and third one. Also, you need to summon the energy to climb steep stairs, only to be mocked by the 'I love Phi Phi' letters at Viewpoint 1.

But after that challenging 20-minute climb, you can enjoy panoramic coastal views. The cashier sells a few drinks, should you need to fuel up. Catch your breath and keep walking along the sun-dappled path for another 10 minutes and you'll be rewarded with picture-perfect vistas of the island shaped like an outrigger boat. There are cafes on the hilltop and the

BEST DAY-TRIP OPERATORS

Here are five Phuket-based operators that offer day trips to Ko Phi-Phi.

Siam Adventure World: To beat the crowds, this Phuket-based tour operator was the first to offer early-bird tours.

5-Star Marine Phuket: This tour agency offers not just day tours but also early-evening bioluminescence and sea canoeing tours.

Sawanu Travel: Based at Royal Phuket Marina, this company offers affordable boat tours to Krabi and beyond.

Seastar Andaman: Facing Coconut Island, this Phuket-based tour operator focuses on quality trips yet strives to include multiple stops.

Love Andaman: This company focuses on small group tours.

EATING IN KO PHI-PHI DON: POPULAR THAI RESTAURANTS

Thai Sea: Tasty cocktails and well-priced Thai food like *pat tai*, papaya salad or fried fish topped with black pepper make this a crowd-pleaser. *10am-10pm* ฿

Pa-Noi Thai Food: Stir-fries for less than 100฿ and ice-cold Chang beer – no wonder this restaurant on Phi-Phi's main strip is popular. *11.30am-9.30pm* ฿

Pad Thai Ja Aed Plaza Phi Phi: Despite resembling a simple stall, this restaurant is popular. Sit on a chair with holes and tuck into shrimp *pat tai*. *10am-10pm* ฿

Mango Garden: Designed like a mango orchard, this cafe serves sweet smoothies, healthy bowls and irresistible fusion desserts. *7am-10pm* ฿฿

BEST BEACHES IN KO LANTA

Hat Nui: Light-brown coarse sand and a castaway feel – wild Hat Nui is quiet all year. There's a bar overlooking the beach; use its stairs to reach the sand.

Ao Kantiang: Home to ghost crabs, this wide-open bay has yet to see a wave of tourists.

Ao Nui: Apart from a peaceful atmosphere disturbed occasionally by monkeys, this beach has turquoise water that gets deep quickly – enjoy swimming.

Hat Klong Khong: Also known as Long Beach, this rocky beach has quiet spots while other sections have bars and restaurants.

Hat Khlong Chak: Fine white sand, a chillax vibe and cosy bars with ice-cold beer make this one of Lanta's best beaches.

boulders are popular selfie spots. Come in the morning for fewer crowds and acceptable temperatures.

Stump up another 20฿ and you can visit **Viewpoint 3** down the hill towards the other side of Phi-Phi.

Ko Hong

TIME FROM KRABI TOWN: **2½HR**

Enjoy picture-postcard scenery

A 360-degree viewpoint that's 109m above sea level, a lagoon and two crescent beaches that look like the wingspan of a bird – Ko Hong, in **Than Bok Khorani National Park**, is the proud flagship of Krabi's karst region.

Get up at an ungodly hour and show up at 7am to beat the crowds. It's worth it. Set foot on Ko Hong's powdery beach and sink your feet into the sand so that it crunches between your toes. After spending some time on the beach, hike the small jungle trail or visit the panoramic viewpoint – a great place to pop the question. The vista of the cove's jungle-clad limestone formations and the karst islets beyond only gets better the further up you are.

If labouring up 417 steps to the lookout sounds like too much work, hop on a kayak and paddle through the emerald lagoon. Or jump off a boat, breathe out and see the bubbles rise.

Back on the mainland at Hat Ao Nang (p552), the jumping-off point for trips to Hat Railay, you can book a 45-minute longtail ride to Ko Hong. Depending on your haggling skills, a return trip costs 3000฿ to 4000฿. Speedboat tours from Phuket with **Siam Adventure World** *(adult/child 4100/2900฿)* or **Love Andaman** *(adult/child 2999/2599฿)* are other options.

Ko Lanta

TIME FROM KRABI TOWN: **1HR 40MIN** 

Eat, shop, drink and chill in Lanta Old Town

Chock-a-block with Chinese merchant buildings, the Old Town is lined with century-old, dipterocarp timber houses. But for every house on stilts sticking out into the ocean, you can see a cafe or shop that hasn't forgotten its heritage.

From sea-gypsy settlement and Malay migrants' home to commercial centre and tourism hub – Ko Lanta has lived many lives. And nowhere on the island is the Chinese influence as woven into the rich tapestry as here in the Old Town, the cultural heartbeat of Ko Lanta.

As you wander along the historic street in the southeastern part of the island – best reached by scooter or sidecar motorbike taxi – you come across souvenir shops selling everything under

DRINKING ON KO PHI-PHI DON: BARS

Camel Rock Bar: A cool place to hang out, this fun, neon-lit bar in the north of the island has swing chairs and painkiller cocktails. *5pm-1am*

Sunflower Beach Bar: Offering happy hours, this beach bar is the place to sip cocktails with friends and listen to the waves crash ashore. *9am-9pm*

Only Bar Bar Phi Phi: The white floorboards blend well with the turquoise sea beneath this chill-out bar. Slump into a beanbag; enjoy the sunset. *24hr*

Bob Bar: Cocktails are on point at this rustic, out-of-the-way bar snuggled into a hillside. Reggae and incense add ambience. *9am-9pm*

ANTONIO LOPEZ VELASCO/SHUTTERSTOCK

Lagoon, Ko Hong

the sun. There are flip-flops made from silk, and hats that celebrate recycled clothes, or Thai-style three-fold cushions.

Thai restaurants serve stir-fries and curries, while gift shops like **Malee Malee** offer a chilled-out mix of cafe, hang-out and art studio. Mix with the locals or sip a cup of tea while lounging in a hammock.

Closed in the low season when clacking heels sound like horse-drawn carriages echoing through the ages, the **community museum** near the pier traces the history of Thai Muslims, *chao leh* and Chinese traders.

Bring your camera – the past and present are glued together at the Old Town pier. Now a shipwreck and popular photo spot, Rawi Warin Grand Ship once took tourists out to sea around Ko Lanta, but was damaged in bad weather a few years ago.

Be a silversmith

Obsessed with sparkly things? Book a workshop at **Silvergypsie** *(facebook.com/silvergypsie; 1/2 persons 3000/5800฿)* and surprise your crush with a new ring. Situated close to Hat Khlong Noen on the west coast, Silvergypsie is run by Jessi and Tak, a German-Thai duo who lost their hearts to silver.

Inlaid with semi-precious gemstones, the couple's silver jewellery is playfully designed. The two of them are more than happy to show you each step of silversmithing in a four-hour workshop from 11am to 3pm, where you solder and polish

BEST ISLANDS NEAR KO LANTA

Ko Jum: Formerly unknown, this islet still has beaches without a soul in sight, a haven for those seeking peace and quiet.

Ko Si Boya: An under-the-radar island without pretty beaches, but with more villagers than tourists, outnumbered though by cows.

Ko Pak Bia: Long-tail boats bobbing on crystal water and a beach framed by limestone rocks – this island is for chilling out.

Ko Lao Lading: Part of the Hong Archipelago, this cove delivers a picture-postcard beach flanked by coconut palms – perfect for swimming and relaxing.

EATING IN KO LANTA: RESTAURANTS

Hidden Hut Cafe & Eatery: Thai food packed with flavours, fast service and local flair at this spot on the outskirts of Old Town. *8am-8.30pm* ฿

SunMa – Thai food: From stir-fried *pat tai* noodles and tasty burgers to Penang curry, this Hat Khlong Chak spot offers a lot. Fruity *lassis* too. *9am-8.30pm* ฿

Khao Yai Restaurant: Overlooking offshore islets, this spot on Rte 4245 near Old Town has delicious Thai food, while bamboo creates a homely atmosphere. *9am-9pm* ฿

Jeab's Dining: A gorgeous sunset spot on Hat Khlong Khong that offers flavourful *massaman* and veg options. Live acoustic music. *9am-9pm* ฿฿

KO LANTA

EATING IN KO LANTA: CAFES

Tuesday Morning Small Talk Cafe and Chill Out: A must-visit for the atmosphere alone. Try avocado mash and sip a healthy drink at this cafe near Hat Khlong Hin. *9am-6pm* ฿฿

Heaven Hill & Seascape Lanta Cafe: Overlooking Ko Lek on the east coast, this coffee shop has hot and iced coffee, frappes, smoothies and ice-cold beers. *8.30am-5.30pm* ฿

Auntie Mae's Bakery & Coffee: Enter via a red London telephone box at this quirky Hat Khlong Tob cafe, with all-day breakfast and confectionery. *8am-6pm* ฿฿

BaanPhutawan Lanta Viewpoint Cafe: This cafe in the island's north has views of mangrove forests sloping into the sea – great for coffee and alfresco dining. *6am-8pm* ฿

SIGHTS
1 Ao Kantiang
2 Ao Nui
3 Baan Tae-Leng
4 Community Museum
5 Hat Khlong Chak
6 Hat Klong Khong
7 Hat Nui
8 Ko Lanta Lighthouse
9 Ko Talabeng
10 Laem Ngu Viewpoint
11 Monkey Point
12 Viewpoint on the Bay

ACTIVITIES
13 Cooking with Mon
14 Following Giants Koh Lanta Ethical Elephant Sanctuary
15 Lanta Kayak for Rent & Long Tail Boat
16 Lanta Kayaking
17 Lanta Zipline
18 Leam Tanod Nature Trail
19 Silvergypsie
see 11 Thung Yipeng Tourism Community Koh Lanta

SLEEPING
20 Baan Purada Lanta Seaview
21 Natty&Nanny's House

EATING
22 Arthaya Cafe
23 Auntie Mae's Bakery & Coffee
24 BaanPhutawan Lanta Viewpoint Cafe
25 Escape Cafe
26 Heaven Hill & Seascape Lanta Cafe
27 Hidden Hut Cafe & Eatery
28 Jeab's Dining
29 Khao Yai Restaurant
30 Lock Lack Coffee (Slow Bar)
31 Siam Home Cafe & Bakery
32 SunMa – Thai food
33 Tuesday Morning Small Talk Cafe and Chill Out

DRINKING & NIGHTLIFE
34 Ga Ru Da Bar & Restaurant
35 Krit Friendly Bar & Diner
36 Sound Shack Bar
37 Why Not Bar

SHOPPING
38 Malee Malee

until you're satisfied. To try your hand at making a ring or bracelet, you need to book a day or two in advance. Note that the daily classes are private; only two people can join. The price includes lunch, drinks and lots of laughs.

Cooking with Mon

You'd better arrive with an empty stomach. Mon's motto is 'Cook like a local; eat like a local', which translates to lots and lots of food.

Mon is assisted by his wife, Maayan, as well as Cakkie and others. These culinary masters run a hands-on **cooking school** *(cookingwithmon.com; adult/child 1600/1200฿; 10am-9pm)* near Hat Phra Ae on Ko Lanta Yai, the more developed of the two Lanta islands. The school is about making everything from scratch, including sourcing ingredients locally.

Typically, you can choose from stir-fries, curries and desserts, but the menu may vary on a daily basis as the first people who book the class get to choose their favourite meals. Others can join in if they find them appealing.

Nothing formal, the 4½-hour cooking classes feel like an auntie-teach-me-how-to-cook experience. If you get something wrong, they offer substitutes, keeping the atmosphere

BEST ACTIVITIES IN KO LANTA

Lanta Zipline: Fly through the jungle, strapped into a harness hanging from a pulley – the sea views are amazing.

Lanta Kayak For Rent & Long Tail Boat: Kayaking tours through sea caves and mangroves, promising close encounters with wildlife.

Following Giants Koh Lanta Ethical Elephant Sanctuary: This animal protection organisation cares for its pachyderms, offering riding-free interactions with the gentle giants.

Thung Yipeng Tourism Community Koh Lanta: Enjoy views of tangled mangroves.

Leam Tanod Nature Trail: Hike the 4.5km loop trail to spot oriental pied hornbills and shy, dusky langurs; a lighthouse is nearby. Rent a scooter to get there.

DRINKING IN KO LANTA: BARS

Ga Ru Da Bar and Restaurant: A mother and daughter duo runs this place off the main drag of the Old Town, serving delicious curries and drinks. *9am-6pm* ฿

Why Not Bar: Bamboo and peace surround this rustic Ao Kantiang bar with tasty drinks and evening fire shows – steps from the lapping waves. *11am-2am* ฿

Sound Shack Bar: Amazing Thai and Mexican food at the northern end of Hat Khlong Khong. Sunset views, good music and happy hours too. *noon-2am* ฿

Krit Friendly Bar & Diner: An idyllic Hat Khlong Khong bar that serves drinks and Thai and Western favourites at bamboo beach tables. *9am-midnight* ฿

BEST KO LANTA SIGHTS

Laem Ngu Viewpoint: This scenic spot on Ko Lanta Noi looks out over huts on stilts and offshore islands beyond.

Baan Tae-Leng: This eye-popping Ko Lanta Noi structure sits in a quiet location. There are graves and a cafe on site.

Viewpoint on the Bay: A short scooter ride from Old Town, this hilltop viewpoint offers sweeping vistas of rubber trees and offshore islets.

Monkey Point (at Tha Tung Yee Peng): Watch naughty macaques prowl for food at the mangrove-lined estuary of Lat Bo Nae in the island's northeast.

Ko Lanta Lighthouse: Sitting on a headland at the southern tip of Ko Lanta, this lighthouse overlooks Ao Waterfall and a rock jutting out of the sea.

PIXHOUND/SHUTTERSTOCK

Kayaking, Ko Talabeng

fun and chatty. There's a large long table, so you can see what others are doing and ask, 'How did you do this or that?' Once you finish the first of three meals, you eat and take a rest.

Mon and his helpers know the recipes inside out. They can tell just by looking what you need to add or remove. They take photos and videos and encourage you to judge by taste as well, so you'll end up constantly tasting your food. You'll leave with a full stomach, a recipe book and priceless memories.

Paddle around Ko Talabeng

Just off the coast of Ko Lanta, **Ko Talabeng** has a hidden beach sandwiched between rocks, which stand over 100m tall. Legend has it that pirates used to hide in the islet's caverns, which today make great kayaking.

On a guided one-day trip with **Lanta Kayaking** *(lantakayaking.com; adult/child 1500/1000฿; 9am-5pm)*, you first venture into the tangled mangroves of Thung Yee Pheng before heading to Ko Talabeng, an island home to playful macaques and monitor lizards. Sitting in the hull of a sit-on-top kayak – a design that makes it easy to get on and off – you glide on emerald water, then paddle into sea caves full of stalactites that glisten like diamonds.

After enjoying stir-fries on the beach, the tour ends with leisure time you can use for getting a tan or bathing in the warm water.

EATING IN KO LANTA: CAFES

Siam Home Cafe & Bakery: Sip coffee in this makeshift collection of floorboards, the most rustic cafe on the island, 4km north of Ao Kantiang. *1-5pm Thu-Tue* ฿

Escape Cafe: Serves irresistible gelato and muffins as well as coffee from Doi Chang, Chiang Rai, this Long Beach cafe focuses on quality. *8am-6pm* ฿

Lock Lack Coffee (Slow Bar): Smoothie bowls and a relaxed atmosphere in a garden setting on the main road in Sala Dan. Indoor and outdoor available. *8.30am-4.30pm* ฿

Arthaya Cafe: Rustic meets chic at this cafe on the main road near Secret Beach. Try a crepe and you're in for a treat. *8am-6pm* ฿

Trang Province

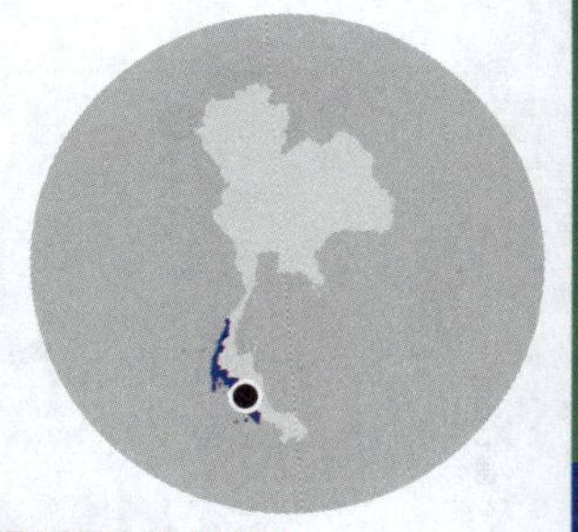

PEACE AND QUIET | NATURAL WONDERS | BREAKFAST CULTURE

From port city and mining town to the birthplace of rubber in the kingdom and the laid-back place it is today, Trang has moved through many eras. Wedged between mountains and the Andaman Sea, Trang's geography is beautifully varied, with enough attractions to woo travellers. Yet the 4918-sq-km province hasn't been overrun by tourists, as it has been overlooked in favour of islands further north and south.

Foodies and history buffs should plan a weekend in Trang city at least. The city's Old Town delights with museums and Sino-European shophouses, while the rest of the provincial capital is a jumble of hawker stalls, photogenic cafes and restaurants dishing up sponge cakes and local-style roasted pork. Chinese-influenced Trang city is infatuated with the morning meal; vendors open as early as 4am.

Those keen to see inland reaches can embark on cave adventures, visit waterfalls and soak in hot springs. Trang Province also has beaches and islands to write home about.

TOP TIP

If the province's extensive mainland reaches are on your itinerary, you'd better rent a car at the airport because public buses don't shuttle you to far-flung destinations, and taxis can be difficult to find in rural areas.

Hop on a Frog-Head Tuk-Tuk

MAP P572

Gaze at street art

Loud and fast, tuk-tuks in themselves are a fun part of the Thailand experience. In Trang city, those three-wheeled, motorised taxis have a quirky addition: a frog head. Make a beeline

GETTING AROUND

Trang city is 6km north of the airport; minibuses and taxis are available near the arrival hall. To get around fast, rent a scooter at one of the travel offices near Trang city's train station. However, the town itself is delightfully walkable. While the markets are within walking distance of the railway station, you can get motorbike taxis and the visually appealing frog-head tuk-tuks. A ride to the town costs 20฿ or 40฿, respectively. Trang's tuk-tuks are also available at Trang Bus Terminal. The blue city bus and blue-white *songthaew* run frequently. Starting at the train station, they go around town in circles.

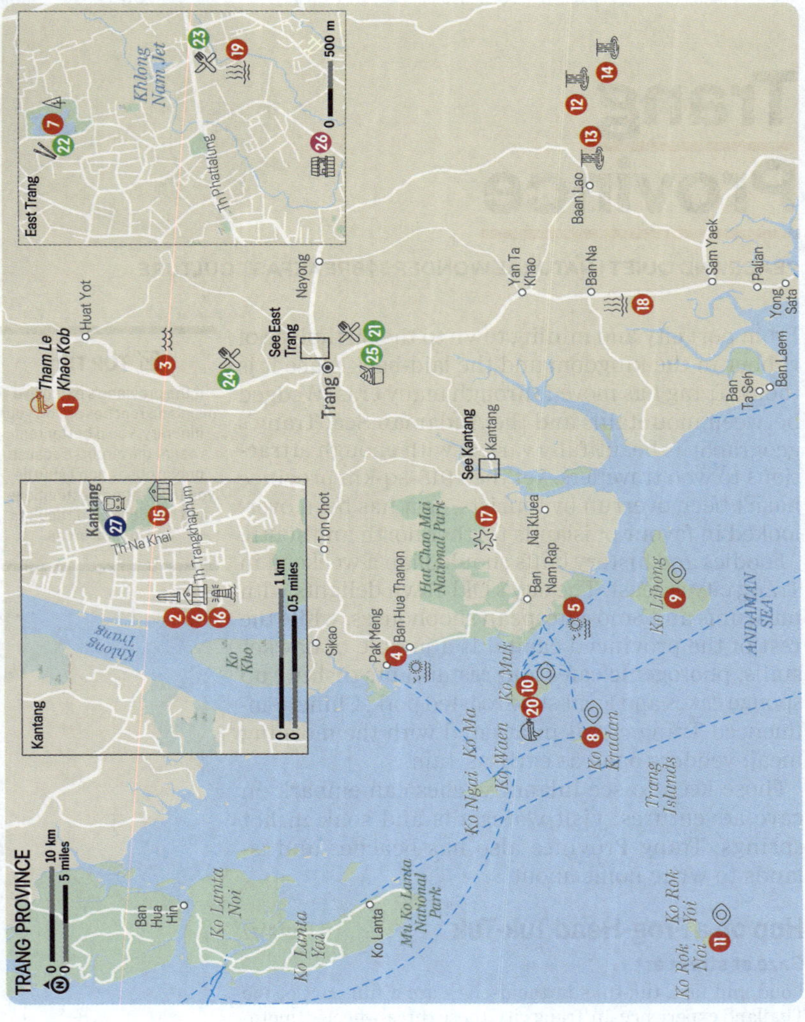

EATING IN TRANG CITY: OUR PICKS

MAP P570 & P572

Manila Cafe & Eatery: A rustic timber building fronted by a Vespa scooter with inexpensive Thai food and a quiet atmosphere. *7.30am-5pm* ฿

Tuta Bah Kut Teh: A Chinese restaurant offering homemade pork dim sum and broths infused with herbs and spices. *7.30am-2pm Tue-Sun* ฿

Mona's Restaurant & Homestay: Come here for the home-cooked food, kitties, brickwork tones and a vintage Coca-Cola couch. *11am-10pm Mon-Sat* ฿

Khun Pum Restaurant: Try *ka nom jeen* noodles for breakfast. But come early – Pum's pearly-white rice noodles topped with curry are gone by 9am. *6am-noon* ฿

HIGHLIGHTS 1 Tham Le Khao Kob **SIGHTS** 2 Dugong Statue 3 Emerald Pool 4 Hat Pak Meng 5 Hat Yong Ling 6 Kantang History Museum 7 Kapangsurin Park 8 Ko Kradan 9 Ko Libong 10 Ko Muk 11 Ko Rok	12 Nam Tok Nhan Sataw 13 Nam Tok Phan 14 Nam Tok Ton Tae 15 Phraya Ratsadanupradit Mahison Phakdi Museum 16 Trang Lighthouse **ACTIVITIES** 17 Kantang Hot Spring Forest Park 18 Kuansra Saline Hot Springs 19 Let's Relax Spa 20 Tham Morakot	**EATING** 21 Cafe'43 @Trang see 21 Gooddays.Cafe 22 Khun Pum Restaurant 23 Pier 88 Restaurant & Bar 24 Pirunyaa Local Cafe 25 Pon Kim Wan Homemade Bakery **SHOPPING** 26 Trang City Center Market **TRANSPORT** 27 Kantang Train Station	

for Trang's iconic train station and hop on one of these wacky vehicles. A ride across town costs 200฿. Tell the driver you want to check out the street art, and be filled with wonder as you putter along through Th Ratchadamnoen, Soi Ratchadamnoen and around the city's municipal park.

Well worth seeing, the murals trace the life and times of Trang. Take the **Sri Trang painting** at the junction of Soi Ratchadamnoen and Th Phet Kasem. The three-dimensional mural that depicts a park with blossoming trees is just one of the city's photogenic illustrations.

Likewise, the **Tham Morakot Mural** eternalised on a wall in the *soi* between Th Phet Kasem and Th Huai Yod 2. The mural provides a fabulous, three-dimensional perspective of Ko Mook's Tham Morakot (p576; emerald cave), with the sun peeping through a sinkhole.

Visit History Museums

MAP P570

Understand Trang's present

Showcasing Chinese influence, **Kantang History Museum** *(free)*, a 20-minute taxi ride from Trang city, is a symphony of Sino-European styles resulting from the tin boom in the late 19th century. While all information is in Thai, the photographs and distinctive rectangular columns, colourful stained-glass windows and a balustraded parapet are worth the taxi ride. To reach the museum, you can also hop on a *songthaew* at

TRANG PROVINCE SIGHTS

Trang Clock Tower: This Trang city landmark close to the train station is an eye-catching sight.

Dugong Statue: Representing Trang Province's mascot, this iconic sculpture is located right next to the history museum in Kantang.

Kapangsurin Park: Centred on a small lake, this state park in Trang city is a great place to chillax and watch the world go by.

Trang Lighthouse: Rising above the Kantang History Museum, the lighthouse looks out over Kantang's picturesque Old Town, which stretches to the coast.

Kantang Train Station: One of the camera-friendliest sights in Trang Province, Kantang's old timber train station appears straight out of a retro film.

DRINKING IN TRANG CITY: CAFES

MAP P572

Si Esperanza: White, clean and bright, this tiny cafe on Kantang Soi 4 boasts award-winning latte art as well as hot and iced coffee. *8am-4pm*

la'-ong Coffee x Arabica: Plants, chatty vibe, piano and tasty *es-yen* (iced espresso) at this homely cafe. *7.30am-5pm Sun-Fri, to 4.30pm Sat*

Trik or Treat: Near the Clock Tower, this coffee shop has Ethiopian coffee, local desserts and dark roast Arabica coffee from Songkhla. *8am-6pm Tue-Sun*

Gray 18 Cafe: A coffee shop with an industrial vibe, Gray 18 has live folklore music from Friday to Sunday and Brazilian, medium-roast drip coffee. *9am-5pm*

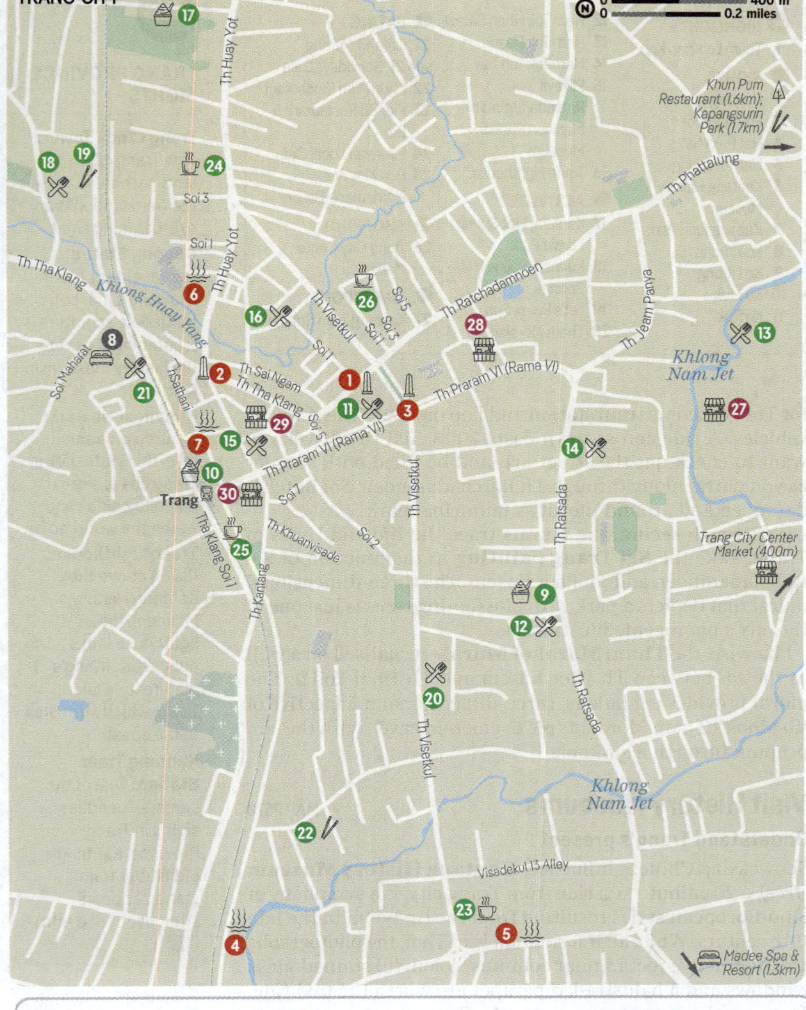

SIGHTS
1 Sri Trang painting
2 Tham Morakot Mural
3 Trang Clock Tower

ACTIVITIES
4 Isira House
5 Kanchana Massage for Health
6 Lily Spa & Massage Trang
7 Yapa Hattawet Traditional Thai Massage

SLEEPING
8 Sleeper House

EATING
9 Bua Loi Khoy Fan Desserts
10 Cake Rot Lert
11 Casa del Vino Est 1956
12 Chen Jia Dim Sum Cafe
13 D-Craft Trang
14 Early Bird & Night Owl
15 Hidden Something
16 Jeeb Khao Dimsum
17 Khanom Pia Soi 9
18 Manila Cafe & Eatery
19 Mona's Restaurant & Homestay
20 Terrang Dim Sum@ Trang
21 Ton Cha
22 Tuta Bah Kut Teh

DRINKING & NIGHTLIFE
23 Gray 18 Cafe
24 la'-ong Coffee x Arabica
25 Si Esperanza
26 Trik or Treat

SHOPPING
27 Cinta Garden
28 Da Laht Center Point
29 Trang City Municipality Market
30 Trang Railway Station Walking Street

Trang's bus terminal, while the train to Kantang should only take 20 minutes.

Less than a kilometre from the history museum is another stunner: **Phraya Ratsadanupradit Mahison Phakdi Museum** *(free)*. To get to this museum, catch a *songthaew* to Th Na Kai and walk the last few metres uphill. This museum is housed in the former residence of Ko Sim Bee. The illiterate but multilingual Bee was Trang's former governor, and was in office when Kantang was the capital of Trang Province. Remembered as the father of Thailand's rubber industry, Bee saved the south's economy by introducing rubber almost single-handedly, giving Chinese labourers hope and a future when cheap plastic heralded the demise of tin. The mansion, which is more than 100 years old, comes complete with the old typewriter of Bee's secretary and chocolate-coloured Victorian furniture. Basic English information is available at the museum.

Relax in Trang's Hot Springs

MAP P570

Time out for me-time

Rich in minerals like sulphites, fluoride, magnesium, calcium and potassium, the therapeutic springs of **Kantang Hot Spring Forest Park** *(adult/child 100/50฿)* are great for letting any lingering jet lag melt away. Local guide Patchanee 'Um' Kunlok says the water has bubbled up from underground since the Ayuthaya period between the 14th and 18th centuries, though the solar-lit forest park only opened in 2000.

Covering 324 *rai* (almost 52 hectares), the jungle-surrounded area welcomes you with a clear pool and water that's 70°C – fine for dipping your feet in, at best. Worry not. Further downstream, there's a natural pool with water well over 40°C. Should algae and piping-hot water not float your boat, the 20°C pool will. And let's not forget the chorusing cicadas and the exotic tak-tak calls coming from the jungle. Other great stress-relievers are artificial hot-spring baths and the on-site massage parlour.

As well as a car park and toilet block, there's a roofed area for socialising and a cafe selling drinks, post-soak nibbles and honey from the forest.

Best reached by car or scooter, the remote location just 15km west of Kantang Old Town is outside the service network of buses and *songthaew*.

BEST TRANG CITY MASSAGE PARLOURS

Let's Relax Spa: The leading spa at Trang Rua Rasada Hotel offers various treatments, including Thai facial massages.

Kanchana Massage for Health: Besides foot and Thai massages, aromatherapy rewards await at this health spa within walking distance of Lotus mall.

Isira House: Situated on the banks of Nam Chet canal, this spa and massage parlour has outdoor and air-con indoor sections.

Yapa Hattawet Traditional Thai Massage: With pressure-point charts on display, the certified Thai and Swedish massage therapists know their craft.

Lily Spa & Massage: Various treatments are available, from body scrubs and facials to Thai massages, including aromatherapies with essential oils.

EATING IN TRANG PROVINCE: PHOTOGENIC CAFES

MAP P570 & P572

Pirunyaa Local Cafe: Geometrically patterned floors and Arabica-robusta blends awake your senses; it's en route to Tham Le Khao Kob. *9am-6pm* ฿

Early Bird & Night Owl: Trang city spot offering Western meals, Asian delights like Hong Kong congee, homely interiors and an outdoor garden. *7am-9pm* ฿฿

Cafe'43 @Trang: Living-room interiors and murals at this cafe near Trang airport. The vanilla black coffee and tangerine cakes are tasty. *8.30am-4pm Mon-Fri* ฿

Gooddays.cafe: Walls for polaroid photos, stickers with butterflies and peace signs, and an old analog TV make this a truly photogenic cafe near Trang airport. *7am-5pm* ฿

TRANG CITY'S MARKETS HAVE CHANGED

Monaphat Bock, originally from Isan but Trang-based since 2019, is the owner of Mona's Restaurant & Homestay (p570).

After Cinta Trang turned quiet during the COVID years, many food and clothes vendors moved to **Da Laht Sritrang**. Customers like everything that's new, so Sritrang, located at the City Center Market, has become more popular.

Trang is generally quiet, probably because flights to Trang are more expensive than other Thai destinations. Trang has beautiful old homes and lacks the messy electrical cables of Phuket or Bangkok.

If you want to visit a peaceful beach, go to **Hat Yao** in Kantang. It has fine sand and a beautiful limestone rock at the southern end of the beach.

VORAVUDS/SHUTTERSTOCK

Boat tour, Tham Le Khao Kob

Visit Trang's Beaches & Islands

MAP P570

Experience real remoteness

If there's one thing Trang's beaches and islands have in common, it's that they're far from cities and blaring beach clubs.

Take **Hat Pak Meng**, 41km west of Trang city. Apart from a handful of resorts and sea-view restaurants, there's nothing here on this casuarina-lined beach. Pak Meng's water isn't the clearest in Thailand, but the chill atmosphere and views of limestone monoliths are priceless.

Using public transport to get here isn't practical, so rent a scooter or hail a cab in Trang city.

A 30-minute drive down the coast on Rte 4162 hides **Hat Yong Ling** *(tourismthailand.org; national park fee adult/child 200/100฿)*. Running parallel to a pine forest, this Kantang beach has muddy sand but is super-quiet. It also has a cave and a nature trail, though be aware that hungry and naughty monkeys like to steal food and water.

On remote **Ko Libong** – best reached by long-tail boat from Hat Yao (90 minutes; shared boat 100฿ to 150฿) – you'd be hard-pressed to find a bar with incessant whump-whumps. Likewise, 21st-century amenities aren't exactly available on **Ko Kradan**, **Ko Rok** and **Ko Muk** (loved for its 80m-long tunnel opening to a hidden lagoon), though day-trippers pouting for selfies have heard of these heavenly islands. The best departure point for these islands is Hat Yao.

EATING IN TRANG CITY: DESSERT SHOPS

MAP P570 & P572

Bua Loi Khoy Fan Desserts: This shop sells *bua loy* – chewy rice-flour, sweet potato, pandan-leaf balls bathed in homemade coconut milk. *1-9.30pm* ฿

Cake Rot Lert: Calling all sweet tooths! This dessert shop sells the sponge cakes Trang is known for: fluffy, fruity cakes with holes in the centre. *6am-9pm* ฿

Khanom Pia Soi 9: Offers baked rice-flour cookies with sweet fillings. Locals leave with bags of taro cookies; signature *khanom pia* sell out by noon. *6am-4pm* ฿

Pon Kim Wan Homemade Bakery: This bakery on the fringes of Trang wins you over with its chocolatey, nutty desserts. *10.30am-5.30pm Tue-Sun* ฿

Summon Courage for the Dragon's Spine

MAP P570

Tham Le Khao Kob

Hidden underneath the massive Khao Banthat mountain range, a 35-minute drive from Trang city beyond public transport, runs a stream only for the brave. Lying flat on your back in a rowing boat, you visit with two boatmen, who push you through a 500m-long cave using their hands as you graze the rocky, upper wall.

Welcome to **Tham Le Khao Kob** *(tourismthailand.org/eng/cave-exploring/tham-le-khao-kop; boat for 4 passengers 300฿; 8am-5pm)*, likely Thailand's most thrilling adventure, considered to be a must-do-but-once-is-enough experience even by non-claustrophobic people.

The tour is done in stages. It starts with a short boat ride down a shallow stream framed by tropical jungle. But then, lying down as you approach the entrance into the cave, you get a flavour of what lies ahead. Inside, you get off to explore the humid cave on foot with one of the two boatmen, who points out dripping Buddha- and ice-cream-shaped stalactites over the squeaking of bats and the duck-like sounds of cyclophorid snails. There's also a cavern with a brightly decorated shrine, plus a mini-version of Ko Samui's genitalia-shaped rocks in stalagmite form.

Locals call the last part of the adventure Dragon Cave due to the ceiling resembling a dragon's spine. The boatman behind you tells you to keep your hands down, and your chest nearly touches the rocky surface of the dragon's backbone above you. You're in a one-way tunnel for 10 minutes before seeing the light of day again.

The whole tour takes 50 minutes. You can squeeze your way through that narrow cave on a rowing boat year-round. Tham Le Khao Kob is only closed when driving rain has flooded the cave. Call **Rescue Khaokob** *(075 500 117)* to be sure it's open.

The Beauty of Nam Tok Phan

MAP P570

Soak in refreshing pools

Be sure to come with a charged camera to capture this pretty, fast-moving waterfall gushing into a fairy-tale world of shallow rock pools – all fine for a dip. Hiding deep in Tambol Palian, this less-known waterfall is well worth visiting if only to escape the crowds that overwhelm more popular waterfalls in the region. With stone tables, benches and

BEST MARKETS IN TRANG CITY

Da Laht Center Point: Night market with street snacks like crispy *ka nom beu ang* crepe filled with shredded coconut and golden egg-yolk threads.

Trang Railway Station Walking Street: A weekend night market with local prices. Fresh fruits and fermented *ka nom jeen* rice noodles available.

Trang City Municipality Market: Come to this central fresh market for crispy Trang pork, veggies and fruit as well as seafood and Thai desserts.

Cinta Garden: Cinta Garden is all about food, particularly spicy seafood salads.

Trang City Center Market: Cinta's successor, now the centre of the action, is a large market with Thai food, clothes and a smidge of nightlife.

EATING IN TRANG CITY: DIM SUM RESTAURANTS MAP P572

Ton Cha: Chinese roadside eatery offering pork roast, curried vermicelli noodles and bite-sized morsels of fried or steamed pork dumplings. *6am-1pm* ฿

Chen Jia Dim Sum Cafe: Marble-topped tables, stools with Chinese patterns, and dim sum served in bamboo baskets. *7am-3pm Thu-Tue* ฿

Terrang Dim Sum@ Trang: A Halal favourite, this Muslim eatery has given dim sum its own spin by offering entirely pork-free dumplings. *6-11am & 4.30-9pm* ฿

Jeeb Khao Dimsum: Popular with locals, this hole-in-in-the-wall with plastic stools serves white, pork-filled dumplings that sell out by 8am. *6am-11.30am* ฿

TRANG PROVINCE NATURAL ATTRACTIONS

Emerald Pool: This peaceful place 20km north of Trang city is for relaxing and picnicking – just don't swim in the treacherous water.

Nam Tok Nhan Sataw: Framed by boulders great for picnicking, this small waterfall in Tambol Palian, a 50-minute drive from the city, has water all year.

Kuansra Saline Hot Springs: Free to use, these hot springs hiding some 40km south of the city have three pools of varying degrees, averaging out at about 42°C.

Tham Morakot: A two-hour drive from the city, Ko Muk's emerald cave opens to a hidden lagoon rumoured to have inspired Alex Garland to write *The Beach*.

Nam Tok Ton Tae: An hour's drive from Trang city, this multi-tiered waterfall cascades from rocks sitting at 320m.

NOK_HAPPINESS/SHUTTERSTOCK

Tham Morakot

wooden platforms overhanging the pools, it's also a great place to spend the day picnicking and get some respite from Thailand's tropical heat.

Nam Tok Phan *(075 208 908; adult/child 100/50฿)* is a 50-minute drive from Trang city. It's best reached by car or scooter, as it takes *songthaew* and public buses a good two hours to get to Palian, and public transport users will struggle to find a taxi to take them from Palian to the waterfall.

Apart from a car park, there's a clean toilet in the area. After paying the entry fee, you can walk the circular path that leads to the pools cascading through the forest. Clear in the sunny season and milky-green after rain, the water's appearance doesn't detract from the beauty of this tiered waterfall. If the white, frothy cascades and the mystical, snake-shaped roots and branches don't persuade you into a swim, you can kayak down the run-off instead. Kayaks are available for hire on site.

EATING & DRINKING IN TRANG CITY

MAP P570 & P572

D-Craft Trang: This hang-out is a nice place to have a beer, play pool and listen to Thai music; singers whip out acoustic guitars. *5.30pm-midnight* ฿

Hidden Something: Situated close to Trang's train station, this homely rooftop bar and bistro has grilled meats and delicious salads. *6-11pm* ฿฿

Pier 88 Restaurant & Bar: A restaurant with stylish interiors, great live music and delicious river prawns – near the bus terminal. *5pm-midnight* ฿฿

Casa del Vino Est 1956: Come here to sip a glass of wine and soak up the chill atmosphere as a local singer plays acoustic guitar. *5pm-midnight Thu-Tue* ฿฿

Satun Province

NATURAL WONDERS | GOOD EATS | CRAFT COFFEE

Satun Province draws tourists from near and far. The appeal is in its paradisiacal beaches. Most travellers regard the southernmost region of the Andaman Coast as a gateway to Ko Lipe or elsewhere in the Adang-Rawi Archipelago, which stretches in a horseshoe shape from Lipe to Ko Batong. But this low-key corner of Thailand has plenty of its own natural wonders, with an all-encompassing geopark sloping from Thung Wa's mountains to the provincial capital, Satun town.

In a province where an estimated 80% are of Malay descent, it's no wonder that Islam is a way of life. Muslims sip coffee as late as 11pm – reason enough for craft coffee shops to open in Satun town and in remote districts close to Trang Province too. Apart from a handful of pizza joints, the quiet provincial capital has countless halal restaurants.

So yes, with viewpoints, waterfalls, caves, beaches and even a 'time traveller's zone', Satun is worth a day or 10.

TOP TIP

Rent a motorcycle in Satun town and visit the waterfalls on two wheels while coffee-tasting your way around the province. Once you're out of the city, the rural roads of La-Ngu and beyond are easy to navigate.

GETTING AROUND

Downtown Satun is walkable. You can find plenty of tuk-tuks and honking *songthaew* (30฿ to 50฿). Or flag down a motorcycle taxi on the main roads or at 7-Eleven near Mambang mosque. Motorcycles (250฿ to 300฿) and bicycles (150฿) are available for rent.

Getting to Malaysia by land is possible via border crossings like the Wang Prachan Boundary Post, some 40km south of Satun in Thale Ban National Park. The post is also worth visiting for the Thai-Malaysia Border Weekend Market. Public transport isn't available, but you can hail a cab in Satun. To catch a ferry to Langkawi, Malaysia, wait at 7-Eleven north of Satun's clock tower. There's a *songthaew* bound for Tha Tammalang, from which ferries depart.

Camp & Make Kopi

Try your hand at coffee-making

More than a craft coffee shop, **Kopi Naka** offers coffee-making workshops in Naka village, where coffee recipes have been passed down for generations. Twenty-five minutes from **Pak Bara**, the jumping-off point for Ko Lipe, Kopi Naka lies beyond the service network of buses, so rent a car or scooter. From Satun town (53km away), it's a one-hour drive.

The approachable husband and wife duo Anucha and Rujeenok 'Nok' Samrea live here amid coffee plants, roasters and solar panels as well as durian and jackfruit trees. They make coffee from scratch, and you can try your hand at it for 300฿. The price includes an overnight stay in a tent plus an aromatic cup of rich, earthy and syrupy *kopi*, also called *cafe boran* or ancient coffee.

HIGHLIGHTS
1 Satun UNESCO Global Geopark

SIGHTS
2 Hat Hin Lak Si
see 1 Khao To Ngai Geological Time Boundary
3 Masjid Mambang
4 Prasat Hin Pun Yod

ACTIVITIES
5 Kopi Naka

SLEEPING
6 Navakiri Boutique Resort Satun
7 Sabaidee Resort

DRINKING & NIGHTLIFE
see 7 Aroma Cafe Chalung & Aroi Malay
8 Coffee Engineering
9 D'oasis Cafe
10 Kopi Rim Khlong By.Khumracha

SHOPPING
11 Thai-Malaysia Border Weekend Market

TRANSPORT
12 Pak Bara Ferry Terminal
see 11 Wang Prachan Boundary Post

LEMARET PIERRICK/SHUTTERSTOCK

Prasat Hin Pun Yod (p581)

After pointing out seedlings and good agricultural practices (GAP) approved by Thailand's Ministry of Agriculture – including drying coffee beans in a solar drying cabinet – Nok lets you stir a boiling mixture of ground coffee beans and brown sugar with a wooden spatula. After 30 minutes of hard work and billowing smoke, the Nutella-like broth turns black like tar. You let that sit for half an hour, then pound the solid mass with a club-like pestle; sucking on those bitter clumps as though they were sweets is allowed.

Interestingly, those fine black pieces turn brown again as you sift them to get a powder. Nok doesn't speak much English, but laughs are guaranteed in this two-hour workshop.

THAILAND'S BEST CUP OF JOE

Rujeenok 'Nok' Samrea, coffee farmer, barista and co-owner of Kopi Naka.

Our signature coffee is grown in **Satun Geopark**, a mountainous area with Ordovician limestone and soils full of minerals, which gives the coffee a rich taste. We take care of every step in the coffee production process, from fertilising and nourishing to harvesting. To get full-bodied coffee with a strong taste, we only collect red beans. Yet we have a zero-waste policy. We use coffee berries for tie-dye bags and bark and leaves for tea and tie-dye fabrics. The remaining waste can be turned into organic compost.

Try natural process medium roast Satun robusta. Our variety has been passed down for four generations.

DRINKING IN SATUN PROVINCE: CRAFT COFFEE SHOPS

D'oasis Cafe: A 15-minute drive from the city centre, this cafe serves fruity morning elixirs like durian coffee or date latte coffee. *10am-6pm Mon-Sat*

Kopi Rim Khlong By.Khumracha: Serves drip and moka pot coffee or latte on the rocks, near Satun Geopark Gateway. *7am-11pm Sat-Thu, from 2pm Fri*

Coffee Engineering: A top-notch cafe serving drip coffee in a garden 20 minutes northeast of the city; local and international varieties. *9am-6pm Sat-Thu*

Aroma Cafe Chalung & Aroi Malay: This cafe in Tambol Chalung specialises in coffee with unique flavour profiles. *6-10.30am & 4-9.30pm Wed-Mon*

KUNANON/SHUTTERSTOCK

Khao To Ngai Geological Time Boundary

TOP EXPERIENCE

Satun UNESCO Global Geopark

Satun UNESCO Global Geopark, covering Amphoe Thungwa, La-Ngu, Manang and part of Mueang Satun, was the first in Thailand, perhaps surprisingly. After all, Satun is better known for its beaches. Yet spread across this coastal province are sites of geological importance, from places where red sandstone and limestone meet to colourful discs washed ashore and polished by the ocean for aeons.

DON'T MISS

- 1000-spire stone castle
- Khao To Ngai Fault Plane
- Bridge overlooking red sandstone and limestone
- Fossils and sea caves
- Hat Hin Lak Si

Geological Time Boundary in Plain Sight

The concept of time travel is nothing new – but here it's real. All you have to do is take a peaceful, 20-minute stroll along an 800m-long bridge framed by two distinctly different forms of rocks: red sandstone dating from the Cambrian period (485 to 541 million years ago) and limestone from the Ordovician period (444 to 485 million years). The bridge sits just 7km southeast of Tha

PRACTICALITIES

● tourismthailand.org/attraction/mu-ko-phetra-national-park ● open 24hr ● Free entry ● Long-tail boat trips to Prasat Hin Pun Yod bookable at Pak Bara

Pak Bara, the jumping-off point to the island of Ko Tarutao in the Tarutao Marine National Park. These rocky areas, known as the **Khao To Ngai Geological Time Boundary**, give you an entry point into different geological eras – 'time travel', you might call it.

Hop on a rented scooter or motorcycle taxi, tell the ranger guarding the security gate you want to visit the 'Time Traveller's Zone' and get the camera out. The area's red rock and limestone merged here due to cracking and moving of the Earth's crust and the Andaman Sea flooding the area. Keep an eye out for fossils camouflaged in the limestone walls as you walk through eras that are millions of years apart, and enjoy the dull booms of saltwater sloshing through sea caves, echoing as it froths.

Hat Hin Lak Si

Within walking distance and also part of Satun UNESCO Global Geopark is Hat Hin Lak Si, or Colourful Stone Beach. While food and drink or facilities such as showers are non-existent here, the beach is totally worth a visit. Best viewed at low tide early in the morning before the heat or at noon when a tree offers shade, the beach features conspicuously coloured pebbles polished by waves for thousands of years, from red and pink sandstone gravel rich in iron to quartz crystals and grey limestone.

Prasat Hin Pun Yod

Known in Southeast Asia as the Land of Palaeozoic fossils due to its abundance of diverse fossils and the world's oldest succession of fossil remains, Satun Geopark is characterised by mountains in the north and east of the province, while beaches and islands prevail on the Andaman Coast.

One such coastal island is **Ko Khao Yai** just off Pak Bara. This island has arguably the most visually appealing site in the geopark: Prasat Hin Pun Yod (known as the 1000-Spire Stone Castle). This is a huge sinkhole encircled by a ring-shaped fortress of ridged limestone rocks. Inside, a milky-grey lagoon with a quartz- and tourmaline-flecked beach appeals to tourists.

A private ride on a wobbly long-tail boat from Pak Bara Ferry Terminal costs at least 1400฿, plus a 100฿ national park fee; cheaper package tours are available in high season. Look closely as you approach the stone castle; there are faces in the giant, crenellated rocks. The lagoon is fine for a dip, but do wear water shoes as the sea floor is rocky.

FOSSILISED REMAINS & 'RUST' ON LIMESTONE

The rust-like stains you see on limestone rocks on the way to Prasat Hin Pun Yod is oxidised iron. Limestone may contain iron, which usually turns reddish-brown when it's exposed to oxygen due to a chemical reaction. At the lagoon inside the 1000-spire stone castle is a 475-million-year-old fossil that looks like a fish skeleton, covered by sandy grains rich in minerals.

TOP TIPS

- Bring your own food and drinks – there's only a pop-up cafe near the security gate to the Time Traveller's Zone.
- Prasat Hin Pun Yod is only accessible by boat from Pak Bara, and you can't go inside the 1000-spire stone castle in rough seas.
- You can book a trip to the 1000-spire stone castle at B&D Travel, located right at Pak Bara Ferry Terminal (ask for Ms Naree 'Bee' Wanbilai 086 964 2623); tell her you want to leave early in the morning to beat the crowds.
- Ask your paddle guide to take you into the bubbling sea caves of the 1000-spire stone castle and show you the fossil on the beach – tips are appreciated.

Satun Islands

Reggae bars, dive sites and white-sand beaches make Ko Lipe a tourist draw.

GETTING AROUND

Getting to Ko Lipe requires flying or riding a train or bus to Hat Yai. That's followed by a two-hour minibus ride to Pak Bara and a 90-minute speedboat tour. To get around the 4-sq-km island, you can walk or ride a tuk-tuk, scooter or bicycle. Reaching Bulon is trickier. Fewer speedboats go there from Pak Bara (p578) and long-tail boat captains challenge your haggling skills. But you won't (yet) have to pay a national park fee, and once you're there, you can cross the island on foot.

First settled by sea gypsies over 150 years ago, Ko Lipe had a quiet existence until fishermen followed by arms and drugs dealers rocked up. Meanwhile, the tiny island has been transformed into a tourist magnet. White-sand beaches, dive sites and reggae bars are reasons why up to 3500 travellers visit this island near Malaysia daily. Nevertheless, the island, which is part of Tarutao National Marine Park, is still paradise, with crystal waters and colourful soft corals.

Closer to Pak Bara is Ko Bulon Le, a jungly speck that's ripe for exploration. Most of its inhabitants are sea gypsies who live in dilapidated bungalows. This isn't the place for creature comforts, but look forward to unparalleled castaway vibes.

Ko Lipe

TIME FROM PAK BARA: **1HR 30MIN**

Kayak Ko Lipe's offshore islets

Paddle silently, gliding into the quiet cove as crystal water laps ashore and enjoy the odd boop-boop-boop of a coucal piping up from a hidden corner. As if Ko Lipe wasn't beautiful enough, kayaking is a wonderful what's-around-the-bend experience.

Going all the way around Ko Lipe when the sun beats down is a tough ask: it would take two to four hours, depending on the number of beaches you visit. But if you set your sights lower, **Ko Kra**, 300m from **Hat Sunrise**, is within reach.

While the 20-minute kayak across to the tiny islet is child's play, the short climb to Ko Kra's rock isn't a walk in the park. There are no ropes for safety, but the panoramic views of Ko Lipe, **Ko Adang** and the surrounding seascape are worth it. Also, be careful when you go swimming, as sea urchins lurk even in Ko Kra's shallow water.

Possibly the cheapest place to rent a kayak is **Jakun Boat Rental and Restaurant** *(086 964 2988; 1/4hr 150/300฿; 8am-5pm)* on Hat Sunrise. The well-maintained kayaks have been painted in Thailand's conspicuous national colours – blue, white, red – so you won't get lost. **Castaway Resort Ko Lipe** *(kohlipe.castaway-resorts.com; per hr 200฿)*, further south on Hat Sunrise, also rents out kayaks.

FOKKE BAARSSEN/SHUTTERSTOCK

Ko Lipe

TARUTAO NATIONAL MARINE PARK TOURS

The national park includes Ko Lipe and surrounding sea and islands, most notably Ko Adang, Ko Rawi and Ko Tarutao.

B&D Travel Pak Bara: Whether you need a private long-tail boat or a package tour, Khun Bee at Pak Bara can help.

Castaway Resort Koh Lipe: This low-key resort on Hat Sunrise has a reliable tour desk.

AdangSeaTour: This travel agency at Tha Pak Bara offers customised itineraries from fun dives to snorkelling tours.

Koh Lipe Star Travel: Situated on Walking Street, this agency offers reasonably priced snorkelling and sunset tours.

Wichit Tour Koh Lipe: Operator offering anything from fishing trips to snorkelling the colourful corals at Ko Jabang.

Fishing with Bulon's sea gypsies

If you're very lucky, a *chao leh* might allow you to ride along when they go out to fish. It's pure kindness and not a service. As such, the provision of these trips can't be relied on. Payment can be a sensitive topic.

It starts with a puff of smoke as Mr Malek fires up the engine of the long-tail boat around 9am. Then a helper uses a bamboo push pole to get the rickety boat out of the shallows. As **Ko Bulon Le** shrinks into miniature, you can enjoy the salt sprays as the boat rocks side to side. Moments later, these sea gypsies of the Urak Lawoi tribe let down nets.

Fishing with tourists is a secondary pursuit for many of Thailand's *chao leh* today, but for those roughly 100 'people of the sea' who live in Ko Bulon Le, money and material

DRINKING IN KO LIPE: BARS

OMG! Sports Bar & Restaurant: One of the first bars to open in Lipe, OMG! has live music in high season and flexible opening hours. *9am-midnight*

Jungle Bar: A chill place for a late-night beer in high season, this bar is embellished with fishing rods and wood from long-tail boats. *10am-2am*

Jimmy Bar: Open year-round, this reggae bar has relaxed vibes. The owner, Jimmy, whose hair is a hurricane-struck mane, says he's from the moon. *4pm-2am*

Zodiac Bar: Cool vibes, tasty cocktails and chill house beats make this sunset bar overlooking Ko Kra a tourist draw. *11am-11pm*

WHY I LOVE KO BULON LE

Philipp Meier, Lonely Planet writer

I'll never forget the day I first set foot on Bulon's deserted School Beach. I was the only traveller to jump from the speedboat, and it was starting to drizzle. Yet that white sand under my feet, the empty beach, crashing waves and the pine forest – for me this was paradise.

Walking up the hill in search of a place to sleep, I still didn't see a single soul. I was warming to the idea of staying in an abandoned bamboo bungalow when I finally met roaming roosters and eventually: *humans*.

My tip? Come in mid-May at the end of the season. That's when Bulon's tiny existence is bigger than mass tourism.

PHILIPP MEIER/LONELY PLANET

OMG! Sports Bar (p583)

goods are unimportant. Before the fishing trip, ask the boat's captain whether or not he'd be offended if you offered a tip.

Pop up in **Ao Mango**, about a 10-minute walk from anywhere on the island, and find Mr Malek. He's a darkly tanned guy who likes to wear a sarong. Use hand gestures to communicate across the language barrier, show interest in what he does and you might be invited on a fishing trip the next day.

Mr Malek and his friends use a technique called drift netting, where nets hang vertically in the water and drift with the current. The guys collect the nets two days later, before the first inkling of light.

Should you want to get some fun pictures, bring your own mobile, protected in a waterproof zip-lock bag, because Mr Malek is happy with his tiny, nostalgic Nokia version.

KO LIPE ON FOOT

Dive into Ko Lipe's reggae bars, souvenir shops and local Thai restaurants with this walking tour across the island.

START	END	LENGTH
Zodiac Bar at Zodiac Sun Resort	Jimmy Bar	2km; one hour

Overlooking Ko Kra, Zodiac Sun Resort's 1 **Zodiac Bar** (p583) makes a perfect start to the walking tour across the island. After slurping a tasty cocktail at twilight, pass Irene Resort Koh Lipe and saunter along the peaceful soi towards 2 **OMG! Sports Bar** (p583), in time with the slowly croaking frogs.

Then continue past the turn-off to Walking Street and visit 3 **Seasick Flagship Store**. From tie-dye tees to notebooks depicting white-sand beaches, this souvenir store has more than postcards from paradise. Wiggle your way out before it's late, walk back and swing left into 4 **Walking Street,** with its bars, shops and restaurants galore.

Pit-stop at a streetside vendor for some sweet banana-topped *rodee*. Another crowd-pleaser is the bubble tea store of 5 **Owl Cha** further down the road, which has prices in the tens. To get a proper meal after pre-fuelling with sugarball drinks and pan-fried flatbread, retrace your steps along Walking Street to 6 **Hua Mum Seafood** opposite the 7-Eleven, and tuck into freshly caught fish from Lipe's sea gypsies. End at 7 **Jimmy Bar** (p583) in an unnamed back alley and soak up its laid-back reggae vibes.

Places We Love to Stay

฿ Budget ฿฿ Midrange ฿฿฿ Top End

Phuket

Map p516 & 518

Green Dreams Guesthouse ฿
฿ Within walking distance of the Surin Circle Clock Tower, this guesthouse offers excellent value for money, with tiny but clean rooms and friendly staff.

Memory at On On Hotel ฿฿
Wrapped in Phuketian heritage, movie location On On has rectangular columns, whitewashed walls, a balustraded parapet and roof-free inner courtyard like in the old days.

Space House Hotel Phuket ฿฿
Wood and neon lights combine the rustic with the modern at this avant-garde, Rawai-based capsule hotel with a pool.

Blu Monkey Hub & Hotel Phuket ฿฿฿ Located a kilometre from the Lard Yai Sunday Night Market, this posh Phuket Town hotel has awesome city views and tubs on balconies.

Ranong

Map p533

Yes No Hotel ฿ With vintage furnishings including a comfortable bed, clean and spacious rooms with balconies plus unbeatable value for money, the answer is definitely yes! South of Ranong town.

A Day Inn Ranong Hostel
฿ This boutique hotel in downtown Ranong has only six rooms. Brick tones, a Sino-colonial building and the community lounge all add to the homely atmosphere. Dorms available.

Sook Hotel ฿฿฿ The rooms of this quiet downtown Ranong hotel are centred on the pool, and free snacks are provided all day. There's also a cafe.

Ko Phayam

Bamboo Bungalows ฿฿
Enjoyable save for the cold shower, this quiet Ko Phayam hotel has a beachfront restaurant and a laid-back vibe, complete with hammocks overlooking the sea.

Ziggy Stardust Resort ฿฿ This Ao Yai resort boasts wooden beach huts that come with en suite bathrooms, hot showers and hammocks strung on the verandas.

Ko Chang

Crocodile Rock Bungalows
฿ Don't be surprised if you end up staying longer. Clinging to a hillside, crocodile's bungalows with their porch hammocks are a haven of tranquillity.

Rattana ฿฿ Tucked away in Ko Chang's northwest, Rattana has spotless huts with porch hammocks. Hornbills visit occasionally, and food and drink is available.

Phang-Nga Town

Home Phang-Nga Guest House ฿฿ Reasonably priced rooms with mountain views characterise this centrally located guesthouse. Tours are bookable on site, and there's a restaurant in a garden setting.

Rachawadee House Phang Nga ฿฿ Backdropped by limestone rocks, Rachawadee sits in a quiet location close to everything. Rooms are spacious and come with verandas and good wi-fi. Dorm available.

Hink Poshtel PhangNga ฿฿฿
Concrete and wood add ambience to this chic yet rustic place. Beds are heaven, as are the views and the atmosphere. There's an on-site cafe.

Khao Lak

Sunflower Bungalows ฿฿
A tranquil spot yet close to everything, this cheap and cheerful bolthole has an intimate atmosphere, a pool and garden and on-site cooking classes.

Poseidon Bungalows ฿฿
Poseidon hides in a sandy cove in the verdant embrace of the surrounding trees. Creature comforts are available, as are a pool and tour desk.

Ko Phra Thong

Aromdee Homestay ฿฿
Located on a beach in the south of Ko Phra Thong, this peaceful homestay has thatched-roof huts and a ramshackle bar for sundowners.

Horizon Eco Resort (p543)
฿฿฿ Nuzzling up to Hornbill Hill, this eco-resort is planted in the heart of nature, with spotless bamboo bungalows that blend in. Kayaks available.

Khao Sok

Khai Jungle Experience (p546)
฿ With tents and bamboo bungalows, accommodation is simple. But Maew's culinary skills, Khai's thrilling jungle tours and chatty vibes make this a worthwhile hideout.

Anurak Community Lodge
฿฿ This eco-resort offers bungalows and safari-style tents amid a sea of palms. With a rainforest rising programme, sustainability is high, and eco-adventure packages are available.

Krabi Province

Map p550 & p554

Chill Out Bar & Bungalow ฿ Taking it easy is at the heart of this chill-out village near Hat Ao Nang, a collection of simple bungalows with a bar for ice-cold beers. Langurs visit, too.

Play Poshtel Krabi ฿฿ Design and community spirit are high at Play Poshtel in Krabi town. Play board games or foosball at the cafe and sleep in a dorm or private room.

Blu Monkey Pooltara Krabi Hotel ฿฿฿ Peace and quiet await in Blu Monkey's tranquil corner, half an hour's drive from Hat Ao Nang. Rooms are bright and spacious, and there's a pool and free bicycle rental.

Ko Phi-Phi

View Hostel ฿฿ This hostel's boast is the view. Snuggled into the hillside of Ao Loh Dalum, it has cheap bunk beds, free nibbles, coffee and snorkelling gear.

Phi Phi Banyan Villa ฿฿ The unique pull of this four-star hotel is the location close to Tha Tonsai. But it also makes our list because of the atmosphere – quiet despite its central location, with a beautiful pool and garden.

Ko Lanta

Map p566

Natty&Nanny's House ฿ Natty&Nanny's rooms have kitchen amenities and cosy verandas. It's located in the northeast of Ko Lanta Yai; the peace is only interrupted by the 'baeee' of a goat.

Baan Purada Lanta Seaview ฿฿฿ This six-room hotel near the Old Town offers cooking classes. Bamboo tattoos are offered on site, and you can meet people at the lounge.

Trang City

Map p572

Sleeper House ฿ This hotel near the train station has a wacky Thai, Chinese-Peranakan colour scheme. Stay in the dorm or book a private room; bicycles available.

Madee Spa & Resort ฿฿ Formerly called Merry Spa & Resort, this wellness hotel with a pool offers heavenly massages, an on-site cafe and a good night's sleep in a quiet corner near Lotus mall.

Satun Province

Map p578

Sabaidee Resort ฿ Get the best bang for your buck at this out-of-town Chalung resort with modern conveniences, just 14km north of Satun town. Thai food and excellent coffee are available across the street.

Navakiri Boutique Resort Satun ฿฿฿ White, clean and bright, the rooms of this splurge-worthy resort in Tambol Chalung are popular with Malaysians. It's centred around a long saltwater pool. Enjoy southern flavours at the restaurant.

Ko Lipe

Chic Lipe ฿฿ This chic hostel offers private rooms as well as female and mixed dorms. Facilities include a restaurant, two pool tables and a library.

Castaway Resort (p582) ฿฿ The rustic bungalows of this 46-room resort are scattered around Hat Sunrise – all have hammocks; none are air-conditioned. Dives and yoga are bookable.

Ko Bulon Le

Chaolay Homestay ฿ A no-frills homestay with barely more than a handful of simple huts, this place has an on-site restaurant and friendly *chao leh*, who still make a living fishing.

Pansand Resort ฿฿฿ Situated behind swaying palms right behind the white-sand School Beach, this two-star hotel is a collection of pared-back bungalows and an airy beachside restaurant.

VALENTIN BACIU/SHUTTERSTOCK

Phi Phi Banyan Villa, Ko Phi-Phi

TOOLKIT

The chapters in this section cover the most important topics you'll need to know about in Thailand. They're full of nuts-and-bolts information and valuable insights to help you understand and navigate Thailand and get the most out of your trip.

Bo Sang Umbrella Festival (p262), Chiang Mai

PLOYPEMUK/SHUTTERSTOCK

Arriving

Many visitors enter Thailand via Bangkok's Suvarnabhumi Airport or Phuket Airport, but international flights also arrive at Bangkok's second airport Don Mueang, as well as at Chiang Mai, Chiang Rai, Hat Yai, Ko Samui and Krabi airports. There are numerous land and sea border crossings with Cambodia, Laos, Malaysia and Myanmar.

Visas

Citizens of 93 countries can enter Thailand without a visa for up to 30 days, which can be extended for another 30 days. All visitors must complete a digital arrival card before arriving in Thailand.

Onward Travel

Technically, visitors should have proof of return or onward travel on arrival in Thailand. Your passport should be valid for at least six months from the day of your arrival.

Wi-Fi

Almost all airports in Thailand offer free wi-fi. At land borders, you'll need to find a nearby cafe or restaurant for your online fix.

SIM Cards

Local SIM cards and data packages are cheap. They can be bought at any airport with international arrivals or at convenience stores and phone shops. Make sure your phone is unlocked and bring your passport.

Transport from Airport to City Centre

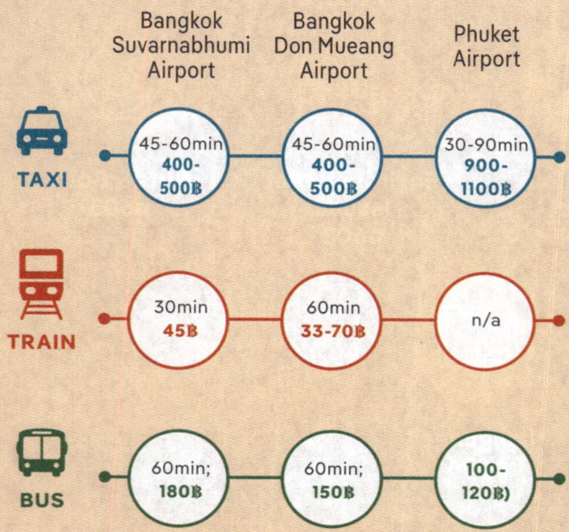

	Bangkok Suvarnabhumi Airport	Bangkok Don Mueang Airport	Phuket Airport
TAXI	45-60min 400-500฿	45-60min 400-500฿	30-90min 900-1100฿
TRAIN	30min 45฿	60min 33-70฿	n/a
BUS	60min; 180฿	60min; 150฿	100-120฿)

LAND & SEA BORDER CROSSINGS

There are over 20 land and sea border crossings between Thailand and Cambodia, Laos, Malaysia and Myanmar, but not all of them are open for foreigners. At the time of writing all Thailand–Cambodia land border crossings were either closed or operating reduced hours due to an ongoing border dispute. It's normally straightforward arriving in or departing from Thailand by land or sea; just ensure your passport is valid for at least six months. Note, too, that you can only enter Thailand by land or sea twice a year without a visa, a result of authorities cracking down on foreigners living in Thailand without visas.

FROM LEFT: FUSE/GETTY IMAGES, GOGLIK83/GETTY IMAGES

Getting Around

Planes, trains, buses or boats are the principal ways to get around Thailand, but you can also hire a car or motorbike.

TRAVEL COSTS

Car rental
900-1500฿/day

Motorcycle rental
200-500฿/day

Bicycle rental
100-500฿/day

Bangkok–Chiang Mai sleeper train
758-1653฿

Air

Budget airlines like AirAsia and NokAir and an extensive network of airports make it easy and cheap to hop around Thailand by plane. Bangkok's Don Mueang Airport is the budget hub and has daily flights to all corners of the country.

Bus & Minivan

Buses head everywhere and are reliable and reasonably quick. Beware of bus companies that operate directly from tourist hubs, like Bangkok's Th Khao San; they're often a rip-off. Minivans have superseded buses in some parts of the country. They're not as comfortable but are faster.

TIP

Download ridesharing app **Grab** *(grab.com)*, the Southeast Asian equivalent of Uber. It's the easiest, and often cheapest, way to get around.

NAVIGATING THAILAND'S ROADS

Thailand's roads are the most dangerous in Southeast Asia, with close to a million traffic accidents a year. Speeding and drink-driving are common, while road rules are routinely flouted. Many visitors hire motorbikes or scooters, but bear in mind that motorcycles are involved in more than half of all traffic accidents. Wear a helmet, remember that roads can be in poor condition, and give way to any vehicle bigger than yours.

Train

All trains out of Bangkok now depart from the newish terminus at Bang Sue, apart from a few local and commuter services. Services head north to Chiang Mai, south to Sungai Kolok, northeast to Isan and east to Aranya Prathet. Trains are scenic and relaxed, but slower than road transport.

Boat

A range of vessels, from ferries to wooden long-tail boats, connect the mainland with the islands, and also act as public transport along rivers and canals in Bangkok and elsewhere. Boats to some islands are less frequent in the June–October rainy season.

Car & Motorcycle

Cars can be rented via international chains or local companies in cities and at most airports. Drivers under 25 are often asked to pay a surcharge. Motorcycles can be hired wherever there are tourists. Visitors planning to drive should have an International Driving Permit, as well as a driver's licence.

DRIVING ESSENTIALS

Drive on the left.

Speed limits: 60km/h urban centres; 90km/h open roads; 100–120km/h highways and expressways.

International Driving Permit not needed for car rental, but if stopped by police they'll probably ask to see one.

Money

CURRENCY: BAHT (฿)

ATMs

ATMs are everywhere and most will accept foreign debit or credit cards, although there's a local fee of 250฿ for each withdrawal, as well as the fee your bank will charge. 20,000฿ to 30,000฿ is the maximum daily withdrawal limit at most ATMs.

Credit Cards

Hotels, shops and restaurants increasingly accept credit cards, but most places still accept only cash or digital payments. Visa and Mastercard are the most widely accepted credit cards.

Digital Payments

Local banks and digital wallets have embraced paying via phone, but Google Wallet is the only international digital payment system currently accepted in Thailand.

Tipping

Hotels 30-50฿ for bag carriers in smart places.

Restaurants Leaving behind small change is appreciated.

Taxis Not expected, but a small gratuity is welcomed.

Service Charges High-end hotels and restaurants add a 10% service charge.

HOW MUCH FOR A...

Bangkok Metro or Skytrain
17-62฿

Museum admission
100-500฿

National park entry
100-500฿

Local lunch
50-80฿

HOW TO... Avoid Touts

In Bangkok and Chiang Mai especially, some tuk-tuk drivers will offer you a 'city tour' that invariably results in high-pressure sales situations in jewellery, silk or handicrafts shops. Others may attempt to steer you towards guesthouses or hotels that will pay them a commission. Be wary of any 'new friend' who offers to accompany you on a shopping or sightseeing trip.

LOCAL TIP

Super Rich, a chain of moneychangers with branches in Bangkok and Chiang Mai, offers better currency exchange rates than the banks, especially if you're changing Asian currencies into baht.

DON'T STEP ON THE KING

Thailand has some of the strictest lese-majeste laws in the world. Insulting, defiling or disrespecting the king is a serious offence punishable by a long prison sentence. When it comes to the Thai currency that means it is technically illegal to step on banknotes or coins that have fallen on the floor because they all have the king's image on them. It is also considered disrespectful to keep banknotes in your back pocket: you're not supposed to sit on the king.

Accommodation

Boutique Glam

An ever-growing collection of stylish boutique hotels populate Bangkok, Chiang Mai, Phuket and Ko Samui especially. But there are also many budget and midrange places, as well as plenty of four- and five-star options. Hotels are a good deal in Thailand, with midrange rooms available from 800฿ per night. Spend more than 1500฿ and you can be very comfortable.

Budget Digs

There's been an explosion of new hostels in the most popular destinations and some now tempt travellers with swimming pools and rooftop bars. Hostels are social, with communal activities on offer. Dorms are the principal accommodation. Most hostels also have private rooms, although they cost about the same as a room in a midrange hotel.

Guesthouse Stays

The arrival of budget hotel chains in Thailand means that there are fewer of the family-run guesthouses that once dominated the low-end accommodation scene. You'll most likely find them in smaller destinations or towns off the tourist trail. Fixtures and furniture tend to be old-fashioned, but you still get air-con. Expect to pay from 500฿ per night.

Experience a Homestay

Homestays can be found across Thailand but are especially prevalent in rural areas. They're a less commercial budget choice, where you stay in a family home and meals are included in the price. Homestays are an excellent way of immersing yourself in the country and are often more sustainable than other accommodation options, as well as benefiting the locals directly.

HOW MUCH FOR A NIGHT IN A...

Boutique hotel
3000฿

Hostel dorm
350฿ and up

Homestay
500฿ and up

Get Back to Nature

Thailand has numerous ecofriendly places far from the hustle of the cities and big-ticket destinations, ranging from cabins on the banks of the Mekong River to hidden-away retreats on the islands or in the forests and mountains of northern Thailand. Most national parks also offer basic bungalows or have campsites where you can rent a tent.

HIGH SEASON & BOOKING AHEAD

Thailand's peak season for visitors runs from December to March, which is when accommodation prices are highest. It is highly advisable to book in advance at this time, both to secure the best deals and to guarantee a room. You'll also need to book accommodation in advance if you're planning to attend any big event, such as the Full Moon parties on Ko Pha-Ngan. Prices drop in the July–October monsoon season, especially on the islands, and great bargains can be found, as long as you don't mind the daily rain.

CLOCKWISE FROM TOP LEFT: J-ALONE/SHUTTERSTOCK, SIHASAKPRACHUM/SHUTTERSTOCK, FAT JACKEY/SHUTTERSTOCK

Family Travel

Thailand is a great place for family adventures. Thais love kids – some young children can find the attention they attract from the locals a little overwhelming – and playmates await everywhere. The beaches, wildlife encounters, outdoor activities, adventure parks, bustling markets and fun museums means that there's something for every age range to enjoy here.

Sights & Activities

Some museums and attractions offer half-price tickets for children under 12 or free entry for kids under three. Children under three and up to 100cm in height travel for free on the State Railway of Thailand and Bangkok's Metro and Skytrain networks. Older children get discounted fares up to the age of 12 or 14. Buses and boats don't charge for babies and toddlers.

Getting Around

Pavements in Thailand are often narrow and uneven, or just plain nonexistent, making them a challenge for pushchairs (prams) and strollers. A back carrier to transport tots is a good idea. If you're renting a car, note that car seats for kids are not always available. An increasing number of cycle shops and bike-tour outfits rent bicycles and helmets for children.

Animal Encounters

Kids love seeing Thailand's many monkeys in action, but remember that they are wild animals and they do bite. Be careful around stray dogs on the islands and in rural areas; they can be aggressive and disease-ridden.

Eating

Some resorts have menus for kids, but most places don't. Thai food is known for being spicy, but there will always be child-friendly dishes staff can recommend. High chairs for toddlers and nappy-changing facilities are rarely available.

CHILD-FRIENDLY PICKS

Children's Discovery Museum

Learning disguised as fun at this Bangkok museum aiming to spark children's creativity. (p130)

Vana Nava

Epic water slides and rides and tons of flora at this Hua Hin park touting itself as Asia's first 'water jungle'. (p425)

Chai Lai Orchid

Children are captivated by the elephants at this ethical community-based project southwest of Chiang Mai. (p299)

BEST BEACH DESTINATIONS FOR KIDS

Hua Hin (p421) The long and wide beaches at this mainland resort town are perhaps the most kid-friendly in all Thailand.
Ko Chang (p364) Thailand's second-biggest island has shallow and gentle seas that are ideal for children.
Ko Kut (p372) Super-soft sand, lots of coves to explore and waterfalls in the interior of the island.
Ko Lanta (p564) Stunning beaches line the west coast of one of the most family-orientated islands.
Ko Samui (p456) Hat Chaweng and Lamai have plenty of activities for kids.

Health & Safe Travel

INSURANCE

Travel insurance that covers you for theft, loss and medical issues is an excellent idea. Make sure that your policy covers emergency evacuation by air. Some policies specifically exclude 'dangerous activities', which can mean scuba diving, hiring a motorcycle or even trekking. If your policy requires you to pay doctors or hospitals directly and claim later, make sure to keep all relevant documentation.

Mosquito-Borne Diseases

Malaria and dengue fever are two potentially fatal diseases that are carried by mosquitoes and present in parts of Thailand. Your best protection is to avoid getting bitten, so use repellent and wear long clothing at night. Malaria and dengue-fever cases spike in the July–October rainy season, but most travellers will experience nothing more than some itchy bites.

Keep Cool

Most people need a couple of weeks to adapt to the heat and humidity of Thailand. Make sure to stay hydrated by drinking lots of water and avoid doing strenuous activity in the middle of the day. The sun is strong even if there's cloud cover, so apply a SPF30+ or greater sunscreen and wear a wide-brimmed hat.

TAP WATER

Thais don't drink the tap water (although the authorities deem it safe) and neither should you. Stick to bottled or filtered water.

SWIM SAFELY

Red flag Not safe to swim

Yellow flag Potential hazards in the water

Green flag Safe to swim

Yellow and red flag Lifeguards on duty

Black and white flag Surfboard and watercraft zone

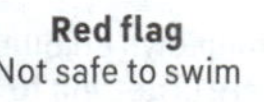

Stay Out of Jail

It's now legal to buy and use cannabis in Thailand, but that doesn't mean other narcotics have been decriminalised. Possessing or trafficking amphetamines, cocaine, ecstasy, heroin, magic mushrooms, methamphetamines or opium remains illegal and punishable with prison time, or a death sentence for the most serious smuggling cases.

POISONOUS SNAKES & JELLYFISH

Thailand is home to 60-odd species of venomous snakes, but they're mostly shy and nocturnal – or sea snakes – and travellers rarely encounter them. There have, though, been a handful of fatal incidents in recent years involving poisonous box jellyfish off Ko Samui and Ko Pha-Ngan. Some beaches have vinegar stations to treat jellyfish stings. Always check local conditions before swimming.

FROM LEFT: AVN PHOTO LAB/SHUTTERSTOCK, KORNIENKO ALEXANDR/SHUTTERSTOCK

Food, Drink & Nightlife

When to Eat

Ask a Thai their favourite thing to do and they will often reply 'eating'. The locals love their cuisine and all its variations so much that they don't restrict themselves to three meals a day, preferring instead to graze throughout their waking hours. Street food is available until late at night in big cities and popular destinations, but most restaurants close around 10pm.

Where to Eat

Restaurants

Range from hole-in-the-wall eateries to very sophisticated places. All cuisines can be found in big cities and major tourist destinations; elsewhere it's mainly Thai food in all its wondrous variations.

Food Stalls

Thailand's street food is delicious, cheap and consumed by people from all walks of life from early morning to late at night.

Markets

Many markets have food stands, so locals can eat while they shop.

Cafes

Thailand has a strong coffee culture and cafes can be found in all cities and towns.

MENU DECODER

A roy Delicious
Ba mee Wheat-and-egg noodles
Bet Duck
Blah Fish
Dom yam Thailand's sour and spicy soup
Gaang Curry
Gaang mat sa man A mild coconut-milk-based Thai-Muslim curry
Gai Chicken
Goo ay dee o Noodle soup
Ka nom Thai-style sweet snacks
Kow Rice
Kow kah moo Braised pork leg served over rice with greens
Kow man gai Thai-Chinese chicken rice
Kow mok Thai version of biryani (rice and chicken dish)
Kow nee o Sticky rice
Larb Minced-meat 'salad'
Moo Pork
Nam deum Drinking water
Nam pla Fish sauce
Nam prik Chilli-based dips
Pak Vegetables
Pat Fried
Pat see ew Wide rice noodles fried with pork and greens
Pat tai Thin rice noodles fried with egg and seasonings
Pet Spicy
Pon la mai Fruit
Prik Chilli
Rahn ah hahn Restaurant
Som tam Papaya salad
Tort Deep-fried
Yam Thai-style salad

HOW TO...

Identify Regional Cuisines

The different regions of Thailand all have their own unique take on food. Part of the fun of travelling here is getting to taste some of those variations. In fact, visitors can identify which part of the country they are in by the dishes they're being served, so here's a quick guide to distinguishing regional cuisines.

Southern Thai cooking is undoubtedly the spiciest (and saltiest) regional cooking style in a land of fiery regional cuisines. Seafood plays a major role.

The people of central Thailand favour sweet/savoury flavours and many dishes include freshwater fish, pork, coconut milk and palm sugar – common ingredients in the central Thai plains.

Northern Thai food is the least spicy regional cuisine and is more reliant on bitter flavours and dried spices. It's also very seasonal, reflecting the local love of veggies. *Kow nee o* (sticky rice) is the traditional accompaniment (as it is in northeast Thailand, too).

HOW MUCH FOR A...

cocktail
250-450฿

dom yam
80-400฿

gourmet dinner
2000-5000฿

noodle soup at food stall
50-70฿

pat tai
60-120฿

small bottle of local beer in a shop
38-45฿

som tam
70-100฿

Thai coffee
25฿

HOW TO... Eat Like a Thai

Sweet, sour, salty and spicy are the parameters that define Thai food, and although many people associate it with fiery heat, virtually every dish is an exercise in balancing these four tastes. This balance might be obtained by a squeeze of lime juice, a spoonful of sugar and a drop of fish sauce, or a tablespoon of fermented soybeans and a strategic splash of vinegar. Bitter also factors into many Thai dishes, and often comes from the addition of a vegetable or herb.

To achieve a balance of four clear, vibrant flavours and textures, a group might order a curry, steamed or fried fish, a stir-fried vegetable dish and soup, taking care to balance cool and hot, sour and sweet, salty and plain.

Whether at home or in a restaurant, Thai meals are always served 'family-style' – that is, from common serving platters. Put no more than one spoonful onto your plate at a time. Heaping your plate will look greedy to Thais.

To dine the Thai way, take a single spoonful of food from a central dish and ladle it over a portion of your rice. Use your fork to push a mouthful of food on to your spoon. Then use the spoon, not the fork, to lift the food into your mouth.

Chopsticks

Chopsticks are reserved for eating Chinese-style food from bowls or for eating in Chinese restaurants. If you fancy travelling with your own chopsticks, reusable (non-wooden) ones can be bought in most supermarkets or markets.

DRINK LIKE A LOCAL

Thailand has a very distinct drinking culture, although that's not always apparent in the big cities and major tourist destinations, where Western-style bars and cocktail lounges proliferate.

Elsewhere, you'll be drinking in local bars. They tend to be big, semi-open-air spaces that cater for groups – drinking in Thailand is a communal activity. There will often be some form of live music and, of course, food to accompany the imbibing.

The drinks will mainly be beer and whisky. Thailand's most popular brands of beer are Chang, Leo and Singha. Leo is the sweetest and Chang the strongest, while Singha is the most expensive. The most favoured brands of whisky are SangSom, Hong Thong and Mekhong. All are distilled from sugar cane and rice, which means they are technically rum. Very popular in rural areas is *lao khao*, which is Thai moonshine and made from fermented sticky rice or molasses.

Rather than buying individual drinks, Thais will order a beer tower and/or a bottle of whisky to share, along with soda water and cola as mixers and buckets of ice. It's polite to top up your companions' glasses as well as your own, or to add some ice to their drinks when they need it. A common toast is *chone gaow* (literally 'touch glasses').

Drinking in Thailand is all about having fun, rather than getting smashed. Staggering around drunk, shouting or fighting are all considered a big loss of face. So smile, get used to putting ice in your beer and watch out for those SangSom hangovers.

Responsible Travel

Climate Change & Travel

It's impossible to ignore the impact we have when travelling; Lonely Planet urges all travellers to engage with their travel carbon footprint, which will mainly come from air travel. While there often isn't an alternative, travellers can look to minimise the number of flights they take, opt for newer aircraft and use cleaner ground transport, such as trains. One proposed solution – purchasing carbon offsets – unfortunately does not cancel out the impact of individual flights. While most destinations will depend on air travel for the foreseeable future, for now, pursuing ground-based travel where possible is the best course of action.

The **UN Carbon Offset Calculator** shows how flying impacts a household's emissions

The **ICAO's carbon emissions calculator** allows visitors to analyse the CO2 generated by point-to-point journeys

Be a Trash Hero

Join the Trash Hero volunteers who clean up litter across Thailand, and who partner with communities on education and sustainability projects that aim to reduce and better manage plastic waste in particular. *(trashhero.org)*

Diving Without Damage

Thailand has world-class dive sites and many come here to learn scuba diving. But with so many divers around, coral and reefs can be damaged and marine life disturbed, so be careful when you're underwater.

Chiang Rai–based NGO **PDA Tours** offers sustainable treks to minority villages and ploughs the profits back into community projects including HIV/Aids education, mobile health clinics and village banks.

A good way to tour Chiang Mai is taking a slow, culturally immersive ride by *samlor* (three-wheel pedicab). **Chiang Mai on Three Wheels** *(chiangmai-alacarte.com)* can connect you with a driver and English-speaking guide.

CHOOSE A HOMESTAY

Consider staying with a family rather than in a hotel or hostel. Homestays are generally the most sustainable accommodation option, as well as directly benefiting the locals, and they're a great way to experience Thai culture.

MOVE OFF THE TOURIST TRAIL

Overtourism is a serious problem in Thailand, with some islands especially suffering from the adverse environmental impact from millions of visitors. Getting off the tourist trail and searching out little-seen destinations is one way of countering that.

Ethical Elephant Encounters

Both the **Phuket Elephant Sanctuary** and **Chai Lai Orchid** (p299) near Chiang Mai offer the chance to observe pachyderms up close, without any of the circus-like rides or shows that are harmful to their welfare.

Get Involved in Forest Conservation

Help preserve and restore forests, work with local communities and get involved in wildlife conservation with **Conserve Natural Forests** *(conservenaturalforests.org)*, which runs projects in north and south Thailand.

Respect Thailand's Hill Peoples

Treks to ethnic minority villages in northern Thailand are perennially popular, but remember that hill peoples have their own distinct cultures and many still follow animist traditions. Talk to your guide about acceptable behaviour in the villages.

Travel by Train

The **State Railway of Thailand** *(railway.co.th)* heads north, south, northeast and east of Bangkok. Trains won't get you everywhere, but using them drastically cuts emissions compared with a flight or bus ride.

Volunteer

There are myriad volunteering opportunities in Thailand, ranging from ecotourism and wildlife projects to assisting migrants and teaching in rural regions. Do some research before signing up to ensure you are joining a reputable organisation.

Hit the road on a bike tour with **Chiang Rai Bicycle Tour** (p207) or **Spice Roads** (p208).

Help out on the farm at **Muang Pon Homestay Program** (p190). a remote homestay south of Mae Hong Son.

Development

Thailand leads all countries in Southeast Asia in the push to achieve the United Nations Sustainable Development Goals by the 2030 deadline. The kingdom scores especially well in poverty reduction and clean water and sanitation.

RESOURCES

volunteerworkthailand.org
Nonprofit resource for grassroots-level volunteering opportunities.

wfft.org
Wildlife rescue centres and conservation projects that welcome volunteers.

trashhero.org
Volunteer-led movement to rid Thailand of plastic waste.

FROM TOP LEFT: JOSE PARDOS/SHUTTERSTOCK, SIRASTOCK/SHUTTERSTOCK

LGBTIQ+ Travellers

Thai culture is relatively tolerant of male and female homosexuality. There is a prominent LGBTIQ+ scene in Bangkok, and fairly high-profile ones in Phuket, Pattaya and Chiang Mai; all hold annual gay Pride events. In regard to dress and mannerisms, the LGBTIQ+ community are generally accepted without comment. However, public displays of affection – whether homosexual or heterosexual – are frowned upon.

Nightlife

Bangkok, Phuket, Pattaya and Chiang Mai are by far the most vibrant destinations for nightlife. In Bangkok, the Silom neighbourhood is especially busy, with many bars and clubs that attract a good mix of locals and foreigners. Chiang Mai has fewer venues, mostly located around its Night Market. In Pattaya, Jomtien is the place to head to, while Patong is the centre of gay nightlife on Phuket. A few other destinations, such as Ko Samui and Ko Samet, have much smaller scenes that are limited to a handful of bars.

PHUKET PRIDE FESTIVAL

Phuket's Pride Festival was first staged in 1999 and is now considered one of the best Pride events in Southeast Asia, attracting locals and visitors, both gay and straight. Usually held in June, the week-long event features beach parties, cabaret shows, sports events and beauty contests, before it all ends with a parade with floats through Patong and an evening concert and party.

Drag Shows

Drag artists take to the stage at a number of venues in Bangkok and Chiang Mai, as well as Phuket and Ko Samui, but the performances staged in Pattaya – such as the extremely popular Tiffany's Cabaret Show – are considered the most flamboyant and fun.

GENDER EQUALITY

Thailand passed the *Gender Equality Act* in 2015, the country's first law to provide protection from unfair gender discrimination. But while transgender and third gender people are quite visible in Thailand, they continue to face discrimination in the workplace and when dealing with branches of the government.

Gay Travel Websites

Travel Gay *(travelgay.com)* Comprehensive guide to the gay scene across Thailand.

Utopia *(utopia-asia.com)* Posts useful information on Thailand for LGBTIQ+ travellers.

Gay Passport *(thegaypassport.com)* Lists LGBTIQ+ nightlife venues in the most popular destinations.

GENDER ROLES

Perhaps because Thailand is still a relatively conservative place, lesbians generally adhere to rather strict gender roles. Overtly 'butch' lesbians, called *tom* (from 'tomboy'), typically have short hair and wear men's clothing. Femme lesbians refer to themselves as *dee* (from 'lady'). Visiting lesbians who don't fit into one of these categories may find themselves met with confusion.

NEW AFRICA/SHUTTERSTOCK

Accessible Travel

Thailand has better facilities for travellers with access needs than any country in Southeast Asia, bar Singapore. However, high kerbs, uneven and crowded footpaths and nonstop traffic make navigating Thai cities a challenge for those with a vision or mobility impairment. Accessing attractions, transport and islands can also be problematic.

Public Transport

In Bangkok, the Skytrain and Metro are accessible for wheelchair users. However, long-distance trains are a bit of an access lottery, while buses and boats to the islands are difficult for people with a disability.

Airport

Bangkok's Suvarnabhumi Airport has decent facilities for travellers with disabilities, with lift service, accessible toilets and air-bridges for boarding and disembarking planes. At other airports, make sure to advise your airline in advance that you require assistance.

Accommodation

Most midrange and top-end hotels have accessible rooms, but most budget hotels, guesthouses and many boutique hotels lack accessible facilities. However, they will do their best to meet your needs if you're able to be adaptable.

BLIND MASSAGE

There are several initiatives in Thailand aimed at assisting visually impaired people, including training them in the fine art of Thai massage. You'll find blind massage places in most major destinations and they are worth supporting.

Shopping Malls

All cities and many towns have at least one modern shopping mall, and this is the place to head for hassle-free shopping and eating, as well as an accessible toilet.

Moving Around

The poor state of pavements in Thai cities and towns, or the complete lack of them, means that wheelchair users will often find it easier to take to the roads.

GETTING TO THE ISLANDS

The biggest challenge with accessing Thailand's iconic islands is getting safely on and off boats and ferries that dock at sometimes rickety piers. Choosing an island with an airport is the most realistic option.

RESOURCES

Accessible Thailand Tours *(accessible-thailand tours.com)* Tours for those with age-, sight- or disability-related issues.

Wheelchair Travel *(wheelchairtravel .org/bangkok)* How to access Bangkok's attractions, hotels and transport.

Disabled Holidays *(disabledholidays. com)* Info on Thailand for travellers with disabilities.

Wheelchair Holidays Thailand *(wheelchairtours. com)* Tours for elderly travellers and those with disabilities.

Wheelchair Taxi Thailand *(transport-disabled-bangkok. weebly.com)* Based in Hua Hin; offers countrywide taxi and tour services.

Few taxis are set up for people with access needs. Many run on natural gas with the tank in the boot, limiting space for a wheelchair or mobility aid. A small number of fully wheelchair-accessible taxis are available in Bangkok and Hua Hin.

Environmental Issues

Thailand has made positive steps in addressing environmental challenges. Giant new solar farms are part of the kingdom's drive to be carbon neutral by 2050, while deforestation has been checked and animal conservation efforts are improving. But declining air quality is an increasingly critical problem, especially in Bangkok and northern Thailand.

Air Pollution

On 16 March 2025, Chiang Mai's air quality was officially rated the world's worst, beating notoriously polluted cities such as New Delhi and Faisalabad. Every year between February and April (known as the 'haze season') Chiang Mai and much of northern Thailand is blanketed in a toxic smog, largely caused by farmers using fires to clear undergrowth and fertilise crops. Air pollution is now a growing issue across the kingdom, with some Bangkok schools forced to close at certain times of the year. In 2024, Thailand's average annual PM2.5 levels were 4.8 times higher than the WHO's recommended standard, while it was estimated that over 12 million Thais were suffering air-pollution-related health issues.

Deforestation

Natural forest cover constituted about 38.7% of Thailand's land area in 2022, according to World Bank figures, up from 27.4% in 1990. Thailand has set the goal of reaching 55% forest cover by 2037. Forest loss has now slowed to about 0.2% per year. In 1989 all logging was banned. It's now also illegal to sell timber felled in Thailand, but this law is frequently flouted.

Flooding

Seasonal flooding is common in parts of Thailand due to monsoon rains. But high-level property-damaging floods have increased in recent years, induced in part by climate change. The record-busting 2011 floods resulted in 815 deaths and an estimated US$45.7 billion in damage. In August and September 2024, floods across 37 provinces left 49 people dead and affected over 180,000 households. The floods in parts of Chiang Rai Province were the most severe for 100 years.

Endangered Species

Thailand's most famous animals are also the most endangered. A century ago, around 300,000 Asian elephants roamed the country. But habitat loss and poaching means there are now estimated to be no more than 3000 to 3600 wild elephants. Nevertheless, the number of wild elephants is slowly increasing.

Some 179 to 223 wild Indochinese tigers stalk remote parts of Thailand, according to the WWF. Poachers continue to kill the cats for the overseas wildlife trade, but Thailand has stepped up its tiger conservation efforts and is the only country in Southeast Asia where the wild tiger population is rising.

CLIMATE CHANGE

- Thailand is considered highly vulnerable to the impact of climate change, even though the country's ranking in the 2025 Global Climate Risk Index improved from ninth place to 30th. Rising sea levels are especially an issue for the kingdom, thanks to Thailand's long coastline and numerous low-lying regions, including Bangkok. If sea levels rise by a metre by the end of the century, as has been widely predicted, most of Bangkok will be under water by 2100, and over 3000 sq km of coastal land and around 17% of the population will be impacted by catastrophic flooding.
- Extreme heat is another major issue for Thailand, as the March–May hot season grows ever warmer. April 2024 was the hottest month recorded in the kingdom, with Sakhon Nakhon Province in northeast Thailand experiencing 47.7°C on 28 April, the highest temperature ever recorded in Thailand.

Nuts & Bolts

OPENING HOURS

Bars and clubs close for certain religious holidays and during elections, when alcohol sales are banned.

Banks 8.30am–4.30pm Monday to Friday; ATMs 24 hours

Bars 6pm–midnight or 1am

Clubs 8pm–2am

Government offices 8.30am–4.30pm Monday to Friday; some close for lunch

Restaurants 8am–10pm

Shops 10am–9pm

Internet Acccess

Almost all accommodation and airports, most cafes and many shopping malls and bars offer free wi-fi.

Weights & Measures

Metric system, except for land measurements. Gold and silver weighed in *baat* (1 *baat* = 15g).

Smoking is banned in indoor places and on public transport, as well as on beaches and in parks. Vaping is widespread, but note that it is technically illegal to bring a vape or e-cigarette into Thailand.

GOOD TO KNOW

Time zone
GMT/UTC+7

Country code
66

Emergency number/tourist police
191/1155

Population
71.6 million

Electricity

Type A
120V/60Hz

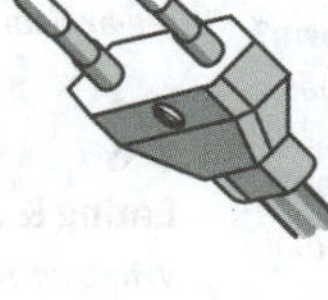

Type C
220V/50Hz

PUBLIC HOLIDAYS

Banks, embassies and government offices close for national holidays/festivals.

1 January New Year's Day

February/March (varies) Makha Bucha; Buddhist holy day

6 April Chakri Day

13–15 April Songkran Festival

1 May Labour Day

4 May Coronation Day

May (varies) Royal Ploughing Ceremony

May/June (varies) Visakha Bucha; Buddhist holy day

3 June Her Majesty the Queen's Birthday

28 July King Maha Vajiralongkorn's Birthday

July/August (varies) Asanha Bucha; Buddhist holy day

12 August Queen Sirikit's Birthday/ Mother's Day

13 October Late King Bhumibhol's Memorial Day

23 October Chulalongkorn Day

5 December Late King Bhumibhol's Birthday/ Father's Day

10 December Constitution Day

31 December New Year's Eve

Language

Standard Thai is actually a dialect spoken in Bangkok and the surrounding provinces. Most Thais understand it – but many speak another dialect.

Basics

Hello. สวัสดี. *sà-wàt-dee*

Goodbye. ลาก่อน. *lah gòrn*

Yes. ใช่. *châi*

No. ไม่. *mâi*

Please. ขอ. *kŏr*

Thank you. ขอบคุณ. *kòrp kun*

Excuse me. ขออภัย. *kŏr à-pai*

Sorry. ขอโทษ. *kŏr tôht*

What's your name? คุณชื่ออะไร. *kun chêu à-rai*

My name is ... ผม/ดิฉันชื่อ... *pŏm/dì-chăn chêu... (m/f)*

Do you speak English? คุณพูดภาษาอังกฤษได้ไหม. *kun pôot pah-săh ang-grìt dâi măi*

I don't understand. ผม/ดิฉันไม่เข้าใจ. *pŏm/dì-chăn mâi kôw jai (m/f)*

Directions

Where's...? ... อยู่ที่ไหน. *... yòo têe năi*

What's the address? ที่อยู่คืออะไร. *têe yòo keu à-rai*

Could you please write it down? เขียนลงให้ได้ไหม. *kĕe·an long hâi dâi măi*

Can you show me (on the map)? ให้ดู (ในแผนที่) ได้ไหม. *hâi doo (nai păan têe) dâi măi*

Signs

ทางเข้า Entrance
ทางออก Exit
เปิด Open
ปิด Closed
ที่ติดต่อสอบถาม Information
ห้าม Prohibited
ห้องสุขา Toilets
ชาย Men
หญิง Women

Time

What time is it? กี่โมงแล้ว. *gèe mohng láa·ou*

Morning เช้า. *chów*

Afternoon บ่าย. *bài*

Evening เย็น. *yen*

Yesterday เมื่อวาน. *mêu·a wahn*

Today วันนี้. *wan née*

Tomorrow พรุ่งนี้. *prûng née*

Emergencies

Help! ช่วยด้วย. *chôo·ay dôo·ay*

Go away! ไปให้พ้น. *ƀai hâi pón*

I'm ill. ผม/ดิฉันป่วย. *pŏm/dì-chăn ƀòo·ay (m/f)*

Call a doctor! เรียกหมอหน่อย. *rêe·ak mŏr nòy*

Call the police! เรียกตำรวจหน่อย. *rêe·ak đam·ròo·at nòy*

Eating & drinking

What would you recommend? คุณแนะนำอะไรบ้าง. *kun náa-nam à-rai bâhng*

Cheers! ไชโย. *chai-yoh*

That was delicious. อร่อยมาก. *à-ròy mâhk*

I'd like (the menu), please. ขอ (รายการ อาหาร) หน่อย. *kŏr (rai gahn ah-hăhn) nòy*

NUMBERS

1
หนึ่ง *nèung*

2
สอง *sŏrng*

3
สาม *săhm*

4
สี่ *sèe*

5
ห้า *hâh*

6
หก *hòk*

7
เจ็ด *jèt*

8
แปด *ƀàat*

9
เก้า *gôw*

10
สิบ *sìp*

THAI SCRIPT

The elegant characters of the Thai script are a source of fascination for those experiencing the language for the first time. The curved symbols seem to run together but they are all divisible into distinct alphabetical units. There are 44 consonants. Vowels are indicated by symbols that may appear before, after, above, below or even around the consonant.

Tone

In Thai the meaning of a single syllable may be altered by means of different tones. In standard Thai there are five: low tone, mid tone, falling tone, high tone and rising tone. The range of all five tones is relative to each speaker's vocal range, so there is no fixed 'pitch' intrinsic to the language.

Close Relations

Thai belongs to the Tai language group, meaning that it is closely related to a number of languages spoken outside the borders of present-day Thailand. Some of these are Lao (Laos), Khampti (India) and Lue (China). The Isaan dialect, spoken in the northeast of Thailand, is linguistically identical to Lao.

Street Talk

A·ròy Delicious
Bāan bāan Nothing special
Chon gâew Cheers
Fa·ràng Foreigner
Gin khâo rĕu yâng? Have you eaten?
Hi-so High society
Taách Cool/very good
Ron mâk Very hot
Tíng-tòng Wacky, eccentric
Wa ngâi What's up

A TOWER OF BABEL

Most of the languages spoken in Thailand belong to one of four major language families: Tai (a subfamily of Tai- Kadai languages), Mon-Khmer (a subfamily of Austroasiatic languages), Austronesian, and Sino-Tibetan.

WHO SPEAKS THAI?

Thailand's official language is the dialect spoken and written in central Thailand, which has become the lingua franca of all Thai and non-Thai ethnic groups in the kingdom.

THE THAILAND

STORYBOOK

Our writers delve deep into different aspects of Thai life

Ordination Hall (p63), Wat Phra Kaew, Bangkok

LARCSKY789/SHUTTERSTOCK

A HISTORY OF THAILAND IN 14 PLACES

Through archaeological wonders, royal legacies and ancient cities, these historical locations tell a story of Thailand's evolution, from ancient civilisations to modern-day marvels. By Aydan Stuart

THAILAND'S STRATEGIC LOCATION in the heart of Southeast Asia has made it a crossroads of diverse cultures and civilisations throughout history. As a geographical centrepoint for animals and humans, the fertile lands and favourable climate made it a prime location for trade, migration and cultural exchange.

From the time of the dinosaurs to *Homo erectus* fossils, *Homo sapiens* migrations and the rise and fall of kingdoms, the land that is now Thailand is home to an enormous amount of ancient and modern historical sites. Venture through archaeological wonders, royal legacies and ancient cities, embracing the vibrant past of Thailand in real-life locations. Era by era, these historical places tell a story of Thailand's evolution, from ancient civilisations to modern-day marvels that captivate the mind and share insight into where the Land of Smiles really began.

1. Khon Kaen

THE TRUE ORIGINS OF T-REX

Research and fossil records in Thailand and other regional locations suggest that *Tyrannosaurus rex* originated right here in Asia. Northeast Thailand is full of fossils, with most dating to the Jurassic and late-Triassic eras, providing the oldest such evidence of dinosaurs living in Southeast Asia.

To see these giant beasts for yourself, Khon Kaen is the de-facto dino destination of Thailand, with the Phu Wiang Dinosaur Museum housing the country's best dinosaur remains and the nearby Phu Wiang National Park still displaying actual dinosaur bones in situ, encased in sandstone and dating back more than 130 million years. If you're dino mad, stop by Kalasin on your way and visit Thailand's very own 'Jurassic Park', the Sirindhorn Dinosaur Museum.

For more on Phu Wiang Dinosaur Museum, see p325.

2. Udon Thani

THE RICE BOWL OF ASIA IS ESTABLISHED

Around 5000 to 4000 years ago, the Neolithic period saw the emergence of settled agricultural communities in Thailand. As people began cultivating crops and domesticating animals, more permanent villages and societies emerged.

The fertile plains and valleys around the Mekong provided ideal conditions for the growth of early civilisations. Ban Chiang archaeological site in Udon Thani offers a glimpse into Thailand's prehistoric past, with some of the region's best-preserved evidence of early human pottery, tools and other artefacts. This site is the most important prehistoric settlement so far discovered in Southeast Asia, marking the beginning of the wet-rice culture that still feeds the region today.

For more on Ban Chiang, see p335.

3. Buriram

RISE AND FALL OF POWERFUL EMPIRES

As messiahs rose and fell in the Middle East, Southeast Asia turned to metallurgy and cross-continental trade, which connected it with neighbouring regions, such as the Indus Valley and China.

The influence of Indian culture began to spread to Southeast Asia, affecting art, language and religion. By the 6th to 11th centuries, the Dvaravati and Khmer empires held sway over great parts of Thailand, leaving behind impressive architectural marvels. Phanom Rung Historical Park in Buriram is where the Khmer empire first left its mark with Thailand's oldest Hindu-Khmer temple complex built on the edge of a (now extinct) volcano. Phimai Historical Park in Nakhon Ratchasima has incredibly well-preserved Khmer temples.

For more on Phanom Rung Historical Park, see p318.

Sukhothai Historical Park (p240)

KARASEV VIKTOR/SHUTTERSTOCK

4. Lamphun

A 600-YEAR CIVILISATION

According to legend, a wandering hermit founded the city of Hariphunchai in the 7th century, inviting a Mon princess to rule a kingdom that would flourish for more than 600 years.

What we know is that the Hariphunchai kingdom became a major centre of Dvaravati culture in northern Thailand, spreading Theravada Buddhism far beyond its relatively modest borders. During its golden era, artisans crafted exquisite bronze and terracotta works, while engineers designed remarkably sophisticated reservoirs and moats. In 1281, the kingdom was peacefully annexed into King Mengrai's expanding Lanna realm after he founded Wiang Kum Kam just a few clicks north, gradually absorbing Hariphunchai's political and cultural influence.

For more on the Hariphunchai kingdom and Wiang Kum Kam, see p279.

5. Chiang Mai

ANCIENT NORTHERN THAI CULTURE

In 1296, Chiang Mai was founded by King Mengrai as the biggest and final capital of the Lanna kingdom, the kingdom of a million rice fields. At Three Kings Monument, marvel at the historical account of traditional life at Lanna Folklife Museum or visit the city's oldest temple, Wat Chiang Man for its spectacular *chedi* (stupa) encircled by elephants and a Sri Lankan Buddha image said to hold powers to bring rain.

Previous kingdom capitals include Chiang Saen, Fang, Chiang Rai and Wiang Kum Kam, each home to relics and temples that hold secrets of this impressive kingdom, which by 1557 fell into Burmese rule for over 200 years before being liberated by Siam.

For more on Chiang Mai, see p252.

6. Sukhothai

CENTRE OF CREATIVITY

Often called the birthplace of Thai culture, the Sukhothai kingdom marks a significant period in Thailand's history. Founded in the 13th century, Sukhothai was a centre of artistic and cultural creativity, much of which can be seen in the well-preserved ruins of Sukhothai Historical Park.

For 200 years the kingdom ruled the plains of modern-day Thailand, bringing with it the invention of the Thai language and the adoption of Theravada Buddhism. To the north, the city of Si Satchanalai stood as a defence against the Lanna and Burmese armies to the north, while Kamphaeng Phet sat on the edge of Mae Nam Ping, a major trade route during the Middle Ages.

For more on Sukhothai Historical Park, see p240.

7. Surat Thani

CULTURAL CROSSROADS

When it comes to Thai history, the southern strip is often relegated to the footer. However, the Malay Peninsula (connecting Malaysia, Thailand and Myanmar) was once a key cultural crossroads, with traders and cultures crossing paths in Surat Thani, Nakhon Si Thammarat and Songkhla for over 2000 years.

Learn about the Hindu-Buddhist Srivijaya empire, which ruled most of the region from the 7th to 13th centuries, at Chaiya National Museum in Surat Thani, which also tells of how Arab traders introduced Muslim beliefs to the region. Neighbouring ancient city Ligor was one of the largest of this era in Thailand, with a rich history of war and peace that can be unearthed at the National Museum of Nakhon Si Thammarat.

For more on Surat Thani, see p468.

8. Ayuthaya

THAILAND'S SECOND KINGDOM

Established in the 14th century following Sukhothai's reign, the Ayuthaya kingdom quickly became one of the most prosperous and influential kingdoms in Southeast Asia and later was officially known as Siam's second capital. By the 18th century, it had become one of the world's largest and most cosmopolitan urban areas and a centre of global diplomacy and commerce.

At Ayuthaya Historical Park, you can still see remnants of this once-mighty empire, reflecting its grandeur and international stature. Despite being sacked by the Burmese in 1767, its legacy lived on, reunified by King Taksin who established a new capital in Thonburi and later Bangkok.

For more on Ayuthaya, see p140.

9. Thonburi & Chanthaburi

ALMOST FORGOTTEN RULER

King Taksin was the one and only ruler of the Thonburi kingdom that led Thailand from 1767–82. Liberating Ayuthaya from the Burmese earned him the right to rule, and although warfare occupied most of his reign, his attention to politics, unification, economy and welfare earned him respect. The King Taksin Monument in the centre of Bangkok's Wong Wian Yai roundabout is a tribute to his reign. After just 15 years on the throne, he was executed by a lifelong friend who subsequently founded the Chakri dynasty that rules Thailand to this day.

For more on Thonburi, see p56.

10. Kanchanaburi

MORE THAN THE BRIDGE ON THE RIVER KWAI

Thailand was neutral during WWII until it was invaded by the Japanese, who persuaded the nation to join the Axis Powers. Thailand maintained its sovereignty (mostly) in exchange for allowing Japanese troops to invade British-held Malaya and Burma from its land.

Kanchanaburi became a Japanese stronghold during the war, with many places bearing witness to the era. Hellfire Pass Interpretive Centre pays tribute to the history of Death Railway, built by Allied prisoners of war and forced local labour. Kanchanaburi War Cemetery honours those who died. You can catch a train from the city across the bridge, made famous by the film The Bridge on the River Kwai.

For more on Kanchanaburi, see p150.

11. Bangkok

ONE KING, 10 COUPS, 17 CONSTITUTIONS

Thailand has seen its fair share of coups and revolutions during the last hundred years, the first being the Siamese revolution of 1932, which effectively ended 700 years of absolute monarchy, replacing it with a constitutional monarchy and parliamentary system. By 1976, war had passed, as well as five coups d'état, leading to the 6 October massacre, a violent crackdown by Thai police and right-wing paramilitaries against leftist protesters at Thammasat University. Today, the October 6 Museum Project hosts an annual commemoration

'Death Railway', Kanchanaburi (p150)

of those events at the university (military officials permitting) with lectures, discussions, film screenings and performance art. In total, the reign of King Bhumibol Adulyadej witnessed 10 coups and 17 constitutions.

For more on Bangkok, see p48.

12. Jim Thompson House

SILK AND SPECULATION

In 1950s and '60s Bangkok, American businessman Jim Thompson entered Thailand's elite, becoming one of Asia's most famous foreigner. He wore many hats, as an architect, a retired army officer, a one-time spy, a silk merchant and a renowned collector of antiques. Yet he was most famous for singlehandedly reinventing Thailand's silk industry and lifting thousands of Thailand's poorest out of poverty through progressive employment. Although he mysteriously disappeared while hiking Malaysia's Cameron Highlands, never to be found again, his legacy lives on at House on the Klong – a mansion made by Thompson using parts of old up-country houses – now home to the Jim Thompson House museum.

For more on the Jim Thompson House, see p105.

13. Grand Palace

PIVOTAL MOMENT

On 13 October 2016, the world's longest-reigning monarch, King Bhumibol Adulyadej, passed away aged 88 and a year-long period of mourning was announced. For months, entertainment venues remained closed, while anything 'joyful' was avoided and normal TV was replaced with 24-hour coverage of the late king and royal events.

After the cremation in Sanam Luang (an open park designed for royal ceremony near Th Khao San), the king's remains and ashes were taken to the Grand Palace and enshrined at the Chakri Mahaprasat Throne Hall, the Royal Cemetery and Wat Bowonniwet Vihara Royal Temple. Almost every province is home to a memorial or museum dedicated to the king and his legacy.

For more on the Grand Palace, see p62.

14. Ancient City

ALL OF THAILAND'S HISTORY IN ONE PLACE

The Ancient City in Samut Prakan is often called the 'world's largest outdoor museum', and is home to near-to-life-size replicas of Thailand's most famous historical and architectural landmarks. The park is designed to mimic the map of Thailand, with the addition of land dedicated to the Buddhist heavens of Suvarnabhumi and ancient lost civilisations of gods and deities, complete with mythical serpent temples and towering godly stupas. A great way to get all your history in one fell swoop if you can't face travelling across plains and mountains to find it.

For more about the Ancient City, see p133.

MEET THE THAIS

Thailand's reputation as the 'Land of Smiles' is true to some extent, but don't be surprised when we express other emotions – we aren't *always* smiley. Choltanutkun Tun-atiruj introduces her people.

OF THE ROUGHLY 71 million people living in Thailand's 77 provinces, the nation's capital, Bangkok, has a population of over 10 million. The rest of the country is nothing like Bangkok, and Bangkok is nothing like the rest of the country. However, you'll be able to find a little piece of each province of Thailand in Bangkok, as many Thai people have had to move here for job opportunities. These people speak different dialects and eat different types of cuisine from all over the country.

Because Bangkok's traffic is pretty bad, we are always late, and the bad traffic is commonly used as a reason (or excuse) for our lateness. Never expect a Thai person to be on time. In fact, if a Thai person ever shows up on time, ask them if everything is OK.

The Thais are not at all confrontational. Confrontation is considered rude, and we don't believe in rocking the boat; we prefer to just let all of those waves of emotion float underneath the surface, without expressing them. We keep everything in, and we put on our best smiles when talking to people, even if we're not happy with them (hence the 'Land of Smiles' moniker). But trust me when I say that you don't want to hear what we say behind closed doors!

The Political Climate

Thailand has had 13 successful coups in its history, and the country is trying to ensure that everyone can coexist: younger Thais are fighting for a better future and discarding old beliefs; older Thais are trying to maintain the old ways.

It's pretty normal for you to see us trying to play with toddlers, even if we've never met them: we want to hold babies and snap photos of them! This is nothing to worry about. We just find babies cute, that's all.

Thais love to take care of their guests and make sure that they've eaten. A typical Thai family wouldn't appear as affectionate towards each other as a typical Western family would. But a mother asking if you've eaten yet and making sure there's food in the kitchen before she leaves for work? That's considered the equivalent of saying 'I love you'.

There are so many ways to address another person in Thailand, and *all* of these ways are based on age; 'P' is used to address someone who's older than you; 'Nong' is for someone younger; 'Naa' is for someone younger than your mum; 'Ar' is for someone younger than your dad; 'Paa' is for a female and 'Lung' is for a male who is older than both your mum and dad. You'll hear these words used to address people (usually in conjunction with the addressee's name) on a daily basis. Confusingly, their use doesn't always reflect age. Someone older than you might call you 'P' for the first time without knowing your name. This is done to low-key imply that they respect you (hierarchy stuff).

CLOCKWISE FROM TOP LEFT: NAYPONG STUDIO/SHUTTERSTOCK, OLEGD/SHUTTERSTOCK, FOTOGLEE/SHUTTERSTOCK, FERRYWIDJAJA/SHUTTERSTOCK

KRENG JAI

There's a term in Thai that we Thais have been struggling to find an English equivalent for, and that term is *kreng jai*. It's an adjective used to express a trait of consideration with a hint of shyness, arising mostly out of the fact that you don't want to trouble the other person. For example, it's late, and you're leaving a house party. A friend offers you a ride home, even though she doesn't live in the same area as you. In response, you say, 'No, it's OK, I'll get a taxi. I'm *kreng jai*.' This is a truly classic trait of the Thais.

If I'm being honest, the 'Land of Smiles' doesn't resonate so well with me. We have other emotions, and honestly, none of us are smiley all the time – but *kreng jai*? It definitely lies at the core of each of us.

CHILDREN IN THAILAND

What Thailand's affection for children says about Thai culture and hospitality service. By Choltanutkun Tun-atiruj

YOU'VE JUST SAT down for a meal when your baby is suddenly whisked away. In some parts of the world, this would provoke panic. In Thailand, it's simply part of the culture.

Cooing and exclaiming *'narak!'* (Thai for 'cute' or 'adorable'), the waitress gently bounces your baby on her hip, smiling as if she's known your offspring since birth. Within minutes, you're eating in peace, the baby giggling somewhere nearby.

A TikTok clip with nearly 12 million views captures this perfectly: a Thai waitress walks away with a foreign couple's baby resting happily on her shoulder, the text on the video reading 'Another day, another Thai woman steals your baby'. Scroll a little further and you'll find dozens more. Compilation videos can be found on YouTube of hotel staff, massage therapists and restaurant servers – each joyfully taking turns holding or entertaining someone else's child.

To outsiders, it might look like exceptional hospitality service. But for Thais, this isn't about hospitality policy or customer satisfaction. It's something far deeper, like an instinct woven into daily life. Loving, protecting and making children happy isn't just an act of kindness; it's a cultural reflex.

In Thailand, the idea that 'it takes a village to raise a child' isn't just a quaint saying. It's deeply rooted in the culture and everyday life. Children are seen as shared joy and shared responsibility. Whether it's a niece, a neighbour's toddler or a tourist's baby, a child's presence naturally draws attention, laughter and gentle interaction. In homes, markets, temples and cafes, adults instinctively include children in the flow of social life. A crying baby doesn't disrupt the room; it invites someone – anyone – to soothe them.

LOVING, PROTECTING AND MAKING CHILDREN HAPPY ISN'T JUST AN ACT OF KINDNESS; IT'S A CULTURAL REFLEX.

This sense of communal care stems from a worldview where happiness is collective. A happy child means a happy moment shared by all. Protecting them, keeping them safe and entertained, isn't a duty. It's simply just joy in motion.

This also has something to do with *nam jai,* a Thai concept of doing something for someone out of kindness without expecting anything in return. When a waitress offers to hold your baby, it's not for tips or praise. It's because caring for children, even for a few moments, genuinely makes them happy.

This openness can surprise visitors from countries where children are more shielded from strangers. In many parts of the world, even smiling too long at a stranger's baby can feel like crossing a line, or make them feel anxious or unsafe. By contrast, Thai people abroad might feel puzzled by those invisible boundaries as well. Both perspectives come from love, expressed in very different ways.

Stay in Thailand long enough and you'll start to see it everywhere: a fruit seller handing a toddler a piece of mango, a massage therapist braiding a child's hair while the parents are getting a foot massage, or a stranger playing peekaboo with a child on a stroller while riding on a crowded train.

For travelling parents, these moments can become some of the sweetest memories of a trip. Your baby might return with a flower tucked behind their ear or a new Thai nickname. But if you'd rather keep your little one close, a polite smile and a gentle *'mai pen rai',* Thai for 'no worries' or 'it's OK', will set the tone perfectly. In Thailand, boundaries can always be drawn with kindness, and kindness will always be returned.

Of course, not every Thai person will be this hands-on, and travellers shouldn't expect that someone will whisk their baby away the moment they sit down to eat. And while these gestures usually come from genuine kindness, parents should always keep an eye on their children, just as they would anywhere in the world. Still, when these moments do happen, they reveal something tender about Thailand: it's a glimpse into Thai hospitality and how it isn't just about service, but something that reflects the heart of Thai culture.

KATERINA KODYAKOVA/SHUTTERSTOCK

WILD ENCOUNTERS: THE ETHICS OF THAILAND'S WILDLIFE

Thailand's wild side draws travellers in – but the magic hides a complex truth. By Olivia Pozzan

IN NORTHERN THAILAND'S morning haze, elephants wade into a river, trunks raised, spray catching the light. On the bank, tourists film the idyllic bathing scene, seemingly capturing the harmony between people and wildlife. Yet that magical close encounter often comes at a cost to the animals. Understanding responsible wildlife travel can make all the difference.

Allure of the Wild

A global review by World Animal Protection found that roughly three-quarters of wildlife tourist attractions involved some form of animal abuse. In Thailand, many travellers seeking ethical experiences unknowingly support venues that exploit animals.

Elephants, icons of the nation's identity, have borne the greatest impact. Elephant riding was once considered an essential Thai adventure, until growing awareness revealed the harsh realities behind the scenes.

Many young elephants endure *phajaan* – the 'training crush' – where they are confined, deprived of movement and beaten into submission. Once their spirit is broken, they become safe to handle, destined for work, entertainment or the tourist trade. As adults, they often develop chronic wounds and joint injuries from carrying heavy saddles and tourists on repetitive rides. When not working, many are tethered by ankle chains that lead to foot problems.

Elephant bathing programmes, promoted as an ethical alternative, can perpetuate the same cycle of control. Repeated washes also impose an unnatural routine that can irritate the skin and take place whether or not the animals wish to bathe.

Any form of hands-on interaction with wildlife is inherently unnatural. The animals that tolerate it have been trained, restrained or sedated to allow such contact. Compliance, in most cases, is not consent.

The same is true for young animals taken from the wild, separated from their mothers, and hand-reared for use in tourist activities. Performing monkeys and orangutans are often harshly trained, sometimes through food deprivation or beatings, to ride bicycles, play instruments or perform bizarre acts in the name of entertainment.

Above left: Asian palm civet; Right: Elephants, Khao Yai National Park (p314)

At tiger temples, tigers are sedated, leaving them docile and sluggish as tourists pose beside them for photos. Some are even declawed. Another popular selfie prop, the slow loris, is a nocturnal creature displayed in daylight for photos, its teeth removed to allow safe handling.

Across parts of Thailand, civets are kept in cramped cages at cafes and small farms and force-fed coffee cherries to produce *kopi luwak*. Made from civet dung, it's the world's most expensive brew – costly both in price and in freedom. These nocturnal creatures are also often exhibited in broad daylight, and stressed by frequent handling and caffeine overload.

Sanctuaries: Hope or Hype?

For travellers seeking ethical encounters, wildlife sanctuaries may seem like the answer. Many rely on visitor donations or paid volunteer programmes, and volunteering can be deeply rewarding. Yet in the absence of formal regulation, some refuges fail to meet basic welfare standards. Knowing what to look for helps travellers distinguish genuine sanctuaries from those that merely adopt the name.

A reputable facility is evident in the details. They make their conservation aims clear, and direct profits towards animal care and habitat protection. Animals appear healthy and relaxed, with space to move and express natural behaviours. Enclosures are clean and offer shelter from the weather. Appropriate diets, enrichment and veterinary care are standard. There should be a clear rehabilitation and release programme for rescued animals unless injury or trauma makes release unsafe. Above all, responsible operations enforce a strict no-contact policy for visitors.

Some venues offer guided elephant walks, where rescued elephants roam freely and visitors follow at a distance. These experiences are ethical only if elephants are never forced to walk or chained once tourists leave.

Any wildlife centre that promotes handling sessions, or captures wild animals for display or long-term captivity, is exploiting those animals. In the rare cases where captive breeding takes place, it must serve species preservation or a conservation purpose aimed at eventual release. Breeding without such intent usually means animals are bred for tourism or trade.

Even in well-kept settings, behaviour and routines reveal a great deal. Repetitive pacing or swaying can signal stress or frustration. Showing nocturnal animals in daylight, overfeeding to suit tourist demands, or prolonged exposure to people is unnatural. For some animals, rescue isn't always rescue.

Keeping it Wild

Responsible wildlife travel begins with the awareness that even seemingly innocuous choices can have lasting impacts. Buying souvenirs made from shells, coral, ivory or fur contributes to the wildlife trade. Coral jewellery may be beautiful, but coral forms the basis of entire marine ecosystems and can take decades to recover. Traditional medicines made from animal parts – such as tiger bone, rhino horn, bear bile or pangolin scales – also fuel demand for the illegal wildlife trade.

Ethical choices at the table matter too. Declining bushmeat or exotic animal dishes helps prevent wildlife population loss and reduces the risk of zoonotic disease. Where possible, supporting local or sustainably farmed food strengthens communities while protecting local wildlife.

Traditions that seem harmless can also take a toll. Wild songbirds are captured and sold at markets for singing contests, or at temples for release as a merit-making ritual. While the act of release is born of compassion, it drives demand that sees many birds trapped solely for this purpose.

Every choice travellers make – from where they visit to what they buy – affects the welfare of Thailand's wildlife. The most ethical encounters are those that leave animals untouched and undisturbed. Observing animals in their natural environment, from a respectful distance and on their terms, offers a far richer experience by allowing them to live as nature intended. Wild and free.

Wildlife Friends Foundation Thailand (WFFT; *wfft.org*) accepts and investigates reports of wildlife abuse and illegal trade, forwarding verified cases to the authorities. Travellers can also report suspected trafficking via the Wildlife Witness app or directly to local officials.

Food vendor, Bangkok (p48)
AUSTIN BUSH/LONELY PLANET

THAILAND'S UNITED NATIONS OF CUISINES

The flavours, ingredients and influences that make up Thai food are more varied and regional than you might imagine. By Austin Bush

FISH SAUCE, CHILLIES, coconut milk, rice noodles: for many of us, these ingredients scream Thai food. But Thai cuisine is less of a singular entity than many visitors realise, and these elements show up in varying degrees in different parts of the country. Although decades of Bangkok-based rule, the proliferation of 7-Elevens and an obsession with Michelin stars have led to increased homogenisation in recent decades, Thai cuisine can still be said to originate from four distinct regions.

Central Thai Cuisine

When people think of Thai food, often what they picture are the dishes, ingredients and flavours of central Thailand, which includes Bangkok. Green curry, pad thai, noodle soups: these are the Thai dishes that have been the most promoted outside of Thailand, thanks largely to the Thai government's so-called 'gastrodiplomacy'. Starting in 2002, the Global Thai programme provided culinary and business instruction and grants for those willing to cook a central Thai-leaning version of Thai food abroad, a campaign that was incredibly successful.

The food of central Thailand revolves around long-grained rice, which is paired with dishes with subtly sweet, rich-leaning, herbaceous yet carefully balanced flavours. Fish plays a large role in central Thailand's cuisine, including in the form of fish sauce, made from anchovies caught in the Gulf of Thailand. The centre is the region of Thailand with the strongest influence from China. Today, Chinese ingredients such as noodles, soy sauce and tofu, Chinese cooking techniques such as wok-frying and deep-frying, and dishes of Chinese origin have become virtually indistinguishable from their Thai counterparts. Other influences on central Thai cooking include the region's Muslim and Mon (an ethnic group who today mostly live in neighbouring Myanmar) communities and even the Portuguese, who introduced a variety of sweets when they were the first Europeans to have diplomatic and trade relationships with central Thai people, starting in the 16th century.

A notable element of central Thailand's culinary legacy is the influence of the royal court. Thailand's kings employed an army of chefs and cooks who created dishes often revolving around exotic and/or indulgent ingredients, and with sophisticated presentation. This decadence arguably reached its apex in the form of central Thailand's jewel-like desserts, items such as *tong ek,* egg yolks and sugar shaped into flowers and topped with gold leaf, or *ka nom praphai* – multi-coloured, flower-scented balls of rice flour filled with mung bean paste.

Bangkok is, of course, the natural place to try central Thai cuisine, while the cities of Ayuthaya and Phetchaburi also have excellent culinary reputations.

AROIJANG

Southern Thai Cuisine

Looking for some heat? Then look south. The dishes of Thailand's southern provinces are by far the country's spiciest, with many based around herb pastes that include dried and fresh chillies, as well as pungent ingredients such as black pepper and ginger.

Like the cuisine of central Thailand, southern Thai cuisine revolves around long-grained rice, but paired with ample seafood and salty seafood-based ingredients such as shrimp paste, fresh turmeric, coconut milk, black peppercorns and pungent ingredients such as so-called 'stink beans'. The curry stall is the classic southern Thai eatery, and a typical spread might include a tart, spicy soup of fish and green papaya, minced pork stir-fried with an incendiary herb paste, a rich coconut milk-based curry, and a fiery dip based around chillies and shrimp paste – among other items.

There's a palpable Chinese influence in Thailand's south, which has resulted in a sub-cuisine: Baba food blends southern Thai, Malay and Chinese cooking techniques, ingredients and dishes. These days you can find these dishes in Phuket, Trang and Takua Pa. But the south's most significant culinary influence comes from its Muslim community. Dishes such as biryani and flatbreads, which can be traced back to the Middle East, are commonplace in southern Thailand, which is also home to dishes with influences from neighbouring Malaysia and even Indonesia.

Phuket Town is a microcosm of southern Thai cuisine, while the cities of Trang and Nakhon Sri Thammarat also have very strong culinary reputations.

Northern Thai Cuisine

The Thai people are thought to have descended from southern China, so it stands that the food of Thailand's north is among its oldest and most traditional.

In the north, the staple is sticky rice: short, chubby grains of glutinous rice that are steamed rather than boiled. This is eaten, typically by hand, with dishes that are often grilled, steamed or boiled. The food of Thailand's north is probably the least spicy of the regional cuisines, emphasising instead herbs, mouth-numbing dried spices and bitter, savoury flavours. These days, northern Thais are big meat eaters, and pork, beef and even water buffalo are grilled, stuffed into sausages and even eaten raw in the form of *larb* (spicy, herbal mince-meat salad) and other dishes. Northern Thais are particular fans of *nam prik*, Thai-style dips that are found in every region of the country; in the north they range from spicy, stringy, smokey pastes of grilled chillies to a bolognese-like mix of minced pork and savoury tomatoes.

Groups that have influenced the cuisine of the north include the Burmese, who ruled the region for centuries; Chinese Muslims, who criss-crossed the region as traders; and more recently, the region's so-called 'hill tribes', ethnic minorities who cultivate crops such as chayote and corn that have entered the northern Thai repertoire.

Chiang Mai is hands-down the north's culinary capital, while the cities of Chiang Rai and Phrae also have strong local food scenes.

Northeastern Thai Cuisine

Thailand's most rustic regional cuisine is that of its northeastern region, often called Isan. The people here also eat sticky rice, often pairing it with soups, dips and grilled dishes. The northeast is the country's poorest region, and its cuisine is notable for the use of ingredients that can be gathered or harvested, such as frogs, birds and even insects. Isan is home to yet another full-flavoured regional cuisine, and salty, funky flavours often come from *plaa raa*, an unfiltered fish sauce made via fermenting freshwater fish along with rice. A highlight of the northeastern Thai kitchen is *tam*, salad-like dishes made by bruising ingredients with a clay or wood mortar and pestle. The most famous example of this is *som tam*, which revolves around strips of green papaya pounded with tomatoes, long beans, chilli, peanuts, lime juice and fish sauce. Another headlining northeastern dish is *gai yahng*, grilled chicken, typically served with a tart/spicy dip based around tamarind – a dish now available across Thailand.

There's a very subtle Chinese influence on northeastern Thai cuisine, and it's also possible to find dishes with roots in neighbouring Laos and even Vietnam.

In recent years, Udon Thani has emerged as the unofficial culinary capital of Isan.

SMELLS LIKE THAI SPIRIT

Thailand's liquor laws had left almost no room for small distillers. Now, independent producers are making spirits that people across the country are noticing. By Craig Sauers

IF YOU ORDER a G&T in Bangkok today, there's a good chance your gin came from a distillery an hour or two away rather than halfway across the world. That kind of proximity – not to mention quality – would've been rare just a few years ago.

Community Liquor Licences

For most of the modern era, Thailand offered almost no room for small producers. As craft spirits boomed elsewhere, the Thai system still favoured power players like ThaiBev, the mass producer of Sang-Som and Mekhong – the stuff poured into buckets at beach parties.

On paper, anyone could apply for a distilling licence. In practice, the rules demanded a minimum production capacity of 30,000L per day, millions of Thai baht in capital investment and hard-to-acquire environmental certifications.

There was one other option, though: a community liquor licence.

Meant for small-scale, traditional spirits like rice wine, those licences came with

Chalong Bay rum, Distillery Phuket (p519)

GINA SMITH/SHUTTERSTOCK

major constraints. You could only have six employees, there was a 5HP ceiling on machinery and blanket bans prevented naming any products gin, rum or vodka. Everything had to be labelled as *lao khao* (white spirit) or *lao see* (brown spirit).

Of these two, *lao khao* was considered a country drink. Cheap booze that gets you drunk, moonshine that might leave you blind – not something you savour in a cocktail. '*Lao khao* was always considered poor man's alcohol,' says Thanawit 'Tiger' Limlertcharoenwanich, founder of Onson, a boutique distillery in Sakhon Nakhon that specialises in *lao khao*.

Tiger is a proud entrepreneur who has worked hard to change minds about his homeland, the rural northeast known as Isan. But it has not been easy. The 5HP limit, he says, 'isn't even enough to run a hair dryer', let alone equipment to control fermentation.

Still, a community licence became a viable entry point for people like him who have plenty of spirit but no high-level backing. In the early 2020s, aspiring distillers began using this licence to make spirits that have nothing in common with industrial liquor: clean, vodka-like distillates made from coconut sugar or sticky rice, grassy *rhum agricole* pressed from fresh sugar cane, and gins infused with *makhwaen* (prickly ash), lemongrass and other native botanicals.

Even if every bottle still had to be labelled a 'white spirit', it was clear they were on to something bigger. Once these new spirits began circulating, the reception was immediate.

Local Spirits Find Support

The rise of these artisanal spirits didn't happen in isolation. As distillers began using the community licence loophole, a younger generation was also redefining Thai identity, taking pride in products that older consumers had written off as cheap or unworthy simply because they were made domestically rather than imported.

Meanwhile, the progressive Move Forward Party had pushed alcohol liberalisation into the national conversation. Thai-made spirits started to draw attention. Venues in Bangkok began making space for their bottles. Travellers started asking about them.

Lao khao **(white spirit) production**

AMNAT30/SHUTTERSTOCK

By the time the initial frenzy faded, the producers who remained were working with far more skill and consistency.

'When [former Move Forward leader] Pita Limjaroenrat brought the "free Thai spirits" movement into the public sphere, a lot of people jumped into production,' says Jeen Snidvongs, co-founder of Choeng Doi, an artisanal distillery that opened in 2024 in Chiang Dao, a growing creative community one hour north of Chiang Mai. 'The producers who are still here have gotten better at making spirits, and they've gotten much better at marketing their product. Before, Thai producers were struggling to copy foreign-style spirits. Now, they're proudly defining their own new categories.' Choeng Doi is one of them. The distillery produces 'spirits that are tied to our land and our culture', as Snidvongs puts it – a 'contemporary version of *lao khao*' made from sticky rice and *rhum agricole* pressed from Chiang Dao sugar cane.

THAI PRODUCERS WERE STRUGGLING TO COPY FOREIGN-STYLE SPIRITS. NOW, THEY'RE PROUDLY DEFINING THEIR OWN NEW CATEGORIES.

Rice wine cocktail

JM TRAVEL PHOTOGRAPHY/SHUTTERSTOCK

Bars across Thailand, from Bangkok's Vesper to Chiang Mai's Bar Not Found, now stock their spirits alongside an expanding lineup of local rum, gin, vodka and rice wine. Some places, including Chiang Mai's popular Nophaburi, build entire menus around products like these.

Local flagships like Issan Rum, Chalong Bay and Iron Balls Gin are easy to find in Bangkok and Phuket, as well as many smaller destinations. Newer producers are emerging, too. Day Drinkers Collective in Chiang Dao are making mead from local honey; Sanpatong is producing eau de vie infused with mango, longan and coconut flowers just south of Chiang Mai; and Onson, one of the pioneers of the artisanal movement, continues to sell out nearly every batch it releases.

The Law Catches Up

Snidvongs believes the best is still ahead, in part because the law has recently begun to catch up with the culture.

In June 2025, the long-anticipated Community Liquor Act finally received royal approval, making it law. It allows farmer groups, community enterprises and small-scale entrepreneurs to apply for commercial alcohol production licences and possess distilling equipment.

The law sounds technical, but its implications are not. It's supposed to avoid the kind of discriminatory, monopoly-friendly conditions that once kept the industry in the hands of a few big players. Licences under this section last three years – enough time for a serious producer to prove they belong. Not just in Thailand, either, but perhaps on the world stage.

In 2026, Choeng Doi plans to export to Singapore and Hong Kong, as well as a few nations further afield, including Switzerland, France and Australia.

'We want to be the flag bearer for Thai spirits on the international market', Snidvongs says, noting that Choeng Doi isn't alone in this goal. 'I don't think we'll have to wait very long to see Thai spirits popping up all over the world', he adds. 'Our peers are all preparing to export, and with the rise of Thai bars in the 50 Best lists, I think Thai spirits are in a prime position to make an entrance on the global scene soon'.

INDEX

Map Pages **000**

O

P

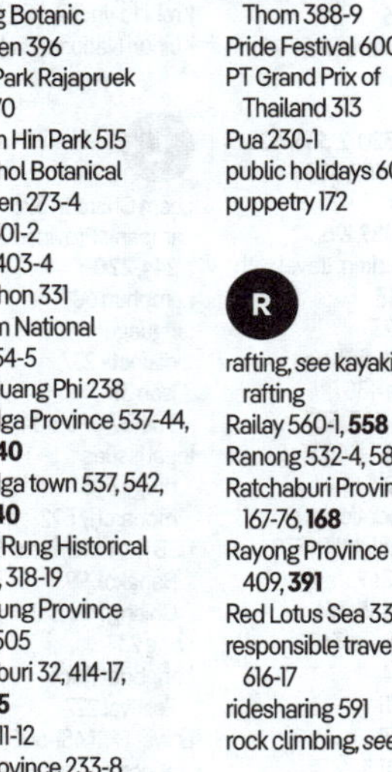

R

"With its talcum-white coves and camel-shaped karst peaks jutting out of green water, Ao Nang (p552) is a bay of ravishing beauty, studded with some 200 islets."

"The largest weekend market in the world, Chatuchak (p126) is a vast warren of 15,000-odd shops and stalls, and with every conceivable item on sale."

Mapping data sources:
© Lonely Planet
© OpenStreetMap http://openstreetmap.org/copyright

THIS BOOK

The 20th edition of Lonely Planet's Thailand guidebook was written and researched by David Eimer, Austin Bush, Philipp Meier, Chawadee Nualkhair, Aydan Stuart and Choltanutkun Tun-atiruj. This guidebook was produced by the following:

Destination Editor
James Pham

Production Editor
Kate James

Image Researcher
Clara Monitto

Cartographer
Valentina Kremenchutskaya

Coordinating Editor
Simon Williamson

Assisting Editors
Janet Austin, Natalie Butler, Nigel Chin, Shauna Daly, Anita Isalska, Jennifer McCann, Jenna Myers

Cover Researcher
Katelyn Perry

Cover Researcher
Melanie Dankel, Darren O'Connell

Paper in this book is certified against the Forest Stewardship Council™ standards. FSC™ promotes environmentally responsible, socially beneficial and economically viable management of the world's forests.

Published by Lonely Planet Global Limited
CRN 554153
20th edition – August 2026
ISBN 978 1 83869 967 3

10 9 8 7 6 5 4 3 2 1
Printed in Malaysia